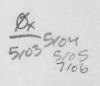

∅x
5103 5104
5105
7106

D0056715

WITHDRAWN

R F K

R F K

A CANDID BIOGRAPHY OF ROBERT F. KENNEDY

C. DAVID HEYMANN

A DUTTON BOOK

DUTTON
Published by the Penguin Group
Penguin Putnam Inc., 375 Hudson Street,
New York, New York 10014, U.S.A.
Penguin Books Ltd, 27 Wrights Lane,
London W8 5TZ, England
Penguin Books Australia Ltd, Ringwood,
Victoria, Australia
Penguin Books Canada Ltd, 10 Alcorn Avenue,
Toronto, Ontario, Canada M4V 3B2
Penguin Books (N.Z.) Ltd, 182–190 Wairau Road,
Auckland 10, New Zealand

Penguin Books Ltd, Registered Offices:
Harmondsworth, Middlesex, England

First published by Dutton, an imprint of Dutton NAL,
a member of Penguin Putnam Inc.

First Printing, October, 1998
10 9 8 7 6 5 4 3 2 1

REGISTERED TRADEMARK—MARCA REGISTRADA

LIBRARY OF CONGRESS CATALOGING-IN-PUBLICATION DATA

Heymann, C. David (Clemens David).
    RFK : a candid biography of Robert F. Kennedy / C. David Heymann.
    p.   cm.
    Includes bibliographical references (p.   ) and index.
    ISBN 0-525-94217-3 (cloth : alk. paper)
    1. Kennedy, Robert F., 1925–1968.   2. Legislators—United States—
    Biography.   3. United States.   Congress.   Senate—Biography.
    I. Title.   II. Title: Robert Francis Kennedy
    E840.8.K4H49   1998
    973.922′092—dc21
    [B]   98-13392
                                                                         CIP

Printed in the United States of America
Set in New Caledonia
Designed by Stanley S. Drate/Folio Graphics Co. Inc.

This book is printed on acid-free paper.

To Georges and Anne Borchardt

CONTENTS

CONTENTS

Bobby is always there when you need him.

—Jacqueline Bouvier Kennedy Onassis

Give me a place to stand and I will move the world.

—Archimedes

It must be understood that a prince, and especially a new prince, cannot observe all those things which are considered good in men, being often obliged, in order to maintain the state, to act against faith, against charity, against humanity, and against religion. And, therefore, he must have a mind disposed to adapt itself according to the wind, and as the variations of fortune dictate . . . not deviate from what is good, if possible, but be able to do evil if constrained.

—Niccolò Machiavelli, *The Prince*

PROLOGUE

THE FUNERAL TRAIN

At one o'clock on the afternoon of June 8, 1968, twelve hundred men and women boarded a specially reserved twenty-one-car passenger train at New York's Pennsylvania Station to accompany the body of Senator Robert F. Kennedy to the recently slain politician's final resting place at Arlington National Cemetery. Drawn by a black locomotive (No. 4901), the train burrowed deep under the Hudson River's currents, emerged in the heat of the Meadowlands, then lumbered across New Jersey and Pennsylvania, Delaware and Maryland before reaching its destination, Union Station in Washington, D.C., from which RFK's remains would be driven by hearse over the Potomac River to the Virginia graveyard. Lasting eight hours and symbolizing the end of an era, the journey struck one intimate Kennedy family friend, Kirk LeMoyne "Lem" Billings, as "almost interminable, a traveling Irish wake without end."

"The Funeral Train," as the commemorative transport came to be popularly known, meant many things to many people. To Russell Baker, who covered the journey for the *New York Times*, the trip represented "a constituency of sorrow along 225 miles of track": the throng of men, women and children who lined the rails to pay their last respects to a hero. Their tributes were painfully touching: burly men in shirtsleeves held their gray hard hats over their hearts; Little Leaguers grasped their baseball caps across their chests; uniformed men saluted; women from every echelon of society stood and cried; black men in overalls waved tiny American flags; a clutch of longhaired teenagers held aloft a home-made banner that read: "REST IN PEACE, BOBBY."

The transport's only stops before reaching Washington were Philadelphia, Wilmington and Baltimore. Soon after departing New York, as the

1

train approached Elizabeth, New Jersey, an accident occurred. A northbound train speeding in the opposite direction struck and killed two people who had wandered too close to the tracks. The tragedy was later blamed on the noise and confusion caused by a half dozen press helicopters that had been hovering just above the melancholy procession.

Looking back on the afternoon, Stewart McClure, chief clerk on a number of Senate subcommittees and a friend of RFK's since the early 1950s, recalled that "few of us on the train realized there had been an accident. We were too caught up in our own horror over Bobby's assassination. Coming as it did only five years after John F. Kennedy's death, it seemed almost a replay, a mind-boggling continuum of terror. Yet despite the grief, there were those of us who retained a modicum of hope. Out of all this craziness, something (or somebody) of promise had to emerge. But the person who emerged, ironically enough, was Richard M. Nixon, the next president of the United States."

Political journalist Dan Blackburn saw the train journey as "the last gathering of what had truly been a rainbow coalition, not what it later came to symbolize under Jesse Jackson, but a genuine coming together of men and women of all races and backgrounds. Indeed, this particular group of people, the mourners on the train, never gathered en masse again, not even when Ted Kennedy ran for president in 1980. Bobby's untimely death at age forty-two signified the end of a line, in many respects the gasping death of liberalism, the last hurrah."

Joseph Crangle, former New York State Democratic chairman, remembered the heroic actions of Bobby's oldest son, Joe, as the sixteen-year-old (wearing one of his father's suits) marched the length of the train shaking hands with each and every guest. "The poignancy of his presence," observed Crangle, "only deepened our agony and misery over Bobby's demise. Joe looked a great deal like his father—it was a difficult moment to accept."

Jacqueline Bouvier Kennedy also passed through the train, "looking sort of icy," according to journalist Pete Hamill, who was accompanied by his then-companion, actress Shirley MacLaine. The latter recalled that Jackie and RFK's widow, Ethel, came through the train together, "Jackie first, very regal, as only she can be, with this marvelous sense of sort of anticipatory dignity. She was always able, somehow, to anticipate when the train was going to lurch or when it would bump, and queen-like, take hold of something so that when the bump came, she wasn't disturbed or dislodged."

Ethel, by contrast, ashen, shaken, her voice and face revealing the strain of her ordeal, could barely maintain her balance. The difference in the manner of the two women was understandable: Jackie had had nearly half a decade to recover from her husband's murder; Ethel's husband had become the family's latest martyr not four days before.

Having made her rounds, Ethel retired to the train's last car. There, covered by an American flag, resting on chairs in a lounge, lay RFK's coffin. It was watched over by changing guards of silent friends who steadied the casket as the train rounded each bend. At one point in the journey, John Glenn and the other pallbearers practiced folding the flag as they were to do that evening at Arlington. On the observation platform at the rear of the car, members of the family sat in the warm breeze and gestured back at the crowds. In the last hours of the trip, except for the sounds of singing from outside, the lounge was quiet as Ethel Kennedy, head bowed and body motionless, knelt beside her fallen husband's coffin.

1

BEGINNINGS

The Fitzgeralds and the Kennedys, like many other Irish immigrant families, fled their homeland in desperation, leaving behind the tyrannical oppression of English landlords and the mass starvation caused by a potato blight. In the famine years, 1845–55, more than a million Irish bought twenty-dollar tickets to clamber aboard rickety freighters—"coffin ships"—for the six-week crossing to Boston. In one year alone, more than thirty thousand of the one hundred thousand who attempted the exodus perished en route.

Once in America, the survivors were confronted by a new kind of oppression: racial and religious prejudice on the part of Yankees. Irish job seekers in Boston were greeted by window signs that read "Americans Only" and "Irish Need Not Apply." In 1882 a Boston newspaper ran a cartoon deriding a disheveled Irish ditchdigger laying city sewer pipe while others of his nationality ineptly carried hods, tamped stones and troweled bricks. The womenfolk of these despised laborers were ridiculed by the cartoonist as taking in the neighborhood wash and toiling in sweatshops for minimal pay.

Shut out of the professions and the mainstream of "polite" society, Irish Americans—their numbers swelling rapidly in their waterfront "Riviera" slums—kept predominantly to themselves and improved their principal skill, politics. From 1885 they ruled Boston without serious opposition for seventy-five years. One of the city's mayors was an archetypal politician named John Francis Fitzgerald. Others of Irish heritage began to achieve success in the fang-and-claw world of commerce, among them Patrick Joseph Kennedy.

Together, "Honey Fitz" and "P. J.," as they came to be known, created a clan that was to fulfill all of the immigrant dreams—and then some—that the Irish had brought to these distant shores.

John Francis Fitzgerald was born in Boston's overpopulated North End, not far from the old North Church, on February 11, 1863. The fourth son of Irish immigrants Thomas and Roseanna Cox Fitzgerald, he worked in his father's grocery store while attending Eliot Grammar School. At age fifteen (about the time his mother died during her thirteenth pregnancy), he earned a scholarship to the prestigious Boston Latin School, from which he graduated in 1884 to enroll directly in Harvard Medical School, a practice then prevalent only among the area's most brilliant Brahmin students. John's dream of becoming a doctor was not to be realized, however, for at the end of his first year of medical school his father died. In order to keep the family together, John quit school and went to work, hiring a housekeeper to look after his younger siblings. He took a job as assistant to Democratic ward boss Matthew Kenny, which afforded an invaluable education in the inner workings of Boston politics. John subsequently became a chief clerk in the customhouse and won office as city councilman in 1892. Later that year he was elected to the state senate, where one of his colleagues was P. J. Kennedy, whose son Joe would eventually marry Fitzgerald's daughter Rose.

In 1889, John married Mary Josephine Hannon, his second cousin, and the couple had six children. By now nicknamed "Honey Fitz"—for the syrupy sweetness of his blarney—John was elected to the Congress in 1894 and served until the summer of 1900. After a five-year hiatus from elective office—spent as publisher of a small Boston Catholic weekly—he ran for the post of mayor of Boston.

"The people, not the bosses, must rule," John Fitzgerald's campaign posters proclaimed. He won the election and took office January 1, 1906. Defeated for reelection two years later, he soon found himself testifying before a grand jury investigating reports of corruption in his administration. Yet, campaigning under the slogan "Manhood Against Money," and frequently breaking into his theme song, "Sweet Adeline," Honey Fitz was returned to the mayoralty in 1910, by the slim margin of fourteen hundred votes.

At the end of his second term as Boston's chief executive, Fitzgerald's political career was over. Thereafter, until his death in 1950, he spent the majority of his time with his family. One of the highlights of his later years was to see his grandson Jack elected to Congress, a triumph he celebrated by jumping on a table and leading the singing of a medley of Irish ballads. Next to him on the same table, singing just as proudly and just as loudly, stood another grandson, Jack's younger brother Robert Francis Kennedy.

The Boston political formula was a simple one—judiciously distributed food, clothing and shelter—and it held the key to victory in the fierce Yankee-Irish scraps at the turn of the century. Employing this formula by assiduously tending to the needs of his fellow Irish, Patrick Joseph "P. J." Kennedy began his career as a saloonkeeper but elevated himself to become a bank president and a member of the state legislature.

Born in Boston on January 8, 1858, P. J. (like Honey Fitz) was the offspring of Irish immigrants. His father, Patrick Sr., died when his infant son was less than a year old. Bridget Murphy Kennedy, P. J.'s mother, helped support the family by becoming a clerk in, and later co-owner of, a small notions shop. Financial need forced young Kennedy to quit school at age fourteen and procure a job as a packer on the Boston docks. Somehow, he managed to save enough of his earnings to acquire a tavern in Boston's Haymarket Square, where business was so prosperous that he invested the profits in two additional saloons. In 1887, on Thanksgiving Day, he married Mary Augusta Hickey, with whom he had four children, one of whom died in infancy.

Well-to-do from his three saloons, P. J. Kennedy entered the political arena. From 1885 to 1891 he served in the state house of representatives, in 1892 he won a seat in the state senate, and on three occasions he represented Massachusetts as a delegate to the Democratic National Convention. He served Boston as both fire commissioner and commissioner of wines and spirits, in addition to working behind the scenes as a district boss for the city's powerful Democratic machine. During his public-service years, he continued to tend to his private holdings, expanding his revenue by investing heavily in real estate. In 1895 he helped organize the Columbia Trust Company, the bank of which he was to become president (in time to be followed in the same position by his son Joe).

After the death of his wife in 1923, P. J. moved in with his daughter Margaret and her husband, businessman Charles Burke. Kennedy died of liver disease in May 1929, while his only son happened to be in California producing a film starring his mistress, Gloria Swanson. It was the old man's grandson, Joseph P. Kennedy, Jr., who attended the funeral in Joe's place, along with honorary pallbearer, in-law John F. Fitzgerald.

A hotshot first baseman for Boston Latin School, Joseph Patrick Kennedy, P. J.'s boy, found the going a bit rougher once he matriculated at Harvard and failed to make the varsity. Nevertheless, he won his baseball letter. Popular legend has it that his influential father threatened to withhold a theater franchise from the Harvard team captain unless Joe played in the Yale game. Off the ball field, young Kennedy's searing ambition led him to the world of high finance.

Graduating from Harvard with a B.A. in 1912, Joe entered the business world with five thousand dollars earned by owning and driving a sight-seeing bus during his summers at college. After eighteen months as a bank examiner for Massachusetts, the impatient would-be financier increased his stake with borrowed money in order to buy stock in Columbia Trust, the bank which his father had helped found. In 1914, Joe was elected president of the bank. He was only twenty-five, the youngest bank president in the nation.

On October 7 of the same year, following an on-again, off-again seven-year courtship, twenty-six-year-old Joe Kennedy married Rose Elizabeth Fitzgerald, Honey Fitz's twenty-four-year-old daughter, the bell of Irish society in Boston. Sensing a decided moral defect in young Joe, Honey Fitz initially opposed the marriage, condoning it in the end only because of his friendship with the groom's father. Despite Joe Kennedy's declarations of devotion to his bride, the marriage proved difficult from the start—on at least two early occasions, Rose left her husband and returned briefly to her father's side. Before long, the couple settled for what can at best be termed an arrangement rather than a marriage.

By early 1915, having overextended his finances by investing in an array of small businesses, Joe Kennedy had gone deeply into debt. Gambling on his own brains and luck, he borrowed money from a New York bank and bought a small but sturdy green-frame house at 83 Beals Street in Brookline, a largely affluent suburb of Boston. There, despite their icy relationship, Joe and Rose set about their duty as Catholics: Joe Jr., Rosemary and Jack (their first three children) were all born in the house. Joe Kennedy, Sr., repaid his loan by procuring a lucrative position at a shipyard in Quincy, Massachusetts. Overseeing the urgent production of World War I submarines and battleships, Joe also supervised the construction of housing for shipyard personnel. And, with his uncanny eye for a dollar, he found time to organize, operate, and profit from an on-site cafeteria.

In the early 1940s, long after amassing his fortune, Joe Kennedy told his two oldest sons, Joe Jr. and Jack, that "bit businessmen are the most overrated men in the country. . . . And here I am, a boy from East Boston, and I took 'em. So don't let 'em impress you."

The remark, like Joseph Patrick Kennedy himself, was full of pride, self-promotion and not a little of the same blarney that had marked

Honey Fitz, his famous father-in-law. But the advice was purposeful, for Joe Kennedy believed that the training of his children superseded all other endeavors. Even more diligently than he accumulated great wealth, he poured into his sons everything that he learned and wished for himself.

The first Irish mayor of Boston had been elected three years before Joe's birth in 1888. But, as Richard Whalen wrote in his biography of Kennedy, *The Founding Father,* "it soon was clear that the Yankee would not be easily overcome. He had, as it were, simply retired from the antechamber and double-locked the doors beyond, which, by reason of their peculiar construction could not be forced. For Joseph Patrick Kennedy, life would center on the search for the key."

From the first, Joe Kennedy understood that the avenue to the key lay in power—in political and social position—and not in money. But if the building of a fortune was subsidiary to that end, it was clearly not incidental to it. It was, in fact, the best and only way of attaining what he desired for his offspring.

Joe Kennedy's business acumen led him after the war into a variety of enterprises, including real estate and the stock market. However, his first major financial success came only in the late 1920s—in the nascent motion picture industry, through which he also achieved his first public notoriety. He acquired two movie studios and a mistress, Gloria Swanson. After personally producing several films, he then merged the companies with the Radio Corporation of America and cashed in his stock, harvesting a $5 million profit in less than three years.

In the stock market, he similarly showed great savvy. One of the few speculators to anticipate the crash of 1929, he managed to bail out in time while others continued to invest furiously until the collapse. In the frenzied maneuvering that followed, Kennedy grew wealthier still through his role in a "pool," a consortium of profiteers who manipulated a given stock's price via calculated rumors and trading. A short time later, as the first chairman of the Securities and Exchange Commission, he enforced federal regulations against the very practices in which he had engaged.

Nor were fine points of law an obstacle for Joe Kennedy when opportunity arose from another national trauma. During Prohibition, he became the United States "distributor" for several British distillers, purchasing and importing thousands of cases of spirits under "medicinal" licenses issued in Washington, where his riches were beginning to buy the power he so ardently sought. A local police official also helped to ensure the operation's success: Sheriff Homer Large of Palm Beach,

Florida, allowed Kennedy to safeguard his liquor supply by stowing it in a prison in the affluent resort town, where the rising tycoon had earlier acquired an expansive oceanfront property.

The moment Repeal took effect in 1933, Joe Kennedy seized the opportunity and sold his vast inventory of alcohol—for millions more than he had originally paid for it. Interrogated by the press regarding the legality of the transaction, he responded: "What do you expect? I'm a capitalist."

True to that calling, Kennedy plowed his "bootlegging" profits and other liquid assets into a new series of ventures, including several Manhattan-based apartment buildings and town houses (one of which he kept for his family's use), office buildings in Boston, the Merchandise Mart emporium in Chicago, as well as Florida's Hialeah Race Track (of which he became a major stockholder). In addition, he purchased another spacious dwelling, the family compound at Hyannis Port, Massachusetts, where he retained the main cottage and built separate residences for each of his children. Before he was done, Joseph P. Kennedy's personal fortune was estimated to be worth in excess of $500 million, a not inconsiderable sum for this grandson of indigent Irish immigrants.

For all his wealth and burgeoning influence, Joe Kennedy remained shockingly parsimonious. Judge James Knott, former director of the Palm Beach Historical Society, considered the Kennedy patriarch "incredibly frugal. I don't mean frugal in a strict financial sense, though that, too. He used his fortune only to enhance the family's power base. But beyond this, he was ungiving in a general way—he never entered wholeheartedly into the social life of Palm Beach, or any of the other communities where he lived. He didn't have public vivacity or wonderful anecdotes he wanted to share. He was just a businessman, very successful and clever, but without social aspirations or habits of any kind. His only discernible cause was the enhancement of his own family's interest."

Joe Kennedy did embrace another cause: adultery. He had always been an ardent womanizer, but his dalliances grew so embarrassing to both sides of his family that one day his father-in-law took him aside and advised him to be more discreet. Honey Fitz, whose doubts about Joe began when the young man was still courting his daughter, was incensed at the shame Joe's behavior was inflicting on Rose; curiously, the aging politician insisted only that his son-in-law be more judicious in feeding his craving, not that he curb it altogether.

Joe ignored Honey Fitz's admonition; indeed, his tireless pursuit of women became more notorious with time. The best known of his sexual adventures involved movie queen Gloria Swanson, whom he met at a Hollywood party in the fall of 1927 when the star was at the height of her fame. He seduced her in the privacy of his Palm Beach estate while his wife sat in another room and Swanson's husband, the Marquis Henri de la Falaise, was off deep-sea fishing for the day. He took the actress in the manner of "a roped horse, rough, arduous, racing to be free," she wrote in her autobiography, *Swanson on Swanson*. "After a hasty climax he lay beside me stroking my hair." Somehow, she sensed, "the strange man *owned me*."

The affair continued for three years, during which time Kennedy formed a movie company, Gloria Productions, that produced Swanson's first talkie. He acted as her financial counselor, installed and maintained her in a private bungalow on Rodeo Drive in Beverly Hills, gave her costly presents (which she later learned he had secretly charged to her expense account), and introduced her to his children. He even brought her along when he and his wife traveled to Europe by ocean liner. Gloria subsequently took Rose shopping, introducing the Bostonian to the first couturiers in Paris. "If [Mrs. Kennedy] resented me," wrote Swanson, "she never gave any indication of it." In short, Gloria must have asked herself whether Rose had the makings of a fool or a saint, or was simply a better actress than she (Swanson) happened to be.

Throughout their romance, Gloria Swanson feared becoming pregnant. Brazen enough to believe he could withstand further scandal, Kennedy wanted a child by her—in his pleadings he declared himself "faithful" to her, offering as proof of that fidelity the entire year the fecund Rose had gone without conceiving. Such "tender" feelings did not, however, prevent him from dumping Swanson when he met Nancy Carroll, also an actress, who bore a striking resemblance to the woman she replaced.

Swanson and Carroll were just two of many. As Palm Beach art dealer George Vigouroux noted, "There were hundreds of women in Joe's life. He thought nothing of inviting a date home for dinner. This was the model that served to nourish the voracious appetites of his four sons."

"Joe Kennedy was vulgar," recounted Doris Lilly, who once "had the misfortune of dating Joe. He was the horniest, most disgusting man I ever knew. One night he took me out to El Morocco in New York. Then he escorted me back to my hotel. It was a hot, humid summer night. He wanted to come up to my room. When I told him I was tired, he grabbed me by the shoulders and forced his tongue down my throat. I gagged. I then hurried to my room by myself and proceeded to vomit."

Joe Kennedy's longest-lasting affair—nearly seven years—involved a statuesque blonde showgirl named Day Elliot, who happened to be a friend of Doris Lilly. Assigning pseudonyms to both Joe and Day, Doris Lilly portrayed their liaison in a January 1963 article for *Cosmopolitan* magazine. Expanding on the article in an interview with this author, Lilly remarked: "Joe Kennedy bought her a duplex in a town house on Beekman Place, which is where all the wealthy men 'kept' their mistresses. It was popular in those days because there wasn't much street traffic and few pedestrians. He also gave her a lot of jewelry and other gifts, including a Goya print and several etchings by Rembrandt. They went on vacations together. On one occasion he chartered a yacht and they sailed to Bimini, where they stayed at the Bahamian Club and gambled. In New York, they would sometimes taxi down to Chinatown and after eating take in a grade-C western at a Times Square movie theater.

"She absolutely fell in love with him. Although he saw other women, she refused to date other men. They frequently saw one another in company with his friends—nobody mentioned the fact that he was married to another woman."

Although relatively civil toward Day Elliot, Joe Kennedy's treatment of women was generally egocentric, callous and, at times, amazingly crude. Literary agent Marianne Strong recalled an incident involving Kennedy and two teenage models he took to dinner at New York's La Caravelle: "My late husband and I knew that Joe Kennedy frequented this restaurant, was even rumored to be part-owner, so it came as no surprise to find him seated next to us. He had these two beautiful and slim girls on either side, and it soon became clear that he was pleasuring one of them under the table. He had his hand in her panties and a hard, ugly smirk on his face. And while he was doing that, he was eating dinner with his other hand.

"My husband summoned the maitre d'. 'We didn't come here to be entertained,' he said. 'May we please have another table.'

"The hapless maître d' couldn't find an empty table anywhere in the restaurant. We could therefore either stay and keep our mouths shut or leave. We stayed and endured the remainder of Joe Kennedy's pornographic performance."

Doris Lilly concurred with the notion—shared by most who knew the family—that Rose Kennedy didn't care how many girlfriends her husband had, because she had her children. Lilly reasoned that Joe and Rose had intimate relations only for the purpose of procreation; once the family was complete, she maintained, the couple no longer engaged each other sexually.

Palm Beach socialite Mary Sanford, for years Rose Kennedy's closest friend and confidante, offered a conflicting point of view. "Rose was gravely wounded by Joe's constant philandering," she said. "Whenever he stepped out on her, she would break down and cry. Then she'd drag herself to a cocktail party and shamelessly flirt with every man in the room.

"She eventually took her revolt a step further. In 1930 she met and began an affair with investment broker Earl E. T. Smith, who was then married to Consuelo Vanderbilt. Conveniently, Earl eventually acquired the estate next door to the Kennedys' on North Ocean Boulevard in Palm Beach. He was very tall—about six feet five inches—and very handsome. A playboy extraordinaire, he was a dozen years younger than Rose. From 1957 to 1959, when Fidel Castro came to power, he served as American ambassador to Cuba. Later he became mayor of Palm Beach.

"The fling lasted several months, but to the best of my knowledge only a handful of people knew about it. Two who found out may have been Jack and Bobby. By strange coincidence, the late president later became involved with Florence Pritchett, Earl Smith's much younger second wife—they were married in 1948. Presumably, Flo learned of the assignation with Rose and transmitted the information to Jack who, in turn, no doubt informed Bobby. That, I surmise, is precisely where the buck stopped."

"I'm not the kiss-and-tell type," asserted Earl Smith when probed about the affair. "Let's just say that Rose Kennedy and I were great friends at one point."

During the middle stages of John F. Kennedy's thousand days in office, Hugh Sidey—then Washington correspondent for *Time* magazine—sent his editors in New York a memorandum detailing the administration's sumptuousness and sensuality. "One weekend when JFK and his staff were in Palm Beach," the dispatch related, "even the President's . . . mother, Rose Kennedy, was part of the high life," attending a party with an escort that Sidey had overheard being referred to as "her gigolo."

Rose Kennedy apparently went to the party in question with none other than Earl E. T. Smith, although their secret affair had long ended and Smith, wealthy and prominent in his own right, could never accurately be called a gigolo.

Time never published the story. Within days of the memo's submission, Attorney General Robert F. Kennedy summoned Sidey to his office, where a copy of the report sat on his desk. Someone in the administration had intercepted it and turned it over to Bobby. "If you ever run this in *Time*," warned the president's brother, "we'll sue your ass for slander and libel." The nation's chief law-enforcement official then proceeded to dismiss the journalist with a flick of his hand.

2

RFK: THE THIRD SON

The oldest of six children, Rose Fitzgerald realized well before she married Joe Kennedy that she wanted a large family. Childbearing formed only part of her ambition, however, for she aspired to more than being the humdrum wife of a run-of-the-mill Boston businessman. Shyness had kept her mother at home and out of the public eye, but Rose, who learned early to savor the bright lights of politics as well as its bare-knuckled infighting, happily began accompanying her father on his official rounds. Together, Honey Fitz and his daughter toured Europe, traveled to Washington and threw out the first ball at Boston's Fenway Park. When Rose, at fifteen, graduated second in her class from Dorchester High School—and was presented with her diploma by her father the mayor—the event made the city's front pages.*

Rose's adolescence "may well have been the high point of her life," contended Mary Sanford. Still, the years that followed were not without satisfaction. Despite the trials of her marriage to Joe Kennedy, Sanford claimed, "she did come to relish his escalating wealth, his connections, as well as his interest in politics and everything that went with it. He was a rover, yes, but he cared about family, particularly about his children."

The Kennedys had nine children: Joseph Jr., born in 1915, John (1917), Rosemary (1918), Kathleen (1920), Eunice (1921), Patricia (1924), Robert (1925), Jean (1927) and Edward (1932). Of the four

*Although Rose was accepted at Wellesley College, Honey Fitz—pressured by a church official—sent her to convent schools in Boston, Holland and New York City. She resented her father's decision. "It was always my greatest regret not to attend college," she informed Doris Kearns Goodwin, author of *The Fitzgeralds and the Kennedys*. "I would have given my eyeteeth to have been allowed to go to Wellesley."

boys, Rose and Joe's seventh child, Robert Francis Kennedy, born November 20, 1925, would most resemble the mother in appearance and the father in temperament. Comparing his first and second sons to his third, Joe Kennedy later ventured: "Joe Jr. and Jack go as far as mortal man can; Bobby goes a little further. I like to think he takes after his old man."

By the end of 1920, having outgrown their Beals Street home, Joe and Rose Kennedy had paid seventeen thousand dollars for a larger house at 131 Naples Road, also in Brookline. The new residence boasted twelve rooms and a more elegant facade, as befitted a family that had begun to prosper and gain recognition. Built in the then-popular shingle style and covered with ivy, the Naples Road House had a capacious veranda on which the children could frolic on rainy days.

It was in this house that Bobby Kennedy was born. Attending Rose at the birth were her longtime obstetrician, Frederick L. Good, and a youthful nurse, Barbara Guest, who later described Bobby as "a delicate baby with blond hair and blue eyes; he weighed only six pounds when born, but he possessed a loud, shrill, piercing cry that stopped only when his mother breast-fed him. Otherwise, he slept little and wailed almost continually, often through the night. Strangely enough, he also stopped crying on those rare occasions when his father would appear in the nursery. The two of them, father and son, would invariably lock eyes and engage in a protracted staring contest."

Bobby Kennedy had nearly turned two when, in the fall of 1927, Joseph P. Kennedy moved his family from Brookline to the New York City neighborhood of Riverdale, in the Bronx just outside Manhattan. The rented house at 5040 Independence Avenue, located by Joe's personal aide, Eddie Moore, had thirteen rooms and a vertiginous view of the Hudson River. A year and a half later, in the spring of 1929, Joe Kennedy uprooted his family again—he purchased a house at 294 Pondfield Road in Bronxville, a posh New York suburb a few miles north of the Bronx. The new place, a country estate situated on six acres with separate cottages for chauffeur and gardener, cost Kennedy a quarter of a million dollars.

Built of brick in the Georgian style, the Bronxville home had originally been constructed for the man who founded the Busch brewing empire. Its long list of amenities included an outdoor swimming pool, lush formal gardens and a basement projection room where Joe Jr. could show the latest Hollywood products to family and friends. Peter Barton, who grew up nearby, recalled watching cartoons one inclement Saturday afternoon with his neighbors: "There was minimal heat in the projection room, although it was mid-winter and half the Kennedy children were suffering from nasty colds. Bobby Kennedy's seemed by far the worst. Only four or five at the time, he kept spewing up green phlegm. A wisp of a lad—his brothers and sisters had nicknamed him 'the runt'—he had what seemed to be either a deadly virus or a serious case of pneumonia. Despite thunderous warnings from his mother to go to bed, Bobby stayed and watched the cartoons, drowning out the soundtrack with his raucous, hacking cough."

While living at Pondfield Road, Joe Kennedy, Jr., attended the Riverdale Country Day School, a private academy, as did Jack, who completed grades five through seven there before leaving in 1930 for boarding school at Choate. Bobby Kennedy completed kindergarten and grades one and two at a public school in Riverdale, then was transferred to the Bronxville public school system prior to entering Riverdale Country Day School, departing only in 1938, when his father became American ambassador to Great Britain and moved the family temporarily to London.

Whether the Kennedys resided in England or the United States, the responsibility for disciplining the children inevitably fell to Rose. "Mother would have made a great featherweight," Teddy Kennedy once said. "She had a mean right hand." Witnesses have confirmed Teddy's description: she used her right hand often and with great authority, utilizing a variety of implements to drive home her point—hairbrushes, coat hangers, belts, shoes. Occasionally she dispensed with such tools and relied on her bare hand, once slapping young Bobby's face so viciously that she punctured his eardrum and split his lip.

"Rose was not one to say, 'Wait till your father gets home,'" observed Lem Billings. "Justice was immediate. The slightest infraction on the part of any of her children usually resulted in harsh reprisal."

This stern regime was aimed at curbing more than mere childish mischief. Axel Madsen, author of *Gloria and Joe*, an account of the Gloria Swanson–Joe Kennedy romance, wrote that Rose "taught her children a certain emotional repression or detachment, which they would come to resent. Any emotional display was discouraged. By her own example and through frequent admonition, she taught her children to hide their true feelings, fearing that if they showed their emotions too openly it would make them vulnerable to taunts and attacks." John Kennedy is cited by Madsen as having remarked about his mother: "She was never there when we really needed her. . . . [She] never really held me and hugged me. Never."

Adding to this dismal picture of corporal and psychological punishment was the fanatic frugality demonstrated by both Rose and Joseph Kennedy. Judge James Knott observed that "the Kennedys didn't care what their homes looked like. They were too parsimonious to put money into home improvement. As a result, their dwellings were all in dire need of repair. Joe would have the front of the Palm Beach residence painted but not the back or sides, because people saw only the front."

Just as Peter Barton had noted the chill air in the Bronxville projection room, Mary Sanford was struck by Joe Kennedy's refusal to heat the Palm Beach swimming pool. "He was too cheap to install a heater," said Sanford. "Consequently, Rose would come over to my house for a swim and would invariably arrive at noon. I would be entertaining friends over brunch when suddenly the nude form of Mrs. Kennedy would appear and make a mad dash for the pool. My guests never knew what to make of it, and I had long before stopped bothering to explain."

Rose pinched pennies as obsessively as Joe, if not more so. Robert Green, proprietor of Green's Pharmacy in Palm Beach, recalled: "Here was a woman who at times attended Mass every day of the week yet never put more than a single dollar bill into the collection plate. Father Jeremiah O'Malloncy of St. Edward's tolerated her actions because the family had a name. But even he eventually grew disgusted with her paltry donations and began to castigate her in front of the entire Palm Beach congregation. She couldn't have cared less. She and her daughters packed their own lunch to the weekly church picnic rather than buy what the church had to offer in the way of food. She would storm around her house turning off light switches to save electricity, mark the liquor bottles to prevent the help from knocking off the booze behind her back, dock the servants a dime for every bottle of Coca-Cola they took from the pantry between meals. The servants were miserably paid. Their name for the Kennedy home was 'The House of the Minimum Wage.'

"I remember when we raised the price of a cup of coffee at Green's, which had a breakfast-and-luncheon counter, from a nickel to a dime—Rose went berserk; she complained, she railed, she remonstrated. After that, she refused to come in. Oh, her children continued to frequent the pharmacy—that's because they never had any money. Joe Jr., Jack and Bobby would hike to the drugstore from their home, barge in and stuff their pockets with candy bars when they thought nobody was looking. We'd add the cost of the candy to their father's bills, but it generally took months for his business office in New York to pay."

"Rose pulled other stunts," said George Vigouroux. "For example, she often gave gifts and later asked the recipients to return them. One Christmas she presented me with three neckties from Saks Fifth Avenue. Six months later, I received a letter from her: 'Do you remember the ties I gave you? I need them back.' Rose had developed a reputation for buying expensive clothes from certain boutiques, wearing them, then returning them for reimbursement. So I have to believe she sent the ties back to Saks. One local merchant, Martha Phillips, owner of Martha's, a tony women's clothing chain, eventually banned Rose from her stores.

"Rose Kennedy indulged in some strange habits. For years, she refused to hire her own chauffeur. Joe had one, but she didn't—not until Jack ran for president. She either hitched rides or took taxi cabs. She always tried to share taxi cab rides with strangers to cut the cost of the fare—that's how chintzy she could be."

In her 1974 autobiography, *Times to Remember*, Rose Fitzgerald Kennedy mused over her role as family matriarch: "I have had nine children. If I had my time over again, I would have liked eleven. There was a long time between Bobby and Teddy. If I'd had another son, then . . ."

Of his position as third son and seventh child, Bobby remarked, "When you come from that far down you have to struggle to survive." At the time of Robert's birth, Joe Jr. was ten and John was eight, and in a family that exalted physical activity Bobby spent his childhood trying to keep up with the older boys. His future wife, Ethel Skakel Kennedy, noted that "the major difference between Bobby and his brothers is that Bobby always had to fight for everything." "He was the smallest and thinnest," his mother commented, "and we feared he might grow up puny and girlish. We soon realized there was no chance of that."

John Kennedy remembered Bobby as a four-year-old repeatedly hurling himself into the ocean to learn to swim. Once he'd mastered the skill, he continued to do his utmost to compete with his reckless brothers. "Joe Jr., Jack and Bobby would swim a mile or two into the Atlantic," Robert Green recalled, "even when there were storm warnings or shark sightings. The more dangerous the conditions, the more they enjoyed the challenge."

Nor were Bobby's brothers the only objects of his fierce sibling rivalry. Eunice Kennedy, four years Bobby's senior, once threw a plate of chocolate pudding at the five-year-old across the dining-room table. The youngster jumped from his chair and raced at his sister, but was deterred from his goal when his forehead collided with the table's edge. Fifteen stitches were required to close the gash that resulted.

As aggressive and determined as young Bobby was, close acquain-

tances also discerned in him a pronounced kindness and sweetness—
qualities that the bitter opponents he made later in life might have been
hard-pressed to detect. One of the family nurses, Luella Hennessey,
deemed Bobby "the most thoughtful and considerate of the Kennedy
children." June Carter, a second-grade teacher, remembered him as "a
restless but loving freckle-faced little fellow, his light brown hair long and
tousled. He was a regular, though intelligent, boy, and it seemed hard
for him to finish his work at times. But he was a perfectionist, and the
assignments he did complete were almost always on the mark." *New York
Times* journalist and family friend Arthur Krock found Bobby "gentle,
affectionate, thoughtful and responsible. From his earliest years, he was
a shy, quiet child who had difficulty making close friends his own age. I
suppose the frequent changes of school must have discouraged those
friendships."

"What I remember most vividly about growing up," Bobby later recalled, "was going to a lot of different schools, always having to make new
friends, and that I was very awkward. I dropped things and fell down all
the time. I had to go to the hospital a few times for stitches in my head
and my leg. And I was pretty quiet most of the time—I didn't particularly
mind being alone."

For a boy raised in the shadow of two accomplished older brothers,
in a family often on the move, frequent mishaps may have represented
an unconscious appeal for attention and affection. Bobby Kennedy's
"struggle to survive" started early and never abated. Indeed, his unusual
combination of reticence and assertiveness may have been the most dis-
tinctive feature of his mature personality. "As an adult he was the least
poised, the least articulate and the least extroverted of the Kennedy
brothers," wrote journalist Jack Newfield. "He was also the most physical,
the most passionate and the most politically unorthodox."

Joe Jr. pointed to RFK's seeming dichotomy—his hushed solemnity
versus his exuberant physicality—when he called his younger brother
"somebody with either a lot of guts or a person with no sense at all,
depending on how you regarded it." At not quite five feet ten inches in
height, compared to three brothers all six feet or over, Bobby in his adult
years often expressed his intense need to test and prove his courage
through dangerous exploits of skiing, rapids shooting, mountain climbing
and jungle exploration. His obsession with valor suggested a zest for adventure and a longing for heroic vindication, mixed with undertones of
self-flagellation and self-destruction.

U tterly brave, Bobby could also be prudent. As a boy, he and the son of his father's chauffeur once made sheets into parachutes for jumping off the Hyannis Port roof. The servant's child jumped first and broke a leg. Bobby refused to follow suit, declaring the game "foolhardy and stupid."

A rchitect William Uris, a childhood friend of Joe Kennedy, Jr., said of Bobby: "He was the typical little brother, the one who constantly got beaten up by his big brothers. As he came of age, this predicament was always on his mind, and he often remarked that he intended to bring up his own children differently. When he was little, it was always, 'Robert, go fetch the ice cream.' Or, 'Robert, take the dogs for a walk.' He and Jack would always fight over what to listen to on the radio. For instance, Bobby loved jazz, especially Benny Goodman, and Jack didn't.

"Bobby was bullied by his elder brothers but he managed to retain a savage individuality. At whatever athletic endeavor or sport it was, this boy was always trying to defeat one of the older boys, trying to overcome the age difference. He didn't often succeed, but he did put up a battle. His determination became evident to anybody who knew or met him."

Ruth Blackburn Leonovich, who lived next door to the Kennedys at Hyannis Port, remembered how ardently Bobby competed with his siblings at sailing: "Each of the brothers and sisters had his or her own sailfish, and they would race each other around Nantucket Sound. Bobby never won, but he always placed second or third—that's when he was still a youngster; later on, he rarely lost. I recall the father telling his sons, 'You either win or lose—there's nothing else in life. If you don't place first, you may as well come in last.'

"My other recollection is that the Kennedys were very insular, they never socialized with the wealthy summer crowd that came down to Hyannis Port from Boston every year. If somebody in the neighborhood gave a party, they didn't attend. Also, they never hired blacks—all the household help were of Irish descent. You had the feeling that Joseph P. Kennedy didn't trust anybody else."

Another Hyannis Port neighbor, Ruth Holmes Korkuch, reminisced that Bobby Kennedy "did on occasion play with other children in the area. We would go exploring together. There was a scuttled boat at the end of the Sea Street jetty which served as a speakeasy for the summer folks. During the day, when the boat was closed, we would clamber aboard and look around. At night, we would hide out at various spots on the jetty and watch the people dancing and drinking on deck.

"Once in a while I would go swimming with Bobby and others at the

Hyannis Port Yacht Club. A heavyset girl, whose name I no longer recall, lost her eyeglasses in the water. Bobby kept diving until he finally recovered them. He seemed to be sensitive to the feelings of other children, especially the less privileged kids who hung around with the rest of us. In fact, his best friend—probably his only male friend—was Austin Bell. His parents were of American Indian heritage."

3

LIKE FATHER, LIKE SON

By the age of ten, Bobby Kennedy had developed a robust enthusiasm for the field of American history. The walls of his bedroom in Bronxville were covered with photographs of the most popular presidents. His bookshelves were crammed with volumes on the Civil War. He collected U.S. postage stamps and received a note of appreciation from fellow philatelist Franklin D. Roosevelt, whose second presidential inauguration he would attend in January 1937. Dated June 1935, the one-sentence letter was framed and mounted in Bobby's bedroom at Hyannis Port:

> Dear Bob:
>
> Your father has told me of your interest in stamps and I want you to know that I am a stamp collector too, and the next time you are in Washington I hope you will stop by and see me.

At age eleven, Bobby procured a summer newspaper route, folding and delivering the Hyannis morning daily, not on bicycle but from the backseat of his father's chauffeur-driven limousine. He would rise at dawn, distribute the paper, then join his father and brothers at the breakfast table, where Joseph P. Kennedy invariably held forth on current political issues. At the end of the meal, Joe would assign each of his sons a separate subject for study during the day, and at dinner that evening each boy would lead the entire family in his topic's discussion.

These freewheeling nightly exchanges afforded Joe Kennedy's children the opportunity to enjoy not only an individual relationship with their father but a group connection as well. Bobby Kennedy later told historian John Jay Hooker that his father's assignments both stimulated his interests and gave him a set of values by which to live. "For example," noted Hooker, "Bobby told me that at the dinner table they never were permitted to discuss money; the subject was taboo. If anyone mentioned the cost of something, the topic would be discarded either by Joe or Rose and another theme substituted—they would talk about family activities or vacations."

Throughout these conversations, the father permitted, even encouraged, his offspring to express their own views and convictions. He did not insist, commented Hooker, that they necessarily agree with him. He did demand that they comprehend the issue and formulate a sensible opinion, then voice that opinion in a succinct and meaningful manner.

This attitude toward his children, Hooker maintained, won Joe Kennedy "what I thought was almost total respect from them. In their eyes he was a tremendous human being—they were very much involved with him and they wanted to please him. But at the same time they had been . . . permitted the luxury of disagreeing with him, so that what they felt for him was not fear of reprisal or fear of arbitrary discipline, but respect for his opinion, respect for his feelings, love and a deep sense of identity."

On October 12, 1937, President Franklin D. Roosevelt announced the selection of Joseph P. Kennedy to the post of American ambassador to the Court of St. James's. Kennedy, whose vigorous support of Roosevelt had included generous financial contributions to both presidential campaigns and the writing of a 1936 book *I'm for Roosevelt*, had sought appointment as secretary of the treasury during FDR's first term. When that job ultimately went to Henry Morgenthau, Kennedy had to console himself with other assignments: first as chairman of the Securities and Exchange Commission, then as head of the U.S. Maritime Commission, and finally as representative to Great Britain, where he became the first Irish Catholic from the United States to serve as envoy to his ancestral homeland's historic oppressor.

He arrived in London the following March to present his credentials to King George VI at Buckingham Palace. The entire Kennedy family, including all nine children, moved into the ambassador's residence at 14 Prince's Gate, a huge house in Knightsbridge that had been given to the American government by financier J. P. Morgan. Equipped with a fleet of cars and two dozen servants, the dwelling allowed the family to continue its custom of luxurious living.

Joseph Kennedy enjoyed strong popularity his first months in England, and his intimacy with Prime Minister Neville Chamberlain made him an effective diplomat. Another asset was Rose, as the British press gushed over her charm and good looks. "She's as slim and young-appearing as a sixteen-year-old," wrote one reporter. A columnist for another daily admired her as "looking like a vivacious screen star, yet possessing all the sagacity of a dowager." Still a third paper spouted that it was nearly "impossible to tell her apart from her daughters whenever a group photograph is seen."

The family spent its first weeks in London visiting the usual sites: Trafalgar Square, Hyde Park, Ascot, the London Zoo in Regent's Park. Joe Jr. and Jack, both on leave from Harvard, audited a seminar in political science given at the London School of Economics by noted socialist Harold Laski.* Although his own politics were miles apart from Laski's, Joe Sr. approved of his sons' taking the course, for he respected the professor's intelligence and presentation. The Kennedy girls, meanwhile, were distributed among London's wide array of convent schools. Bobby and Teddy, aged thirteen and six, were sent to the Gibbs School for Boys at 134 Sloane Street. Dressed in flannel slacks, maroon jackets and cherry red hats, they were driven to school each morning by embassy limousine.

Cecil Parker, a classmate of Bobby's, recalled that "young Kennedy disliked the Gibbs School. He particularly hated Latin, did poorly in the subject and eventually dropped it. He also never quite got the hang of cricket, although he did his utmost to keep up with the rest of us. Finally, I remember his refusing to join the English Boy Scouts because he would have had to say a pledge of allegiance to the throne. He didn't want to appear unpatriotic to the United States. He did, however, lay the cornerstone for a new boys' club in London, and the entire class attended the ceremony."

England's enthusiasm for the Kennedys did not last. In Ascot, at a house the family had rented for weekends, Rose had the misfortune of encountering Lady Diana Cooper, a leading British socialite. Lady Diana described her colonial hostess as "a social climber, very crude, rude, pretentious, her face smeared in make-up. She wishes only to rub shoulders with the elite and even affects a British accent so as to appear more polished. Her sole interest in life appears to be in slipping off to Paris whenever possible to go shopping for the latest fashions." The ambassador and his wife began receiving fewer and fewer invitations to London social events.

Less popular than Rose was her eldest son, who with others had started a pro-isolationist club for students at Harvard. Joe Jr. espoused

---

*Both boys had studied with Laski at the London School before—Joe Jr. in 1933–34, Jack in 1935–36.

his political views, which echoed those of his father, to everyone he met in England. Alexander Schnee, a young American also studying with Harold Laski at the London School of Economics, spent a week with Joe Jr. in Ireland. Schnee recalled his traveling companion as "full of arrogance, constantly deriding England, an overexuberant drinker who stalked every girl who looked his way. He had no respect for women, but rather only wanted to be serviced by them. He was like every other male member of the boorish family."

But most of Britain's growing disdain for the Kennedys focused on the family's head. An appeaser and an apologist for Neville Chamberlain, Joseph Kennedy won approval from his sons but not from Winston Churchill, who had replaced the discredited Chamberlain as prime minister in May of 1940, some eight months after the start of the Second World War. Churchill loathed Kennedy, whom he denounced on many occasions as a liability to both Britain and America. The U.S. envoy, charged Churchill, was advising members of Parliament that President Roosevelt was nothing but a puppet of the Communists and Jews; he was arguing that democracy in England was doomed and Adolf Hitler and fascism would soon take hold. When Kennedy went so far as to suggest that America and Britain strike a secret trade agreement with Germany, Churchill insisted that MI5, the British counterintelligence agency, place him under surveillance—in Churchill's eyes, the American ambassador was operating as a German spymaster.

British investigators did uncover an American cipher clerk, Tyler Kent, who while employed at the U.S. embassy was passing highly classified information to German officials. Kent, it turned out, had been close friends with Joe Kennedy. When the clerk was apprehended and returned to the States to stand trial for espionage, Joe Kennedy reacted by granting an interview to Louis Lyons, a reporter with the *Boston Globe*.

"I'm going to spend all I've got to keep the United States out of the war," vowed the American ambassador. "There's no sense in our getting in. We'd only be holding the bag. What would we get out of it?

"I know more about Europe than anybody else in America. . . . Democracy is finished in England. It isn't that she's fighting for democracy. That's the bunk. She's fighting for self-preservation."

The diplomat also noted Winston Churchill's fondness for brandy, King George's speech impediment and the queen's dowdy wardrobe.

Perhaps his most damaging indiscretion, politically speaking, was his discussion of Eleanor Roosevelt. "She bothered us more on our jobs in Washington to take care of the poor little nobodies than all the rest of the people down there put together. She's always sending me a note to have some little Susie Glotz to tea at the embassy."

Instead of "Susie Glotz," Joe Kennedy invited Barbara Hutton to the American embassy. Hutton, the beautiful five-and-dime heiress with dark brown eyes and shiny blond hair, was then living in London. Ostensibly, Kennedy called her in to recommend that she return to the States because of the war. Minutes into the meeting, however, he revealed a different intent: he chased her around his desk and proposed that she become his mistress. She declined.

The *Boston Globe* interview, the Barbara Hutton incident, the overall demeanor of the man were all part of the picture: President Roosevelt had long since begun to conduct his relations with the government of Great Britain—and with Winston Churchill, in particular—without involving his ambassador. A confrontation between Roosevelt and Kennedy did not remedy the embarrassing situation, and in October 1940, under pressure from the White House, Kennedy resigned. Nevertheless, for the rest of his life he insisted on being addressed as "Ambassador."

Portsmouth Priory (today called Portsmouth Abbey) was the Catholic boys' preparatory school in Portsmouth, Rhode Island (overlooking Narragansett Bay, eight miles north of Newport), in which Robert F. Kennedy enrolled in the fall of 1939, after Rose Kennedy and her children had returned to the United States on the eve of war.* With morning and evening prayers, as well as mass on Sundays and three times during the week, the Benedictine monks who operated Portsmouth mandated for their students an ascetic regime similar to their own. Bobby spent two and a half years there, the only one of the Kennedy sons to attend Catholic boarding school for more than a term—Teddy later attended Portsmouth for a few months—before transferring at age seventeen to the Milton Academy.

Bobby performed well in athletics at Portsmouth, but not in academics, at one juncture eliciting an appropriately stern letter from his mother: "I am so disappointed in your report. . . . Please get on your toes. . . . You have a good head and certainly you ought to use it. You owe it to yourself as well as to me to make the most of your advantages. Remember, too,

---

*Joseph P. Kennedy, waiting until his resignation as ambassador became official, returned by himself on October 28, 1940. He and Rose took up residency once again at their home in Bronxville, New York. RFK hagiographers should also note that before entering Portsmouth, Bobby had spent two months at St. Paul's, a preparatory school in Concord, New Hampshire. Not liking the atmosphere at St. Paul's, Bobby asked his mother to switch him to Portsmouth.

that it is a reflection on my brains, as the boys in the family are supposed to get their intellect from their mother, and certainly I do not expect my own little pet to let me down."

"The most unsociable of my sons," said Rose of Bobby during those years. "He didn't make friends easily," concurred Pierce Kearney, a classmate at Portsmouth. "Those of us who did befriend him called him Bob—never Bobby. I remember him as scrawny for his age, short and thin, but he was agile and strong for his size. On the other hand he demonstrated a very serious demeanor, a kind of altar-boy disposition.

"He and I lived in the same dormitory at Portsmouth, and our housemaster was also our Latin teacher. Neither Bobby nor I did very well in Latin, but we would plug away at our textbooks before exams. Well, one day somebody in the dorm found a mimeo copy of the next morning's Latin exam in a wastebasket, obviously tossed there by our housemaster. We passed the exam around and when it reached me, I took it into Bob's room. He's at his desk, hunched over his Latin text, studying Caesar as hard as he can.

"So I waltz in and say, 'Look what we've got, Bob, tomorrow's Latin exam.' He starts shaking like a leaf, he's so nervous, and I can see he's truly bothered. There's this debate going on in his mind. 'Should I or shouldn't I?' He's actually trembling. He looks at me for two or three minutes and says nothing, but finally he acquiesces. He grabs the exam and makes some notes, and then hands it back. We all passed the exam, but I never knew if he was being one of the boys or simply yielding to temptation.

"Near the end of his stay at Portsmouth, he and I had a huge falling-out. A photograph of Rose Kennedy had appeared in *Life* magazine when I was home on vacation, and I recall my mother saying, 'She has so much lipstick on, she looks like a Hollywood star.' So at some point during the semester I repeated this, as a teenager would, to Bob. He went out of his mind. I can still hear him: 'How can you say such a thing?' He became so angry, and I didn't think it was so terrible. As a result he chased me outside around the dormitory. He had this streak of loyalty to his entire family, and the merest slight sufficed to set him off.

"Before I knew it, he had jumped on top of me and we were rolling around on the ground. I took the wrangle as a kind of joke, but Bob was completely into it. It ended our friendship, but then I knew him again when we were both students at Harvard, and he had cooled off. He didn't hold a grudge against me, which made me the great exception in his life. He seemed on the whole to have a memory like an elephant, and he rarely forgave anybody he felt had crossed him."

In mid-1941, while Robert was still at Portsmouth, Joseph Kennedy authorized a specialist to perform a prefrontal lobotomy on Rosemary, his eldest daughter, who had been exhibiting behavior problems. The surgery, which Joe approved without consulting Rose, failed horribly: it left Rosemary profoundly retarded and slightly paralyzed on her left side. Her father immediately made arrangements for her to enter a Catholic home for the mentally retarded in Wisconsin, where she has remained ever since. Occasionally, the nuns would take her to visit her mother.

The family created a mythology to explain Rosemary's abrupt disappearance. Future biographers would tell of Rosemary's "mood swings" and her increasingly unpredictable demeanor. They would trace her problems to damage done when Rose's legs were held together to delay childbirth until the doctor could be found. In reality, the young woman suffered from dyslexia and was unable, or unwilling, to conform to the clan's exuberant lifestyle.

According to Martin Evarts, an acquaintance of Joseph P. Kennedy, "the event left Bobby—and several of the other children—in a state of uncertainty. They were traumatized by Rosemary's sudden banishment. Although they adored their father, they began to see him as a sometimes ruthlessly controlling taskmaster. Rosemary's tragedy left a lifelong impression: one false move—or rather a pattern of erratic behavior—and you would be permanently removed from the family annals."

In September 1942 Robert Kennedy, then a junior, transferred from Portsmouth Priory to Milton Academy because his father believed Milton would better prepare the boy for an education at Harvard. At his new school, which was located just south of Boston in Milton, Massachusetts, Bobby lived in Forbes House, in a room that had once been occupied by T. S. Eliot. The student body at the "nonsectarian" institution consisted of a handful of Catholics, two or three Jews and the rest Protestants, most of Anglo-Saxon background.

His contemporaries at Milton recalled Bobby's shyness, his determination and his self-mocking sense of humor. The academy included a girls' school and, while there was no coeducation, there was social contact. "He used to walk with his head way down, buried in his neck, like a bird in a storm," remarked Mary (Piedy) Bailey, a student there at the time. "Appealing, funny, larky, separate and a little bit solitary. . . . Bobby mostly stood on one foot with the other one resting on top, his hands way down in his pockets." "Moonfaced" in those days, he "had a forelock that drooped over his right eye."

Bobby's shyness with women soon diminished. Samuel Adams, a classmate of Bobby's at Milton who became a Boston attorney, recalled an English girl named Jane Hodges, whom RFK dated his senior year. "We both liked her," said Adams, "but he was quicker about it than I was. One day we were thinking about going over to her dorm for tea, but Bobby said we shouldn't, we had some work to do. This seemed sensible, so I went to the library. Later, after I'd come home, in walked Bobby, his hair soaking wet. He was smiling. He'd been out in the rain, walking around with Jane. He loved that one-upmanship."

Adams first met Bobby through football. "We both made the second backfield in the fall of 1942, but in those days the first backfield played both ways and we saw action only as substitutes. Bobby ran every practice play and tackled and blocked dummies as if he were in a hard-fought game. To another sixteen-year-old kid this gung ho attitude seemed a little weird. But gradually, I became aware of the characteristic of Bobby's which I admired most—his ability to ridicule himself and his efforts and still go all out."

Football also provided the backdrop for Bobby's friendship with David Hackett, one of the best athletes ever to attend Milton. "Hackett had such glamour," said Mary Bailey, "that the littlest kids from the lower school would just mill around as though there were tin cans tied to him every place he went. . . . He'd never push you around or anything or be arrogant. He just had this incredible way about him so that people would stop and their jaws would hang open."

Hackett and Kennedy became the closest of comrades. In an oral history for the John F. Kennedy Library, Hackett said, "I think maybe my first impression of him was that we were both, in a way, misfits. He was a misfit because he'd come in toward the end. . . . My interests were, at that time, primarily in athletics and not in academics; I think, therefore, I was a little bit of a misfit. I think he was a bit of a misfit because of coming in both late and also because of who he was—he didn't fit into Milton easily."

Hackett later told Arthur M. Schlesinger, Jr., for *Robert Kennedy and His Times*: "He was neither a natural athlete nor a natural student nor a natural success with girls and had no natural gift for popularity. Nothing came easily for him. What he had was a set of handicaps and a fantastic determination to overcome them. The handicaps made him redouble his effort."

The two boys spent a lot of time in each other's rooms, wearing each other's clothes, wrestling, throwing things out the window. As Schlesinger observed, "Robert Kennedy was identified in the school as Hackett's friend, his best friend. This gave him status among his classmates. It also no doubt gave him new and needed reassurance about himself."

Bobby needed such encouragement, for he could not have reaped much confidence from his barely passing grades. In his second term at Milton, RFK received a C in English along with the remark: "He writes poorly; needs to learn the elements of expression; but he has a refreshing habit of asking 'How' and 'Why.' " French, C. Math, D: "Bob has been handicapped by a weakness in fundamentals." Physics, no grade: "Impossible to give any grade at this time for much is yet to be made up. On work of past two weeks, Bob is below the average of the class."

This undistinguished record earned Bobby a letter from Joe reminding him that Rose had received honors in school. "I don't know where I got my brains," answered Bobby in a rueful letter home, "but its [sic] quite evident I received them from neither my father nor my mother." In the same letter he joked about his poor performance in mathematics: "On the first day of school, the math teacher made a small speech to the class in which he said that two great things had happened to him: one that Rommel was surrounded in Egypt and 2nd that Kennedy had passed a math test."

Mathematics had long been a difficult subject for Bobby. George B. McCutcheon recalled the math teacher, Albert Norris, frequently looking at the lad and saying, "Kennedy, your mouth's open." Never an RFK admirer, McCutcheon further observed, "I was aghast when later Robert Kennedy obtained influence and a certain amount of power in this country. It came as a jolt to me. I wondered what this country was coming to."

Nor was McCutcheon RFK's only detractor at Milton. Classmate Nathaniel Preston reflected, "He seemed to me—surly is perhaps too strong a word, but it would apply from time to time. . . . I don't think it was an active, conscious thing on his part, but he wasn't interested in being helpful, he wasn't interested in being humane. . . . I found myself shaking my head in wonderment years later when I heard about this great friend of the downtrodden and that this was the same kid. There was nothing of that visible then."

Another classmate, Samuel Campbell, Jr., said of Bobby, "I think he had a lot determination. I don't think he was very gregarious. I don't think he went out of his way to make friends. He was sometimes reserved, I guess. I wouldn't say he had a chip on his shoulder, but he didn't get along with everyone. I think he was short-tempered, not hot-tempered. I think he irritated some people. I think some people thought he had a chip on his shoulder, a short fuse. . . . He was not a politician in the usual sense of the word, he wasn't looking for votes."

Hugh M. Watson, later an eminent physician, put it directly: "My impressions at the time were that I did not think of Bobby as someone who was destined for greatness. If you'd have asked me to pick out who in the class would be successful, he probably would not have been my choice. He seemed to me to be a late bloomer. I think—we're going back to when we were sixteen or seventeen years old—it came hard to him but I remember him as being steady and persistent though not brilliant, and I imagine some of the brilliance came out afterward at a time when I didn't know him."

B y the time Robert Kennedy began his senior year at Milton in the fall of 1943, both of his older brothers were engaged in hazardous World War II action as members of the navy: Joe was flying missions over the English Channel and Jack was serving on PT boats in the South Pacific.* Even Kathleen Kennedy had left for London to work in the rest-and-recreation clubs sponsored by the Red Cross for American GIs in England. Bobby longed to follow in his siblings' patriotic footsteps.

That October, therefore, six weeks before he turned eighteen, Bobby enlisted, signing up for a naval officers' training program. The program specified a year of college before starting military training, which would lead to a commission. A photograph of Bobby at the induction center (accompanied by his father) appeared in the press—"Kennedy's Third Son in Navy," read the headline in one paper.

Still a student at Milton when he enlisted, Bobby received a note about the publicity from Jack:

> The folks sent me a clipping of you taking the oath. The sight of you up there, just as a boy, was really moving, particularly as a close examination showed that you had my checked London coat on. I'd like to know what the hell I'm doing out here, while you go stroking around in my drape coat, but I suppose that what we are out here for—or so they tell us—is so that our sisters and younger brothers will be safe and secure. Frankly I don't see it quite that way—at least if you're going to be safe and secure, that's fine with me, but not in my coat, brother, not in my coat. . . .

*Jack's fabled *PT-109* exploit took place on August 1, 1943, when a Japanese destroyer rammed the boat he was commanding. According to legend, as described in books and on film, Kennedy personally saved most of the twelve-man crew. However, several eyewitnesses eventually emerged to throw doubt on the story, attributing it to exaggeration and outright fabrication.

Through his father's intervention, Bobby matriculated at Harvard in March 1944 and entered the university's V-12 naval training unit. In June he graduated formally from Milton Academy. During the ceremonies he could speak of nothing but his desire to join in battle on behalf of the Allies.

I n July 1944, Lieutenant Joseph P. Kennedy, Jr., volunteered for a perilous mission piloting a specially modified version of the cargo plane known as the PB4Y Liberator. In an effort to stop the V-1 rocket bombings that were inflicting so much damage on England, the PB4Y was to be loaded with explosives at an English base and flown toward the German rocket base in France. Just before the aircraft arrived at its target, the pilot and copilot would parachute into the Channel, where waiting boats would retrieve them; the plane would then be guided for the remaining few miles by a remote-control device located in an escort fighter.

On the morning of August 1, Joe Jr. and his copilot, Lieutenant Wilford J. Willy, took off in the Liberator, code-named "Zoot-Suit Black." They reached the coastline at an altitude of about two thousand feet, minutes from the position at which they were to parachute to safety. But suddenly a massive explosion engulfed the plane. Now, two of Bobby's siblings had been taken from him.

Years later, analysis of Nazi war documents revealed that the mission would have been pointless even if it had been completed: the German rocket base had by then been moved to another location. In 1972, one of Zoot-Suit Black's wings, and a piece of its fuselage, were discovered buried in a wood on the English coast. The bodies of the fliers were never found.

4

HARVARD DAYS, RESTLESS NIGHTS

When Robert F. Kennedy appeared at Harvard in March of 1944, the regular rhythms of academic life there had been disrupted. Combining regular course work with military training, students arrived at unusual times in the academic calendar and departed according to the obligations of service. Harvard Yard bustled with uniforms—naval uniforms, in particular—as the elite institution did its part to aid the nation's war effort.

The recruits in the mysteriously named V-12 program were placed in two "houses," as dormitories are called at Harvard: Kirkland and Eliot. Living in Eliot House among his fellow trainees, Bobby nonetheless, as at his previous schools, found social contact difficult in the new environment. "I am now sitting in my room by myself with no friends, wishing I were back at Milton," he wrote to David Hackett, who still attended the prep school.

The homesick freshman also stayed in close touch with his parents, sending frequent letters describing life in and out of the lecture hall. Of his roommate he quipped: "His name is Hans Anguelmueller so you can see he is not very Irish." Concerning his studies he expressed anxiety; his father replied with words of reassurance and encouragement:

> I think you have developed a maturity in the last year that is surprisingly good. Previous to that time I don't think any real strides had been made. I don't think I'd be thinking too much about what's going to happen three, four, or six months from today. The important thing is to do a good job now and every day. After all, you've got your life ahead of you and heaven knows it's going to require all the brains anyone has to work out a satisfactory existence, and the only way to do that is to be well prepared, so stick in there and work as hard as you possibly can.

Before long, Bobby began making friends. As always, new acquaintances were struck by his love of athletics and by the relentless energy and enthusiasm he employed to compensate for his short stature. Edward Zak, a student at the time, observed: "I knew Robert Kennedy at Harvard in 1944, the only year I spent there. We met at a party at Eliot House. He was on the small side—five nine, one hundred forty pounds—but he was an avid sportsman who played football, tennis, even golf. He and I played golf together once. He shot about a ninety; I must have shot nearly twice that, I figure.

"Like many other Harvard students of the time, Robert attended the V-12 program. Nobody knew quite what V-12 meant, but it was the equivalent of NROTC, the Naval Reserve Officers' Training Corps. In those days, because of the war, you did the program and went straight into the navy. And that's exactly what RFK wanted. He seemed impatient to serve. He didn't like the idea of training. He wanted to see some action."

D day came and went. Joe Jr. was killed. Meanwhile, the dead hero's restless kid brother continued to train and to wait. In the early fall of 1944 he invited several of his companions in the V-12 unit to Hyannis Port, where an atmosphere of grief hung over the Kennedy residence. "Several of us went up to Bobby's house on the Cape," remembered Paul Alcott, one of the visitors. "The family was still in mourning over Joe Jr.'s recent death. The father spent hours in his bedroom listening to the operas of Richard Wagner. I thought this rather odd since Joe had died fighting the Germans. Anyway, several of us, including Bobby, were outside tossing around a football. I guess we were making too much noise, because his mother appeared and told us to tone it down. She then turned her stare to Bobby and bellowed, 'Don't you have any respect for your dead brother?' Thoroughly embarrassed, he went white as a sheet."

In November 1944, Apprentice Seaman Robert F. Kennedy, Class V-12, United States Naval Reserve, was transferred to Bates College, in Lewiston, Maine, for further V-12 training. The nineteen-year-old spent the winter on the icy campus, which the navy had appropriated for its wartime needs. Whereas at Harvard Bobby's course work included both civilian and military subjects, here his classes were strictly naval: advanced seamanship, damage control and engineering, piloting, celestial navigation.

Another change from Harvard came in the form of good grades, which earned him the praise of his father: "I congratulate you on your marks," wrote Joe. ". . . By the look of some of those subjects of yours, I know that I would never be able to get even an E." Bobby won the respect of his outfit, too, receiving appointment as a platoon leader. His spare time was filled with activity: he went to mass at a local church, he played basketball, he joined his unit's ski team, he dated a number of girls. Still, he itched to enter the fight. When he heard that a friend might soon ship out, he wrote David Hackett that "the possibility makes me feel more & more like a Draft Dodger."

Haven W. Hammond, another Bates trainee, initially perceived RFK "as a puny little kid in a white sailor suit. He seemed isolated and despondent when he first arrived, no doubt because of the death of his brother. Later his bitterness wore off and he became more sociable.

"But, as I say, at the beginning he was in his cups and quite disturbed about being at Bates. He wanted to get out to sea. He wanted to be in the war because one older brother had died in the war and the other was still fighting. He had to show his father he was as tough as they were.

"There was another factor at work as well. I think Bobby felt inferior to the rest of us in the program because we already had some sea experience behind us. In addition, he came from a moneyed background and most of us didn't, so he felt as though he had bought himself a commission. It added to his feeling of uncertainty. And it didn't help that we were always borrowing money from him. The moment our checks would come, he'd be on top of us: 'Hey, give me back my five bucks.'

"He was seeing a girl from Pittsburgh named Betty Blackburn, whom he'd met on the Cape. She went to Sarah Lawrence College. I remember once going to a party with him and Betty, and he became extremely agitated because she was dancing with some other guy. He occasionally dated other girls as well. But if you asked him about his dates, he clammed up and got very defensive.

"Bobby had a Jekyll and Hyde nature. You never knew quite what to expect. I was master of arms in our dormitory, and one day when his room was rather messy I said to him, 'You better straighten up that room, or you might get reported.' He looked at me. He was the platoon leader, and he didn't like my tone. 'If you report me,' he snapped, 'then you'll probably be out of step when we march.' He had already developed that venomous bite for which he would later become famous."

In June of 1945, with the war in Europe at an end, Robert Kennedy was moved back to Harvard for yet more officer's training. Months later, after Japan's surrender, hope finally emerged for the anxious youth to get to sea. During autumn, the navy commissioned a new destroyer named after Bobby's late brother. On February 1, 1946—again through the intercession of his father—Bobby left the NROTC unit, forgoing his commission, and joined the *Joseph P. Kennedy, Jr.* as a seaman on its maiden voyage.

The vessel set sail, headed for the American naval base at Guantánamo, Cuba. Rough seas the first day out produced "a very sea sick crew," Bobby wrote his parents, "but your No. 7 passed the test in true Kennedy fashion & held on to his stomach." After reaching Cuba, the ship cruised the warm waters of the Caribbean around the island. Meeting the other crewmen, most of whom were southerners and unlike the people he generally knew, produced in RFK a revelation: they "have a lot of something, a lot of those guys at Harvard lacked," he wrote a friend.

Disappointed that the war had passed him by, the young sailor held no illusions of heroism. About halfway through the cruise, he wrote his parents that he'd been shifted "from the lowest grade of chippers, painters & scrubbers, the 2nd Division, up into one of the highest grades of chippers, painters & scrubbers, the I [for Intelligence] division. . . . I am sure if the fact that Robert Kennedy was in the Intelligence Division of one of the U.S. Navy's fighting ships was made known to the public women & children would sleep more comfortably in their beds." By early spring, he was rotated back to the States.

Despite his ardent desires, Robert Kennedy never had the chance to equal his brothers' combat records. His service to his country during the Second World War consisted of some two years of training at New England colleges and some dozen weeks of swabbing decks aboard a ship sailing little more than a hundred miles off the U.S. coast, months after the conflict had ceased.

On May 30, 1946, the navy issued him an honorable discharge.

With his eldest son dead, Joseph Kennedy anointed the next in line to lead the family's younger generation into the world of politics. In 1946, therefore, with the eager support of his father, John F. Kennedy announced his candidacy for the United States Congress. Jack had lived most of the last twenty years in and around New York City, but for the run he returned to the Boston area, where he and his father had been born, and where both his grandfathers had practiced the political trade.

One of those grandfathers had lived to see the baton's passing. Ever energetic at eighty-three, Honey Fitz maintained an active presence in the campaign, chomping on his cigars and spinning yarns for his cronies and anyone else who'd listen. The more consequential relative was the candidate's father. Joe engineered the campaign from headquarters at the Ritz Hotel, where he worked the phones and doled out the funds, channeling his anguish over Joe Jr. into ambition for Jack.

As Bobby Kennedy's stint in the navy wound down, he, too, began to spend time on the family project. At first, the candidate expected little from his younger brother. Paul "Red" Fay, Jr., a friend of Jack's from the navy, recounted Robert's first visit to the campaign:

"One day word came that Bobby Kennedy had gotten leave from the Navy and was coming up to help Jack in the campaign for the weekend," wrote Fay in his memoir of JFK, titled *The Pleasure of His Company*.

> "It's damn nice of Bobby wanting to help," Jack told me, "but I can't see that sober, silent face breathing new vigor into the ranks. The best plan is to make it known to the press. One picture of the two brothers together will show that we're all in this for Jack. Then you take Bobby out to the movies or whatever you two want to do."
>
> "Fine," I said. I decided I would take Bobby to a movie house in Boston that also featured vaudeville.
>
> Young Bobby arrived. I knew he was there only because I could see him. Words came out of his mouth as if each one spoken depleted an already severely limited supply.
>
> When I suggested the movie and vaudeville, his reply was a quiet, expressionless "All right." Off we went, with me trying my best to make conversation. Bobby's total contribution was an occasional "yes" or "no."
>
> Once we reached the theater, the movie gave me a chance to break off the struggle to keep communication alive. Then the vaudeville began. After several tumbling and juggling acts, a comedian came on stage. He was hilarious. Certain that I had made a good choice for a place to entertain my ward for the evening, I looked over to make sure he was enjoying this as much as I was. From his expression, he might have been paying his last respects to his closest friend.
>
> I turned back toward the stage, with my enthusiasm markedly reduced. When three more uproarious jokes failed to raise a chuckle from my partner for the evening, I suddenly found all my own pleasure draining away. About ten minutes of this was all I could handle.
>
> "Shall we go?" I asked Bobby.
>
> Without hesitation, he got up and the two of us filed out in absolute silence.
>
> As we came out of the theater that day, I would have cheerfully taken bets against the possibility that I would ever volunteer to spend an hour with Bobby Kennedy again.

The key to the race in the overwhelmingly Democratic Eleventh Congressional District was the June primary; the general election in November served only to ratify the party's nominee. The district encompassed parts of Boston proper—East Boston and the North End—and extended into the neighboring municipalities of Charlestown, Somerville and Cambridge. Laboring full-time in the campaign once his commitment to the navy ended, Bobby opted to work in Cambridge, "the place where Jack Kennedy was least known," recalled David F. Powers, a local man who joined the '46 run and remained a Kennedy political aide on into the White House. "At least it was the place where our number one opponent was the strongest. The candidate from Cambridge was Michael Neville, and he had been mayor of Cambridge and a member of the legislature, and all of your pros were already with him. And it was strange, you know, Bobby could have worked in Charlestown with me or he could have worked in Somerville . . . but he wanted to go to Cambridge where he thought it would be the toughest. He volunteered for that area and he was assigned it."

Jack gave over Bobby to the care of Lem Billings, who headed the operation's Cambridge office. Jack's closest friend from Choate, the Connecticut prep school JFK had attended from 1928 to 1933, Billings found Bobby less than docile in accepting his authority. "I remember Bobby showing up and he was still in his sailor suit," he later commented. "He wanted to do something and it's funny that Bobby showed his aggressive strong nature even then. Bobby and I were great friends—I'd known him ever since he was a kid. He came and started working with me in Cambridge. He didn't want to work under me in Cambridge. Very shortly he wanted to go out on his own."

Of eleven wards in the city, noted Billings, Bobby "took over three. Those were his and he didn't want me to get into them at all. . . . As I recall, it was the poorest part of Cambridge. I'll never forget it—Bobby wouldn't let me near the place."

Joe and Honey Fitz handled the traditional pols, but Jack and his cadre of inexperienced, avid young workers tailored their message to a different audience. Detecting opportunity in the district's large number of newly mustered-out veterans, they saw that every one of them received a reprint of John Hersey's 1944 *Reader's Digest* article about the *PT-109*. To appeal to women, Jack depended on his good looks, as well as the help of his sisters Jean and Eunice.

John F. Kennedy had filled his staff with friends; Jean and Eunice enlisted personnel, too, including Ethel Skakel, of Greenwich, Connecticut. RFK had met Ethel, Jean's roommate at Manhattanville College, the previous Christmas vacation—Jean had brought her along on a family ski holiday at Mont Tremblant in Quebec. Now Ethel and her older sister

Patricia assisted Bobby, doing chores around his tiny East Cambridge office, handing out leaflets with him, ringing doorbells.

Mostly Italian and working-class, Bobby's wards were not considered friendly territory to a candidate who'd graduated from Harvard courtesy of a millionaire father, or to the office seeker's sheltered, unproven brother. Jack and Joe would have been satisfied with a four-to-one margin of defeat in East Cambridge against local favorite Neville. But Bobby defied expectations. He worked the streets tirelessly, eating spaghetti with the adults, playing sports with the children. The locals were impressed. "When Bobby showed up in East Cambridge," recalled Joe DeGug, the area's political boss, "I assigned my brother Lawrence to go around with him in the three wards we were supervising. What they did, they went around and met the kids, and played a lot of touch football with them. It had the effect of proving the Kennedys weren't snobs—that Bobby was willing to pal around with them. And Bobby made a lot of friends in East Cambridge."

When the primary vote was taken, JFK nearly beat Neville in Bobby's sectors. With large pluralities in other parts of the district, Jack swept to a victory.

The election constituted a success for Robert Kennedy as well. He surprised not only the poor residents of Italian neighborhoods; he also caught off guard the members of his own family. Ironically, the activities that gratified his relatives took place when he was out from under their gaze. As he'd started to learn during his months aboard the navy destroyer, Bobby had an affinity for people of social classes lower than his own. In his first taste of politics, taciturn, awkward Bobby had seemingly drawn water from a stone. He'd begun to earn the respect of his brother and his father.

With Joe Jr. gone and Jack launched on a public career, it was Bobby's turn to grow up. He had been at college and served in the military; now he set out to remake himself in the image of the father whose approval he longed for so intensely. Joseph Kennedy frowned on the expression of emotion, so the gentle, vulnerable boy began to form a leathery shell. Tenderness submerged beneath caution, diffidence was hidden away in competitiveness that grew even more fervent. He allowed his feelings to surface only if couched in self-mockery—the sole acceptable way, according to the Kennedy code. From these days to the end of his life, he revealed his inner self only to his most intimate acquaintances—and not even always to them.

After the primary, with the summer free before his scheduled return to Harvard in the fall, RFK embarked on a grand tour of Latin America—his first lengthy trip, with the exception of his naval cruise, taken without members of his family. As described by Arthur Schlesinger in his RFK biography, Bobby traveled with Lem Billings—they visited Brazil, Uruguay, Argentina, Chile, Peru, Panama, and Mexico. Billings found Bobby a bit vexing at times. At Rio de Janeiro, their first stop, Bobby annoyed his friend by bathing late at night at deserted Copacabana Beach. Billings, who liked to drink, found it cloying that his companion would imbibe nothing stronger than Coca-Cola, one reason being his desire to claim the two-thousand-dollar reward his father offered to any of his children who refrained from the use of tobacco and alcohol until their twenty-first birthday.

In late summer, the two travelers arrived in New York. Their brief stay provided the opportunity to take care of the one vital element still missing in Bobby's assent to manhood, Kennedy-style. Joseph P. Kennedy's antipathy toward whiskey and cigarettes did not carry over to another vice. He delegated responsibility to Billings, who'd proven himself capable once before:

"There was a cat house on Sugar Hill at the edge of Harlem," said Billings years later, "where I had once taken Jack when he lost his virginity. It was a rite of passage the old man, Joe Kennedy, Sr., approved of. He kept telling his sons to get laid as often as possible, married or not. Naive and innocent, Bobby was nearly twenty-one and still a virgin—in his father's eyes, that simply wouldn't do.

"So I took him to the same cat house where I had taken Jack. The girl was different. Bobby's was a light-skinned Negro, very tall, very slender. But beautiful. She had the figure of a ballerina. I paid her and told her to be gentle. I knew the old man would want a blow-by-blow description, but Bobby didn't talk much about it afterwards. He said only that he could feel her rib cage and that it wasn't all it had been cooked up to be. 'It wasn't bad, but it wasn't fabulous either,' is all he kept saying.

"The old man reimbursed me the money I'd laid out."

In September 1946, the campus of Harvard College teemed with veterans. With war's end, every dormitory suite held at least one extra man, and those who'd arrived in Cambridge late slept for a time on cots arranged on a basketball court. Lines were the norm at the dining hall and at the library; in classrooms, individuals jockeyed for choice seats in the aisles and on windowsills. Students varied widely in age and experience, so that thirty-year-olds who'd trudged through the Ardennes now strolled to study hall next to boys who'd barely begun to shave.

With partial credit granted for his V-12 course work, Robert F. Kennedy reentered Harvard as a junior and was assigned to a room in Winthrop House. For the next two years, his studies again failed to excite him. Registered for the lectures of a number of well-known professors—C. H. McIlwain, Roscoe Pound, Payson S. Wild, Bruce Hopper, among others—he cut class often, leaving virtually no impression with his professors. At Bates, he'd earned good marks; now he reverted to form, scoring "gentleman's C's," coupled with D's in Anglo-American Law and in the Principles of Economics. He spent much of his junior year on academic probation.

Officially, RFK's field of concentration at Harvard was government. In fact, he majored in football, living and breathing the sport, forming most of his friendships among his teammates. One of those players was Kenneth P. O'Donnell, the younger brother of the team's captain and the son of the football coach at Holy Cross. O'Donnell, who became a lifelong confidant to Bobby and served as Jack's presidential appointments secretary, depicted Bobby's football career in *That Shining Hour*, a collection of reminiscences about the Kennedys edited by Patricia Kennedy Lawford: "I met Robert F. Kennedy in September, 1946, in the locker room of the Dillon Field House. I had just returned from Europe, with the end of the war. . . .

"By this time, the G.I. Bill allowed even the poorest of boys to seek an education in our best universities and Harvard was overflowing with the finest collection of athletes to be found anywhere. The Harvard squad was inundated with transfers from all over the United States—most of the boys had played some one or two years at Notre Dame, Wisconsin, etc. When Bobby reported for practice, he found himself faced with the biggest and most talented group of ends that the University had ever gathered. Because of Bobby's size, the coach exhibited very little interest in him, and consigned him to sixth or seventh squad which is, as generally understood in college football, the end. The varsity coaches never see you again."

Bobby persevered. He arrived for practice an hour before the others and stayed an hour later. During scrimmages he blocked and tackled ferociously. By midfall, he'd risen to the varsity. By season's end, he'd impressed his teammates sufficiently to be made a member of the Varsity Club.

Bobby's congeniality with his fellow ballplayers, most of whom hailed from poor families, took time to develop. Initially, they dismissed the ambassador's son as a pest, an inferior athlete who had no business hanging around them. Even as his determination won them over, they remained puzzled by the behavior of a rich kid who affected poverty. "We'd go on trips," said one teammate, "and he never had any money and whatever it was I'd pay." His apparel hardly matched his economic status. "His clothes were awful," recalled Wally Flinn, another player. "He never wanted anybody to think he was a stuffed shirt. He never got dressed up. You know, he'd have a tweed sport coat, but he might not have a necktie on unless he was going someplace special. We all wore sweaters occasionally—his would have holes. And he wore sneakers. Let me tell you, if you saw him walking through Harvard Square, you would have died laughing. He looked like a bag of rags."

Nor did Bobby's car evince his wealth. "It was an old Chrysler convertible," said Flinn. "His father bought all of his cars from the Chrysler Corporation in those days. And this thing was a wreck.

"Now, Bobby had one very bad habit, he drove too fast. And he made me terribly nervous. I remember driving down to Cape Cod one time, just the two of us. We were going down there under the pretense of studying for our finals that particular semester. Bobby informed me that the tires of this jalopy were practically bald. He told me that under the law of averages, either he or his brother Jack would be killed in a car accident. 'Well,' I asked him, 'please do it sometime when I'm not with you.' That was the end of that conversation."

For his final year at Harvard, Bobby moved into the Varsity Club. His roommate there was Paul Lazzaro, who later called him "one of the sweetest fellows I ever knew, not at all the ruthless politician he supposedly became but genuinely kind and caring." Charles Glynn, also a football player, accompanied Bobby on monthly visits to his illustrious grandfather's suite at the old Bellevue Hotel in downtown Boston. "Honey Fitz was a well-known Bostonian character," recollected Glynn. "He had a lisp, but he talked up a storm. He and Bobby had a wonderful relationship. He would take his grandson down to the bar and order drinks, but Bobby didn't like alcohol. Honey Fitz would kid him: 'What kind of Irishman are you?' Anyway, Honey Fitz would drink and to everyone's delight would tell one dirty joke and story after another. He could talk for hours. But he would tell the dirty stories in a soft whisper. It was very funny, and there was something extremely touching about Bobby and his grandfather."

Evenings, Bobby and his friends would gather around the training table and discuss, in Ken O'Donnell's words, "football, politics and girls. Occasionally, the order was reversed." Well prepared by his boyhood of conversations around Joe Kennedy's dinner table, Bobby, along with O'Donnell, led the debates. The two rarely agreed: O'Donnell, the all-out New Deal liberal, saw things differently than Robert, who generally adhered to the views of his isolationist father.

In the fall of 1947, the dinnertime chatter turned from the theoretical posturing of undergraduates to the consideration of a practical problem. Scheduled to play the University of Virginia, the team booked rooms in a Charlottesville hotel. However, the inn refused accommodations to one team member, a tackle named Chester Pierce, because he was black. The white players, including Robert Kennedy, united around Pierce, threatening to cancel the game if all of them weren't allowed to sleep under the same roof. The hotel relented and the team made the trip.

For the 1947 opener against Western Maryland, Bobby was promoted to the starting lineup. While he had many close friends on the team, some still resented him: it "was a gyp," one complained; "there were better players on the team." Dick Harlow, the head coach, thought little of the grumbling. "He had more zip," he later said, "he was the toughest kid, pound for pound, and what he didn't do with his body he did with his heart. That's why he played regularly."

RFK's season began with promise—during the Western Maryland game he caught a touchdown pass from O'Donnell, and the team won, 47–0. But just days later, he got hurt. "We were scrimmaging," recalled O'Donnell, "and he and I were playing side by side, missing block after block. The coach was raging at me, and I was raging at [Bobby]. After nearly half an hour, Bob collapsed on the field. He had been playing with a broken leg all of that time." Bobby sat out the rest of the season, except for the finale, against Yale, when Coach Harlow inserted him for the last few plays so that he could earn his letter. Despite the huge cast covering his leg, Bobby threw himself onto the closing pileup. Robert Kennedy, like his first-baseman father, had lettered at Harvard. His older brothers had not.

RFK's love life at Harvard won him no awards. The closest he had to a steady girlfriend was Patricia Skakel, whose sister Ethel he also saw occasionally. The younger girl resisted the role of second fiddle—when Bobby invited Pat to Palm Beach during his senior year, Ethel finagled her own invitation from Jean Kennedy.

Among the other women Robert dated, one unwittingly made clear that the prostitute in Harlem had omitted some points from his lesson. "Bobby was strange about girls," chuckled Charles Glynn. "I recall a female he took out—her name was Shirley Flowers and she was Miss Lynn, Massachusetts, of 1946. Five or six of us gathered in the Varsity Club and Bobby was very nervous: 'What should I do? Where should I take her? How do I handle it?' He had never done much dating. So we said, 'What you do is, you take her to the movies'—in those days it was a big thing to do—'and then you take her out for a drink.' 'I don't drink,' he said, and he didn't at the time. 'Well, take her somewhere,' we replied.

"So the next day he reports to us. 'How did it go?' we asked him. 'I don't know. She kisses funny.' 'What do you mean she kisses funny?' 'Well, she put her tongue in my mouth.'

" 'Bobby,' we said, 'you've got it made.' "

In March 1948, the same month he graduated from Harvard, Robert F. Kennedy departed for a tour of Europe and the Middle East. Ostensibly traveling as a foreign correspondent for the *Boston Post*—Joe Kennedy had pulled the necessary strings—Bobby, accompanied by college friend George Terrien, visited Israel and Jordan during the British withdrawal, Greece during its civil war, Czechoslovakia just after the death of Jan Masaryk, and Berlin during the airlift. Other ports of call included Istanbul, Brussels, Amsterdam, Vienna, Copenhagen, Stockholm, Dublin, London and Rome. Over the course of the journey, the fledgling reporter filed some half dozen dispatches back to Boston.

The two young men were staying at the Grand Hotel in Rome when they received tragic news: Kathleen, Bobby's captivating twenty-eight-year-old sister, had perished in a plane crash near Lyons, France, on May 13.

While serving with the American Red Cross during the war, Kathleen Kennedy—nicknamed "Kick"—had met and fallen in love with William Cavendish, the Marquess of Hartington and eldest son of the Duke of Devonshire. Rose Kennedy opposed the match—not only was Cavendish Protestant, relatives of his had been viceroys in Ireland during British rule. Nonetheless, on May 6, 1944, with the reluctant blessing of the bride's parents, the couple were wed in a civil ceremony in London. By September, the groom was dead, killed in action in Belgium.

The young widow returned to her family in America, but just after the war she went back to London, where she bought a town house in Smith Square and began an affair with another wealthy Protestant aristocrat. By her parents' standards, eighth earl Peter Fitzwilliam made an even less suitable mate than Billy Cavendish: the new beau was married, with a daughter, and had a notorious reputation as a playboy. With the earl resolved to divorce his alcoholic wife, Kathleen pleaded with her scandalized family to approve their betrothal. Rose stood fast, threatening never to see her daughter again if she went through with her plan. Desperate, Kick petitioned her father, who agreed to meet the pair in Paris.

While waiting for Joe to arrive in France, Kathleen and Peter decided to fly to Cannes for a few days on the Riviera. En route, the small private plane encountered a thunderstorm and crashed, killing both passengers as well as the pilot and copilot.

Joseph P. Kennedy escorted his daughter's body from France to London for a May 20 funeral at the Immaculate Conception Church. Later that day, Kathleen was laid to rest in a graveyard at Chatsworth, her late husband's ancestral estate in the Derbyshire countryside. Hundreds of mourners had attended the rite, including Anthony Eden, Randolph Churchill and Lady Astor. Of Kick Kennedy's immediate family, the only representative was her ashen-faced father.

Shortly after the burial Bobby arrived in London, where he met William Douglas-Home, a British playwright who'd been a friend of Kathleen's. Hoping to lift the spirits of the bereaved young American, the dramatist gave Bobby tickets to see his long-running play *The Chiltern Hundreds*. Backstage at the Vaudeville Theatre after the show, RFK was introduced to Joan Winmill, the female lead. Their ensuing romance is detailed by Jerry Oppenheimer in *The Other Mrs. Kennedy*, an intriguing biography of Ethel Kennedy.

Bobby was smitten by the blond-haired, hazel-eyed starlet. Although only twenty-one, she was sexy and sophisticated, a far cry from the girls he'd dated at Harvard. For her part, she later professed to have felt love at first sight for the freckle-faced young man with the toothy grin. Bobby suggested dinner the next evening; Joan accepted without hesitation.

As their relationship progressed, word seeped back to Bobby's father. Joe exploded, fearing that publicity over the entanglement might do harm to Jack's future in Washington. But the enraptured young man treated his father's remonstrations with scorn. Bobby had worked in politics, he'd lettered at Harvard—what better way to further emulate his famous father than to carry on with an actress?

All the same, Bobby exercised discretion. He and Joan rarely ventured out where they might draw the attention of the press. Instead, he routinely picked her up at the theater after each night's performance. Crossing the street to the Savoy Hotel, they would dine in a quiet corner of the restaurant. The two would then adjourn to Kathleen's house in Smith Square.

The liaison continued the entire summer, interrupted only by Bobby's brief return to the Continent to complete his stint as journalist. In August, about to board the *Queen Mary* for the voyage back to the States, Bobby embraced his lover and told her not to cry, he'd return to England the following summer. He couldn't stay away from her, he declared.

He never saw her again.

5

ETHEL SKAKEL KENNEDY

Robert F. Kennedy completed his bachelor's degree without a clear blueprint in mind for his future. Despite his summer as roving reporter, he never seriously considered a career in journalism; rather, he settled on law school as a logical, if uncompelling, next step. His atrocious grades precluded admission to Harvard Law—even considering his family's influence at the institution*—so he applied to business school and even joked about pursuing dentistry. The University of Virginia School of Law, however, known as a magnet for the less-than-accomplished sons of well-heeled parents, saved him from a life in the boardroom or behind a drill. With his academic transcript offset by his birth certificate, he was accepted to begin there in the fall.

When RFK arrived in Charlottesville in September 1948, he did not present an imposing figure. Gerald Tremblay, who also enrolled at that time, remembered Bobby's first day on the Virginia campus: "He showed up in a rather old convertible, a Chrysler that his father had given to him. He was dressed in an old pair of khakis, and he . . . looked like a young guy in his first year of college, more than a young guy coming down to law school."

Bobby's accommodations were as modest as his appearance. To start, he rented a flat at the Jack Jouett Apartments. Then, he and a roommate "moved out to a little tiny tenant house . . . ," recalled Tremblay, "which was about, oh, maybe, thirty or forty feet from the railroad track. Every

---

*Joseph Kennedy's connection to the law school in particular was striking: the dean, James M. Landis, had worked for Joe at the SEC and now served as a trustee of several Kennedy trust funds. Bobby's grades must have been low indeed, compared to those of the average applicant, for his father to have been unable to work his usual magic.

time a train went by, the whole place shook. It didn't have central heat. It just sort of had a space heater. It had a little kitchen, a living room . . . and two rather small bedrooms. That was it, a little tin-roofed place. He always had a dog. At that time he had a great big . . . German police dog."

The study of law came no more easily to Bobby than had the undergraduate study of government. But this time, Bobby applied himself. "It was like everything he had done, it was like trying to make the football team at Harvard all over again," commented Charles "Chuck" Spalding, a family friend. "I don't think it was easy for him. I was conscious that he was spending long hours studying, that it was tough going." Although he never rose to the highest ranks of academic achievers, RFK did succeed in shedding the happy-go-lucky jock image of his Harvard years. Mortimer M. Caplin, then a professor of corporate finance and taxation who went on to serve as commissioner of the Internal Revenue Service in the Kennedy administration, recalled that Bobby "didn't volunteer much in discussions. He was a tough-minded sort of fellow, quiet—he didn't really sparkle in class. But he was likable, in a tough sort of way, and he was a good, strong student."

If Bobby didn't scintillate as an attorney-in-training, his years in law school were exciting nevertheless, for in the fall of 1948 he began in earnest his courtship of Ethel Skakel.

Bobby's lukewarm romance with Patricia Skakel fizzled when she became enamored of a young Irish architect by the name of Luan Cuffe. Shedding few tears over the lost attachment, Bobby quickly turned his affections to the boisterous, irrepressible girl he had barely noticed previously. Without delay, Robert and Ethel fell in love. Soon they were spending almost every weekend together, with Bobby coming to be a familiar face at the Manhattanville campus and Ethel growing equally recognizable on the grounds of UVA. The exuberant coed brought animation to the life of the young law student—a refreshing new spirit he urgently needed. "As a couple, they were vibrant and such fun!" remembered Lem Billings. "And it was Ethel who provided most of the vibrancy. Bobby remained distressed for many months about the death of Kathleen, coming as it did after Joe Jr.'s demise. The Kennedys had now suffered two great losses—three, if you include Rosemary—and it told on all of them. Nobody said anything, but there was an air of heaviness. I remember Bobby lightening up only when he and Ethel were together.

"Ethel had a good effect on Bobby. She was two years his junior but seemed more mature in certain ways. She had a lot of spunk and a biting sense of humor. In that respect, she resembled the other Kennedy girls.

She wasn't beautiful, but she had a great smile, a lot of teeth, tremendous verve and energy. She also had athletic ability. To Bobby's chagrin, she regularly beat him on the tennis court. She could sail, play touch football, hit a softball as well as, if not better than, any of the guys. Once, while Bobby was at quarterback, she blocked Teddy so violently that he sprained an ankle and displaced an elbow. In other words, she could put you out of commission."

She fit into her new family immediately. "She wasn't afraid of Joe Kennedy," Billings continued. "He liked to heckle both his kids and their friends, but Ethel heckled him right back. 'Instead of jeering from the sideline, Joe,' she once said during a game, 'why don't you come out here and toss the ball around with us?' He admired her for it. She had guts. She and all the other Kennedy girls were always falling over each other to get hold of the football. It was a far cry from the kind of rarefied antics Jackie Bouvier later brought into the family. No fox hunting or china collections for Ethel. And she preferred hot dogs and barbecued chicken to pâté de foie gras and finger sandwiches."

Ethel Skakel was born on April 11, 1928, in Chicago, Illinois, to parents who both hailed from dysfunctional families. George Skakel, born in Chicago in 1892, hated his alcoholic father, Curtis, a wretched failure in business who beat his wife, Gracie, in front of their three children. At age fourteen, George left his family in Tyndall, South Dakota, where they had lived for a decade, and returned to the Windy City to stay with his wealthy uncle, whose success the boy would replicate many times over. Outgoing, bright, and ambitious, George didn't bother to finish high school, but instead set about making his fortune. In his first full-time job, he worked as a freight-rate clerk for the Chicago, Milwaukee & St. Paul Railway. Then he became a salesman for a coal supplier, the William Howe Company, where he impressed not only his employer but also a fellow employee by the name of Ann Brannack. The pretty blonde secretary made an unlikely sweetheart for George for two reasons: first, her height—she towered over him; second, her religion—she was a devout Roman Catholic, and George's staunch Protestant parents despised followers of the pope.

Margaret Brannack, Ann's mother, had been born Episcopalian, but she converted to Catholicism when Ann was ten and thereafter raised the girl to be a passionate soldier for the Church. Ann's father, Joe, offered little to the family aside from his surly drunkenness—the strapping Irishman held a series of menial jobs and eventually moved out of the family apartment on Chicago's blue-collar South Side. When not attending mass with Ann and Ann's younger sister, after whom Ethel would be named, Margaret would tutor the girls in the domestic arts, teaching them sewing and cleaning, holding contests to see who could bake the most delicious cakes. Ann finished high school, then entered a secretarial institute, where she excelled in typing and shorthand.

Curt Skakel died a drinker's death in January 1917, but Gracie Skakel was still alive and she bitterly opposed her son's intention to marry a Catholic. Ann refused to be defeated. Recognizing George's potential, she persisted in her pursuit of the prize and eventually won it. George adored his funny, rambunctious girlfriend, and anyway had already begun to distance himself from his parents' bigotry. With no strong religious convictions of his own, he even acceded to Ann's demand that they be married by a priest. Father Edward Mallon performed the ceremony on November 25, 1917, at St. Mary's Church. A simple meal followed.

The newlyweds set up housekeeping—together with George's mother-in-law, who would reside with the couple the rest of her life—in Chicago's Irish ghetto. The following spring, with the nation at war, George joined the naval reserve. By the time he came home eight months later, he and Ann had a two-month-old daughter. They had named the baby Georgeann, after themselves, because at the time they planned on only one child. The strategy was short-lived: over the next fifteen years the couple added six more offspring, for a final total of three boys and four girls.

George's old job at the William Howe Company was waiting for him when he returned from the service, but he stayed barely long enough to clean out his desk. In May of 1919, he and two partners each put up a thousand dollars to form their own coal distributorship, the Great Lakes Coal & Coke Company. The enterprise prospered immediately, its swift start ensured by the connections of one of George's colleagues, who signed the Standard Oil Company as the new venture's first customer. Within a few years, George had made enough money to buy his wife a lakefront estate and a brand-new Packard, which she drove to daily shopping sprees at Chicago's most elegant shops. The former typist, who had been trained by her mother to iron and cook, soon became a favorite client of the city's antiques dealers.

Thanks largely to the phenomenal business acumen of George Skakel, the Great Lakes Coal & Coke Company mushroomed into one of the largest privately held companies in America. All his life, George remained secretive about his wealth, refusing interviews, shunning all press coverage. But by the time Ethel was a little girl, her father was rumored to be one of the richest men in the country. Like the Kennedys, the

Skakels noticed the depression only in the lowered wages needed to attract good servants.

The opulence of the family's surroundings, however, came at a price to its psyche. The limitless energy that George poured into his business, along with Ann's increasingly frenetic whirl of social activities, meant that the Skakel children were raised mostly by a series of nurses and governesses—the only constant family authority was provided by the youngsters' live-in grandmother. When George wasn't burning the midnight oil at the office he was on the road, seeing to accounts nationwide. His wife usually accompanied him, shopping her way across the country, so that the children often didn't see their parents for two to three months at a stretch.

More and more, the trips took the couple to New York, until George finally decided to relocate there, booking space for his executive offices in the newly constructed Empire State Building. (The company's operations departments remained in Chicago.) In June 1933 he hauled his family east, including five-year-old Ethel, her five older siblings and her four-month-old sister. The brood spent the summer on the Jersey shore, then moved to a furnished mansion in Larchmont, a wealthy community in Westchester County. Set on some dozen acres, the vast house became the site of one never-ending party, as George and Big Ann, as she was now known—she'd added girth to her height and weighed in at close to two hundred pounds—lavishly entertained clients and friends practically round the clock. People would stop by for breakfast, lunch and dinner, for cocktails that lasted long into the night, for an eye-opener before a morning of hunting, for a round of highballs after a round of golf. The Skakel estate functioned as a full-time public-relations arm of George's commercial behemoth.

The seven children acted as props in George and Ann's productions. The parents would parade their progeny before the guests to prove that beneath the captain of industry's dynamic veneer glowed a warmhearted family man. The children exhibited their fine manners by helping clear the dishes; in the kitchen, even the tiniest of them would imbibe the liquor the grown-ups had left in their glasses. Alcohol flowed freely those years in Larchmont, as the legacy of Curt Skakel and Joe Brannack began to tighten its grip over their descendants. George became an alcoholic; Big Ann almost kept up with him. Drinking afflicted a number of Ethel's siblings in the years to come.

In 1935, after two years in Larchmont and a brief stay in nearby Rye, George moved his family across the state line in search of lower taxes. He purchased "Rambleside," a magnificent home on Lake Avenue in

Greenwich, Connecticut. The elite town's WASP aristocracy hardly rolled out the welcome wagon for the self-made millionaire and his tumultuous Catholic family. Fighting to establish their social position, George and Ann stepped up their partying—and the discipline of the children disintegrated further. The boys, in particular—Jim, George Jr. and Rushton, then teenagers—became notorious for their arrogant, rowdy antics. According to biographer Jerry Oppenheimer, each child who reached driving age would receive from George a new automobile of his or her choice. A neighbor, George Crossman, remembered how Jim Skakel mixed motoring with "the way of the bottle": "He was coming out of the Greenwich Country Club one night with a load on. He had a brand-new—I mean, those Skakels were wasteful bastards—a brand-new something-or-other, I guess it was a Lincoln. And he backs up to pull out of the parking lot, and then he hits a tree. So he puts it in forward, and then he hits another tree. This big tree.

"So he loses his temper. And he goes back, forward, back, forward, until that shiny new car was totaled. I mean, those guys were legends!"

George bought guns for his sons, too, and not just rifles like the ones he took hunting. Aiming .45-caliber pistols out the car window, the boys would shoot up mailboxes and street signs as they sped along sedate Greenwich streets at ninety miles an hour. The unamused local police chief frequently stationed a patrol car at the bottom of the family driveway in hope of catching any one of the pack in a violation. However, the town authorities did not prove uncooperative when Greg Reilly, a chum of the boys, sustained a gunshot wound to the shoulder while playing on the Rambleside grounds: the police made little effort at investigation and kept the incident quiet. The circumstances of the shooting, which most likely occurred accidentally, have never been revealed.

Ethel grew up a tomboy, demanding as a toddler that her brothers teach her to throw a football and swing a baseball bat. A skinny girl with an insatiable appetite, in Larchmont she attended the Dominican Day School, a progressive institution designed for the spoiled children of upper-class Westchester Catholics. When the family resettled in Connecticut, she and sister Pat switched to the nonsectarian Greenwich Academy, one of the East Coast's most prestigious schools for girls. Her father had lobbied his religious wife for the change—by acquiring a secular education, his daughters would assist in his campaign of assimilation into the community. Ethel adjusted smoothly to her new environment, but she never abandoned the Catholic ardor she had inherited from Big Ann. The schoolgirl slept with a cross and rosary over her bed and devotional texts on her nightstand.

If Ethel did not adopt the religious customs of her Protestant classmates, she did embrace another tenet of their ethos: a fixation with horses. Within months of the move to Greenwich, she took part in her first equestrian competition and began lessons with the area's top instructor. By her adolescence, the walls of her bedroom were covered with photographs of her riding the several mounts she owned over the years and with the ribbons and citations she had earned in competitions throughout the Northeast. She rode fearlessly, jumping the highest obstacles and performing perilous stunts like leaping from one horse to another. Big Ann hated horses, but she tolerated her daughter's expensive obsession because it kept the ungovernable girl out of her mother's hair. When Ethel and friends would trot their steeds through the house, trampling the priceless oriental rugs, Ann would barely lift an eyebrow.

Ethel thrived at Greenwich Academy, to which she was driven each morning by a chauffeur armed with a loaded revolver to ward off the possibility of any kidnap attempt. She showed little talent for math or geography, but she shone in athletics, setting the standard for her class in field hockey and tennis. Incorrigible at home, her behavior at school was not better. With fellow hell-raisers Pixie Meek and Pan Jacob, she formed the PEP Girls, so named after the initials of their first names. The three pranksters delighted their schoolmates, and terrorized their teachers, by practicing perpetual mischief.

When not on horseback, Ethel would frolic with the Skakels' menagerie. The grounds of the estate were home to a goat and several sheep, a pair of pigs, a flock of chickens, dozens of rabbits, and hordes of mongrel dogs. (The neighbors disdained the breeding lines of the dogs almost as vehemently as they scorned the ancestry of the mutts' owners.) As she got older, Ethel turned for amusement to her red convertible. She drove no more sensibly than did her brothers—at night she would sometimes drive with the lights off—although she did not, apparently, open fire upon the roadside property.

As Ethel finished tenth grade, Big Ann decided the fifteen-year-old should complete her high school education at a Catholic institution. So in September 1943, Ethel began her junior year at the Convent of the Sacred Heart, Maplehurst, a five-day-a-week boarding school in the Bronx attended by the daughters of prominent Catholic families. While the nuns of the convent helped fortify Ethel's religious passion, the youngster otherwise picked up where she'd left off at Greenwich, playing field hockey and talking nonstop about horses, quickly earning a reputation as the most audacious of the thirteen pupils in her class.

After graduating Maplehurst in June 1945, Ethel matriculated that

September at Manhattanville College of the Sacred Heart, then located in New York's Harlem. Within a week, she met Jean Kennedy, and the two rapidly became best friends. Jean hatched plans that fall for Bobby and her new pal, but the scheme was temporarily confounded when Ethel returned from Christmas at Mont Tremblant mesmerized by Bobby's debonair older brother. Friends soon prevailed upon her to lower her sights—never considering herself glamorous, she realized she couldn't measure up to the sophisticated women favored by Jack. Her heart would belong to Bobby, if her sister would only get out of the way.

Robert and Ethel saw each other occasionally the next couple of years as he went out with her sister. For both Pat and Bobby, their dating never generated much passion, and after she jilted him for her Irishman, Bobby finally opened his eyes to her sister. Whereas Pat was quiet, feminine and studious, Ethel was brassy, athletic and funny. She and Bobby had much in common, starting with their love of sports. Both belonged to sprawling Irish Catholic families headed by rich, strong-willed fathers. Even their birth orders were similar: Bobby came seventh out of nine children, Ethel sixth of seven.

After her weekends at Charlottesville—where she slept, in proper Catholic fashion, at the nearby farm of a girlfriend—Ethel would rhapsodize to her Manhattanville dormmates about the man she intended to marry. She had little else on her mind: an indifferent student, she had never harbored career goals for herself other than bearing children for a husband who would depend on her love and support. But in mid-1949, staying at home in Greenwich after her college graduation that June, she developed cold feet. During her long hours in the saddle, she began to feel intimidated by the Kennedys and by the new life that beckoned. Her anxiety became so intense that she even considered joining the church and becoming a nun. "How can I fight God?" pondered Bobby.

But late in the year the plucky young woman regained her nerve. At Thanksgiving, she flew to Charlottesville to give her patient boyfriend the good news in person. The couple agreed on a June wedding.

The other extracurricular highlight of RFK's time at UVA consisted of his work with the Student Legal Forum, which had been established to bring distinguished citizens from outside to speak at the law school. Serving as president of the forum for two semesters, Bobby drew upon his connections to supply a string of stimulating lecturers: a former ambassador, Joseph P. Kennedy, and a current congressman, John F. Kennedy, as well as a number of Joe's friends, such as Supreme Court Justice William O. Douglas, journalist Arthur Krock and Joseph R. McCarthy, United States senator from Wisconsin.

Bobby's invitation to African American diplomat Ralph Bunche provoked a controversy at the university, where a few years earlier Harvard's black tackle had caused a stir. When RFK (in his continuing vein of youthful individualism) proposed the booking, some objected. The criticism escalated when Bunche wrote to inquire if the audience would be segregated; if so, he would decline to appear. One professor suggested that the university evade Virginia's statute forbidding racially mixed seating simply by marking separate sections, then neglecting to enforce the designation. Bobby rejected the compromise. He took his case to a meeting of the student government, where all present agreed with him but, to his bewilderment, the boys from the Deep South refused to support him publicly. Incensed, Bobby and the Student Legal Forum wrote the university president, Colgate Darden, that insistence upon segregation for Dr. Bunche's lecture would be "morally indefensible." Darden, who personally opposed segregation, found a way out: citing a recent Supreme Court ruling mandating the admission of blacks to a Texas law school, he pronounced Bunche's speech an educational event that required an integrated audience. Bunche kept the date.

Arranging lectures was not the only task at UVA for which Bobby sought his family's assistance. He also attempted to draw upon Kennedy resources to help with his homework. Mary Davis chronicled a visit from the would-be lawyer to Jack's Capitol Hill office, where she worked as the lawmaker's secretary: "I'd never met him, and I remember he came busting into the office one day and he said, 'You're Mary.' And I said, 'Yes, I am.' And he throws a sheaf of paper down on my desk, and he says, 'You've got to type this up for me right away. It's one of my papers for school.' And I looked at him and I said—there were pages of this thing—'I can't do that.' And he says, 'You have to. I'm Bob Kennedy, you know. . . .' And blah, blah, blah. . . . 'Well, I just don't have the time to do that. . . . If Jack says that I have to do it, then I'll do it. But I can't do it.' Of course, Jack wasn't there at the time when he came busting in. And he says, 'No, no, no. You've got to put everything aside. You have to do this because there's a time limit on it.' . . .

"Jack finally came back, and I asked him. And he says, 'You don't have to do a thing for him. You have enough work to do. He's got a hell of a nerve coming in and asking you to do this.' "

In January 1950, publications around the country announced the engagement of the ambassador's son to the industrialist's daughter. In detailing the couple's backgrounds, the article noted that Robert Kennedy had served in the navy for three years during the war and that he had traveled extensively as a writer of newspaper articles. In placing the story, Joseph Kennedy had apparently considered Bobby's résumé insufficiently impressive without selected exaggerations. He felt even more strongly about the credentials of his future daughter-in-law: added to her diploma from Manhattanville was an all-but-completed, and utterly fictitious, postgraduate degree at Columbia University.

Bobby and Ethel did not shop together for an engagement ring. Instead, he sent a representative from Cartier to the Skakels' home with a huge tray of rings from which the bride-to-be chose a large, but tasteful, diamond. She had her first chance to show off the ring at the engagement party her parents threw just after New Year's. Two hundred guests celebrated the betrothal at the Lake Avenue home over a sumptuous meal. Ethel also giddily displayed the expensive bejeweled compact she'd received from Bobby's mother.

As soon as the ashtrays from the January bash had been emptied, Big Ann sprang into action, organizing the dazzling affair that would be her daughter's wedding. She supervised the sending of some twelve hundred invitations and hired scores of servants for the reception. She contracted with the area's costliest caterers and ordered an enormous tent to be erected on the Rambleside grounds to protect the guests in case of rain.

In charge of preparing the groom's side of the bridal party was the best man, who in his spare time served as United States representative from the Eleventh District of Massachusetts. Mary Davis, Jack's secretary, may have balked at contributing her time to typing Bobby's law school papers, but now she helped ready his nuptials, earning her government salary by processing a ream of correspondence sent out over her boss's signature. On May 22, she mailed the ushers the schedule of events, with precise instructions as to attire:

Black calfskin low shoes, highly polished
Plain black silk socks and garters
Dark gray striped trousers
  Morning coat and light gray double breasted waistcoats
  Striped four-in-hand and light gray gloves will be provided
White shirt with French cuffs, detachable stiff turned-down collar.
  Please see that cuffs show three-fourths of an inch below coat
  sleeves.
  The best man has the same clothes as the groom and his tie is
  identical to the groom's.
The ushers have the same clothes as the groom. Their tie is different
  from the groom's; all ushers have identical ties.

[Handwritten] Ties will be provided on arrival.

In the cover letter, issued on House of Representatives letterhead, Jack noted that morning suits would be rented for those not owning one and asked each usher to send Ethel his glove size. When one attendant failed to provide the statistic, Ethel's nervous request for it arrived on the congressman's desk.

Jack also cooked up his brother's bachelor party. The roasting would take place at the Harvard Club in New York, two nights before the wedding. The groom's remembrance of his penultimate evening of liberty would be a silver cigarette case inscribed with the autographs of all who came to honor him. The best man wrote to each contributor asking that he forward his signature on a "plain piece of white paper"; the cost to the participants was $10.87 per capita. The night of revelry turned out to be more festive than intended. The Skakel boys mixed it up with Bobby's football pals, and a few weeks later a sheepish JFK had to ask the pardon of the Harvard Club's management. He also had to fork over $1,040 for damages incurred.

Early in the day on Saturday, June 17, 1950, a crew of hairdressers assembled on Lake Avenue to beautify the women who were to take part in the glorious event later that morning. Much of the careful work of the stylists had to be redone, however, after a number of the bridesmaids wandered outside to mingle with the Skakel and Kennedy boys and soon found themselves thrown into the swimming pool. Rose Kennedy, who had slept in Hyannis Port, arrived in Greenwich for breakfast. Her husband appeared later, coming from New York, where he had spent the night breaking the vows his son would this day recite.

By 11:30 A.M., some two thousand guests had filled St. Mary's Roman Catholic Church in Greenwich. In front of the sanctuary, which had been adorned with white peonies, lilies and dogwood, an excited crowd had gathered hoping to catch a glimpse of some of the famous politicians, performers and socialites seated inside. To music provided by Michael O'Higgins of the Royal Academy of Music, Dublin, the procession began. The matron of honor, Patricia Skakel Cuffe; the maid of honor, the bride's baby sister, "Little Ann"; as well as the six bridesmaids— Georgeann Skakel, Bobby's sisters Jean, Eunice and Pat, plus Ethel's sister-in-law and a cousin—all wore dresses of white Chantilly lace over taffeta, with matching jackets, and hats of white organza trimmed with pink gardenias and baby's breath. Treading stiffly in their morning suits were the fifteen ushers, who included Ethel's three brothers, Ted Kennedy (then a student at Milton), George Terrien, David Hackett and a significant portion of Harvard's 1947 gridiron squad. Occupants of the pews could almost feel the building shake as the beefy linemen stomped down the aisle.

George Skakel gave the bride away. Wearing a white satin gown made with a fitted bodice finished with an off-the-shoulder neckline and a bertha of pointe de Venise lace embroidered with pearls, she carried a bouquet of Eucharist lilies, stephanotis and lilies of the valley. Her white satin mitts were embroidered with seed pearls and her full-length tulle veil was fastened to a headdress of matching lace trimmed with orange blossoms. The Reverend Terence L. Connolly of Boston College performed the ceremony and the Reverend Alexander C. Wollschlager read the blessing from Pope Pius XII. (New York's archbishop, Francis Cardinal Spellman, had offered his consecration the previous morning in a private mass at his Madison Avenue residence.)

After the service, the guests returned to Lake Avenue, where they dined on lobster and shrimp, and listened to the singing of Morton Downey, the Irish American tenor and close friend of Joe Kennedy from Palm Beach. Bobby toasted his new bride, announcing that he had found the girl of his dreams. Ethel blushed and kissed the groom on the lips.

The couple flew to Hawaii for their honeymoon. Georgeann's husband had made the arrangements, booking the lovebirds into bridal suites at Hawaii's most luxurious hotels: the Royal-Hawaiian on Waikiki Beach and the Hanamaui on the island of Maui. Each morning the pair received a fresh supply of orchids and a magnum of champagne.

After six weeks, Bobby and Ethel flew to Los Angeles, where they borrowed Pat Kennedy's car and drove it cross-country, stopping in Salt Lake City and Denver to visit friends. By late August, Mr. and Mrs. Robert Francis Kennedy arrived in Charlottesville, Virginia. There they took up residence as the new husband began his last year of law school.

"I thought that she was a wonderful influence on him," remembered William Guerry, a UVA classmate who later became a judge. "Before, he didn't shave very often and came to class in an old sweatshirt and khaki pants. He looked like he'd just rolled out of bed or had been playing touch football. But when he married, he completely changed. He started wearing a coat and tie.

"We took a trial practice class together, and Ethel came frequently to act as a witness or play a role or sit on the jury. She was almost always there."

Bobby's dedicated wife bettered more in his life than merely his wardrobe. No longer did he live in a rooming house without central heating; now the newlyweds rented a one-and-a-half-story Colonial-style home in an affluent section of Charlottesville. Forming a small circle of friends, they entertained often, but Ethel depended on the women of the group, as well as on her black servants, to make her meals edible—Big Ann had never passed on her own mother's lessons in home economics.

Visitors to the whitewashed brick residence were met with an unpleasant aroma: when Toby Belch, the couple's recently acquired English bulldog, wasn't salivating on the furniture, he was relieving himself on the carpets. The guests, most of them students and their wives struggling to make ends meet, may also have been put off by Ethel's complaints about her living conditions. The whole house could fit in one room of a Rambleside guest house, she moaned. Bravely, though, she vowed somehow to make do until Bobby received his degree.

"Ethel was like a born Kennedy," observed June B. Birge, an acquaintance of the period. Her informality, and the unashamed flamboyance with which the twenty-two-year-old took her wealth for granted, drew the attention of her husband's more humble classmates. "Every morning she would drive up in their Cadillac convertible," remembered Harry J. Hicks. "She'd be in her pajamas, with her hair in curlers, and he'd get out and walk into school." She didn't always stay in the car. "She'd come to the law school in outfits the other wives wouldn't have dared to wear outside the home," noted Thomas Wilson, "like a housecoat or bathrobe. And she'd run into the building to give him something he'd forgotten."

On weekends, Bobby and Ethel left their friends behind and flew, on planes owned by George's company, to Hyannis Port, Greenwich or Palm Beach. Nor could their fellow students afford to belong to the Farmington Country Club, a verdant golf-and-tennis facility where no Jews were allowed and where the only blacks wore white coats and carried trays of mint juleps and cream-cheese canapés.

The refined surroundings, however, did not dampen the competitive fire each brought to athletics—or to contests of any sort. "When Bobby and Ethel had guests at their house, they would play charades," recalled Arthur Scott, a member of the country club. "Ethel had to win, and she became downright vindictive when she lost. She was the same way on the tennis court, in fact at anything she endeavored to do. She didn't know how to have fun or relax, and neither did Bobby. It was blood sport. They played to win and were terribly sore losers.

"I remember one tennis match Bobby was playing, and he was losing. Suddenly, in the middle of the match, he just walked to the center of the court and lowered the net. As it fell to the ground, he turned and walked off without saying a word."

Bobby finished the University of Virginia School of Law with a respectable, albeit hardly illustrious, academic record: he ranked fifty-sixth of 124 graduates and carried a grade point average of 2.54. He did not linger for the June commencement ceremony, however. A few weeks earlier he and his wife had flown north and moved into one of the two guest houses at Lake Avenue, where they eagerly awaited the birth of their first child.

The pregnancy was not an easy one. As the mid-June due date approached, Ethel grew increasingly anxious, frightened at the prospect of motherhood and privately angry that she'd had to spend most of the gestation in Charlottesville, far from her family's support. She was thoroughly overwrought by the time labor began, three weeks past the expected day. Ethel suffered an excruciating delivery, but gave birth on July 4, 1951, to a healthy girl of nine and a half pounds. The new parents named their daughter Kathleen, after Bobby's late sister.

As Ethel emerged from the delivery room exhausted and still distressed, Bobby felt helpless to comfort her. He turned to his mother, whom he telephoned in Hyannis Port. Rose advised him to call Luella Hennessey, the Kennedy family nurse since the late 1930s. Starting with young Kathleen, Hennessey would attend some twenty-six of Rose's newborn grandchildren, including all belonging to Bobby.

Mother and child remained in the hospital for two weeks as Ethel recovered from a torn perineum and a painful internal injury caused by the child's size. George Skakel paid the bill the day they went home, since Bobby was out of town attending to Kennedy family business, but the financial largess of Ethel's father was not matched by emotional generosity on the part of her mother. According to Hennessey, when Ethel arrived at Lake Avenue, Big Ann registered little sympathy for her daughter's physical and psychological condition. The cold reception didn't deter Ethel from a warm gesture to the baby's other grandmother: she ordered a dozen red roses sent to Mrs. Kennedy—a tradition she would keep for the birth of each of her succeeding children.

The new parents stayed in the main building, while the infant slept in a guest house alongside her nurse. Hennessey would bring Ethel her baby each morning, then take the child back to the cottage for naps and bedtime. After a few weeks, Luella Hennessey was permitted to return to her home, and Bobby and Ethel resumed their place in the guest house, where Bobby spent the summer studying for the Massachusetts bar exam. Before long, they announced their choice for their firstborn's godfather: Senator Joseph McCarthy.

By mid August, Ethel and Bobby longed for relief from the stresses of recent events. Leaving the baby behind in Connecticut in the care of another nurse they'd hired, they set out for Salt Lake City, where they had spent part of their honeymoon. They were joined in Utah by several friends of Bobby's, including fellow Harvard graduate Dean Markham. The group, numbering five, hit the road, driving through the Mojave Desert and visiting a ranch in Arizona owned by Ethel's family. They were back in Greenwich just after Labor Day.

The new father didn't stay at his wife's side for long. In early September of 1951 he went to San Francisco, where representatives of fifty nations had convened to conclude the Allies' peace treaty with Japan. His stated purpose was to cover the gathering for the *Boston Post*—an assignment again procured by Joe. Returning home, RFK remained not much longer than it took to unpack his bags before he repacked them anew, this time to accompany Jack on a congressional junket to the Near East and Asia. With their sister Patricia, they left in early October, stopping first in Israel, then moving on to India, where they met with Prime Minister Jawaharlal Nehru, who paid more attention to Pat than to her brothers. Disappointed by Nehru's evident lack of warmth, the trio departed for their next port of call: Vietnam. As they walked the streets of Saigon, the Kennedys heard gunfire exchanged at the city's outskirts between French forces and the Vietminh guerrillas of Ho Chi Minh.

After seven weeks abroad, Robert arrived in Greenwich only to move his new family to Washington, D.C. Joseph P. Kennedy and Joseph R. McCarthy were both heartily disliked by President Harry Truman; nonetheless, the isolationist onetime ambassador and the red-baiting Republican senator together had enough pull to land Bobby a job in the Criminal Division of the Democratic administration's Justice Department. Heading the division was Assistant Attorney General James A. McInerney, a friend of Joe Kennedy's who did legal work for the Kennedy family after he left the public sector years later. After a routine FBI check of Bobby's background, in which the agents found "no criminal record and credit rating satisfactory," Ethel located a three-bedroom town house at 3214 S Street in Georgetown; the novice lawyer started at $4,200 a year in the Criminal Division's internal security section, which worked to ferret out supposed Soviet spies who'd infiltrated the capital.

Although he enjoyed his first job, RFK had still not settled on the course of his professional life. According to J. Walter Yeagley, a later employee of the Justice Department, Bobby often discussed with colleagues "what direction he should aim for; whether it should be in government, whether or not it even should be legal, or whether it might be in business. And of course not having money problems, he seemed to have quite a potential choice. . . . Bobby never came to a decision during these months as to just what he really wanted to do in the long term for a career." Bobby got along well with his fellow employees, who found him "a delightful person to work with, . . . very informal around the office. As a matter of fact, . . . he frequently took his shoes off and worked in his stocking feet."

Soon, Bobby moved again. On February 28, 1952, the attorney general transferred him to the Eastern District of New York to assist in the prosecution of "numerous cases of frauds upon and conspiracies to defraud the Government of the United States." While he was at this posting, his most significant task was to help present evidence to a Brooklyn grand jury investigating two former Truman officials who faced corruption charges.

For the next three months, RFK spent most of his time in New York, heading back when he could to his frustrated wife in Georgetown. He resigned from the Justice Department on June 6. Two days later, in a lengthy article on the departure, the *New York Times* assessed Bobby's brief tenure: "Young Kennedy, good looking and 26 years old, has been a particular favorite around the Brooklyn Federal Building. Even the civil service employees have been calling him by his first name, although witnesses leaving the grand jury room have been heard to mumble as they left that he was a 'tough' inquisitor."

James McInerney, the paper noted, promised his former subordinate "that there would always be a place on the Attorney General's staff if he decided to return to public life" (although just how high a place on that staff Bobby would assume when he did come back, McInerney could not have imagined).

Robert Kennedy himself gave the reason for his exit. "I hate to leave such an interesting assignment as I have had in Brooklyn," he told the *Times*. "But I think I owe it to my brother Jack to return to Massachusetts and do my part before the Democratic primary in September. Of course, I think Jack is going to be the Democratic nominee and the new United States Senator from Massachusetts."

6

McCARTHY & CO. (Part One)

John F. Kennedy had assumed a formidable task in 1952. Although in the primary he faced minimal opposition, in the general election he would have to unseat Henry Cabot Lodge, Jr., a popular legislator who had first entered the Senate in 1936. If the Kennedys were coming to be the first family of Irish, Democratic Massachusetts, the Lodges were long established as the leading dynasty among the state's Brahmin Republicans. Lodge's grandfather and namesake had served Massachusetts in the United States Senate for over thirty years—in his 1916 reelection campaign his unsuccessful foe was none other than Honey Fitz. Lodge's great-great-great-grandfather, George Cabot, represented the Bay State in the Senate during the administration of George Washington, when the Kennedys and the Fitzgeralds were digging for potatoes on the other side of the Atlantic.

Joseph P. Kennedy, relishing the opportunity to tweak the Yankee noses while at the same time furthering his son's career, joined the effort with his customary open wallet and overbearing attitude. But his dated grasp of political maneuvering carried even less relevance to the statewide race than it had to the local bid six years earlier. Mark Dalton, who led the 1946 run, had again signed on as campaign manager, but a faction in the organization rapidly came to believe him inadequate to the job. Joseph Gargan, a cousin to RFK, remembered Ken O'Donnell's recognition that only one person could curb the candidate's domineering father and thus keep the entire enterprise from a catastrophic collapse: " 'This isn't gonna work,' said Kenny, 'we need a family member running this campaign.' And he went to Bobby in New York and said, 'It's gotta be

63

you, Bobby.' Bobby said, 'I don't want to, I'm just not ready for that.' Not that he wouldn't want to help Jack, but he was in a stage of his life where he wanted to do his own things. But they prevailed upon him and he became the campaign manager."

Although he had flourished as a prosecutor—and thrived on his independence from his father—Robert Kennedy could not resist the call to family duty and promptly left for Boston, where headquarters had been established in a run-down former warehouse at 44 Kilby Street. Amid the ancient desks and creaky chairs, Bobby set to organizing a campaign like none other Massachusetts had ever seen. With little faith in the established Democratic Party apparatus, he resolved to circumvent it by designing his own machine statewide. He delegated its formation to O'Donnell and to Lawrence O'Brien, a political operative from Springfield who would over the years remain a top Kennedy aide. "The key to the Kennedy organization in 1952," O'Brien explained, "was the network of three hundred local campaign directors we recruited, the Kennedy secretaries, as we called them. The title was significant. We could have called them Kennedy chairmen, but that might have offended the local party chairmen, who in theory were still chairmen of everything—our campaign included."

As in 1946, the Kennedys actively courted the female vote. Polly Fitzgerald, a cousin, and Helen Keyes, a family friend, arranged a series of teas for women around the state. As the ladies sipped, the candidate's mother and sisters would sing his praises. Occasionally, JFK himself would show up at such events, after which enthusiastic listeners would line up to enlist in the cause. Women volunteered in droves, remarked O'Brien: "The old ones wanted to mother Jack, the young ones to marry him. I'm sure every girl was hoping he'd notice her."

The women did more for the handsome young politician than moon over him. "We'd sent nomination papers out all over the Commonwealth," Gargan remembered, "because there was a goal of getting something like two hundred fifty thousand signatures. And I would have the girls in the afternoon or during the evening sit down and write out thank-you postcards to each person that had signed one of those petitions." The nominating drive achieved its purpose superbly, for JFK captured the primary with 75 percent of the ballot.

In addition to its dogged contact of voters one by one, the campaign made use of a brand-new medium to communicate with the electorate en masse. Adapting the format of the teas, albeit with a change of beverage, the organization sponsored two editions of *Coffee with the Ken-*

nedys, a television program that showcased a variety of family members and made Rose a favorite in every corner of the state.

RFK came to the race well aware of his youth and his relative inexperience in politics. To make up for these shortcomings, he set the campaign's example for diligence, arriving at headquarters first and departing last, as he had done on the football field at Harvard. When a laborer refused to place a Kennedy poster atop a drawbridge, Bobby grabbed the sign and climbed the forty-foot ladder himself. By Election Day, the fifteen-to-twenty-hour days had caused a dozen pounds to drop off his already slender frame.

Bobby's most precarious job during the run had to do not with heights, but with the "care and feeding" of the operation's obstreperous financier. "Bobby, at twenty-six, usually stood up to his old man," said Larry O'Brien. "In fact, as I recall, they always seemed to be arguing." The constant quarreling notwithstanding, Joe shared with Jack an unshakable trust in Bobby's judgment. The ambassador toed the line and paid the bills. His single largest expenditure was a loan of half a million dollars to the *Boston Post*. As soon as the check cleared, the paper made its endorsement for United States senator from Massachusetts: it backed the Democrat.

As November drew near, the Kennedy campaign ascended to a level of frenzy. The army of female volunteers left literature on the seats of buses and taxicabs. The workers stuffed mailboxes and knocked on doors, taking care to reach every home in their assigned areas. Altogether, the women hand-distributed nine hundred thousand copies of JFK's leaflet. Equally comprehensive, the telephone canvass targeted each voter in the state for at least two calls.

"Bobby's best work took place behind the scenes," noted Ken O'Donnell. "He wasn't at all personable, had little finesse, and hated speaking in public." RFK did give a few speeches, but remained a reluctant orator. His best-known address was, in its entirety: "My brother Jack couldn't be here. My mother couldn't be here. My sister Eunice couldn't be here. My sister Patricia couldn't be here. My sister Jean couldn't be here. But if my brother Jack could be here, he'd tell you that Lodge has a very bad voting record. Thank you."

Actually, Lodge's voting record hardly figured as an issue, for the Kennedy brain trust deemed the senator's studiously middle-of-the-road positions to be immune to attack. The central point of dispute in the race became who could more effectively bring home the federal bacon. "He Can Do More for Massachusetts," JFK's placards proclaimed. "He Has Done the Most for Massachusetts," Lodge's read in turn.

Bobby proved a productive campaign manager. His lack of finesse won him few friends, but he didn't mind; indeed, the legend of Robert Kennedy as hatchet man had its inception in 1952, as he displayed little tolerance for the state's older politicians and their quaint but inefficient ways of electioneering. One day he threw an elderly labor leader out of the office because he was sitting around and telling jokes. Another day fisticuffs nearly broke out between an experienced, sixty-year-old state legislator and the intense young campaign boss who insisted that his orders be obeyed.

JFK appreciated his brother's readiness to play the heavy and thereby insulate the candidate from distasteful necessities. When Paul Dever, the Democratic governor running for reelection, proposed combining his own political apparatus with that of the Kennedys, Jack wanted no part of the idea; he knew such a merger could only drag him down. (Dever had run well short of JFK in the primary.) However, Jack didn't reveal his opinion to Dever in person; he assigned the deed to Bobby, who incurred the governor's anger at a face-off filled with shouting. It was left to the elder Kennedy to smooth Dever's ruffled feathers, but the apologies Joe delivered on behalf of his precocious child were anything but sincere. On the contrary, the parent marveled at his pitiless young son's nerve. RFK was a chip off the old block: "Bobby's my boy," Joe boasted later. "When Bobby hates you, you stay hated."

Robert Kennedy's iron focus ensured that his operation was all business, whereas the other side possessed no such driving force. The incumbent refused to take his young opponent seriously—the senator was fifteen years Jack's senior—and considered the entire Kennedy endeavor an elaborate waste of Joe's riches. Like Bobby, Lodge also managed a campaign that fall—the presidential effort of Dwight D. Eisenhower—and he blithely neglected his own race to stump for Ike.

Lodge boasted to the *New York Times* that he would bury the upstart by three hundred thousand ballots, and he had reason to be confident. General Eisenhower carried Massachusetts by two hundred thousand. Dever lost the statehouse by fifteen thousand. One of the few Democrats in the country to withstand the Republican landslide was John F. Kennedy. National Democratic leaders took note as the new scion defeated the old by seventy thousand votes.

For much of the 1952 campaign, Robert Kennedy shared rooms in a Boston boardinghouse with cousins Joe and Mary Jo Gargan. The quarters at 4 Marlborough Street were too modest to accommodate

Bobby's family—the furnishings were simple and there was no kitchen—so Ethel, while her husband busied himself getting her brother-in-law a new job, remained mostly at their house in the District of Columbia. Langdon P. Marvin, Jr., an aide to JFK during the race and afterward in the Senate, described how Bobby coped with the loneliness of being separated from his wife:

"Bobby always struck me as a kind of Junior G-man type, but in many ways he was like his father. There was this perpetual myth about Bobby not being a ladies' man. This couldn't have been further from the truth. All the Kennedy men were like dogs: whenever they passed a fire hydrant they had to stop and take a leak. That's how they regarded women—they were there for the taking. Bobby may have been less prolific than his brother Jack; his affairs tended to be longer-lasting and more serious, without so many one-night stands. But he certainly had his share of extra-marital relationships.

"During the '52 campaign, I bearded for him one weekend at Old Saybrook, Connecticut. There were five of us, three men and two women, one of whom was named Elizabeth Okrun. We stayed in a rooming house in five separate bedrooms, but Bobby spent both nights with Elizabeth and then snuck back to his room early the next morning. The first evening, we attended a formal dinner dance at the Old Saybrook Yacht Club. We took turns dancing with the girls so there would be no raised eyebrows—just five friends out for a good time. The next evening, Bobby and Elizabeth separated from the group and went out on their own.

"Elizabeth Okrun was a beautiful young debutante who eventually married a New York investment broker and, to the best of my knowledge, lived happily ever after. But throughout the '52 race, she and Bobby were an item. She worked on the campaign, so they saw a good deal of each other. He was married and had started a family, so there was never any question as to the affair being more than it was. But Robert and Elizabeth had a deep mutual fascination and, from the sound of it—I was in the room next door—a passionate sexual attraction."

"Bobby didn't need sex as a daily fix the way Jack did, but he knew how to get it," professed Morton Downey, Jr. "It was more of a macho thing with Bobby, as if he had to prove himself. This macho business extended to other areas as well."

Downey, who achieved minor notoriety during the 1980s by hosting a confrontational television talk show, was the son of the Irish tenor who was Joe Kennedy's best friend. The Downeys lived most of the year in Palm Beach, but they also owned a summer house in Hyannis Port.

"One of my favorite remembrances," continued Downey, "was of a softball game on the Cape when I learned that you can win and still lose with the Kennedys. Bobby was catching, I was playing first base, Jack was in right field with crutches that he dropped when he had to go get a ball. There was a guy named Torby [Torbert H.] McDonald, Pat Kennedy was playing—anyhow, the positions were filled with Kennedys and their friends.

"There was a kid standing on third base, I think his name was Gareth Skenk. He was about nineteen years old, I was eighteen and Bobby must have been twenty-five or twenty-six. The ball was hit, Jack threw it in, Gareth slid into home plate and Bobby tagged him. 'You're out, Gareth,' said Bobby. 'I'm safe,' argued Gareth—he was kind of a spoiled kid. 'No, you're out.' 'I was safe.' Jack, forever the peacemaker, said from out in the field, 'Gareth, why don't I have my *brothah* throw the ball back out *heah*, and *Moht* will count one, two, three, and at two, Gareth, you *staht* running, and at three I'll throw the ball to *Rahbeht*.'

"So it was done. I went one, two, Gareth started running; three, Jack threw the ball; four, Gareth slides across the plate—Bobby steps aside to let him do it; five, Bobby plants the ball in Gareth's mouth and knocks out his front tooth. And Gareth is writhing on the ground, crying and bleeding, and Bobby looks at him and says, 'You're right, Gareth, you were safe.' "

Joseph P. Kennedy may have beamed with pride over the job one son had done to elect the other, but he did not give the victorious campaign manager long to rest on his laurels. With the family gathered in Hyannis Port in November to celebrate Jack's advancement, Joe spoke to Robert soberly: "You haven't been elected to anything. Are you going to sit on your tail and do nothing now for the rest of your life? You'd better go out and get a job."

Bobby had little time to pursue the want ads, however, before his concerned father took matters into his own hands. In early December, Joe Kennedy placed a telephone call to Joseph Raymond McCarthy. The junior senator from Wisconsin had just won a second term, and his list of financial supporters included the father of the newly elected junior senator from Massachusetts.

Joe McCarthy began his political career as a circuit judge in Wisconsin and won election to the U.S. Senate in 1946. McCarthy's early years in Washington went largely unnoticed until February of 1950, when he seized the nation's attention with a speech in Wheeling, West Virginia. Charging with no evidence that the State Department was infested by Communists, he that night initiated the campaign of menace and intimidation that would lend his name to an era in American public life. By the fall of 1952, fueled by the solidification of Communist control in Europe and Asia, and by the outbreak of the Korean War in June 1950, McCarthy's crusade had gathered steam. It would enter a more vigorous, more rampant phase following the election: with Republicans recapturing Congress on Ike's coattails, McCarthy would in January assume the chairmanship of the Permanent Subcommittee on Investigations of the Senate Government Operations Committee.

McCarthy's tactics of falsehood and innuendo did not deter the Kennedys from admitting him to their circle of closest friends. He claimed to have run across JFK in the Pacific during the war, when the Midwesterner served as a marine captain, but the association more likely took hold in 1947, when the two freshman Catholic legislators both arrived on Capitol Hill. McCarthy soon became a frequent visitor to Jack's residence in Georgetown. Eunice Kennedy, who shared the house with her brother, dated Joe McCarthy for a while, eventually passing him along to her younger sister Patricia. McCarthy quickly made his way up the family ladder to Joe Kennedy, who savored the outspoken Irishman's coarse energy and admired his frank ambition. By the time Bobby and Ethel honored him as Kathleen's godfather, Joe McCarthy had enjoyed many weekends at Hyannis Port and Palm Beach.

John F. Kennedy did not yearn to have his family's connection with McCarthy publicized—Tail Gunner Joe (as he called himself) had aroused many influential detractors in Massachusetts—but Joe Kennedy displayed no such reluctance in asking that Bobby be named chief counsel to the Permanent Subcommittee on Investigations. McCarthy replied that he had already filled the position, with a twenty-five-year-old lawyer from New York named Roy M. Cohn, but he hired Bobby as assistant counsel. Technically, Bobby would work not under Cohn, but for Francis Flanagan, general counsel to the subcommittee. When reporters asked McCarthy to clarify the lines of authority between his general counsel and his chief counsel, each of whom had a separate staff, the senator said merely, "I don't know." In fact, the older Flanagan's presence was intended as respectable window dressing while the chairman and his attack dog chased lurid headlines. Flanagan didn't last long under the arrangement—in early 1953 the office of general counsel was vacated and Bobby thereafter reported to Cohn.

"Roy Cohn was a little bastard," recalled Flanagan; "nobody liked him. And Bob hated him." Cohn returned the feeling—"Roy told me he considered Bobby the most vicious man he ever met," said Tom Bolan, who worked as Cohn's law partner in later years—and the mutual enmity between the two attorneys would last the rest of their lives. RFK was predisposed to dislike Cohn even before they met: "Roy had been given the job as chief counsel that Robert Kennedy had wanted," claimed Bolan, "the job for which his father had recommended him. When Bobby lost out, he could never get over it. He could never forgive the slight." Bobby had been passed over, by a family friend, in favor of a man eighteen months his junior. And Bobby was not used to his father's generosity being underappreciated.

Judge Albert Cohn of New York's Supreme Court had likewise been instrumental in his son's rise, and the competition between the two younger men sprang, at least in part, from their similarities. "Both were young, ambitious, driven," Bolan contended, "not angry, but power-hungry and out there to get people. In a psychological sense, Bobby may have looked at Roy Cohn and seen a bit of himself there, so it could even have been a kind of self-loathing."

Not all the loathing was self-directed; Bobby found much to despise in Cohn that was alien to his own personality. Whereas Bobby had slogged through his education, Roy Cohn had been a boy wonder with a photographic memory, graduating from Columbia University Law School at nineteen, two years shy of the requisite age for taking the New York bar exam. Thanks to Judge Cohn's connections, Roy awaited his twenty-first birthday as a clerk-typist in the office of the United States attorney for the Southern District of New York, then was sworn in as an assistant U.S. attorney hours after being admitted to the bar. RFK's interest in politics had been practical, concerned more with winning elections than with promoting any dogmatic agenda; Cohn waged ideological warfare, coming to McCarthy's attention because of strong affiliations with activists of the far Right.* Although Bobby did not emulate his father's anti-Semitism, Cohn's New York Jewish sensibilities must have rankled the young Catholic patrician with New England roots. Bobby did inherit his father's aggressive brand of manhood, however, and found himself repulsed by the homosexuality that Cohn barely tried to hide. Kenneth Crawford, an army lawyer who knew RFK from the University of Virginia, recalled speaking with Bobby at the time: "He didn't get along at

---

*Cohn gained an early reputation by assisting in the prosecution of the controversial Rosenberg spy case, which resulted in the conviction and electrocution of Julius and Ethel Rosenberg.

all with Cohn, they were just at loggerheads. And I finally wheedled out of Bob what he was sore about: it appears that Roy had referred to him as 'that cute kid.' He didn't like that at all."

While Cohn and McCarthy clamored after Reds in the State Department and the Voice of America, Robert Kennedy was assigned the more tedious task of researching Western trade with Communist China, whose troops were fighting on the side of America's enemy in the police action still under way on the Korean peninsula. Bobby brought his usual informality to the office: LaVern Duffy, the investigator designated to assist him, noted that "Bobby looked like Joe College with his ruffled hair, ruffled white shirt, ruffled slacks, penny loafers, and white athletic socks."

According to Arthur Schlesinger, the two men were soon wading through old newspaper clippings, insurance company shipping indexes, court transcripts and reports from American intelligence agencies. In doing so, RFK and Duffy soon established that vessels sailing under the flags of American allies accounted for some 75 percent of all ships delivering cargo to China. At the same time, many of these transport companies were also reaping hefty profits from the United States government for carrying foreign-aid shipments to Western Europe. The shipping concerns, Bobby believed, were playing both sides of the fence: the assistance to Europe was designed to buttress America's allies against the same Communist expansion U.S. soldiers were resisting with their lives in Asia.

If McCarthy was surprised that Robert Kennedy's efforts had netted such productive results, he nonetheless made the most of the findings. On March 28, 1953, in a televised press conference with Bobby standing beside him, the senator announced that he had personally negotiated an agreement with a number of Greek shipowners, who promised that their 242 cargo vessels would no longer call at Chinese or Soviet-bloc ports. "I didn't want any interference by anyone," McCarthy said in explaining his bypass of normal diplomatic channels. All members of the permanent subcommittee voiced support of their chairman's startling accomplishment.

The administration, however, was livid. Harold Stassen, director of the government's foreign-assistance effort, accused McCarthy of usurping the prerogative of the executive branch to conduct foreign policy. Officials were working behind the scenes to dissuade Western nations from trading with China, protested Stassen, and Senator McCarthy's grandstanding was undermining those fragile overtures. Moreover, the State Department revealed, the government of Greece had several days earlier already consented to halt the shipments.

To quell the brewing feud, the White House dispatched Vice President Richard M. Nixon, who hosted a luncheon for McCarthy and Secretary of State John Foster Dulles. After the meal, the two men issued a joint statement in which Dulles effectively disowned Stassen by commending McCarthy for his "first-rate" work. For his part, the senator conceded the president's primacy in the management of foreign affairs and pledged to turn over to the administration any new information he received regarding East-West commerce.

McCarthy had been pleased by the initial labors of his assistant counsel. Four days after the news conference, Bobby's annual salary went from $4,952.20 to $5,334.57 in recognition of the "energy, judgment and imagination [he had] exercised in the conduct of this inquiry." Bobby, in turn, supported his chairman in the press, informing the *Boston Post* that he had been amazed by the manner in which McCarthy's detractors had ambushed him. "I don't know," Kennedy is quoted as saying. "I really don't. I had supposed that it just didn't make sense to anybody in this country that our major allies, whom we're aiding financially, should trade with the communists who are killing GIs."

RKF's stance on McCarthy provoked criticism. "I called and told him that McCarthy was bad news, a terrible tyrant," said Larry O'Brien. "Frankly, I thought he was a little rat bastard," remembered Red Chandor, a New York socialite who occasionally crossed paths with the Kennedys. "I mean, here he was on the McCarthy committee. He was a political prostitute."

Bobby's work for Joseph McCarthy reached its most public moment on May 4, when he testified as the chairman's lead witness in a subcommittee hearing. His voice trembling, RFK presented a synopsis of his research into ships engaged in "enemy trade": in 1952, 193 vessels owned by allied nationals had made 445–600 voyages to Red China; 82 of those ships had simultaneously earned "good profits" transporting American cargoes overseas. He conveyed similar statistics concerning business done between the West and the Soviet sphere. The following day, the *New York Times* accompanied its article on the proceedings with a photograph, one column by two and a half inches, of the assistant counsel who had had his first occasion to testify before Congress.

Witnesses from various government agencies voiced support of McCarthy's stance in favor of a complete cutoff of the shipping operation. But the State Department's representative, John M. Leddy, argued that the situation could not be so simply disposed of. The allied nations in question considered such trading arrangements to be in their national interest, and while State was seeking to decrease the commerce, the administration had priorities more deserving of the expenditure of precious diplomatic capital. The chairman showed no patience for such striped-pants niceties. In the middle of Leddy's statement he rose from his chair and began to storm from the room. Before adjourning the hearing, however, he demanded to know whether Leddy's opinion represented official State Department policy. Breaking whatever truce he had reached with Dulles at their tête-à-tête a month before, he insisted that the answer come directly from the secretary of state himself.

In the following weeks, Joe McCarthy pressed his advantage. On May 14, he fulminated on the floor of the Senate, singling out the United Kingdom for particular scorn:

> "We should . . . keep in mind the American boys and the few British boys, too, who had their hands wired behind their backs and their faces shot off with machine guns—Communist machine guns, Mr. President—supplied by those flag vessels of our allies. . . . Let us sink every accursed ship carrying materials to the enemy and resulting in the death of American boys, regardless of what flag those ships may fly."

Five days later, McCarthy again confronted the Senate, this time moderating his tone, omitting any call for American torpedoes: "We can [stop these transactions] by simply telling our allies that they will not get one American dollar while any of their flag ships are plying this immoral, dishonest, indecent trade."

During that speech McCarthy thanked the Democrats on his subcommittee for lending him "for the day, the very able minority counsel, Mr. Kennedy." In fact, Bobby was not counsel to the minority; at the time, all subcommittee staff worked for the body as a whole, not for either side. Probably not coincidentally, the following day a member of the subcommittee, Democratic senator Stuart Symington of Missouri, did McCarthy a favor. Acting on testimony that indicated Defense Department backing for McCarthy's position, Symington suggested that a letter be sent to the president inquiring whether the administration favored more assertive measures to limit allied trade with China. With Symington's proposal, McCarthy could bring the dispute to Eisenhower's doorstep and, to some extent at least, blame the Democrats for forcing his hand.

Robert Kennedy was assigned to draw up the letter, which he hand-delivered to the Oval Office. The missive's polite language didn't mitigate its impact: Ike was fed up. McCarthy's meddling threatened to upset the delicate balancing act the administration was performing in trying to keep both domestic and foreign critics at bay and at the same time negotiate an end to the Korean hostilities. Once more, President Eisenhower called on his subordinate whose anti-Communist credentials were most unimpeachable, Richard Nixon, who prevailed on McCarthy to back off. The senator retracted the letter and his assistant counsel played along, denying (for the sake of the press) that he had ever set foot near the White House.

On July 1, RFK submitted his interim report to the Senate. As he had during the dispute over Ralph Bunche's appearance in Charlottesville, Bobby implored those in power to be governed by absolute standards of right and wrong. Whether or not United States authorities could actually end the pernicious practice "of fighting the enemy on the one hand and trading with him on the other," he wrote, action needed to be taken: allied shipping firms would have to be more carefully regulated. The document (according to many of RFK's later supporters, including Arthur Schlesinger) was unique among texts issued under McCarthy's aegis in that it relied upon well-substantiated assertions and never impugned the morality of American policymakers. Overall, Bobby's work for the subcommittee generated "unusual lapses into silence among the egghead set which never expected to see documented evidence flow from a McCarthy source," clucked the *Boston Herald*.

For his fine performance, Robert Kennedy received still another raise. But the extra $2,007.43 per annum could not keep him at McCarthy's side. In later years, RFK maintained that he quit because he "disagreed with the way that the Committee was being run." As he recalled in *The Enemy Within*: "I thought Senator McCarthy made a mistake in allowing the Committee to operate in such a fashion, told him so and resigned."

In those subsequent accounts, Bobby laid most of the fault for McCarthy's errors at the feet of Roy Cohn. By and large, wrote RFK, "no real research was ever done. Most of the investigations were instituted on the basis of some preconceived notion by the chief counsel or his staff members and not on the basis of any information that had been developed." Cohn and G. David Schine, a young man hired by Cohn to serve as a consultant to the subcommittee, showed McCarthy "all those wonderful things. He destroyed himself for that—for publicity. He had to get his name in the paper."

How much Bobby's departure had to do with principled disapproval of Cohn's methods, and how much with the two lawyers' reciprocal personal rancor, is unclear. An FBI memorandum from the period hints at the reason for Bobby's quitting: RFK "braced Cohn on an administrative matter and brought it to a head by stating that it was either he or Roy Cohn. The matter was resolved in Cohn's favor and Kennedy resigned."

The memo yields no clue as to the nature of the "administrative matter" on which McCarthy sided with Cohn and against Bobby.

Upon his leaving, Robert Kennedy received generous notes of commendation from several of the subcommittee's Democrats. On July 29, 1953, he tendered his resignation to his daughter's godfather. The armistice ending the Korean War had been signed two days earlier.

Again thanks to his father, Robert Kennedy didn't stay unemployed for long. Joseph P. Kennedy had served two years (1947–1949) on a Commission on Reorganization of the Executive Branch, headed by former president Herbert Hoover; in 1953, Dwight Eisenhower revived the blue-ribbon panel for another two-year stint, and Joe was reappointed. Although in his letter of resignation to McCarthy Bobby had cited his "intention to enter the private practice of law," he had by now settled on a career in government. He joined the Hoover office in August 1953 as Joe's chief aide.

The second Hoover Commission, created by Congress "to promote economy, efficiency, and improved service in the transaction of the public business" by the various arms of the federal government's executive branch, was composed of a dozen men: two senators, two representatives, the attorney general, an official of the Defense Department and six distinguished private citizens. The eminent pedigrees of the members did little to further the commission's objectives—few in Washington paid much attention to the body, and Hoover spent much of his time lamenting the apathy. "President Eisenhower's heart is in the right place," he complained, as recounted by Theodore C. Klumpp, a staff assistant. "Wouldn't you think he'd do more to implement the Commission's recommendations?"

The eighty-year-old ex-president also bemoaned the indifference of Congress to his efforts, and expressed special dismay over a lawmaker with a family interest in the work: "I am particularly disappointed that Senator Kennedy has not introduced a single bill to implement the Commission's recommendations. In supporting the Commission's findings and recommendations, wouldn't you think he would see to it that the necessary legislation was introduced?"

Bobby was in a "sorry state," recalled Lem Billings. "Always ambitious, he felt his present position lacked glamour." He had bigger plans; with little to do of substance, he chafed at being drawn into the petty squabbles that broke out among the autocratic Hoover and his assortment of graybeards. Perhaps most depressing, RFK was working under his father, who, Billings commented, "tended to treat him as he would a young boy."

Billings found Bobby contentious and sour-tempered during these months, but his mood, and his employment, would soon change. In February 1954 he returned to the Permanent Subcommittee on Investigations. This time, though, he would serve not the interests of Joseph McCarthy, but rather those of the senator's adversaries.

7

McCARTHY & CO. (Part Two)

On May 23, 1953, in the midst of the imbroglio over the letter sent to the White House, Robert Kennedy and Joseph McCarthy had taken time out to travel to New York for the nuptials of Eunice Kennedy and R. Sargent Shriver, Jr., a thirty-seven-year-old Maryland native descended from a signer of the Declaration of Independence. Joseph P. Kennedy spared no extravagance for the wedding, the first he'd thrown. Held at St. Patrick's Cathedral, the ceremony was conducted in candlelight by Francis Spellman, who in his seven years as cardinal had never before joined two hands in holy matrimony unless one of the hands belonged to a member of his immediate family. Following the service, the seventeen hundred guests walked east on Fiftieth Street to the Waldorf-Astoria, where luncheon on the Starlight Roof featured ornate fountains that flowed with pink champagne as the newlyweds danced to "April in Portugal." Joe neither confirmed nor denied press reports that the affair set him back a hundred thousand dollars.

Two other young individuals of wealth and prominence quickly followed Sarge Shriver in acquiring RFK as a brother-in-law. Jacqueline Bouvier, a glamorous postdebutante who had worked as an "inquiring camera girl" for a Washington newspaper, became the wife of Senator John F. Kennedy on September 12, 1953, in Newport, Rhode Island. A crowd of three thousand watched from the street as thirteen hundred guests entered St. Mary's Church for the nuptial mass conducted by Richard Cushing, archbishop of Boston. Bobby served as best man for his brother in a ceremony marred only by the absence of the twenty-four-year-old bride's father: John V. "Black Jack" Bouvier had earlier that morning been discovered drunk in his room at the Viking Hotel, and

Jackie's mother, Janet, warned her ex-husband that he would be forcibly ejected from the sanctuary if he dared show his face there. Janet's current spouse, Hugh D. Auchincloss, walked his stepdaughter down the aisle in Black Jack's place. "Uncle Hughdie" also hosted the reception at Hammersmith Farm, his family's estate overlooking Narragansett Bay.

Peter Lawford, who had parlayed his British accent, good looks and negligible talent into a successful Hollywood career playing male ingenues, married Patricia Kennedy on April 24, 1954. Pat, a California resident working in television production, had begun dating the movie star two years earlier and had assented to his proposal only after he agreed to forsake the Protestant faith of his fathers for that of his prospective father-in-law. Joe Kennedy footed the bill for the wedding day, which began at the Roman Catholic Church of St. Thomas More on East Eighty-ninth Street in New York City, but Peter's receiving of the sacraments did not assuage the ambassador's displeasure at his daughter's choice: "If there's anything I'd hate as a son-in-law," he grumbled, "it's an actor; and if there's anything I think I'd hate worse than an actor as a son-in-law, it's an English actor."

Eventually, Joe came to appreciate the English actor, for he would serve as the family's conduit to show-business money and celebrity. Although the Kennedy men may have belittled Peter's acting ability, they would value him for another gift: his skill as a procurer of starlets for their enjoyment and entertainment.

Sargent Shriver did not cater to the carnal needs of his new family, but he contributed nonetheless. Son of a wealthy financier, he received undergraduate and law degrees from Yale before serving in the navy during World War II, eventually rising to the rank of lieutenant commander. He met Eunice at a Washington dinner party in 1946. Working then as assistant to the editor of *Newsweek*, he seemed a perfect candidate for a post Eunice's father had been looking to fill—that of editor of Joe Jr.'s letters for private publication. The former gunnery officer impressed Joseph Kennedy, who soon dispatched him to Chicago to oversee the Merchandise Mart, the huge office building Joe had purchased for a song in 1945. Shriver, who was working as the Mart's manager when he wed Eunice, soon became a trusted cog in the Kennedy political machine. He accepted his first government appointment in 1961, when his relative in the White House named him to head the newly created Peace Corps.

The most warmly welcomed of the three new in-laws was Jackie Bouvier, who Joseph Kennedy believed would prove an asset to her husband's career. Bobby shared his father's assessment. Jack's bride, he sensed, would help to spring the Kennedys from the back pages of America's newspapers, via the society pages, to the front pages. RFK enjoyed the company of his new sister-in-law, whose sophisticated manners and rarefied tastes contrasted so distinctly with the less elevated ways of his own wife. Fluent in French, Jackie had attended the Sorbonne after two years at Vassar. She grew up primarily among refined French Catholics, so her background had little of the Irish raucousness that marked the Kennedys and the Skakels.

Ethel resented her husband's admiration of Jack's icy wife—she took RFK's warm regard for Jackie as an insult to herself. How could Bobby be taken in by such a snob? Ethel, eager to knock the princess off her pedestal, didn't disguise her scorn for the family's new darling. When Jackie mentioned that she had dreamed of becoming a ballerina, Ethel cocked a head toward her sister-in-law's size-ten-and-a-half pumps and cracked, "With those feet, kiddo, you should have been a soccer player." Jackie disdained her shorter, plainer counterpart. She laughed as she watched Ethel roughhousing with the Kennedy boys on the football field "like a monkey in heat." Ethel's deficiencies in wit and elegance did not detract from her one indisputable forte: Bobby's mate, quipped Jackie, functioned as a supremely efficient "baby-making machine."

And the machine continued to hum. Joseph Patrick Kennedy III was born on September 24, 1952; Robert Francis Kennedy, Jr., joined his brother and sister on January 17, 1954. To accommodate his three children, Robert Francis Kennedy, Sr., moved his family to O Street—still in Georgetown and only blocks from the old address.

The added burdens of the larger house, and the larger brood within, did not inhibit Bobby from striking up a new romance. His partner in the affair had been a flight attendant and now worked in the offices of National Airlines in Miami. Tall, brunette Amy Brandon bore a startling resemblance to the other new woman in Bobby's life, Jacqueline Bouvier Kennedy. "Bobby and I used to meet in Palm Beach and in New York," Brandon recalled. "He spoke only in passing about his marriage to Ethel. I had the impression he was in love with her but not in a very passionate way. He reserved his fire for me. Our relationship was a lusty one, based completely on sex. Bobby was like a young boy—he had amazing powers of recuperation. He would reach climax, and two minutes later he would be ready to go again. He could keep it up all night.

"My impression of Bobby was that of a man possessed. He was full of that famous Kennedy ambition. 'One day,' he told me, 'my brother Jack will be president and I'll be senator from Massachusetts. Teddy will be elected senator from Connecticut. Those are the long-term plans.' Old

Joe Kennedy had mapped it out, and Bobby fully believed it to be in the cards. He was as driven in politics as he was in bed."

In July 1953, as Bobby Kennedy was composing his letter of resignation to Joe McCarthy, the subcommittee's three Democrats walked out in a huff. Denied a voice in the hiring of staff, Senators Stuart Symington of Missouri, John L. McClellan of Arkansas and Henry M. "Scoop" Jackson of Washington boycotted the panel's workings for the rest of the year. They relented in January after McCarthy, seeking to ensure the full Senate's approval of his ever-expanding budget, granted them the right to hire one staff member. The Democrats decided to take on a minority counsel, and they chose for the job the man to whom the chairman had mendaciously given the title the previous spring. Anxious to put the unhappy months at the Hoover Commission behind him, Bobby accepted instantly.

On February 23, 1954, Robert F. Kennedy reported for duty as chief counsel for the minority, Senate Permanent Subcommittee on Investigations. "I'm looking forward to the task," RFK informed Larry O'Brien. Bobby had returned to McCarthy's orbit just in time to be part of one of the most extraordinary episodes of political theater in the history of the Republic.

The dispute between the United States Army and Senator Joseph McCarthy, a brawl that would hold a nation spellbound and bring about a demagogue's downfall, arose because a young man received a letter from his draft board. G. David Schine had not been bred to be a buck private. J. Myer Schine, owner of several radio stations and 150 movie theaters, had sent his son to Andover and then, in 1945, to Harvard, where he anointed the boy vice president of the family's central holding, Schine Hotels, a nationwide chain of lodgings. The young executive did not lead the life of the average college student. He cruised Cambridge in a black Cadillac convertible equipped with a then-unheard-of radio telephone. As a pedestrian he also advertised his riches, strolling through Harvard Yard one sunny day giddily showing passersby a suitcase filled with eleven hundred dollars. To aid in the management of the hotel business, he hired a secretary, whom school authorities permitted in Schine's dormitory room only during standard parietal hours. The schedule was sufficient for her not only to type letters to suppliers of linen and cutlery, but also to transcribe the shorthand notes she'd taken at the classes her hardworking boss couldn't spare the time to attend.

Schine's flaunting of his wealth hardly endeared him to his fellow undergraduates. ("I'm signing a check for three thousand dollars," he informed one roommate. "Have you ever signed a check for that much?") But his most egregious offense was to masquerade as a veteran. After two terms away from school because of bad grades, he returned bragging that he'd been "a lieutenant in the army," when in fact he'd drawn a lieutenant's pay as a civilian in the Army Transport Service. His unamused neighbors in Adams House, most of whom had actually spent time in the trenches of Europe and the Pacific, soon stopped talking to him. Schine complained to the dorm's headmaster, who beseeched the boys to be nicer to the lonely heir. They didn't strain themselves trying.

Dave Schine left his insensitive classmates behind in 1949, when his graduation present from his father was a promotion within the family business. Aside from escorting actresses and beauty queens to the Stork Club, the junior industrialist's most notable accomplishment in the years just after college was to write *Definitions of Communism*, a tract he published privately in 1952 and had placed at every family-owned bedside— "Offered as a public service," the pamphlet's back cover proclaimed, "by the Schine Hotels—G. David Schine, President and General Manager." The six pages of scholarship, for which Cohn and McCarthy would later pronounce Schine an "expert" on communism, placed the 1917 Russian Revolution in 1916, confused Stalin with Trotsky and gave Lenin the wrong first name. These and other errors did not diminish Roy Cohn's ardor to make the author's acquaintance. "We hit it off immediately," Cohn later wrote, recalling his initial meeting, in Miami Beach, with the tall young innkeeper whose sleepy eyes and sleek blond hair gave him the appearance of a bandleader.

On Easter Sunday, 1953, just after the investigation of the Voice of America had ended, the subcommittee's chief counsel and its unpaid "chief consultant" showed up in Paris. Roy and Dave spent the next ten days on a whirlwind tour of European capitals, scanning the shelves of embassy libraries for subversive literature, meeting with marginal local politicians and generally terrorizing American diplomats. European newspapers avidly followed the pair of twenty-six-year-olds, gleefully reporting such escapades as Schine chasing Cohn through a hotel lobby while swatting him over the head with a rolled-up newspaper. Only later did journalists write of the many careers ruined by the reckless trip, and of the lasting damage done to the morale of the foreign service. In between press conferences in Vienna, Schine found time to visit a tobacconist's shop for items to place in his cigar museum, which housed, he boasted, the largest and most varied collection of cigars in the world.

In July, when the selective service notified Schine that he would soon be required to take up arms, Roy Cohn swung into action. The first call he made was to Major General Miles Reber, the army's chief liaison with Congress, who arrived at Joe McCarthy's office to hear of the senator's interest in a direct commission for the draftee. When that request was denied, Cohn urged the brass to consider a reserve commission for Schine. A position in intelligence was also explored. The secretary of defense, the director of the Central Intelligence Agency, a host of generals—all took part in seeking suitable employment for the "exceptional" Ivy Leaguer. Schine himself invited Robert T. Stevens, secretary of the army, to his suite at the Waldorf Towers in New York. As the two later rode in Schine's car, the avid and energetic Red hunter complimented the secretary on *his* anti-Communist activities. "He thought," Stevens later recounted, "I could go a long way in this field. And he would like to help me. He thought that it would be a much more logical plan for him to become a special assistant of mine [than] to be inducted into the Army." Schine's reasoning impressed Stevens no more than did his Cadillac, and the hotel president began his life as a GI on November 3.

Roy Cohn did not take lightly the insult of his friend's mistreatment. A few weeks before Schine's induction, in a meeting with the army's top lawyer, John G. Adams, Cohn threatened to "expose the Army in its worst light and show the country how shabbily it is being run." His vehicle for revenge was a set of hearings into alleged treason at Fort Monmouth, the New Jersey base where the Signal Corps had been conducting sensitive research into new forms of radar. From autumn until spring, witnesses were hauled before the subcommittee. In seeking a villain, the subcommittee's grillers could come up with nothing better than an army dentist named Irving Peress. In the tooth puller's promotion from captain to major, thundered McCarthy, lay "the key to the deliberate Communist infiltration of our armed forces."

The chairman plunged into the Fort Monmouth investigation with Cohn's enthusiasm, but not with the chief counsel's motive. Joe McCarthy had little interest in the fate of David Schine. On several occasions he told Adams that he considered Schine a pest and a publicity hound; the army, affirmed the senator, should deal with Schine as it would any other conscript. But he never repeated that opinion to army officials in the presence of Cohn; he would either second the lawyer's stormy demands or remain silent. McCarthy craved action, and Cohn's rage, whatever its source, had exciting consequences.

In the months following Schine's induction, Cohn hectored Adams almost daily about Schine, who had been sent to Fort Dix, New Jersey. In "vituperative" and "abusive" language, according to the army's subsequent description, Cohn tirelessly insisted on special favors for Schine:

weekend and weeknight passes, assignment after basic training to a post near New York—all so that the valuable specialist might continue his work for the subcommittee. In November, McCarthy and Cohn suggested their protégé be transferred to First Army headquarters to sniff out Communist leanings in textbooks at West Point. In January, Cohn and Francis P. Carr, Jr., the subcommittee's executive director, spent most of two days searching by telephone for Adams, whom they finally tracked down in Amherst, Massachusetts. The reason for their frantic mission was horror at Schine's scheduled performance of KP duty the following afternoon. Peeling potatoes was just not G. David Schine's calling. One rainy day, while the soldier's comrades in Company K were practicing their riflery on the firing range, his commanding officer discovered him sitting inside a truck. Private Schine, recalled Captain Joseph Miller, declared that he was studying logistics and other things so as "to remake the military along modern lines."

When Robert Kennedy rejoined the permanent subcommittee, he resumed the pattern of relationships he'd begun the year before: blind hostility toward the chief counsel, loyal affection toward the chairman. Cohn recalled that RFK made his feelings known immediately: "Well, Bobby did come back. . . . But . . . he didn't come back to fight McCarthy, he came back to fight me." One day, Cohn continued, the minority counsel "went up to Senator McCarthy's office looking for him. He couldn't get him. Then he asked for Mary Driscoll, who was the senator's longtime secretary. And he . . . finally found her in the beauty shop at the Senate Office Building. And . . . he said, 'I couldn't find Joe, but I want you to give him a message. In these hearings, I'm going to do nothing to hurt him. In fact, I'm going to protect him every way I can, and I still feel exactly the same way as I always have about him. But I'm really out to get that little son of a bitch Cohn.' And of course, Mary related this to Senator McCarthy and then he called her in and had her tell it to me, and any doubts I had as to where Bobby stood . . . were eliminated at that point."

One session in the Fort Monmouth inquest led to Robert Kennedy's first clash with an antagonist he would battle often in the years to come. After the subcommittee's pointless interrogation of an army Teletype operator, Senator Symington dispatched Bobby to FBI headquarters for further data on the woman. Louis Nichols, an assistant to J. Edgar Hoover, refused to grant RFK access to the files. Kennedy persisted, urging that the matter be resolved by the director himself. Hoover, who had been funneling information to Cohn and McCarthy, took note of the presumptuous young attorney; in a memorandum to Nichols, he said:

"Robert Kennedy has got to be watched. He is a dangerous fellow." The memo easily could have been applied to Al Capone.

In mid-March, the army, tired of McCarthy's harassment, struck back. It released an accounting, drawn in painful detail, of Cohn's efforts on behalf of Schine. The resulting uproar led to calls for a full airing of the controversy, and on April 22, 1954, Karl E. Mundt, Republican senator from South Dakota, gaveled the Permanent Subcommittee on Investigations to order in what immediately became known as the Army-McCarthy hearings.

Mundt, who presided because McCarthy was a party to the dispute, laid out the issues: the army charged that McCarthy, Cohn and others had "sought by improper means to obtain preferential treatment for one Private G. David Schine"; McCarthy and Cohn countered that the army, in the persons of Robert Stevens and John Adams, "made constant attempts to trade off preferential treatment for Private Schine as an inducement to the Subcommittee to halt" the Fort Monmouth probe. The hearings quickly proved the army's case and refuted McCarthy's. Hardly had the army held Schine "hostage" in order to "blackmail" the subcommittee, as the Wisconsin senator and his chief counsel contended; the shakedown had in fact come from Cohn and McCarthy, who throughout their campaign for Schine made plain the link between their associate's fate and the severity of their witch-hunt.

But the issues paled before the spectacle of the personalities. The army had signed on as its chief counsel a sixty-five-year-old Boston lawyer named Joseph Welch. A lifelong Republican, whose calm authority bespoke his eminent career and whose earnest, flat inflection divulged his Iowa roots, Welch was cast as leading accuser of McCarthy, the street-corner bully with the abrasive voice and the arrogant laugh. Washington hostesses canceled parties and jockeyed for admission to the audience. All over America, citizens chose up sides as they watched the confrontation unfold on television—broadcast live, the hearings consumed 187 hours over thirty-five days and attracted 20 million viewers.

Beneath the jousting of Welch and McCarthy, Robert Kennedy and Roy Cohn quietly pursued their feud. Cohn described the role his nemesis played: "When I was testifying as a witness, or out at the other end of the table, I could see him feeding questions to the Democratic minority. And whenever I said anything or tried to do anything, he would always have this smirk on his face, which I suppose was designed to get under my skin and did get under my skin."

Finally, the vendetta erupted onto center stage one Friday when the witness was Joe McCarthy and the topic was a "psychological warfare" plan Schine had concocted to combat communism around the globe. "Bobby," according to Cohn, "provided Senator Jackson with a bunch of questions, each of which poked fun at Dave's plan. And every time Kennedy fed him another question, Jackson burst into laughter. I became more and more pissed—at both of them." Schine's scheme called for enlisting the help of the Elks and the Knights of Columbus. Where, Jackson wanted to know, were the Elks lodges in Pakistan and Africa? "The crowd tittered," reported the *New York Post*. And Cohn snapped.

After the hearing had been recessed—and the television cameras shut off—he approached Bobby; in his hand he held a folder labeled "Jackson's record." "You tell Jackson," Cohn fumed, according to Bobby's account that day in the New York *Daily News*, "that we are going to get on his case on Monday. We will bring up stuff on him. He's been writing favorably on Communists."

"He sounded as though he was about to explode," RFK continued. "He was speaking through his teeth. I told him he had a [fucking] nerve coming to me and threatening a Democratic senator. I told him: 'You started with the army and if you have a threat to make to Senator Jackson you carry it to him yourself.' "

The minority counsel, Cohn said later, "was very heated, white in the face. I said, 'Well, Bob, you have a personal hatred. Your hatred is showing right now.' "

As Cohn further recalled, "One word led to another and finally he was screaming at me and I was going back at him, so finally I said, 'Well, look, this is no place to have an argument. You want to settle it, let's step outside and settle it.' " The rivals didn't wait to leave the Senate Caucus Room before they raised their fists, but they were separated before any blows could be exchanged.

The bad blood between the two young counsels constituted one undercurrent of the hearings; a more pervasive subtext was sex. While the public at large was ignorant of Roy Cohn's personal life, Washington insiders knew plenty. "During the time he worked for McCarthy," recalled Doris Lilly, a society columnist for the Hearst chain of publications, "Roy sublet a town house in Georgetown. He used to throw parties there, inviting judges, lawyers, politicians—some of the town's most powerful citizens. There was a decidedly gay crowd at these parties as well—little eddies of hangers-on who were present for Roy's amusement. He made no secret of his homosexuality."

Considering Cohn's erotic preference, his extraordinary advocacy on behalf of Schine set tongues wagging about the nature of their friendship. Lillian Hellman labeled Cohn, Schine and McCarthy "Bonnie, Bonnie and Clyde." Joseph Welch referred obliquely to the subject at one point during the hearings. Pressing an uncooperative subcommittee aide on the origin of a photograph Schine possessed showing the army private meeting with the army secretary, Welch asked sardonically, "Did you think this came from a pixie?" Welch had begun to move on when Mc-Carthy interrupted to ask that he define the word *pixie*. The courtly bow-tied lawyer was pleased to comply: "I should say, Mr. Senator, that a pixie is a close relative of a fairy." The knowing audience howled with delight. The laughter was even more deafening at Welch's next question, directed to Cohn and referring to the New Yorker's prior description of the photo "as representing Mr. Stevens smiling at Schine."

The conjecture did not stop at Cohn and Schine. Ralph Flanders, senator from Vermont, took the floor of the Senate not only to speculate about the two young principals, but also to implicate their boss in the entanglement. When, the septuagenarian Republican asked, would the hearings then in progress investigate the "real heart" of the situation? It was time, he declared, to solve the "mystery concerning the personal relationships of the army private, the staff assistant, and the senator. There is the relationship of staff assistant to the senator. There is the relationship of the staff assistant to the army private. It is natural that he should wish to retain the services of an able collaborator, but he seems to have an almost passionate anxiety to retain him. Why? And then there is the senator himself. Does the staff assistant have some hold on the senator?" Flanders's question has never been answered.

The Army-McCarthy hearings ended on June 17. Robert Kennedy, in concert with Harvard Law dean James M. Landis, wrote the minority's report. McCarthy and Cohn, the Democrats pronounced, had been guilty of "gross misconduct" in the matter of G. David Schine. Furthermore, the charges made "against Secretary Stevens and Mr. Adams which impugned their patriotism and loyalty, were totally unsubstantiated and unfounded." The Republicans disagreed, finding no wrongdoing on the part of their colleague from Wisconsin.

The acquittal by the subcommittee's majority notwithstanding, Mc-Carthy was convicted by the larger jury watching in living rooms coast to coast. The public had no trouble discerning the hypocrisy in the efforts of the senator and his lawyer, two self-styled superpatriots, on behalf of a semicrackpot goldbricking brat. And in Joseph Welch, McCarthy the public performer met his master. In turn kindly, appalled, humorous, austere, the army's counsel played the high drama, and low comedy, of the proceedings with unerring virtuosity. A sizable portion of the nation still supported Joe McCarthy after the hearings. But most Americans concurred with Welch when, after McCarthy had leveled an especially gratuitous smear at a young associate in his Boston law firm, the jurist asked the senator, "Have you no sense of decency, sir, at long last? Have you left no sense of decency?"

The subcommittee's reports were not filed until September 1, but by then the full Senate had already moved in response to the public mood. On July 30, Ralph Flanders introduced a resolution of censure, and three days later the body voted, 75–12, to create a select committee to report on Resolution 301:

> Resolved, that the conduct of the Senator from Wisconsin, Mr. Mc-
> Carthy, is unbecoming a member of the United States Senate, is contrary
> to Senatorial traditions, and tends to bring the Senate into disrepute.

The panel of six senators opened for business on August 31. Throughout his trial, McCarthy was on his best behavior—at the insistence of his counsel, Edward Bennett Williams, and the committee's chairman, Senator Arthur Watkins of Utah, he curbed the habit of interruption and insult that had so ill served him during the spring. But his politesse did him no good: on September 27, Watkins and his associates recommended that the Senate denounce its wayward son.

Robert Kennedy, seizing the opportunity to again strike out at McCarthy's former chief counsel (and at McCarthy as well for placing him in that spot), likewise recommended censure. The minority report demanded that McCarthy take full responsibility for Cohn's wrongdoing and encouraged the Senate to "take action to correct the situation."

Taking action was not a course one senator looked forward to with pleasure. McCarthy had dated John F. Kennedy's sisters, employed his brother, bent elbows with his father. But Jack squirmed less at the personal aspects of the issue than at the political: many Irish Catholics in Massachusetts had taken Joseph McCarthy to their hearts and even now refused to let go. With Theodore Sorensen's help, Senator Kennedy penned a speech by which he might tiptoe through the minefield: he denounced the Wisconsinite, but only to uphold the presumed "dignity" of the Senate—not necessarily because of any shortcomings on the part of McCarthy himself. If questions of character existed, JFK (or so he wrote) wasn't the person to evaluate them.

Jack never gave the speech—"he had a little luck there," as Charles Spalding later joked. On October 21, a team of four physicians at New York's Hospital for Special Surgery performed a fusion procedure on JFK's spine in the hope of correcting a congenital defect aggravated during the war. Within days, as the doctors had feared, adrenal insufficiency due to Addison's disease led to infection and other complications. Last rites were given, and the patient languished in critical condition for three weeks.

Jack remained hospitalized until December 20, by which time the Senate had already recorded its judgment of McCarthy. JFK had released no statement at the time of the vote, and Spalding recalled the senator's strategy for continuing to avoid comment the day he left his sickbed to be flown to Palm Beach for Christmas: "I was up in the hospital room as they were preparing to take him downstairs and he was looking, sort of tapping his tooth with his finger, and he said, 'You know, when I get downstairs I know exactly what's going to happen. Those reporters are going to lean over my stretcher. There are going to be about ninety-five faces bent over me with great concern, and every one of those guys is going to say, "Now, Senator, what about McCarthy?"' And he said, 'Do you know what I'm going to do? I'm going to reach back for my back and I'm just going to yell, "Oow," and then I'm going to pull the sheet over my head and hope we can get out of there.'"

On December 2, 1954, the United States Senate, by a ballot of 67 to 22, condemned Joseph McCarthy for conduct "contrary to Senatorial traditions." The vote formalized the end of McCarthy's reign as animator of America's id. He remained in the Senate, but overnight his influence vanished. Whereas the year before only one senator had dared oppose his budget, in 1955 he actually could not get a postmaster approved for his hometown. Editors reassigned correspondents who had previously reported his every sneer, and his friends drifted away. Roy Cohn had been one of the first to leave—only weeks after Army-McCarthy had closed, Bobby's archenemy had returned to New York to enter private practice.

Joseph McCarthy died, of causes related to alcoholism, on May 2, 1957. Funerals were held at St. Matthew's Cathedral in Washington, in the Senate Chamber (the first there in seventeen years) and at St. Mary's Roman Catholic Church in Appleton, Wisconsin, where the body was interred on a bluff atop the Fox River.

Robert Kennedy attended all three services.

8

THE McCLELLAN COMMITTEE

Robert F. Kennedy," announced the *Washington Daily News* on January 18, 1955, "whose tousled hair and Irish charm make him look even younger than 29, will take over this week the job of chief counsel of the Senate Investigations subcommittee." Two years after he'd been slighted by his father's friend Senator McCarthy, Bobby finally achieved the position to which he'd aspired. He owed his good fortune to an election, and to a new patron.

John McClellan became the subcommittee's chairman after his party recovered command of the Senate in the 1954 midterm elections. The Arkansas Democrat chose as chief counsel a man with whose work he had become well acquainted the last twenty-four months: not only had McClellan been ranking minority member of the subcommittee under McCarthy, he'd also served with Joseph Kennedy on the Hoover commission. He later recalled his early opinion of Bobby: "Although he was then a young attorney and just beginning his professional career, he was mature beyond his years. I was attracted and impressed by his keen intellect and capacity to research and organize material and to make an analytical presentation of facts and proposals."

Grandson of a sharecropper, fifty-nine-year-old John L. McClellan had served in the Senate since 1942. Although his formal education did not extend past tenth grade, he'd learned the law as a youth while traveling a three-county judicial circuit with his father. Ike McClellan, who had studied for the bar by night while teaching in a one-room country schoolhouse by day, took his son in as partner when the boy was only seventeen. After passing an oral examination given by local counselors, John became the youngest practicing lawyer in the history of his state.

From early childhood, the quick-witted future senator had settled on a career in politics—Democratic politics, since in the white South of the early twentieth century Republicans were as unappreciated as they were in Irish Boston of the same time—and after service in World War I he became active in his local party, winning election as a prosecutor in 1926 and as a congressman in 1934.

Few outside Arkansas noticed Senator McClellan before Army-McCarthy, but the televised hearings brought attention to the "man of dour visage, of dark and funereal aspect," as the *Saturday Evening Post* characterized him. His sober, lawyerly questions, asked in an intonation so deep that journalist Mary McGrory once dubbed it the "Voice of Doom," stood out amid the general circus. His performance won praise from the Senate's liberal Democrats, who previously had never considered forgiving the conservative southerner for the enmity he directed at Harry Truman through most of the Missourian's presidency.

Army-McCarthy had enhanced Robert Kennedy's stature, too, and in January 1955 he traveled to Louisville, Kentucky, to be honored as one of the Ten Outstanding Young Men of 1954 by the nation's Junior Chamber of Commerce. "McClellan understood that he had a good thing in Bob Kennedy," recalled Dr. Bob Riley, a close friend of the senator's who served as lieutenant governor of Arkansas during the 1970s. "He knew that as Bobby's reputation grew, so would his own."

The serious-minded son of poor rural Dixie took the serious-minded son of wealthy urban New England under his wing. "Senator McClellan was very high on Robert Kennedy," Riley continued, "as high as you can get—they got along splendidly. He found out that Bobby was the best person on his staff; he saw something in the young man that was true, something that was going to help his cause, and it did."

Perhaps the older man's affection for his young associate was enhanced by an element common to their otherwise divergent backgrounds: family tragedy. John McClellan's mother had died when he was only three weeks old, and during the 1940s he lost two sons: one succumbed to illness while serving in the army during the North Africa campaign; another perished in a traffic accident a few years later. To the senator, RFK was not just another employee. "John got himself convinced that Robert Kennedy was the total article he was looking for and never changed his mind," said Riley. "And when Bobby would question witnesses during a hearing, the senator would beam like a proud father."

Upon assuming authority, the subcommittee's decorous new chairman set out to rid the panel of the excesses it had suffered under the uninhibited former leader. His first step was to commission Bobby to draw up a new set of rules that would preclude the abuse of procedure, and of witnesses, so often practiced and condoned by McCarthy. The new guidelines protected the rights of those giving testimony, granted the minority a greater voice in subcommittee proceedings and banned McCarthy's habit of conducting hearings with no other member present. Also, to be sure he eliminated all vestiges of the old regime, McClellan cleaned house, hiring not only a new chief counsel, but virtually an entire new staff, and he trimmed the number of employees to nineteen from 1954's high of twenty-five.

The most decisive break with the events of the previous two years came in the agenda. Before McCarthy had turned the subcommittee into his personal garden of anti-Communist delights, it had been concerned with the investigation of less sensational government corruption, that is, with graft and waste, not treason and intrigue. McClellan determined to return the panel to its initial mission, and declared he would leave the uncovering of Communists to its properly mandated forum, the Internal Security Subcommittee of the Judiciary Committee.

Before the shift could take effect, however, unfinished business beckoned. Writing McClellan in December, Robert Kennedy had recommended a reevaluation of the Peress case: "If there is a rotten situation in the Army it should be exposed; if there is not, the bogeyman should be put to rest." Eight days of hearings in March revealed evidence of a bevy of oversights and errors in the Army's original investigation of the matter. Still, where the former chairman had detected "deliberate Communist infiltration," the current subcommittee ascribed the hapless dentist's "promotion and honorable discharge" mainly to military bureaucracy and lack of judgment.

Another bit of "unfinished business" involved the reopening of McCarthy's previous inquiry into alleged espionage at American defense plants. In May, a number of so-called "security risks" were summoned to appear before the subcommittee to explain their alleged ties to the Communist Party. Those willing to cooperate were permitted to confess their sins behind closed doors; the unrepentants were exposed in full public glare. Four employees of the Westinghouse Corporation—one who pleaded the Fifth Amendment, three who refused to testify—soon lost their jobs.

"McClellan was a stern taskmaster," recalled LaVern Duffy, RFK's staff assistant, "and commanded an awful lot of respect. He and Robert Kennedy had a close relationship. The senator let Bob do a lot of things he would never let anyone else do." With purity ensured at Westinghouse, Senator McClellan's chief counsel finally steered the subcommittee in the more prosaic direction his boss had earlier outlined. The panel shifted its focus to supposed illegalities and kickbacks in such areas as the construction of grain elevators, the manufacture of naval uniforms, the importation of Swiss watches, the exportation of wheat and wheat products.

As unglamorous and petty as the hearings of 1955 were, they nonetheless gave Robert Kennedy a chance to cut his teeth as an interrogator. He soon earned renown as "a very forceful examiner," in the words of Paul Tierney, a former FBI agent whom Bobby hired for his staff. "Some people," Tierney contended, "criticized Bob for being *too* forceful, for being a little too abrupt in his questions. I didn't think so. Remember, in those days we had a mission in mind, we were all gung ho. It depended on what side of the fence you were on." From journalist Bob Novak's side, "a lot of the proceedings were staged. They would give Bobby a long leash. Senatorial hearings to this day are not a textbook case in fairness, and McClellan was no civil libertarian. I think he sometimes played the good cop and Bobby was the bad cop." Ralph Dungan, an assistant to JFK, considered Bobby a bad cop, indeed: "At that time, when he worked for the McClellan committee, he was a little fascist."

RFK's burgeoning cocksureness caused him to collide again with the director of the FBI. When Bobby suggested that the subcommittee look into wiretapping in the nation's capital, one of Hoover's aides wrote that Kennedy's views seemed to be at odds with those of the Bureau. Hoover's ire was relayed to James Juliana, the subcommittee's minority counsel, who conveyed the message to Bobby and the Democrats, and the probe was shelved.

His missteps with Hoover notwithstanding, RFK was learning the ropes. Russell Baker, who covered Capitol Hill during this period, wrote in his memoir *The Good Times* of Bobby's rapid development:

> At first it was easy to dislike this rich, favored, young Kennedy. As a committee counsel, he was clearly incompetent. He stammered, got confused in his questions, blushed, got angry, lost his poise, seemed childish, a boy trying to do a man's job. Except for the famously rich father, I thought, he would be lucky to find work as a file clerk.
>
> I moved to covering other things and didn't come back to his committee for several months, and was surprised to discover he had grown up, and had done it very quickly. Now his questioning was calm, shrewd, and to the point. He had picked up the self-confidence needed to keep him in control of touchy situations in the hearing room. Surprising in a daddy's rich boy, he had a sense of irony, a sharp wit, and the gift of

humor. I began to forgive him, then to admire him. . . . I began thinking
he was wasting his life as counsel on a rather shabby Senate committee.
I thought he had a bright political future, and wondered why he didn't
start working on it.

The obscurity of the subcommittee's affairs did give way briefly for
five days of hearings in July. Charles Bartlett, Washington reporter for
the *Chattanooga News* and friend of the Kennedys (it was he and his
wife who first introduced Jack and Jackie), told Bobby that he suspected
Harold Talbott of using his position as Secretary of the Air Force to benefit Paul B. Mulligan & Company, an engineering consulting firm of which
he controlled fifty percent of the stock. The fact that Joe Kennedy had
played golf with Talbott a number of times in Palm Beach did not deter
RFK from launching an all-out investigation. The investigation and ensuing hearings resulted in Talbott's resignation.

"Bobby was the driving force behind the McClellan committee," asserted Ken O'Donnell, "he and John McClellan and, eventually, Irving
Ives [Republican senator from New York]. But as chief counsel Bobby
asked most of the questions. He could be a bit like a bull in a china shop
the way he charged forward with his questions, but he got the job done.

"There was the sense that Bob was out to prove himself because
he was so young. And he obviously succeeded, because he gained the
admiration of his staff and the other members of the committee. In my
opinion, his work for McClellan was what put him on the political map.
Because of the subcommittee's success, Bobby became a force to be
reckoned with."

On July 27, 1955, the same day the Talbott hearings concluded, Robert
Kennedy left Washington for Paris aboard Pan American Airlines
Flight 116. He did not remain long in France—after only an hour at Orly
Airport he boarded a plane for Tehran, where he met up with William
O. Douglas to begin a monthlong tour of Soviet Central Asia.

An intrepid traveler, the Supreme Court justice had previously visited
non-Communist states in the region and wanted to be able to compare
conditions under the opposing political systems. Four previous applications for a visa had been denied—in 1949 *Pravda* had curiously branded
him a CIA agent—but in 1955, with Stalin dead and relations with the
West beginning to thaw, the Kremlin finally granted permission. For
Bobby, John McClellan's permission was needed as well; the chairman
obliged, promising RFK that the job of chief counsel would not be filled
in the young man's absence.

According to Bobby's later account, the idea of his going along came from Douglas. When the jurist had come to Charlottesville to address the University of Virginia law students, RFK explained, "we were talking about some of his trips, and he said he was hoping to go to Central Asia and asked if I would be interested. I said I would, and he had been trying every year since then to get visas."

In fact, Bobby had been foisted on Douglas by the young man's father, who had begun the justice's Washington career by luring him from Yale Law School to work for the SEC during the 1930s. As Douglas later wrote, "Joe Kennedy telephoned me and asked if I would take Bobby to Russia with me. He said, 'I think Bobby ought to see how the other half lives.'

"I told Joe that I would be happy to take his son. Joe was a crusty reactionary and a difficult man, but he was very fond of me and he cared a great deal about his boys. He had big plans for Bobby and probably thought that the Russian trip would be important in his education."

Douglas's wife at the time, Mercedes, argued against taking the young hothead. "I felt that Bobby was not really very admirable," she later remembered, "that anybody who worked for Joe McCarthy was actually pretty terrible." As vehement a defender of the First Amendment as the senator from Wisconsin was its foe, Bill Douglas nonetheless felt he could not refuse the man to whom he at least in part owed his seat on the High Court: "Anything that Joe wants," he told his wife, "I must do because Joe is my friend."

Following a meeting with the shah, the travelers left Tehran by taxi for the Iranian port city of Bandar-e Pahlavi, on the Caspian Sea. There they boarded a Soviet freighter bound for Baku, capital of the Azerbaijan Soviet Socialist Republic. Landing in Baku, RFK and Douglas were informed that, contrary to their expectations, no interpreter would be provided. Realizing that their hotel accommodations would be outfitted with listening devices, the two Americans conceived an ingenious solution to their predicament: "We went to Justice Douglas's room," Bobby later reported, "and on the way we had a whispered conversation as to our strategy." Alone inside the room, "in rather loud voices, we discussed what an obvious mistake these people in Baku were making; that although we hated to do so we would have to telephone Nikita Khrushchev to tell him of the very bad treatment we had received and that certainly Khrushchev would be very upset with those people who were treating us in this manner. Within an hour . . . [tourism officials were] knocking at our door and explaining that they had just made arrangements with Moscow to have a special guide furnished to us and that they were going to do everything possible to facilitate our forthcoming trip, and we were sure that we had everything to make us comfortable."

Through Azerbaijan, Turkmenistan, Uzbekistan, Tajikistan, Kazakhstan, Kirghizia and western Siberia, the pair were shown the highlights of socialist society: collective farms and steel mills, textile plants and power stations, libraries and universities, folk festivals and operas. And "at almost every stop and at every introduction," wrote Douglas, "Bobby would insist on debating with some Russian the merits of Communism." RFK informed the growers of wheat that their counterparts in Nebraska achieved superior output per acre and he pressed labor leaders about their unions' right to strike. The learned judge grew abashed at the behavior of the nearly thirty-year-old prosecutor more than a quarter century his junior: "I said, 'Bobby, that's whistling in the wind. You never can argue with these fellows, so why don't we just forget about it . . . rather than . . . try to convert some guy who will never be converted?' "

In Alma-Ata, Kazakhstan, the duo met with representatives of the local secret police. According to RFK, the MVD, as the organization was then called, had never before granted an interview to foreigners. Thus, the officials could not have been prepared for their relentless grilling by Bobby, who treated them as though they were witnesses before his subcommittee: How many prison workers were there in the Soviet Union? In Kazakhstan? How many MVD agents operated in uniform as opposed to plain clothes? Was the organization active outside the Soviet Union? The helpless provincial gendarmes, unaccustomed as they were to the receiving end of an interrogation, answered each query politely but evasively. Whether they took notes on the young American's inquisitorial technique is unknown.*

After the episode in the Baku hotel, Bobby wanted to know about the MVD's use of wiretapping. "They said that they frowned upon that 'disgraceful' practice," Bobby recounted back in Washington, "that they never touch mail either; that it was most despicable for anyone to do that sort of thing." (Apparently, Robert F. Kennedy was not a person with whom officials on either side of the Iron Curtain wished to discuss electronic surveillance in 1955.)

Bobby marveled at the number of women toiling on farms—"in their

---

*What is known, however, is that the KGB documented RFK's visit. Newly released KGB files describe Bobby as "a brash, outspoken, dangerous opponent" of socialism, who on "more than one occasion during his stay" asked his interpreter to "provide him with women of loose morals." According to the files, the interpreter did not comply with what presumably was a request on Bobby's part to see a prostitute.

bright red and blue dresses busily working in the field"—noted with distaste the placement of children in state-run nurseries for day care, and shook his head at the statues and pictures of "Lenin and Stalin everywhere, until it comes out of your ears." He took a particular interest in the Bolsheviks' suppression of religion. Noting that most houses of worship in the once devoutly Islamic region had been shuttered since the advent of Soviet rule, Bobby visited what mosques, and churches, he could find. A professor in Frunze, Kirghizia, told him that Communists "look upon people who practice religion as backward people." The brave Catholic tourist wore his backwardness with pride: "Everywhere he went," wrote Douglas, "he carried ostentatiously a copy of the Bible in his left hand."

The Soviet citizens did not hesitate to return Bobby's criticisms with challenges of their own. At each location, he later recalled, "after our question period was finished, we always asked our hosts . . . if they had any questions for us. Almost invariably they spoke about the discrimination against Negroes in the U.S. and asked whether they were being mistreated and whether there were any lynchings taking place. They were critical of segregation in the U.S., even though it is practiced to a much greater extent in the Soviet Union." (Bobby was pleased to report back to his countrymen that the "schools of Central Asia are segregated," with the "white" European Russians attending one institution and the "dark" native inhabitants another.) By the time he'd resumed his work in Washington, RFK had devised a solution to what he considered the Soviets' misimpression of American race relations: "I think it would be a wonderful thing if the Harlem Globetrotters would consider going to Russia and touring the country for a month. . . . However, I doubt if the Russians would give them permission, as that would help the U.S." RFK did not say whether he had raised this idea to his traveling companion, who the previous year had voted in the Supreme Court's unanimous decision, in *Brown v. Board of Education,* to integrate American public education.

After several days in the Tien Shan mountain range, the travelers prepared to depart for Russia's capital. Flying across western Siberia toward Moscow, RFK became, as Douglas wrote afterward, "very, very sick. I felt his forehead and was sure that his temperature must be at least 105 degrees. We got off the plane at Omsk and went immediately to a room which our interpreter had reserved for us at the airport. I told Bobby I was going to call a doctor. He said he would have nothing to do with one because Russian doctors were Communists and he hated Communists. I told Bobby I had promised both his father and his wife,

Ethel, that I would bring him back in a safe and sound condition and that whether he liked it or not, I was getting a doctor."

Douglas put his sickly charge to bed and slipped away to send for a physician. Soon, a woman dressed in white, Bobby's age, arrived to examine the by-then delirious cold warrior. The doctor reported to Douglas, "Our patient is very disturbed." "How right she was," wrote the judge; "for nearly two months he had been on a veritable crusade that was charged with great emotion." Using medicine Douglas had been carrying, she administered doses of penicillin and streptomycin. She didn't leave the ailing American's room for thirty-six hours, and would accept no payment on her departure. Douglas remained in Omsk for four days, then flew to Moscow. His recovering companion, embarrassed to have had his life saved by an admirer of Karl Marx, followed two days later.

On September 2, the sojourners were greeted in the Soviet capital by Bobby's wife and two of his sisters, Jean and Pat. The party of five visited Moscow for six days, dining with the American ambassador and seeing *Swan Lake* at the ballet, then moved on for a brief visit to Leningrad. The week in Russia permitted Ethel to add her voice to her husband's frank condemnation of communism's evils. She gave "one woman's opinion of religion" to an atheistic Russian guide and took umbrage at the local method of tending youngsters during the workweek—"Speaking as a mother," she harrumphed upon her homecoming, "I was shocked by the way they take children . . . and put them into State nurseries. The mothers don't get to see them until about 8 in the evening." (She doubtless would later repeat that opinion to her own children, now including three-month-old David Anthony Kennedy, born June 15, who spent Ethel's Russian trip in the care of hired help back home.)

The Kennedys parted company with Douglas—who left for Helsinki—and journeyed to Warsaw, which Bobby thought "100 percent better off than any place I saw in Russia. . . . The big thing is that the Polish people are a stubborn people. They have a natural dislike for the Russians, and the Communists are having a hard time getting through a large number of their theories. For instance, you can't get into a church on Sunday because they are so crowded." After a couple of days, Robert, his wife and his sisters reentered the Free World, taking a train to Berlin, then making their way to the south of France, where they spent a week recovering from their tour of the workers' paradise and enjoying the fruits of the laissez-faire system their fathers had so profitably mastered.

The Kennedys crossed the ocean on the *Ile de France* and landed in New York on September 22. Bobby, after a quick trip to his Washington office, followed his family to Hyannis Port. There he reported to his father the details of the trip not already related by Bill Douglas, who had arrived on the Cape a few days earlier at Joe's invitation.

In October, a reporter asked Bobby if he would like to visit the USSR again someday. "I had enough of it," the traveler replied.

B obby returned to his job with Senator McClellan. On most weekdays, Bobby would compile copious legal briefs and conduct detailed examinations of witnesses as he ferreted out fraud and subversion in the halls of power. On days off and on weekends, he would fly to New York, where he learned another side of law enforcement.

"The Federal Bureau of Narcotics,"* asserted Howard Diller, today a leading criminal-defense attorney, "was a cross between the KGB, the FBI and the Gestapo." Precursor to today's Drug Enforcement Administration, the FBN employed 240 agents, most of whom operated out of New York headquarters at 90 Church Street in lower Manhattan and undertook drug busts throughout the city's five boroughs. "Nobody really knew about the group, not even in government," said Diller, who served as an FBN agent at the time. "It was all very hush-hush. It was led by Harry J. Anslinger, a man who wore the same suits for thirty-five years. His appearance was incredible—he resembled a wrestler I remember called the Swedish Angel. Anslinger was about six two, two hundred sixty pounds, with a head that was completely cueball. When you saw him, you started to shake."

RFK found a home with the FBN. "There used to be the phenomenon of the buff," Diller continued. "A detective squad might have a seventy-year-old Irish guy who'd go for coffee or sharpen pencils. Obviously, he wouldn't get paid for the errands; the reward would be that he'd get to ride in the radio car. A fire department buff would get to ride in the ladder truck. So, in a sense, Bob Kennedy was a buff, a groupie. He'd enjoy the company of the agents. They were tough, they drank, they played around—he thought he was like that, too."

Anslinger and the other top officials of the Federal Bureau of Narcotics didn't mind accommodating the taste for adventure of an up-and-coming Washington attorney with a famous name and strong ties to Congress. Moreover, Bobby's run-ins with J. Edgar Hoover made the FBN a natural school for his continuing education. "In J. Edgar Hoover's portfolio," noted Diller, "there was no such thing as organized crime. He

---

*The Federal Bureau of Narcotics, known today as the Drug Enforcement Administration (DEA), had several different names over the years, including the Bureau of Narcotics and Dangerous Drugs (BNDD). It has grown in size to a veritable megaforce.

pooh-poohed Anslinger, who did focus on the mob. As for Bobby, he started to believe in the existence of organized crime from the beginning of his service on the McClellan committee. Since the FBI wouldn't give Bobby the time of day, he gravitated toward us." "Bobby had a romance with the Bureau of Narcotics," maintained William G. Hundley, then employed in the internal security section of the Justice Department and during the Kennedy administration Bobby's top assistant for organized crime and racketeering. "I believe the Bureau of Narcotics represented his first true exposure to organized crime. Before that, he'd barely heard of the Cosa Nostra."

The existence of organized crime was not the only point of departure between the two bureaus. "The FBN's agents were quite different from those who worked for the FBI," Diller maintained. "We were freewheeling and undisciplined; many of us were college graduates but at heart we were cowboys and renegades. In those days you didn't need a subpoena or search warrant to enter a house in which you suspected the use of drugs, you just went in with guns drawn. We'd push the people against the wall, arrest them and confiscate the drugs. We did a lot of wiretapping, too, all of it illegal.

"The notion that Anslinger had, and that was consistent with what Robert Kennedy ultimately stood for, is that as long as you got the bad guys, it didn't matter how you did it. So you commit some crimes, you kick a little ass, you have a little fun, you kill somebody—in the end, good would be achieved."

Always well informed, J. Edgar Hoover got wind of Bobby's moonlighting ventures. The news that the chief counsel of the Senate Subcommittee on Investigations was tagging along on operations of what, to the FBI chief, seemed a rogue agency soured Hoover's appraisal of Bobby even further. "I knew about it," said Hoover's longtime aide, Courtney A. Evans, "and I was amazed by it. To actually become involved in the knocking down of doors! Those were the kind of madcap antics that always made the director suspicious of RFK's character, and probably for good reason. He resorted to many of the same ploys after he became attorney general."

Knocking down doors would become the least madcap of Bobby's antics. "Robert Kennedy went along for more than just the ride," recalled Diller. "Pretty soon, he began participating in some of the more illicit aspects of these drug busts, which might involve opium, heroin, hashish and/or cocaine. Other agents who hung out with Bobby, fellows named Jimmy Ceburi and Arthur Krueger, would purportedly come back with reports of him seizing bags of coke for his own use or, more probably, for distribution among his buddies.

"It was an era when New York State in particular did not have any laws against search and seizure. But this tremendous power was not abused across the board—otherwise there'd have been a revolution. It was only abused as to blacks and Hispanics. Most of the people we busted were drug abusers, in places like Harlem and the South Bronx. During the raids, the men would be taken to one room in the apartment, the women to another. It wasn't uncommon for an agent to indulge in sex with one of the women, sometimes more than one. In exchange for their sexual favors, the women were often let go and not carted off to jail. Bobby caught on fast. I think he enjoyed the anonymous sex, because that way he wasn't really cheating on Ethel—or at least that's how he could rationalize it. Bobby thought nothing of fondling these women or having intercourse with them. Or he'd force them to engage in fellatio. Then, afterward, he'd brag about it, just like the agents.

"In the Federal Bureau of Narcotics, Bobby discovered a kind of fantasy existence that enabled him to escape the vagaries of his humdrum workaday life. Amazingly, nobody has ever mentioned or even written about RFK's close ties to the Bureau of Narcotics. What is truly ironic about his secret activities with the bureau is that soon thereafter he was named attorney general of the United States, the top law-enforcement officer in the country. Yet here's a man who raped and pillaged and stole, a man who presumably took drugs. Bobby loved that James Bond bullshit, the 007-type of stuff, and all the dirt that went with it. He struck me as basically schizophrenic, a man capable of great good and, at the same time, incredible evil. The Roman emperor Caligula seemed mild by comparison."

Robert F. Kennedy did not rely solely on the marauders of the Federal Bureau of Narcotics to take him prowling the mean streets of New York City. "Bobby and I were friendly from the late forties when I was working as a photographer for the *Daily News* and did the night beat on crime," recalled Mel Finkelstein. "Bobby would come up from D.C. and we'd ride together, chasing down crime stories with the police radio blaring.

"We'd stop at Horn & Hardart for coffee with the rest of the midnight-shift reporters. Bobby loved to bullshit with these guys, most of whom are now dead, I imagine. He had this fascination with crime and criminals. He also had an intensely homophobic reaction to gays. He could be sweet, but at other times was mean-spirited and Machiavellian.

I once told him that the little criminal, the drug pusher in the alleyway, wasn't important. It was the kingpin, the importer, who had to be rounded up. But he didn't seem to differentiate—big guys, little guys, if they were criminals, they were all the same to him.

"We once heard a radio call about some black guy in a sixth-floor walk-up in Harlem hurting his live-in girlfriend's baby. We got there just as the cops did. The guy had this two-year-old girl on a bed and he was making her do fellatio on him—of course, the baby didn't know what she was doing. Bobby went into the other room to try to console the girl-friend, who had been beaten up and was hysterical. Then he joined us back in the bedroom, where one of the four cops opened the window and the other three took this black guy and heaved him out of it. Bobby must have been shocked, but he never said a goddamn word.

"Another time we were in a seedy midtown bar on the West Side of Manhattan. Somebody there recognized Bobby from the newspapers— this was when he was working for McClellan. So this bloke, who was more than a little tight, started spouting off to Bob about 'rich kid' this and 'Boston Irish' that, and about how Bobby's father was a piece of shit. Then he began to push Bobby around. He was a big motherfucker, white guy, maybe six four, two hundred fifteen pounds, a construction worker, and RFK was maybe five nine, a hundred thirty-five pounds. As they got up to go outside I thought, Christ, this gorilla's going to murder Bobby. I tried to intervene—I said, 'Hey, Bob, forget it'—but he just pushed me aside. The hard hat reached the sidewalk first, and as soon as he turned around, Bobby sucker punched him—it's the old streetfighter's trick. He broke the guy's nose. There was blood everywhere and this guy was out of it.

"I also saw Bobby take advantage of hookers. He loved hookers, he loved New York City street life. He screwed the women for nothing by threatening to run them in if they didn't come across, and that's some-thing he did until the day he died. Robert Kennedy was a strange admix-ture. He'd also pick up bums on the street and buy meals for them at that restaurant his father co-owned, La Caravelle.

"One of the most unusual men I've ever known."

9

HICKORY HILL

We've come a long way since McCarthy—I'm happy with the rules that govern the subcommittee," Robert F. Kennedy said to LaVern Duffy. As he approached his thirtieth birthday, Bobby was a man who, to outward appearances, lived according to well-defined, time-honored rules. He occupied a highly visible position as a morally certain enforcer of his nation's laws. Obeying the commands of his church, he had brought into the world the beginnings of a large family of Catholics.

Yet he was driven to abide outside the rules of both God and man. The accountable government attorney took advantage of his position to force himself on frightened, indigent women in trouble with the authorities. The father and husband guiltlessly conducted extramarital affairs. The educated son of wealth and privilege got into bar fights with little hesitation. In his late teens and early twenties, RFK had been shy, diffident. Uncomfortable around his social peers, he sought refuge on a football field among boys of humbler background. Ill at ease with women, he received his sexual initiation at an age embarrassingly late for a son of Joseph Kennedy. The rebellion against society's bonds that had not occurred during Bobby's adolescence took place later; the confidence acquired in the intervening decade, combined with the power of a man embarked on a career of influence, gave his behavior a dangerous, aggressive edge. He was embracing, and acting upon, the sense of invulnerability conferred upon him by his rule-breaking father.

Politically, he hadn't veered far from Joe Kennedy's place in the right flank of the Democratic Party. Although capable of individual acts of conscience toward African Americans—as in his principled stands regarding his Harvard teammate and Ralph Bunche—Bobby remained essentially untouched by the growing movement for black equality that was beginning to take hold of the nation's agenda. His break with Joseph McCarthy had been more over the tactics and personality of Roy Cohn than over the senator's assault on intellectual freedom, and the year after the Wisconsinite's humiliation Bobby had been happy to separate four ordinary citizens from their jobs with a defense contractor. Indeed, America's citizenry may owe Joe McCarthy a debt of gratitude for his choice of Cohn over Kennedy in December 1952; had the senator initially hired as his chief aide the politically astute young conservative lawyer, instead of the politically oblivious young conservative lawyer who would confuse a personal relationship with an issue of national urgency, he might never have self-destructed so spectacularly. Who knows what devastation the demagogue might have wrought under the guidance of a mind as shrewd, and a will as determined, as Bobby Kennedy's?

For Bobby was shrewd and he was determined. In 1952 he had engineered a groundbreaking electoral campaign that foreshadowed the broad changes that would overtake American politics in the last half of the twentieth century—changes he would be instrumental in shaping. As he entered his fourth decade, Robert Kennedy was decisive, righteous, loyal, brilliantly analytical. He was also violent, immoral, promiscuous, uncontrolled. He was a man of great promise and a man of intriguing contradictions. The word *ruthless* has often been used to describe him. No wonder.

I n the early afternoon of Monday, October 3, 1955, the parents of Ethel Kennedy drove to Connecticut's Bridgeport Airport. Stepping aboard a converted B-26 bomber, which George had purchased for his corporate fleet after the air force had decommissioned it, the couple took off on a business trip to Los Angeles. Pilot Joseph Whitney, who was captain of the company's aviation department, and copilot John McBride flew the twin-engine craft southwest, touching down that evening for refueling in Tulsa, Oklahoma. Back in the air for only half an hour, Whitney radioed the control tower at Oklahoma City that he needed to make an emergency landing. Within two minutes, however, people on the ground in nearby Union City noticed a plane, flying at an unusually low altitude, with flames shooting from the engines. Moments later, they saw the aircraft consumed by an explosion. When officers of the Oklahoma State Highway Patrol examined the wreckage, they found the bodies burned almost beyond recognition. The troopers identified the party by means of the pilot's wallet and George Skakel's Diners Club card.

George and Big Ann left seven surviving children, six of whom promptly converged on the family's Greenwich home. Ethel, as Jerry Oppenheimer noted in his biography of her, wished to join her siblings at Rambleside in making arrangements for the Friday funeral. But Bobby, perhaps to shield his wife's feelings, perhaps to keep her from the alcohol he knew would be flowing freely in the Skakel household, would not permit her to go. Ethel would not assist in the burial's planning, RFK told George Skakel, Jr., who had called the Kennedys' Washington home to discuss the ceremony; she would be present only to attend the funeral. The dutiful wife obeyed her husband, to the outrage of her brothers and sisters.*

When the Kennedys arrived Thursday night, they found themselves in the midst of a traditional Irish wake, with the traditional Skakel abundance of liquid refreshment. On Friday, October 7, hundreds of friends and acquaintances crowded into St. Mary's Roman Catholic Church, where Bobby and Ethel had been wed five years earlier, to hear Requiem High Mass. After the interment at St. Mary's Cemetery, the guests wended their way to Rambleside, where the cocktail-party atmosphere continued.

Ethel longed to remain in Greenwich for a few days, but Bobby overruled her once again. They left that evening for New York, where they dined at Le Pavillion and slept at the Carlyle Hotel, where Joseph Kennedy leased for his clan a penthouse suite.

In the aftermath of her parents' sudden death, Ethel Kennedy turned to her family's standard antidote for the relief of pain. She was "regularly arrested" for drunken driving during this period, noted Howard Diller. Also, according to journalist Bob Novak, she was several times caught shoplifting small items from Georgetown stores. As the Greenwich police had done for her brothers after the Rambleside shooting years before, authorities conspired to keep Ethel's offenses quiet. Apart from "regular" lectures by judges, and occasional suspensions of her driver's license, no punishment was ever meted out.

Robert Kennedy, knowing a thing or two about death and aircraft, sought to ease his wife's anguish. He learned about a facility in Vancouver, British Columbia, where psychiatrists were experimenting with a then little-known drug, lysergic acid diethylamide. A number of film stars had undergone several weeks of LSD therapy at the appropriately named Hollywood Hospital. One of the participants in the ten-year-long study of the hallucinogen was Cary Grant, who credited the experience with

---

* George Skakel, Jr., would also perish in an airplane. Piloting a small Cessna in September 1966, he crashed in the mountains of western Idaho.

changing his life. "Before taking the drug," said the late actor, "I was a self-centered boor; afterward, I grew up."

Ethel Kennedy has never commented publicly on her psychiatric treatment with LSD. Cary Grant, however, admitted that "Bobby contacted me to ascertain whether the program at Hollywood Hospital might help Ethel regain her footing. 'Well, LSD is preferable to brain surgery,' I told him. I don't know whether Ethel went—I think she did. I do know Bobby and I remained in contact the rest of his life."*

John McClellan's subcommittee accomplished little during the fall of 1955 and the first half of 1956. Despite the chairman's previously stated goal of targeting government fraud, the cold war provided the backdrop for several of the body's investigations, as Bobby and staff cast about for subjects that would capture headlines. In January, the subcommittee heard testimony regarding four vocational schools, attended by veterans of World War II and Korea, reportedly owned by Communists. The rationale for the inquiry lay in the $3 million paid by the Veterans Administration to the various institutions, and in the possibility of amending the GI Bill to exclude such educators from further government munificence. In May, the chairman made public an ongoing probe concerning "what has been called 'brainwashing' " of American prisoners of war during the Korean conflict. "The many phases of this program," noted McClellan, "from personal mistreatment to intensive indoctrination or schooling, resulted in numerous cases of prisoners signing peace petitions and false confessions." Open hearings would serve to educate the public as to the Communists' "inhumane methods" and give insight into how such practices might "be counteracted in the future." Neither investigation attracted much attention: Red trade-school operators were obscure, uncompelling villains; Chinese and Korean jail keepers were distant, unimmediate villains. The subcommittee returned to a familiar subject, hoping to make fresh hay.

The investigation that occupied most of Robert Kennedy's time during these months was an extension of the probe he'd begun, three eventful years before, as an eager new employee of the then-high-riding senator from Wisconsin: East-West trade. Seeking to reignite interest in

---

*According to Canadian health officials, Hollywood Hospital's medical records were destroyed in a fire in 1975, a year after the facility itself closed its doors. A note of interest, however, is that in May 1966, Senator Robert Kennedy [D.-NY] led an inquiry into federal agency involvement in LSD experimentation and therapy. He took the unpopular position that programs and projects in this area ought to continue.

the issue, Bobby and his chairman seized on a year-and-a-half-old statement by Harold Stassen, who in mid-1954 had led the State Department's team in negotiations on the topic with America's allies. Those talks resulted in the reduction, by almost half, of the types of goods embargoed for export to Communist countries. The Europeans had insisted on the reduction, threatening otherwise to drop the sanctions entirely. "I am convinced," said Stassen on his return from the discussions, which had been held in Paris, "that this revision . . . will result in a net advantage to the free world of expanded peaceful trade and more effective control of the war potential items. It is a move in the best interests of the United States." The subcommittee's majority hoped to prove Stassen's prediction wrong by pointing to recently increased commerce between East and West in strategically significant items—"indispensable in time of war"—such as copper, used to make shell casings, motors and communication conductors, and the horizontal boring and milling machine, used in the production of "large hydraulic turbines, ship engine parts, tank turrets and other heavy equipment."

The Eisenhower administration, unwilling to endure further insult on an issue it considered long closed, refused to cooperate with the inquiry. Citing the need to protect national security, it declined to provide classified information; citing the need to protect the policymaking process, it declined to provide "working-level papers"—in other words, practically everything else. The stonewalling frustrated the subcommittee's Democrats, particularly RFK. But with the Korean War long over and Joe McCarthy's once-shaking fist effectively crippled, the public this time showed little concern over the disputed trade and cared even less about the seemingly abstract constitutional issue of executive-branch accountability to Congress. The probe went nowhere.

By the end of the year, John McClellan and Robert Kennedy would land upon a topic that would return them to the spotlight. Meanwhile, Congress took its midsummer recess. Nineteen fifty-six was a presidential election year, and the parties were set to hold their nominating conventions.

On July 1, 1956, John F. Kennedy spent his Sunday morning at the Washington studios of the Columbia Broadcasting System. "I am not a candidate for vice president," he told his questioners on *Face the Nation*. He went on to speculate that Adlai Stevenson, who by then had sewn up his party's second consecutive presidential nomination, would hardly select a running mate who was Catholic and only thirty-nine years old. To balance Stevenson's own strength in the Northeast, JFK surmised, the former Illinois governor would most likely select a southerner when the Democratic National Convention convened in Chicago on August 13. The senator from Massachusetts was quick to add, however, that he would be honored to be asked and "of course . . . would accept if nominated."

Jack had already gone to great lengths to attain that unsought honor. He'd endorsed Stevenson for the nomination the previous October and had thereafter helped to purge anti-Stevenson elements from the Massachusetts Democratic leadership. In case Stevenson appreciated these efforts sufficiently to consider him for the second slot, JFK in early 1956 moved to ensure that his most trusted lieutenant would be in a position to mobilize support at the crucial time. For that arrangement, he turned to the man who had succeeded him as U.S. representative from the Eleventh District. "As a member of Congress," Thomas P. "Tip" O'Neill wrote in his memoirs, "I was in charge of naming four delegates from my district to the Democratic National Convention. I selected three local politicians and kept the fourth spot for myself.

"After I made the appointments, Jack called and asked me to name Bobby as a delegate. But the positions were already filled, and besides, Bobby didn't even live in my district.

" 'I'm sorry, Jack,' I said, 'but I've already notified the delegates.' And I told him who I had picked.

"But Jack would not be denied. 'Tip,' he said, 'my brother Bob is the smartest politician I've ever known. He's absolutely brilliant. You know, lightning may strike at that convention, and I could end up on the ticket with Stevenson. I'd really like to have my brother on the floor as a delegate so he could work for me.'

" 'If you feel that strongly about it,' I said, 'I'll make sure he gets there.' So I took myself off the list and put Bobby on instead."

The party's regular slate of delegates was to be confirmed in the April 24 primary, but in March the plan met an unexpected snag in the person of George P. Donovan, a twenty-eight-year-old from East Boston. Filing a last-minute petition with the State Ballot Law Commission, Donovan appealed for RFK's candidacy to be disqualified on the grounds that he failed to meet residency requirements. As did Jack, Bobby lived close to his work in Washington, and like Jack, he listed his voting address as 122 Bowdoin Street, Boston. "How the senator and his wife, plus Robert and his wife and children could squeeze into this two-room furnished apartment is beyond me," groaned Donovan, who was on the ballot in opposition to those named by the organization. The commission took a week to consider the matter, then allowed itself to be persuaded by JFK's lawyer that the fly of Donovan's protest should be swatted on a technicality. After the ritual of April's voting, Bobby was free to pack his carpetbag to attend his first national convention.

Although Tip O'Neill had given up his own seat in the Massachusetts delegation to Bobby, the senator's brother never thanked him. "I once mentioned this to the old man," O'Neill recalled, "and I'll never forget what he said: 'Tip, let me tell you something. Never expect any appreciation from my boys. These kids have had so much done for them by other people that they just assume it's coming to them.' . . .

"Of all the brothers," O'Neill reflected, "I knew Bobby the least. We weren't friendly, and to be blunt about it, I never really liked him. I'm sure the feeling was mutual. To me, he was a self-important upstart and a know-it-all. To him, I was simply a street-corner pol."

On the eve of the convention's Monday opening, the Kennedys arrived in Chicago hoping for the nod from Stevenson. Jack, Bobby and Teddy checked into a downtown hotel, while the senator's wife, seven months pregnant, bunked with the Shrivers at their luxury Lake Shore Drive apartment that came with Sarge's job as manager of the Merchandise Mart. Regardless of his immediate future vis-à-vis Adlai Stevenson, John F. Kennedy had been cast at the convention as one of the party's rising stars. Before hearing the keynote speech by Frank Clement, governor of Tennessee, the delegates learned of their party's history by viewing a twenty-minute film, produced by MGM and narrated by JFK. Jack, who had gone to Los Angeles in July to record the documentary's voice-over, had been suggested for the job by CBS anchor Edward R. Murrow—Kennedy was "young, bright, charismatic and definitely on his way up," Murrow told screenwriter Norman Corwin. The following night, the party faithful listened again to the handsome senator's voice, this time live, as he delivered the speech placing the name of Governor Stevenson in nomination.

As expected, the Democratic Party named Stevenson its standard-bearer on the first ballot. But the nominee then departed from script. He and his staff had been unable to decide among three senators to fill the bottom half of the ticket: JFK; Hubert H. Humphrey of Minnesota; and Tennessee's Estes Kefauver, whom Stevenson had bested in the primaries. Late Wednesday evening, therefore, instead of submitting his running mate of choice for the convention's ratification, the ex-governor broke with tradition and threw open the decision to the delegates.

Stevenson's surprise electrified the convention. Jack, disappointed that he hadn't been named outright, couldn't resist a challenge and decided to campaign actively for the vote to be taken the next day. His first order of business was to assign Bobby to relay the developments to their most senior adviser. Joseph Kennedy, vacationing in Val-sur-Mer on the French Riviera, exploded upon receiving RFK's phone call. For months, the ambassador had tried to dampen his son's interest in the vice presidential nomination. "Stevenson can't take Eisenhower," he'd cautioned earlier in the year. "Jack's better off without it. If he runs with Stevenson, they'll blame the loss on his being a Catholic. Besides, if you're going to get licked, get licked trying for first place, not second. He's better off running for the top spot in '60."

With a late-night meeting in Jack's hotel room, the Kennedy machine, tested in local and state campaigning, launched its first venture into national politics. Following the conference, Bobby, Teddy, Sargent Shriver, Theodore Sorenson, Ken O'Donnell, Charles Bartlett and others fanned out to hunt for votes. The candidate remained in his room, where he worked the telephones until early morning. Senator George Smathers of Florida remembered picking up the receiver by his hotel bed at 2:30 A.M.: "It was Jack, asking me to nominate him for vice president. I told him to get Connecticut governor Abe Ribicoff. He said he already had Ribicoff, but he wanted me to second the nomination. 'Kefauver has it wrapped up,' I told him. He insisted on running, said it would be wide open. I finally agreed, just to get some sleep.

"When I walked out there the next day at 8:00 A.M., the convention center was half empty. I didn't know what the hell to say. When Jack started in Congress, he was still basically a young upstart, a whippersnapper with big ideas and a wealthy father. Advancing to the Senate, he was not especially industrious or influential as a legislator, and seemed excessively preoccupied, for such a junior senator, with higher office. The ambition was unmistakable, but it was an ambition almost totally devoid of any purpose for the country. The object of winning was simply to win. I didn't think he stood a chance of getting the vice presidency. Well, I started talking about John F. Kennedy as World War II hero—*PT-109* and all that. The guy hadn't done anything politically really. So next I talked about his distinguished family. I repeated this bit three or four times. Suddenly I felt an excruciating pain in my back and chest. I thought I was having a heart attack—right out there on television in front of the world. It was Sam Rayburn, the convention's chairman, poking his gavel into my ribs to let me know that my two minutes were up. 'McCormack's here,' he whispered into my ear. [Massachusetts congressman and House majority leader] John McCormack was to give the other seconding speech, and I was glad as hell to get away from the microphone."

As the day wore on, Bobby roved the arena, visiting various state delegations, pursuing backers with his usual directness. G. Mennen "Soapy" Williams, Michigan's governor, and from 1961 to 1966 assistant secretary of state for African affairs, described a brief but intense encounter with the brash young operative: "As I was leaving the floor . . . suddenly I heard somebody say, grabbing me by the arm, 'Why are you against my brother?' I looked down and was amazed to see a very exercised Bobby Kennedy. And I was just flabbergasted because we had actually, at that point, no animus either for or against Kennedy. We had come as Kefauver supporters. That Kennedy was running didn't affect our strategy or our loyalties one way or another; and to be asked why I was against Jack Kennedy made no sense at all to me."

Bobby's boldness failed him, however, when he was assigned a more familiar figure to cajole. When the Kennedys first asked John McCormack to follow Smathers in seconding the nomination, the congressman demurred, fearing that by taking sides in the vice presidential race he would offend individuals who had assisted him in a prior procedural wrangle. He soon overcame his reluctance, though, and sent one of his state's delegates to fetch RFK. "I went to the back of the convention hall," recalled Peter Cloherty, "and I found Bobby, and he was talking with some people. And as soon as I got a chance to get him aside for a second, I mentioned to him, I said, 'Would you like to have John McCormack second Jack's nomination?' And Bobby, who seemed to be very perturbed about it, said, 'We already asked him, and he refused.' . . .

"I said to him, 'I think if you ask him again, that he will do it.' And I walked down the aisle with him to where the Massachusetts delegation was seated. Congressman McCormack was talking to another member of Congress, and he didn't break it off immediately, and Bobby started to walk away. . . . I said, 'Aren't you going to ask him?' He said, 'He turned his back.' I said, 'He's talking to a member of Congress that he serves with, Bob.' I said, 'Just wait a minute.' "

McCormack finished the chat with his colleague, Cloherty continued, then "turned and he said, 'Yes, Bob.' And Bob was a little hesitant about asking again. I don't know whether he felt there'd be a refusal or he wasn't quite as aggressive a young man as he has become since that time. And I said, 'Mr. Leader, they would like you to second Jack's nomination.' He said, 'That right, Bob?' [RFK] said, 'Well . . . Congressman, yeah, it would be very helpful.' So he said, 'All right come on.' And with that, he went down the aisle with him to have Rayburn recognize him to second Jack's nomination."

The balloting began with the outcome in doubt. Despite Jack's forecast that Stevenson would turn to a man of the South, a number of delegations from that area went for Kennedy because his indifference to civil rights contrasted with the records of his main opponents. Kefauver was considered by many a traitor to his region because of his refusal to stand with his fellow southern legislators in opposition to school desegregation. Humphrey had first gained national attention in 1948 when, as mayor of Minneapolis, he had delivered to the Democratic convention a rousing oration in support of the civil-rights plank in the party platform—an address that helped precipitate that year's walkout, and subsequent independent candidacy, by South Carolina's Strom Thurmond and his "Dixiecrats."

JFK's religion made him unacceptable to some. Ken O'Donnell recalled visiting the Minnesota delegation and asking Congressman Eugene McCarthy, Hubert Humphrey's campaign manager, whether Minnesota would support Kennedy if Humphrey, the state's favorite son, dropped out: "McCarthy, himself a Catholic, looked me in the eye and said, 'Minnesota has too many Protestants to go for Kennedy.' So then I went to see Sam Rayburn, the Speaker of the House, to try and convince him to swing the Texas delegation. 'The last thing we need is a Catholic,' he said. In the end, Lyndon Johnson, then Senate Majority Leader, delivered the Texas vote, but it wasn't enough to get us in. Everything considered, we did pretty well."

Estes Kefauver won his party's nomination for vice president on the first ballot by a mere thirty and a half votes over John Kennedy. The second-place finisher then took the podium to ask that the Tennessean be chosen by acclamation. Jack's speech impressed those assembled in the hall and those watching around the country. "He lost so gracefully," commented Dave Powers, "that from then on, he looked like the all-American boy. He made more friends in losing. . . . You know, the world loves a loser up to a point, and he was the ideal loser that day."

Vying for, then losing the vice presidential slot turned out to be the best of all possible worlds for John F. Kennedy in 1956. He was saddled with no blame for Stevenson's trouncing in November at the hands of the popular incumbent, yet his prominent place in the convention's dramatic events introduced him to a nation hungry for new faces. Around the country during the fall campaign, if either of the party's top two candidates was unable to attend a rally, noted Powers, "Jack Kennedy was the most sought-after speaker. . . . And after Stevenson and Kefauver lost in '56, and it was Stevenson's second time, and we all felt it was the end of the road, these people remembered Jack Kennedy." The compressed run for vice president further fueled the senator's already blazing ambition.

"In twenty-four hours' work," JFK said, "we almost won the second spot. If we work for four years, we can pick up all the marbles."

Following the convention, Jack and his wife flew to Boston. Exhausted by the week's tumult, a heavily pregnant Jackie decided to recuperate at Hammersmith Farm with her mother and stepfather. Her husband, with Teddy, soon left for France. The two brothers had previously made plans with Senator Smathers for a European sailing excursion. Despite her approaching due date, Jackie insisted that the men leave as scheduled. " 'You all worked so hard,' " she said, according to Smathers, " 'especially Jack. He deserves a rest.'

"So we went," the Floridian continued, "but Jack should have known better. Jackie had suffered a miscarriage only the year before, which meant there might be complications. Also, she'd nursed JFK back to health following his back surgery. Now that she needed him he seemed to be deserting her."

Jack and Teddy visited with their father for a few days at Val-sur-Mer, then moved on to Cannes, where they connected with Smathers. The trio of vacationers there chartered a forty-foot sailing vessel that came complete with skipper and galley cook. Evenings, the passenger cabins were crowded, for the men were not alone. One of the women on board, a beautiful American socialite who called herself "Pooh" but was known to others simply as "P," was used to traveling with JFK: she had accompanied him in July when he flew to Los Angeles to record the convention film's narration. "To P—/In memory of times together/In past and future/ John Kennedy," read the inscription in her copy of Jack's new book, *Profiles in Courage*.

On August 23, while her husband and his mistress were enjoying the Mediterranean sun, Jacqueline Kennedy experienced severe abdominal cramps due to an internal hemorrhage. Rushed by her mother to Newport Hospital, she underwent an emergency Cesarean. Doctors extracted a lifeless baby girl.

As she regained consciousness following the surgery, the first person upon whom Jackie laid eyes was her brother-in-law Robert, who had driven to Newport from Hyannis Port after Janet Auchincloss had called him with news of her daughter's condition. Before leaving the Cape, Bobby had tried to reach Jack by transatlantic telephone, but the amenities with which Jack's boat was equipped did not, apparently, include a ship-to-shore radio. It was Robert Kennedy who informed Jackie of her infant's fate.

The dead child's father did not speak to his heartbroken wife for three days. After telephoning her from Genoa, Italy, he expressed mild annoyance but no intention of cutting short his pleasure cruise. George Smathers set him straight: "You better haul ass back to your wife if you ever want to run for president." After two more days enjoying P's company, JFK finally flew home.

Smathers understood the political necessity of a serene marital facade. The truth behind the smiling photographs, however, had little effect on a husband's electoral success during the 1950s, and Jack's growing renown for chasing skirt was a nonfactor in his unsuccessful vice presidential bid. Indeed, the winner of that brief contest had a reputation perhaps surpassing that of his young rival in notoriety—and not just for womanizing. "I always thought Kefauver was a little bit of a phony," offered Edmund G. "Pat" Brown, who attended the 1956 convention as a delegate from California and was elected that state's governor two years later. "He was drinking very heavily at times. He had a little bottle in his pocket and he'd keep drinking it. That's the thing that finally killed him. He was a very heavy drinker. It got worse. He was an absolute alcoholic at the end, I think. . . . He was a terrific guy with the women too. He'd sleep with anybody who came along the pike."

Jack Kennedy would sleep with anybody, also, including his wife's sister. According to writer Gore Vidal, whose mother had preceded Janet Bouvier as the wife of Hugh Auchincloss, JFK conducted a torrid affair with Lee Bouvier, then married to her first husband, British-born Michael Canfield. Lee, whose relationship with the older Jackie had always been more competitive than cooperative, flaunted her fling with her sister's husband—during lovemaking with Jack, she made so much noise that people nearby were made well aware of the activities taking place behind closed doors. The affair and her marriage both ended, after which she wed Prince Stanislas "Stas" Radziwill, a Polish-English real estate magnate and an active womanizer in his own right.

From the time of his honeymoon, John F. Kennedy's appetite for adultery was insatiable, as though he'd consciously set out to outdo the record of his father, and succeeded. Jackie suffered no illusions about her husband's fidelity, but, sharing his ambition to occupy the White House, she would not seriously contemplate divorce. After they lost their second child, the marriage of John and Jacqueline Kennedy deteriorated. It encompassed outward glamour but no inner warmth; there was joviality among others but not happiness together. In time, husband and wife would grow to accept each other's frailties, and their union would be infused with newfound intimacy. Jackie would regard Jack's wanderings as an inevitable feature of upper-class wedlock. Also, she would respond with several affairs of her own, including a liaison with actor William Holden.

The events of late August 1956 had shaken Jackie's confidence in her husband. But she believed in his brother: "You knew that, if you were in trouble, he'd always be there," she said later. Jacqueline Kennedy did not learn until some time after her child's stillbirth that Bobby had arranged for the infant's burial in the family plot at Holyhood Cemetery in Brookline.

As Adlai Stevenson prepared for the fall campaign, his staff invited Robert Kennedy to join the candidate as he toured the country. According to John Sharon, an organizer for the Democratic Party, the idea of including Bobby came from Jim Finnegan, Stevenson's campaign manager: "Jim was very sensitive—I thought he was hypersensitive—but he was extremely sensitive about the Catholic issue, the fact that John Kennedy had lost. I think it was Finnegan's view that it would be useful to have some member of the Kennedy family traveling with the governor just to be sure that the Stevenson people didn't create the image that they had defeated Kennedy. I thought it was sort of a tragic sight because whenever the governor would appear, Bobby would stand up and take a bow to the cheers of the crowd, but he never did anything. If I had been Bobby, I would have been frustrated as hell if all I did was sitting around, traveling, standing up, and taking bows. Bobby's an industrious, hard-working fellow, and they didn't give him anything to do that I know of."

"He was always a loner," recalled Eugene Anderson, a Stevenson campaign aide who would become JFK's ambassador to Bulgaria, "and he quite often was included in a little group that would meet with Adlai in his suite . . . but he was always sort of sitting in a corner and acting rather uncomfortable." With no assignment of substance from the Stevenson organization, the road show's ornamental Catholic found his own way to make good use of his time. "He seemed more like an observer than a participant," Anderson remarked. RFK watched and he analyzed. And whether slumped in a rear seat of a bus lumbering between towns or sitting on a railroad track while the candidate spoke during a whistle stop, he filled the pages of his journal.

Bobby's real master during the fall of 1956 was not Adlai Stevenson. Although Joseph Kennedy held a low opinion of the year's Democratic nominee, his objection was not ideological. Instead, he considered Stevenson vacillating and overly intellectual—Stevenson was that most contemptible of men in Joe Kennedy's eyes: "an inept, ineffectual politician." The ambassador approved of Bobby's attachment to the Ste venson caravan, however, for he wanted his son to learn everything there was to know about running a presidential campaign. "It's worth noting," said George Smathers, "that after the convention Joe Kennedy paid to have a study conducted of the sentiment regarding Catholics in the United States—could there be a Catholic president? The study concluded there could." In four years, Joe assumed, Robert would be managing his older brother's campaign for the White House; Joe wanted him to be prepared for the job.

Minding his own business—or rather, the business of his father and his brother—the pensive traveler made few friends among his companions. "I formed a rather bleak impression of him," recalled George Ball, who was Stevenson's law partner and would serve as undersecretary in JFK's State Department. "I thought him rather surly and not very helpful." And to the injury of Bobby's peripheral status, members of the public added the insult of mistaken identity. "He was in an angry mood all the time," observed Ball, "because people mistook him for his brother."

Robert Kennedy's autumn-long funk lifted momentarily in Lewiston, Pennsylvania. An enthusiastic crowd had greeted the campaign train at the station, but the candidate couldn't be heard above the din created by a band of frolicking schoolchildren. To no avail, Stevenson's aides entreated the youngsters to be quiet until, finally, Bobby Kennedy came to the rescue. Leaping from the train, he yelled, "I can beat anyone from here to the lamppost!" The youngsters followed as he raced away. At a safe distance from the rally, the lighthearted family man gathered the boys and girls around him. While the grown-ups conducted their business, the young people formed a circle and listened in rapt attention as their Pied Piper told them stories. Robert Kennedy had saved the day.

His ebullience was short-lived. "Bobby found it depressing to work for Stevenson," said Ken O'Donnell. "Like Joe Kennedy, he found Stevenson's indecisiveness very disturbing. 'He's got no balls,' he used to say about the Democratic candidate. 'He sits around with his staff for hours talking about nothing. He can't even give a speech—he has to read it aloud from a script. There's no organization in the camp—nobody knows what anybody else is doing. He can't make up his mind about anything, and he doesn't know how to delegate responsibility. Basically, I've learned how a campaign shouldn't be run.' One evening Bob called me up and said, 'I think Adlai's a faggot.' "

"Adlai Stevenson had little rapport with the public," remarked Larry O'Brien, "but he wasn't quite as bad as Robert had it. After six weeks, he quit the campaign and telephoned me. 'I feel I'm alive again,' he said. 'That asshole was absolutely killing me.' "

Honey Fitz was fortunate to have met his Maker in 1950, for had he lived another six years, he would have witnessed the unthinkable: a grandson of his voting Republican. On Tuesday, November 6, 1956, Bobby cast his ballot to reelect Dwight Eisenhower and his running mate, Richard Nixon.

As Joseph P. Kennedy became more interested in making his son president, he became less interested in enlarging his fortune. On May 19, 1956, when Jean Kennedy wed Stephen E. Smith, the family gained someone who would help free up the ambassador's time.

Born in Brooklyn in 1927 to wealthy Irish Catholic owners of a fleet of Hudson River tugboats—"My family had money before the Kennedys had money," he once boasted—Steve Smith became an air force lieutenant during World War II and then attended Georgetown University. His marriage to Jean Kennedy was performed at St. Patrick's Cathedral by Francis Cardinal Spellman, but the affair otherwise departed from family custom—Jean wanted a small affair, so the ceremony took place not in the main sanctuary packed with a thousand-plus associates and dignitaries but rather in The Lady Chapel before seventy-five close friends and relatives. The reception ensued at the Plaza.

Although he showed no talent for touch football, Smith's facility with money endeared him to his in-laws. By the time of the wedding, he'd already been in Joe's employ for two years, and would before long assume effective direction of the family's finances. From Joe's office on lower Park Avenue in Manhattan, Smith would attend to matters large, like lucrative real-estate deals, and small, like the unpaid minor bills various Kennedys forwarded to him. (Sometimes he paid them, sometimes he didn't.)

Smith fit into the family easily, becoming perhaps the in-law most happy to submerge his identity beneath that of the Kennedys. His marriage fit into the family, too—although long-lived, it was not particularly happy, and both husband and wife pursued extramarital diversions.

Joseph Kennedy concerned himself little with the level of conjugal faithfulness shown to his daughter by his new son-in-law. In Smith the old man had found an utterly trustworthy surrogate to manage the empire he'd forged. In the mid-1950s, estimates of the family's net worth ran as high as several hundred million dollars.

Not long after their wedding, John and Jacqueline Kennedy moved from their residence in Georgetown to a Georgian manor just across the Potomac River in McLean, Virginia. Set on nearly six wooded acres,

Hickory Hill, as the property was called, had last been owned by Robert H. Jackson, the recently deceased Supreme Court justice who had also served as chief prosecutor at the Nuremberg Tribunal following World War II. JFK paid Jackson's estate $125,000 for the home, which had been constructed just after the Civil War; in June of 1956 he would, for tax purposes, sell it to his father for $10.

With its two and a half stories, the white-brick house at 1147 Chain Bridge Road seemed perfect to accommodate the young couple's goal of raising a large family. The grounds already included features essential to gracious living: stables, tennis courts and a swimming pool. Jack and Jackie added a nursery, then awaited the babies to occupy it.

When she had recovered sufficiently to leave Newport Hospital, Jackie returned to Hammersmith Farm. After her second failed pregnancy, and with her marriage so troubled, she could not bear to see the Virginia home in which she'd invested so much hope and longing. Adding to her despair was the contrast between her own childlessness and the fecundity of her in-laws: by the fall of 1956, the Shrivers had two children, as did the Lawfords, and Bobby and Ethel counted five with the arrival of Mary Courtney on September 9.

Robert, Ethel, Kathleen, Joseph III, Robert Jr., David and Mary Kennedy took up residence at Hickory Hill soon after John and Jacqueline left. The sprawling grounds suited the sprawling brood. After the family had lived there only a few months, a Washington gossip columnist painted a picture of contentment: "The Kennedys employ two nursemaids, three other servants and a groom to minister to the Irish riding horses and a pony. Papa Joe still owns the house, of course." Robert Kennedy was never technically master at Hickory Hill—Joe retained title until 1965, when he recovered his ten-dollar investment by selling the property to Ethel for that same price. But over the years, as his wife added children, Bobby added to the comforts of their home: an old stone barn was equipped as a playhouse; a north wing was constructed containing two bedrooms, a living room and a family room; a pool house that doubled as a movie theater was built.

As the responsibility and influence of Robert Kennedy increased, Hickory Hill became a frequent gathering place for Washington's powerful. Writer George Plimpton, a family friend, recalled the home and the hospitality: "The house stood back from the road up a steep incline, with a steep U-shaped driveway that went up past the front door and was always choked with cars. When they had the big affairs, the cars were parked for a hundred yards along Chain Bridge Road. The guests would walk through the house out onto the back terrace and see the tables set down the hill by the swimming pool. You'd get a drink on the terrace and amble down past the big hickory that had a swing hanging from one of the high boughs, and a tree house in which there was usually a Kennedy child watching you go by, owl-like, with grave, proprietary eyes."

Robert Kennedy would reside at Hickory Hill the rest of his life.

10

HOFFA

The way they talked about him being so tough," laughed James P. Hoffa about his father Jimmy, "you would have thought he was six feet eight inches. In reality he was five five and weighed one hundred eighty pounds." Having dispatched Roy Cohn to an early retirement from government service, Robert Kennedy now fastened upon a new object of his disdain: a labor leader who consorted with gangsters and abused the trust placed in him by the ordinary workers he represented, a rough-cut working-class potentate who held in his pinkie-ringed hand the alarming power to bring the nation's commerce to an abrupt halt. "I'm boss of an outfit that wins," the man boasted, although Robert Kennedy would judge him more properly identified as chief malefactor in a nationwide "conspiracy of evil." Jimmy Hoffa was the giant, and Bobby would set out to slay him.

RFK had had a faint whiff of union corruption in connection with one or two earlier McClellan committee investigations and hearings. But when Washington journalist Clark Mollenhoff urged him to undertake a wide-ranging probe of labor's misdeeds, he at first demurred. As uncourageously as the Labor Committee had shrunk in the face of the union movement's political clout in recent years, that body, Bobby argued, not the Government Operations Committee (or its Investigations Subcommittee), held Senate jurisdiction over union affairs. Mollenhoff persisted, however, eventually persuading the rising lawyer that crookedness in the labor movement, which then held $25 billion to $30 billion in its pension and welfare funds, would present an urgent story to tell the American people. Under the pretext that unions filed various tax and financial reports with the federal authorities and were thus involved in government operations—as, indeed, anyone could be considered who filed, or was supposed to file, a tax return—RFK in August 1956 convinced John Mc-Clellan to sanction an initial probe. The week following the November election, Bobby traveled to Los Angeles to launch in earnest his investigation of the International Brotherhood of Teamsters, Chauffeurs, Warehousemen and Helpers of America.

Founded in 1903 when the Team Drivers International Union merged with the Teamsters National Union, the International Brotherhood of Teamsters had been led from 1907 to 1952 by Daniel J. Tobin, a Bostonian who was known, unlike his successors, for his zealous guardianship of union funds. With a background in old-fashioned craft unionism, Tobin disparaged mass organizing; nonetheless, the union's membership grew under his leadership from forty thousand to over a million, in large part because of the strategies of regional bosses like David Beck, whose diligence in bringing autonomous locals together had shaped the Western Conference of Teamsters into a dynamic negotiating network. While Tobin had been an avid supporter of FDR, Beck, who replaced Tobin as president, catered to the Republican White House with his espousal of "business unionism," the idea that unions should be run like any industrial enterprise, using the same principles of modern management employed by America's largest corporations and eschewing any broader goals of societal progress. Beck's philosophy of cooperation, not confrontation, had helped build on Tobin's record: by 1956, when Bobby Kennedy visited the West Coast to dig up Beck's home turf, the Teamsters were America's largest and richest union, with 1.3 million members and nearly a quarter of a billion dollars in welfare and pension assets.

Bobby's traveling companion on the trip was Carmine Bellino, formerly the FBI's top accountant, now working as a fiscal adviser to Congress. A specialist in uncovering financial improprieties from within the dense pages of ledgers and bank statements, Bellino would help RFK understand the inner workings of union economics.

In Los Angeles the pair heard tales of Teamster-delivered extortion plots and beatings. Flying next to Portland, they learned of an intricate web of associations connecting the union's officials to local mobsters and politicians. In Seattle, where Beck had lived, informants seduced them with descriptions of the labor leader's generosity to himself courtesy of his union's treasury. By Christmas week, the trail led to the Chicago office of Nathan W. Shefferman, a labor-relations consultant who had handled Beck's finances. Bellino's examination of Shefferman's records confirmed RFK's suspicions of Beck's criminality and corruption.

Back at work after the New Year, Robert Kennedy and John McClellan decided to capitalize on their exciting discoveries by initiating a full-scale probe into labor racketeering nationwide. The astute chairman knew the political risks such a course would entail, so he sent Bobby to seek the sanction of George Meany, the cigar-chomping ex-plumber from the Bronx who headed the American Federation of Labor and Congress of Industrial Organizations. Astonished by RFK's revelations regarding Beck, Meany promised to look into the matter. At a late January meeting in Miami, the AFL-CIO executive council promised its full cooperation with a congressional probe and ruled that any union leader who pleaded the Fifth Amendment against charges of alleged corruption had no right to continue in office. The only vote of dissent belonged to Dave Beck.

With McClellan as chairman and Robert Kennedy as chief counsel, a new panel—the Select Committee on Improper Activities in the Labor or Management Field—was authorized and formed by the Senate. The Republican members of the group were Joe McCarthy, Barry Goldwater, Karl Mundt and Irving Ives; in addition to McClellan, the Democratic senators on the committee were Sam Ervin, Patrick McNamara and John F. Kennedy. The presence of both Kennedy boys on the same labor investigations group infuriated their father. "All you're doing," he told them, "is jeopardizing future votes. One of you on such a panel would have been one too many. But both of you—forget it! You're committing political suicide."

For once, Joe Kennedy's prediction proved false. The Rackets Committee, as the panel soon became known, turned out to be vastly successful. "For one thing," said Ken O'Donnell, who was asked to become the committee's chief of staff, "RFK hired a number of investigators who became lifelong devotees, starting with Carmine Bellino and LaVern Duffy. He added former FBI agent Walter Sheridan to his staff. Bellino's sister-in-law, Angie Novello, was engaged as Bobby's private secretary and started working eighteen-hour days. Pierre Salinger, a correspondent for *Collier's* magazine, signed on in an official capacity, while journalists like John Seigenthaler and Edwin Guthoran became unofficial, unpaid advisers—the latter two later joined the Kennedy Justice Department, while Salinger became JFK's White House press secretary. Within a year of the committee's inception, the staff consisted of exactly one hundred and one employees. By coincidence, we worked out of room 101 in the [old] Senate Office Building."

The hearings opened with an elaboration of the leads RFK had developed on his trip to the West Coast. The committee's key witness was James Elkins, a fifty-six-year-old Portland wiseguy whom more than one reporter covering the session would describe as "Runyonesque." Before Bobby asked Elkins to comment on recent events, he engaged him in an account of his checkered past. The chief counsel began the review with a question about the witness's youth in Aberdeen, Washington:

KENNEDY—Did you get into difficulty there?
ELKINS—Yes, I did.
KENNEDY—What was your difficulty?
ELKINS—Making moonshine.

Bobby asked about further "difficulty" in Arizona involving a 1931 charge of assault with intent to kill. He then shifted focus back to the Northwest:

KENNEDY—And did you have some difficulty with the law in the state of Oregon?
ELKINS—I did, yes, sir.
KENNEDY—What was that in connection with?
ELKINS—I picked up a package at the American Express office for a friend and got fifteen months in Alcatraz for possession of narcotics.
KENNEDY—And that was in what year?
ELKINS—Nineteen thirty-eight.
KENNEDY—And you served your year then?
ELKINS—That is correct.
KENNEDY—A year and a day. Then did you have any difficulty after that?
ELKINS—Not after that. I had more difficulty before that, though.
KENNEDY—Approximately how many difficulties?
ELKINS—Well, I don't believe I could say exactly. . . . A few, four or five.

Elkins, known to operate gambling and bootlegging "joints," as the witnesses, lawyers, senators, and press called such establishments, then narrated the efforts of Teamster personnel from Western Conference headquarters in Seattle to muscle in on Portland's action. Led by a hefty union "enforcer" named Tom Maloney, the out-of-towners supplied assistance, much appreciated at first, in establishing houses of prostitution and organizing a monopoly on the city's pinball machines, as well as in securing the cooperation of Portland's mayor, Terry Schrunk. When the racketeers succeeded in electing as district attorney Elkins's former partner, William Langley, who promised a tip-off service before all raids the sheriff might perform, the teaming of local mobsters and visiting union men seemed a happy marriage, indeed. But the blissful partnership hit the skids when the invaders moved to cut the locals out of the newly flourishing commerce. Elkins and his friends petitioned Frank Brewster, who had joined Dave Beck in the union's executive offices as district president, to call off Maloney—"Get that gorilla back to Seattle and back into his cage," one Portlander begged the union chief. Brewster was not moved. "I make mayors and I break mayors," he answered, according to Elkins. "I make police chiefs and I break police chiefs. Nothing scares me. If you embarrass my boys, you'll find yourself walking across Lake Washington with concrete boots on."

His Eden vanished, Elkins salved his disappointment by cooperating with the authorities, but few of his former associates joined him in song. Brewster, Maloney, Langley and a host of other gamblers, public officials and union strongmen took the witness stand in the Senate Caucus Room to make liberal use of their right to remain silent. Mayor Schrunk and DA Langley were indicted within weeks, but Bobby had already snagged a bigger fish, and now moved to reel him in.

Dave Beck's appearance in late March capped the West Coast phase of the committee's inquiry. The nation's top Teamster opened with a statement on the United States Constitution, explicating the document's relevance to the committee's conduct—such an investigation, he declared, was forbidden by the doctrine of separation of powers found in Articles 1, 2, and 3; moreover, the Bill of Rights offered him privileges which he refused to waive. Following Beck's Madisonian discourse, the Republican members treated him to a round of sympathetic questions, to which he responded in statesmanlike tones. When Robert Kennedy took over the examination, however, the heavyset labor leader's bald dome began to drip with perspiration. Working from notes developed through a wide variety of sources, Bobby concentrated not on the involvement by Beck in the Portland rackets, but rather on the union president's personal enrichment via his organization's coffers: Had Beck taken $36,000 from the Joint Council of Teamsters in Seattle to pay off a bank loan in 1946? Had Beck taken $4,812.39 from the Western Conference of Teamsters in 1949 and deposited it in his private bank account? Had Beck paid a Seattle builder named John Lindsay $196,516.49 out of union funds for work done on his own home and other real estate that he owned? Had Beck taken $85,119.92 from union funds between 1949 and 1953 to pay his own personal bills?

The flustered witness had no answer to the avalanche of questions, so, as promised, he retreated to the refuge of his civil liberties. He cited the Fourth Amendment as well as the Fifth, invoking the latter more than fifty times before the day was done. Wasn't Beck bound, asked Sena-

tor John F. Kennedy, by the AFL-CIO's January ruling that any union
official who asserted the Fifth Amendment in response to such allegations had to forfeit his office? "I certainly am not!" the witness shouted
back at Kennedy. "I am bound only by the international law of the Teamsters union!" The laconic chairman grew weary at Beck's repeated legalisms. "There comes a time," McClellan sighed, "when patience ceases to
be a virtue. I'm tired of the broken record; but let Mr. Beck take the
Fifth all he wants and get any dubious pleasure he can."

Aired on national television, the proceedings, which culminated in
Beck's downfall and eventual imprisonment, catapulted Robert Kennedy
into sudden prominence. It was a show that one individual, the president
of the Central States Conference of Teamsters, watched with particular
interest. Born in 1913 in Brazil, Indiana, James Riddle Hoffa had led a
childhood a world apart from that enjoyed by Robert Kennedy. Hoffa's
father, an Indiana coal driller, died when his son was only seven. Before
long, the boy was working part-time to help his family, and, shortly after
finishing ninth grade, he took his first full-time job as a department-store
stock boy. By 1932 he was leading a strike at a Detroit grocery chain, and
soon thereafter was brought to Minneapolis to work with Farrell Dobbs,
the Trotskyist head of the Central States Drivers Council, whose particular goal was to organize long-haul interstate truck drivers. Jimmy Hoffa
would emulate his mentor's distrust of capitalism. But the younger man
channeled his suspicions not into any leftist utopianism, but rather into
a cynical, caustic opportunism. When Dobbs left the union in 1939 to
concentrate on the Socialist Workers Party, Hoffa rose to the leader's job
and was free to pursue his own theory of the working class: that morality
was a scam by which the powerful sought to instill passivity in the weak,
that only fools observed the niceties of the law, that force had to be
repaid with interest. By the late 1940s, Jimmy Hoffa controlled Teamster
locals in more than twenty states. Elected a vice president of the international in 1952, he had been investigated by various arms of law enforcement but had never been pinned with a major scandal. In 1957, he was
poised to take advantage of Dave Beck's pending downfall.

On February 19, as Bobby's investigation of the West Coast Teamsters
was gathering steam, he and Jimmy Hoffa sat down to dinner at the
Washington home of Edward Cheyfitz, an associate of Hoffa's attorney—
and Bobby's buddy—Edward Bennett Williams. Cheyfitz, who had been
feeding the committee leads about Dave Beck, thought he might persuade RFK that the rising labor leader from Detroit could be an ally in
the fight against union corruption. "The meeting nearly dissolved into a
fist fight," said LaVern Duffy. "Bobby kept peppering Hoffa with ques-

tions, until Hoffa finally said to him, 'What is this, the Inquisition?' After that, it was all downhill. 'He became extremely belligerent,' Bobby told me. 'He was defensive because my family has money, and his didn't. That's not my fault. He also holds against me my Harvard education. What does that have to do with the price of beans?' "

"It was at that very first meeting," claimed James P. Hoffa, "that Robert Kennedy saw that my father was not an easy mark. He was clever and argumentative, and Robert Kennedy realized he could not manipulate Jimmy Hoffa."

"Jimmy delighted in showing people, particularly people with substantial education, that he was their equal or better," recalled Joe Konowe, an associate of Hoffa's who would head Teamster Local 733 in New York. "And he was able to do this because, notwithstanding his ninth-grade education, he was a quick study. With the seriousness of the depression, the loss of his father, the enormous workload that his mother undertook—doing washing and housecleaning—and with the children helping out, Jimmy always had a soft spot for the so-called underclass and a great disdain for people who were not only well educated but who came from wealthy families. And that was the cause of the fight, the ongoing vendetta between Kennedy and Hoffa."

The feud would take on epic proportions in the months and years to come, but its basic framework had been set that snowy night: both men were, and would remain, utterly convinced of the rightness of their position, and neither would give an inch. Hoffa's defense of Teamster "paper locals" in New York City left RFK unimpressed—he knew that such phony union offices existed only to connect with mob money and muscle. Nor was the prosecutor swayed by Hoffa's bellicose attitude. "He assured me he was as tough as hell," RFK later told LaVern Duffy, "but guys who talk that way aren't usually tough at all." On that point, Bobby was mistaken. Robert Kennedy fancied himself tough, but his spirited tackling on the football field in Cambridge and his occasional dealings with the Federal Bureau of Narcotics in New York could hardly compare to the life story of Jimmy Hoffa, who, in the vicious labor struggles of the 1930s, had experienced the wrong end of a nightstick and the right end of a blackjack. None of the union leader's justifications could move the moralistic investigator. "From Kennedy's point of view," maintained Konowe, "Hoffa and the other Teamster officials were racketeers who preyed on the workers. Bobby was going to be the avenging angel and wipe out this calamity for the labor movement."

"Maybe I should have worn shoulder pads and a helmet," Bobby responded to Hoffa's swaggering. The unionist did not smile at the joke.

"As far as my father was concerned," insisted James Hoffa, "there were the Kennedys, going from Palm Beach to Hyannis Port, from Peter Lawford's California beach house to Las Vegas. And at the end of each month the credit-card bills would be sent to Steve Smith, who sat in his Park Avenue office doling out the money. It created a complete air of unreality. These people had no idea whatsoever about the real-life hardships of the average working man.

"Also, my father was a puritanical type of guy. He didn't smoke or drink, he didn't run after women. He watched them, the Kennedys. He saw the photos of the touch football games, he saw the pictures of the family gatherings, but he knew differently. He knew the Kennedy men were chasing every skirt and he was disgusted by it.

"My father left that dinner thinking to himself, 'This Kennedy kid is nothing more than a spoiled brat.' "

Bobby's smug comportment that night may have been fed by his knowledge of, and participation in, a trap into which his adversarial dinner partner was about to walk. Early in February, a Washington lawyer named John Cye Cheasty had received a message that Jimmy Hoffa wished to see him. Cheasty traveled to Detroit, where the union chief offered him eighteen thousand dollars in cash if he could get a job on the new Senate select committee and supply confidential information on the investigations under way. With a down payment of a thousand dollars in his pocket, Cheasty returned to Washington and promptly—a week before the dinner—reported Hoffa's proposition to Bobby, who notified McClellan, who met with J. Edgar Hoover. The chairman and the director agreed to collaborate in a sting, and over the next month, Cheasty met several times with Hoffa or an intermediary to hand over internal committee documents, most of them relating to the financial misdeeds of Dave Beck. At 11:10 P.M. on March 13, after meeting Cheasty outside Washington's Dupont Plaza Hotel and exchanging two thousand dollars for an envelope full of committee files, Jimmy Hoffa walked through the building's lobby and headed for the elevator. Before he could reach his hotel room he was met by FBI agents who handcuffed him and took him away.

At the federal courthouse after midnight, waiting to be charged with bribery and conspiracy, the captured man saw a familiar face and fixed on it. "He kept looking at me, his eyes full of disdain," RFK later reported to LaVern Duffy. With those eyes now opened to Bobby's awareness of the sting all along, Hoffa eventually broke the silence to renew the confrontation. "Listen, Bobby," he said, "you run your business and I'll run mine. You go on home and go to bed, I'll take care of things. Let's don't have any problems." RFK, Hoffa noted with pleasure, seemed a bit put out "because I called him Bobby." The labor leader further annoyed the younger man by steering the conversation toward the subject of physical fitness. "Hoffa said, 'I can do fifty one-handed push-ups,' " related Tom Bolan, Roy Cohn's law partner. " 'How many can you do?' From that day forward, Bobby practiced doing one-handed push-ups, until he could do a hundred on each side."

At Hoffa's trial, which began in late June, Bobby used his hand not to do calisthenics, but to take his oath as witness. Attending the trial, Larry O'Brien found RFK "an able witness, but not as able as Hoffa's lawyer, Edward Bennett Williams, who convinced the twelve-man jury (eight of them black) that his client had thought he was hiring Cheasty as an attorney, that the money he had paid him represented legal fees (not a bribe), and that in return Cheasty had turned over legal documents. It helped that several newspapers in the Washington area depicted Hoffa as pro-worker and pro–civil rights." Moreover, during a break in one day's testimony, the jurors were treated to the sight of the defendant being embraced by Joe Louis. "My father brought Louis in on purpose," James Hoffa explained. "They were born a year apart and had been friends for many years back in Detroit, where they both lived as youths. With a jury two-thirds black, my father thought Joe Louis would gain him some sympathy." On July 19, whether swayed by the emotion of the former heavyweight champion's appearance or by the grace of Edward Bennett Williams's courtroom style, the jury returned a verdict of not guilty.

Humiliated, Bobby struck back. Less than three weeks after the trial ended, he advised the press that his committee would begin another set of hearings into labor racketeering among the Teamsters. Speed was essential: with the acquittal, and with the AFL-CIO's suspension in March of Dave Beck as a member of its executive council, the election of Jimmy Hoffa as president of the International Brotherhood of Teamsters at his union's September convention seemed inevitable. Naively, Bobby believed that by exposing Hoffa's wrongs he could influence that gathering's delegates to deny the candidate his prize.

"Can Bobby Kennedy take Jimmy Hoffa?" asked Edwin A. Lahey in the *Detroit Free Press* on the eve of the August 20 opening of the hearings. RFK did score points at his opponent's expense in what Lahey called the "main bout" of the labor rackets investigation. After the senators posed mild queries to Hoffa—getting the hard-nosed leader of workers to attest to such controversial beliefs as support of the free-enterprise system and dislike of socialism—Bobby attacked. Whereas he had exposed Dave Beck merely as a man caught with his hand deep in a well-stocked cookie jar, RFK portrayed Beck's presumed successor as a partner in organized crime with some of the nation's most notorious characters. Playing recordings of some of Hoffa's telephone conversations (which had been made by Frank Hogan, the district attorney of Manhattan), Bobby attempted to force the witness to confess his ties to the mob. Hoffa did not make Beck's mistake of pleading the Fifth Amendment. Instead, the autodidact suffered deep memory lapses, answering one question after another with sentences like, "To the best of my recollection, I must recall on my memory, I cannot remember." RFK accused Hoffa of suffering from "self-induced" amnesia.

But neither Bobby's accusations nor the witness's questionable tactics persuaded Hoffa's union brethren to abandon him. Nor were the delegates to the Miami Beach convention particularly disturbed by the Senate testimony of close Hoffa associates—people like Owen "Bert" Brennan, president of Detroit Local 337, whose police record contained fifteen arrests, with six convictions, for bombing, conspiracy, assault, and violation of antitrust laws, and who took the Fifth Amendment 107 times before McClellan's panel. Two pending indictments of Hoffa in New York—one for wiretapping, the other for perjury—only served to enhance his legend. The rank-and-file laborers did not begrudge him his mob connections any more than they resented his expensive suits or his Cadillacs. Known until now as a hard bargainer who secured profitable contracts for the workers he represented, Jimmy Hoffa was adding to his reputation by thumbing his nose at authority, at the same time making fools of some of the most prominent dignitaries of the political and legal establishment; by acting out the fantasies of ordinary truck drivers, the pugnacious leader was validating his constituents' working-class rage. The September convention cheered for its hero as it voted overwhelmingly to make him the international's new president, replacing the fallen Dave Beck, who from 1959 to 1964 languished in prison on charges of grand larceny and federal tax evasion.

Bobby's moral ardor for the investigation of the Teamsters was real, but the target, a union allied with the Republican Party, was politically convenient for a pair of Democratic brothers aiming for the White House. The select committee's Republican members, particularly Barry Goldwater and Karl Mundt, thought the proceedings too convenient for their political rivals and insisted the panel pursue a labor leader who sided with Democrats, someone who the GOP senators believed to be "the most dangerous man in America."

Walter Reuther did not use his position as president of the United Auto Workers to acquire such things as either Dave Beck's large bank account or Jimmy Hoffa's roster of shady friends. His salary was modest and his habits frugal. Rather, his sin in Republican eyes lay in his integration of union activism into an overall liberal vision. Hoffa taunted his counterpart by labeling him "the Czar of Soviet America," a reference also to the fact that Reuther had worked briefly in Russia during the 1930s. Nevertheless, the UAW head boasted a solid résumé of Americanism: during World War II he'd helped ensure labor peace and had originated the "Reuther Plan," a program for mass production of aircraft in automobile factories; in 1946 he assumed the UAW's presidency after a bitter struggle against the union's Communists. Like Hoffa, he had come up the hard way, quitting school in his hometown of Wheeling, West Virginia, to work as an apprentice at a tool-and-die shop. Fired for trying to organize the workers in protest of Sunday hours, he moved to Detroit, where he became a shop foreman with Ford; his union activities cost him that job, too. After traveling through Europe and the Far East, he and his brother Victor returned to Detroit in 1936 to found UAW Local 174. Walter Reuther participated in most UAW sit-down strikes until 1942, when he was elected the union's vice president. Beaten up in the Ford Factory Strike of 1941, he was severely wounded by a shotgun blast into his Detroit home in 1948. In 1952 he became president of the CIO and three years later he helped to engineer its merger with the AFL, becoming vice president of the new federation under George Meany. Whereas Jimmy Hoffa continued to espouse Dave Beck's "business unionism," maintaining cordial relations with employers while avoiding any agitation for meaningful political or economic change, Reuther fought for his workers forthrightly and took the liberal side on any question of civil rights or social-welfare legislation. Conservatives throughout America despised him.

By calling for an investigation of Reuther, the Republicans hoped not only to cripple an enemy unionist; they also aimed to embarrass the Kennedys, who, they suspected, were hoping to ride the Teamster probe all the way to 1600 Pennsylvania Avenue.

John McClellan had no taste for Walter Reuther's politics, but he knew of the UAW president's spotless reputation for personal probity. Still, after months of fending off Republican charges that he and the Kennedys were protecting Reuther, the chairman finally agreed to initiate an inquiry into the union and its role in a two-year-old strike action against the Kohler Company, a concern that produced kitchen and bathroom plumbing fixtures; their main plant was located in Sheboygan, Wisconsin. McClellan's hand had been forced by the panel's makeup: unlike almost all standing Senate committees, on which the majority party holds the majority of seats, the current select committee was evenly divided between Republicans and Democrats. In July 1957, the chairman and his chief counsel agreed that John McGovern, a Republican staff member hired at Goldwater's insistence, would conduct the investigation.

For the next three months, McGovern issued regular reports to the committee's Republicans but supplied no communications to the Democrats or to Bobby, who was, ostensibly, his direct superior. In October, McGovern wrote McClellan a 20,000-word memorandum. RFK read the document and found it to be little more than a reiteration of the work of the National Labor Relations Board, which had just released a report on the strike. McGovern's memo included the NLRB's findings of transgressions committed by workers, such as illegal mass picketing, as well as violence and vandalism, and ignored the board's conclusion that management had refused to negotiate in good faith.

Despite McGovern's lack of original material, Goldwater and his fellow Republican colleagues continued to press for hearings, still claiming, preposterously, that the UAW practiced the same brand of racketeering as did the Teamsters. Reuther, hesitant about trusting Robert Kennedy—the McCarthy connection had led him to support Kefauver for the vice presidential spot in 1956—sent an assistant, Jack Conway, to confer with RFK. Conway suggested that Bobby fly to Sheboygan to view working conditions there; Kennedy wasted little time, boarding an airplane within hours of Conway's visit.

LaVern Duffy, accompanying Bobby on the trip, recalled the "incredible" scene that awaited them in Sheboygan: "The conditions at the Kohler plant were astonishing. It was a dark, dingy factory with vermin and rats and open furnaces and hundreds of heavily perspiring workers standing around in heavy boots and protective face masks. They weren't given a lunch break, they were forced to eat while they worked. There were no fire doors, no emergency exits. There was no ventilation and some of the work spaces were hotter than hell. The UAW labor organizers wanted to raise wages, institute decent lunch breaks and modernize the plant—at least make the environment safe. You had to sympathize with their cause."

At the hearings, which began at the end of February, both Kennedys parried Republican attacks against Walter Reuther and his union. The other Democrats on the committee offered little backup; during testimony by Kohler management, only the two brothers posed nettlesome questions, with Jack handling Herbert V. Kohler and Bobby taking on Lyman Conger, the attorney for the Kohler Company. Conger's arrogant defense of his corporation's lunch policy made Bobby "madder really than when witnesses took the Fifth Amendment. . . . To hear a reputable American businessman, in 1958, matter-of-factly advocate a two- to five-minute luncheon period—well, until then I had believed that that kind of thinking had long since disappeared from the American scene."

Joseph Rauh, the civil-liberties lawyer Reuther had hired as the UAW's counsel for the proceedings, recalled working closely with RFK at the time. "Bobby was very cooperative," said Rauh; "he couldn't have been more fair to the UAW. He was really on our side during the 1958 hearings, and he and his brother had a political reason for that: Jack was going to run for president and he was going to need the union's support. But I always thought there was nothing wrong with that. You had to make up your mind who was the villain in that fight, Reuther or Kohler, and they decided Kohler was.

"I was quite happy with the cooperation I enjoyed with both brothers. Every night we'd go downstairs from the hearings—the whole affair lasted about a month I think—and by the time I got there Bobby had his coat off and he and Kenny O'Donnell were lobbing a football back and forth, and then we'd all discuss the next item on the agenda. I remember, he had a good sense of humor. I came down one day and I was pretty depressed because the other side—that was Goldwater, Mundt and Curtis,* the anti-UAW crowd—had done a job on Emil Mazey, the UAW secretary-treasurer. He had made a slip, uttering a pretty badly anti-Catholic remark [about priests in Sheboygan who had signed a statement supporting management]. And when I entered Bobby's office, he said to me, 'Don't look so blue, Joe, the Pope hasn't been in touch yet.' We had a pretty close relationship during those hearings."

By late March, it was time for Walter Reuther to testify. The UAW president, while admitting some past mistakes, furnished a cogent defense of his organization's actions in the Kohler strike and an eloquent justification of his working-class philosophy. McClellan, who had been muttering in the Senate cloakroom that his colleagues never should have bothered with Reuther in the first place, soon gaveled the hearings to a close. Far from driving a wedge between the Kennedys and labor, the Republican members of the panel had provided the ambitious brothers an opportunity to prove to the unions their good intentions.

With Reuther cleared, Robert Kennedy once again turned his guns

---

*Carl Curtis, a conservative senator from Nebraska, replaced Joe McCarthy on the committee after the Wisconsinite's death in May 1957. Other changes in membership were Frank Church of Idaho for Pat McNamara in 1958 after the UAW sessions and Homer Capehart of Indiana for Irving Ives in 1959.

on Jimmy Hoffa. The president of the Teamsters had beaten the rap in both New York indictments: the perjury charge had been dismissed and the wiretapping case, after an initial hung jury, had ended in an acquittal at retrial. Nor was he any longer constrained by the scruples of George Meany and Walter Reuther—in December, an AFL-CIO convention had expelled the Teamsters from beneath its umbrella. With Meany's blessing, RFK entered upon a new set of hearings, which began in July 1958.

The hatred between Robert Kennedy and Jimmy Hoffa dominated this round even more than the last. "It seemed like they were two scorpions in a bottle," recalled Russell Baker. "They just detested each other." "Whenever Bobby asked a question," Joe Konowe remembered, "Jimmy would say, 'You don't know what you're talking about. You were born with a silver spoon in your mouth. You're picking on me and the Teamsters for the publicity.' " The witness also used nonverbal tactics to irritate his foe, applying to the chief counsel what Bobby described in *The Enemy Within* as a "stare of absolute evilness," maintaining the gaze for thirty minutes or more. Then he'd punctuate the exercise with a wink. "I used to love to bug the little bastard," Hoffa later guffawed. "Whenever Bobby would get tangled up in one of his involved questions, I would wink at him. That invariably got him."

Just about everything Jimmy Hoffa did got to RFK. "One night after a hearing," recollected Tom Bolan, "Bobby and an assistant or two were headed home at about eleven when they passed the Teamsters Building at 25 Louisiana Avenue. The lights were on and they could see Hoffa and his boys working away. Bobby ordered his limo to turn right around and take them all back to their office. 'If Hoffa's working at this hour,' he said, 'we'll work, too.' "

The rivalry between the two men grew into a mutual obsession, and the public was fascinated. "One day," Joe Konowe remembered, "I said to Jimmy, 'You know, if I could rent Madison Square Garden and persuade you and Bobby to get into the ring, it would be an enormous draw,' and Hoffa said, 'I'd kill him.' Then I saw Bobby several days or a week later and I said, 'Bobby, how would you like an opportunity for you and Hoffa to take on a fight for charity in Madison Square Garden?' And he said, 'Oh, I'd knock his block off.' I was impressed by the fact that, despite the differences between these two men, there was also a great similarity. Both perceived themselves as unbeatable, and it made for a natural antagonism."

In addition to Hoffa, the committee also heard from some of gangland's most illustrious citizens: Barney Baker, an ex-con and Teamster organizer who had associated with Bugsy Siegel and Meyer Lansky; Joey

Gallo, an official of a New York union and a suspect in a murder case; Joseph Glimco, Chicago's "jukebox king" and boss of Teamster Taxi Local 777, who had been arrested thirty-six times; Tony "Tony Pro" Provenzano of New Jersey's Local 360, believed to be a capo in the Genovese crime family; Momo Salvatore "Sam" Giancana, involved with the Brotherhood of Electrical Workers and considered by law enforcement to be Chicago's top don, who had evaded the committee's subpoena for a year. The men formed a colorful procession of coarse accents and manicured hands; together they took the Fifth hundreds of times. Jimmy Hoffa would never repudiate his unsavory pals, nor would he apologize for placing convicted men in positions of authority. "Hey muscles, that looks like Acapulco," *Life* magazine quoted him as cracking about the suntan of Raymond Cohen, the thrice-arrested, once-convicted secretary-treasurer of Philadelphia Local 107 whom the McClellan committee accused of using union funds to purchase and maintain a yacht in Florida. About another associate's long police record, Hoffa merely quipped, "He's just had bad write-ups." But Bobby had reason to take Hoffa's associations more seriously—in March of 1958 the FBI had informed him of threats, emanating from the Teamster camp, against Ethel and the children.

Hoffa's mannerisms annoyed Bobby. His choice of friends earned RFK's censure. But no action of Jimmy Hoffa's made the committee counsel's blood boil more furiously than his announcement that he would seek to link his organization to two others: the International Longshoremen's Association, recently expelled from the AFL-CIO for its corruption, and the International Longshoremen's and Warehousemen's Union, banished in 1949 from the CIO on charges of a Communist taint. Robert Kennedy responded with a lengthy article in *Look* magazine: "The worst elements of the American labor movement," the essay began, "are creating an unholy alliance that could dominate the United States within three to five years." Continuing, Bobby described the unbounded power wielded by such a coalition's dominant partner, "the Teamsters' union and its general president, James R. Hoffa":

> At birth, it is a Teamster who drives the ambulance to the hospital. At death, a Teamster who drives the hearse to the grave. Between birth and death, it is the Teamsters who drive the trucks that bring you your meat, milk, clothing and drugs, pick up your garbage and perform many other essential services.
>
> The individual truck driver is honest, and so are the vast majority of local Teamster officials—but they are completely under the control and domination of certain corrupt officials at the top. Picture this power,

then, and the chaos that could result if these officials were to gain control also over sea and other transportation outlets. Such a force could conceivably cause anyone—management and labor alike—to capitulate to its every whim. . . .

With Hoffa at the controls of the union that will dominate the transport alliance, *this power would certainly be in the wrong hands.*

The sinister capacity of the Teamsters to bring America to its knees—with or without the help of other unions—was a frequent theme in press accounts throughout the period of the rackets hearings. In April of 1957, *Newsweek* warned that "with their absolute control of the nation's wheels, the Teamsters hold almost a life-and-death power over other unions, and business as well." Two years later, in a three-part series on Hoffa and his organization, *Life* published a stylized map of Manhattan that ominously illustrated everyone's worst nightmare about labor's defiant bad boy. At the inbound side of each bridge and tunnel leading to the island, a huge backup of trucks was held at bay by sign-carrying men. Rail lines were halted, as well. "WHAT HOFFA, HIS MEN, HIS ALLIES COULD DO TO NEW YORK . . . IF THEY DARED TO TRY," blared the heading of the map that depicted Teamster picketers strangling the homes and business of America's commercial nerve center.

Jimmy Hoffa never tried to immobilize New York. At times, in fact, he downplayed his might. "I recollect walking through a passageway in an airport with Jimmy," said Joe Konowe, "and the reporters said to him, 'Bobby Kennedy said the Teamsters must be broken, that if the Teamsters chose to call a general strike, they could paralyze the country.' And Jimmy looked at the reporters and said to them, 'You know, Bobby doesn't know what he's talking about. Even if I were to call a general strike, there's no way it could be a hundred percent effective. Remember, I travel. I don't control the airlines. We don't control the boats, we don't control the railroads. What is he talking about? That's nonsense. A man would have to be crazy—and I'm not—to think in terms of a national strike.' " Yet on other occasions, Hoffa seemed pleased to stoke his countrymen's fears: "We are the transportation of America," he stated, "and we control because raw materials must be transported in and finished products must be transported out."

In September of 1959, with committee investigations still in progress, Robert Kennedy submitted his resignation to John McClellan. The press reported that the retiring counsel planned to write a book about the work that had consumed him for almost three years. The press also noted that on Bobby's next-to-last day on the job he'd "denounced as a fraud" continuing Republican efforts to tar the UAW. RFK was proud of the "notable public service" performed by the committee: by "bringing to the attention of Congress and the people many of the deplorable conditions existing in the current labor-management field," Bobby wrote to McClellan, "a climate has been established which will make it easier for the force of clean unionism to thrive, allowing the labor movement to proceed toward its much needed goals of aiding working men and women throughout the United States."

Through nearly three hundred days of testimony, the rackets committee had seen 1,526 witnesses, 343 of whom had asserted their constitutional rights in refusing to answer questions. In addition to its probes of the Teamsters and the UAW, the panel had investigated such unions as the Meat Cutters, the Carpenters, the Sheet Metal Workers and the Hotel and Restaurant Workers. Leaders of the Bakers, the Operating Engineers and the United Textile Workers had joined Dave Beck in the ranks of the unemployed. Justifying the penultimate word in its full name, the Select Committee on Improper Activities in the Labor or Management Field had not only inspected the behavior of the Kohler Company, it had also forced Sears Roebuck to admit, and back away from, the union busting it had pursued with the help of Beck's money launderer, Nathan Shefferman.

The hearings had also led to the passage in 1959 of the Landrum-Griffin Act, by which Congress took steps to ensure the integrity of union finances and elections. The bill had originated the previous year as the Kennedy-Ives Act, written after consultation with Meany and Reuther, and had passed the Senate 88–1 only to die in the House. JFK tried again the following year, and Bobby supported the proposed legislation with articles, speeches and television appearances. When his own bill again seemed doomed, Jack worked in conference to see that the eventual, more stringent, law would be minimally tolerable to most of labor.

For his personal fortune, the rackets hearings had, firmly and forcefully, established Robert Kennedy as a national figure in his own right. For the fortunes of his family, the proceedings had once again proved him to be a remarkably deft politician. Navigating perilous shoals, he had relentlessly pursued one segment of the labor movement while establishing important friendships in another.

Still, Robert Kennedy was not fully satisfied by his work for John McClellan's committee. For all the corruption uncovered, the hearings resulted in the conviction of only three persons by the Department of Justice. And, most gallingly, while much of labor had "taken forceful action in a number of cases to rid itself of racketeers and crooks who were exposed by the committee," as RFK wrote his chairman upon leaving, one group refused to reform: "Only in the Teamsters Union did there seem to be a reluctance to clean up." To Bobby's mind, he had proven that Jimmy Hoffa had operated with illegal autocratic control, had commanded the use of physical violence, perhaps even murder, against union opponents, had misappropriated at least $9.5 million in union funds, and had exchanged favors with employers in order to pad his own wallet. To cement his supremacy, he had employed the services of known criminals; to avoid jail he had tampered with the judicial process.

"Bob Kennedy never wavered or faltered," John McClellan said years later of his chief counsel's work, "but with courage and fidelity vigorously assailed evil and exposed wrongdoing with a determination to see that right and justice prevailed." But right and justice had not prevailed—not entirely and not yet. Robert Kennedy was a man who believed in absolute standards of good and evil, and Jimmy Hoffa represented absolute evil. Yet far from toppling the giant, RFK's efforts only enlarged the giant's stature in the perception of his followers.

11

"EMOTIONAL, JUVENILE BOBBY"

Even with the births of Michael Lemoyne Kennedy (on February 27, 1958) and Mary Kerry Kennedy (September 8, 1959), the human inhabitants of Hickory Hill did not outnumber the members of other species. By the time Bobby left his job at the Senate, the Kennedys of McLean had amassed a zoo that exceeded even the collection at Rambleside during Ethel's childhood. Mammals (goats, pigs, cats, rabbits and horses) lived side by side with birds (chickens and ducks) who shared the premises with reptiles (turtles and snakes); all conspired with the seven bouncing children and the two sportive parents to give the house and grounds all the decorum of a nonstop carnival-cum-insane asylum.

Dominating the estate's animal kingdom were the dogs. Canines of every size, shape and color filled Hickory Hill with their barking and their play (as well as their randomly placed droppings). Former FBI agent Paul Tierney related that Bobby's favorite, a Newfoundland named Brumus, would often devour the meals of guests: "Francis Flanagan, who knew Bobby from the McCarthy committee, was over there one evening having dinner outside on the patio and they were serving steaks. So Francis got his food, put it down and took a seat. And when he looked back at the plate, the steak had disappeared. Then he saw that huge dog. . . .

"The dogs and the other animals had free rein among the Kennedys. That's the way the family was. They would have Easter parties and invite all the kids of Bobby's staff. I remember our kids would come home with chickens and rabbits. The chickens were colored red, white and orange. Live rabbits! Our kids just loved it. Of course, the rabbits died in our den.

"But that was typical of them, they were animal lovers. At that house

137

there was freedom, freedom of anything around, animals and kids. Bobby loved his children, adored them. There was no doubt about that, he was a family man."

He was also a Kennedy man. When he wasn't frolicking with his off-spring amidst the rustic abundance of Hickory Hill, he would romp with older playmates in the urban elegance of another family residence—the pied-à-terre at New York's Carlyle Hotel. One woman whom he invited to share the penthouse suite was Jade Stewart, owner of a swanky Manhattan jewelry shop. Well over six feet in heels, the tall brunette loved being seen around town with her shorter friend, although for the seven months of their affair Bobby kept most of their meetings discreet.

Socialite Mary Sanford, a confidante to Stewart and a witness to several of RFK's liaisons, recalled that the energetic attorney earned from his lover a nickname appropriate to a man whose home was the site of so much animal husbandry: "Jade was extremely pretty, although somewhat naive—she actually thought that Bobby would abandon his relationship with Ethel to be with her. She called him 'the rabbit' because he came so quickly."

Whether setting beds afire high atop Madison Avenue or burning the midnight oil in Washington to keep pace with Jimmy Hoffa, Robert Kennedy had little time to spend at home. Journalist Lee Rainey, who has written extensively on the younger generation of Kennedys, noted that the family would make the most of the father's infrequent appearances: "When he came home it was 'Hail, the conquering hero!' It was similar, I would guess, to the way Joe Kennedy was in his own children's lives. In other words, physically he was not around a lot, but when he *was* around, he was emotionally quite connected. Part of it was that the kids were so desperate for his love and attention that whatever they got they really enjoyed. Still, my impression is that those occasions were not that numerous because he was away so much.

"What his kids talk about now that they're grown up is those Sunday dinners where they had to recite poems or tell a little history lesson or something like that, which is straight out of Joe Kennedy's playbook. I mean, it's straight out of Joe's basic parenting style. And the kids appreciated it and took away pleasant memories."

If RFK remembered his father's model of tutelage, he forgot, or perhaps consciously rejected, the harsh discipline that had been his mother's pattern. Pandemonium prevailed at Hickory Hill. To help manage the chaos, Bobby and Ethel would summon to their suburban domicile women who supposedly worked for RFK only at his downtown office. "The Kennedy Justice Department was full of secretaries who were all pretty and smart and well-spoken," remembered Polly Feingold, an aide to Bobby during the sixties. "Certainly, if they were starting out now, they would not be secretaries. Sometimes these cute young things became home helpers for the Kennedys. They would go off to Hickory Hill and baby-sit not only the eleven or ten children, or however many it was at the time, but mommy and daddy as well, because those two were like kids in a Boy Scout or Girl Scout troop. They were—*irresponsible* isn't the word. No, they had the rich people's attitude of 'Someone will take care of that.' "

The Kennedys had need of constant part-time domestic help, for few employees would consent to work full-time under such anarchic conditions. "They went through household help as fast as Saddam Hussein went through generals," commented Lee Rainey. "They just tore them up and spit them out. There was one woman, though, I forget her name, an Irish woman. They really liked her a lot. She waited on Bobby and Ethel and made sure they didn't kill themselves. She's been there forever and is probably a candidate for sainthood."

"The only reason those kids survived was that they had this marvelous Costa Rican nurse named Ena Bernard who was absolutely wonderful," said Sam Neel, a neighbor. "The children adored her and they would obey her. She was the rare full-time employee."

"Ena did all the shopping and everything else," remarked Arthur Arundel, another nearby homeowner. "She was the glue that held that house together."

The merry bedlam of Hickory Hill made the home an island unto itself in this very prosperous suburb. "I believe they had few friends in the neighborhood," Arundel maintained. "They inhabited another world." As Rose and Joe Kennedy had rarely socialized with other inhabitants of the Cape, so Ethel and Bobby paid scant attention to their neighbors in McLean, Virginia. "This was a very friendly community," stated Sam Neel, "with strong local involvement. But for the Kennedys, the community was not a place they desired much to do with. They simply were such a family unit that they weren't interested in establishing any local ties. They were oriented either to Massachusetts or to their political people, and their house became a place to entertain politically. If the Kennedys ever gave a party that wasn't political in nature, I would be surprised. They never entertained in the neighborhood."

President of the McLean Citizens Association, Neel was often obligated to contact Bobby and Ethel regarding issues like fence repair and trash collection. He did not find them cooperative: "They had some security around, which was a pain in the ass, and they had an unlisted number. So if you had a problem, (*a*) it was difficult to get hold of them and (*b*) they weren't interested if you *did* get hold of them. In any matter concerning the neighborhood, I would have a very hard time getting any action out of them or even getting them to listen. They didn't want to be bothered. The Kennedys were self-centered. They were extremely inconsiderate in many, many ways.

"It was different during the short period Jack lived here. He was such a consummate politician that even if he didn't know you well, you perceived him as being somebody that could and would be your friend. For example, when the county was going to widen Chain Bridge Road, and all the trees would have had to come down, the Citizens Association asked me to talk to the senator. He was not difficult to see. I explained the situation to him and he said, 'It would be as bad for me as for anybody else. I think it's terrible and I will make a telephone call.' Which he obviously did because the plan was eventually aborted."

With Bobby so seldom present, it was left to Ethel to set the tone of the children's upbringing, and she brought to the task the example provided by George and Big Ann. In its madcap atmosphere as in its menagerie, Hickory Hill duplicated the Skakels' Greenwich home, to which Ethel had moved at age seven. The replica was not exact; it omitted the original's wanton abuse of alcohol. Still, like Rambleside, the McLean household suffered from a dearth of responsible adult supervision. Sam Neel and his wife often found themselves looking after the offspring of their famous neighbors. "Their younger children came over a good deal," said Neel. "Our property adjoined theirs and we had a riding ring and they had ponies. Or they came over to play in the barn—our barn was close to theirs and in those days we had hay. The children were perfectly all right. They were completely undisciplined and nobody ever told them no in their lives, but we had pretty good rules here and they complied. Their parents didn't pay too much attention to them. On one occasion when I was away, Mrs. Neel rescued one of the little ones from the middle of Chain Bridge Road. She rescued another one who was caught between the rails of a fence and she pulled still a third out of the pond. Their helper, Ena, was conscientious, but Bobby and Ethel were careless toward their children, just like I guess the other Kennedys are in their Massachusetts compound. Of course, Bobby was away a lot of the time."

If the neighbors tolerated the freely roaming Kennedy offspring, they were less magnanimous when visited by Kennedy canines. "Among their many dogs," Neel continued, "were two big Newfoundlands. One of them, Brumus, was Bobby's dog and he took him to the office a lot. The dogs wandered all over the vicinity, even though there were leash laws and the like. We were raising small dogs at the time; on several occasions the Newfies actually attacked the little stud dog we had. That was when I actually went to the mat with the Kennedys, but I never did get them to control those dogs. Even today, the dogs that they have are not kept in at all. They're out on the road a lot, and they bother joggers and people who go by.

"The most careless thing they ever did, though, was to build an enormous swimming pool and pool house right on the edge of their lot, backed up to the property of my friend Harry Ormiston. Harry was an architect in modest circumstances, no children, and when they put that pool up they also installed an outdoor audio system that they would blast during their parties. It was so loud, particularly in the summertime, that I don't know how Harry stood it. The rest of us had a hard time with it, too, and finally it got to the point where on several occasions I even got the police out here to get them to turn it down. We finally got the message across, but it was only after a lot of upheaval. They would have been astonished, I'm sure, to know that there was a rule that they shouldn't have the sound over a certain level. Their attitude was not one of hostility, just complete indifference. Once a year for many years they had a circus over there and Art Buchwald came out as the master of ceremonies. There would be hundreds of people, politically connected people. But they never invited the neighbors.

"I would say that from a neighborly point of view, on a scale of one to ten, they were about one point one."

Amid the confusion of his home, Robert Kennedy was somehow able to concentrate on his book about the rackets committee investigations. Written with the help of journalist John Seigenthaler, the text interspersed narrative accounts of the panel's work with a jeremiad about the "tentacles of corruption and fear" that penetrated even the highest offices of labor, business and government. The volume's title, *The Enemy Within*, was meant to place the internal threat of crime and corruption on a par with the external menace of world communism. The name also revealed the growth in RFK's thinking: while working for Joe McCarthy, the youthful investigator would have likely followed his boss's lead and named left-wing subversion as the nation's imminent domestic danger. Bobby's increasing focus on racketeers rather than Reds would not ease relations with J. Edgar Hoover in the years to come.

Published in early 1960, *The Enemy Within* made the best-seller lists briefly; royalties went to the care of retarded children. One admirer of the volume was the well-known producer Jerry Wald, who in 1961 called the nation's new attorney general to discuss purchasing film rights to the book. The deal made, RFK and Wald agreed that the ideal screenwriter for the project would be Budd Schulberg, creator of *On the Waterfront*, the 1954 movie (starring Marlon Brando) exploring union corruption along a New Jersey dockside. Schulberg, who saw the assignment as a chance to write a sequel to the previous film, met Bobby at Hickory Hill, then spent several months poring over committee transcripts and working with a union informant provided him by Walter Sheridan.*

Schulberg's script never reached the screen. After the sudden death of Jerry Wald, Twentieth Century-Fox withdrew from the project. Still reeling from the financial catastrophe of *Cleopatra*, studio executives were in no mood to take risks after they had received a visit from a union representative who warned "that if the picture was ever made drivers would refuse to deliver the prints to the theaters. And, if they go there by any other means, stink bombs would drive out the audiences."

With RFK's approval, Schulberg undertook to produce the film himself and shopped it to a number of studios. Unwilling to confront the project's adversaries, most companies declined the offer. The cowardice spread beyond the offices of the moguls to those who performed in front of Hollywood's cameras: "One film star," Schulberg reported, "telephoned to say he loved the script, then came to my house drunk to tell me he was afraid he might be killed if he did it." Finally, Columbia Pictures, which had distributed *On the Waterfront*, inquired, and a meeting was scheduled between Schulberg and studio management. But on the eve of the conference, the studio received a letter from William Bufalino, a lawyer for the International Brotherhood of Teamsters. In the note, Schulberg recalled, the attorney "stated flatly that 20th Century-Fox had wisely abandoned the project as soon as all the possible eventualities had been pointed out to them, and he felt confident that Columbia would be smart enough to do likewise. On the morning of the meeting, a studio secretary called to tell me that it had been canceled, indefinitely. Apparently Hoffa and Bufalino had decided what the American people could and could not see."

One can imagine Jimmy Hoffa winking in the direction of the Justice Department as he gave Bufalino his orders.

---

* In 1972, Sheridan wrote *The Rise and Fall of Jimmy Hoffa*, a book for which Budd Schulberg penned the introduction. See that introduction, as well as Budd Schulberg, "RFK—Harbinger of Hope" (*Playboy*, January 1969), for information on the would-be film version of *The Enemy Within*.

"**A**ll right, Jack," said Robert Kennedy to his brother during a Palm Beach vacation in December of 1959. *The Enemy Within* behind him, Bobby had assumed his job as manager of JFK's upcoming bid for the presidency. "What has been done about the campaign, what planning has been done? Jack, how do you expect to run a successful campaign if you don't get started? A day lost now can't be picked up at the other end. It's ridiculous that more work hasn't been done already."

Perhaps Bobby couldn't imagine that serious campaign activity could take place without him, but during the previous year and a half, while RFK was occupied fighting crime through Senate hearings and the printed word, the Kennedy forces had hardly been sitting on their hands. Their first task had been the 1958 bid for reelection to the Senate. To boost his stature for the presidency, Jack needed—and got—a landslide victory, thanks to a campaign headed by baby brother Ted.* Although the '58 operation relied on the innovations introduced by Bobby in 1952, RFK took no part in the campaign except to fly to Boston for the election-night celebration. The following spring, Lawrence O'Brien began touring states that would hold primaries, looking for information and allies.

The candidate had spent his time establishing his credentials as a leader and statesman. His involvement in congressional oversight of labor, thanks in large part to the prosecutorial urges of his younger brother, sharpened his focus on domestic issues. Concerning international affairs, Jack made speeches in the Senate and around the country so as to mold a forceful profile as a plausible commander in chief. Leaving behind the conservatism and isolationism of his father, and abandoning his own nondescript earlier record, he at once joined and transcended the mainstream of his party's cold war liberalism with dire warnings of a "missile gap" and idealistic calls for the export of American democratic principles to Third World nations such as newly independent South Vietnam. Liberal intellectuals like Arthur Schlesinger, Archibald Cox and John Kenneth Galbraith came to support a man they'd previously

---

*Twenty-six-year-old Ted had little time to rest after his political baptism, for on November 30, 1958, he would stand at the altar of St. Joseph's Roman Catholic Church in Bronxville, New York, to recite wedding vows under the guidance of Francis Cardinal Spellman. His bride was Virginia Joan Bennett, daughter of a New York advertising executive who had moved his family to Bronxville just as the Kennedys were leaving the town for Joe's diplomatic assignment in England. Joan, twenty-two, had met Teddy while a student at Manhattanville—all the Kennedys had come to the campus to dedicate a gymnasium donated by the Joseph P. Kennedy, Jr., Foundation and named in memory of Kathleen, who had also attended the school. A striking blonde, Joan had made her debut at the New York Debutante Cotillion and had worked as a model before her college graduation.

scorned as callow and insubstantial, but who now resembled their former standard-bearer, only with more nerve—"Stevenson with balls," columnist Joseph Alsop called him.

Less cerebral citizens were taken with the senator's handsome young face and disarming wit, as well as his dazzling young wife and adorable baby daughter—Jackie had finally given birth, to Caroline, in November 1957. Feature articles, with happy family snapshots, appeared often in popular periodicals, particularly women's magazines. Joseph Kennedy knew the value of his son's emerging charisma. "I'll tell you how to sell more copies of a book," he told an interviewer. "Put his picture on the cover. Why is it that when his picture is on the cover of *Life* or *Redbook* they sell a record number of copies? You advertise the fact that he will be at dinner and you will break all records for attendance. He can draw more people to a fund-raising dinner than Cary Grant or Jimmy Stewart."

While the ambassador was only too pleased to gush publicly over his son's better-than-movie-idol glamour, his more consequential role lay behind the scenes. He spent 1959 in full campaign mode, writing checks, as always, and working the phones to political bosses and potential contributors from coast to coast. His base of operations was an outdoor office in Palm Beach. Next to his swimming pool, he'd built a simple enclosure—four walls, no roof—and furnished it with only a deck chair and a telephone. Joe used "the bullpen," as he called his open-air phone booth, instead of just sitting on the main patio, because of a personal idiosyncrasy. America's rich and powerful had no idea that the multimillionaire on the other end of the line, laboring to have his son elected president of the United States, wore not a stitch of clothing as he conducted his business.

Despite the unbuttoned comfort of his oceanfront mansion, Joe would desert the Florida sun whenever necessary to ensure his boy's future. "My older brother Roger had met Jack during World War II and become friends with him," recalled Joseph Foley, then a political operative in Nevada. "And when Jack's father came out here in late '59 to see whether he could line up support for the presidential run, Roger, who was then state attorney general, made the rounds with him. This was LBJ territory here, with our senators supporting Johnson, but at the convention we got more votes for Jack than for everyone else combined. My brother had never met Joe before he walked into his office here, but when Roger was appointed to a federal judgeship by Jack in 1962, Bobby sent word to me that that was the only federal appointment old Joe Kennedy ever asked for.

"Joe was pretty widely known around here in business circles. I believe he went hunting and fishing, and the likes of that, with several of our leading financial people in the northern part of the state—bankers and brokers and gamblers and so on. E. L. Cord was one whom Kennedy knew—he was the one who developed the Cord automobile. Also, there was a man named Norman Blitz, a real estate developer who had big interests in ranching and other areas."

Nominally a Republican, Norman Blitz applied the full weight of his monetary influence to members of both parties. Married at the time to Esther Auchincloss, the sister of Jackie's stepfather, he found in Joe a comrade in money and drive, a scoundrel who spoke his language of power. Taking the ambassador's cause as his own, Blitz brought into Jack's camp people like Wilbur Clark, owner of the Desert Inn in Las Vegas and a leader of the state's Democratic apparatus. By November 1960, Step-uncle Norm had raised for JFK's effort a reputed $15 million.

While out West weaving the web of his contacts, Joe Kennedy often stopped to mix business with pleasure at the Cal-Neva Lodge, a resort hotel overlooking the scenic north shore of Lake Tahoe. The California-Nevada state line ran down the middle of the log cabin–like structure, and the offerings were located accordingly: slot machines and gaming tables in Nevada, food and entertainment in California. On some visits there Joe would see his son-in-law Peter Lawford. Or he would share a table with his son-in-law's friend Frank Sinatra, who owned a share of the operation. Or he would chat with Sinatra's friend, another part-owner, Sam Giancana.* When the ambassador retired for the evening, the establishment's management saw to it that his bed did not lack for human warmth to protect against the cool lake winds.

No matter where Joe might spend his nights, his presence was felt at Kennedy events far and wide. "I was a fund-raiser for John Kennedy's campaign in Rhode Island," recalled Perry Gildes, "and around Christmas in 1959 we held an event at the Watch Hill Inn, along the coast near the Connecticut border. Bobby Kennedy was there, but he didn't so much as say thank you for the hundred thousand dollars we raised. His sole interest that night was trying to meet all the blondes he could find at the private beach club. Toward the end of the evening somebody called his father a Nazi and Bobby spat in the guy's face. Some diplomat!"

---

* Joe Kennedy had met Giancana in Chicago several months earlier through the intervention of associates, and the two men apparently discussed the possibility of Giancana's helping to deliver votes in such states as Illinois and West Virginia. After further meetings with the mobster at Cal-Neva Lodge, Joe asked Frank Sinatra to carry notes back and forth. Sinatra acquiesced.

RFK may have lacked Joe's ambassadorial tact, but he was persuasive all the same. When Michael DiSalle of Ohio got cold feet about being the nation's first governor to endorse JFK, Bobby, accompanied by Connecticut Democratic leader John Bailey, paid him a visit. As Ken O'Donnell later put it, "Bailey subsequently told me that Bobby was all over DiSalle, 'like a fly on shit.' He gave him a real tongue-lashing, and in the end DiSalle capitulated." On January 6, 1960, four days after JFK formally announced his candidacy, DiSalle promised his state's convention delegation to Jack.

As effective as the Kennedys were in soliciting the support of party activists and professionals, the results, whether achieved by Joe's scheming or Bobby's hammer, were only provisional; to win among the pols, Jack would have to prove he could win among the voters. In 1960, the system for choosing each party's presidential candidate was, in the words of former Maryland senator Joseph Tydings, "much more reasonable, much more civilized" than the grueling process of nonstop primaries and caucuses that prevails today. Most delegates to the summer conventions were still selected through state party organizations, and of the sixteen states that staged primary elections, several would use the contests to anoint a favorite son* The Kennedys thus needed to run in only a handful of primaries. Those races would in themselves yield few delegates, but they would test JFK's strength and send signals nationwide to bosses as yet unimpressed by the wife, child or ideological positionings of the forty-two-year-old senator with little history of legislative accomplishment and the unpredictable burden of a Catholic baptism. "The approach to the campaign was very simple," explained David Hackett, the prep school friend whom Bobby hired to work on Jack's correspondence. JFK would "demonstrate his vote-getting ability, his popularity in those primaries," then work with the bosses "in the big states, where those blocks of delegates . . . were controlled."

"I kept waiting for the opposition to show up," said Larry O'Brien of his early visits to the primary states, "but it never did." Only Hubert H. Humphrey, the voluble liberal from Minnesota, would risk slugging it out with Jack in the preliminary rounds. Other potential candidates waited on the sidelines, thinking to fill a breach which Kennedy and Humphrey

---

* A "favorite son" was an esteemed local figure (usually a governor) who would enter the primary not as a legitimate candidate for the presidency, but in order to win control of the state's delegation and then use that authority as leverage with the bona fide contenders. With the hyperdemocratic reform of the nominating mechanism that began after the cataclysms of 1968, the favorite-son tradition has withered away.

would open by inflicting each other with mortal wounds. Lyndon Johnson, the Senate majority leader, hoped that his support in Congress would be mirrored among convention delegates; Adlai Stevenson, ever the darling of the seasoned liberals, longed for one more chance from a party he'd twice led to abysmal defeat; Stuart Symington of Missouri, known for his lack of enemies and for little else, prayed for a miracle.

JFK breezed through the New Hampshire primary in March without serious opposition, then moved on to Wisconsin to face Hubert Humphrey. Wisconsin's "third senator," who used his formidable presence on Capitol Hill to fight for the agricultural interests of his neighboring state, Humphrey attacked his opponent's support of Republican farm policies: "rural America," proclaimed a nine-page Humphrey pamphlet, "found [JFK's] legislative record on agricultural issues far from prepossessing."

If milkers of cows found language like "far from prepossessing" opaque—the senator from Minnesota certainly had no prose stylist to match Ted Sorensen—they had less difficulty comprehending the Kennedys' anti-Humphrey innuendos. Jack delivered few of the coded insults himself, maintaining instead the dignified tone recommended by his pollster: "At all costs," read Louis Harris's memorandum, "Kennedy must avoid being looked upon as a politician. Anything approximating name-calling can only hurt Kennedy. He must make every effort to resist taunts and barbs thrown by Hubert Humphrey." But while JFK was expounding philosophically upon his theories of the modern presidency, his campaign workers were selling insignias of the *PT-109* at a dollar apiece, thus reminding voters not only of Jack's valiance, but also of his rival's well-known failure to have worn the uniform of his country. And while John Kennedy quoted from icons—Jefferson, Hamilton and Lincoln—Robert Kennedy invoked the name of the devil: Jimmy Hoffa, he repeated over and over, would spend anything to beat Jack. (Just as RFK never stated that the Teamsters president actually *was* putting a dime into the election, neither did Humphrey have to mention any names to get his message across in response to Bobby's charge: "Whoever is responsible deserves a spanking. And I said spanking because it applies to juveniles.")

The slur about Hoffa's money particularly riled the senator from Minnesota, who bumped along country roads in a rented campaign bus while the Kennedys cruised the skies in their private airplane, the *Caroline*. Not only could John Kennedy afford Lou Harris's exclusive services, he could also put the pollster's counsel into effect through an unavoidable wave of broadcast, print and door-to-door advertising. Matched up against the money of the Kennedy father, as well as the cadre of Kennedy aides and the touring band of Kennedy relatives, Humphrey, a pharmacist's son who had put himself through college, complained that he felt like an independent merchant competing against a chain store.

Two days before the vote, the Minnesotan known for fits of uncontrolled talkativeness let his frustrations fly before an audience at a Jewish community center in Milwaukee: "They say the Humphrey campaign is disorganized—but I want you to know that the most organized thing that ever happened almost destroyed civilization." Humphrey, once a teacher of political science, knew that his listeners were wary of John Kennedy because of the ambassador's pro-German leanings two decades earlier. Robert Kennedy, always defensive of his father's honor, could not have appreciated Humphrey's pejorative remarks.

Whether Wisconsin's Jews accepted Humphrey's implied comparison of the *Caroline*'s punctual performance to the Teutonic efficiency of Hitler's war machine, their misgivings about JFK were less significant than those of the primary's Protestant voters. While distrust of the pope no doubt motivated many Wisconsinites, liberal Protestants were reluctant to take John Kennedy's side because of a figure closer to home. "We from Wisconsin were, of course, very concerned about Joe McCarthy," recalled Robert Lewis, then an activist on farm issues who worked for the Kennedy campaign during the fall. "McCarthy, who'd been our senator, had been a guest in the Kennedy home in Massachusetts and we viewed these people with a great deal of suspicion. The fear was, there was a reactionary element in the Catholic Church that was very responsive to Joe McCarthy."

To fire up Jack Kennedy's presumed supporters, someone sent Catholics all over the state an antipapist tract ostensibly authored by Humphrey's side. Infuriated by the anonymous trick, the Minnesotan and his staff suspected it was the work of Paul Corbin, an "incredible guy," according to the often sarcastic Senator Daniel Patrick Moynihan of New York, "a genuine, veritable original from Wisconsin." Corbin, a man gifted with a voice and manner as imposing as his conscience was meager, attached himself to Robert Kennedy during the Wisconsin primary. In return, Bobby gave Corbin a long leash and would make ample use of him in years to come. Moynihan, who would work with Corbin during the fall campaign, judged RFK's new friend to be "one of the worst manner of men in American politics, utterly cynical and full of energy and absolutely sort of infuriating in various ways. . . . We never really knew with Corbin [what] he was selling—how much bullshit, how much truth." Paul Corbin's closeness to Bobby—he would later convert to Catholicism only because he wanted RFK and Ethel for godparents—gave the Humphrey people yet another reason to hold the manager of the Kennedy campaign in contempt.

When the votes had been counted on the evening of April 15, they gave John Kennedy a narrow victory. Wisconsin had split along religious lines, with Jack sweeping the Catholic districts and Humphrey taking the Protestant. The result was inconclusive for the Kennedys—despite JFK's victory, he had not shown an ability to draw non-Catholic support—but neither had Humphrey shown strength among Catholics. If the Minnesota senator was unable to carry a state next to his own, how could he be taken seriously as a national nominee? Humphrey was finished, and everyone knew it except the candidate, who intimated that his weak showing was the result of voting by Catholic Republicans, who Wisconsin rules permitted to cross over into the other party's primary.

Ignoring his staff's advice as irrelevant, a seething Hubert Humphrey could not resist taking the fight to West Virginia, where crossover voting was not allowed and Catholics were both scarce and unpopular. His decision to continue to run exasperated the Kennedys: Humphrey, they felt, no longer had any realistic shot at the nomination; his only role now was as a stalking horse for other candidates. Jack and Bobby were not alone in that assessment. By campaign's end, LBJ would appear in the town of Clarksburg, one of Humphrey's state managers would admit he was actually for Stevenson or Symington, and Senator Robert Byrd, an avowed supporter of Johnson, would urge his fellow West Virginians to vote for Humphrey with a strategic eye to the continuing contest: "If you are for Adlai Stevenson, Senator Stuart Symington, Senator Johnson or John Doe, this primary may be your last chance to stop Kennedy."

As Bobby flew to West Virginia, he knew that his long quest to put his brother in the White House depended on the state's election results. Still, he had other matters on his mind. "Bobby's friend from Milton Academy, Dave Hackett, was joined in West Virginia by the writer John Knowles," said film producer Lester Persky. "Hackett was very close to Knowles, who had used Hackett as the basis for a character in his novel *A Separate Peace*. Knowles knew how important the state was and assumed Bobby would be very tense, very focused when he got there. Knowles accompanied Hackett to the airport to greet RFK when he arrived and was surprised at the attitude of the supposedly businesslike campaign manager upon disembarking: 'So, do you have any girls for me?' Bobby wanted to know."

The pressure of the campaign quickly darkened RFK's mood. Charles Peters, who helped organize in the state and would go on to found and edit the *Washington Monthly*, gave Bobby the bad news about Robert

Byrd's opposition. Years later, he described his boss's reaction: "He just got angry at me and started berating me. And that made an impression on me—I disliked him. I admired Jack but I did not admire Bobby. I respected him; he was a hardworking political manager who, when the right things were pointed out to him, usually did them. But as a guy you like—no, I just disliked him."

Bobby's agitation was understandable, for his situation appeared bleak. In a Harris poll conducted the previous December, JFK had been favored by a margin of 70 to 30; that survey was now meaningless, a campaign worker told Bobby: "No one in West Virginia knew you were a Catholic in December. Now they know." Hubert Humphrey did not press his advantage explicitly. Still, he made the most of the difference in doctrinal allegiance by adopting as a theme song the old revival song with the refrain "give me that old-time religion." Unable to run from the subject any longer, Jack and Bobby huddled, and opted for a more outspoken approach. Their decision to tackle the religion issue in a direct and head-on manner became a major turning point in the campaign. "Nobody asked me if I was a Catholic when I joined the United States Navy," Jack declared in his next address, leaving it to others to wonder if anybody had challenged Hubert Humphrey's old-time religion when the Minnesotan had spent the war at home.

Jack and Bobby were not content merely to address the problem; they embraced it until they had wrung it dry. "Let me put it this way," recalled Herbert C. Little, who covered the primary for the Associated Press, "the Kennedy people seemed determined to make a bigger thing out of the religious issue than it really was. They tried to convey the idea that JFK was an underdog fighting against great odds. It was the rare case among political campaigns where a candidate's handlers would take offense if you wrote something suggesting that he might be the favorite. His people would keep reminding reporters how badly Al Smith got beaten in West Virginia.*

"When JFK would appear before an audience, he would often solicit questions at the end of his speech. And after a while, nobody was bringing up the matter of his Catholicism. So, about midway through the campaign, he changed his tactic: he began bringing up the issue himself. The Kennedys played the underdog role to the hilt."

The senator from Minnesota may have had God on his side, but the

---

*Before 1960, Governor Alfred E. Smith of New York was the only Roman Catholic ever nominated for the presidency by a major party. He ran against Herbert Hoover in 1928 and lost in a landslide.

senator from Massachusetts had Joe Kennedy, and the ambassador not only had more money than God, he was willing to spend it. While Humphrey struggled for exposure, Jack dominated the airwaves as the courageous war hero, the prizewinning author, the tenderhearted family man. ("We'll sell him like soap flakes," Joe had burbled.) The financial fight was even more one-sided than it had been in Wisconsin, as Humphrey's previous sources of funds evaporated. Mainstream labor, which had for years esteemed Hubert Humphrey as its champion, gave up on his candidacy after the Wisconsin defeat. And, thanks to the hardball politics of the Kennedys, other spigots closed, too. Backers of Adlai Stevenson were warned that if they continued to bestow gifts on Humphrey, their real favorite would receive no consideration as JFK's secretary of state—the job Stevenson coveted as a fallback if he failed to land in the Oval Office himself. In Connecticut, *Encyclopaedia Britannica* publisher and U.S. senator William Benton, who had donated five thousand dollars to Humphrey's war chest earlier in the year, was informed by state boss John Bailey that any further largesse would send Benton home from Congress and back to his reference library.

Humphrey tried to make a political virtue of his financial necessity by appealing to the class interests of the poverty-stricken state's populace: "I don't think elections should be bought," he maintained with foreboding. "Let that sink in deeply." Only one Democratic candidate was not a millionaire, he noted, only one had experienced poverty, only one had watched his mother "crying when our family home had to be sold." Humphrey had reason to shed tears now. RFK had made visits around the state looking for residents who would make up the strongest delegate slate in each county; then, Lawrence O'Brien would dole out "campaign expenses" to the people Bobby had chosen. "I'm being ganged up on by wealth," Humphrey protested. "I can't afford to run around this state with a little black bag and a checkbook." He tried—Humphrey's aides had been to the same courthouses and greasy spoons visited by RFK and O'Brien, but had been outbid.*

Humphrey was playing "fast and loose with smears and innuendos," volleyed Bobby. Hubert returned fire: "Jack will have plenty of chances to speak for himself without handouts through brother Bobby. Politics is

---

*O'Brien later wrote, "Neither Jack nor Bob Kennedy knew what agreements I made—that was my responsibility." Considering RFK's obsession with detail—the *Baltimore Sun* reported that file cards at Kennedy headquarters in Charleston contained the "name, address, telephone number, and other pertinent data on every one of the Kennedy enthusiasts" statewide—O'Brien's claim, at least with regard to Bobby, is difficult to credit.

a serious business, not a boy's game where you can pick up your ball and run home if things don't go according to your idea of who should win." Loquacious Hubert Humphrey could not find enough words to express his slight regard for "that young, emotional, juvenile Bobby": "Anyone who gets in the way of teacher's pet—I should change that to Papa's pet—is to be destroyed. Bobby said that if they had to spend half a million to win here, they would do it. I don't have any daddy who can pay the bills for me."

JFK himself, descending from the lofty perch on which he'd been set by Lou Harris, joined in the name-calling: Hubert Humphrey "cannot win the election. He cannot be President of the United States. So why, you might ask, is he conducting a gutter campaign against me here in West Virginia? Why is he letting himself be used as a tool by the strangest collection of political bedfellows that has ever joined to gang up on one candidate? And why should he ask West Virginians to waste their votes on him?" Humphrey's side sneered in response that they refused to recognize "the divine right of the Kennedys" to select the Democratic Party's nominee.

The preference of the deity in the 1960 West Virginia Democratic primary must have by this time seemed unclear to the average citizen of that state, but Robert Kennedy no doubt considered it a gift from God when West Virginia's Teamsters came out for Humphrey. The move, said the former committee counsel, confirmed what he'd been saying all along about the intent of the union's general president; the endorsement was a purely local decision, shot back the opposing camp, which had "nothing to do with Hoffa, regardless of how the Kennedy forces try to distort it." "This is just cheap, low-down gutter politics," sputtered Humphrey. Bobby was reverting to the "guilt by association" tactics he'd learned "while working for the late Senator McCarthy's committee during its heyday."

Humphrey's relentless attacks flustered the Kennedys, but the charges did not stick. The coal miners and farmers of West Virginia came to like the wealthy senator from New England. Hubert Humphrey, a true son of the depression who had known hardship and hunger during his youth and had championed the causes of the poor his entire career, could not match the sincere sorrow and amazement John Kennedy displayed when he encountered the poverty of the West Virginia hills. "Imagine, just imagine kids who never drink milk," said JFK, who had never wanted for anything and, in his political life to this point, had rarely bothered to consider anyone who did. Bobby, too, despite his friendships with working-class teammates at Harvard and his fascination with high-level criminals, had never before been confronted by an America that existed side by side with the bounty and comfort of his spacious suburban home. "We were all shocked, and moved," recalled Helen Keyes; "we had not seen poverty like this before. The people were living on lard and flour."

The voters of West Virginia enjoyed catching sight of the splendid Kennedy sisters and the buoyant Kennedy mother who waved from platforms around the state. The voters didn't even mind the roguish Kennedy paterfamilias. The candidate joked, "I got a wire from my father that said, 'Dear Jack, Don't buy one more vote than necessary. I'll be damned if I'll pay for a landslide.' " Jack's charm and energy allowed ordinary citizens to overlook Joe's money and machinations.

As usual, Robert Kennedy led the way in detecting the campaign's inner dynamics. When he proposed that Jackie appear by her husband's side at rallies, everyone else in Jack's brain trust objected. The miners' wives in their simple dresses would despise the debutante in the Parisian suits, the advisers all argued. But Bobby insisted and was proven right. "There was no question," maintained Charles Peters, "that instead of identifying with the woman who was like them—Muriel Humphrey— they identified with the Princess. You could just tell they wanted Jackie. They had a wondrous look in their eyes when they saw her. After the dowdiness of Eleanor Roosevelt, Bess Truman and Mamie Eisenhower, they were looking for an aristocratic image. And the Kennedys did a superlative job of merchandising that image." It was Bobby's intuitive political genius to realize that rather than resenting the wealthy, radiant Kennedys, West Virginians—and Americans—would choose to live vicariously through them.

The most powerful weapon in Bobby's arsenal had an even more famous patrimony than his own. Although his mother supported Adlai Stevenson, Franklin Delano Roosevelt, Jr., had met with Jack, Bobby and Joe at Palm Beach following the Wisconsin primary and had offered to aid the cause in West Virginia. A younger version of arguably America's greatest president, FDR Jr. traveled to towns and villages where the New Deal was still as much gospel as the Bible read from every Sunday in whitewashed Baptist churches. By his speeches, he gave the imprimatur of his lineage to the candidacy of the rich young senator with the strange northern accent and the likewise strange Roman religion. Yet again, Hubert Humphrey, the rightful inheritor of the New Deal mantle, had been trumped by the "aristocratic" Kennedys, arrivistes to the cause.

But for Bobby, the junior Roosevelt's support of Jack was not enough; he needed the late idol's scion to curse the enemy. Two weeks before the vote, FDR Jr. struck: "Hubert Humphrey has always been a loyal

Democrat, but I don't know where he was in World War II." With the Kennedy camp finally proclaiming out loud what it had been implying for months, Hubert Humphrey was beside himself: Roosevelt's charges "are the lowest kind of campaigning. He has been a friend of mine for the last fifteen years and he knows my public and private record." Rejected by both the army and the navy because of a heart murmur, Humphrey insisted that he was no draft dodger. The gallant hero of the Pacific claimed innocence in the affair. "I have not discussed the matter of war records," declared Jack, "and I'm not going to. Mr. Roosevelt is down here making his speeches. I'm making mine." Four days before the balloting, Roosevelt sharpened his indictment: Humphrey had requested deferments to teach school, to manage a political campaign and to handle labor relations for a Minnesota company. JFK again denied any knowledge of the situation: "Any discussion of the war record of Senator Hubert Humphrey was done without my knowledge or consent. I strongly disapprove the injection of this issue into this campaign." The future president's disavowal was not the first lie a politician had ever told. "Of course Jack knew," FDR Jr. said years later. "But I always regretted my role in the affair. Humphrey, an old ally, never forgave me for it. I did it because of Bobby. Only in his mid-thirties, RFK was already a full-blown tyrant. You did what he told you to do, and you did it with a smile."

On primary night, Tuesday, May 10, while RFK awaited the returns anxiously at campaign headquarters in Charleston, Jack went to the movies in downtown Washington. (He and Jackie, joined by *Washington Post* editor Ben Bradlee and his wife, Toni, saw a soft-porn feature entitled *Private Property*.) Tabulations were slow in the mostly rural state, but by ten o'clock the results were clear: county after county went solidly for Kennedy. As Jack flew down on the *Caroline*, Hubert Humphrey huddled with his staff at the Ruffner Hotel in Wheeling. At 1:15 A.M., a quarter of an hour after receiving Humphrey's telegram of concession from a Western Union messenger, Robert Kennedy walked into Hubert's suite. After kissing Muriel Humphrey on the cheek, he greeted his now fallen rival, whom he then accompanied to Humphrey headquarters. The passionate liberal choked back his emotion as he spoke to the few supporters who had remained through the long, disheartening night: "I have a brief statement to make. I am no longer a candidate for the Democratic presidential nomination." Robert Kennedy, his eyes as moist as those of everyone else in the room, walked over and put an arm around Humphrey's shoulder, then led the downcast senator back out into the rain, toward the Kanawha Hotel to hear Jack claim victory. The months of invective were forgotten. The foe, now vanquished, was forgiven.

"My initial reaction to Robert Kennedy was that there didn't seem to be one ounce of warmth in him," said Philip Hoff years later. Hoff, a former governor of Vermont, encountered RFK during the 1960 campaign and worked with him on civil-rights issues in the early sixties. "He was direct, he was to the point, but he was absolutely humorless and almost chillingly cold.

"Over a period of time, I got to know the other side of Bobby Kennedy. It made such an interesting combination: on the one hand, he was so terribly businesslike, so coldly, almost grimly, efficient, while on the other hand he had so much compassion. It was a fascinating time. He was one of the most honest people I ever met."

John F. Kennedy entered and won seven primaries in 1960: New Hampshire, Wisconsin, Indiana, West Virginia, Nebraska, Maryland and Oregon. But West Virginia was the key. Had Lyndon Johnson and Adlai Stevenson been more astute in their desire to "stop Kennedy," they would have seen to it that the fast-rising New Englander ran in that primary uncontested. For only by his trouncing of the good Methodist Hubert Humphrey did John Kennedy demonstrate to Democratic power brokers his appeal to voters outside his own communion. "I think we have now buried the religious issue once and for all," Jack told the press in Charleston after his victory speech.

With the Bible Belt triumph, the campaign's tone changed overnight. More work needed to be done before the Democratic National Convention, set to begin July 11 in Los Angeles, and the Kennedys traveled frenetically to nail down delegates at party gatherings from coast to coast. But no longer was JFK the junior candidate vying to upset the party's older, more proven leaders, and the remaining primaries, previously expected to oblige continued slogging in the arduous marathon, turned into victory laps. Senator Joseph Tydings, then a member of the House and the local campaign manager for Maryland, recalled the instant transformation: "Our primary was scheduled ten days after West Virginia's. We had felt he would lose West Virginia, then we'd have to bail him out here. However, when Senator Kennedy won there, everything changed. I mean, all of a sudden, he became the favorite. And when he came into Maryland it was almost like night and day, with all the politicians running out, wanting to get their pictures taken with him.

"The Sunday before the voting we had a big reception for the ladies at the Emerson Hotel in Baltimore. It was one of those famous Kennedy teas. There were so many ladies who came that we didn't have enough chairs—there must have been close to a thousand. Jackie Kennedy was there, and Ethel. We also had Jean Smith, and we had Bobby. He and Jackie were going to do the speaking. All the Kennedys were late in arriving—the ladies had been on their feet for about an hour before they got there. Then they came in, shook hands around a bit, and came up on the podium. Jackie was pregnant at the time and didn't want to say anything, so I said a few words on her behalf. Then I introduced Bobby, who started giving one of those long-winded campaign speeches. And he went on and on. Finally, I stuck a note in front of him saying, 'If you'll be quiet and sit down, we can win this election; if you talk much longer, we're going to lose it.'

"He sat down. We won."

12

HONORARY BROTHER

On June 9, 1959, while still John McClellan's chief counsel, Robert F. Kennedy had sat across from Sam Giancana in the Senate Caucus Room:

> KENNEDY—Would you tell us if you have opposition from anybody that you dispose of them by having them stuffed in a trunk? Is that what you do, Mr. Giancana?
>
> GIANCANA—I decline to answer because I honestly believe any answer might tend to incriminate me.
>
> KENNEDY—Would you tell us anything about any of your operations or will you just giggle every time I ask you a question?
>
> GIANCANA—I decline to answer because I honestly believe my answer might tend to incriminate me.
>
> KENNEDY—I thought only little girls giggled, Mr. Giancana.

The evasive demeanor of Chicago's murderous *capo di capi* may have reflected his knowledge that not everyone in RFK's family held him in the low esteem evidenced by the snarling inquisitor himself. Some months before, Giancana had received a phone call from Bobby's father: Would the don care to be of assistance in Jack's upcoming presidential campaign (the ambassador wanted to know). Intrigued by the suggestion, Giancana over the next year and a half held a series of meetings and telephone conversations with Joe (and very possibly Jack) in which he promised not only to add funds to the Kennedys' already bottomless treasury, but also to assist in ensuring friendly vote totals in his hometown. In return, the Massachusetts political family offered better days to the Illinois gangster and his crime clan: Joe and Jack, Giancana is reported to have said, would see that their crime-fighting relative was not allowed to carry his crusade into a Kennedy administration. "Bobby doesn't even know what Jack and I have been talkin' about," the mafioso supposedly chortled. "He's out of the picture. He'll be just another goddamned law-yer soon. They've promised me they'll take care of him."

Giancana's mirth at the witness table may have had another source. At around the same time Joe Kennedy made his initial inquiring contact, the don arranged to purchase a controlling interest in the Cal-Neva Lodge. Not only would the resort complement Giancana's other holdings in the gambling business, it would also give him a means of ensuring that the Kennedys kept their end of the bargain. Through his own presence at the club and through the reports of others, the mobster knew that neither the prospective Leader of the Free World nor the former ambas-sador to the Court of St. James's was ever likely to refuse a good time at the Lake Tahoe resort, which both had been visiting for years. As owner of the facility, Giancana could see that the amenities the men enjoyed— the plush carpets and firm beds on which they attended to their gratifica-tion—were augmented by less pleasurable furnishings: hidden cameras and microphones. According to subsequent FBI reports, Giancana boasted of a safe-deposit box overflowing with tape recordings, films and photographs of Joseph and John Kennedy taking carnal delight in the company of women for whom affection was strictly a cash business.

In order to fool, or perhaps just appease, the Nevada Gaming Com-mission, Sam Giancana did not buy the Cal-Neva openly, but instead hid behind the ownership share of his friend of almost thirty years, Frank Sinatra. The singer had no need to be secretive, as did the gangster, in associating with the Kennedys. Sinatra had met Jack in the early fifties and since that time the two men had shared generously with each other their respective connections—Sinatra supplied telephone numbers of Hollywood actresses to the starstruck, randy politician, while JFK repaid the favor with introductions to members of Congress for the entertainer lustful for proximity to power. The connection was personified by Peter Lawford, who had received induction into the "Rat Pack," the Sinatra-led nonstop floating crap game and exercise in male bonding, Vegas style, that also included Sammy Davis, Jr., Joey Bishop and Dean Martin. In early 1959, when the singer's support of the senator's ambitions was so spirited that he renamed his social circle the "Jack Pack," Sinatra traveled to Palm Beach with the friend he now called "brother-in-Lawford" to meet with Joe. The ambassador assigned to Sinatra the task of raising funds among the singer's thousands of close personal friends in California and Nevada, then requested that he record a campaign theme song. Sina-tra would choose to transform a recent hit, "High Hopes," with special lyrics he commissioned from his personal arranger, Jimmy Van Heusen, and the tune's author, Sammy Cahn. By Election Day of 1960, the tune would be omnipresent along the campaign trail and could be heard on jukeboxes in all corners of the nation.

Although busy in the financial and entertainment wings of the Kennedy enterprise, Frank Sinatra did not neglect his duties as social director. On February 7, 1960, at a party at the Sands Hotel in Las Vegas held to celebrate the completion of *Ocean's Eleven,* the legendarily atrocious film starring the entire Rat/Jack Pack, the singer introduced the senator to Judy Campbell, a raven-haired twenty-five-year-old whose successful partying career had taken her places she had only imagined during the brief years of her failed acting career. Although Sinatra and Campbell had only just concluded the affair they'd begun the previous November while visiting Hawaii with the Lawfords, the singer was delighted to nurture the chemistry that stirred so obviously between JFK and his new acquaintance, and offered the patio of his hotel suite to the pair for lunch the next day. The smitten senator pursued the seduction slowly: a three-hour meal, followed by frequent telephone calls over the next month, before consummation at New York's Plaza Hotel on March 7.

Despite the senator's triumph, Frank Sinatra had not yet finished expanding Judy Campbell's circle of acquaintances. A week after her debut in Kennedy's bed, Sinatra invited the lissome brunette to Miami Beach to see his act at the Fontainebleau, where, between shows, he introduced her to another music fan who happened to be visiting, Sam Flood. Campbell would soon come to accept cash and expensive gifts from Mr. Flood; just as quickly, she would learn his real surname: Giancana. For the two and a half years of her affair with the senator-then-president, Campbell would remain an intimate of the underworld kingpin. Years later, as Judith Campbell Exner, she would tell her story. One of her claims is that she served as courier between John Kennedy and the Mob.*

Judy Campbell connected Frank Sinatra to Jack, but another woman would link the singer to Bobby. "Barbara Marx was without a doubt one of the most popular, beloved women I've ever met," recalled socialite Mary Harrington. "At this time she was only in her thirties, and she walked on the most beautiful pair of legs imaginable. (She had been a successful showgirl.)" Marx lived next door to Frank Sinatra in Palm

---

*Robert Kennedy knew of his brother's liaison with Judith Campbell from the start, but received "official" notification only after he became attorney general. An FBI memo dated 8/17/62, noted that J. Edgar Hoover had "previously" apprised RFK of the affair.

Springs, California, with her husband, Zeppo Marx, the less hilarious brother of Groucho, Harpo and Chico. "He was so much older than she was, an elderly gentleman then, and he spent most of his time playing poker with his cronies on a small boat he kept in Acapulco. That suited his wife just fine because Barbara was the party girl of all time; there wasn't a shindig given in Palm Springs that she didn't attend. Her taste ran to lots of pancake makeup and bleached blond hair—she had no chic about her at all, yet no one noticed it because everyone adored her."

In the early sixties, a time came when Marx began to absent herself from the Palm Springs scene. Harrington continued: "Barbara would say to me, 'Mary, I'm going off for three or four days but I'll call you when I get back.' I never questioned her, but when she returned from these trips she'd be so sad. After this had been going on for a while she finally said to me, 'You know, I've really fallen in love and I'm afraid of it.'

" 'Does he love you?' I asked.

" 'Yes, but he's not only married, he's also from a very powerful family. Every time I see him it takes me three days to get emotionally ready and three days to recover.'

"One day we were over in Vegas and Barbara was very nervous about getting dressed. I had never seen her this way. 'My goodness, Mary,' she said, 'he's here. You're going to know who it is. Stay close to me. You're single, you can bear the brunt of it. If anything comes out in the press, I want you to be the one mentioned. I can't lose my marriage.'

"So we went down to the show—it was Sinatra, Dean Martin and Sammy Davis. The entire world was there, a whole crowd of celebrities. Every now and then she would touch my hand—her hand was clammy— and all of a sudden there was Bobby Kennedy. He was watching her and she was watching him. It was like they had a magnet. They started toward each other and met in the middle of the dance floor. They were in each other's arms and I said to myself, 'Mary, what are you going to do?' So I pushed in between them and said, 'Oh, Bobby, I'm so happy to see you!' I gave them a moment to regain their composure. She had tears in her eyes. Later we asked him back to our table, and I shifted my chair around close to Bobby's and reached over and linked my arm in his and let everybody see it. What are you going to do? You've got to protect your friends.

"Later that evening Barbara disappeared and I didn't see her until the next morning. After that night I was deeply intertwined in their relationship, and when she wanted to see him she would ask me to join them."

Over the next few months, Harrington would accompany the couple in public, as if to suggest that the two women and one man were no more than carefree buddies enjoying dinner or a show in Las Vegas, Palm Springs or Los Angeles. But before long Bobby came to regard Harrington as more than just convenient camouflage. "I had an apartment in New York at the Carlyle," Harrington said, "and whenever Bobby came to town he'd call and we would have lunch. I always thought we were just friends. Then one weekend I was in Jamaica—I'd told him where I was going—and I received a telephone call from one of his aides who said Bobby was at the Half Moon Club and wanted to see me. I went down there and we started dancing. Pretty soon, I thought to myself, 'Oh, my glory!' I became extremely attracted to him, so I made up an excuse and fled back to the house where I was staying.

"When I got back to New York, Bobby started calling me, saying he could no longer see Barbara because she was becoming so emotional. Then, after I had checked into New York Hospital for phlebitis, he sent a lovely note up to my room along with flowers and a gold bracelet from Cartier. His aides had been coming by to see how I was doing, but one night, around one a.m., he showed up himself. I was seeing a doctor on the staff, but Bobby charmed the night-shift nurses and doctors to keep quiet about his visit. Following that first appearance, he would come to see me two or three times a week.

"One evening not long after I got back to my apartment, he sent red roses and called to say he was having dinner sent in. He came to my door thinking, 'Ah, another conquest.' But when he got there I had to say, 'Sorry, I'm on these crutches.' He looked at me—it was very amusing. And that was the end of it. I was violating my friendship with Barbara and he was a married man. It was against all my principles.

"Bobby had animalistic vibrations about him. The word *charismatic* was, I'm sure, created for him and his brother. But Bobby, because he wasn't as handsome, conveyed much more sincerity. He had style, he was cultured. And when he talked to a woman, he would not only look directly at her, he would also speak in a soft, low tone. It was as though he was caressing you with his voice. He was far better with the ladies than Jack."

RFK's affair with Barbara Marx would last over a year. While the liaison was in progress, word of it reached the entertainer who had aided the Kennedys during their run for the White House. The blue-eyed song stylist would always resent Bobby for his romance with the onetime showgirl, who several years after Bobby's death would become Mrs. Frank Sinatra.*

Jacqueline Kennedy, pregnant and tired, stayed in Hyannis Port during the 1960 Democratic convention and followed the proceedings on television. But not all the week's activities made the network news broadcasts.

JFK first met Marilyn Monroe in 1957 at the lavish Santa Monica beach house belonging to the Lawfords. On that occasion, the senator took a long walk along the shore with the actress, discussing movies and politics. He postponed a more intimate knowledge of her until 1959, when he arranged to spend several days in her company at the Palm Springs home belonging to the singer who was his friend and her ex-lover.

Frank Sinatra also owned Puccini's, the Los Angeles bistro where Jack and Marilyn, along with Ken O'Donnell and Peter Lawford, dined the second night of the convention. "Of all his 'other' women," Lawford reflected, "Marilyn was perhaps the best for him. They were good together. They both had charisma, and they both possessed a sense of humor. Marilyn proclaimed that night that Jack's sexual performance was 'very democratic' and 'very penetrating.' She also came up with that memorable line, 'I think I made his back feel better.'

"Jack liked to pat and squeeze her. He was touching her here and there under the table when this bemused expression suddenly crossed his face. Marilyn said later he had put his hand up her dress and discovered she wore no underwear."

Joe was at the Cal-Neva Lodge in June when Jack called from Washington. The Pennsylvania delegation, which had been a special project of Joe's, had come around. "Well, that's it," the ambassador responded. "We've got a majority."

---

*On December 8, 1997, "Page Six" of the *New York Post* published an article in which Barbara Marx denied ever having been involved with Bobby Kennedy. "I was never that lucky," she said. "But I got even luckier than that when I married Frank Sinatra in 1976." Barbara Marx's non sequitur notwithstanding, the source for the Bobby-Barbara relationship as well as several other anecdotes in the book was the well-known and well-connected socialite Mary Harrington, who gave many interviews for this project, all of them taped. Known to high society as "Magnolia" (a name given to her by Jacqueline Susann), Mary died in July 1997. Because the RFK-Barbara Marx relationship has been grouped thematically with the Judith Campbell-JFK affair, it has been transmogrified slightly in chronological terms. The details of the relationship are precisely as "Magnolia" related them.

The Kennedys' main rivals were unwilling to face that reality. Several weeks before the convention, JFK had visited Adlai Stevenson in Chicago to ask for his endorsement. The former Illinois governor refused, citing LBJ's then still undeclared candidacy: "If you are elected, you will need somebody to be a liaison between you and Johnson because he's very mad at you, and, therefore, this would be the role that I would take. So, as a result, I think it's important for me to stay in a position of neutrality at this point." The transparency of the two-time nominee's desire for a third shot was not lost on John Kennedy, and it ruined the Midwestern-er's prospects for becoming the nation's top diplomat. "I'm turned down ten times a day by people around the country," Jack told Charles Bartlett, "and it doesn't really bother me. But his bothered me because it was such a silly idea to think of Adlai Stevenson as a liaison between me and Johnson. If he couldn't come up with a better one than that, he certainly wouldn't make a very good secretary of state."

The lack of respect between the former nominee and the current front-runner was mutual. "That young man never says please," Stevenson complained. "He never says thank you, he never asks for things, he de-mands them." Although Stevenson had had word by late June of Kenne-dy's insurmountable lead, an enthusiastic welcome at the Los Angeles airport on convention eve helped keep the ex-governor's hopes intact. That night, Stevenson aide William McCormick Blair, Jr., attended a din-ner at the Lawfords'. "I sat between Judy Garland and Nat King Cole," Blair remembered. "As I came in I saw Mr. Kennedy, Sr., whom I'd known very well over the years—as tough a fellow as I'd ever hoped to meet—and I thought to be polite I'd just go up and say good eve-ning . . . and he looked at me and said, 'Your man must be out of his mind.'

"I said, 'Well, maybe this isn't the time to talk about it. As you know, I've always been hoping that Mr. Stevenson would support Jack,' at which he took his fist and clenched it . . . and said, 'You've got twenty-four hours.' "

JFK seemed to Blair less disturbed by the situation, but the candi-date's brother was smoldering: "Bobby was looking very darkly at me and the next day called me in the morning and said, 'Jack wants to know if the governor will nominate him.' I said, 'I'll urge him again, but I'm sure the answer is no.' And when I got back to Bobby and told him he slammed down the phone, very angry about it."

Nor was Lyndon Johnson ready to throw in the towel. He had only just tossed his ten-gallon hat in the ring, finally ending his charade of noncandidacy with an announcement at the Senate Office Building on

July 5. With only six days remaining before the convention's opening, the Texan immediately began conducting his campaign for the presidency by orchestrating an all-out smear campaign of his rival. Theodore H. White, author of the *Making of the President* series, recalled the spreading of one rumor: "A person very high in Johnson's Administration now"— White was speaking shortly after JFK's assassination—"called me about five days before the Los Angeles convention and said, 'I think you should know that John Kennedy and Bobby Kennedy are fags.' I said, 'You're crazy.' He said, 'We have pictures of John Kennedy and Bobby Kennedy in women's dresses at Las Vegas this spring at a big fag party. This should be made public.' I said, 'I'll print it if you give me the pictures.' He said, 'I'll get you the pictures within twenty-four hours.' He never delivered the pictures to me."

Arriving in Los Angeles, Lyndon Johnson also joined in the general merriment. Associating the former ambassador to England with the British prime minister who had sought to appease the Germans, Johnson told a reporter for the *New York Times,* "I was never any Chamberlain umbrella policy man. I never thought Hitler was right."* Johnson aide John Connally informed a writer for the *Chicago Daily News* that John Kennedy, presented to America as the embodiment of vigorous youth, actually suffered from Addison's disease. Ted Kennedy countered by noting LBJ's recent heart attack, but Bobby went further. "You've got your nerve," he said to LBJ staffer Bobby Baker. "Lyndon Johnson has compared my father to the Nazis and John Connally . . . lied by saying my brother was dying of Addison's disease. You Johnson people are running a stinking damned campaign and you'll get yours when the time comes. We'll fucking kill you."

Better humor prevailed at a "debate" between LBJ and JFK before the Texas delegation early in the convention week. The joint appearance had been Johnson's idea; Jack, despite his father's advice to stay away, couldn't resist the challenge. "Look," Jack told Ken O'Donnell, who agreed with the ambassador, "I know Lyndon like no one knows Lyndon, and I can't wait to get there." The candidates avoided serious disputation, and Jack won the day by outcharming the Texan among the Texans, cracking, "You're a great majority leader, and I hope you'll be the same

---

*Two years later, Vice President Johnson said to Attorney General Kennedy, "I know why you don't like me. The reason you don't like me is because I made those remarks about your father at the press conference." LBJ then claimed he'd been misquoted. Although Bobby protested disingenuously that he didn't know what the vice president was talking about, the next day he checked with John Seigenthaler to confirm that the Texan had been quoted accurately. He had.

for me." Even Johnson's people couldn't help but laugh. "He went in, and I think that was the end of Lyndon Johnson," said O'Donnell later.

Robert Kennedy did not share his brother's cool confidence. By the time Frank Sinatra opened the convention's first night with a jazzy rendition of the national anthem, the campaign manager had been in town for a week, working feverishly from a command post established in room 8315 of the Biltmore Hotel. As the balloting neared, RFK got less and less sleep, and he expected his subordinates to take his family's cause just as seriously as he did. "He wanted everybody to work hard," commented Joseph Tydings. "I mean, he was tough. I was one of the thirty-two coordinators on the floor who worked directly for Bobby—we each had a delegation or two. And every morning at seven o'clock we had a meeting at which we gave status reports—what each delegate was thinking about, whether he was for us, agin us, undecided—whatever we knew.

"Now, in order to really cover the delegations, you had to stay out late at night because there were all sorts of parties and receptions going on. So you wouldn't get to bed till two or three in the morning. And of course, nobody's getting paid. Nobody's even getting expenses covered—everyone's out there on his own. So during one morning meeting, a guy straggled in at around seven-thirty and Bobby said, 'Look, if it's too much for you to get here at seven when we get here, just let me know and you'll be excused.' "

At the heart of RFK's operation was a comprehensive database consisting of over three thousand blue, three-by-five-inch note cards—one for every person included among the convention's delegates and alternates. As David Hackett noted, the cards, compiled over the course of the previous year and a half of campaigning, listed "basic information" like "what the candidate called the person, when RFK had first met him, how important the person was." And each of the delegates was assigned a numerical ranking in accord with his or her presidential preference. "A ten, for example, was a person who—there was no question—was a Kennedy man. To get a ten we'd require that at least two people designated him as a ten. We'd never rely on one person's judgment." In the final days of the Los Angeles effort, the tracking of the vote grew even closer, with floor coordinators ordered to communicate to Bobby's headquarters without delay any change in a delegate's status. The workers had to call in *"immediately,"* as one of them told the *New York Herald Tribune,* "not in five minutes." None of the other camps had an operation that could remotely approach Bobby's in its tenacious attention to detail and its disciplined plan of action.

Beginning each day on the eighth floor of the Biltmore, RFK would gather his army of aides and advisers, workers and followers, address them en masse, then lead them to the Los Angeles Memorial Sports Arena to take part in the jawboning. Film producer Dore Schary, a Stevenson loyalist, remembered that RFK and his "squads were operating in full flight. They would move in and surround an indecisive delegate. And there'd be eight fellows around and you could see Bobby in there working on him." Lyndon Johnson, contended Hackett, had "just worked with the senators. Bob Kennedy, with his basic political instinct, did the hard, difficult, boring work, and that was the state-by-state count."

"There's no tomorrow," RFK said at the morning meeting on Wednesday, the day the vote would be taken. "If we don't win this evening, we're gone." Among state leaders offering to make deals for votes on a second ballot was Carmine de Sapio of New York, who proposed to funnel thirty votes to Johnson for the first round only. "To hell with that," Bobby replied, "we're going to win it on the first ballot." Were the initial vote not conclusive, the Kennedys' carefully constructed aura of inevitability might begin to fade; Johnson did have support in the South and among leaders of Congress, and many of the delegates still held Adlai Stevenson close to their hearts, as evidenced by the convention's emotional outpouring at Eugene McCarthy's impassioned nominating speech of him.

"We had the votes on the first ballot," Ken O'Donnell later insisted, "the second ballot, the third ballot or the tenth ballot. We had the votes." In the end, it was Bobby's anxiety, his refusal to take a single vote for granted, that vindicated the optimism of the others. By the time the first roll call reached the last state in alphabetical order, JFK was still 13 votes short of the 761 needed to win. Jack, watching television in the apartment he'd rented for the week from actor Jack Haley, saw his youngest brother in the midst of the Wyoming delegation. Network microphones did not pick up the words Teddy was shouting above the din, but Tracy S. McCraken, Wyoming's national party committeeman, heard them clearly: "You have in your grasp the opportunity to nominate the next president of the United States. Such support can never be forgotten by a president." McCraken did not let the moment go by, and announced that Wyoming would cast all 15 of its votes for John F. Kennedy.

The presidential nominee of the Democratic Party quickly left for the Sports Arena. Before entering the hall to make a brief address to the delegates, he met with his campaign manager in an outer corridor. As the two brothers walked away from reporters to share their victory in private, Jack smiled. Bobby, his head bowed, hit his right fist into his open left palm.

At precisely eight the next morning, Pierre Salinger, who was the campaign's press secretary, visited room 8315 of the Biltmore, soon to be followed in by Ken O'Donnell. "Robert Kennedy was in the usual Kennedy place," O'Donnell remembered; "he was in a bathtub. Pierre said, 'He just told me to add up all the northern states we thought we could carry and add Texas.' I said, 'You mean Johnson?' He said, 'Yes.'"

Despite the mud LBJ had been slinging JFK's way, the political calculus of the general election dictated that the Texan be named Jack's running mate. Already well positioned to capture several segments of the traditional Democratic coalition—with his natural attraction to Catholics and his adroitly crafted appeal to labor and liberals—Jack needed to shore up another important party stronghold, the white South. Although many in Kennedy's camp had been recommending Scoop Jackson or Stuart Symington, Joseph Kennedy pushed for LBJ, notwithstanding the glee Johnson had been taking in dredging up the ambassador's past. For once, Bobby's personal bias could not stand in the way of his cold political eye; he was forced to swallow his hatred for an enemy and yield to the logic of the choice. The final decision actually belonged to the nominee. And unlike his younger brother, whose public career had been characterized by one savage vendetta after another, Jack refused to hold a grudge against his self-interest. "I don't believe in personal feuds," JFK had said; "there's no percentage in them."

On Tuesday night, while RFK was still sweating out the delegate count for Wednesday's presidential balloting, the untroubled candidate had moved discreetly to ensure Johnson's place on the ticket. Among a crowd gathered outside Chasen's restaurant, where the United Steelworkers were throwing a party, JFK conferred with Tip O'Neill, who that night was acting as messenger for Speaker of the House Sam Rayburn. Johnson's mentor, Rayburn had previously expressed opposition to the Texas senator's accepting the second slot, but he offered a different opinion once O'Neill told him that Jack had the nomination sewn up. Handing O'Neill his phone number, the Speaker said, "If Kennedy is interested in Lyndon being the vice presidential nominee, you have him call me and by golly, I'll insist on it." When Jack was given the news, O'Neill recalled, "he was delighted. 'Of course I want Lyndon,' he told me. 'But I'd never want to offer it and have him turn me down. Lyndon's the natural choice, and with him on the ticket, there's no way we could lose. Tell Sam Rayburn I'll call after the session tonight.'"

Advance word of Kennedy's upcoming invitation did not sweeten Lyndon Johnson's temperament as the convention proceeded. And late

Wednesday night, whether angry at Bobby and his family over the slurs traded between camps or suspicious that RFK opposed Jack's decision, or perhaps simply chagrined at his own second-place finish in the just-completed presidential balloting—he'd gotten only half as many delegates as the victorious upstart from Massachusetts—LBJ was in a foul mood. "I went up to the seventh floor of the Biltmore where Johnson was staying," reported Gene Scherrer, then head of VIP security for the Los Angeles Police Department. "Johnson was in the hallway, ranting and raving about the Kennedys, saying things like, 'Those motherfuckers,' and 'I'd like to piss on Bobby.' He didn't have a shirt on and his fly was open. He was very drunk and *very* obscene. Of course, the next day, he was named John Kennedy's vice presidential candidate."

By the time Bobby climbed out of his bathtub on Thursday morning, Ken O'Donnell was demanding to see Jack. "I'm not about to stand still on this one," said O'Donnell, the campaign's labor liaison at the convention to labor. O'Donnell knew that union officials had little use for the Senate majority leader. "Lyndon Johnson had been the chief obstacle to many of the bills that labor had been interested in," O'Donnell later explained, "and Walter Reuther and George Meany had gone to Johnson for seven years and received nothing." Many in the party also resented what they saw as Johnson's inferior record on race issues, never forgiving his role in watering down the Civil Rights Act of 1957. In JFK's suite, the nominee sought to calm his aide's anger by asserting, preposterously, that he'd chosen Johnson in order to get him out of the way—the Texan would be much easier to control as vice president than as majority leader of the Senate. Pacified by this rationalization, O'Donnell was then ordered to visit his delegates. "You get your tail over there and see your labor friends," barked Jack. "You get them and tell them this is the way it has got to be. I don't know whether he'll take it or not, but I've offered it to him and I'm hopeful he'll take it."

O'Donnell was not willing to walk into the lions' den alone. "I'm not that big," he told Bobby, "but you and I will go over and see them. I know them all, but you're the candidate's brother and you've got the muscle. I don't have it."

By the time O'Donnell and RFK reached the delegates, word of the selection had already been announced on television. "I was working in Reuther's suite at the hotel where the labor people met," recalled Paul Schrade, labor vice chairman of the campaign. "And they were just jumping out the fuckin' windows." The candidate's brother did not find a cordial reception. "I don't think Robert Kennedy ever was so savagely attacked in his life," recalled O'Donnell. The unionists, who had succumbed to Jack's wooing during the primaries and before, now felt double-crossed. Governor G. Mennen Williams of Michigan, head of the convention's most ardently prolabor delegation, was threatening to offer his name in nomination in opposition to Johnson. Bobby was "ashen," O'Donnell said. "We were all ashen."

By the time the shaken pair arrived back at campaign headquarters, LBJ had accepted Jack's offer, but the reports of disaffection caused Jack to reconsider. As always, the senator called upon his brother to do his dirty work. As RFK entered the outer room of Johnson's seventh-floor suite he encountered Sam Rayburn, who walked into the bedroom to announce the visitor's arrival. LBJ, conferring with his wife, Lady Bird, and with Phil Graham, a Johnson backer and publisher of the *Washington Post,* angrily refused to see Bobby and told Rayburn he wished to speak to the young campaign manager's older brother. Once Bobby left the suite, Graham telephoned Jack, who reassured him that LBJ's presence on the ticket was still welcome.

Upstairs, the grumbling intensified. Labor activists like Walter Reuther and Jack Conway had called upon the nominee to voice their discontent. To compensate, Jack summoned to the suite a parade of people known to be favorable toward Johnson—big-state pols like Carmine de Sapio of New York, John Bailey of Connecticut and Mike DiSalle of Ohio—who were dispatched to delegate caucuses to make LBJ's case. But opposition to the selection could not be contained, and Bobby was once again dispatched to the seventh floor.

This time, LBJ met with the emissary. Bobby began by explaining that resistance to Johnson had unexpectedly developed among the liberals, and Jack was eager to spare his Senate colleague the ordeal of a bitter floor fight. The campaign manager then offered LBJ a consolation prize if he would withdraw: the chairmanship of the Democratic National Committee. The offer of the figurehead position to the majority leader in love with power may not have been intended as an insult, but it was taken as one. "Piss off!" was Sam Rayburn's reply. "Who's the goddamn candidate," asked John Connally, who'd joined the discussion, "you or your big brother?" Phil Graham telephoned upstairs. "Jack," he said to the nominee, "Bobby's down here and he's saying that there is opposition and that Lyndon should withdraw." "Forget it," the senator replied. "Bobby doesn't know what's going on." Graham then handed the receiver to Johnson, who heard the message himself. The instant RFK walked out the door, LBJ called him "that fucking little piece of shit, that squirt-assed cunt."

The Kennedys had outmaneuvered LBJ from before the primaries through the convention's presidential vote, but on Thursday, Jack and Bobby had been bested by the stubborn Johnson. By day's end, both brothers were claiming that they'd offered the slot to the Texan only as a matter of courtesy, never imagining he would actually accept it. Yet that explanation didn't hold up: O'Neill's account of JFK's dealings with Rayburn on Tuesday night, as well as O'Donnell's account of his conversations with both Kennedys on Thursday morning, make clear that the savvy brothers would never have been so reckless or so naive.

Once Johnson had forced their hand, the Kennedys made their choice official. Labor and liberal delegates, with Thursday afternoon to calm down, saw the inevitability of Johnson's nomination and called off their protest. That night, LBJ was nominated by acclamation.

Several hours after Bobby had left Lyndon Johnson's suite for the second time that day, Texas oil baron H. L. Hunt and his wife paid a visit. Lady Bird, in tears over the day's indignities, threw herself into Mrs. Hunt's arms. "I didn't want him to take it," she kept repeating. In the bedroom, her husband was on the telephone, talking to a reporter about a story quoting RFK as saying that LBJ had been invited onto the ticket only because of pressure from the Texan's camp. "I'll be goddamned if I'll deny. Let the sonofabitch deny it."

According to Arthur Schlesinger's RFK biography, Bobby evidently would have been proud to have been known as his brother's "sonofabitch," a person "prepared to do what the candidate should not have done." "I'm not running a popularity contest," Schlesinger quotes RFK saying to *Time* magazine's Hugh Sidey. It didn't matter to Bobby whether they liked him or not. "Jack can be nice to them, but somebody has to be able to say no." That somebody was Robert F. Kennedy.

The only business remaining in Los Angeles was Jack's speech accepting the nomination. California's state Democratic chairman had earlier convinced the national committee to stage the address not in the Sports Arena, where the first four days of the convention were to take place, but in the Los Angeles Coliseum, where the party could claim the nominee to be speaking before the largest crowd ever assembled to hear any speech of any kind. The stadium's capacity of a hundred thousand spectators gave JFK's campaign manager pause. Joan Braden, in charge of filling the Coliseum's seats, recounted a phone call she received from Bobby just before the convention: " 'If,' came the voice from the other end of the line, 'my brother speaks to empty seats, I will shoot you.' And he hung up." Jack spoke to empty seats, but not many. Eighty thousand people heard the Democratic nominee for president proclaim that "we stand today on the edge of a New Frontier—the frontier of the 1960s—a frontier of unknown opportunities and perils—a frontier of unfulfilled hopes and threats."

If Richard M. Nixon had any advisers as perceptive as John Kennedy's campaign manager, he surely had none as close to him as Bobby was to Jack. Thus, there was no one to convince the Republican nominee of the foolishness of his pledge, made in his speech accepting the nod at his party's Chicago convention in late July, to visit all fifty states by Election Day. An exhausting autumn of crisscrossing the nation would find the vice president spending precious days in transit to Alaska and Hawaii, while his rival could focus on key industrial states such as Ohio and New Jersey.

Nixon had other problems, too. A kneecap banged on a car door in North Carolina became infected and landed him in Washington's Walter Reed Hospital from August 29 to September 9, his leg in traction while John Kennedy was on the road. The Republicans' choice for vice president did not measure up to the Democrats': while Lyndon Johnson was expected to give Jack Texas, Henry Cabot Lodge, who had served as ambassador to the United Nations since losing his Senate seat to JFK in 1952, had little hope of swinging his home state of Massachusetts against the local hero at the top of the opposing ticket.

The Republican candidate did enjoy one key asset, however: his Protestant faith. Norman Vincent Peale, the proponent of "positive thinking," joined on September 7 with other prominent Protestant clergymen to question whether any Catholic who sat in the White House could remain independent of the occupant of St. Peter's Throne. "Our American culture is at stake," the group warned.

The prejudice of his fellow citizens weighed heavily on Bobby. William A. Geoghegan, a Cincinnati lawyer (who would subsequently join Bobby's staff in the Justice Department), remembered a visit RFK made to that city in early September to open a campaign office: "At this time the religious issue was at its very peak and he had cut through a part of Indiana which was known as the Bible Belt . . . where the Klan had been quite active as recently as the late twenties. He had been hit the day before with one question after another about the religious issue. . . . He was obviously distraught about this and I got the impression that this was by far the most important issue in the campaign as he saw it at that particular time." When Bobby rose to speak, he began by discussing the matter of his family's faith "very candidly." "People have often said that Bob Kennedy is, you know, without emotion," Geoghegan continued, "without sympathy, is cold . . . that he never cries. Well, this time Bob Kennedy did cry and he broke down as he was giving that talk. I was sitting right beside him and got up and had to take over. It was a very emotional experience I think for everybody there present. . . . Many people thought that this was just a grandstand effort but nothing, I'm sure, could be further from the truth. I can recall the words that he spoke, the last words that he spoke following which he could not go on with his talk. He said, 'I can't imagine that any country for which my brother Joe died could care about my brother Jack's religion when it came . . .' Then he stopped."

A few days later, the candidate himself addressed the question before the Greater Houston Ministerial Association, a Protestant group that had invited him to defend the right of a Catholic to be president. "I believe in an America," he told the unfriendly audience, "where the separation of church and state is absolute—where no Catholic prelate would tell the president (should he be Catholic) how to act, and no Protestant minister would tell his parishioners for whom to vote." "By God . . ." said Sam Rayburn, watching on television, "he's eating 'em blood raw!" The following day Nixon agreed that religion should not be an issue in the campaign. Before long, Peale backed down.

Jack's gutsy performance neutralized his faith as an issue nationally, but in localities with large concentrations of Catholics the Kennedys were eager to keep the matter alive. Bobby and his staff had determined, as they had earlier in West Virginia, that the campaign had nothing to lose by mentioning the issue—since devout antipapists would never vote for a follower of Rome, the Kennedys might as well maximize support among Jack's coreligionists. Pat Moynihan was among those who received marching orders. "I . . . made a lot of speeches up and down New York State," he remembered, "where . . . there was only one message, just one thing we said up and down, and we said it was time for a Catholic to be president. That's what we said."

After the Houston speech, the candidate let his supporters handle the doctrinal wars, while he pounded away at Nixon on the cold war. John Kennedy promised to increase defense spending and to expand America's presence among Third World nations emerging from colonialism into the global struggle between East and West. The Democrat vowed as well to speed the growth of the nation's economy by abandoning the Republican policy of tight budgets and high interest rates. While Nixon based his campaign on Eisenhower's record of peace and prosperity, Kennedy painted the GOP as complacent, the nation as stagnant. Although only four years younger than Nixon, JFK sought to project an image of youthful optimism and vigor in contrast with the tired rhetoric of the Republicans. "It's time to get the country moving again" was his mantra.

Jack's call to stir the nation's energy found public resonance after the night of September 25, when the two candidates met in a Chicago television studio for the first of four debates. While Richard Nixon won the event on paper and on the radio, those who watched the broadcast saw a Republican exhausted from his hospitalization and travel, beads of perspiration streaking the "Lazy Shave" makeup applied to cover his heavy beard. Nixon scored debating points, but the Democrat, crisp and controlled, addressed his broad themes not to the rival standing across from him but to the 70 million Americans watching from barstools and easy chairs across the country. Nixon had wanted to contrast his experience—he was, after all, the man who had faced off against Khrushchev in the "kitchen debate"—with the lack of substance many perceived in Kennedy. After the Chicago encounter, however, JFK was a lightweight no more. Instantly, crowds at his campaign stops became larger and more frenzied. Women tore at his clothes and ripped out his cuff links; he ended his days with hands and forearms bleeding. The politician as television celebrity had been born.

If John Kennedy seemed more relaxed during the debate than Richard Nixon, perhaps the Republican had not prepared as effectively as the Democrat. "We had recently returned from New Orleans," recalled Langdon Marvin, "where Jack spent twenty minutes making love to stripper Blaze Starr in the closet of a hotel suite while her fiancé, Governor Earl Long, held a party in the next room. In the closet, Jack found the time to tell Blaze the story of President Warren G. Harding's making love to his mistress Nan Britton in a White House cloakroom.

"The night before the debate," continued Marvin, "Jack said to me, 'Any girls lined up for tomorrow?' So I called Bobby and we made arrangements to have a girl waiting for him in a room at the Palmer House. I took him down there about ninety minutes before airtime, rode up in the elevator with him, introduced him to the girl (she'd been prepaid for her services), then stood guard in the corridor outside the hotel room. Jack evidently enjoyed himself, because he emerged fifteen minutes later with an ear-to-ear grin on his face.

"During the debate he looked the picture of self-assurance and good health. Nixon, meanwhile, looked like an escaped convict—pallid, perspiring, beady-eyed. Jack was so pleased by the results he insisted we line up a girl for him before each of the next three debates."

Conquering the still-young medium of television—if helped along by conquests in the oldest medium of all—was only one of the pioneering accomplishments of the campaign headed by RFK. As Joe Gargan contended, "Nobody ever ran for president before the way the Kennedys ran in 1960; it just had never been done. And the things they did in the 1952 campaign for the Senate, and the things they learned, were what they brought to the '60 run." As he had done in Massachusetts eight years earlier, Bobby sent his own people to supervise, and at times supersede, local party leaders who were considered insufficiently reliable—a "very considerable invention," Pat Moynihan called the practice. To keep the regular party's involvement to a minimum, Bobby's coordinators would work with groups of local volunteers called Citizens for Kennedy, headed in each area by an in-state person with a Kennedy connection and directed nationally by Byron "Whizzer" White, a Denver lawyer and a man the Kennedys could appreciate—a PT boat veteran, he'd been an all-American running back at the University of Colorado.

As before, RFK made information his tool as others had never thought to, and by 1960 he had new technology to facilitate its use. Newspaper editor Ralph McGill wrote that the Kennedy campaign "had a great deal of the electronic age in it. [Robert Kennedy] used polls, computers and many IBM machines. His efforts were exacting, painstaking and careful."

Joe's infinitely deep pockets represented another aspect. John Richard Reilly, an operative out of Chicago who would go on to serve in Bobby's Justice Department, recalled a meeting at which Dave Hackett noted that the coffers were bare of funds used to supply the "bumper stickers, placards . . . tie clips, etc." needed around the country: "We finally got down to the point where Dave said, 'Well, we need, to do what we really should do, seven hundred thousand dollars, and we don't have it.' So everybody was kind of looking around the room at one another. I mean, it was a staggering figure. Bob Kennedy was kind of sitting with his head down, and all of a sudden he looked up and he said, 'Jeez, does anybody know anybody with seven hundred thousand dollars?' Of course, the room broke up because he was the only guy in the room that had seven hundred thousand dollars or could even touch it."

For most of the fall, Joe worked behind the scenes—"Jack and Bob will run the show / While Ted's in charge of hiding Joe," ran a Republican piece of doggerel—but the other family members pitched in for all to see. Ted stumped out West, performing daredevil stunts like riding bucking broncos. Eunice and Ethel appeared in Texas, although they refused Lady Bird Johnson's request that they don cowboy hats. Rose, Pat and Jean visited women's clubs, while a pregnant Jackie managed to publish a weekly "Campaign Wife" column syndicated in hundreds of small newspapers around the country. The Campaign Wife made another, less domestic, contribution. Disgusted by the manners of Frank Sinatra and his pals, she convinced her husband and brother-in-law that the Rat Pack should disappear from the campaign. Naturally, Bobby was assigned the unpleasant task of speaking to his brother's friend; the singer, aware that his slightly sordid image might not jibe with the wholesome family portrait the Kennedys wished to convey, complied without complaint.

Relatives and money, computers and television, a team of handpicked "Kennedy men" spread nationwide—all these elements were needed to complete the image of a successful Kennedy campaign and offered Bobby the opportunity to contact people. When the New York Reform Democrats, a liberal faction supported by such personages as Eleanor Roosevelt and former governor Herbert Lehman, were slow to lay down arms in their continual war with the party regulars, JFK's campaign manager snapped, "Gentlemen, I don't give a hoot if the state and county organizations survive after November, and I don't give a hoot if you survive. I want to elect John F. Kennedy."

However affronted the New Yorkers were at RFK's heavy-handedness, they did not return the belligerence with the verve shown by George Smathers. "Bobby and I had a lot of run-ins when Jack was campaigning for president," said the former senator from Florida. "Jack asked me to handle all the southern states, so I did. But Bobby was constantly calling, saying, 'I don't like the schedule you've worked out for Jack,' and so on and so on. I said, 'Why don't you go to hell?' He'd never been in the South. I told him, 'You come down here with that Irish Massachusetts accent, they'll tar and feather you, boy.'

"He didn't like that, naturally, and we didn't get along very well at all. As a matter of fact, one time, in an Atlanta hotel, we had a fight, a physical fight. Now, the newspaper reporters wanted to say it was over some great big issue—that he was for the poor people and I was for the rich, something like that. Well, damn it, this was over whether Jack was going to Tallahassee or to Jacksonville. That's about how big it was."

Bigger was Bobby's appearance on a New York radio program on Labor Day. When he criticized southern Democrats in the Senate for blocking progressive legislation, party leaders in Florida and South Carolina threatened secession from the national campaign. To squelch the uproar, Bobby agreed not to set foot in either state for the remainder of the fall.

Not content to inflame the passions only of white segregationists, RFK on the same broadcast managed to provoke one of black America's greatest heroes, Jackie Robinson, the Brooklyn Dodger who had broken baseball's color line. Earlier in the year, the Kennedys had ardently courted Robinson's endorsement, but the former athlete, presently working as personnel director for a chain of New York coffee shops, had just come out for Nixon. RFK attacked Robinson for questioning Jack's commitment to civil rights, then implied that the ex-ballplayer was supporting the Republican only to curry favor with his boss at Chock full o'Nuts. Robinson's reply was withering: "If the younger Kennedy is going to resort to lies, then I can see what kind of campaign this is going to be. I don't see where my company has anything at all to do with his brother's having had breakfast with the head of the White Citizens Councils and the racist Governor of Alabama. . . . To me, the most revealing part of the whole attack was Robert Kennedy's reference to 18 million Negro Americans as 'his Negroes'—meaning Jackie Robinson's. Apparently young Bobby hasn't heard that the Emancipation Proclamation was signed 97 years ago. I don't run any plantation and I suggest to Kennedy that he stop acting as if he did."

Robinson campaigned almost full-time for Nixon throughout the autumn, but Jack Kennedy did win the support of Harry Belafonte, then one of the country's most popular entertainers and a leading activist in the civil-rights movement. The alliance led to perhaps one of the fall's more embarrassing moments when JFK and Belafonte appeared together in a short campaign film. "It opened with a great fanfare," recalled John Seigenthaler, "Harry Belafonte and Senator Kennedy walking down a street in Harlem and you had the music in the background. . . . They walked down this street and into this house, a Harlem tenement, and sat down and talked with these people. [JFK] told them how he felt about the problems of the Negro and what he wanted to do for the Negro." Through a snafu by a young volunteer, the film was televised in Mississippi immediately following a pro-Kennedy speech by John Stennis, the state's ultrasegregationist senator. Stennis was livid, Mississippi Democrats were aghast. Anxious Kennedy aides tracked down copies of the film elsewhere in the South before they could be aired, but the electoral votes of Mississippi were lost.

In seeking the votes of African Americans, the Kennedys could not afford to sacrifice those of white southerners. Thus, while they arranged a conference on black issues in Harlem, they declined (at the advice of Byron White) to use the term "civil rights" in the event's title. They established an Office of Civil Rights in the campaign—led by Sargent Shriver in concert with Harris Wofford, a white law professor at Notre Dame, and Louis Martin, a black journalist from Chicago—but hid most of the group's activities from the the general public. And all the while, Lyndon Johnson toured Dixie, reassuring nervous citizens and politicians that the Catholic nominee posed no threat to their time-honored way of life.

Robert Kennedy detected the political gold that lay in the untapped voting strength of America's minorities. The day after Jack's nomination in Los Angeles, RFK herded his troops into the ballroom of the Biltmore Hotel to begin work on a massive registration drive. Believing that new voters would split two-to-one for his brother, Bobby concentrated his efforts in the ghettos and barrios of the nation's cities. Old-fashioned pols did not appreciate the endeavor. "Kennedy is an asshole for sending in all these jerks to register the niggers," a St. Louis labor boss told Tip O'Neill. In New York, the Kennedys recruited Herman Badillo, who would later serve in Congress and as the city's deputy mayor. "The Kennedys had come to the conclusion that if Jack Kennedy was going to win the presidency, he had to carry New York State," said Badillo. "And the only way he could do that was if there was a campaign to register more blacks and Puerto Ricans. The Kennedys knew that politicos such as Carmine de Sapio would do nothing to register minority voters because these people would later turn against them. So they set up a Citizens for Kennedy office, which competed with the regular party, in a mansion at 277 Park Avenue that apparently belonged to Bobby's father.

"They found out that I was a young lawyer, about twenty-eight years of age, that I was known as a young Puerto Rican who was articulate in both Spanish and English, and that I wasn't committed to the party organization but was only interested in getting more Puerto Ricans to register and vote. After I was interviewed at great length by Steve Smith and Robert Kennedy at 277 Park Avenue, I was put in charge of the campaign for East Harlem. They gave me money to open up a political clubhouse at 115th Street and Third Avenue, which I called the East Harlem Kennedy for President Committee.

"Believe it or not, I had the highest percentage increase in voter registration in the state: forty-eight percent. And it turned out that Bobby Kennedy was right. JFK won by a narrow margin in New York State, and primarily because the blacks and Puerto Ricans voted for him."

While Bobby's astutely conceived and carefully executed plan for increased voter participation helped his brother's cause, Jack's success with black Americans in the election of 1960 turned on an event over which the Kennedys had no control: the arrest of Martin Luther King, Jr. When John F. Kennedy asked Harry Belafonte in the spring to provide access to black entertainers, the singer recommended that JFK get to know

King. "Why do you see him as so important?" Kennedy asked. "What can he do?" The importance of Martin Luther King to the nation's discourse had not yet become impressed upon the minds of most white Americans, and the senator from Massachusetts was no exception. When King and Kennedy met in June, the former considered their exchange pleasant but judged the senator to lack a "thorough understanding" of civil rights.

On October 19, less than three weeks before Election Day, Martin Luther King was placed in Fulton County Jail for staging a sit-in at the segregated restaurant of Rich's Department Store in downtown Atlanta. Thanks to the city's moderate mayor, the thirty-five fellow demonstrators who had joined King in jail were released five days later, but their leader remained behind bars at the request of Judge Oscar Mitchell of adjacent DeKalb County. The previous May, Mitchell had dealt King a one-year suspended sentence for driving with an Alabama license three months after he had moved to Georgia; now the magistrate ordered a hearing on whether the arrest at Rich's constituted a violation of the probation granted in the earlier case.

On October 25, King, in handcuffs and leg irons, was seated next to a ferocious German shepherd in a police car and driven to Decatur, where Judge Oscar Mitchell held court. Mitchell showed no mercy to the nemesis of his region's white establishment: he sentenced the future Nobel laureate to four months at hard labor on a state road gang, starting immediately. Bail was denied.

King's supporters were horrified. His wife, Coretta, six months pregnant, was petrified. Lynching was no distant memory at the time, and the admirers of Martin Luther King feared for his life.

Harris Wofford drafted a statement for Senator Kennedy to release in objection to the sentence, but Ernest Vandiver, Georgia's segregationist governor and a Kennedy supporter, promised to secure King's release if the Democratic candidate remained silent; Wofford's statement was never issued. Yet Vandiver's pledge proved hollow. In the middle of that night, King was taken from his cell at DeKalb County Jail and moved to Reidsville State Prison, a maximum-security facility 230 miles away in rural Georgia.

Concern for the safety of black America's much admired young leader intensified, and the next day, October 26, the Washington headquarters of the campaign's Office of Civil Rights was inundated with telephone calls. Harris Wofford and Louis Martin had given up on their candidate making a public statement, but they conceived of a more indirect gesture: a telephone call to Coretta King.

Wofford tracked down his immediate boss, Sargent Shriver, at Chicago's O'Hare Airport, where the candidate had just addressed a meeting of Illinois businessmen and was now waiting with his entourage in a VIP holding suite near the runway. "If the Senator would only call Mrs. King and wish her well," Wofford pleaded with Shriver, "it would reverberate throughout the Negro community." Shriver approved the idea but waited until the candidate was alone to approach him. O'Brien, O'Donnell, Sorensen and the rest, who privately ridiculed Shriver as the "house Communist," would never stand for any move that might cost white votes. Indeed, among the Kennedy family the liberal Shriver was nicknamed "Boy Scout." Even so, JFK, resting in the airport suite's bedroom, was receptive to his brother-in-law's proposal. "What the hell," he replied. "That's a decent thing to do. Why not? Get her on the phone." The candidate for president took two minutes to express his concern for the well-being of Coretta King, her husband and her soon-to-be-born baby, then boarded his plane for Detroit while Shriver slipped out the suite's back door.

En route, JFK mentioned the call to Pierre Salinger, who contacted Bobby from midair. The campaign manager telephoned Sargent Shriver in a rage. "You dumb shit, you've blown the election," he screamed. He then demanded to see Wofford and Martin, to whom he continued the stream of invective. When Bobby paused, Martin defended himself by noting that King had received four months on a chain gang for a petty traffic violation and had been refused bond.

"How could they do that?" RFK asked. "Who's the judge? You can't deny bail on a misdemeanor." Robert Kennedy had conducted legal examinations at the highest levels of government, but he understood little of the way southern courts dealt with black defendants. "They wanted to make an example of him as an uppity Negro," Martin patiently explained.

Louis Martin continued to explain the situation to the horrified campaign manager. "I told Bobby," Martin recalled, "that Jackie Robinson and Nixon were going to . . . hold a press conference and blame the Democrats. This is the line that we gave Bobby and Bobby was quite excited about it. I must say his first reaction was very vigorous—the fact that a guy [could] be jailed for having the wrong . . . driver's license. I don't think he got the civil rights impact until the second thought." Martin had known RFK only a short time, but his story about Robinson, a fib he'd made up on the way to Bobby's office, hit its mark. The ballplayer and the senator's brother had exchanged venomous words, and Bobby Kennedy did not forget his enemies.

After ordering the civil rights section to keep out of trouble for the remaining thirteen days of the campaign, RFK asked John Seigenthaler to drive him to the airport, where he would catch the shuttle to New York to give a speech. In the car, Bobby wondered aloud if he might in some way act as a lightning rod in the affair for Jack; Seigenthaler advised that he take no further action. The following day, however, after King had been released on fifteen hundred dollars bond, reports indicated that the judge's change of heart had come about because of a telephone call from Bobby. "But don't fret," Seigenthaler told RFK. "I asked [press aide Roger] Tubby to issue a denial."

"Well," Bobby responded, "you'll have to make sure he retracts it." Whether because of his moral outrage over a miscarriage of justice or his political concern that a racist judge was, as he told Seigenthaler, "screwing up my brother's campaign and making the country look ridiculous before the world," RFK had telephoned Judge Oscar Mitchell from a New York phone booth. Calmly and politely, RFK told the judge that he was calling not in his role as presidential campaign manager, but simply as a lawyer who opposed the "disgraceful" abuse of a defendant's rights. If the call was not the only reason for Mitchell's release of King, it was certainly a contributing factor. When Robert Kennedy phoned Louis Martin late that night to tell what he had done, the veteran African American journalist conferred on his boss a distinction neither man would have thought possible a day earlier. "We can now make you an honorary brother," Martin said.

Armed with the active involvement of both Kennedys, the Office of Civil Rights moved cautiously to exploit their political advantage. Richard Nixon had remained silent on the King controversy; although his record on civil rights was credible, and his party's platform on the subject strong, the Republican had been seduced by enthusiastic southern crowds in August and had thereafter decided to mute his support of civil rights in order to vie for Dixie's electoral votes.* As the Kennedy campaign had hoped, white Americans remained largely unaware of the brothers' moves on behalf of King—in the *New York Times* Jack's call merited only two inches on page 22—but Wofford and Martin strove to get the story out to blacks. Seeking to supplement the coverage in the black press, the two strategists proposed to print pamphlets on the subject. Shriver approved the plan and promised he would find the funds, but ordered Wofford and Martin not to mention the idea to RFK. Entitled

---

* Richard Nixon did not prosper in the region in 1960. Eight years later, however, his "Southern Strategy" would begin the realignment of the nation's electoral map that has lasted to the present day.

" 'No Comment' Nixon Versus a Candidate with a Heart, Senator Kennedy," the tract reported Jack's telephone call but omitted mention of Bobby's. Some 2 million copies were disbursed at black churches the final Sunday before Election Day.

The black vote in 1960, which had gone 60–40 for Eisenhower four years before, split 70–30 for John Kennedy. In addition, JFK won 81 of the Old Confederacy's 128 electoral votes. As they had in the labor rackets hearings, the Kennedys played, and won, both sides of a delicate situation. Robert Kennedy, whose most notable mention of the civil rights issue before 1960 was his suggestion that the Harlem Globetrotters visit the Soviet Union, had directed an effort to swell the power of minority voters and had personally intervened to rescue the nation's premier civil rights activist from the perils of Jim Crow justice. Still more pragmatist than crusader, RFK was oblivious of black America no longer.

Martin Luther King, Jr., refused to back anyone for the presidency. His father had previously joined fellow Baptist preachers in supporting Nixon, but now he switched his allegiance. "I had expected to vote against Senator Kennedy because of his religion," King Sr. told a crowd of worshipers at Ebenezer Baptist Church. "But now he can be my president, Catholic or whatever he is. It took courage to call my daughter-in-law at a time like this. He has the moral courage to stand up for what he knows is right. I've got all my votes and I've got a suitcase, and I'm going to take them up there and dump them in his lap."

The final weekend of the campaign, John Kennedy worked his way from West Coast to East, ending with a 3 A.M. rally in Waterbury, Connecticut. On Monday night, the candidate spoke before a full house at Boston Garden, then rose on Election Day to cast his ballot at the West End Library in Boston, near the 122 Bowdoin Street flat he still called his legal home.

Jack and Jackie then left for Hyannis Port, where Bobby's house in the Kennedy compound had been equipped with telephones, televisions, Teletype machines, as well as ten secretaries and the top members of the campaign's brain trust. In the week before the election, Bobby and his lieutenants had wired campaign workers around the country with telephone numbers to be called as returns trickled in. Key districts were given particular attention. "NEED SPECIAL COVERAGE IN PRECINCT TWENTY-TWO TUCSON," Larry O'Brien's telegram to Arizona congressman Steward Udall had read. "PLEASE MAKE ARRANGEMENT TO HAVE CAPABLE PERSON CALL DIRECTLY WITH RESULTS FROM THIS BAROMETER PRECINCT ON SPRING 5–5549 (FIVE-FIVE-FIVE-FOUR-NINE). PLEASE

CONFIRM BY WIRE." Jack walked on the beach and napped while his brother spent the day receiving reports on voter turnout.

As the polls began closing, calls went back and forth between Hyannis Port and the more populated states as Bobby, always impatient, always hungry for information, sought to learn the results faster than the television networks could discover them. The news from Chicago seemed encouraging. Mayor Daley, to counter the strong showing he expected from downstate Republicans, had rousted the graveyard vote to ensure a citywide margin of 450,000 votes. "I was a Republican poll watcher that day in a South Side precinct," noted George McCutcheon. "And in that neighborhood there was a good deal of urban renewal going on. Many people had been displaced, so there were only twenty-two people on the official polling sheet for the precinct. At the end of the day somebody went around and looked in the back of the big voting machine and announced that there were a total of three votes for Richard Nixon. Being a mathematics teacher, I thought I knew how many there would be for Kennedy. But when the vote for the Democrat was announced, the number was seventy-one. That's when I realized there was a new political arithmetical formula first in the country: if there were twenty-two voters, it was perfectly possible to have three vote one way and seventy-one the other."*

Early returns around the nation were favorable, but as the evening proceeded the race tightened. "We're being clobbered," Bobby groaned. Ethel replenished the snacks for the anxious staff as the phones continued to ring and the television sets continued to blare, but by early morning the staffers had all retired to their respective hotel rooms. The candidate walked back and forth between his own house and his brother's, finally settling in next to Bobby at 2 A.M. At four, still a handful of electoral votes short of the 269 needed to win, Jack got up to leave. "What am I going to tell the press?" asked Pierre Salinger, on his way to the Hyannis Armory to brief reporters. "Tell them I went to bed," Jack replied. "Wake me if anything happens."

While his brother slept, Robert Kennedy, tireless, dogged, loyal,

---

* Daley-controlled wards went for Kennedy in unprecedented numbers as Jack carried the state by less than nine thousand votes of over 4.75 million cast, but wards run by the mob did not deliver for the Democrat nearly as robustly. The mayor's machine "interpreted this disappointing performance as a mild rebuke by the syndicate people who had been mercilessly pounded by the presidential candidate's brother, Robert," wrote Len O'Connor in *Clout: Mayor Daley and His City*. The vote totals seem to contradict Sam Giancana's alleged boast, reported by his family in *Double Cross*, to have handed JFK Chicago, and thus the White House.

watched the flickering screens alone. At 5:35, the networks called the 20 electoral votes of Michigan for Kennedy, and the race was decided. Ten minutes later, a team of Secret Service agents who had been shadowing the candidate and his family—as a similar group had been following the Nixons in Los Angeles—moved to implement full security at the compound.

Robert Kennedy had begun his career in politics in 1946, eating spaghetti in the Italian wards of East Cambridge. Fourteen years later, he had fulfilled his brother's ambition, his father's desire, his grandfathers' dream. John F. Kennedy, a Catholic three generations removed from the green hills of Ireland, would be America's next president.

13

ATTORNEY GENERAL

Robert Kennedy was out of a job.

Since graduating from law school in 1951, he'd held a variety of legal positions in the government and managed two successful political campaigns, but his career had not proceeded along any well-defined path. For a decade, Bobby's overriding goal had been to see his brother elected president. Now that he had accomplished that feat, it was finally time, at age thirty-five, to confront the question he'd avoided so long: what did he want to be when he grew up?

At Hyannis Port, in the wake of their victory, Jack had broached to Bobby the possibility that the victorious campaign manager might now lead the Justice Department. RFK wasn't for it. "In the first place," he said later, "I thought nepotism was a problem. Secondly, I had been chasing bad men for three years and I didn't want to spend the rest of my life doing that." Also, Bobby's newly awakened awareness of black Americans and their struggles led him to fear that as attorney general he would saddle his brother with "a burden he doesn't need." "There's going to be another Civil War in this country," he told Larry O'Brien, "and somebody is going to have to make some very unpopular decisions. My being attorney general would only compromise and cripple my brother's ability to govern."

The president-elect was willing to take no for an answer. The first father–elect was another story. In Palm Beach just a few days after the election, Jack suggested to Joe that Bobby be made second-in-command at the Defense Department. It was a good job, JFK argued: the Department of Defense had the largest budget in Washington, and Bobby would be well situated to move to the top spot in a second Kennedy term. The ambassador would have none of it: "Damn it to hell, Jack, Bobby busted his ass for you." Only one job was suitable for the son who had brought the family so far, and only one job would keep that son close enough to the older son who would need his support over the next four to eight years. "My old man wants him to be attorney general," a helpless JFK lamented to George Smathers.

Resistant to his father's importuning, Bobby considered his options. His aides from the McClellan committee, Pierre Salinger and Ken O'Donnell, were joining the president's team as press secretary and appointments secretary, respectively, but working with them on the White House staff would place RFK too close to his big brother. "Jack's Senate seat would now be open," said Ken O'Donnell. A phone call from the new president to the governor of Massachusetts, and the younger Kennedy would receive appointment to serve out the term. However, RFK would not accept the favor. He would serve only if he ran and won.

"Ethel, by the way, wanted Bobby to wait until 1962 and then run for governor of Massachusetts. Until that point, he could do something like run a foundation or a university. The one thing Bobby didn't want to do was go into private law practice, which he saw as too confining." RFK had by no means given up the possibility of working in government; still, his key concern in accepting any post within the bureaucracy was not his well-being but that of Jack. As John Seigenthaler remembered, Bobby would accept a job only "where he could serve his brother and not be controversial and at the same time be in a position where, if there was a problem or a failure, he'd be able to take the responsibility for that problem without transmitting it to his brother."

While Bobby brooded, his brother had an administration to staff. Jack's first appointments were *re*appointments—just two days after the election he announced he was asking J. Edgar Hoover, director of the FBI, and Allen Dulles, director of the Central Intelligence Agency, to continue in office. While many of JFK's advisers had lobbied for the dismissal of both men, Jack, who had won the White House by fewer than 113,000 votes out of some 103 million cast, was not about to risk alienating either the internal or the external security apparatus he would need to operate his new government. (He'd also begun to appreciate the full, salacious detail with which his personal life was documented in Hoover's personal files.)

To gather names of candidates for other top positions, Jack called on his reliable in-law, Sargent Shriver, and he asked Lawrence O'Brien to do the same for secondary slots. The new chief executive made few important appointments without consulting his brother, and it was Bobby who dissuaded Jack from his initial choice for secretary of state. In addition to his chairing of the Senate Foreign Relations Committee, William Fulbright of Arkansas had become known for his vigorous opposition to civil rights; RFK theorized that the nation's international credibility would suffer were Fulbright named. "Any time we took a position against any of the nations of Africa," Bobby later maintained, "or any time that we would take a position that was unpopular . . . the Russians and the others would be able to say, 'Well, this is all done because we have a Secretary of State who feels that the white man is superior to the Negro.'" The job did go to a southerner—albeit to one without Fulbright's racial baggage: Dean Rusk, president of the Rockefeller Foundation and a native of Georgia who, as assistant secretary of state for Far Eastern affairs from 1950 to 1952, had been instrumental in convincing Harry Truman to intervene in Korea. To head the National Security Council, which the new president would look to in order to circumvent the inoffensive Rusk and the slow-moving ways of the State Department, Jack hired McGeorge Bundy, a former dean of Harvard College who had graduated first in his class at Yale. Adlai Stevenson, miffed at losing out to Rusk for the top job in the State Department, took his time in accepting JFK's offer of the ambassadorship to the United Nations—a post Jack considered significantly insignificant to serve as a parking place for the ex-governor who had so annoyed him and his family over the past several years.

To reassure the financial markets, Jack chose for Treasury a Republican, Wall Street's own C. Douglas Dillon, who had served in Eisenhower's State Department and was a pillar of his family's investment banking firm, Dillon Read. Interior went to Arizona congressman Stewart Udall and Labor to AFL-CIO counsel Arthur Goldberg. South Dakotan George McGovern, just defeated in his bid for the Senate, was considered for the position of secretary of agriculture, but was opposed by farm-state members of Congress as insufficiently experienced. The office went to Orville Freeman, governor of Minnesota, and McGovern was placed in charge of Food for Peace, the agency that distributed surplus food abroad.

For Defense, JFK selected Robert McNamara, who had only weeks before been promoted to the presidency of the Ford Motor Company. Known as one of the bright corporate "whiz kids" of the fifties, McNamara had had prior experience in the management of armaments during World War II, when he'd worked to improve the efficiency of the army's analysis of its bombing campaigns. Despite asking his new commander in chief whether *Profiles in Courage* had been ghostwritten, McNamara passed his job interview with flying colors. Not only did he get the job, he also was granted what other cabinet officers were not: a free hand in staffing his department. As McNamara would hardly be interested in having the president's brother breathing down his neck, Robert Kennedy's future as defense secretary-in-waiting had thus evaporated. The new secretary took the autonomy he'd been given seriously: despite entreaties from both Kennedy brothers, he refused to make the savior of West Virginia, Franklin D. Roosevelt, Jr., secretary of the navy. He did, however, relent sufficiently to appoint Jack's PT-boat comrade and man-about-town, Red Fay, the navy's undersecretary.

Filling the office of attorney general continued to be the president-elect's principal headache. A few days after the election, JFK invited Connecticut's governor, Abe Ribicoff, to Palm Beach. "We had lunch and then we went out and played golf," Ribicoff recalled. "Then he offered me the attorney general's job. I said I didn't want it. He said, 'God, that's the best job. I thought you wanted to be attorney general, then get on the Supreme Court.'

"I said to him, 'I'll tell you why I don't want it, Jack. The biggest problem you're going to be facing as soon as you're elected is the problem of civil rights, and it's going to be a very tough go. And as I look at this, the first Irish Catholic president doesn't need a Jewish attorney general to shove changes down the throats of the white Anglo-Saxon Protestants and the blacks of the South. I'm thinking about the impact it would have on anti-Semitism in the United States.'

"He said, 'God, I never thought of that, I never thought of that at all. Whom would you suggest for attorney general?'

"I said, 'Put in Bobby. Jack, I've watched you people over a half dozen years. You both came out of the same womb. Every time there's been a crisis, every time you've had a problem, you've automatically turned to Bobby. He's your right hand. You can't be president without him playing a major role—you're going to have problems and you're going to have to turn to him. The worst thing that could happen for you is, every time you want to see your brother, he comes in through the kitchen door. The public won't go for that. No, the only way you can do this is for him to have a prominent role. Whenever you want to see him, he has to come in through the front door; the public and the newspapers have to know that he's coming in to talk to you and that he's attorney general.'

" 'But people won't go for it,' the president said. 'They'll charge nepotism.'

"I said, 'So what? People will get used to it.' "

Asked what position he *did* want, Ribicoff chose to head the Department of Health, Education, and Welfare.

Despite Bobby's initial demurral, John Kennedy continued to consider his brother a candidate for the attorney generalship, and in mid-November he decided to test public reaction to the idea. On a plane taking the president-elect and his party to Palm Beach from Texas—they had visited the LBJ Ranch, where the new vice president had rousted Jack from bed at 5 A.M. to kill a deer—William H. Lawrence of the *New York Times* sidled up to Jack for a conversation about the new administration. As the discussion turned to the Justice Department, Jack asked the reporter, "How do you feel about Bobby as attorney general?"

"Do you think you can get away with it?" Lawrence inquired in return.

"Why not? I don't see why I should discriminate against him just because he's my brother."

The next day, when Lawrence called JFK's secretary, Evelyn Lincoln, to make sure he was authorized to print the piece, Jack gave his consent, but only on the condition the reporter not reveal the story's source. The new chief executive likewise insisted on another stipulation: "Make the point," Lincoln told Lawrence on her boss's order, "that he is not going to discriminate against his brother because he is his brother."

The *New York Times* reacted to its own story by running an editorial (November 23, 1960) noting that the job of attorney general "ought to be kept completely out of the political arena." Naming a "bright young political manager" would be "simply not good enough." Bobby agreed. When he returned after Thanksgiving from a brief vacation in Mexico, he reiterated to Jack his unwillingness to take the post.*

For a month following his election, Jack wavered on how far to push the reluctant Bobby and how firmly to resist the pull of the unrelenting Joe, who continued to insist on the appointment. Harris Wofford, working with Sargent Shriver on personnel decisions, remembered hearing initial rumors that Bobby would head Justice: "I thought it was an appalling idea. I couldn't believe they were actually considering it. Subsequently I discovered that they were. So we didn't do anything about Attorney General. Sargent would regularly read JFK his names for various jobs and then Kennedy would say, 'Well, who have you got for Attorney General?' Shriver responded, 'Well, I understood you planned to have Bobby.' Jack said, 'No, Bobby's not going to take it. Why would you

---

* Although Bobby still didn't have a job when he returned to the States, he did have a new nephew: John F. Kennedy, Jr., born by cesarean section on November 25, 1960.

sit on your ass just because you hear some stories that it's going to be Bobby? Bob doesn't think it makes any sense. . . . Get me an Attorney General.' "

Shriver and Wofford went to work assembling a list. "We whittled it down to three or four," said Wofford, "and we had several hot ones. So then Shriver called Kennedy and remarked, 'Well, there are four people who seem well-suited for Attorney General.' And Kennedy said, 'Attorney General? Bobby's going to be Attorney General. Why are you bothering me with the Attorney Generalship? That's all cleared up. Forget that.' A week later, going through everything, Kennedy would say, 'Well, who have you got for Attorney General now?' And Shriver would say, 'You said Bob had it.' 'No, Bob's not going to have it.'. . . It feels to me now as if there were about five times when we were told he was it and then he wasn't it. I must have spent hours and hours and hours discovering who were the best men to be Attorney General."

A government decision had turned into a family dilemma, and the man who would soon have his finger poised above the nuclear button could not face his father. Since Bobby, Jack's usual choice for difficult assignments, shrank before the old man no less fearfully than did his big brother, the president-elect called upon Clark Clifford to serve as ambassador to the ambassador. The prominent Washington-based lawyer and renowned fixer had come to Palm Beach to work on the transition, and one day around the swimming pool he advised JFK against choosing a campaign manager as attorney general. A few hours later Clifford found himself called into the house for yet another meeting. "I agree with what you have said about the job; so does Bobby," Jack told him. "I think my father might listen to you. He speaks highly of your contribution to the campaign and the family, and you have good standing with him. I'd like you to go to New York and talk to him about this. But don't tell anyone else about it."

Clifford accepted the assignment, but told an associate, "*This* is truly a strange situation—the President-elect asks a third party to try to talk to his father about his brother. Only the Kennedys!"

Clifford traveled to New York to try to convince Joe Kennedy that appointing RFK to head Justice would not be in the interest of either brother. "Bobby is very valuable," the emissary concluded. "He is young. . . . Give him the chance to grow. He will be outstanding."

As Clifford remembered, "I was pleased with my presentation; it was, I thought, persuasive. When I had finished, Kennedy said, 'Thank you very much, Clark. I am so glad to have heard your views.' Then, pausing a moment, he added, 'I do want to leave you with one thought, however—one firm thought.' He paused again, and looked me straight in the eye. '*Bobby is going to be Attorney General*. All of us have worked our tails off for Jack, and now that we have succeeded I am going to see to it that Bobby gets the same chance that we gave Jack.' "

Worn down by the irresistible force that was Joe Kennedy, JFK transmitted the pressure to his brother, but Bobby held his ground. "If you announce me as Attorney General, they'll kick our balls off," RFK told Jack on December 12. "You hold on to your balls," replied the president-elect, "and I'll make the announcement." Bobby remained unconvinced.

At 7 A.M. two days later, with John Seigenthaler in tow for support, RFK waded through the group of reporters camped out amid four inches of snow in front of Jack's Georgetown house. Over bacon and eggs, the three men chatted about various cabinet appointments. Finally, RFK turned to his brother and asked, "Well, Johnny, what about me?"

"Bobby, I need someone I can completely and totally and absolutely rely on, somebody who's going to tell me what the best judgment is, my best interest. There's not a member of the cabinet I can trust in that way. What I really need is someone who's there, available to . . . me. There is nobody. I have nobody." Having offered this declaration of sibling affection and need, JFK looked Bobby in the eye: "If I can ask Dean Rusk to give up a career; if I can ask Adlai Stevenson to make a sacrifice he does not want to make; if I can ask Bob McNamara to give up his job as head of that company—these men I don't even know . . . certainly I can expect my own brother to give me the same sort of contribution. And I need you in this government."

Robert Kennedy had gotten his brother elected president, but that achievement did not satisfy either Jack or Joe. Bobby's wish for a career exclusive of his brother gave way before his brother's inability to do without him and his father's refusal to set him free.

As the Kennedys suspected, the press reacted with disapproval. "If Robert Kennedy was one of the outstanding lawyers of the country," editorialized the *New York Times,* "a preeminent legal philosopher, a noted prosecutor or legal officer at Federal or State level, the situation would have been different. But his experience is surely insufficient to warrant his present appointment." *The Nation* termed it "the greatest example of nepotism this land has ever seen." *Newsweek* found it "a travesty of justice," while *Atlantic Monthly* deemed it "a slap in the face to all law-abiding citizens."

Jack Kennedy made light of the criticism; in a speech before the Washington-based Alfalfa Club, he quipped, "I can't see that it's wrong to give Bobby a little legal experience before he goes out to practice law."

He cracked other jokes of a similar nature before other groups. "How else can I deal with this crap?" he asked his friend Len Billings.

People were definitely talking. Georgia Senator Dick Russell said to Lyndon Johnson, "I think it's a disgrace for a kid who has never practiced law to be named attorney general." "I agree," responded Johnson, "but I don't think Jack Kennedy's gonna let a little fart like Bobby lead him around the ying-yang."

To prepare Bobby for the hearings before the Senate Judiciary Committee, John Richard Reilly was sent to the library. "The criticism, as you recall, was that he had no experience," Reilly later noted, "and 'How can a lawyer who never tried a case be an attorney general?' So I was assigned the task of going through all the biographical background of all former attorneys general to discover if there was anyone who had less experience than him. Well, the fact was that even though I went back to the very beginning, I could find no one who hadn't practiced law. But . . . I finally came up with the fact that Harry M. Daugherty, who was attorney general during the Teapot Dome scandal [in the 1920s], had practiced law for thirty some odd years, so that we decided that experience wasn't much of a qualification anyhow. So at the time of the hearing we planted that question with [Michigan senator] Phil Hart. . . . I was always very proud of having uncovered that particular detail."

Bobby may not always have esteemed Jack's sense of humor, but he enjoyed the irony of the researcher's discovery. "When I finally said," continued Reilly, " 'I can't find anybody that's had less experience, but I found somebody that went to jail that had more,' well, he got the biggest kick out of that. But it turned out to be about the only thing we had to go on."

When RFK appeared before the committee on January 13, 1961, only Roman Hruska displayed outward hostility. "You have as I understand it," jabbed the Nebraska Republican, "never negotiated a settlement, for example, of a litigated civil case for damages or the breach of a contract or tort case." "I doubt," retorted Bobby, "if I am going to be doing that as attorney general." Even Hruska soon came around—when the committee voted on the nomination, the decision was unanimous for approval. When the full Senate took up the issue a few days later, Robert Kennedy was confirmed as the nation's top law official.

At the holidays, the new first couple had given Bobby a copy of *The Enemy Within* that had been rebound in red calf leather. Jackie inscribed the volume, "To Bobby—who made the impossible possible and changed all our lives." Her husband, constrained by the Kennedy code of cloaking feelings within wisecracks, and still exhausted from the struggle to persuade Bobby to take the job at Justice, wrote below, "For Bobby—The Brother Within—who made the easy difficult. Jack, Christmas 1960."

"**H**e believed that his administration of the Department of Justice would be looked at very closely because of his relation to the president—this would be one of the crucial things in judging the administration," remembered Lee Loevinger, who, thanks to a recommendation from Hubert Humphrey, left a job on the Minnesota Supreme Court to be appointed assistant attorney general for the Antitrust Division. The youngest attorney general since the presidency of James Madison, RFK sought to assemble a staff of experienced lawyers who would make up for the shortcomings in his own background.

As his second-in-command, Robert Kennedy chose Byron White, the onetime Rhodes scholar who had clerked for a chief justice of the Supreme Court. To fill the positions next in line—those as assistant attorney general—Deputy Attorney General White turned first to fellow alumni of Yale Law School: Nicholas Katzenbach to head the Office of Legal Counsel; Louis Oberdorfer, Tax Division; William Orrick, Civil Division. Texan Ramsey Clark, son of a former attorney general and current justice of the Supreme Court, Tom Clark, was placed atop the Lands Division thanks to recommendations from William O. Douglas and Sam Rayburn, while Herbert J. "Jack" Miller, Jr., a Republican who had been involved in the battle with the Teamsters, became head of the Criminal Division. Bobby had intended to abolish the Internal Security Division but, in order to avoid antagonizing J. Edgar Hoover, he relented, retaining to lead the unit its previous head, Republican J. Walter Yeagley, a former FBI agent. (Nevertheless, Bobby instructed Yeagley to quietly withdraw the division from prosecutorial activity.) Archibald Cox, the Harvard law professor who during the campaign had advised the Kennedys on issues, became solicitor general.

According to Sargent Shriver, the most qualified man to lead the Civil Rights Division was Harris Wofford. But there was no love lost between Wofford and Byron White: Wofford had lobbied RFK in vain against the appointment of White, whom he considered stubborn and humorless, while the latter persuaded Bobby that Wofford's well-established ties to Martin Luther King and his sympathies for the doctrine of civil disobedience would not sit well with Dixie legislators. So White selected for the post Burke Marshall, a high-powered corporate lawyer and another graduate of Yale Law School. As the new appointee's law partner and friend, Wofford was in no position to protest the choice, even though Marshall's prime qualification in White's mind was his utter lack of experience in civil-rights issues.*

Although Robert Kennedy had organized large staffs for his Senate committees, on those panels he'd employed as his assistants mostly hungry young attorneys. So, when meeting with the seasoned lawyers who would be logical candidates for high Justice positions, the new attorney general exhibited limited hiring skills. RFK was considering Philip Elman, a longtime veteran of the solicitor general's office (who would wind up as a member of the Federal Trade Commission), for the job of assistant attorney general for the Office of Legal Counsel, the post that eventually went to Nicholas Katzenbach. "RFK didn't know how to conduct an interview. The whole thing was very awkward, long pauses. After an interval of silence, his next question was, 'What law school did you go to?' This was 1960, I had graduated from law school in 1939, twenty-one years earlier, I had done a few things in those twenty-one years, and they were considering making me an assistant attorney general. And here he was asking me what law school I had gone to. So, I took a deep breath and said, 'Harvard.' He said, 'How did you do?' and I said, 'I did pretty well.' He wasn't satisfied. He said, 'How well?' So I said, 'I did very well.' You would think that he would have known I was on the *Harvard Law Review* and I had been Justice Frankfurter's law clerk, so I must have done pretty well. Even that wasn't enough. He said, 'What were your grades?' And at that point I thought it was too demeaning that he should ask me what my grades were in law school. So I said, 'That was a long time ago, Mr. Attorney General, a long time ago, I don't remember.' Of course I remembered my grades, you never forget your law school grades, but I said, 'That was a long time ago.' So he said, 'What was your

---

*Wofford had thought he would assist Sargent Shriver in the establishment of the Peace Corps, but in early February 1961 JFK summoned the former law professor to the White House. The president had just concluded a meeting with two members of the Civil Rights Commission appointed by Eisenhower. When the men requested that there be someone on the White House staff to receive their views, JFK improvised: "I already have a special assistant who is working full time on that, Harris Wofford." With no idea what he was being sworn in for, Wofford, then still occupied as a personnel researcher, vowed outside Jack's office to uphold the Constitution, and subsequently met the president, who said little more about his duties than that he should work with Theodore Sorensen at the White House and with the Justice Department. "You're the expert. Get going," said Jack as he hustled the bewildered Wofford out the door. Wofford, a dedicated advocate of civil rights, would find little encouragement among other members of the administration; in 1962 he resigned to take a Peace Corps position in Ethiopia. But he was proven prophetic about Byron White: within two months of the administration's beginning, the deputy attorney general would develop a severe duodenal ulcer.

rank in the class?' And I said, 'It was pretty high.' I just was stubborn, I was damned if I was going to get this job on the basis of my grades or rank in law school. I don't remember how the thing petered out but he dropped the subject, and he didn't have very many more questions to ask. That was my interview with Bobby Kennedy for the job of assistant attorney general."

For his personal staff, Bobby had no need to conduct interviews: he made Angie Novello his secretary and Edwin Guthman his press spokesman, and he brought in John Seigenthaler as his top adviser, giving him the title of administrative assistant. Joseph Dolan, who had worked for Jack and Bobby in the Senate and for White in Denver, was made White's assistant.

In addition to the personnel he needed to occupy the Justice Department's Washington headquarters, RFK had to staff offices around the country. Many candidates for the regional U.S. attorney slots were referred to Bobby and his team by members of Congress, remembered John Richard Reilly, who became executive assistant in charge of U.S. attorneys, "and some of them were not exactly the type of people that Bobby Kennedy wanted to be his arm out in the states. So we had a meeting one of the first days with Byron and Bob and myself in which he made it very clear that political considerations must enter into it, as he recognized, but that he would not stand for any hacks."

Some appointees arrived on the job unsure where their allegiance now lay, but their new boss quickly set them straight. "You have been recommended to us by people involved in politics," RFK would tell them. "You yourself perhaps have been involved in politics and owe your appointment to somebody. But as of this minute you owe your appointment to only one person, and that's the president. . . . If you ever have to compromise, you have one loyalty, and that's to the Justice Department and that's all there is to it. And if it ever happens any other way, you're gone. . . . I will support you constantly . . . and if you run into a problem, you are to talk to me about it, and I'll be available at any time to discuss it. But your loyalty is now to the Justice Department." The lecture was invariably effective. "You know," Reilly commented, "you get those blue eyes staring at you at that point across that desk, and there was not much question that the guy got the message, that he may have some political ambitions or political debts to pay, but he wasn't going to pay them during this administration.

"It was always a very impressive thing to me, and I loved to hear it because I always kind of felt good about it. And the reaction of the U.S. attorney was always just amazing to me. Bob always kept his end of the bargain, also. He did support them constantly. And as a result, I don't think there ever was or there ever will be again an administration with greater loyalty between the men in the field and the attorney general. I get letters today, still, from people."

While Robert Kennedy would not permit disloyalty in his department, he was tolerant of other flaws, many of which he discovered while reading background information collected on candidates by the FBI. "We used to have some rare times reading some of these FBI reports . . ." remarked Reilly. "We had one guy, upon graduation from law school he had gotten a little loaded and went to an amusement park with a bunch of his friends and urinated off the top of a Ferris wheel. Now, this was a big thing in the FBI report: We shouldn't appoint him as assistant U.S. attorney. So I told Bob about it, and . . . he says, 'Jeez, that sounds like just the kind of a fellow I want in there.' "

Career employees at the Justice Department had never seen an attorney general like Robert Kennedy. On the wood-paneled walls of his spacious office at the Justice Department could be found crayon pictures drawn by his children. Next to an imposing fireplace, he placed a stuffed tiger, its front paws in the air, ready to pounce on visitors who disapproved of a shirtsleeved cabinet member who propped his feet up on the Jeffersonian-period desk as he reclined in his black leather armchair. Almost as big as the tiger (which had been given to him by Ernest Hemingway) was Brumus, who made himself at home as unself-consciously as his master. (Regulations prohibited even the presence of dogs in government offices. This regulation was obviously ignored, particularly considering Brumus's habit of relieving himself on the attorney general's rich burgundy carpet.)

Previous heads of the Justice Department rarely, if ever, visited field offices, but Bobby traveled frequently throughout the nation, meeting with U.S. attorneys and their assistants, local FBI leaders, regional administrators of the Internal Revenue Service and any employees of the department's organized-crime section who happened to be on assignment in the area. He also would meet with judges, assuring them that although he had recently been a campaign manager, he was now making no political demands of them.

Bobby made unprecedented visits within Washington, D.C., headquarters as well. A Justice Department lawyer named Patricia Collins told author Ovid DeMaris that she had worked in the Department for years without ever having been personally introduced to an attorney general. RFK changed all that by dropping in on her and conversing with her at length, assuring her he knew what it felt like to be ignored. He charmed her with his sense of humor. "I used to make next to nothing as an attorney for the Rackets Committee," he told her, "and then my brother was elected president. Look at me now."*

One day each week, he would choose a division to visit. "He wouldn't go to see the head of the unit first," said John Seigenthaler, who would accompany RFK on the tours; "he would just start dropping by offices, saying 'Hi, I'm Bob Kennedy, how are things going? What are you working on?' A couple of times we walked in on people who were reading paperback novels, and one of them was terribly embarrassed and burst into tears when the attorney general said it was unfair to the taxpayers and unfair to other people in the department.

"The visits were a great inspiration to those lawyers buried in the bureaucracy, because most of them would never even get to see the head of their division. And here was the attorney general of the United States and brother of the president saying hello to the secretary and then coming into the lawyer's office, asking about things like radiators that didn't work or dirty windows. 'Can't we get you some light in here?' he'd say. He always followed up on those things."

If few attorneys general of the past had ever bothered to notice the working conditions of low-level employees, surely none had ever opened his eyes to a more significant circumstance—a deficiency as glaring to RFK as it had been invisible to others. "One day," Seigenthaler continued, "he said to me, 'Doesn't it strike you as strange that we're going through the Justice Department and we haven't seen a single black person except those doing custodial work?' As a result of his question, I wrote a letter to the head of every division saying, 'Would you please, by the end of next week, give me a count on the number of black people who work for you?' It turned out that there were a couple of lawyers and a couple of secretaries, but otherwise nobody.

"The only person who didn't respond to the memo was J. Edgar Hoover. I sent a second memo, after which he wrote me saying it was a violation of federal regulations to inquire into the race of government employees. We went back and forth on it, and finally, after we'd found out that the most any division had was one, he wrote back to say he had two, and he gave their names. I showed the memo to Sal Andretta, chief

---

*Apparently recovered from his embarrassment over Jack's quip about his inexperience, Bobby used a similar joke to boost staff morale. "I started in the department as a young lawyer in 1950," he told a department gathering. "The salary was only four thousand dollars a year, but I worked hard. [*Pause.*] I was ambitious. [*Pause.*] I studied. [*Pause.*] I applied myself. . . . And then my brother was elected president of the United States."

administrator of the department, who'd been there for years, and he said, 'Hell, they're Hoover's drivers.'*

"At any rate, once we got the results of that survey, we wrote to the deans of every law school in the country saying that if there were minority students who might be interested in working for the Justice Department, we'd welcome their applications. And then Robert Kennedy named for the first time a black U.S. attorney in San Francisco and one in Cleveland. He also sent word to the U.S. marshals that they were expected to employ deputy marshals who were minorities.

"I remember William D. Rogers, Bobby's predecessor, left him two gifts when he departed. One was a fountain pen to sign judicial nominations and the other was a big bottle of aspirin for the headaches he knew he would have. I really admired Attorney General Rogers; he was a terribly nice guy. But I had the feeling that there was a dramatic change of pace when RFK took the job. The place came alive. There was an electric atmosphere."

The eight inches of snow that hit the nation's capital on January 19, 1961, prevented many of the entertainers rehearsing that afternoon at the National Guard Armory from returning to their hotels for dinner. Accordingly, at that evening's presidential gala, which had been organized by Frank Sinatra and Peter Lawford, many of the celebrities appeared in informal clothes instead of in the tuxedos and evening gowns that had been tailored for the occasion. A number of the stars, who included Laurence Olivier, Gene Kelly, Nat King Cole, Harry Belafonte, Janet Leigh, Tony Curtis, Ella Fitzgerald and Leonard Bernstein, among others, had dined the night before at Hickory Hill as guests of the next attorney general and his wife. The blizzard that choked Washington's streets kept half of the symphony orchestra and much of the audience from traveling to the armory, but the show went on—two hours late—as soon as the new first couple arrived. Following the program, most of the performers, as well as the president-elect—although not his wife, who was still recovering from the cesarean she had undergone only two months previously—relocated to Paul Young's restaurant for a party thrown by Joseph Kennedy.

Three thousand workers toiled through the night with snowplows and

---

* Harris Wofford, adviser to JFK on civil rights, noted that "despite RFK's growing attentions to the black situation in general, his approach to the black situation in the Justice Department was seen by some as tokenism: among others, he wanted to bust J. Edgar Hoover's chops. I'm certain that's how Hoover perceived it."

flamethrowers to clear Washington's thoroughfares for the inauguration and parade to take place the following day. At noontime, in the bitter cold, Marian Anderson sang the national anthem and Robert Frost recited a poem—not the one he had written for the occasion, for he was unable to read it in the glare of the brilliant winter sun, but a previously penned poem he knew from memory. Lyndon Johnson swore to defend the Constitution as vice president, and then JFK, his right hand on the (Honey Fitz) Fitzgerald family Bible, took his oath. Seated near the new president were his parents. Joe was dressed in the same morning suit he'd worn twenty-two years earlier when he had presented his credentials to the King of England. (That evening, for the multivarious inaugural balls, Rose would put on the gown she'd worn on that same occasion.)

After Jack exhorted his fellow Americans to ask what they could do for their country, he and Jackie waved to the crowds of well-wishers from the open limousine that led the parade from the Capitol down Pennsylvania Avenue. A few cars back, Bobby stood and waved from the car he shared with Ethel. Then, the two brothers took their positions near the White House to review the rest of the procession. Despite the pomp and ceremony, RFK no doubt considered the responsibilities of his new job, for which he would be sworn in the following day. "I was in the press pool for the inauguration," recalled Robert Novak. "I was right at the reviewing stand with the president and Bobby was there. Stan Tretick, a photographer with UPI and very close to the Kennedys, came up to him and said, 'Well, Bobby, what are we supposed to call you now? Bobby or Attorney General or General or Sir?' And Bobby said, 'Just call me son of a bitch because that's what everybody else is going to be doing.'"

The first of the evening's five official inaugural balls took place at the Mayflower Hotel. The Kennedys then moved to the Statler-Hilton for the next event. Jack and Jackie barely had time to get settled in the box they were sharing with Lyndon and Lady Bird Johnson when Jack excused himself to take an elevator up several floors to where his friend Frank Sinatra was hosting another party. There he encountered Angie Dickinson, who was ostensibly escorted for the evening by Red Fay. Fay, whose wife was vacationing in Europe, had agreed to Jack's request that he accompany the actress to the inaugural events, since it would be unseemly for her to be seen with her real date for the evening, the thirty-fifth president of the United States. JFK and Dickinson, in the midst of an affair, spent twenty minutes in whispered conversation before Jack returned downstairs to the icy glare of his wife.

Another actress at Sinatra's party was Kim Novak. Like Dickinson, she was less interested in her nominal companion for the night, architect

Fernando Parra, than in a high public official in the new administration. Reporter George Carpozi, Jr., related an incident involving the curvacious movie star that occurred during the early 1960s: "Kim Novak had just been to Russia—she'd gotten a visa just when the cultural exchange program began. And when she returned she called me up in New York and asked me to visit her the next day at her suite at the Plaza Hotel. When I went up to her suite, I could smell the remains of a fire. I asked her about it and she showed me a copy of the newspaper, which had a page one photo taken by *Daily News* photographer Mel Finkelstein of her escaping the fire at the Plaza.

"She said, 'George, you'll never believe what happened. When I got back from Russia, the first person I called was Bobby Kennedy.'

" 'Why did you call Bobby?' I asked.

" 'Because he arranged through the State Department for my trip to Russia. Now, don't breathe a word of this. I phoned Bobby to thank him, but I also wanted to complain about his diplomat in Washington who was so rude to the Russians. So I called Bobby in Washington and he said he wouldn't talk to me about it over the telephone, but he'd come to see me in New York immediately.' "

Carpozi continued: "So Bobby showed up that night in her hotel suite. Kim said, 'I'd bought a big Russian fur hat and it was right here on the coffee table in the living room when Bobby and I hear fire engines. We look out and there are several fire trucks in front of the hotel. And sure enough, somebody knocks on my door and says, "Get out, fire!" '

"Bobby says, 'What am I going to do now?' Kim opens the door, looks out and says, 'The coast is clear.' Just outside the door was a staircase circled with opaque glass. Bobby dashes out of the room and down the stairs. Kim shuts the door to her room and starts to dress properly so she can go downstairs herself when there's a knock at the door. It's Mel Finkelstein. 'Put on your furs, Kim,' he tells her, 'and I'll take a picture of you at the fire.'

"If Finkelstein had made it there two minutes earlier, he'd have gotten the picture of a lifetime—at least that's what he told me, and he ought to know."

Meanwhile, on Inauguration Night, Robert Kennedy tagged along with his brother, even sending Ethel with his regrets to a party thrown in his honor at the Shoreham Hotel by industrialist Cornelius Vanderbilt, Jr. Later on, when Jack and Jackie, along with Ethel and Bobby, arrived at the armory for the evening's third and largest ball, the crowd of more than a thousand guests rose and gave them a twenty-minute ovation. Ken McKnight, who would work in the Department of Commerce, recalled the scene: "There they were up on the balcony, and the band played 'Hail to the Chief.' The spotlights shone on JFK, and this was really his first major public appearance as president. He was so pleased—you could see he was just eating it up."

A weary Jacqueline Kennedy did not attend the evening's remaining two balls with her husband. Nor did she or Ethel accompany Jack and Bobby when, well after midnight, the two husbands stopped for a nightcap at the home of columnist Joseph Alsop. There they encountered half a dozen beautiful young women; imported for the occasion, they were the cream of the "Golden Girls"—three hundred Hollywood starlets and Las Vegas dancers who had appeared at campaign functions "to add color, charm, and photographic appeal," as one organizer had written. After the country's new leaders discussed issues of national import with the influential journalist, they trained their sights on the eager ladies. "All six wanted to be with the president," remembered Peter Lawford. "They arranged a lineup as they would at Madame Claude's brothel in Paris, and Jack chose two of them. This *ménage à trois* brought his first day in office to a resounding close. Bobby had his choice of the four lovelorn women his brother had rejected."

It was almost 4 A.M. before the brothers were ready to leave. With reporters gathered around Alsop's front door, however, Jack and Bobby opted for the rear exit. Stepping through the tall boxhedges surrounding Alsop's yard, the president of the United States and the man who in hours would become the nation's top law-enforcement officer scampered past the adjoining house and emerged, their shoes and coats wet from the snow, on the next street. They strolled together for a while before parting company, Bobby bound for his suburban home, Jack for the executive mansion, where he would spend his first night as commander in chief.

14

HIT LIST

*Robert Kennedy was a strange, complex man, easier to respect than
to like, easier to like than to understand; in all, a man to be taken
seriously. His love for humanity, however real, seemed greater in the
abstract than in individual cases. He was no intellectual, but he was
more receptive to other men's ideas than most intellectuals. But even
as you made excuses for his weaknesses, there was the fear that you
were doing more than he would do for you.*

> —Pat Anderson, a press aide in the Kennedy
> Justice Department, writing in *Esquire*, April
> 1965

Robert Kennedy would be no ordinary attorney general. Brother
of the president, he would involve himself extensively in areas of the
administration far afield from his formal responsibilities in law enforcement—in social policy, in defense, in counterinsurgency matters, and in
foreign affairs. Still, his most direct impact was at Justice, where he
would use his unique position as both department head and head presidential confidant to fundamentally redirect the federal law-enforcement
authority. Although he had been a reluctant appointee, once in office
he would act as though he'd never given it a second thought. With
remarkable continuity he would pursue the agenda he had developed
during his years as John McClellan's counsel, an agenda whose targets
included not only the insidious rot he'd identified as infesting the nation's innermost core, but also the several men who had stood atop his
pantheon of private villains.

Remorseless rackets buster and compassionate friend to the poor,
self-effacing colleague to his staff and steely boss, this "strange, complex
man" would bring all aspects of his multifaceted personality to his tenure as attorney general. No contradiction would be more pronounced,
or more difficult to reconcile, than that between the pillar of legal rectitude, blindly serving the national interest, and the nimble political oper-

ator, acting as rigorous protector of the interests of his brother and his president.

"I am getting out of all political activities as fast as I can," RFK told Peter Maas in a *Look* magazine interview on March 28, 1961. "Partisan politics played no role when I was chief counsel for the McClellan Labor-Rackets Committee. They will play no part now." Despite that promise, the new chief at Justice stayed active in party affairs. "During 1961–63 Robert Kennedy was for all practical purposes the head of the Democratic political machine," wrote Pat Anderson. As ever, Bobby relieved his big brother of distasteful but necessary chores, handling such prickly personages as Chicago's Mayor Richard Daley and Harlem's Congressman Adam Clayton Powell, Jr., as well as tending to "the dirtier political transactions with an endless stream of lesser politicos who had some claim to press the Kennedy flesh and bend the Kennedy ear."

Yet according to one witness, the once and (presumed) future campaign manager made at least some effort to erect a wall of separation between his political and governmental roles and had to be tricked into breaching that barrier. "Kenny O'Donnell was a close friend of mine," recalled John Richard Reilly, who traveled with RFK on his visits to regional offices, "and Kenny always used to say, 'John . . . I just heard the other day that the two of you went into Chicago and that Bobby didn't even call the mayor.' I said, 'Yes, that's right. He maintains he's nonpolitical.' And he said, 'Yes, but someday the president's going to have to run again, and he's going to have to be political, or somebody is. And you just can't go into Chicago without at least telling Mayor Daley that you're in town. . . . I'm going to make you responsible for at least checking in with the right people so that they don't read in the newspaper that Bobby Kennedy was there and hasn't even chosen to speak to them.' "

Reilly looked for a way to have his boss speak with a town's political powers while thinking that the pols themselves had initiated the contact: "Let's say that . . . there was a six-thirty-to-seven-thirty cocktail party and then a dinner at which he was speaking. He normally skipped the cocktail party and arrived at the dinner as they were sitting down. And during that period of time we would have had him scheduled so he maybe was arriving at the hotel at six-thirty, quarter to seven. Then he'd immediately fill the bathtub up, almost up to the top, and get in the bathtub and relax in the hot tub and read his speech and so on. So I finally hit upon the idea that while he was in the tub I'd always . . . call whoever I had figured . . . he should speak to in that town, that had been helpful during the campaign, such as Frank Chelf of Louisville, Kentucky—and I'd say, 'Frank, this is John Reilly. I'm traveling with the attorney general. He's just in town for a few hours and wants to say hello.' Frank would say, 'Fine.' I then called Bob. I said, 'Frank Chelf's on the phone. He wants to say hello.' So the two of them would talk, and that would be the end of it, and everything would go off fine. And I'd come back and tell O'Donnell, 'Well, we talked to so-and-so and so-and-so, and everybody's happy.' "

Reilly's scheme worked without a snag over many road trips, until a visit to San Francisco produced a halting conversation between RFK and Mayor John F. Shelley: "Bobby said, 'Hello, Jack, how are you?' The mayor said, 'Fine, Bob, how are you?' There's silence. Bob says, 'What's up?' Shelley said, 'I don't know, you called me.' Bob said, 'No, you called me.' So they go through this whole thing, and he finally hangs up, and he turns to me, and he says, 'You son of a bitch, you've been doing this for two years, haven't you?' He finally caught me."*

However sincere or flimsy the boundary between RFK's partisan and official duties, the two spheres intersected unavoidably in two cases that came to his attention only months after he'd assumed his post: those of a New York judge accused of accepting a bribe and a midwestern mayor charged with soliciting payoffs.

The allegation that Judge J. Vincent Keogh of the Supreme Court of the State of New York took money from a convicted man seeking a light sentence would hardly have troubled the attorney general and his brother had not the judge had a brother of his own. Congressman Eugene Keogh, a longtime friend of Joseph Kennedy and chairman of the House Rules Committee, had been, according to Bobby, one of the "most helpful people to the President in the election." "I can't recall any incident involving a criminal matter which caused more consternation than that early one in the administration," remarked John Reilly. Political people at the White House lobbied Bobby to drop the case, and the new attorney general faced a difficult choice. "I don't think Bob Kennedy ever really recovered from what he had to do, but he had to make a decision early in his administration as to whether or not he was

---

* During his journeys with Bobby, Reilly discovered another of the attorney general's dual identities: the millionaire with an empty wallet. "He never had money with him," said Reilly. "No matter where you'd go, you'd end up paying cab drivers, and you'd end up tipping bellhops, and you'd end up paying checks. . . . For the first couple of weeks I began to think, 'I can't stand this.' Finally, I talked to Angie Novello, and she said, 'Just keep track, and when you come back, tell me, and I'll give you the money. It's been going on for years, John, you're not the first one to have gone through it.' "

going to be a political attorney general or attorney general of the United States and true to his oath."

The matter was complicated because the key witness in the affair, the alleged go-between for briber and bribee, was, in Reilly's words, a man of "bum reputation. . . . It wasn't a . . . cut-and-dried case, that somebody had a picture of somebody handing money to Vince Keogh. . . . It was a questionable thing, and Bob Kennedy could have killed the case, and done so with probably a clear conscience on the basis of the fact that the evidence is not good enough, but he didn't."

Reilly was unable to pinpoint how high in the administration the pressure to forgo prosecution originated. He did, however, catch sight of an incident that provided a hint. The scene was a White House reception for Supreme Court justices and Justice Department personnel. Reilly recounted: "Drinks were served, and everybody drank quite a bit and had a good time, and Mrs. Kennedy and the president mixed with the crowd the entire evening.

"In the front hall of the White House there's a winding staircase, and at one point I remember looking up on the landing. Standing on the landing were the president, Bob Kennedy, Jack Miller, and Byron White. It was a very animated conversation. Only the noise below kept the actual conversation from being heard, but the noise of the conversation was evident, and it was obvious that there was an argument taking place—much gesticulating, etc. I asked Jack Miller after that what was going on, and he said, 'Well, it was the Keogh matter.' . . . It was an extremely touchy and a tough matter, I'm sure, for the attorney general to decide in the very beginning. I would suspect that the president would have preferred that Bobby hadn't done it, but he had no choice."

Prosecuted along with two other men also involved in the case— Elliot Kahaner, a high-ranking official in the U.S. Attorney's operation, and Tony ("Ducks") Corallo, a New York racketeer—Vincent Keogh was convicted and sentenced to two years in prison. Although Gene Keogh attended the annual Army-Navy football game with the president five days after his brother's indictment, the congressman never forgave Bobby; neither did the judge.

George Chacharis, a Greek immigrant who served as mayor of Gary, Indiana, was not the target RFK named to Jay Goldberg, a Justice Department lawyer assigned to investigate rumors of rampant corruption. "He gave me a list headed by Frank Zizzo and followed by the names of other supposed local hoodlums, all those vowel people," Goldberg recalled. "But when I went to Gary, Indiana, I learned that crime and corruption weren't controlled by gangsters but by people friendly to

Robert Kennedy, namely Mayor George Chacharis. Chacharis had played an active role in the nomination of President Kennedy at the Chicago convention of 1956, and had just been appointed ambassador to Greece, pending Senate confirmation. When I notified Washington that the mayor was behind the corruption, all hell broke loose." Goldberg's probe turned up evidence that Chacharis had skimmed over two hundred thousand dollars from city contracts. The mayor hadn't pocketed the money—he'd turned all of it over to his local party organization—but he hadn't reported it on his tax return, either.

"Efforts were made to kill the investigation," Goldberg continued. "First, Ray Madden, the congressman from Gary who was on the Rules Committee, refused to release a farm bill for a vote on the House floor unless Robert Kennedy recalled me from Indiana. But the citizens of Indiana wouldn't stand for it; they sent the White House a hundred coconuts on which they'd engraved the word 'Help' and asked that I remain there.* I was. It was clear to me that I had the full support of the people of Indiana, but was somewhat of a pain in the ass to Robert Kennedy, who would have been more than happy to see Mayor Chacharis pay his taxes and leave for Athens as ambassador. What made matters worse was that Mayor Chacharis had hired as his lawyer Alexander Campbell, who was the Democratic National Committeeman from Indiana.

"As I was getting ready to present the evidence against Chacharis to the grand jury, and having called fifty-six witnesses from all parts of the country to come and testify about the widespread corruption he had led—my case was focused on the shakedowns and extortion involving the construction of the Indiana Toll Road—my secretary came into my office and told me that Attorney General Kennedy was on the phone.

" 'I understand that you have been threatening to indict Mayor Chacharis at a time when Mr. Campbell, his attorney, is going to be in Israel giving a speech.'

" 'I made no such threat,' I told him.

" 'I would like you to put off the grand jury and sit down with Mayor Chacharis and Mr. Campbell and tell them who the witnesses are who will testify against them and show them the documents to be used as evidence.'

" 'I could never do that because it would imperil the security of the people who have stepped forward to testify against the mayor. And it's

---

* The gesture was meant to recall JFK's similar use of a coconut to send for help after the wreck of the *PT-109*.

just not something that one does in the course of presenting a case to a grand jury. It will imperil the grand jury.'

"He said, 'I'm directing you to turn it over.'

" 'I cannot do it.'

"At which point he put his hand on the speaking portion of the phone and said, in a voice that was completely audible to me, 'George, he will not let you see the documents.' George Chacharis, the malefactor, the criminal, the ambassador-designate, the mayor of Gary, Indiana, the close friend of the Kennedys, was actually in the attorney general's office as the attorney general was trying to prevail upon me to compromise the investigation by turning over these documents to the mayor."

The case went forward nonetheless. "There was such a groundswell of support for me in Indiana," Goldberg said, "that there was no real possibility of Kennedy killing the investigation, and Mayor Chacharis was eventually convicted and sent to jail. But on one occasion when I was back in Washington I saw the attorney general. He sat behind his desk. He had a deep tan—and a slim muscular frame. He sat with his feet up on the desk, with drawings by his kids on the walls, and he said to me, 'You know, Jay, my brother said that if we don't stop locking up Democrats he's gonna have to put me on the Supreme Court.' And I said to myself, Is this a joke? Is this real? If he could make him attorney general, he could do anything. I didn't know whether it was meant tongue-in-cheek or whether he was serious, but that's exactly what he said."

Although Goldberg didn't appreciate Bobby's jest, he was surprisingly charitable in his assessment of RFK: "The whole story leaves me with this feeling: Obviously, one thinks of the attorney general of the United States as a prosecutor. On the other hand, attorneys general are often very important political figures, and as such they have political pulls on their decision making. They're far different from a local prosecutor, who, when there's a person who's presumed guilty, will prosecute. When I went on the national scene, I realized how tough it was to press forward against a figure with a great deal of political strength."

Journalist Victor Navasky, editor of *The Nation*, summed up Bobby's balancing of politics and justice this way: "He did about as well, I think, in managing classic conflicts of interest as any other attorney general I can think of in recent memory."

Edwyn Silberling, who headed the organized-crime section and was Goldberg's superior, had a different opinion: "When it came to making a decision, Robert Kennedy's first criterion was, Is it good for my brother? The second criterion was, Is it good for the Democratic Party? And the third criterion was, Is it good for the country?"

For Goldberg, the case of George Chacharis had an unexpected postscript: "Some years later, when Bobby was a U.S. senator and I was out of the Department of Justice, I received an invitation to a fund-raising party at a classy New York apartment. The guest of honor was Richard Hatcher, then running for the spot that had been held by Chacharis. If elected, Hatcher would become the first black mayor of Gary, and one of the first black mayors anywhere in the country. People like John Kenneth Galbraith were there, as well as Ossie Davis, Ruby Dee, and Bobby Kennedy. RFK's hair had grown long, it had curled up in the back with a sort of theatrical look to it, and he had on a navy suit with wide stripes. Hatcher, speaking in the front of the living room, said that but for Robert Kennedy, he wouldn't be there. Then the microphone went to Kennedy, who remarked that although he appreciated all the compliments, he had to give much of the credit to Jay Goldberg, his trusted aide. Even now when I think of it I get goose pimples, because I stood up and I tipped my martini glass in his direction. That was the last time I saw him."

Roy Cohn had prospered in the private practice of law since he left Washington in the wake of Joe McCarthy's disgrace. From the office he decorated with dozens of stuffed animals at the law firm that would become known as Saxe, Bacon & Bolan, he cultivated a list of clients that would come to include New York powerhouses such as real-estate moguls Donald Trump and Samuel Lefrak, church moguls Francis Cardinal Spellman and Terence Cardinal Cooke, and mafia moguls Carmine Galante and Anthony "Fat Tony" Salerno. His list of friends was no less dazzling, ranging from Norman Mailer and William F. Buckley, Jr., to Estée Lauder and Ronald Reagan, and included a legion of lesser-known, if often even more influential, lights of business, government and entertainment. With these contacts, Cohn burrowed deep within New York's (and America's) power structure—and always with his heavy-lidded eye on the prize: "Power means the ability to get things done," he once said. "It stems from friendship in my case. My business life is my social life."

His social life wasn't all business. As he had in Washington during the McCarthy period, he became well known in Gotham for get-togethers attended not only by the town's movers and shakers but also by numbers of young, muscular, attractive men. Partygoers reported that in the midst of an evening's gathering, Cohn and several leather-clad studs would disappear into the bedroom. From behind the closed door, the gray-suited lawyers and their pearl-necked wives could hear what sounded like blows being delivered, followed by moans of pleasure, apparently emanating from their host. The influential lawyer would shortly reemerge, rejoining his more genteel guests as if nothing had happened. Such denial was essential to Roy Cohn's self-image—he continued to publicly disavow his homosexuality until his death from AIDS in 1986.

Not on Cohn's party list was Robert Kennedy, although Cohn occupied a prominent place on another kind of list kept by Bobby. The day RFK was sworn in as attorney general, Cohn telephoned James Juliana, a lawyer who had worked for both men during the fifties. "Jim," said Cohn, "I don't want to bother you with this, I haven't spoken to Bobby in years, I can't imagine he's sitting around thinking about me. But just between us, Jim, what's his attitude towards me?"

"Hoffa's number one," replied Juliana. "You're number two."

RFK wasted little time before launching his pursuit of number two. In late summer 1961, Irving Younger, an assistant U.S. attorney for the Southern District of New York, was summoned to the office of his boss, U.S. Attorney Robert M. Morgenthau. "Behind the desk sat Morgenthau, smoking a cigar," Younger wrote in the October 1976 issue of *Commentary* magazine. At the time of the article, Younger was a professor of law at Cornell University. "In a chair in front of the desk Robert Kennedy fidgeted with a pair of heavy horn-rimmed glasses. Morgenthau introduced me to the Attorney General, who nodded once. It was his only contribution to the conversation. . . .

" 'The Department,' said Morgenthau, 'has a special interest in Roy Cohn.' That was no news to me. It had been the gossip of the office for months. 'The Department thinks it would be a good idea to consolidate all of our Cohn activities in one assistant. I'm designating you. Review the files. Follow up. Go wherever you have to. Your job is to find out whether Cohn is guilty of something. The Department wants Cohn.'

" 'I'll get him,' I said, and nodded to Kennedy, who was still fidgeting with his glasses. Neither he nor Morgenthau spoke as I left the room. That afternoon, I began to read about Cohn."

Over the next nine months, Younger would examine every item in the Department of Justice's records on Cohn, leaving no stone unturned in his effort to put the fiend behind bars. The chief line of inquiry involved a set of shady stock transactions effected through a Liechtenstein entity called Brandel Trust. First, Morgenthau supplied Younger with a copy of Cohn's 1960 tax return, though the document suggested no connection with Brandel. Then, by pressuring a Zurich lawyer who represented the firm in Switzerland, Younger obtained Brandel's books, hoping that those documents would link Cohn to several of the firm's principals who had been indicted the year before. The accounts provided a slag heap of information about illegal conduct, but did not incriminate Roy Cohn. To Morgenthau, Cohn's absence from these records was only further proof of his deviousness: "Well, we know Cohn is smart. Maybe he set the thing up so that the records don't involve him." Morgenthau called in the FBI, whose agents bugged the New York hotel room of the Zurich lawyer, who was in town to testify against the Brandel executives and was expecting a visit from a Cohn associate. The microphone failed, as did the investigation.

By spring of 1962, Younger reported his findings to Morgenthau. "I had been to Europe twice," he wrote, "to Central America once, and to various places within the United States. I had studied every official file in which Roy Cohn was mentioned. I had put Cohn before the grand jury. I had devoted myself single-mindedly to investigating Roy Cohn, and the result was nothing.

" 'I'm licked,' I said. 'If he has violated the law, I can't find it.'

" 'I'll inform the Department,' Morgenthau said.

"I understood that I was no longer the Department's man on Cohn."*

Yet the U.S. attorney for the Southern District of New York and the attorney general of the United States were hardly finished with Roy Cohn. In September 1962, Championship Sports, Inc., a fight-promotion outfit owned by Cohn and his law partner Tom Bolan, staged a title bout between Floyd Patterson, the graceful heavyweight champion, and Sonny Liston, the hard-slugging contender. Although Liston knocked out Patterson in the first round, the dethroned champ may not have been the most stunned person in Chicago's Comiskey Park that night, for by the time the fight had ended, Cohn and Bolan learned that employees of the Internal Revenue Service had seized all the fight's proceeds. The IRS agents, acting on Bobby's orders, took not only the live gate, but also the funds collected at closed-circuit-television locations around the country.

The IRS termed the seizure a "jeopardy assessment," undertaken to ensure that taxes on the proceeds would not be evaded. The government had learned that Cohn had set up a shell corporation through which he would pay Floyd Patterson his purse over a seventeen-year period.

---

*Morgenthau penned a 1,700-word reply to Younger's article, calling the account "absolute fiction from beginning to end," "false both in its small details and its larger suggestions." Morgenthau denied that the described meeting with RFK ever took place.

"There was also information," stated Robert Arum, "that the money was going to be taken by Cohn and deposited in a Swiss bank account." Arum, who later became a boxing promoter himself, supervised the case as head of Morgenthau's tax division. "Under current IRS law, it's okay to pay a performer on a deferred basis. But in 1962, Cohn's plan was against the code of yet-performed services, since the taxes on the full sum might never be paid. Cohn was definitely aware that under the law, as it existed at the time, you couldn't pay out the money that way. His cognizance of the statute was clearly established at the civil proceeding that followed, and the position of the government was vindicated."

Cohn did not concur. Calling the government's action in the case "fascist," he later asserted that the "taxes weren't due until the following year, and no proof existed that we were going to dead-beat the government. Moreover, everybody's end was seized—the fighters', the theater owners', the managers'—in that way, I suppose, Bobby and his boys were very democratic, they screwed everybody equally."*

Cohn and Bolan eventually prevailed—they got most of their money back, although not all of it and not for years. Still, Cohn's outrage over the case, like most of the outrage in his seemingly inexhaustible supply, rings hollow, for he had a lifelong aversion to paying the tax collector. For his legal work he drew an ostensible salary of only a hundred thousand dollars a year, but he lived in opulent fashion thanks to a tax-free expense account that ran as high as a million dollars a year: his law firm supplied him with a rent-free Manhattan town house and paid part of the rent on his vacation home in Greenwich, Connecticut; it saw that he traveled in a chauffeur-driven Rolls-Royce as well as in other luxury cars; it picked up all his tabs at extravagant eateries like Le Cirque and 21. During Bobby's tenure as attorney general, the IRS made Roy Cohn one of its closest acquaintances. "One agent was in the office so much," laughed Tom Bolan, "I thought he was an associate of the firm." Cohn was audited for twenty-three consecutive years. After his death, the IRS sent his estate a bill for $3.18 million in back taxes.

Nevertheless, the actions taken against Cohn by the Kennedy Justice Department and Morgenthau's office, and the attitude toward him that pervaded both agencies, were disproportionate to his sins. "There was a

---

*While most of RFK's indignation in the affair was aimed at Cohn, he did reserve a portion for Floyd Patterson. Before the bout, he'd had an autographed picture of the boxer hanging on the wall of his office. Afterward, whether considering Patterson complicit in Cohn's financial intrigue or simply disappointed that the champ had succumbed so quickly to Liston's crushing assault, he took the photo down.

concerted effort to rein Cohn in at that time," recalled Arum. "He was considered to be a villain. And very often when a man is considered to be a villain, the various agencies of government make a concerted effort to investigate him fully and, if possible, bring criminal charges. Everybody in the U.S. attorney's office thought of him that way. Cohn was the arch-villain. Similar—not identical, but similar—to the way federal prosecutors felt toward John Gotti before he was finally convicted."

The feud that began in December 1952 when Roy Cohn got the job that Robert Kennedy wanted may not have been the only personal vendetta affecting the legal affairs of Joe McCarthy's onetime alter ego. In 1953, Cohn and McCarthy attacked Robert Morgenthau's father, Henry Morgenthau, for his decision as FDR's secretary of the treasury to briefly loan U.S. occupation-currency printing plates to the Soviet Union at the end of World War II. According to Cohn, the younger Morgenthau bore a "mortal grudge" over the improprieties done his father and used his position in law enforcement to exact revenge.

Whatever the motivation of Morgenthau and RFK, Roy Cohn became a prime target in their endless quest for justice. "One day, Charlie, my regular mailman, who used to deliver the mail to my home in Queens, was sick," recounted Tom Bolan. "And so his replacement showed up, looking confused and scratching his head. He held in his hand a yellow card and couldn't figure out what it meant. My wife took a look at it and saw that it was a confidential direction for the mailman to deliver all my mail first to the supervisor at the post office. It was what was called a 'mail cover.'"

Morgenthau and his assistant took charge of the matter; the assistant, Gerald Walpin, later filed affidavits denying knowledge of the mail's interception. At a subsequent hearing, Walpin not only confessed that he had ordered the mail cover on Bolan, but also admitted to prescribing the same arrangement for Cohn. Judge Archie Dawson assailed the government for conduct that "smacks of the Soviet Union rather than the United States," and even the American Civil Liberties Union weighed in on the side of the powerful New York attorney.

The mail cover was brought to light in late 1963, as Morgenthau was preparing to try Cohn on charges of perjury and obstruction of justice. Growing out of an investigation begun by the Eisenhower Justice Department, the government's case alleged a stock swindle involving the United Dye and Chemical Corporation and linked Cohn to Las Vegas mobster Moe Dalitz. With the jury deadlocked eleven to one for conviction, a mistrial was declared when a juror's father died. A retrial three months later resulted in acquittal.

Irving Younger wrote his *Commentary* article as a mea culpa, reproaching himself for cooperating in Kennedy and Morgenthau's pursuit of Cohn. "I am not proud," Younger confessed. Terming the campaign against the controversial attorney an example of "the power of power," he concluded, "If I possibly could, I was going to be the one to do the job the Department wanted done. Not once did I stop to think what it was a Department of."

Roy Cohn was tried twice more in federal court—in 1969 for fraud and in 1971 for bribery—and was acquitted on both occasions. He did, however, finally suffer conviction of a sort. Six weeks before his death in 1986, while he continued to insist he was suffering only from liver cancer (rather than AIDS), a five-judge panel of the Appellate Division of State Supreme Court pronounced his conduct in four legal matters "unethical," "unprofessional" and, in one case, "particularly reprehensible," and disbarred him from the practice of law in New York State.

Eighteen years earlier, when Robert Kennedy was murdered, Roy Cohn is said to have been jubilant.

J. Edgar Hoover, said FBI tour guides in early 1961, "became the director of the Bureau in 1924, the year before the Attorney General was born." Perhaps the director expected his youthful boss to begin his Justice Department education respectfully, joining the awestruck visitors who listened as FBI hosts sang the praises of the nation's number one G-man. But RFK withheld the deference the director considered his due. The new attorney general did not take the tour; nor, once he'd been told what the guides' script contained, did he allow the offending sentence to remain. J. Edgar Hoover would not enjoy working for Robert Kennedy.

RFK and Hoover had clashed more than once during the 1950s. But when Bobby was considering his brother's employment offer late in 1960, he paid Hoover a visit to seek the older man's advice. "Hoover's immediate recommendation was, 'Take the job,'" recounted Courtney Evans, an FBI agent who acted as liaison between the director and the Kennedys. "He could see that here was a conduit to the White House that was more direct and more influential than he ordinarily had. He'd had his own relationships with presidents in the past, but at times they tended to be tenuous. He generally had to depend on the attorney general for the day-to-day presentation of his views at the White House."

Hoover's belief that the special bond between this president and this attorney general would work to his benefit soon yielded to the realization that the connection would give the attorney general an advantage in taking on the FBI and its director. "Bobby had figured out, whether intu-

itively or in a calculated way, how to franchise the Kennedy charisma,"
commented journalist Victor Navasky. "He looked like his brother, he
talked like his brother, he had the same name as his brother, and his
brother delegated the power of the White House to him so when he
called somebody and said, 'The president wants you to do this,' that
somebody had to accept it. He could tell his aides to speak in the name
of the president. No other attorney general was ever able to do that. 'The
president wants it done. Period!' "

Although the FBI was an arm of the Justice Department, and thus
the director was nominally a subordinate of the attorney general, J. Edgar
Hoover was used to operating with little or no supervision. He'd forged
a formidable national reputation fighting outlaws in the thirties, Nazi
spies in the forties and Communists in the fifties. Presidents had found
him impossible to contain, and he was lionized by Congress and in the
press. RFK, however, seeing himself atop Hoover on the organizational
chart, moved quickly to assert his authority. William Hundley remembered sitting in RFK's office in 1961: "He said to me one day—I forget
what we were discussing—'Should I get Hoover over here?' I never had
an attorney general say that. They always used to go over to his office."
Hundley, who had headed the organized-crime section during the Eisenhower administration, remained in the department as a special assistant
to Bobby until reappointment to his old job in 1963. "I was curious more
than anything else, so I said, 'Yeah.' You know, he pushed this buzzer and
[Hoover] came over. I thought I was sitting in on history, and I think I
was."

The installation of the buzzer was only one of the affronts the impu-
dent attorney general visited upon his venerable underling. Within
months of taking office, Bobby invited members of the State Department's diplomatic corps to view an exhibition of FBI marksmanship. John
Richard Reilly recalled that Courtney Evans was assigned the task of
informing the director: "Courtney came back with the information that
the FBI shooting range was closed on Saturday morning. You know, Hoover wasn't going to open it. So Bob said to Courtney, 'You go back and
tell the director that the range is now open on Saturday morning.' In fact,
this was a head-butting mission, and Courtney had to handle it. The
range was open, they did have an exhibition, it was wonderful, and so on.
But poor Courtney had to come back, first of all with the information
that Hoover wasn't going to open the range, and then go back to Hoover
and say, 'You've been directed to open the range.' "

Any show of disrespect, no matter how apparently insignificant, rankled Hoover. "On one occasion," reminisced John Mintz, who served as

the Bureau's general counsel, "the attorney general held a reception for all the regional U.S. attorneys. The director was not invited. Now, even though Hoover hated receptions and parties, he disliked most social interaction and kept his distance from people; he nevertheless called me into his office and said, 'Get me an invitation to that reception.' So I went through my contacts in Kennedy's office and the director did, indeed, get a letter. When it came time for the event, however, Hoover didn't show up. I saw the invitation later. He'd scribbled on it, 'I choose to pass.' "

Staid, entrenched, reserved, the sexagenarian Hoover viewed with contempt the energetic, innovative, informal style of his boss thirty years his junior. Particularly cloying for Hoover was the sight of Bobby in shirtsleeves, his sleeves rolled up, and his tie loosened. Growled the director on one occasion, "It is ridiculous to have the attorney general walking around the building in his shirtsleeves. Suppose I had a visitor waiting in my anteroom. How can I have introduced him?" Another day, Hoover and Clyde Tolson, his aide and longtime companion, met with Bobby in the latter's office. During the entire course of the hour-long meeting, RFK entertained himself by throwing darts into a board he'd fastened to the wall. Each time the attorney general rose from his desk chair to retrieve the darts, Hoover had to bite his tongue. He was infuriated by the seeming lack of respect on the part of a man many years his junior.

Hoover was equally infuriated by the visits Bobby paid to FBI district offices across the country. "Attorneys general didn't ordinarily do that," noted Reilly; "they went through channels, they went through Hoover." Nor did Bobby consult the director before ordering some redecorating. "We'd walk into the special agent in charge's office . . . the SAC's office, and his desk was always clean, always four pencils up in the right-hand corner, always something over in the left-hand corner, you know, neat, clean, everything, a picture of J. Edgar behind him. And after about the third one we visited, Bob said to one of the SAC's . . . 'I don't see a picture of President Kennedy around here.' . . . So Courtney, being very bright, caught this immediately, and from then on we didn't walk into any FBI office anywhere in the country that as soon as you walked into the door, bang, there wasn't a picture of President Kennedy staring you in the face." Perhaps worst of all for the director was the response the visits stirred in his supposedly loyal troops: "The agents loved Bobby," claimed Evans.

Matters of etiquette aside, the sorest point of friction between the director and the attorney general turned out to be the department's mission. For Hoover, the chief threat to the domestic tranquillity—indeed, the *only* threat worth considering—was colored bright red, and from the moment RFK assumed his new post he was inundated with reports from Hoover detailing the perils of the American Communist Party. "Look at this shit," he said in April 1961, showing a typical Hoover memo to Ken O'Donnell. "He was convinced," remarked O'Donnell, "that somewhere along the line Hoover had gone mad. 'He's a fucking cocksucker,' said Bobby. 'Any day now I expect him to show up at work wearing one of Jackie's Dior creations. And then there's that sheer nonsense about the Communist Party. What a supreme and utter waste of time.'"

Rather than waste his own time on Hoover's "nonsense," Robert Kennedy vowed to root out America's real enemy, the all-penetrating virus he had identified in his work for John McClellan: organized crime. He instilled new vigor into the department's organized-crime section, hiring Edwyn Silberling, a veteran of Frank Hogan's Manhattan district attorney's office, to head it. Under RFK's leadership, the crime section's staff of lawyers tripled in number and the time the attorneys spent in the field increased dramatically. Indictments and convictions would soon rise by 70 percent.

Although he'd paid grudging lip service to the existence of organized crime since 1957, when New York state troopers happened upon a convention of dozens of Mafia bosses in the upstate town of Apalachin, J. Edgar Hoover cared little about gangland. The year before JFK's election, the Bureau's New York and New Jersey offices were populated by nearly six hundred agents assigned to the investigation of communist activities, with only a half dozen agents allocated to organized crime. Hoover's willful ignorance on the subject has never been satisfactorily explained. One answer is that he did not wish to expose his agents, bred to be square-shouldered and squeaky clean, to the money the mob might dangle before them. "He was concerned that his men would be corrupted," contended attorney Howard Diller. "This was a nasty business. They could go after communists and kidnappers, but this caused aggravation and he didn't want any aggravation." Perhaps the director also was resolved to steer clear of the tangled web of connections woven by gangsters with local politicians and police departments. Or maybe he feared that his cherished crusade against political subversion would be weakened were he to train the Bureau's efforts on criminal subversion. Whatever had motivated him previously, to acknowledge in 1961 the existence and the extent of organized crime would have been to admit a decades-long mistake. To divine the deepest purposes of J. Edgar Hoover—a man who, after his limousine was rammed during a left turn, forbade his driver from ever again turning left; a man who couldn't abide anyone, particularly agents, standing in his shadow—is, finally, impossible.

Robert Kennedy tried to force J. Edgar Hoover to stand in *his* shadow. To conduct his war on organized crime, Bobby sought to marshal all the resources of the federal government.* "One of his major accomplishments," maintained Ronald Goldfarb, an attorney who worked for RFK at the time, "was to get all the investigative agencies to work together as one police force. It seems like an obvious, fundamental thing, only it had never been done before and there was tremendous resistance from the very powerful J. Edgar Hoover. Only a Robert Kennedy, by the power he had as the president's brother, could have made that happen." Hoover went along kicking and screaming, incensed that the job of coordinating the enterprise went to the Justice Department's organized crime section, not the FBI. But Bobby had the enthusiastic cooperation of at least two agencies contained in the Department of the Treasury: the IRS, at whose head Jack had placed Mortimer Caplin, RFK's law professor at UVA; and the Federal Bureau of Narcotics, led by Harry Anslinger, Hoover's rival and, until Bobby's appointment, the government's leading opponent of the Mafia.

"All the agencies operated as separate fiefdoms," Goldfarb continued. "They were jealous of their own prerogatives and subservient to Hoover. Kennedy came in and said, 'This is ridiculous. From now on we're going to pool our resources and work together. You're all going to be under the supervision of me and my attorneys.' So I'd go out to Cincinnati or Louisville to set up a strike force. We'd call in the local IRS guy, the FBI guy, the Narcotics guy and whoever else we needed. We'd set up a game plan. We were the coach and quarterbacks and they worked for us. It was brand new. In many places we were resisted strongly by local people used to their old ways. They would wait for a sign from Hoover that it was okay. He would eventually give it—his arm was twisted. The standard operating procedures changed.

"If the New Frontier was an exciting place, the organized crime section was one of the hot spots. The attorney general called us about our cases, sat in on meetings. There was a crusade going on. Although I'd been one of those who thought Bob Kennedy was an outrageous choice to be attorney general, my feelings about him changed markedly. He was a man who really grew with power, it brought out the best in him. He

---

* According to Edwyn S. Silberling, an aide to RFK in the Justice Department assigned to investigate organized crime in Chicago, "Bobby took me off the Chicago investigation just when I began to come up with information, the reason being that his father was often mentioned in connection with the Mafia. He was interested in crime busting only to the extent that his family wasn't involved."

managed to do one thing which most administrators take courses to do but don't do, and that is change a huge organization—not only the department, but the other investigative agencies as well, thousands of people spread all across the country. There's no question but that he was a charismatic person. His power coursed through the halls of the department and touched us all."

Hoover's participation didn't come easily. Early in 1961, RFK offered legislation to enhance FBI jurisdiction over matters such as interstate racketeering and gambling; Congress enacted the majority of Bobby's proposals. And he had to allow the director to continue to indulge his obsession with leftist sedition. "Robert Kennedy received credit as the first attorney general to gain control of the FBI," observed Victor Navasky. "He got the Bureau to act on organized crime and civil rights. But what he really did was cede more power to Hoover as his price for doing so. It was a Faustian bargain, because Kennedy allowed the anti-Communist mania that encouraged the Bureau to persist. Although he let the department's Internal Security Division wind down, he didn't put his time and energy into it. And that anti-Communist hysteria that was still part of the American political culture is what later permitted the wiretapping of the phones of Martin Luther King and his associates."

Although the director made motions to placate the president's brother, his cooperation was limited at best; he kept his boss in the dark about most of the Bureau's dealings. Throughout 1962 and 1963, the IRS conducted a broad investigation into racketeering at Las Vegas casinos; at the same time, unbeknownst to RFK, the FBI engaged in its own Las Vegas probe, making extensive use of illegal wiretaps. When the FBI's activities became known, the revelations led to the suppression of much of the IRS's evidence and, as a result, the loss of the prosecutions that might have ensued. The Las Vegas fiasco aside, Hoover, as required by law, generally sought the attorney general's written approval before installing phone taps. An anomaly in federal law, however, also gave Hoover license to plant "bugs"—surreptitious microphones used to monitor nontelephonic conversation—at his own discretion. The director did not hesitate to take advantage of the loophole.

J. Edgar Hoover had ways to ensure that the assertive attorney general went so far and no farther. The dossiers held by the director of the FBI on the personal and professional lives of Washington's elite were no secret in the capital; indeed, the legend of the files exceeded their overflowing reality, and Hoover, as he doled out bits and pieces of information to lawmakers or reporters, always strove to maximize his own notoriety. "Hoover's genius," said Victor Navasky, "was to let everybody believe that he knew of all their indiscretions, whether or not he knew them. And you had to assume, since he would tell you what he had on other people, that he was capable of telling other people what he had on you." One of his favorite tricks was to meet in his office with a congressman or senator (or attorney general) and, while discussing a piece of pending legislation, never make mention of the file folders displayed conspicuously on his desk—folders, clearly labeled, on the visitor, his family and/or his associates.

The Kennedys had long been aware of the director's investigative reach. Early in World War II, Ensign John Kennedy, while working at the Pentagon for the Office of Naval Intelligence, had an affair with Inga Arvad, a Danish journalist working for the *Washington Times-Herald.* Because Arvad had been suspected—incorrectly, it turned out—of being a German agent, the FBI conducted intensive surveillance of the couple, including electronic eavesdropping on their sexual trysts. Joe Kennedy appealed to several of his contacts in the government—including J. Edgar Hoover, a man he called his friend—to see that his ambitious son was not cashiered out of the navy but only transferred from intelligence to PT boats.

Now that the randy young naval officer was president, and his precocious brother attorney general, the director let the family know that he was in on their secrets. He brought to the attorney general a variety of reports—some accurate, some fanciful—on Jack's sexual escapades. The reports made clear Hoover's knowledge concerning the clan's patriarch: "Before the last Presidential election," read a memo Hoover wrote to RFK in mid-1962, "former Ambassador Joseph P. Kennedy was visited at Cal-Neva Lodge, Lake Tahoe, California, by several 'gangsters' [not identified] who have gambling interests."

Still, Hoover's most explosive information concerned the chief executive himself. "Information has been developed," began an internal Bureau memo dated March 20, 1962, "that Judith E. Campbell, a freelance artist, has associated with prominent underworld figures Sam Giancana of Chicago and John Roselli of Los Angeles." The memo went on to list a number of telephone toll calls Campbell had made from Los Angeles and Palm Springs "to Evelyn Lincoln, the President's Secretary at the White House" during the previous several months. "The nature of the relationship between Campbell and Mrs. Lincoln is not known," the memo remarked dryly. But the document also noted the opinion of one informant, a man "of questionable reputation"—the name has been blacked out in the copy released under the Freedom of Information Act—who "referred to Campbell as the girl who was 'shacking up with

John Kennedy in the East.' " The director informed his immediate superior, the attorney general, who in turn informed *his* superior, the president.*

At Justice, news of the FBI's discoveries was not confined within the richly paneled walls of the department head's office. "In mid-1962," recalled Robert Hinerfeld, who worked on organized crime for the Los Angeles U.S. attorney, "I was reading reports prepared by Harold Dodge, the local FBI agent assigned to cover Johnny Roselli. And there were some things in these reports that blew my mind. Every month Dodge would note conversations between Judith Campbell and Roselli in her Beverly Hills apartment. Roselli was also said to have spent time at Frank Sinatra's home in Palm Springs.

"The agents went to the local telephone company to gather the telephone slips for the interstate calls she had made, and there were several made to a number in Washington, D.C. The Washington field office then went to its local phone company to find out whose number it was, and it turned out to be the White House! They were person-to-person calls, and the person called was none other than Evelyn Lincoln. At the time we didn't know who she was, but the Washington field officer identified her: she was the personal secretary of the president of the United States. Whoa! That produced a lot of conversation in the U.S. attorney's office because we assumed this had been passed to Bob, and that Bob had talked to the president. And we both knew that now Hoover really had both the Kennedys by the balls."

Not long after RFK became attorney general, he decided to place a tap on J. Edgar Hoover's telephone lines. Discovering the tap, Hoover had several of his agents wire the attorney general's telephone. During an April 1961 conference between the two men, they began to argue, each accusing the other of illegal interoffice wiretapping. Courtney Evans, attending the meeting, recalled having to step between them to avoid an actual fistfight. Less than a year later, Hoover railed to Richard Nixon about "that sneaky little son of a bitch" who had been installed as his boss. Bobby held his tongue on the subject of Hoover for most of his tenure as attorney general, but by 1964 he was telling reporters that he considered the FBI chief to be "dangerous," "senile" and "rather a psycho."

Bobby entered the Justice Department with a "Hit List," and Hoover

---

* An FBI memo dated 8/17/62, from Courtney Evans to Hoover, confirms that "the Attorney General" had been "made aware" of JFK's relationship with Campbell. No doubt, however, Bobby knew of the liaison long before the FBI informed him.

was on it. For his part, Hoover soon created a "Hate List"—Martin Luther King and Robert F. Kennedy shared top billing.*

Jimmy Hoffa had an interest in two elections held in 1960. The first, in July, turned out well for him—he was reelected to the presidency of the International Brotherhood of Teamsters. The second, in November, did not—he had supported Richard Nixon for the presidency of the United States, and the Republican's loss caused the union chief trouble almost before the last campaign balloons had been popped.

That summer, Attorney General William Rogers, acting on information initially developed by Bobby and the rackets committee, had moved to indict Hoffa on charges of mail fraud involving half a million of his home local's funds and a Florida land development project in which he owned a 45 percent option. But while a Justice Department lawyer was in the midst of presenting evidence to a Florida grand jury, Rogers decided to postpone the case, most likely due to pressure from Vice President Nixon, who valued Teamsters support as a counterweight to John Kennedy's endorsement by most other unions. Nixon's clout—and Hoffa's luck—ran out after Election Day, however, and Rogers brought the indictment by month's end.

After RFK gave up his Senate post in the fall of 1959, he and Hoffa continued to trade jabs. Upon finishing *The Enemy Within*, the author sent the book's star character a signed copy: "To Jimmy," the inscription read. "I'm sending you this book so you won't have to use union funds to buy one. Bobby." In May 1960, following the West Virginia primary, Hoffa filed suit in federal court against Bobby, Jack Paar and the National Broadcasting Company over comments the campaign manager had made during an appearance on *The Tonight Show*. (Hoffa never pursued the case, and it was dismissed two years later.)

Once in office, Robert Kennedy turned his words into deeds, establishing a labor rackets task force and placing it under the command of Walter Sheridan. "Sheridan was one of those dedicated detectives who

*The animosity between RFK and Hoover only increased over time. FBI files reveal that on June 5, 1963, Hoover sent RFK a memo suggesting that the FBI had developed information suggesting that in late 1960 RFK had paid a Palm Beach socialite, Alicia Purdum Clark, $500,000 in settlement of a breach-of-promise suit which dated to 1951. According to Hoover's memo, John F. Kennedy had married Clark in 1951 (before he married Jackie) and the pay-off represented hush money. "This story is so old," an irate RFK wrote back to Hoover, "that it's grown whiskers. There was no marriage, no lawsuit, and no monies were ever paid." Although journalists continue to write about the possibility of this early JFK marriage, the rumor has never been proved.

never gave up," recalled Hoffa associate Joe Konowe. "He kept hammering away. You'd see him everywhere. He could be so active, sometimes I thought he didn't sleep." Within months, the unit—known in the department as the Get Hoffa Squad—had gathered steam, employing lawyers, investigators, FBI agents. Sheridan, himself a onetime G-man, used his many contacts in the FBI to advance his efforts; before RFK and Sheridan were done, they managed to seat some thirteen grand juries in an effort to destroy Hoffa.

Robert Kennedy needed the FBI's help in his pursuit of the foe, but over a July weekend in 1961 at Hickory Hill he held a series of anti-Hoffa strategy meetings to which no Bureau personnel had been invited. Back in the office the following week, after terming his failure to include any FBI representatives in the conferences "strictly an oversight," RFK told Courtney Evans that the assembled officials had agreed upon the need for intensive physical surveillance of the Teamster president and five of his associates. Kennedy's order was carried out, but not without grumbling: "OK," the director wrote dyspeptically at the end of Evans's memo on the subject, "but it is surely a great drain on manpower and money."

"The Attorney General," Evans wrote in a follow-up memo to the FBI director, "recognizes that it is practically a physical impossibility to maintain continuous protracted surveillances of an individual without the surveillance becoming known." It didn't take Jimmy Hoffa long to catch on. In September, stuck with three of his aides in a Chicago traffic jam, the union boss stormed out of his car and began sticking his head in the windows of surrounding vehicles. "In a loud, boisterous, swearing and threatening manner," the Chicago FBI office informed headquarters, "Hoffa uttered a verbal and obscene tirade against the police, the FBI and the attorney general and remarked he may seek injunction against both the police department and FBI for harassing him." One driver Hoffa confronted was, in fact, Special Agent A. Bucar—one of several operatives on the scene—who managed to avoid identifying himself. The members of the surveillance team noted that the union leader appeared "visibly shaken, highly excited, and emotional as he returned to his car and was driven off."

The tantrum did not go unnoticed by Hoffa's nemesis. Meeting with Evans four days after the incident, RFK, while stating that he did not want Hoffa to suppose the attorney general could be intimidated, understood that he himself faced an FBI unenthusiastic about his project—during the discussion, recalled Evans, the operation's cost "was casually mentioned." Bobby defended the undertaking by claiming that it had "served a very definite purpose" but had to admit that "the amount of information gained had not been large." He then ordered that the surveillance be reduced to one day a week; by May of 1962, having yielded little useful intelligence, it was called off entirely.

The intensive surveillance of Hoffa had lasted only two months, but the labor chief's complaints of harassment intensified through the years of the Kennedy administration. He became convinced that the FBI, at Bobby's behest, followed his every move. "They were on top of my father day and night," said James Hoffa. "They tapped his telephone, opened his mail, raided his home and office, audited his taxes. At one point, they stole union records and then accused the teamsters of destroying them." The full extent to which the civil liberties of Hoffa were compromised in the course of Bobby's holy war may never be completely known, but Jimmy Hoffa was on edge. At the Hilton Hotel in Chicago—where, as the FBI discovered, he occupied the three-hundred-dollar-a-day Imperial Suite and slept on the same silk sheets used by the "kings and queens" who usually stayed in the rooms—he was confronted with repeated torment: everywhere he went, someone would have the bellboys page Bobby Kennedy. (Neither Hoffa nor the FBI was able to identify the instigator.) "Apparently," noted the Bureau's memo, "this gets under his skin but the pressure is continuing and whoever is playing this game is hitting the target."

Practical jokes could not irritate Jimmy Hoffa as keenly as indictments, however, and he soon faced a pair. One, brought in Chicago, charged him with milking his union's $300 million Central States Pension Fund for personal gain. Since some of the misappropriated monies were alleged to have gone to bail out the Florida land deal, the earlier charges brought by Rogers were subsumed under this case and the prior proceeding was abandoned.

Nashville was the setting for the second indictment. In 1948, Hoffa had acted to settle a strike against a Detroit trucking firm on terms beneficial to the company. Shortly afterward, his wife and the wife of an associate signed incorporation papers in Tennessee for the Test Fleet Corporation, a truck-leasing outfit that, thanks to fat contracts with the same Detroit trucking firm, would over time net Mr. and Mrs. Hoffa hundreds of thousands of dollars. The Justice Department, bringing to conclusion an investigation begun during Bobby's term at the McClellan committee, charged that the relationship between the two companies amounted to a payoff for the labor leader's help with the strike, thus violating the Taft-Hartley Act. The case illustrated RFK's utter determination to nail Hoffa, for the alleged wrongdoing didn't so much as constitute a felony. "Never in history," wrote Victor Navasky in *Kennedy*

Justice, "had the government devoted so much money, manpower and top level brainpower to a misdemeanor case."

As the Nashville trial got underway in October 1962, the odds seemed to favor Bobby and the Get Hoffa Squad. "When Sheridan had E. G. Partin released from jail, the government had a witness," said Joe Konowe. "Partin, a fellow Teamster, faced all sorts of charges—kidnapping, murder, robbery, rape. They turned him and he became the number one informant against Jimmy." Partin, putting on an Oscar-winning performance, became attached to Hoffa's staff during the latter's trial. "Jimmy used Partin as a sort of guard outside the hotel quarters we occupied in Nashville. It was his job to keep people out who didn't belong there. And all the time he was working for Kennedy and Kennedy's people."

The dispatches Partin passed to his new friends included an assertion that Hoffa had asked the informant what he knew of plastic explosives— the labor leader, Partin maintained, wanted to do away with the attorney general. Neither Sheridan nor RFK believed Partin, despite the fact that the former jailbird had just passed a polygraph test.

Whether or not Partin's tale rang true, Jimmy Hoffa never made an attempt on Robert Kennedy's life. Moreover, as Joe Konowe recalled, he passed up a golden opportunity to strike his rival below the belt: "Jimmy didn't seem interested in attacking Bobby's personal life. One day, a couple of gentlemen came to the office claiming they had hotel and airline bills, as well as other articles, that proved Bobby had a liaison going with a certain female. They wanted ten thousand dollars for the papers. I told them to stay put and I went back into Jimmy's office and told him about this material. I said it could be very effective against Bobby. He said, 'Kick their asses out of the building.' He wouldn't go that route. There was a tacit understanding between Bobby and Jimmy that neither one would bring the other's wife into the dispute. So, just as Josephine Hoffa was never subpoenaed, Ethel Kennedy would never see this kind of thing."

If sexual scandal was essentially out of bounds, governmental scandal was not, and Jimmy Hoffa joined forces with RFK's two other prime enemies in an attempt to provoke an investigation into the attorney general's prosecutorial practices. Intending to discredit Bobby among his liberal allies, J. Edgar Hoover had assembled supplementary files that would paint the nation's top law-enforcement officer as a menace to the Bill of Rights. To keep himself at a distance from the attack, Hoover enlisted Roy Cohn, a close contact since the early fifties, when the director had generously shared intelligence with the McCarthy committee. Cohn telephoned Congressman Cornelius Gallagher, a New Jersey Dem-

ocrat known as a watchful civil libertarian, to arrange a visit to the lawmaker by another conspirator, Sidney Zagri, who earned his living as
Washington's chief lobbyist for the Teamsters. Zagri, said Cohn, would
provide data that "could become the basis for a whole series of hearings."

After taking a night to examine the contents of Zagri's briefcase, Gallagher wanted no part in the plot. Cohn argued that the congressman
could make two important friends if he went ahead: "Mr. Hoover will
consider it a very personal favor if you chair these hearings. He's sick and
tired of the bullshit of Bobby Kennedy." And, "Hoffa—Jimmy—will be
ever so grateful to you, because of what Bobby's doing to him; they'll
support you in any way they can, and they'll even hire your law firm for
$100,000 a year." But Gallagher wouldn't budge: "Who would be silly
enough to get involved in this goddamn war between Bobby and Hoover?" To the congressman, Cohn's motive was clear: "Roy, I think this is
all part of your hard-on for Bobby." In the end, nothing came of Hoover's
supplementary files on RFK, although Roy Cohn, who had also befriended Jimmy Hoffa, gave the Teamster copies of everything.

"Hoffa and I would occasionally dine together in New York," noted
Cohn. "I asked Hoover if I could give Hoffa the RFK files. 'Go ahead,'
he said. When I presented them, Hoffa asked, 'What do I do with them?'
'I don't know,' I responded. 'Save them for a rainy day.'"

The Nashville trial terminated in a hung jury, 7–5 for acquittal. But
as he declared a mistrial, the judge called for an investigation into
whether Hoffa's side had tampered with the panel. When RFK's staff
met to consider bringing such charges, only Ramsey Clark raised a constitutional issue, wondering aloud if the union boss's right to counsel had
been compromised by Partin's "infiltration of the defense."

"I voiced the opinion that it might not be worthwhile going after
Hoffa again at this point, that there would be other opportunities," said
Clark. "But Bobby was adamant—whatever the cost, whatever it took, he
wanted to get Hoffa. 'I'm going after that bastard,' he said." The attorney
general decided to prosecute.

Throughout his legal troubles, Jimmy Hoffa had the support of many
Americans, including some who might have seemed the last people likely
to take the side of a labor leader who had never hidden his delight in
defying authority. "Deans of law schools throughout the country helped
Jimmy," said Joe Konowe. "They sent him information from cases that
had already been adjudicated, and during the trial Jimmy would spend a
good portion of each night reading those transcripts. The next morning,
when his lawyers assembled, he would say, 'How come nobody said anything about *Gray v. United States*, blah, blah, blah?' And they just

dropped dead. 'Where did you hear that, Jimmy? Where did that come from?' It was something sent him by some law school professor. Jimmy had become the underdog in this fight and he gained a lot of sympathy from various members of the legal profession."

Moved to Chattanooga at the request of the defense, the jury-tampering trial began in January 1964. In March, largely on the strength of testimony given by E. G. Partin, Jimmy Hoffa was convicted and sentenced to eight years in federal prison. Three months later, a federal jury in Chicago found him guilty of diverting a million dollars from union pension funds to his own use. He received a five-year sentence. After more than seven years of concentrated effort, Robert Kennedy had finally managed to get Jimmy Hoffa.

H offa was not ready to submit. His attorneys based their host of appeals on the use of Partin as informant and on other purported abuses of prosecutorial power. Hoffa intimate Charles "Chuckie" O'Brian summarized the government misconduct that, according to the labor chief's camp, occurred during the Chattanooga trial: "We uncovered the FBI's surveillance of our attorneys, the illegal wiretapping of our telephones and the bugging of our conference rooms. We even brought forth documented evidence showing the jury had been mishandled by the U.S. marshals. We had proof of the marshals wiretapping the actual jury deliberations as well as affidavits and sworn testimonies that the same marshals furnished alcoholic beverages and prostitutes to the jurors. The government had literally broken almost every law in America."

Even a hearing before the Supreme Court—and even a stinging rebuke of the government issued by Chief Justice Earl Warren in dissent—could not save Jimmy Hoffa from prison. On March 7, 1967, he entered the federal penitentiary in Lewisburg, Pennsylvania.

"Going to visit my father in jail was like going to visit a caged lion," recalled James Hoffa. Jimmy Hoffa spent much of his time stuffing mattresses in a prison factory. The rest he spent attending to union affairs, for he remained Teamsters president until June of 1971, when he gave up the office to Frank Fitzsimmons. Six months later, on Christmas Eve, Richard Nixon granted clemency to his onetime backer, and Jimmy Hoffa went free.*

---

* FBI records reveal that in 1968, while running for president, Nixon received campaign contributions from Teamster officials in exchange for Jimmy Hoffa's eventual pardon. RFK received a similar bribe offer but declined, stating that "I'd rather see Hoffa fry in the electric chair."

Fitzsimmons had taken over his mentor's job on a "caretaker" basis, but Hoffa's commutation order stipulated that he be barred from union activity of any kind until March 1980. "Fitzsimmons double-crossed my father," insisted James Hoffa. "He gave him lip service, but he wanted to be the new union president himself. Nixon tried to ensure the continuing support of the Teamsters rank and file by letting my father out, but he also wanted to do a favor for Fitzsimmons since he seemed to represent new power in the union. That's why the deal was struck."

Following his release, Jimmy Hoffa traveled the country speaking on behalf of prison reform. But his aim was always to regain control of his Teamsters. His efforts toward that end are believed to be the reason behind his disappearance when he was traveling on July 30, 1975, to a meeting with Detroit mobster Anthony "Tony Jack" Giacalone.

Robert Kennedy had been dead seven years when someone managed once again to get Jimmy Hoffa, this time for good.

15

SEX

This administration is going to do for sex what the last one did for golf.

—Theodore Sorensen

I'd rather have a president or an attorney general who does it to a woman than to the country.

—Marilyn Monroe

Young agents newly assigned to President Kennedy simply couldn't believe what they were seeing," recalled Marty Venker, a Secret Service operative posted at the White House, "though they quickly learned to keep their comments to themselves. Kennedy enjoyed having them around. They not only procured for him but partied with him. They were young, handsome, well-educated fellows who enjoyed women and drinking and drugs. This was the James Bond era, and Kennedy was intrigued by the whole mystique of the Secret Service. He identified with us and knew we would never betray him. There was an unspoken agreement within the agency that went something like, 'You protect my ass and I'll protect yours.' They weren't going to talk about his sexual proclivities because they were doing more or less the same thing. That's not to say they didn't wonder about his behavior. After all, he was president of the United States. They couldn't fathom that this sort of thing was actually going on in the White House. They'd say, 'God damn, people are going to find out about this.' But nobody dreamed of talking or going to the press. To do so would have been to betray not only the president but the agency. There would have been an immediate closing of ranks. Any agent who talked would have been off the detail by sundown, and, since it was the plum detail, nobody talked. And had an agent talked, every other agent would have clammed up or denied the stories, which by the way also included Bobby and Ted Kennedy."

As active as the sex lives of Joseph Kennedy's sons had been during the 1950s, the heights of authority presented new opportunities for them to satisfy their libidinal urges. But for the ambassador himself, whose example and teachings had guided his male offspring to the unfettered pursuit of both power and pleasure, the sixties meant an end to his life as a man of affairs (in all senses of the word).

On December 19, 1961, the old man fell ill during a round of golf in Palm Beach. By the time his niece Ann Gargan was able to rush him to the hospital, his right arm and leg and the right side of his face had begun to show signs of paralysis and his speech had begun to thicken. Doctors diagnosed an intracranial thrombosis, a stroke.

Jack and Bobby flew to Florida at once. After their father survived a bout of pneumonia, he returned home to begin the long period of invalidism that would conclude his life. Constant companions during those years would be his devoted niece Ann Gargan; his nurse, Rita Dallas; and his old pal Morton Downey.

"The most frustrating day I ever spent was when I visited Joe Kennedy in Palm Beach after his stroke," remembered George Smathers. "It was hell to watch him try to tell Jack what to do. He couldn't make himself understood. His face got beet red and he would just go 'arrgh,' instead of getting the words out." The only words Joe was able to enunciate clearly were "no" and "shit," although "no" often seemed to mean "yes." JFK, accustomed to hearing his father's advice, would simply nod and say, "Thanks, Dad, I'll take care of it. I'll do it your way." When Joe was brought to the White House, Jackie would wipe the drool from his mouth during meals.

Marty Venker: "Being with John F. Kennedy was like attending a traveling fraternity party. It was always party, party, party. There was this feeling that nothing could ever go wrong. You boarded Air Force One and you were in another world. The plane, which Jackie decorated, was as plush as a mansion. You asked for a barbecued steak and you were served a barbecued steak. It wasn't warmed-over airplane food; it was barbecued before your eyes—steaks three inches thick! The president had his own bedroom facilities where he often entertained women when Jackie wasn't aboard. I was told Jackie was bored by the whole White House experience and enjoyed going off on her own. And of course Kennedy encouraged her to go so he could party."

While her husband explored pleasures of the flesh, Jacqueline Kennedy often indulged in delights of a more material nature, unleashing shopping binges that consumed tens of thousands of dollars spent on jewelry, clothes, antiques. But her deepest consolation came when Jack gave her the funds to build "Wexford," her own weekend retreat in Atoka, Virginia. The land for Wexford was sold to the Kennedys for a pittance by Paul and Bunny Mellon, who carved the parcel out of their own huge estate. The Mellons did Jackie another favor: they allowed her to board her horses at their stables until she built facilities of her own. Friends of the first lady wondered why she preferred the rolling hills of central Virginia to the sandy beaches of Hyannis Port. "I need a place where I can go to be alone," she replied.

Marty Venker: "On arriving at hotels on presidential trips, the president would immediately conduct two meetings, one of a political nature with his chief of staff, the other with the head of the Secret Service detail, usually the advance agent who had been in that particular city or country for at least two weeks prior to the president's arrival. So there were two orders of business: political and social. Kennedy invariably met with the advance agent first, which provides some indication of his personal priorities. He didn't want to know about security but about broads. The agent was supposed to set up dates for the president. If he was new to the job and unaware of this fact, Kennedy let him know pretty quickly. He'd say something to the effect of 'You've been here two weeks already and still don't have any broads lined up for me? You guys get all the broads you want. How about doing something for your commander in chief?' It was said in a semijocular vein, but he meant it. Those in the know knew enough to have the broads lined up for him. Naturally every local beauty wanted to fuck the president. It was her patriotic duty. If we were on foreign soil, they did it for the adventure or novelty of the experience. Think how much fun they had telling their friends they'd just been laid by the president of the United States.

"Bobby Kennedy became quite alarmed about all this womanizing. Of course he engaged in his own extracurricular activities, but he feared that his brother's affairs would bring down the entire administration. He warned JFK to exercise greater prudence."

The officers sworn to protect the president's life were far from his only procurers of women. Jack's British-born brother-in-law, as talented at the art of the party as he was unimpressive at the art of the cinema, applied himself to the provision of a steady stream of companions to feed Jack's appetite for variety. Peter Lawford usually dug up unknown starlets or high-priced call girls, but occasionally he struck gold with a referral that tickled the president's fascination with celebrity. Then second on Hollywood's ranking of sex symbols only to another Lawford-to-JFK connection (Marilyn Monroe), Jayne Mansfield would become one of Jack's most prized conquests. "Jayne looked like a dumb blonde but was by no means stupid," remarked Lawford. "There were three meetings that I know of—one in Beverly Hills, one in Malibu, one in Palm Springs. Jayne, whose marriage to Mickey Hargitay was floundering during this period, used to call Jack 'Mr. K.' Jack spoke of her sexual prowess. She had the best body in Hollywood, long legs, large firm breasts and a minuscule waistline.

"The time they met in Palm Springs Jayne was pregnant with Maria, her fourth child, and Jack wasn't aware of it until they got together. She was visibly pregnant. Her condition apparently turned him on, which frankly surprised me."

John Kennedy was "mechanized and cold," said New York party girl Leslie Devereux, another Lawford find, "with hard glazed eyes and a high-powered smile.* Peter Lawford never explained the situation, just gave me an address and told me to meet him there. It turned out to be the Hotel Carlyle. He and I went upstairs together to a penthouse duplex and there stood the president of the United States. He smiled and said, 'All right, Peter. Disappear.'

"I saw him four or five times at the Carlyle. It was all pretty standard sex at first, later it got more kinky. I'd been with a number of powerful politicians and one thing they always liked was mild S and M. So we did a little of that—I tied his hands and feet to the bedposts, blindfolded him and teased him first with a feather and then with my fingernails. He seemed to enjoy it. He then suggested I see his brother, the attorney general. I refused because I'd heard he was an out-and-out sadist."

"Bobby was more selective than Jack," observed Abe Hirschfeld, a New York real-estate developer who contributed to Kennedy campaigns. "He was more discreet, too."

Although the two brothers' sexual preferences were not identical—RFK was not quite as voracious as Jack and his affairs on the average

---

*Assessments of JFK's sexual persona varied widely. Gunilla Von Post, a stunning twenty-one-year-old Swedish aristocrat who had a fling with Kennedy in 1953 and then wrote about it in 1997 (*Love Jack*), found him "utterly sweet, gentle and charming."

lasted longer—their romantic misadventures sometimes had a common thread. "In 1963 Jayne Mansfield was making a movie in Germany with European singing star Freddy Quinn," remembered Ray Strait, Mansfield's press agent. "Her then boyfriend, Nelson Sardelli, was with her, as well as her two young boys. [Sardelli, who was married at the time, had fathered one of the boys, but both were raised by Jayne and her husband, Mickey Hargitay.] The boys were so sweet that I agreed to stay with them in Germany while Jayne left for Washington, where she was to open her nightclub act on the Fourth of July at the Casino Royal.

"Paul Blaine, Jayne's road manager, told me what happened in D.C. On several nights, Robert Kennedy came to see the show. Mickey was there with Jayne, even though they weren't getting along at all at that point, so Bobby had to make a delicate arrangement to see her. Paul became the emissary between the two, and after some back and forth he offered the use of a suite of rooms that he had at a hotel around the corner. The attorney general had sex with Jayne in the bedroom one night while Paul sat in the living room watching a Western on TV. It's noteworthy that JFK had likewise been with Jayne."

Marty Venker: "The president's private parties when held at the White House usually took place in and around the swimming pool. Because of his bad back, the pool was heated to more than ninety degrees Fahrenheit. His father had commissioned French artist Bernard Lamotte to paint a mural of the harbor of St. Croix for the swimming pool. They installed stereo speakers for music and a special lighting mechanism. One flip of the switch and it was high noon at St. Croix. Another flip and it was midnight with the moon and stars shining in the darkened ceiling above. A door to the pool had been changed from clear to frosted glass to prevent anyone from spying on the president. The parties often involved Kennedy and two or three women. A pitcher of daiquiris would be prepared in anticipation and chilled in a portable refrigerator; little Vienna sausages wrapped in bacon would be kept in a portable heater. The waiters and household staff would either be dismissed for the day or told to stay away from the swimming pool area. When Jackie was away, riding the elevator could be hazardous to one's health. The kennel keeper was on his way to the basement one evening. Just as the elevator door opened, a naked blonde office girl came running out of the lift, practically bowled him over, then stopped and asked if he knew where she could find the president. But even among the staff of the White House there was a conspiracy of silence to protect Kennedy and keep Jackie from divining his secrets.

"The president would keep tabs on his wife by having his Secret Service agent maintain radio contact with Jackie's agent. In this way, he always knew her whereabouts. He would be partying in the pool, and Jackie would be landing at Andrews Air Force Base. Kennedy and the girls would keep at it until the last possible moment when Jackie entered the White House grounds. Naked bodies scattered every which way. An agent or usher rushed in gathering up the drinks and highball glasses and any other telltale evidence. Kennedy would remain in the swimming pool presumably doing his back exercises, while the women would be ushered out of the White House through the back door."

Bobby participated in at least some of the notorious swimming pool parties with Jack," maintained Peter Jay Sharp, a real estate executive who in 1967 bought the Carlyle Hotel. "I was quite friendly in the early 1960s with a girl who used to go down to see Bobby at the White House and also at the Department of Justice, and she reported a kind of orgy in the White House swimming pool with both brothers present.

"I didn't own the Carlyle when John Kennedy was president, but I knew him and visited him at the hotel a number of times. Once, I went up to the family's penthouse suite and found a Secret Service guard in front of the door. He ushered me inside and there was Jack in one of the beds with a blonde and Bobby on the living-room floor with a brunette. I was actually looking for Teddy, but Robert told me he was in the bathroom with another girl. I didn't want to bother Ted, but as I was leaving I asked Bob to tell him to call me when he was finished. Bobby carried on this conversation without missing a beat with his girl, who wasn't paying any attention at all to me. She was concentrating on Bobby—the whole time, she had a finger up his anus.

"A bit later I had a gold plaque made up to commemorate the afternoon; it read, 'RFK Came Here.' I was friendly with the people who then owned the hotel, and they mounted it on the wall of the penthouse suite. The Carlyle was the Kennedy playpen in New York.

"I don't know how much of Bobby's activities Ethel knew or cared about. I was always under the impression that all the Kennedy women, in-laws and otherwise, were like Rose—once they had their children they didn't care what their husbands did so long as it didn't happen in front of their noses, though on several occasions it did."

Not all of Peter Lawford's efforts pleased the president. At one intimate White House dinner party—wives uninvited—Jack turned to an attractive young woman who had arrived with the actor. "What do you do for a living?" asked the president. "I work for Senator Goldwater," she answered.

The promising warmth of the evening instantly turned to chill and the pretty Republican soon found herself in a taxicab leaving the mansion. "For God's sake, Peter!" JFK thundered once the two men were alone. "She works for *Barry Goldwater*! He'll probably be my opponent in 1964! Do you know what he could do with information like that? Don't you find out who people work for before you bring them up here? *Jesus!*"

"When Bobby was going with girls," said Abe Hirschfeld, "it was almost like they were second or third wives. He was loyal to them."

The love of Robert Kennedy's extramarital life may well have been an extremely attractive brunette he met at a Manhattan cocktail party in early 1961. Originally from Norway, Carol Bjorkman wrote a personalities column for *Women's Wear Daily*. "She was not only chic but very bright," remarked Mimi Strong, then society editor of the *World Telegram and Sun*. "She exercised a great deal of influence in the world of fashion."

During much of their year and a half together Bjorkman and Bobby saw each other mostly at the Carlyle. But the attorney general of the United States and his mistress didn't shun all public outings. On several occasions, Hirschfeld accompanied the couple to theaters and restaurants. And Patricia Seaton, later Peter Lawford's fourth and final wife, recalled some common New York gossip of the time: "Bobby used to pick her up at her Madison Avenue hairdresser. He always seemed impatient. 'When are you going to be ready?' he'd say. 'When are you going to be done?'"

Robert Kennedy is purported to have asked Carol Bjorkman to marry him. He would leave Ethel, he promised. She turned him down.

In mid 1961, Robert Kennedy met twenty-six-year-old actress Lee Remick at a Justice Department dinner party in Washington, D.C. The next time he traveled to Los Angeles, Bobby asked Peter Lawford to set up another meeting with Lee. Lawford, who subsequently also became intimately involved with Lee, did more than schedule a meeting—he arranged for RFK and Remick to spend a weekend together at a friend's secluded home in Malibu. The actress evidently fell for Bobby, despite being married at the time to producer-director Bill Colleran, with whom she had two young children. Even after she and Peter Lawford became lovers, she continued to pursue Bobby, whose high energy and take-charge attitude attracted her. RFK and Lee Remick spent a second weekend in each other's company early in 1962, on this occasion at the home of a Kennedy associate in Palm Beach.

"**I** visited the president twice at the White House," continued call girl Leslie Devereux, "the first time for only fifteen minutes in a small room off the Oval Office. His secretaries didn't so much as blink when they saw me. They showed me in and out as naturally as they would the secretary of state.

"On my second visit, I met him upstairs in the family living quarters. A Secret Service agent ushered me into a dark and somber room filled with heavy wood furniture, and said, 'Make yourself comfortable, he'll be with you shortly.' He motioned to an enormous, intricately carved rosewood bed. 'That's where Abraham Lincoln slept,' he said. 'You mean,' I asked, 'I'm to lie down on *that,* on Abraham Lincoln's bed?' 'Lady,' he retorted, 'it's the best we've got.'

"Soon the door opened and a white-gloved butler brought champagne on a silver tray. Then the president appeared and we spent several hours together. I told him it seemed sacrilegious to violate Abraham Lincoln's bed. He laughed and told me about the White House legend that when you made a wish on the Lincoln bed it always came true. 'Make a wish,' I said. He closed his eyes and I mounted him. 'See,' he said, 'it never fails.' "

The romantic liaisons of the youngest Kennedy brother, like those of his elders, ranged in duration from hours to years. One of his longest-lasting alliances involved Helga Wagner, an Austrian-born blonde who operated a shop on ritzy Worth Avenue in Palm Beach selling high-priced jewelry made from seashells. "Whenever Helga traveled," columnist Doris Lilly noted, "she would pack in her suitcase—along with her clothes and underwear and stockings and so on—letters, photographs and telegrams from Teddy. Many of the pictures were of the two of them together. They posed for pictures, those idiots. I saw many snapshots of them." Ted even allowed Wagner to conduct showings of her jewelry at a home he owned in Virginia.

Bobby may have been discreet in his affairs; Ted was anything but. He and Wagner once spent three months together vacationing in Switzerland, making no effort to hide the escapade from his wife, Joan, whose drinking problem intensified as a result. Foreign travel was not the only thing he made little effort to conceal. "I once stayed at a friend's apartment at the Palm Bay Club in Miami," Doris Lilly continued. "All the flats there had terraces overlooking the bay. One evening, around dusk, I was walking to the clubhouse to have dinner when out onto one of the terraces walked Ted Kennedy, stark naked, his little wangle dangling in the breeze. I looked right at him and couldn't believe my eyes. He was staying in a suite there with Helga, and when he saw me he flashed one of those big, toothy Kennedy grins.

"Ted started seeing Helga while Jack was president, and the affair lasted quite a few years. When Chappaquiddick happened, the first person Ted called was Helga."

When a well-known reporter decided to work on a profile of the president, he received an invitation to spend a weekend at Camp David. The generous head of state also invited the newsman's family and, of course, the attractive young woman who served as his children's baby-sitter. Naturally observant, the journalist soon realized that the president and the governess were doing more together at the retreat than admiring the verdant countryside. The newsman never reported the affair, nor did he publish the president's new dress code for the heated Camp David pool: no swimsuits allowed. What he could not report, because he never found out about it, was that the young baby-sitter became pregnant by the president and flew to Puerto Rico for an abortion, which had been paid for by the Kennedys.*

Italian journalist Benno (Gilbert) Graziani, a friend of Jackie Kennedy's and a suitor of her sister, Lee Radziwill, visited the executive mansion as the guest of the first lady. "While Jackie was showing Benno around the White House," said yellow journalist Francis Lara, "she suddenly opened the door to an office in which two young women were seated. Jackie turned to Benno and said, 'Those two are my husband's lovers.'"

The pair were well known to the president's brother Bobby, who referred to them as Fiddle and Faddle. Formerly college roommates, Priscila Weir (Fiddle) and Jill Cowan (Faddle) joined on JFK's campaign drive as pollsters, then went to work at the White House, the former as an aide to Evelyn Lincoln, the latter assisting Pierre Salinger.

---

*Other reports of abortions necessitated by JFK's womanizing have circulated, most notable among them the claim made by Judith Campbell Exner in the January 1997 issue of *Vanity Fair*. According to Exner's account, she was impregnated by JFK in December 1962, the last time they slept together. Upon discovering her condition some weeks later she telephoned the president, who told her she could keep the baby if she wanted to. "We can arrange it," he said. "That's an absolute impossibility because of who you are," Exner responded. "We'd never get away with it!" JFK then asked her to call Sam Giancana to set up the abortion, which she underwent at Chicago's Grant Hospital.

Jackie's response to her husband's philandering varied according to her moods. Sometimes she sought revenge. "At one particular White House gala," remembered Peter Lawford, "Jackie drank too much champagne, discarded her shoes and danced and flirted with every man in sight. She would throw her head back and laugh, or make eyes at her partner. The ploy evidently worked—Jack took notice; so did the other guests at the White House that night."

At other times she seemed resigned, and on occasion she became almost playful. During a Palm Beach vacation, she took a swim with the Lawfords, then returned to the house only to tell her husband, "You'd better get down there fast. I saw two of them you'd really go for." At a White House dinner party she seated Jack between two of his recent conquests and enjoyed watching him squirm.

Marty Venker: "Everybody knows the one about the White House maid who found a pair of black silk panties in the president's bed. Thinking they belonged to Jackie, she returned them to the first lady. The next time Jackie saw her husband, she handed him the panties and said, 'Here, find out who owns these. They're not my size.'"

"**B**obby was always rather bedazzled by Jackie," said Coates Redman, who worked for the Peace Corps in Washington and was a friend of Ethel's. If RFK never intervened to halt the endless humiliation inflicted on the first lady by her goatish husband, he did defend her honor when he perceived it to be threatened by another man one evening in November 1961.

In throwing a party at the White House to honor Lee Radziwill, Jackie had included among the guests Gore Vidal, stepson to Hugh Auchincloss, the sisters' stepfather. After several visits to the well-stocked bar, Vidal had a quiet conversation with Janet Auchincloss, Jackie and Lee's mother, then moved on to more vociferous exchanges with Lem Billings and Robert Kennedy.

Bobby and Vidal parted, but they came together again when the attorney general noticed the writer crouching next to Jackie, balancing himself by resting his arm on her shoulder. RFK approached them and wordlessly removed the arm. He began to walk away but stopped when Vidal rose and barked, "Never do anything like that to me again." Bobby turned away but Vidal kept after him: "I have always thought that you were a goddamned impertinent son of a bitch." At that, RFK stood his ground. "Why don't you go fuck yourself?" he snapped. Vidal: "If that is your level of dialogue, I can only respond by saying: 'Drop dead!'" Saying nothing more, Bobby turned and strode toward the opposite side of the room.

Another partygoer, Arthur Schlesinger, was called in to remedy the situation. Jackie had asked the historian to see Vidal back to his house. With the help of John Kenneth Galbraith and George Plimpton, Schlesinger complied. Accompanied by his three new-found companions, Vidal was escorted out of the White House and driven off into the night.

I n the Washington of the early 1960s, reporters treated knowledge of JFK's sexual high jinks as privileged information to be kept within their cozy men's club; almost nothing was written or broadcast to dispel the popular image of the peaceful, patriotic first family—the glamorous couple as enthralled by each other as they were by the music of Pablo Casals, the youthful husband and wife strolling the beach with two small children in tow. While not all reporters were privy to the truth, many cooperated in protecting the illusion. *Look* feature photographer Stanley Tretick recalled a conversation he once had with Clark Mollenhoff, who wrote for the same publication: "Clark used to tell me to document the girls JFK was sneaking into the White House, and I said how the hell am I supposed to do that? 'Just go to the southwest gate and stand around and watch those delivery vans come and go,' he said. I told him that if the girls were going in that door they were being smuggled in with the baked goods and floral wreaths and things like that. He implied they were."

Ned Kenworthy, a Washington correspondent for the *New York Times,* once spotted Dave Powers walking up the White House stairs toward the president's private quarters with a young woman no more than twenty years of age. The moment Powers noticed the reporter he pointed to a portrait on the wall and loudly proclaimed, "This painting was given to the White House by James Madison." Although Kenworthy was hardly fooled by the impromptu lesson in art history, the story, like many others on the subject uncovered by the *Times,* was never printed.

"Press manipulation was commonplace during the Kennedy years," commented Phillipe de Bausset, Washington bureau chief for *Paris Match.* "The JFK administration was one huge public relations show. I used to think how amazed the country would be to find out that Jacqueline Kennedy, supposedly the most desirable and exciting woman on earth, couldn't satisfy her husband. It wasn't entirely her fault. Kennedy was too intent on enjoying himself. This may not have hindered his ability to run the country, but it didn't help matters either. Had he lived, many of his indiscretions would have become public knowledge. He would not have been reelected. As is, he didn't succeed in carrying out his political agenda. We were prisoners of a myth we helped to create. Professional image makers built an image; journalists bought into the propaganda and were later forced to go along with it."

If John Kennedy's levels of testosterone were ever tested, the results have never been made public. Surely, his libido did not lack natural biochemical foundation. But throughout his administration, both he and his wife would receive a steady diet of mood-altering drugs from an unorthodox New York physician. By her part in the treatments, Jacqueline Kennedy would unwittingly augment her husband's already insatiable hunger for debauchery.

JFK first met Max Jacobson in the fall of 1960, a week after his speech to the Houston ministers and just before his first debate with Richard Nixon. He had been referred to the doctor by two patients: Mark Shaw, a photographer for *Life* then on assignment to take pictures of the first family, and JFK's friend Chuck Spalding. With Jacobson's office cleared of other visitors, the Democratic candidate for president arrived to tell the German-born doctor of the stress and fatigue he was suffering because of the grueling campaign. Jacobson responded that treatment of stress was one of his specialties and picked up a syringe. The injection spread warmth throughout the patient's body. His tension vanished.

Just after the election, Jacobson treated JFK a second time, on this occasion making a house call at Hyannis Port. He did not hear from the president again until May, as Jack and Jackie were preparing to travel to Canada on their first state visit. At this time the doctor was summoned to the Kennedy estate in Palm Beach. There he was informed by the president that since the birth of John Jr. the previous fall, the first lady had suffered bouts of depression coupled with severe headaches. Asking to see the patient, Dr. Jacobson found her in bed nursing a migraine. He gave her a shot that quickly ended the headache and brightened her mood.

Over the next two and a half years, Max Jacobson treated the president and first lady at Palm Beach, Hyannis Port, the White House and the Carlyle. Jack took treatments to ease his nerves and boost his alertness during times of crisis, or sometimes only to relieve the discomfort of a bad back. Jacobson accompanied the first couple around the world, and dosed the commander in chief just before his summit meeting in Vienna with Nikita Khrushchev. From late summer of 1961 to the end of Jack's presidency, the Kennedys availed themselves of Jacobson's healing powers at least once a week. JFK even asked the physician to move into the White House, but he declined, unwilling to give up his other patients.

Max Jacobson, whose office was filled with a jumble of unmarked vials, had contempt for the medical establishment, but his list of patients comprised a virtual who's who of the rich and famous. Politicians like Winston Churchill and Claude Pepper, show-business stellars like Cecil B. DeMille and Greta Garbo, sports personalities like Mickey Mantle and Mel Allen—all relied on "Dr. Feelgood" for his miracle cures. Working eighteen-hour days in a lab coat spattered with blood, he would inject mixtures of placenta and bone, human liver cells, tissue taken from electric eels, even heart cells extracted from a freshly killed elephant. But the main ingredients in the brews he dispensed to Jack and Jackie were amphetamines and steroids. Max Jacobson may have been his own best patient: the injections he administered to himself enabled him often to go without sleep for days at a stretch.

The official White House physician, Janet Travell, tried to discuss amphetamine addiction with the president, but he showed no interest. Nor would Jack listen to Bobby's frequent admonitions. In June 1962 the concerned brother sent four vials of Jacobson's medications to the FBI for analysis. RFK's initial suspicions involved the wrong class of drugs—a Bureau memo notes that the laboratory had been requested to determine "whether narcotics or barbiturates were present"—but technicians eventually discovered the amphetamines and steroids mixed with vegetable oil and water in each tube. Although at least some of the containers were labeled with Dr. Jacobson's name, Bobby did not allow those involved with the testing to know the identity of the patient. After RFK's aide Andrew Oehmann delivered one of the vials to the Bureau, Courtney Evans wrote in a memo that "Oehmann said the Attorney General was anxious about this. He added that the Attorney General had someone with him and Oehmann didn't have the opportunity of asking the Attorney General anything about the bottles of medicine. Oehmann speculates this may have been medicine for the Attorney General's father. He said, however, he is only guessing and reached this conclusion because of the AG's obvious intense personal interest."

Faced with the hostility of RFK and Travell, as well as that of Chuck Spalding, whose opinion of the doctor had changed, Jacobson asked the president if he might cease treating him. "That's out of the question," Jack laughed. Bobby then insisted on sending the medications to the Food and Drug Administration for analysis. Reluctantly, Jack agreed. When the FDA confirmed the FBI's findings of amphetamines and steroids, JFK wasn't concerned. "I don't care if it's horse piss," he told his brother. "It works."

Heavy long-term use of amphetamines has been known to produce memory loss, hallucinations, depression, anxiety, weight loss, paranoia, schizophrenia and hypertension. But the drugs had another effect on John Kennedy. "The combination of steroids and amphetamines no doubt increased Kennedy's sexual drive," said Tom Jacobson, Max's son, who occasionally substituted for his father. Adding artificial chemical stimulus to JFK's naturally monumental sexual metabolism was like putting jet engines on a race car.

Max Jacobson last treated Jack Kennedy on November 15, 1963, in Palm Beach, where the president was preparing for his trip to Texas a week later.

D oris Lilly: "During his brother's presidency, Ted Kennedy took a trip to Europe. One day, finding himself in Antwerp, Belgium, he heard about a dinner party to be given that night by a wealthy couple in honor of the country's king and queen and decided he wanted to attend. Even though the hostess had no desire to have a Kennedy as a guest, she could hardly refuse after the American ambassador called her to request an invitation for the visiting brother of the president.

"They had a grand eighteenth-century house, with Aubusson carpeting on the floors and paintings by old masters on the walls. The mansion abounded with valuable antiques, glittering jewels, polished silver.

"Despite the invitation he'd gone to some trouble to get, Ted didn't show up for dinner. But after everyone had eaten, he arrived, staggering, obviously plastered. With him was a young woman he'd obviously just picked up in the red-light district. She had on a tiny skirt—hardly the kind of thing one wears to meet royalty. They both just stood there, bleary-eyed, swaying to and fro.

"After the hostess hustled the king and queen of Belgium into another room, Teddy and this hooker plopped onto one of the many couches in this large, exquisitely appointed room. As the two of them sat there, thighs touching, with the host and hostess trying to figure out what to do with them, everyone except Ted suddenly realized that liquid was running down this woman's leg onto the beautiful antique sofa. Ted noticed only when the urine, running in a rivulet, wet his own trousers.

"The butler rushed off to find some large towels to try and clean up the mess—she'd really unloaded—but the damage had been done. The hostess resolved never to let a Kennedy into her house again."

P eriodically, the attorney general would travel to Europe. His stated purpose would be to attend to administration business—to discuss defense issues with the French, for example. His actual destination, how-

ever, would not be government offices in Paris, but a boat docked at
Cannes. Bobby and the vessel's owner, buxom blonde actress Romy
Schneider, would sail into the Mediterranean and drop anchor. Following
the custom of the Côte d'Azur, Schneider would remove her bikini top
as the two enjoyed the sun and a bottle of Bordeaux.

D oris Lilly: "One of Steve Smith's most passionate affairs was with Connie Snow, who happened to be the best girlfriend of Teddy's lover
Helga Wagner. Steve and Connie used to have lunch at Lutece in New
York and then go across the street to a sex boutique to buy various adult
toys to spice up the afternoon's lovemaking. In my newspaper column, I
mentioned the shopping habits of the famous Kennedy brother-in-law,
his interest in bondage, male dominance and S and M.

"Soon after the item appeared I encountered Steve Smith at Elaine's
restaurant, on the Upper East Side. I was seated with Lee Guber, the
film and TV executive, and singer Tony Bennett and his wife. Smith was
sitting at a nearby table with some bimbo—not Connie—who had on
white boots and a miniskirt. When he saw me, he rose, came over to our
table and started berating me for writing about him and that kinky sex
shop. He became livid and soon was shouting at the top of his lungs. Lee
Guber just looked at this guy in puzzlement, but Tony Bennett stood up
and said, 'You little piece of Kennedy shit. If you don't shut up, I'm going
to rip your face off.' Smith shut up and sat down pretty quickly after
that."

F rom January 1962 until his death, John Kennedy carried on an affair
with a Washington conceptual artist by the name of Mary Pinchot
Meyer. The pair managed to keep the liaison secret even from Meyer's
sister, Toni Bradlee, wife of Ben Bradlee, executive editor of the *Washington Post.* "I honestly had no idea that Mary was involved with Jack,"
Toni Bradlee said later, after she'd learned of the connection. "And I'm
almost positive Ben knew nothing about it. It came as a shock, though of
course my sister had known Jack since his student days at Choate, and
later when she attended Vassar and he went to Harvard. She was also a
close friend of Jackie's."

Broadcast journalist Blair Clark, who had roomed with JFK at Harvard, remembered a night when he, the Bradlees and Mary Meyer were
all invited to the White House: "Ben Bradlee suggested we all go together and I escort Mary. So I did. There was nothing in the atmosphere
that night to indicate that we were going to a tryst. It was one of those
dancing parties for about a hundred and twenty-five people, mostly

friends. It was a purely social gathering. Yet at a given point during the dancing, Jack and Mary disappeared. They were gone for about half an hour. Inadvertently, I'd served as Jack's 'beard.' "

"She was a free spirit," Toni Bradlee said of her sister, "way ahead of her time." Meyer took it upon herself to free up the spirit of the leader of the Free World. Upon her death, her diary was discovered by her sister, who gave it to James Jesus Angleton, chief of counterintelligence at the CIA.* Angleton, who eventually returned the diary to Toni, spoke of entries he had read that described Meyer's meetings with JFK, "of which there were between thirty and forty during their affair—in the White House, at her studio, in the homes of friends. One of Mary's friends was Timothy Leary, the well-known 'acid head' guru of the 1960s. Mary apparently told Leary that she and a number of other Washington women had concocted a plot to 'turn on' the world's political leaders with pot and acid in order to make them less militaristic and more peace-loving. Leary helped her obtain certain drugs and chemical agents with precisely that end in mind. Later she developed her own source for drugs.

"In July 1962 while visiting the White House, Mary took John F. Kennedy into one of the White House bedrooms, where she produced a small box with six joints in it. They shared one and Kennedy laughingly told her they were having a White House conference on narcotics the following week.

"They smoked two more joints and Kennedy drew his head back and closed his eyes. He refused a fourth joint. 'Suppose the Russians drop a bomb,' he said. He admitted to having done cocaine and hashish, thanks to Peter Lawford. Mary claimed they smoked pot on two other occasions, and on still another occasion they took a mild acid trip together, during which they made love."

F inally tiring of her husband's infidelities and indiscretions, Jean Smith had an affair with an Italian nobleman she met in the south of France.

---

*Mary Pinchot Meyer was murdered at 12:45 P.M. on October 13, 1964, as she strolled along the Chesapeake and Ohio towpath in Georgetown. The crime was never solved.

A homeless black defendant was tried and subsequently acquitted. Evidence in the case suggests that Mary was the shooting victim of either FBI or CIA agents who might have believed that in the course of her relationship with the president, he could have divulged important state secrets. Robert Kennedy, alarmed by the effect that public disclosure of the affair might have on his late brother's reputation and on his own political future, did his utmost to distance himself from the entire matter.

The Italian promised to marry her, and she was ready to walk out on Steve. But the lover then deserted her. Her drinking, long a problem, increased sharply after that disappointment.

"**O**nly once did I see Jackie lose her composure because of another woman," said Lem Billings. "It was over Odile Rodin, the young French wife of Porfirio Rubirosa, the Dominican playboy-ambassador known for his numerous female conquests and marriages to wealthy heiresses Doris Duke and Barbara Hutton. Jack and Rubi had been introduced by gossip columnist Igor Cassini. They had one thing in common: a burning interest in women. They became friends; Jack and Odile became better friends. Rubi, never particularly prone to the vagaries of jealousy, didn't seem to mind; Jackie minded a great deal.

"I couldn't understand what it was about her that infuriated Jackie, unless she simply centered her frustrations on Odile. Jack could be shameless in his sexuality, would simply pull girls' dresses up and so forth. He would corner them at White House dinner parties and ask them to step into the next room away from the noise, where they could hold a 'serious discussion.' Although these women may have been serious, he wasn't. He disappeared with Hjordis Niven, the wife of David Niven, below decks of the presidential yacht for ten minutes or so during his forty-fourth birthday party. One can't draw any hard or fast conclusions from that incident, but it was typical of how he dealt with women."

Coates Redman: "I first met Bobby one summer during the early 1960s at a party on Martha's Vineyard held at a house rented by Art Buchwald and his wife. There were only about three people there who weren't famous—my husband and I, and one or two others. Otherwise, it was the real Kennedy in-crowd: Arthur Schlesinger, the William Styrons, Jules Feiffer, Lillian Hellman, Robert McNamara. I used to be able to name more of them than I can now. It was a very, very glittery group.

"Bobby was there—he just sort of stood by the mantel and held court. Ethel had a short skirt on, one of those cute mini outfits. Jackie had on a pajama suit of white silk crepe, which was *the* thing that year. Jean and Steven Smith were there—she wore a silk crepe outfit like Jackie's, only in jewel green.

"I was trying desperately to make conversation with Dick Goodwin, the Kennedy speechwriter, when Teddy and Jean Smith came down the stairs from where the young people were dancing. Goodwin lit up like a Christmas tree—Ted's appearance meant he wasn't stuck talking to a nobody anymore—and he began joshing Jean and Teddy: '*Wheah* have you two been?' You know, they have those Bostonian accents. 'You've been *upstaiahs*, have you?' They were all kidding, with Jean and Teddy saying, 'Ho, ho, ho, we're having an *affaiah*.' It was really something. The two of them had their arms around each other. And Ted was wearing a pink linen short-sleeve pajama suit. The front was open and he had combed up all his chest hairs.

"Dick Goodwin introduces me—'Senator, Mrs. Smith, this is Mrs. Redman'—very formal, but a bit mocking, too. Now, I was wearing a rather low-cut dress for the evening—my husband thought I was going a little too far, but I told him that with all those people and all those outfits, I wasn't going to be wearing a lily. So Ted looks at me, then leans over and gazes down my front. 'Is *theah* anything down *theah?*' he says. He'd obviously had a lot to drink. I tried to laugh it off. Then Goodwin says, 'Why don't you find out, Ted?' And he drops an ice cube into my dress. 'Go get it, Ted.' So the senator from Massachusetts puts his huge ham hand, his immense hand, down the front of my dress.

"Well, I got wet to the bone, and I fled. I just fled. It was all I could do."

When California restaurateur Peter Fairchild decided to sue his wife, starlet Judy Meredith, for divorce, he hired private eye (and former Los Angeles Police Department officer) Fred Otash to identify her partners in adultery. Otash found that Meredith had consorted with some of the biggest names in show business. But he also learned that one of the actress's admirers was an employee of the federal government. Word of the discovery made its way around Los Angeles, and soon Otash received a telephone call from Johnny Roselli, who wished to meet the investigator. The mafioso was acting, he claimed, "at the request of the attorney general."

The two men conferred at the Brown Derby restaurant in Hollywood. "I'm sitting there with Johnny Roselli," Otash recalled, "and two FBI men are covering the meeting. Roselli says to me, 'Listen, Otash, you've got yourself a problem. You're in trouble. You're fucking around with the White House here. What's this shit that you're gonna name Jack Kennedy as a corespondent in Judy Meredith's divorce case? How can you name the president of the United States in a divorce case?'

"I said to him, 'He fucked my client's wife, that's how! Who the fuck is that cocksucker! Who are you representing, anyway?'

"He said to me, 'I'm representing the Kennedys.' I said, 'Are you kidding me?' I couldn't believe my ears—here's Roselli, a guy who's a fucking *mobster*, intervening on behalf of the White House. I used to have the prick under surveillance. I used to put guys like him in jail, and now he's representing the *president*. I'm sitting there thinking, *Wait a minute. What is this bullshit all about?*"

Several additional meetings took place, at least two with Sam Giancana in attendance. During one such encounter, Roselli asked Otash how they might "straighten things out." "Very simple," Otash replied. "Judy wants a hundred thousand dollars. My client isn't gonna give her shit, because I'm gonna name Frank Sinatra as a guy who was fucking her, Sammy Davis as a guy who was fucking her, Dean Martin as a guy who was fucking her, Jerry Lewis, Jack Kennedy. My client has a real case for divorce, and he ain't giving her a dime. Why don't you have the Rat Pack throw a charity affair, give Judy the money, and the case will go away."

By the scheduled court date for the divorce action, little progress had been made regarding Roselli's concern. Or so thought Otash: "I went into that courtroom, prepared with the documents needed to have the complaint amended and name John Kennedy. I'm in the judge's chambers and I've got all the papers and all of a sudden somebody hands a check to Judy's lawyers. And the matter is settled. She got what she wanted. She sure as hell didn't get it from her husband, my client. She got it from somebody else."

P eter Lawford's generosity toward his in-laws knew no bounds—even after they ceased to be in-laws. Near the end of his life, he offered the services of his wife, Patricia Seaton, to Ted Kennedy (whose sister he'd long since divorced). The cooperative wife called on her husband's ex-relation, who asked that she perform oral sex to relieve his stress. She complied.

N ever as graceful as Jackie, never as untroubled as Ethel, never as adaptable as either one, Joan Kennedy struggled to find her place in the family. When she turned to the president's wife for help in understanding her husband's errant behavior, Jackie advised her, "Kennedy men are like that. They'll go after anything in skirts. It doesn't mean a thing."

A lthough Robert Kennedy and his brothers lived their sexual lives well outside society's norms, the attorney general was content to submit his fellow countrymen to a restrictive code of morals. Publisher Ralph Ginzburg bore the brunt of this double standard.

"The first time I met Robert Kennedy," remembered Ginzburg, "I was twenty-three years old and working at my first journalism job, as circulation and promotion manager of *Look* magazine. He was then counsel for the McClellan committee and they were trying to nail Jimmy Hoffa. *Look* was publishing some inside material he'd fed them and I went down to Washington and met with Bobby in some Senate office to lay plans for promoting the issue.

"Not too long after that, I left my job at *Look* and became a freelance writer, and I was working on an article for *Reader's Digest* called 'The Men Running the Government Are Too Old.' Eisenhower, then president, was rather aged, and the heads of all the major congressional committee were even older. I interviewed Bobby extensively and he took me down to the Senate and showed me some guys actually sleeping in their seats while the thing was in session. He invited me up to Boston where his brother John was running for reelection to the Senate and I spent a day with the family—with Bobby, Jack and Joe Sr. Joe was by far the most intelligent of the Kennedys. He was supposed to be an anti-Semite, and probably was, but he was really a very impressive man. I hate to say that considering his posture, but I'm telling you, he was very smart.

"I was on a first name basis with the Kennedys. I knew them. So I was dumbfounded when Bobby indicted me."

Early in the sixties, Ginzburg founded *Eros,* a magazine, in Victor Navasky's words, "devoted to the joys of love and sex." The periodical and its publisher caught the attention of the attorney general. "I ought to prosecute him," Bobby told Nicholas Katzenbach, "but it will hurt politically.* They will blame it on my Catholicism." After RFK's initial vacillation, *Eros* came out with an issue depicting lovemaking between interracial couples, and the attorney general's boiling point had been reached.

"Bobby had a lot of trouble getting me charged," Ginzburg continued. "He took it to a grand jury in New York. I remember it was rare for a potential defendant to appear before a grand jury, but I requested it. I went before them and persuaded them of the correctness of my motives, and they refused to indict me. Robert Morgenthau found out about it and he refused to pursue the case. So then Bobby went to the U.S. attorney in Newark and he wouldn't touch the case, either, saying I wasn't guilty of anything. So then he went down to Philadelphia, where there was a U.S. attorney named Drew O'Keefe, and I was indicted there on charges of using the U.S. Postal Service to distribute obscene literature.

"After the indictment came down I learned that Bobby was attending

*Nicholas Katzenbach took over as deputy attorney general after JFK appointed Byron White to the Supreme Court in March of 1962.

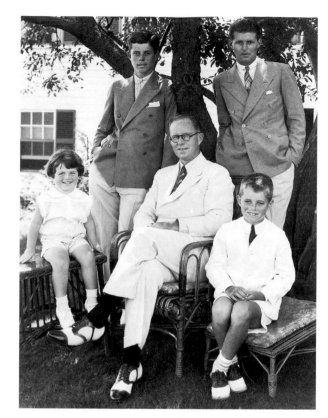

Joseph P. Kennedy and sons *(left to right):* Teddy, Jack, Joe Jr., and Bobby.

Kennedy family *(left to right):* Edward, Jean, Robert, Patricia, Eunice, Kathleen, Rosemary, John, Rose, and Joseph Kennedy.

Young Bobby, Jack, and Teddy in Palm Beach, Florida.

The '47 Harvard football squad: RFK is number 86, and his lifelong friend Ken O'Donnell is number 22.

RFK with family devotee and confidante LeMoyne Billings.

The wedding of the year: Robert F. Kennedy and Ethel Skakel, June 17, 1950. AP/WIDE WORLD

Robert and Ethel went on to have eleven children *(left to right)*: Max, Christopher, Kerry, Courtney, Kathleen, Ethel, Douglas, Bob, Joe, Bobbie, David, and Michael. Rory, the eleventh, was born after RFK's death. ELIZABETH KUHNER/JOHN F. KENNEDY LIBRARY

Senator Joseph R. McCarthy was Bobby's first boss. UPI/Corbis-Bettmann

Roy Cohn and Bobby became
eternal foes after their rivalry
for Joe McCarthy's attention.
Archive Photos

RFK and JFK during the McClellan Committee Rackets Investigation.

Jimmy Hoffa
ranked high on
RFK's hit list.

RFK, campaign manager for Jack, takes a fast-food break during the 1960 West Virginia Democratic primary. JOHN F. KENNEDY LIBRARY

Mobster Sam Giancana, who claimed he helped put JFK in the White House, was one of a number of mafia figures who were later recruited in the CIA's effort to assassinate Fidel Castro.
UPI/CORBIS-BETTMANN

Frank Sinatra, Peter Lawford, and RFK going to a Democratic fund-raiser. Sinatra later blamed RFK for breaking up his marriage to Mia Farrow. RFK also dated Barbara Marx, Sinatra's current wife.
UPI/CORBIS-BETTMANN

Ethel and Robert Kennedy on the campaign trail. Kristi Walker

Eliminating Castro became Bobby's major obsession.
UPI/Corbis-Bettmann

FBI Director J. Edgar Hoover and Attorney General Robert F. Kennedy loathed each other from the first.
UPI/Corbis-Bettmann

Some of the women in Bobby's life *(clockwise from top):* fashion columnist Carol Bjorkman and actresses Claudine Longet, Jayne Mansfield, and Lee Remick. Fairchild Syndication; UPI/Corbis-Bettmann; Archive Photos; Photofest

Candice Bergen *(left)* and Kim Novak were also linked to Bobby.
20TH CENTURY-FOX/PHOTOFEST; ARCHIVE PHOTOS

Mary Jo Kopechne, allegedly
involved with Teddy at the time of
her death at Chappaquiddick in
1969, had actually been Bobby's
lover. UPI/CORBIS-BETTMANN

Marilyn Monroe with the Kennedy brothers following her rendition of the "Happy Birthday" song at Madison Square Garden. After JFK broke off with Monroe, he turned her over to Bobby. CECIL STOUGHTON/TIME-LIFE

Bobby was JFK's closest adviser—almost, some said, his co-president. JOHN F. KENNEDY LIBRARY

November 22, 1963: Bobby and Jackie watch as the slain president is placed in an ambulance at Andrews Air Force Base near Washington, D.C. Their shared grief soon developed into a more intimate relationship.
AP/WIDE WORLD

President Lyndon B. Johnson,
RFK's arch-nemesis. LARRY
STEVENS/GLOBE PHOTOS

Robert Kennedy and journalist-
companion Kristi Witker, during
the 1968 presidential campaign.
KRISTI WITKER

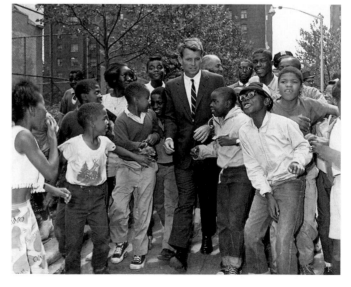

After JFK's death,
civil rights became
Bobby's cause
célèbre.
UPI/CORBIS-BETTMANN

RFK and pal Rudolf Nureyev.
GLOBE PHOTOS

Crowds tear at Bobby's
clothes as he campaigns for
president. BURT GLINN/MAGNUM
PHOTOS

The assassin, Sirhan Sirhan, is led away by police. UPI/CORBIS-BETTMANN

RFK, mortally wounded. BORIS YARO/L.A. TIMES SYNDICATE

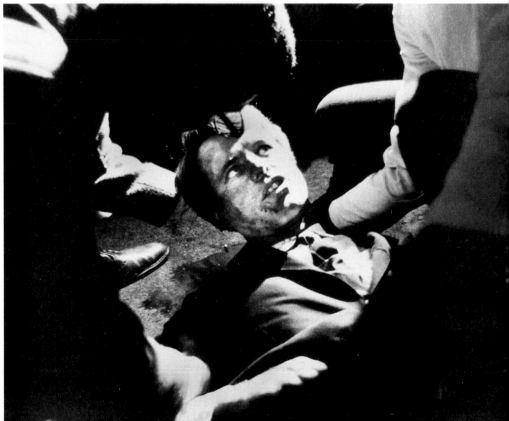

Bearing the coffin *(clockwise from left)*: Stephen Smith, John Seiganthaler *(obscured)*, LeMoyne Billings, James Whitaker, W. Averill Harriman *(obscured)*, Rafer Johnson, C. Douglas Dillon, Bill Barry, John Glenn *(obscured)*, Lord Harlech, Robert McNamara *(partially obscured)*, David Hackett, and Robert F. Kennedy, Jr. *(at center)*.
DECLAN HAUN/BLACK STAR

Crowds lined the tracks to greet the funeral train transporting RFK's body from New York to Washington, D.C., for burial. UPI/CORBIS-BETTMANN

Robert F. Kennedy, 1925 1968.
ARCHIVE PHOTOS

a luncheon at a New York hotel. I found him and cornered him. I said, 'Hey man, what the fuck are you doing?' He said, 'Ralph, I'm sorry, I'm not at liberty to talk to you about it.' That constituted our entire discussion.

"*Eros* was an extraordinary magazine. It won the gold medal from the Art Directors Club of New York, the most prestigious award you can win in all of design. The magazine contained photographs which weren't at all explicit. They were less explicit than you'd find in an issue of *Vanity Fair* today.* And at the very time I was indicted, *Eros* was included in a State Department exhibit of exemplary American periodicals. It was part of the United States Information Agency exhibit that was traveling around the world to show the best of American publishing!"

The specific edition of *Eros* that so infuriated RFK featured an article illustrated with photographs of naked black men touching and holding groups of naked white women. Ginzburg considered the layout artistic in nature, but according to Nicholas Katzenbach's later assertion, the publisher "promoted" an interracial issue "all across the South at the height of the country's racial tensions in the aftermath of the integration of Ole Miss." "Pure balderdash," Ginzburg commented, "pure and unadulterated! I never for a moment thought of any political implications. I'm an expert at magazine circulation and promotion and I safely say we tried to avoid the South, not because of any racial concern but because the South was a rotten mail-order market for all my publications. Don't ask me why, but that always had been the case.

"The problem was that my magazine wasn't puerile, unlike *Playboy*, which was really thriving then. It was a serious publication and it was very hard to put down as insignificant or trash, because it wasn't. The intelligentsia of the country knew *Eros* was going to strike a powerful blow for sexual freedom, and that, I think, was what my enemies, including Bobby, really feared—intuitively and unconsciously, because they never articulated it. This was when the country was truly rocked by the sexual revolution, and I was an absolutely irresistible target, a loudmouth kike from New York. 'Baby, let's get this fucker, he's a pushover.' I was the kind of guy they could muck up with impunity.

"Bobby felt getting me was politically necessary. He may not have thought I was ruining the country's morality, but the Catholics whispering in his ear thought so. The Catholic Church was then much more of an influence on America than it is today. They were concerned about me.

---

* By later standards, the sexual content of *Eros* was mild, indeed. For example, while it contained photographs of naked women, almost nothing was seen below the waist.

The magazine never had any real clout but it was beginning to have some and this bothered them."

Believing his case to be strong, Ginzburg opted for a nonjury trial but the strategy backfired and he was convicted and sentenced to five years in prison. Three appeals, including one to the U.S. Supreme Court, were each in turn defeated. "I served eight months in jail. I got out so early because there were all kinds of protests, full-page ads in the newspapers placed there by the American intelligentsia—Norman Mailer, Arthur Miller, a lot of other names that were big then, but are now dead— protesting my imprisonment."

Ginzburg went on to publish a series of other magazines, including *Moneysworth, American Business* and *Better Living,* and to work as a photographer for the *New York Post.* But he considered his career "wrecked" by the *Eros* case. "If I may say so, I was a highly innovative, creative publisher. I was the first to publish many major figures in American arts and letters, and I was very proud of it. *Eros* had class—it was nothing like the image the government successfully portrayed. You stop anybody on the street, and if they have any recollection of the *Eros* case, they think of it as a grimy publication. But if you see the periodical itself, you understand that it was nothing like that.

"If you're a convicted felon, you don't just pay the draconian fines or spend the time behind bars as I did. You carry the label of 'convict' for the rest of your life. Dealing with other publishers, trying to get ads into all kinds of media—for publications completely unrelated to sex— became very difficult for me afterward.

"I have a sister, she's nine years older than I am. She's been blind all her life and now she's in an old people's home. When I went to visit her recently she told me about an eye doctor who examined her. She said, 'He asked how you happened to switch from pornography to photography.' My own sister thinks of me as a pornographer."

United States Government
Memorandum

DATE: 8/20/62

TO: Mr. [Alan] Belmont*
FROM: C. [Courtney] A. Evans

SUBJECT: MEYER LANSKY

* Assistant director of the FBI and a top aide to Hoover.

ANTI-RACKETEERING*

The Attorney General was contacted and advised of the information
we had received alleging he was having an affair with a girl in El Paso.
He said he had never been to El Paso, Texas, and there was no basis in
fact whatsoever for the allegation.

He said he appreciated our informing him of it; that being in public
life the gossip mongers just had to talk. He said he was aware there
had been several allegations concerning his possibly being involved with
Marilyn Monroe. He said he had a least met Marilyn Monroe since she
was a good friend of his sister, Pat Lawford, but these allegations just
had a way of growing beyond any semblance of the truth.

In early June of 1963 Lord John Dennis Profumo resigned as the United
Kingdom's minister of war following his confession that he had been
intimate with Christine Keeler. The fetching twenty-one-year-old had
been introduced to him by London osteopath Stephen Ward, who had
made a hobby of supplying attractive young playthings to gentlemen of
position and power. Although Profumo was a married man—his wife was
actress Valerie Hobson—the chief count in his disgrace was not adultery.
Rather, he'd committed a grave breach of security, for one of Keeler's
other sex partners was Evgeny "Honeybear" Ivanov, naval attaché at the
Soviet embassy in London and a known spy, who had asked the sociable
young woman to find out from Her Majesty's enamored war minister the
date for the installation of nuclear warheads in West Germany. The scandal rocked the government of Prime Minister Harold Macmillan, who
resigned in October, pleading poor health.

On the other side of the Atlantic, another head of government followed the British scandal with ardent attention. JFK "devoured every
word written about the Profumo case," noted Ben Bradlee. "He ordered
all further cables on that subject sent to him immediately." In March
1963, when UK opposition leader Harold Wilson visited the White
House, he was scheduled to see the president for only a few minutes but
wound up spending two hours with him. "I couldn't believe it," Wilson
said upon leaving the Oval Office. "The man talked and talked about the
Profumo business. He really grilled me on what I knew." JFK's interest
was more than just prurient, for England's uproar threatened to cross the
ocean and engulf his presidency.

*The claim addressed in this memo was made by the gangster to an associate acting
as an FBI informant.

Suzy Chang possessed an exotic lure for the all-American president. A native of China who resided in London, the aspiring young actress and model posed for pictures wearing flowers in her hair and skintight Asian-style silk dresses over her well-proportioned body. In and out of the United States between 1960 and 1963 to see her ailing mother, she became Jack's occasional dinner companion in New York. "We'd meet in the 21 Club," she said later, referring to the restaurant separated from the Carlyle by only a short cab ride up Madison Avenue. "Everybody saw me dining with him. I considered him a nice guy, very charming. What else can I say?" When in England she was often seen taking her meals in the company of Dr. Ward and other principals in the Profumo case.

Chang may or may not have worked as a prostitute, but there is no doubt about the profession of Mariella Novotny, a member of Ward's stable before she relocated to the States in 1960 at age nineteen. That December, according to information she supplied to Scotland Yard two years later, she met her new country's president-elect at a party hosted by singer Vic Damone at his suite in a New York hotel. Dependable Peter Lawford made the introduction, and the politician and the call girl quickly repaired to an empty bedroom to further their acquaintance. The ambassador's son used his knowledge of his new friend's homeland to break the ice. "He talked about England briefly," Novotny recalled, "but locked the door and undressed as we chatted." The statesman-to-be must have enjoyed the encounter, for, after his inauguration, his brother-in-law recruited the lively blonde again. This time, Lawford requested that she arrange "something a bit more interesting for the president." So, at her apartment on New York's West Fifty-fifth Street, Novotny and two other hookers, one dressed as a doctor, the other as a nurse, ministered to JFK, a "patient" in need of healing treatments not contained in Max Jacobson's little black bag.*

More alarming than Jack's merely coincidental connection to the Profumo case was an element that might have produced a homegrown facsimile of the British scandal. Novotny's live-in companion in New York, and co-administrator with her of a call-girl ring employing fifteen women, was Harry Alan Towers, a British television producer rumored to be on the KGB payroll as a provider of information on American public figures. In 1962, when Novotny returned to Britain, Towers fled the United States and wound up behind the Iron Curtain.

---

*According to her later claim, Novotny also serviced Robert Kennedy, although at the time she didn't realize he was the president's brother. The encounter took place at UN Headquarters in New York, perhaps the most decisive act ever performed in that building. Novotny described Bobby as "very boyish and cheerful in bed."

As always, J. Edgar Hoover kept himself well informed of the president's doings. And on June 28, 1963, as the furor over the Profumo case reached its peak in England, he struck. That day, the *New York Journal-American,* a Hearst newspaper with close ties to the FBI director, ran an article that began: "One of the biggest names in American politics—a man who holds a 'very high' elective office—has been injected into Britain's vice-security scandal." The attorney general immediately telephoned his brother, in Europe on a journey that would be known for his Irish pilgrimage and his declaration in West Berlin: "Ich bin ein Berliner." Jack was in London when Bobby phoned—he interrupted his dinner with Harold Macmillan to take the call.

Within forty-eight hours, the two authors of the story found themselves on the receiving end of a torrent of invective in Bobby's Washington office—they had been rousted from their New York homes and flown to the capital on the *Caroline.* RFK asked the reporters to identify the "very high" elected official mentioned in the piece; they admitted that the reference was to the president. Bobby demanded that they reveal the source of the allegation, but the journalists refused to name names. Before dismissing the unhappy pair, RFK informed them that he was considering bringing an antitrust suit against the Hearst organization. The paper's editors chose to kill a follow-up story.

J. Edgar Hoover's people, however, circulated details of the would-be scandal within the agency's ranks, and the director continued to see that any time the FBI got hold of a scoop, the news was disseminated—albeit to an extremely select audience. A month after the *Journal-American* story appeared, Courtney Evans informed Bobby of the Bureau's findings concerning both Novotny and another woman said to have traveled "on pre-election rounds with the presidential candidate" in 1960. (The latter may have been Chang, but the name has been blacked out in the released copy of Evans's memo.) As he had the previous year when confronted with the alleged El Paso affair, RFK played dumb: "The Attorney General," read an Evans memo to Hoover, "was appreciative of our bringing this matter to his attention personally. He said it did seem preposterous that such a story would be circulated when a presidential candidate during the campaign travels with scores of news reporters. He added that with the next presidential election now less than 18 months away, he anticipated there would be more similar stories and he would like for us to continue to advise him of any such matters coming to our attention on a personal basis, as he could better defend the family if he knew what was being said."

Bobby need not worry. The FBI would indeed "continue to advise him" of other "such matters."

British author Anthony Summers revealed to this author that he had once spoken to a reporter who worked on the popular television program *20/20.* "The reporter told me," said Summers, "that he had done a TV interview with Pierre Salinger, President Kennedy's former press secretary. Off camera, Salinger bitterly commented that one day he had come home only to find his wife, Nicole Gillman Salinger, in bed with Bobby Kennedy." According to a November 1997 article in *Vanity Fair,* Salinger repeated the story for the benefit of journalist Seymour Hersh. The article went on to say, however, that Nicole, now divorced from Salinger, denied her former husband's allegation: "It's true that Robert Kennedy had affairs—unfortunately not with me."

"What I don't understand," Truman Capote once mused, "is why everybody said the Kennedys were so sexy." He explained, "I know a lot about cocks—I've seen an awful lot of them—and if you put all the Kennedys together, you wouldn't have a good one. I used to see Jack in Palm Beach. I had a little guest cottage with its own private beach, and he would come down so he could swim in the nude. He had absolutely nothin'! Bobby was the same way—I don't know how he had all those children. As for Teddy—forget it."

16

CASTRO

On the evening of Tuesday, April 18, 1961, with the American-sponsored contingent of 1,543 Cuban exiles known as La Brigada pinned down on the beaches of their homeland's Bahía de Cochinos, Robert Kennedy stepped onto the White House dance floor to grab the elbow of George Smathers, who was visiting the executive mansion for a white-tie reception honoring members of Congress. "The shit has hit the fan," the attorney general told the Florida senator. "This thing has turned sour like you wouldn't believe." The fiasco of the Brigade's invasion at the Bay of Pigs, which occurred just three months into the new administration, rattled the confidence of the optimistic purveyors of the New Frontier. The shocked president, vowing never again to be led astray by his government's foreign-policy apparatus, would thereafter make his chief adviser on Cuba the one member of his administration he trusted utterly, his brother. To the domestic duties already on his list of responsibilities, RFK would add foreign affairs. And to the domestic individuals already on his list of enemies, he would add a foreign foe, Fidel Castro, the Cuban premier who had so humiliated his brother before the nation and the world.

On March 11, Richard Bissell, the CIA's chief of clandestine operations, had arrived at the White House cabinet room to brief JFK on the latest blueprint for the invasion the Agency had begun planning during the last year of the Eisenhower administration. "Too spectacular," said the new president of the proposal to storm a beach near the Cuban port of Trinidad. "It sounds like D day. You have to reduce the noise level of this thing." Seeking to minimize political risk at home and abroad, JFK hoped to avoid overt American military involvement and thus preserve his own "plausible deniability" of the covert CIA role; that is, if the Agency's actions became publicly known, Kennedy wanted to be able to disclaim knowledge of them without appearing to be an obvious liar. Bissell soon came up with a scaled-back design to land at the Bay of Pigs, with the only air support supplied by a set of antiquated B-26 bombers flown by Cuban exiles from a CIA-run airbase in Nicaragua.

Enamored of intrigue and impatient with bureaucracy, the Kennedys accepted the new CIA plan with few questions and refused to listen to dissenting voices within the government. Bobby enforced his will on advisers considered unreliable, such as Undersecretary of State Chester Bowles, the former Connecticut governor who had been a Stevenson ally. "You're for the invasion," RFK told Bowles in the White House as he jabbed three fingers into the older man's stomach; "remember that, you're for it. We're all for it." CIA bigwig Richard Bissell, used to imparting information through winks and nods, never fully briefed his commander in chief on the risks of the operation, which depended on the tiny invasion party, outnumbered by Castro's forces more than one hundred to one, to spark a popular rebellion on the island—an outcome even the Agency's own analysts deemed unlikely. Three days before the invasion was scheduled to begin, JFK ordered the "noise level" down yet a further notch, cutting in half the already paltry number of B-26 missions.

Disaster struck the Brigade instantly as it approached the Cuban shore early Monday morning. Landing craft foundered on coral reefs that appeared as seaweed on CIA maps as the exiles struggled to the beach under punishing fire from Castro's tanks and planes. By midafternoon, the hapless "liberators" were clearly on the verge of defeat. JFK authorized additional B-26 runs from Nicaragua, but the outdated planes were no match for Castro's T-33 fighters, which had originally been a gift from the United States to Castro's predecessor, Fulgencio Batista.* Even with the invading forces facing imminent destruction, President Kennedy insisted on muting his country's role, ordering navy ships out of shooting range of the shore, thus rendering them useless as a means of defense.

---

* Many of the Cuban B-26 pilots, exhausted and afraid, refused to fly the sorties, and Bissell, contrary to presidential orders, permitted American airmen to go up in their place. Four of the Americans were killed. The participation of the U.S. fliers did not become public knowledge until many months later, when word appeared in a midwestern newspaper. According to *New York Times* reporter Hanson Baldwin, Arthur Sylvester, an aide to Robert McNamara, was ordered by RFK to deny the story. "Goddamn it," Sylvester told Baldwin, "I've got to be a liar just because of Bobby Kennedy." Sylvester did as he had been told, but the involvement of the Americans was later confirmed.

JFK finally allowed one air operation by U.S. Navy jets—six planes, their markings painted out, were sent to fly cover for the B-26s; at the last minute, however, a decision was made to abort the mission. By Wednesday, Castro's forces had prevailed. Twenty-six of the exiles, clinging to floating debris for two days, were fished out of the water by U.S. naval vessels. Over three hundred members of the Brigade were killed and the rest were captured by the loyalists.

Ultimately, the president assumed full responsibility for the debacle; privately, he seethed at the CIA, the military, the State Department—everybody he could find to blame. Bobby had played almost no part in the operation's planning; now Jack turned to him as the only person on his team with no ambition of his own. JFK "knew that his brother was absolutely for him, that his advice was entirely unslanted by any consideration except the desire to serve his brother," commented General Maxwell D. Taylor, brought out of retirement by Jack to head a committee investigating the failed invasion. Taylor, a hero of D day, had resigned as army chief of staff in 1959 because President Eisenhower had refused to endorse his concepts of counterinsurgency and limited war. Sitting on the committee with Taylor were three current officeholders: two whose positions dealt with matters of foreign policy, the director of the CIA and the navy's chief of operations, and one whose portfolio was supposedly bounded by the nation's shores, the attorney general.

If unfamiliar with the committee's subject matter, Robert Kennedy found himself at home in the panel's process. "Bobby impressed me from the outset because he was what I would call a constructive activist," Taylor continued. "He was impatient as a young man would be with red tape and government jargon; and above all manner of fuzzy thinking. We had to interrogate many, many witnesses in connection with the Bay of Pigs. I suppose it was his training first of all as a lawyer, and secondly in his own investigative capacity in the Senate that led him to be an excellent interrogator. I was impressed with how quickly he could go to a point and brush aside all the nonessentials and the rubbish that gets into testimony, particularly of reluctant witnesses. After knowing him for a while I told him I would pay him the highest compliment I could make. I thought that he would qualify for membership in the 101st Airborne Division because I was sure he would either take a hill or loot a town with the same abandonment as my parachutists."

On the committee and off, RFK took it upon himself to shift fault for the failure. Hanson Baldwin, then military editor of the *New York Times*, remembered a conversation with the attorney general: "I talked to Bobby Kennedy over the phone and, of course, he was trying to get the onus off his brother. . . . He said: 'Well, have you looked at the role of the Joint Chiefs of Staff in this? They're the ones to blame. You ought to investigate that.' And I said, 'I have and I will.' In fact, I'd talked to all the Joint Chiefs . . . and it was pretty clear that it was a botched-up operation all around. [John] Kennedy had lost his nerve. He never really understood what he was doing, I guess. He took it on too soon."

Jack asked his brother to begin attending meetings of the National Security Council.* At a gathering of the group only a week after the Bay of Pigs, Bobby's favorite whipping boy, Chester Bowles, read a State Department paper asserting that Fidel Castro could not be dislodged from power except by a full-scale U.S. invasion. "That's the most meaningless, worthless thing I've ever heard," RFK howled. "You people are so anxious to protect your own asses that you're afraid to do anything. All you want to do is dump the whole thing on the president. We'd be better off if you just quit and left foreign policy to someone else."

The president sat quietly, tapping a pencil against his front teeth as his brother raged. Speechwriter Richard Goodwin witnessed the scene: "I became suddenly aware—am now certain—that Bobby's harsh polemic reflected the president's own concealed emotions, privately communicated in some earlier, intimate conversation."

"One aspect of [RFK's] relationship to the president struck me from the outset as most unusual," Maxwell Taylor observed. "Although the younger brother, he had a certain protective outlook towards his brother. He was always trying to anticipate his troubles, watching for those things which might hurt the president in some way, and anticipating them and allaying them. It seemed to be rather the reverse of the usual fraternal relationship of the big brother looking after the little brother."

The disaster at the Bay of Pigs did not end the Kennedys' efforts to dethrone Fidel Castro.† On the contrary, the embarrassment they suffered among their fellow citizens, and among their fellow politicians in both Congress and the Kremlin strengthened their resolve to evict the cigar-smoking revolutionary and his Communist regime from the tiny island so near the American coast.

---

*The National Security Council's formal members are the president, the vice president and the secretaries of state and defense. The director of the CIA and the chairman of the Joint Chiefs of Staff, plus the president's national security adviser and the adviser's deputy, generally attend meetings as invited guests. (Other officials, as well as staff members, are also often present.)

†One objective of the invasion had been to take Fidel Castro alive. Had this not been possible, CIA plans called for his assassination, as well as the evacuation of his brother Raul Castro and the capture or death of Che Guevara.

Disgusted with the CIA for leading him to his folly, John Kennedy lamented that he hadn't established control over the Agency from the beginning: "I never should have made Bobby attorney general," he told Ken O'Donnell. "He ought to be running the CIA. Nobody else around here seems capable of that prodigious feat."* Agency chief Allen Dulles was on his way out—he and Bissell took the fall for the botched assault—and Jack considered handing the directorate to RFK.† However, the attorney general quickly talked the chief executive out of the idea: with the president's brother and universally recognized chief confidant as the CIA's boss, presidential deniability of unsavory Agency operations would be anything but plausible.

Although Robert Kennedy would have no formal role at the CIA, he would become its active supervisor, particularly with regard to Cuba. Since outright invasion had failed to oust Castro, Bobby prescribed a program of low-level harassment, featuring sabotage, meddling and infiltration. "Counterinsurgency" became the Kennedys' watchword. On one occasion Bobby invited a contingent of army Green Berets to Hyannis Port. RFK and his brother the president watched the unconventionally trained soldiers display their prowess at hopping from one tree branch to another.

The chief instrument in the intended destabilization of the Cuban regime was to be Operation Mongoose, a joint project of the Pentagon and the CIA run out of the White House. (As a mongoose kills a cobra—exhausting the snake by striking repeatedly while nimbly dodging its fangs—so would the operation attempt to bring down Castro.) To head the program, Jack and Bobby called General Edward Lansdale back to Washington from Saigon, where he was the top American adviser to

---

*On February 21, 1998, the CIA released "The Inspector General's Survey of the Cuban Operation," a highly critical internal inquiry into the Central Intelligence Agency's Bay of Pigs invasion. The 150-page report, written by the CIA's inspector general, Lyman Kirkpatrick, six months after the failed invasion, states that "the fundamental cause of the disaster was the CIA's incompetence, rather than President Kennedy's failure to follow through with the air raids in support of the commandos." The Agency misled the president by not informing him "that success had become dubious and [by failing] to recommend that the operation be therefore canceled."

†In informing Bissell of his fate, JFK admitted in a note the seriousness of his administration's missteps in the affair: "In a parliamentary government, I'd have to resign. But in this government I can't, so you and Allen [Dulles] have to go." To avoid appearing to violate his own public profession of responsibility for the invasion—and to keep the Republican Dulles around to deflect heat over the matter from Republicans in Congress—the president allowed a decent interval to pass before accepting Dulles's and Bissell's resignations. Nevertheless, by early 1962, the two scapegoats were gone.

South Vietnam's president, Ngo Dinh Diem. The enterprise would be overseen by another new entity, the recently established counterinsurgency unit, otherwise known as Special Group (Counterinsurgency). (This panel, on which RFK would sit, was formed as an outgrowth of the Special Foreign Investigations Group, a longstanding committee, composed of high-ranking national-security personnel, charged with oversight of intelligence activity.) Placed in charge of the special counterinsurgency unit was Maxwell Taylor, whom the Kennedys had convinced to stay on in Washington as a personal military adviser to the president.

Ed Lansdale was a man the Kennedys admired. The model for Colonel Edwin Hillandale in the best-selling novel *The Ugly American*, he had achieved renown during the 1950s as leader of American efforts supporting the successful suppression of a Communist rebellion in the Philippines. During that conflict he had employed methods not found in army training manuals: one tactic (according to author Evan Thomas) had been to drain the blood from the bodies of fallen enemy guerrillas, then leave the corpses around the countryside so as to suggest the work of vampires. He was no less creative when it came to Cuba, making plans to ruin the country's sugar crop by spraying agricultural workers with incapacitating biological-warfare agents at harvest time. He also proposed to bombard the island with rumors of the Second Coming. A submarine would then surface off the Cuban coast and light up the night sky with fireworks, causing the awestruck Catholic population to regard its new premier as the Antichrist. The general predicted that by November 1962, the date of U.S. congressional elections, he would lead a glorious march into Havana, executing what he called his "touchdown play."

Although Lansdale and Taylor were the blood and bones of the antiCastro effort, Robert Kennedy provided the brains and spirit. Unseating the Caribbean Communist, he declared, was the administration's "top priority. . . . No time, money, effort or manpower is to be spared." RFK's pursuit of Castro was not merely a function of cold war geostrategic politics; it was personal. Both the president and the attorney general, remarked Lansdale, wanted "to bring Castro down. . . . But Bobby felt even more strongly about it than Jack. He was protective of his brother, and he felt his brother had been insulted at the Bay of Pigs. He felt the insult needed to be redressed rather quickly." Roswell Gilpatric, deputy secretary of defense, spoke of "the righteous anger and determination displayed by Robert Kennedy in an effort to wipe out this blot on the Kennedy administration, the Bay of Pigs. He was determined to overthrow Castro's regime, to remove him as a viable threat. It was almost like a religious fervor. I mean, he had this sense of mission, a ruthless kind of drive. It was black and white."

With RFK riveted on the project, CIA operatives added to Lansdale's wild ideas, coming up with proposals for attacks not just on the island's economy or military structure, but on the person of the leader himself. One CIA officer, after learning that Castro enjoyed scuba diving, suggested eliminating him by sending him a poisoned diving suit. The Agency's Technical Services Division finally constructed such a suit; it worked by contaminating the body with fungus spores that caused a chronic skin disorder and injected tuberculosis bacilli into the mouthpiece of the breathing apparatus. Desmond FitzGerald, who succeeded Lansdale as operations director of the enterprise, asked the technicians to create a seashell that would explode when the Cuban dictator picked it up.* How, one CIA agent asked with derision, would they make sure Castro chose the right shell? "Put a flashing neon sign on it and have it play Beethoven's Fifth?"

Considering the pressure applied to the CIA by Bobby, suggested navy captain Alex A. Kerr, then a Pentagon official, "it's no wonder they came up with some screwball ideas. They'd pretty soon run out of sound ones." The urgency of the situation was felt in even the most unlikely parts of the nation's defense establishment. "Counterinsurgency became almost a ridiculous battle cry," recalled Robert Amory, deputy director for intelligence for the CIA. "It meant so many different things to so many different people. The extreme kind of reaction to Bobby Kennedy's insistence that everybody get gung ho about it was that word went out from the chief of staff of the U.S. Army that every school in that branch of the military service would devote a minimum of twenty percent of its time to counterinsurgency. Well, this reached the Finance School and the Cooks and Bakers School, so they were talking about how to wire typewriters to explode in one's face . . . or how to make apple pies with hand grenades inside them."

While most of the harebrained schemes never found their way off the drawing board, the Kennedy administration's campaign to destabilize Communist Cuba seemed hardly theoretical. Commando raids—at the eventual rate of nearly one per week—were launched against elements of the island's infrastructure: power plants, sugar mills, oil refineries. And

---

* Operation Mongoose was abandoned, and Lansdale sacked, in late 1962 following the Cuban missile crisis. But soon thereafter, the effort was reconstituted under the rubric Special Affairs Staff. With the exception of a few personnel changes, the project continued as before.

whereas at the Bay of Pigs the CIA's combat role had been predominantly limited to ferrying Cuban fighters ashore, on many of these later forays Agency operatives executed the mission in full cooperation with their Cuban confederates.

To accommodate the activity, the CIA station in Miami grew to be the largest in the world. Called JM WAVE, the post employed a permanent staff of over four hundred American employees who controlled several thousand Cuban agents and supervised a network of secret naval bases, training facilities and safe houses dotting South Florida and the Keys. The effort shortly spread around the globe, every major CIA station in the world having at least one case officer assigned to the Cuban operation and reporting to the Miami office. In Latin America, the Agency's Cuban specialists were charged particularly with counteracting potential Cuban subversion of local regimes. Operatives in Europe focused on disrupting the island's trade: they convinced a German producer of ball bearings to manufacture a faulty supply of its wares and export them to Cuba; and they sabotaged a set of English buses to be shipped there.

Behind all these efforts was Robert Kennedy, possessed of the zeal that arose from his characteristic moral certainty, relentlessly goading all working on the project to do more to bring the detested foreign leader to his knees. "I remember that period so vividly," said Ray Cline, then the CIA's chief analyst. "We were so wrapped up in what the president wanted. Bobby was always extremely emotional [about Cuba], and he always acted as though he occupied the Oval Office, and he really did in a way. He was perpetually on the CIA's case about the Cubans." Fidel Castro's presence on the island was a continuing affront to Bobby's standards of right and wrong, good and evil. By the simple act of holding power, the Cuban premier made daily mockery of the brother to whose well-being RFK had consecrated his life.

"Bobby wanted boom and bang all over the island," recalled Sam Halpern, a top CIA assistant on Cuba. Richard Helms, who succeeded Richard Bissell as the Agency's top spook, likewise remembered the attorney general's ardor for the project: "I attended meeting after meeting after meeting with Robert Kennedy. I had telephone call after telephone call after telephone call with him. All about blowing up this Cuban munitions plant, trying to put that structure out of commission. Maybe *obsession* is too strong a word, but it certainly was his preoccupation." RFK, said Helms, "wanted Castro *out* of there."

For all Bobby's attention to the affairs of Cuba, the secret war had little effect. Some Cubans were killed, some shipments sabotaged, some structures detonated. "But," said Maxwell Taylor, "in a strategic sense [such efforts] weren't anything more than just pinpricks." Nor is it likely that the CIA wreaked havoc on the island's supply of natural resources by its instruction to the meager Cuban underground to leave faucets running and lightbulbs burning.

Far from toppling the Cuban government, the Bay of Pigs and the secret war made Fidel Castro an even more painful thorn in America's side. By his defiance of the *yanqui* imperialist, the Cuban leader built his legend among his people and rallied them to their homeland's defense. Moreover, U.S. aggression drove Castro, a diffident Communist at best before the American invasion, deep into the arms of the Soviet Union. The campaign of sabotage was ended by Lyndon Johnson shortly after he became president. But by their demonization of a man and their fanatic inflation of the threat presented by a small Caribbean island, the Kennedys locked American administrations to this day into a pattern of ineffectual saber rattling against a leader whose beard and battle fatigues symbolize the impotence of the hemisphere's behemoth to swat the gnat buzzing about its own backyard.*

Unlike Roy Cohn or Jimmy Hoffa, Fidel Castro would not in any way succumb. The Kennedy administration's campaign to overthrow the premier of Cuba—a policy founded in grandiose delusions and foolish rage—was an abject failure.

R obert Kennedy's participation in his country's foreign policy began with Cuba but did not end there. At Jack's behest, he continued to attend meetings of the National Security Council. Although he never again hijacked the panel's proceedings as he had following Chester Bowles's presentation on the Bay of Pigs, his presence was hardly ceremonial. "RFK was one of the most important members of the NSC, even though, technically, he wasn't a member at all," contended Edward McDermott, who attended meetings as director of the U.S. Office of Emergency Planning. "It would be highly unusual for him to participate in the

---

*The Bay of Pigs had other ramifications as well. The weakness Nikita Khrushchev discerned in JFK's conduct of the invasion may well have emboldened the Soviet leader to erect the Berlin Wall four months later. And in order to compensate for such perceptions on the part of allies and adversaries alike, the U.S. president moved to toughen his stance in Southeast Asia. The day after the Brigade's defeat he spoke before the American Association of Newspaper Editors. Proclaiming that America would not hesitate to intervene abroad to fight Soviet influence, he vowed, "We dare not fail to see the insidious nature of this new and deeper struggle. We dare not fail to grasp the new concept, the new tools, the new sense of urgency we will need to combat it, whether in Cuba or in South Vietnam." Following the speech he established a secret Vietnam Task Force.

discussion unless a question was directed to him by the president or another of the senior officials there. He said very little.

"But in most instances, the first person to see the president after the meeting was the attorney general. Bob would follow his brother from the cabinet room, where the meetings were generally held, into the Oval Office, and they would, obviously, discuss what had transpired. The president relied heavily on Bob's advice."

Jack gave Bobby a more formal role when he asked him to head still another "Special Group," the Special Group for Counterinsurgency and Strategic Services. "The organization," recalled Justice Department aide John Nolan, "which was set up at RFK's suggestion, was supposed to counter what at that time were called wars of national liberation, which made up the key facet in Khrushchev's strategy for prosecuting the cold war and keeping America off balance. Bob Kennedy was up to his eyeballs in all that counterinsurgency stuff. I'd gone to the Naval Academy and had been in the Marine Corps, so one day he said, 'Come on, we'll go over there. I want you to keep an eye on it.'

" 'Over there' meant the Executive Office Building. Although Rusk and McNamara were on the committee, they generally sent undersecretaries in their stead. The other people who went, however, were the heads of their agencies: Ed Murrow of the U.S. Information Agency, Dave Bell of the Agency for International Development, John McCone [Dulles's successor] of the CIA."

The seniority of the group's members did not deter Bobby from asserting his authority as their chairman—and their commander in chief's brother. "He could sack a town and enjoy it," said Maxwell Taylor after one display of RFK's temper. "He was arrogant," remarked Thomas Parrott, a committee staffer; "he knew it all, he knew the answer to everything. He sat there, tie down, chewing gum, his feet up on the desk. His threats were transparent. It was, 'If you don't do it, I'll tell my big brother on you.' "

When he wasn't railing at his colleagues, Bobby busied himself by offering them information. "He'd bring in some returning ambassador from Southeast Asia," recalled Roswell Gilpatric, "or some expert in the British forces on counterguerrilla activity. He tried to stimulate original thinking, to get away from military stereotypes. We picked through the issues and Bobby was the one by whom the group's recommendations moved forward to the president." To one meeting RFK brought Courtney Evans, who represented the FBI in a discussion of the Police Assistance Programs, a U.S.-run undertaking aimed at training foreign law officers in counterinsurgency techniques.

The versatile attorney general of the United States even got a chance to play at being 007 when he was contacted by Georgi Nikitovich Bolshakov. Equally adept at drinking his American friends under the table or beating them at arm wrestling, Bolshakov was every Washingtonian's favorite Russian spy. Although officially attached to the Soviet embassy in a low-ranking press position, Bolshakov's true role as Khrushchev's personal eyes and ears happened to be no secret around town. And when, just after the Bay of Pigs, the Soviet premier desired a back channel to the Oval Office, Bolshakov told Frank Holeman, a reporter for the *New York Daily News,* "I'd appreciate it if you would introduce me to Robert Kennedy."

Holeman contacted Ed Guthman, who spoke to Bobby, who spoke to the president. Jack, aware that Bolshakov was an agent of the KGB, authorized RFK to meet with the Russian.

The meeting took place in Bobby's office at the Justice Department. Over the next eighteen months, the two men saw each other on more than fifty occasions. To avoid the eyes of the press, and those of Soviet and American intelligence officers, Holeman would generally pick up Bolshakov in a cab and take him to the Virginia countryside. Occasionally, their encounters took place in seedy bars, coffee shops, or parks, and once at the Washington zoo, where they took turns pouring beer down the elephant's trunk. They discussed Thailand, Laos, Berlin and Russian-American relations. They made preparations for the summit to be held in Vienna. "Bobby liked Bolshakov," noted Lem Billings, "because the Russian was so damn eccentric."

"After my retirement, whenever I returned to the Justice Department, I could hardly believe my eyes," said John Nolan. "People were literally pushing papers around and it was like a morgue. When Bob Kennedy was there, it became the center of the most vibrant activity in the world. I had an office in between the reception area and the attorney general's office, and there were people streaming through there all day long.

"The stuff that I worked on was what he worked on, and it didn't have a lot to do with the Department of Justice. With a few exceptions, the only major areas with which RFK concerned himself were organized crime and civil rights. So far as the routine operation of the department was concerned—the Tax Division, the Civil Division, the administrative office, the appointment of judges, the courts, all of that—this was predominantly handled by other people.

"Bobby's range of activities kept him going. Angie Novello, his personal secretary, would type up his telephone messages: Averell Harriman [JFK's special roving ambassador] called about Thailand; the Soviet ambassador hopes to see you next week; so-and-so wants you to attend an event in Cleveland. There was always something.

"It was an extraordinary place. I was dazzled, dazzled!"

In mid 1960 (during the last months of the Eisenhower administration), after CIA operatives had laced a box of Fidel Castro's favorite cigars with botulism-producing poison, Richard Bissell realized he lacked the means to deliver the lethal smokes to their intended consumer.* He took his dilemma to Sheffield Edwards, head of the Agency's Office of Security, who suggested they contact none other than the Los Angeles hood Johnny Roselli. The United States government was about to undertake a foreign-affairs mission in partnership with the Cosa Nostra.

Edwards had made the mobster's acquaintance the year before at a party hosted by Robert Maheu, a former FBI agent who had done free-lance undercover work for the CIA (and who in later years worked for Howard Hughes). Maheu would be merely a middleman, whose job it was to distance the Agency from the operation. In September, Maheu and Roselli met for drinks in Hollywood at the Brown Derby. On behalf of the CIA, Maheu offered Roselli $150,000 (half in advance) to murder the Cuban leader; the gangster, citing love of country, offered his services gratis.† A few weeks later in Miami, Roselli introduced Maheu to two associates: Santos Trafficante, who had been Havana's kingpin before the revolution, and Sam Giancana. Giancana and Trafficante were as patriotically motivated as Roselli, but all three had other motives for cooperating with the plot: a supposed history showing they had helped the CIA would hopefully serve them well when other arms of the government took a prosecutorial interest in their less public-spirited activities, including tax evasion and union racketeering. In actuality, these Mafia dons were no more fond of Castro than the ideologues of the Agency were: by eliminating mob-run drug running, gambling casinos and houses of prostitution in the newly revolutionary state, the Cuban premier had cost the syndi-

---

*Kennedy supporters such as Arthur Schlesinger have long claimed that the JFK Administration inherited the absurd CIA-Mafia kill Castro plot from Eisenhower. While this is partially true, it is likewise clear that the Kennedys attempted to see the scheme to its illogical conclusion.

†Roselli, who was part owner of the Sands Hotel in Las Vegas, also evidently offered his services gratis to John F. Kennedy, whom he had met in the late 1950s. After JFK became president, Roselli made available to him a private cottage on the hotel grounds and several comely prostitutes who provided the chief executive with entertainment. Such are among the disclosures of the most recently released FBI files.

cate as much as a billion dollars a year, to say nothing of a hotel, restaurant, and resort trade from which the mob also derived a healthy cut.

With the contact established, Bissell let Giancana know he favored an old-fashioned mob-style hit, the target to be shot in the back of the head, perhaps while he sipped coffee at a café or had a meal with some aides. Giancana wanted nothing so dramatic; he demanded poison pills that would dissolve in Castro's drink. After the several months it took the Agency's Technical Services Division to concoct the tablets, the mob began to arrange for their use; however, the plans dissolved faster than would have the pills: a senior official in Castro's government volunteered to perform the dirty deed, but he lost his job and consequently his access; a waiter in a restaurant was then engaged but Castro decided he no longer favored the establishment's cuisine and stopped eating there. Discouraged by these missteps, and by the disaster he had wrought at the Bay of Pigs, Bissell in May 1961 suspended the CIA-Mafia scheme.

In the meantime, John Kennedy and his brother had assumed office in Washington. On May 22, 1961, the attorney general received a memo from his always knowledgeable subordinate, J. Edgar Hoover. The document outlined the activities of Edwards and Maheu, and noted that Giancana was cooperating "in attempting to accomplish several clandestine efforts in Cuba." For the most part a summary of statements Edwards had made earlier in the month to the FBI, the memo did not indicate that the operation was about to be terminated. It said instead: "Edwards added that none of Giancana's efforts have materialized to date and that several of the plans still are working and may eventually 'pay off.'"

The document contained no explicit reference to a possible assassination, although a previous memo sent to Hoover by one of his field agents and dated October 18, 1960, had reported that Giancana was boasting of his intention to murder Castro. That earlier memo made no mention of the CIA, but surely the conspiratorially minded director of the FBI had no trouble putting two and two together. And whether or not Hoover shared with his boss all elements of the equation, RFK had more than an inkling about the exact nature of what the May memo, quoting Edwards, called a "dirty business."

With his ceaseless clamoring to "solve the Castro problem as quickly as possible," the attorney general no doubt knew the CIA would seek to eliminate the Cuban leader by whatever means possible. Why else would the Agency have called in some of the nation's most notorious criminals if not to take advantage of the mob's expertise in murder? Richard Bissell had no trouble interpreting Bobby's insistence: following a particularly shrill tongue-lashing in November 1961, he reactivated the Mafia contacts.*

Still, while the CIA he rode so mercilessly worked with the Mafia on Cuba, Robert Kennedy pursued organized crime through his Justice Department as no attorney general ever had before (or has since). Indeed, some of the mobsters the department went after most vigorously were the same ones involved in the Cuban venture. "Here I am," complained Johnny Roselli, "helping the government, helping the country, and that little son of a bitch is breaking my balls." The hopes of Roselli and Giancana for easy treatment from Bobby's prosecutors in exchange for "helping the government" were never realized. A personal memorandum from J. Edgar Hoover to RFK conveyed information that "Giancana complained bitterly concerning the intensity of investigation being conducted of his activities." Giancana had apparently asked Frank Sinatra to speak either to the president or to the president's father regarding the situation. The memo concluded: "[Giancana] allegedly made a donation to the campaign of President Kennedy but is not getting his money's worth. He will not donate a penny toward any future campaign."

Giancana's Cuban assignment and his legal troubles may have been among the subjects discussed by the don and the president in the notes they allegedly passed via Judith Campbell. The lady's inconsistencies led to doubts about her veracity: she made public her professed role as courier only in 1988, claiming that inclusion of that part of the tale in her 1977 published memoir would have put her life at risk.† There is no doubt, however, that telephone records link her to the Kennedy White House. There is no doubt that Bobby found out about her, and her ties to both the president and the mob (whatever the president knew, Bobby also knew—the brothers shared every dream, whim, inspiration and disil-

---

*According to one high-ranking CIA official, RFK himself communicated with Roselli (and other Mafia chiefs involved in the Cuban operation) via an Agency operative named Richard Ford. Ford, who worked for William Harvey, a subordinate of Richard Bissell, became a middleman between the attorney general and the mob. His exact role, however, is not known. What is known is that Harvey, together with CIA agent Gerry Droller, had helped organize back-channel operations at the failed Bay of Pigs invasion, and that both men came to detest the Kennedys. Harvey, now dead, has been accused in certain quarters of having been involved in JFK's assassination. The truth may be revealed in the year 2029, when the CIA's JFK assassination files are finally opened.

†Campbell's fear during the 1970s seems to have been justified, for she had just lost two close friends. In June 1975, Sam Giancana took seven bullets in the throat and mouth as he was frying sausages in his Chicago kitchen. Thirteen months later, authorities found Johnny Roselli's body, hacked to pieces, in an oil drum that had been tossed into the ocean off Miami.

lusion). There is no doubt that RFK was likewise aware of direct communication between the White House, the Justice Department, the CIA and the Mafia. It was Bobby, in fact, who ultimately suggested that Kennedy family attorneys and Mafia lawyers be used to transmit messages from one faction to the other.* The lawyers for both sides complied, assuming the part that Judith Campbell claimed for herself. And while Campbell may or may not have also been a conduit, the Kennedys knowingly and willingly utilized the mob to conduct their far-fetched, ludicrously contrived Machiavellian murder plot.

RFK was not *officially* briefed by the CIA on the involvement with the mob until May 1962. The briefing came about only because the Agency had attempted to suppress a Justice Department prosecution of Robert Maheu for wiretapping: with CIA approval, he had arranged to bug a Las Vegas hotel room frequented by a Giancana girlfriend whom the mobster suspected of infidelity. The Agency had to explain to Bobby the embarrassing facts such a trial might reveal—for instance, the hiring of a known mafioso by the United States government for the purpose of "doing in" a foreign leader. (Although one of the participants later claimed that he had briefed the attorney general "all the way," RFK had evidently been told only that the mob connection had ended the previous May, but not that it had been renewed six months later.) According to Lawrence Houston, the Agency's general counsel, the briefing's recipient did not take the news happily. On the other hand, Bobby did not pass judgment upon the operation itself, nor did he forbid further contact with the mob. Houston left the meeting with the distinct impression that RFK knew more than met the eye.

In a memorandum following the briefing, J. Edgar Hoover, who also attended, wrote to Courtney Evans: "I expressed great astonishment at [the Mafia link] in view of the bad reputation of Maheu and the horrible judgment in using a man of Giancana's background for such a project." The director's "astonishment" was expressed over a situation of which he had become aware the year before. Were he and Bobby playing an elaborate game with each other about facts each knew but wasn't sure the

---

* One self-proclaimed Mafia lawyer who acted as a conduit between the White House and the mob was Frank Ragano, whose client list included Santos Trafficante and Carlo Marcello. He also served for fifteen years as Jimmy Hoffa's personal attorney. In his 1997 book, *Perfect Villains, Imperfect Heroes*, former Justice Department special prosecutor Ronald Goldfarb quotes Trafficante on RFK following JFK's assassination: "We shouldn't have killed John. We should've killed Bobby." In the same volume, Marcello is quoted as saying to Trafficante: "You . . . and me are in for hard times as long as Bobby Kennedy is in office. Someone ought to kill that sonofabitch."

other knew? Or was Hoover, as suggested by Anthony Summers in *Official and Confidential*, a biography of the director, creating a paper record to provide the attorney general with plausible deniability of the affair, thereby placing the Kennedys further in his debt?

Lem Billings recalled having lunch with Bobby at the latter's Carlyle suite in New York in June 1962. "Bobby seemed in an excellent mood that day," said Billings. "He spoke and even laughed about the Mafia's involvement in trying to do away with Castro. He remarked that when the CIA had recently told him of renewing its ties to the mob, he'd done a better job of feigning shock and anger than Burt Lancaster. 'Of course, I knew,' he said. 'I'm the guy who developed the goddamn plot. But Hoover [J. Edgar Hoover], he's a whole other ball game. He deserves a fucking Oscar.' "

In the foggy aftermath of this doomed operation, the CIA's movements were rarely documented. Even within the Agency, people spoke of their bloodiest deeds in a bloodless code, so that when Richard Bissell, for example, initially approached Allen Dulles with information concerning the cooperation between the CIA and the Mafia, no mention was made of a plot to assassinate Castro. Code names were used, and Bissell referred to a hierarchical progression that went from himself to Edwards to Maheu to Roselli as "X to Y to Z to Mr. R."

Plausible deniability aside, Robert Kennedy's well-established views of the imperatives dictated by absolute right and absolute wrong are consistent with using a great evil, the mob, to erase a greater evil, Fidel Castro. RFK's desire to purge the Free World of the Cuban revolutionary is commensurate with Henry II's intentions regarding Thomas Becket when he cried out, "Who will free me from this turbulent priest?" Neither the twentieth-century U.S. attorney general nor the medieval English king could have harbored many illusions about the consequences of his importuning.

"When Robert Kennedy wanted something," observed Lem Billings, "he tended to be rampant on your tail. You wanted him off your tail. I happen to believe, however, that in using gangsters to try to assassinate Fidel Castro, Bobby and Jack went much too far. In essence, they were digging their own graves."*

---

*Ken O'Donnell remarked that Bobby "became quite nutty at times when talking about Castro. He once told me about this idea he had to blow up an American civilian airliner and then blame the dirty deed on Castro. 'We'll say the Cubans did it.' 'Come on, Bobby. Get real,' I told him. 'You're going to kill innocent American civilians and then blame it on Castro? You've got to be nuts. Does your brother know about this?' 'Of course not,' he said. 'He'd never approve.' "

After the daring soldier of fortune William "Rip" Robertson spoke at length with Robert Kennedy in mid-1961, he informed the Cuban exiles he was leading on commando raids that the attorney general was "an all-right guy." As Robertson had been one of the few Americans to land on the beach at the Bay of Pigs, and as he was thought to despise all politicians, his opinion impressed the Cubans. Bobby, by his efforts on behalf of the nearly 1,200 members of La Brigada still languishing in Cuban prisons, would live up to the commandos' expectations.

Fidel Castro had opened negotiations for the prisoners' release a month after the invasion with his request for five hundred bulldozers. The administration, concerned that bulldozers might be used for military construction instead of agriculture, offered five hundred tractors. Castro suggested $28 million, the cost of the bulldozers. Republicans, rabid in their outcry against acceding to blackmail, intimidated John Kennedy into refusing that easy deal.

In March 1962, nearly a year after the invasion, the prisoners were put on trial. The Cuban Revolutionary Tribunal sentenced each man to thirty years of hard labor. Castro's price for their collective release rose to $62 million. In mid-April, he liberated sixty sick and wounded prisoners for $3 million. RFK decided, in conjunction with his brother, to bring in a negotiator and turned to New York lawyer James B. Donovan, who had recently engineered the exchange of captured Eastern Bloc spy Rudolf Abel for Francis Gary Powers, the American U-2 pilot downed by the Soviets. Domestic politics dictated that the administration not appear to be contemplating payment of a ransom, so Donovan nominally worked for a private group, the Cuban Families Committee for the Liberation of the Prisoners of War.

Donovan commenced discussions with Castro, and over the summer and into the fall, each side's position began to soften. RFK remained passionately committed to a successful outcome, and as a result he tried to ensure that his colleagues in the administration harbored an interest that was not only as avid as his own, but just as pure. "Around the end of September 1962," recalled Milan "Mike" Miskovsky, like Donovan a New York lawyer brought in to work on the release, "Jim Donovan came back with the idea that a deal might be struck. So Bob Kennedy called a meeting. It was in the White House, in the National Security Council area, and was attended by representatives from Defense and the CIA, as well as by McGeorge Bundy and Dean Rusk. Bob sat at one end of the big table and I was happy to be sitting at the other end.

"The secretary of state began with some comments that amounted to little more than a geography lesson on Cuba. Then General Ed Lansdale began describing still more geography, talking about the location of the Isle of Pines where the prisoners were being held. At this point I'm watching Bob Kennedy, and he had an expression on his face that said, 'Fellas, who are you kidding? What are you telling me? Nothing.'

"So it went around the room and it finally got to McGeorge Bundy. And he says, 'Well, this is an issue we ought to consider in terms of the congressional elections coming up in November. It might result in some Republican victories.'

"Bob Kennedy had a yellow pencil in his hand, and he started, not tapping it, but just sort of moving it. And he looked at me, and then he tossed the pencil onto the table, over which it skidded right into my hands. He stood up and glared at the secretary of state, Defense people, McGeorge Bundy, and he said, 'As long as I'm attorney general, we have a moral obligation to those people in that jail. And I don't care if we lose every election that will ever be held. We're going to get those guys out.' And with that he stalked out of the room. He just turned and left. I mean, he was boiling."

As important as the prisoners were to Bobby, their freedom would have to wait. Just two weeks after the White House meeting, photo interpreters from the CIA made a discovery that would for thirteen days seem to hold prisoner humanity itself.

The visit of Richard Helms to the attorney general's office on the morning of Tuesday, October 16, 1962, had been scheduled to discuss a recent Soviet defector. But Bobby's first words to the CIA official pertained to another topic. "Dick," he asked, "is it true they've found Russian missiles in Cuba?"

"Yes, Bob, they have."

"*Shit!*"

Robert Kennedy did not need Helms to tell him the news, having been informed earlier in the day by an ever more reliable source, Jack. The president had gotten word at half past eight when he received McGeorge Bundy in the White House master bedroom. Eating breakfast in his nightshirt, JFK listened to the national security adviser describe U-2 reconnaissance photographs taken the previous Sunday that showed a missile base under construction. Following Bundy's presentation, JFK's first phone call went to his brother—there's "great trouble," the president said. Bobby's initial reluctance to believe the report reflected the fact that he didn't *want* to believe it. A bank of Soviet nuclear missiles on the island of Cuba meant that American cities and military installations could be destroyed with almost no warning. If the missiles were allowed to remain, the brothers believed, their administration would face disgrace at home and discredit abroad. No American president could tolerate the placement of Soviet strategic weapons just ninety miles from American soil. War between the superpowers, always dreaded from afar, now seemed an imminent possibility.

To avoid political pressure and public panic, JFK ordered that the crisis be kept secret from the citizenry and the Congress while his government studied its options. To that end, he formed an ad hoc panel called the Executive Committee of the National Security Council. "Ex-Comm" was composed of the government's top advisers on defense and foreign affairs, including Dean Rusk, Robert McNamara, Maxwell Taylor (by this time chairman of the Joint Chiefs of Staff), Vice President Lyndon Johnson, Senator Richard Russell, air force chief of staff Curtis LeMay, CIA director John McCone, former secretary of state Dean Acheson (who had been an informal foreign policy adviser to JFK), former American ambassador to the Soviet Union Llewellyn "Tommy" Thompson, and, of course, Bobby. At its first meeting, the group listed three viable options: bombing the missile sites, invading Cuba and forcing the missiles out by naval blockade. "The one alternative we didn't examine was doing nothing," Dean Rusk later wrote. "All agreed that the missiles were simply unacceptable."*

With the Soviet base estimated to be no more than twelve days from completion, the council of wise men began intensive deliberations, and the youngest among them led them in their work. "There was no formal designation, but Robert Kennedy was the de facto leader of ExComm," said Roswell Gilpatric, a member of the body. "John Kennedy didn't attend the meetings, so his brother assumed the role by virtue of his closeness to the president. He was like his brother's shadow and had an intuitive sense of what was formulating in Jack's mind. He was the second most important person in the administration, if not number one.

"Robert Kennedy kept the group in session, often hours at a time,

---

*One day into the Cuban Missile Crisis, JFK asked Robert A. Lovett, defense secretary under Truman, to come to the White House to offer tactical advice. Seated outside the Oval Office, Lovett was surprised when the door to the office opened and RFK's head protruded. "Hey, you!" barked the attorney general. Lovett sat motionless. "Hey, you!" Bobby said a second time. "Me?" asked Lovett. "Yes, you, dammit—come in here!" The president, seated behind his desk (according to Ken O'Donnell), "became exercised at his younger brother and in no uncertain terms told him to 'shut up!' Lovett, after all, had been a distinguished former member of a presidential cabinet. But that was Bobby for you."

each of the thirteen days of the crisis. He tended to be low-key. He didn't have a take-charge, dominate-the-discussion point of view. Rather, he tried to encourage everybody to express himself. He would roam around the room shooting questions or making comments. And he tried not to preclude different opinions. In other words, he wasn't trying to force a consensus. He just wanted everybody to think and talk it out. The atmosphere was one of a brainstorming session.

"We were conscious that everything we said would reach the president through his brother. But it wasn't an inhibiting feeling, he didn't make us feel we were constrained. He encouraged precisely the opposite. He wanted open and free discussion. I believe he conducted himself admirably."

The ExComm advisers soon coalesced into two factions, which those involved called "hawks" and "doves":* the hawks, led by Maxwell Taylor, Curtis LeMay, Senator Richard Russell, and Dean Acheson, advocated prompt and decisive military action, beginning with an air strike to destroy the missile base and possibly continuing with an invasion of the island; the doves, led by McNamara and Rusk, favored a naval blockade to halt shipment of further military hardware, with the threat of an armed response should the Soviets refuse to yield. Bobby sided with the doves. "He brought up the analogy of Pearl Harbor," recalled Gilpatric, a confirmed dove. "He didn't want this country to be in the position that Japan had put itself in with that raid. He felt that a sneak attack would only make us look bad in the eyes of the world, whereas a blockade would gain us the time we needed to make proper decisions."

On Saturday, October 20, President Kennedy called the members of ExComm to the living quarters on the second floor of the White House. Dean Rusk opened the meeting advising "quarantine," as the naval blockade was now dubbed. ("Blockade," a term well identified in international law, carried various restrictions and obligations; "quarantine," a new term for such an action, was used to "allow for maximum flexibility . . ." as Rusk wrote, "partly because no one knew exactly what a quarantine meant.") Robert McNamara concurred, stressing that an air strike would likely lead to a "very major response" on the part of the Soviets. "The outcome could very well entail an all-out war." Maxwell Taylor urged an air attack, and quickly, before the missiles could be camouflaged. Robert Kennedy summarized the views of ExComm's members, then himself endorsed the quarantine. Lyndon Johnson rec-

---

*The crisis, and a *Saturday Evening Post* story about it published shortly afterward, brought the pair of terms into its modern usage (just in time for Vietnam).

ommended that the president take the advice of his secretaries of state and defense.

The counselors to the commander in chief had finished speaking. "And with that," recalled Edward McDermott, "the president stood up and left the living room and walked out onto the Truman balcony, overlooking the Washington Monument. And he was out there alone. He was making his decision, which he was going to announce when he came back in. And there was absolute silence in the room.

"After a while Bob Kennedy got up and went out. It was a very vivid picture we saw through the window, the two of them speaking out on the balcony. After a few minutes Bob came back in. A few more minutes passed, then the president returned and said what he had decided to do and why he had decided to do it."

He had decided to impose the quarantine.

On the evening of Monday, October 22, with American ships moving into position, the president addressed the nation to speak of the circumstances that had for the past six days been filling its leaders with nightmarish visions of cities laid to waste. On Tuesday, RFK met with the new Soviet ambassador, Anatoly Dobrynin. Speaking, as only he could, for the president, Bobby stated that his brother's prior hope of "being able to work with Premier Khrushchev" had been changed by the surreptitious placement of missiles in Cuba, as well as by the construction of missile sites and military encampments. Meanwhile, the U.S. Army's 82nd and 101st Airborne Divisions, plus forty-five thousand marines—one hundred thousand troops in all—were massed in Southern states and in the Caribbean, poised for attack.

On Wednesday, October 24, the Kremlin announced its rejection of the American quarantine and sent submarines to escort its cargo vessels. But on Thursday, Soviet ships suspected of carrying nuclear-headed missiles stopped dead in the water and turned back toward their bases in the Black Sea. The naval action had succeeded. Confrontation at sea had been averted.

The missiles already ashore remained, however, as did the newly completed military installations. Unless the missiles were removed and the sites abandoned, JFK threatened to take whatever measures he deemed necessary to guarantee the security and safety of the United States.

On Friday, October 26, a solution seemed to emerge. John Scali, State Department correspondent for ABC Television News, relayed an offer from the Soviet embassy: the Kremlin would swap removal of the missiles for a public American pledge never to invade Cuba. The same day, an official letter arrived at the White House from Nikita Khrushchev tendering the same proposition.

The Americans considered the crisis all but over. On Saturday, however, another letter from Khrushchev arrived. Whereas the first message had been full of heartfelt personal language about the urgency of avoiding war, the second bore the imprint of a joint effort forced on a dovish premier by a hawkish politburo. Saturday's letter upped the price for withdrawal of the Cuban missiles, calling for not only the no-invasion promise, but also the removal of American Jupiter missiles from Turkey.

To the Kennedys and their advisers, the introduction of the Turkish missiles into the discussion represented a step back toward stalemate: while the president could live with renouncing invasion of Cuba, he could not abandon the defense of Turkey, a NATO ally. Yet the proposal in fact contained the sword that cut the Gordian knot, for the Americans considered Jupiter missiles all but obsolete. JFK had taken steps to withdraw them in 1961, but had been persuaded to leave them so as to avoid embarrassing the Turkish government, which had only recently convinced its parliament to accept the antiquated missiles. New Soviet missiles in Cuba for old American missiles in Turkey, a country bordering Soviet Central Asia just as Cuba neighbored the United States, seemed a reasonable, and not unfavorable, trade—if it could be accomplished discreetly.

On Saturday afternoon, the State Department drafted a letter to the Soviets declaring the Turkish missiles untouchable. But Bobby and others advised a different tack: why not respond to the first letter and ignore the second? Asked by the president to pen another reply, RFK sat down with Ted Sorensen. The letter they wrote restated the initial offer: removal of the Cuban-based missiles for an American promise not to invade. JFK ordered the message cabled to Moscow, then asked his brother to speak again with Dobrynin.

Amid the crayon drawings and the stuffed tiger in Bobby's Justice Department office, the attorney general met with the ambassador. The day before, a U-2 spy plane had been downed over Cuba and its pilot killed. The president, RFK said, though under pressure from the military to take action, had so far resisted, determined to avoid a war that would leave millions dead on both sides. Yet not all American generals were reliable; were a rogue to take matters into his own hands, the outcome could be catastrophic. Bobby encouraged Dobrynin to accept the no-invasion offer forthwith, before the opportunity for a peaceful resolution vanished. Dobrynin responded by inquiring about the Jupiter missiles. Speaking in a terse and straightforward manner, RFK stressed that the

Americans would countenance no quid pro quo but that within six months Turkey would be free of all American-made missiles. "I won't sign on a dotted line," remarked Bobby, "but you have my word." The two men shook hands.

On Sunday, October 28, Premier Khrushchev took to the airwaves in Moscow to announce that his nation's missiles would soon be withdrawn from Cuba under UN supervision. A day later, Ambassador Dobrynin brought Bobby an unsigned letter written by Khrushchev which spelled out the various points of the U.S.-Soviet agreement, including RFK's stated intention to remove the Jupiter missiles from Turkey. "This is not a tit-for-tat situation," Bobby told Dobrynin the following morning, having spent that night mulling over the letter. Unwilling to lose face, the Kennedys wanted the world to know that America simply would not tolerate the presence of enemy warheads only miles from their shore: no conditions (at least none expressed in writing) could be attached to their demand. Khrushchev retracted his letter. America withdrew its Jupiter missiles. World War III had been narrowly averted.

Robert and John Kennedy had precipitated the October missile crisis. The Bay of Pigs invasion and the secret war on Cuba drove Fidel Castro to seek the economic support and military protection of the Soviet Union; in exchange for the Soviets' help, he was willing to play his part as pawn in the superpowers' global game. But as reckless and wrongheaded as they had been toward Cuba before the crisis, during the thirteen October days, when the fate of humanity seemed to hang by a thread, the Kennedy brothers were judicious and astute, showing the savvy and intuition—not to mention raw Irish luck—that had gotten them to the White House in the first place.

And they did it together. Sir Isaiah Berlin, the noted British historian, observed the brothers at a White House dinner not long after the crisis had ended: "They sat quite far away from each other at the table. When either spoke to the other across a distance the understanding was complete, and they agreed with each other, and they smiled at each other, and they laughed at each other's jokes, and they behaved as if nobody else was present. One suddenly felt this absolutely unique rapport, so to speak, such as is very uncommon, even among relations. They hardly had to speak to each other. They understood each other from a half-word. There was a kind of constant telepathic contact between them."*

---

*An unsung hero of the Cuban missile crisis was Ambassador Tommy Thompson, who understood the motives behind Khrushchev's aggressive position and explained them to JFK and RFK: "He wants the West out of Berlin in exchange for Cuban missiles. He also wants it to appear that he saved Cuba—he prevented an invasion. All in all, he can be dealt with in diplomatic fashion."

With the crisis ended, Bobby stepped up efforts to extricate the Bay of
Pigs prisoners. Castro and Donovan agreed to trade the captives for
food, medicine and moneys, with the Cuban leader willing to release the
men as soon as he received 20 percent of the goods plus $2.9 million (in
cash) for the sick and wounded already freed. Since the U.S. government
seemed unwilling to send supplies or pay the bill, RFK set out to raise
the ransom, which would be funneled through the Cuban Families Committee, from private donors. He wanted the men home by Christmas.

The Justice Department went to work. Nicholas Katzenbach became
the project's coordinator, Louis Oberdorfer his lieutenant. As head of the
department's Tax Division, Oberdorfer played a particularly significant
role, for tax policy became the key to unlocking corporate largesse. "The
Cubans basically wanted two classes of stuff," said John Nolan, "drugs
and baby food. There were only a handful of baby-food manufacturers—
Beech-Nut, Gerber, etc.—so we decided on a Friday afternoon in December to have a meeting with their representatives over the weekend
and get them to agree to make a pledge. We sent telegrams to the companies saying that the Cuban Families Committee, which was interested in
obtaining the freedom of the Brigade, was seeking contributions of baby
food. This was a tax-exempt organization, and contributions to it would
be tax-deductible. These telegrams were signed by Bob Kennedy, and
the idea was, 'Come to Washington Sunday at ten a.m. for a meeting
with the attorney general. Bring along someone who knows what your
inventory is and somebody who knows what your tax picture is.'

"There were too many pharmaceutical companies to contact individu-
ally, so we approached them through the Pharmaceutical Manufacturers
Association, then represented by a Washington lawyer named Lloyd Cutler, who had been a law partner of Lou Oberdorfer. We were soliciting
furiously and we took everything we could get. We had seventy-five thousand dollars' worth of Ex-Lax, five hundred thousand dollars' worth of
Listerine. We had something called Gill's Green Mountain Asthmatic
Cigarettes and thirty-seven different kinds of menstrual remedies. It was
a great shelf-clearing operation for the drug companies, and we took all
of this stuff and loaded it either on an airplane or on a ship." One of the
ships that made the voyage was a privately owned vessel that JFK had
renamed the S.S. *Maximus* in honor of his doctor, Max Jacobson (although its cargo is not known to have included either amphetamines or
cells extracted from electric eels, another of Max's favorite "medicinal"
cure-alls).

A massive logistical operation got the supplies to Havana in time, but the cash payment for the earlier release of invalids remained. General Lucius D. Clay, a sponsor of the committee, borrowed $1.9 million on a personal note. For the remainder, Bobby telephoned Richard Cardinal Cushing, the archbishop of Boston who had married the president and first lady nine years before. Cushing later recalled that RFK "wanted to know if I could get them $1,000,000 before the day was over. It was then only a couple of days before Christmas, and they wanted these prisoners in the United States prior to that day. I replied, 'I'll call you back in a few hours.' I did so, and I promised to have the money delivered to him at the White House about 6 p.m. Where did I get the money? I borrowed it from Latin American friends and those in the United States and promised to pay it back within three months."

The Brigade was released on December 22. A week later, the Kennedys attended a rally for the men at Miami's Orange Bowl. The crowd of forty thousand Cubans erupted in shouts and tears as the president inspected the emigre troops. One of the commanders gave Jack the Brigade's flag, which the president unfurled as he stepped to the microphone on the fifty-yard line. "I want to express my great appreciation to the Brigade for making the United States the custodian of this flag," he said. Continuing, he seemed to forget the no-invasion pledge he'd just made to Nikita Khrushchev: "I can assure you that this flag will be returned to this brigade in a free Havana."

In the coming months, the CIA would hold discussions with Rolando Cubela Sccades, a former associate of Fidel Castro who now wished to see the Cuban leader dead. In Paris, a CIA operative would hand the aspiring assassin a weapon, a Paper Mate pen which Agency technicians had rigged with a hypodermic needle to be filled with poison. That delivery took place on November 22, 1963, at almost the exact moment John Kennedy's motorcade passed beneath the Texas School Book Depository in downtown Dallas.

17

CIVIL RIGHTS

Robert Kennedy's blend of moral outrage and political artifice in dealing with the race issue had helped win his brother the White House in 1960. Once in office, the Kennedys would again have to balance the rights of African Americans with the realities of the nation's electoral map. But the requirements of power complicated their task. Whereas the symbolic gesture of two telephone calls had sufficed to free Martin Luther King, Jr., from his jail cell and capture the black vote, now the nation's chief executive and its chief enforcer of the law would be forced to take concrete action, or else to choose unmistakable inaction: "I think if you sat the two Kennedys down in a room and asked them, they would say that racial equality is right," commented Jack Greenberg of the NAACP Legal Defense Fund. "They were pro–civil rights, they wanted to support us. But there were all sorts of reasons why they might have been reluctant to, and we had to take steps which required them to override those concerns." "Honestly," RFK said on one occasion to LaVern Duffy, "before I became attorney general I didn't give a shit about civil rights. It never touched my life." The president and his right hand would have been pleased to ignore the civil rights tidal wave that was about to sweep the nation. Soon, however, they had no choice but to jump in and swim.

Bob Kennedy's earliest statement of principles on the subject came on May 6, 1961, when he traveled to the University of Georgia to deliver one of his first major talks as attorney general. After thanking Georgia for giving his brother "the biggest percentage majority of any state in the Union," he compared the domestic struggle for civil rights to the Free World's fight against communism. Racial incidents such as the discord over school integration in Little Rock, Arkansas, he declared, "hurt our country in the eyes of the world." On the other hand, the recent admission of two black students to the University of Georgia would "without question aid and assist the fight against Communist political infiltration and guerrilla warfare." Bobby vowed forthrightly that his Justice Department would enforce civil rights statues and Supreme Court decisions. "We will not stand by and be aloof," he concluded. "We will move." (He also made clear his intention to desegregate the Justice Department itself.) RFK had intentionally gone deep to the Deep South to present his speech, deciding that to offer such words in a Northern setting would represent an overt act of cowardice. Thus he could not have expected the reaction of the audience of sixteen hundred: a thirty-second standing ovation.

Events quickly tested RFK's promises. In early May, as Arthur Schlesinger describes it in his Robert Kennedy biography, a dozen blacks and whites, under the aegis of the Congress of Racial Equality (CORE) and its director, James Farmer, boarded a bus to confirm recent decisions of the Supreme Court outlawing segregation aboard interstate buses and in the terminals that served them. Heading southward from Washington, D.C., to Georgia, the Freedom Riders encountered some violence but mostly hostile stares as they sat in the vehicle's front seats and on benches in waiting rooms marked "White." Dividing the group in two—half on a Greyhound bus, half on Trailways—they began to hear reports that an ugly public mood awaited them in Alabama.

The reports had not been exaggerated. In Anniston, the buses were met by a mob of white men armed with clubs, bricks, iron pipes and knives. The Greyhound bus was torched; the same renegades then boarded the Trailways coach and beat several of the Riders senseless. In Birmingham, the shaken passengers were greeted by members of the Ku Klux Klan, who subjected them to further acts of violence. When photographs of the carnage appeared on the front pages of every newspaper in America, RFK dispatched John Seigenthaler to the scene.

Seigenthaler telephoned his boss from Birmingham and reported that the Freedom Riders wanted to go on with their journey but that no bus driver would continue. Bobby got in touch with Greyhound's local superintendent. "Well," the attorney general shrilled, "surely somebody at that damn bus company can drive a bus, can't they? . . . I think you . . . had better [get] in touch with Mr. Greyhound or whoever Greyhound is and somebody better give us an answer to this question. I am . . . going to be very upset if this group does not get to complete their trip." With eavesdroppers listening on the line, this last sentence was printed in newspapers throughout the South, confirming for many what they had already suspected: that the attorney general was the secret mastermind of the civil rights movement.

The transportation company complied with RFK's request. The Riders were driven to Montgomery, the state's capital, where they were subjected to a new wave of terror. An angry white mob beat the demonstrators with chains and ax handles, and Seigenthaler, coming to the rescue of an elderly female, was knocked unconscious. To this point Bobby and Jack had been negotiating with Alabama's slippery governor, John Patterson, a sturdy Kennedy man in 1960. "There's nobody in the whole country that's got the spine to stand up to the goddamned niggers except me," Patterson had told Seigenthaler before eventually agreeing to protect the Riders; Bobby regarded the governor's promise as a sham.

"I never thought we would reach the point of having to dispatch troops to troubled areas," RFK told Peter Maas for a *Look* magazine profile. "I cannot conceive of this administration's letting such a situation deteriorate to that level." With such a situation deteriorating to exactly that level, the Kennedys examined their choices. A dispatch of troops from the regular army or the National Guard, a tactic that required a public proclamation of emergency, could have conceivably embarrassed the president before Nikita Khrushchev at their summit in Vienna. A team of federal marshals, which could be sent with only a written notice from the president to the attorney general, seemed a more palatable alternative.

On May 21, Byron White led a force of five hundred marshals, many of them hastily deputized prison guards, to Montgomery, Alabama. That night, some fifteen hundred blacks came to hear Martin Luther King at the Dexter Avenue Baptist Church while twice as many whites gathered on the street outside. Momentarily, one of the whites set a car on fire and the crowd began rushing the marshals, whom Byron White had positioned around the periphery of the building. Bricks and rocks flew as the beleaguered federal forces attempted to repel the surging rioters with clubs and tear gas. Bobby ordered army units placed on alert at Fort Benning, Georgia, then heard that Governor Patterson had proclaimed a state of martial law. After National Guard units under state authority were called in, White placed the marshals under the guard's control, and the guard commander promptly ordered them to depart. The National Guard proceeded to break up the white mob. But when the sermon ended and many of the black churchgoers wanted to leave, they too faced the guard's bayonets: the governor's militia would not permit the blacks to exit the church.

Throughout the night, Robert Kennedy worked the phones to Governor Patterson and Dr. King. James Farmer remembered one contact made by the attorney general: "Bobby called King or King called Bobby—I don't know who initiated the call. After their conversation, King said to me: 'Jim, I've been talking to the attorney general. He would like you to halt the Freedom Ride and have a cooling-off period so he can straighten things out and clear up this matter. Are you willing to oblige?'

"I said, 'No, we've been cooling off for three hundred fifty years. If we cool off anymore we'll be in a deep freeze. So the Freedom Ride will go on.'

"Martin then said, 'Well, Jim, don't you think that maybe the Freedom Ride has made its point and that we should call it off for now?'

"And I said, 'Martin, my purpose is not to make a point, but to end segregation in interstate bus travel. So until that is done I am not justified in calling it off. So I wish you would tell the attorney general that.'

"Martin said he understood and got back on the telephone and passed that message on to the attorney general. And King told me that the attorney general was furious, not only at my rejection of his request but at the flippancy of my language about the 'deep freeze.' Bobby wasn't accustomed to people saying no to him."

Negotiations continued until dawn, when Byron White sent an assistant to the field headquarters of the National Guard's Dixie Division. Amid Confederate (and no United States) flags, the commanding general agreed to escort the blacks to their buses and homes.

A week later, Robert Kennedy petitioned the Interstate Commerce Commission to draft regulations to end segregation in interstate bus terminals. The ICC was reluctant, but in September, after four months of persistent lobbying by the Justice Department, the commission issued the order. It went into effect November 1.

"The Kennedys meant well, but they did not feel it," remarked Farmer. "They didn't know any blacks growing up—there were no blacks living in their communities or going to their schools. But their inclinations were good.

"On Bobby, I had the impression in those years that he was doing what had to be done for political reasons. He was very conscious of the fact that they had won a narrow election and he was afraid that if they antagonized the South, the Dixiecrats would cost them the next election. And he was found to be very, very cautious and very careful not to do that. But we changed the equation down there, so it became dangerous for him *not* to do anything."

The national publicity accorded the Freedom Rides earned James Farmer an invitation to Colorado the following year: "I was moderating a two-week executive seminar sponsored by the Aspen Institute of Humanistic Studies, a great-books course for corporate executives—you know, Shakespeare, Dostoyevsky, Hume, Locke and so on. And at the end of the two weeks the president of the institute, Joseph Slater, asked me if I would stay an additional week because there were some foreign students coming in and they would be meeting with the attorney general. He thought it would be most helpful if I could be there to assist the attorney general, as the students were sure to have questions on the civil rights revolution. I told him I would check my schedule with my office in New York and get back to him right after lunch.

"So after lunch I called Slater and told him I could remain the extra week, but he said, 'Well, Jim, I'm sorry, I'm going to have to withdraw the invitation.'

"I said, 'Why?'

"He said, 'Well, after speaking with you I called the attorney general and told him that there was a possibility that you could stay over and help him field questions. And the attorney general said, "If that sonofabitch Farmer's going to be there, I'm not coming. Cancel him or I'll cancel. I'll bring Thurgood Marshall with me." '

"So I was canceled and he brought Thurgood."

Bobby Kennedy's multivarious readings in history had convinced him that Reconstruction-era efforts to provide blacks with the rights of citizenship had failed because federal officials had gone about the process in the wrong way: they had tried to impose the changes by force instead of allowing them to take root in southern society. So, on Wednesday, September 26, 1962, when James H. Meredith made his third attempt to register as the first African American student at the University of Mississippi, the attorney general sent with him a federal escort of only two men: the Justice Department's John Doar and Chief U.S. Marshal John McShane. Mississippi's Lieutenant Governor Paul Johnson (an opponent of desegregation) was backed by more formidable forces—lines of state troopers and sheriffs—as he awaited the trio by the front gates of the Ole Miss Campus in the picturesque town of Oxford. The would-be student and his two protectors had no choice but to turn back, as white citizens throughout the state exulted.

As the attorney general had conferred with Governor Patterson of Alabama during the Freedom Rides, so now he kept in close contact with

Mississippi's chief executive, Ross Barnett. Some of the conversations were heated, with Barnett railing against a federal "dictatorship" acting at the behest of the "Communist-funded" NAACP, and RFK reminding the governor that he was not just a Mississippi resident, but more important, a citizen of the United States. Generally, however, the two veteran politicians sought accommodation. Barnett wanted to get Meredith's inevitable registration over with while seeming to his state's citizens a model of fiery intransigence; Bobby wanted to install the student without resort to massive federal force. So they worked out a plan whereby Barnett would make a dramatic surrender to two dozen U.S. marshals. The governor, however, found his coscriptwriter's sense of theater insufficient: "I was under the impression," he told Bobby, "that [the marshals] were *all* going to pull their guns. We have a big crowd down here, and if nobody pulls his gun and we all give in, it could be very embarrassing. Isn't it possible to have them all pull their guns?"

On Thursday, Bobby sent Meredith, Doar and McShane, this time accompanied by the marshals, to Ole Miss by car from Memphis. But hearing that Oxford was throbbing with militant jubilation, RFK ordered the caravan to turn back. Reports had it that cars and pickup trucks were cruising the streets with horns blaring and Rebel flags flying; good old boys had come to town from all over the South, beer can in one hand, rifle in the other; radio stations were broadcasting in emergency mode, alternating updates from the university with renditions of "Dixie."

News reports focused on the confrontation. Meanwhile, the Fifth Circuit federal court, which had previously ordered the university's integration, threatened to jail Barnett and his lieutenant governor by the following Tuesday unless Meredith was registered. On Friday, RFK met in the Pentagon War Room with Maxwell Taylor, chairman of the Joint Chiefs of Staff, and Cyrus Vance, secretary of the army, to discuss military options. In place of the maps of Vietnam, Cuba and other Third World hot spots that were usually displayed in that chamber, the three men spread out several detailed road maps of Mississippi.

On Saturday, Bobby deemed the situation serious enough for presidential intervention. "You have a go at him," said the attorney general to his brother as White House operators dialed Barnett's line. Jack took advantage of the delay to rehearse an opening statement: "Governor, this is the president of the United States—not Bobby, not Teddy, not Princess Radziwill." When Barnett got on the phone, the president spared him the jocular introduction but found himself stifling laughter when the Mississippian ended the conversation with thanks for JFK's interest in "our poultry program." Jack and Bobby could not, however, have been amused by the substance of the discussion: asked by the president what he intended to do about the Tuesday deadline, Barnett replied that he needed a few more days to consider the situation. The president's personal authority had been invoked to gain only further delay.

Another scheme—to register Meredith in the state capital of Jackson rather than in the university town of Oxford—fell apart after Barnett attended Saturday's football game between the University of Mississippi and the University of Kentucky. "We want Ross! We want Ross!" the hometown crowd in Jackson's Memorial Stadium began shouting during halftime. The exuberant governor crossed the football field to a microphone that beamed his voice out over a bunk of loudspeakers. "I love Mississippi! I love her people! I love her customs!" he declared, accentuating his words with a raised fist. The cheering fans were euphoric. Whites in the stadium and throughout the Magnolia State were digging in for a last stand on behalf of their race. Barnett, flush with the day's events, called Washington to say he could not go through with the latest deal. That night, President Kennedy signed proclamations placing the Mississippi National Guard under federal command.

Sunday, Barnett was on the phone again, suggesting a new plan of action: he would stand in front of six hundred Mississippi lawmen and civilians—unarmed, he promised—and capitulate to a superior federal force. RFK scotched the suggestion as needlessly precarious, then shrewdly told Barnett that the president was scheduled to speak to the nation that evening and was prepared to reveal that the Mississippi governor had broken the promise he'd made Saturday to register Meredith. The threat served its purpose. Barnett was horrified—not that Americans would believe he had lied to the president, but rather that Mississippians would learn he had been lying to *them* while secretly cooperating in integration efforts. The anxious governor then came up with still another plot: Meredith could be brought to the campus at once. That way, Barnett could continue to rally the state for a Monday showdown and, once the Sunday registration had been revealed, claim he had been tricked by the treacherous Kennedys.

Bobby agreed to the offer and swung the Justice Department into action. Louis Oberdorfer, Nicholas Katzenbach, Ed Guthman, and other Justice Department officials were immediately flown to Mississippi.

Gunfire broke out on campus, and two marshals were hit. They, along with comrades who had fallen in the barrage of flying objects, were taken by ambulance to the closest hospital. Ross Barnett attempted to assure Washington that matters at the university were well in hand. "I haven't had such an interesting time since the Bay of Pigs," joked the president grimly in the White House Cabinet Room, which had become the civil rights command post. Comic relief helped ease the tension but only for a brief span.

Several hours later, word came that rioters had discovered James Meredith's temporary quarters in a university dormitory and were about to storm the building. A lynching seemed possible, even imminent. Three more marshals had been wounded and a British journalist had been killed by a bullet to the back. The marshals, equipped with side arms, began to return fire, as Katzenbach finally told RFK he needed soldiers. The attorney general sadly agreed.

Seventy-five members of the local Mississippi National Guard unit arrived to reinforce the marshals. U.S. Army troops were flown in from Memphis. Their presence more than any other gradually helped restore order. Early Monday morning, soldiers held back a jeering crowd as James Meredith entered the administration building to register for school. That same day, under the guard of federal marshals, he attended his first class.

"I don't think Robert Kennedy understood, when he started out, the extent to which segregation in the South was undergirded by violence and the threat of violence," commented Louis Oberdorfer. By the end of the riots, 160 marshals had been wounded, 28 by gunfire, and a local jukebox repairman had been killed in addition to the English newsman. Robert Kennedy had gone to great lengths to avoid a violent showdown, only to find himself in the middle of a staggering bloodbath. And seeking to show deference to local custom and to the rights of states to self-governance, he allowed himself to be manipulated by a crafty governor with a sweet Dixie drawl. RFK's handling of the crisis pleased no one: not southern whites, to whom the presence of federal troops was a reminder of the post–Civil War occupation; not blacks, to whom Washington's vacillation was a sign that their rights still took second place to white sensibilities. Bobby's actions pleased himself least of all. He blamed himself for failing to resolve the situation without troops, and conversely for waiting so long to call the troops out once they were needed.

Although John Kennedy had previously enjoyed the company of Sammy Davis, Jr., during evenings with Frank Sinatra and Peter Lawford, he was appalled to see him at a reception to celebrate Abraham Lincoln's birthday at the White House in 1963. (He had ordered the entertainer's name stricken from the guest list of some thousand prominent African Americans, but presidential assistant Louis Martin had reinserted it.) Pulling his aides aside, Jack feverishly began looking for ways to keep the entertainer's presence hidden from photographers ready to cover the event. One plan was for the first lady to call Davis aside just before the cameras appeared, but Jackie rejected the idea as insulting and, until her husband spoke soothingly to her, refused to come downstairs for the party. Jack's problem was not with Davis, but with his wife, Swedish actress May Britt. The president feared that photos of him with the interracial couple would not improve his prospects for the coming year's election.

No pictures of Mr. or Mrs. Davis were shot that night at the executive mansion. Nor were any taken of Martin Luther King—because the civil rights leader had boycotted the festivities. King would not attend the party in honor of the sixteenth president because he was disappointed in the thirty-fifth president: after two years in office, Jack had proposed none of the civil rights legislation promised by the Democratic platform in 1960. The president maintained that he could do more for blacks by appointment and executive order than by offering bills to a Congress that would never pass them—an explanation that rang hollow considering that the black community had benefited only sparingly since JFK's entry into the White House.

King and the Kennedys had a good deal of contact in the ensuing months, however, as the preacher led a campaign of protest in Birmingham in April and May. Millions of television viewers watched Birmingham's police force attack demonstrators, including women and children, with German shepherds and water hoses. The operation ended when local merchants agreed to desegregate their businesses—an agreement the Kennedys (to their credit) helped broker both publicly and behind the scenes.

In Birmingham's aftermath, with King and other black leaders showing no signs of relenting, Robert Kennedy took the advice of comedian Dick Gregory and called James Baldwin. The attorney general asked the novelist to assemble some prominent citizens to help him understand the mood of black America. On May 24, at an apartment Joseph Kennedy kept for his family on New York's Central Park South, Baldwin produced a group that included his brother and a cousin, as well as several activists and a number of people from the entertainment field. Martin Luther King had also been invited but because of a prior commitment did not attend.

RFK arrived with Burke Marshall and Ed Guthman. He opened the proceedings with a review of what he considered his administration's unprecedented support of civil rights. When a few listeners cautiously suggested he could accomplish more, the attorney general expressed his puzzlement that the best efforts of the Kennedy administration had met only with rising impatience among blacks. What was worse, African Americans were beginning to succumb to the sway of a new cadre of extremists, exemplified by the Black Muslims, whose growing influence was bound to cause trouble.

One guest refused to be polite. "You don't have any idea what trouble is," barked Jerome Smith, a young CORE activist. "Because I'm close to the moment when I'm ready to take up a gun." Smith, whose participation in the Freedom Rides had won him a stay in Mississippi's notorious Parchman Penitentiary, told Bobby that the administration's problem wasn't with people like Black Muslims, it was with those, like himself, who were tiring of civil disobedience: "I've had enough shit. I'm gonna kiss it off and pull the damn trigger."

Bobby tried to go on with his reasoned presentation, but Baldwin asked Smith if he could imagine serving in his country's armed forces. "Not in a million years! Never!" shouted the young man. "What're you saying?" countered Bobby, visibly shaken by Smith's apparent lack of patriotism. The black activist went on about prisons and police; the white attorney general insisted upon the obligation to military service.

"When Jerome Smith spoke," recalled psychologist Kenneth Clark, "he set the tone for the evening, and that tone was not tempered or deferential. He said, 'I don't identify with a country where people are beaten.' He was extraordinary in the way he zeroed in. It was about as direct, honest and focused a discussion that I have ever heard. Before, or since."

Smith finally said that sitting in the same room with Kennedy made him want to vomit. Insulted, RFK turned away, at which point playwright Lorraine Hansberry (*A Raisin in the Sun*) rose to agree: being there made her sick, too. Harry Belafonte spoke up on the attorney general's behalf, noting the many hours he and RFK had spent together discussing civil rights. Unfortunately, the singer's attempts to pacify the other members of the group failed. When Clarence Jones, an attorney who advised both Baldwin and King, mentioned King's latest idea that the president ought personally to escort students past segregationist blockades, Bobby laughed out loud. Blacks in the room returned the guffaws when the attorney general defended the records of several segregationist judges he had appointed as sops to southern legislators.*

---

*Among the judges was Harold Cox of Mississippi, who from the bench regularly referred to blacks as "niggers" and "baboons." The Kennedys had reason to regret the appointment, as Cox ruled against the Justice Department in a number of civil rights suits.

Robert Kennedy was incensed that those present showed so little consideration for himself, his brother and their respective offices, as well as for the administration's work on behalf of civil rights. "He used the word 'insatiable,'" said Clark. "I guess it seemed as if we wanted everything. As a group, we were hardly impressed by Bobby's assertion that he understood black suffering because of the discrimination his own family had endured as the result of being Irish. After all, they were white."

After nearly four tense hours, Lorraine Hansberry terminated the meeting by leading a walkout. On his way to the front door, Clarence Jones approached Bobby. Patting RFK's shoulder, Jones mentioned that he knew Burke Marshall and the Justice Department's efforts from Birmingham. Bobby responded, "Why didn't you say as much during the meeting?" The attorney general would not forget what he deemed Jones's cowardice.

If Bobby had expected a sympathetic listener in James Baldwin, he was mistaken. "Bobby Kennedy was a little surprised at the depth of Negro feeling," the author said afterward. "We were all a bit shocked at the extent of his naïveté." Yet Kenneth Clark found the attorney general's performance reason for hope: "The intensity and the emotionality that were communicated to him were not lost. He was not totally rejecting it. Although he didn't quite understand what was being communicated to him, he, like his brother, was quite sensitive to the racial problem. The expression on his face was, 'My God, this is something very sincere, a very serious sort of problem.' But I feel at the same time that he was hearing us, he was also protecting us. He didn't cop out and say, 'I'm going to go back to Washington and tell my brother he's got to do all these things you've asked for.' He was trying to get us to understand that what was being said was something that could not be handled tomorrow. Bobby was honest! And I, for one, prefer to work with somebody honest than with a bullshit artist who promises the world and does nothing."

Shortly after the Baldwin meeting, Bobby asked the FBI for information on the participants. Reading over the reports, he noted that Clarence Jones and two others were married to whites; those three, he remarked, must be suffering from psychological "complexes" due to living so easily in the white world. Yet within days he also expressed understanding of the anger he had seen that night, confessing to Ed Guthman that he, too, might feel strongly opposed to his country if he'd grown up black.

Martin Luther King said during this period, "We're through with tokenism and gradualism and see-how-far-you've-comeism. We're through with we've-done-more-for-your-people-than-anyone-elseism. We can't wait any longer. Now is the time."

With the Baldwin meeting, Bobby's comfortable racial world of white men and black servants, a world in which he could take unquestioned pride in his labors on behalf of both America's downtrodden and America's president, began to crack.

B lack dissatisfaction with the Kennedys was exceeded only by Southern white suspicion. David Filvaroff, an aide to Nicholas Katzenbach, recalled the attorney general's reaction to a column written in mid-1963 by reporter James J. Kilpatrick, a Virginian known as an outspoken foe of integration: "The attorney general said, 'I just read this piece by Kilpatrick that all these demonstrations and disruptions were planned by us. You know, it doesn't really bother me that they think we're that venal, but it disturbs the hell out of me that they think we're that stupid.' That wry, very, very sharp sense of self-deprecating humor was typical of the way he would make a point."

One week after the Kilpatrick article appeared, a half dozen blacks were arrested for eating in a bus-station restaurant in Winona, Mississippi, notwithstanding that the federal order outlawing segregation in bus terminals had already brought down "White" and "Colored" signs from most southern stops. When one of the protestors, Annell Ponder, refused to say "sir" to police officers calling her "nigger" and "bitch," the officers beat her furiously. Delivering the blows, they cursed the name Bobby Kennedy.

W hen former amateur boxer George Wallace ran for governor of Alabama in 1962, he declared his intention to oppose integration "to the point of standing in the schoolhouse door." Thus, as the state's chief executive in 1963, he had little choice but to oppose a federal court order to integrate the University of Alabama. Alabama was the only state in the South yet to admit a single black to its state-supported "white" schools, and many of Wallace's constituents cheered his feisty defiance. But a number of the state's leading citizens, weary of racial conflict after the recent events in Birmingham, pressured the governor to stop his antics. Wallace also heard from federal judge Seybourn Lynne, whose stern warnings made clear that a refusal to enroll the students would find the ex-pugilist doing his shadowboxing behind bars.

Robert Kennedy, determined to avoid a repeat of the previous year's disaster at Ole Miss, did not engage in protracted negotiations with Wallace. On June 12, 1963, as Wallace took his position at a lectern placed in front of the university's administration building, he knew that four hundred army troops, specially trained for riot duty, sat in helicopters at

Fort Benning, Georgia, ready to fly to the Tuscaloosa campus at a moment's notice. Nicholas Katzenbach arrived and strode toward the governor. "Stop!" proclaimed Wallace, backed by a cluster of state troopers. After the federal official called upon the governor to give "unequivocal assurance that you will not bar entry to these students," Wallace launched into a lengthy harangue. "I denounce and forbid this illegal and unwarranted action by the central government," he concluded.

Katzenbach then deliberately bumped shoulders with Wallace, forcing the governor to make good on his promise to block the door. After turning away, Katzenbach telephoned Bobby; Bobby telephoned Jack, and the president immediately summoned the Alabama National Guard into service under federal authority. Hours later, a general of the guard ordered Wallace to stand aside, which he did. Two black students—both male—entered the building to enroll. To their surprise, they found a friendly reception. "Hi, there," said a registration clerk to one student. "We've been waiting for you." There were no mobs, no guns, no tear gas.

Bobby had planned the day well. By sending Katzenbach without the students—they sat in cars parked at a distance from the confrontation—RFK permitted Wallace to make his stand without literally turning away the youths, thereby exposing himself to Judge Lynne's threatened contempt charges. The governor was allowed his moment in the (nationally televised) sun, and the registration took place in relative peace.

"The events at Ole Miss," observed Kenneth Clark, "resulted from the fact that the administration attempted to mollify the authorities in that state. The Kennedys didn't understand the depth of racial prejudice there, nor did they realize that nothing they might do could reassure the Mississippians. The whites in that state would fight desegregation to the death, and they did. And so, with all the pussyfooting going on, with all the Kennedys' dillydallying and shilly-shallying, the forces of opposition to integration kept building up and building up, until finally, when the time came for Meredith to enter the university, it was impossible to do it in any peaceful way.

"Well, the administration had learned its lesson by the time the Alabama situation came along. Nobody knew what Wallace was gonna do, but the Kennedys made clear that there would be no backing down. At this point they truly had no alternative except to dissolve the Union. And they didn't want to do that."

As Jack waited to learn the outcome of events in Alabama, he decided to give a speech to the nation that evening on civil rights. His advisers were aghast that such a sensitive topic would be addressed with so little time to prepare. But the president would not be budged, and at 8 P.M. he went on the air. His text, based on a hurriedly written draft by Theodore Sorensen, was unfinished. Much of the speech would be ad-libbed.

"We are confronted primarily with a moral issue," he proclaimed. "It is as old as the Scriptures and is as clear as the American Constitution. The heart of the question is whether all Americans are to be afforded equal rights and equal opportunities, whether we are going to treat our fellow Americans as we want to be treated." Finally, a president of the United States was urging white America to see the condition of its black compatriots as a matter of right and wrong. JFK did not fall back on legalisms, nor did he mention southern heroics with a football. Instead, he declared directly, "Now the time has come for this nation to fulfill its promise. . . . A great change is at hand, and our task, our obligation, is to make that revolution, that change, peaceful and constructive for all." He announced that he would soon submit to Congress a bill calling for the end of segregation in public accommodations.

Martin Luther King, quoted by the following morning's *New York Times* as urging the president to begin speaking of civil rights in moral terms, hastily typed a letter to JFK, calling the speech "one of the most eloquent, profound and unequivocal pleas for Justice and the Freedom of all men ever made by any President." But the jubilation of King and others in the civil rights movement did not last long. That night, as he entered his home in Jackson, Mississippi, Medgar Evers was shot in the back by an assassin who stood in a honeysuckle thicket some fifty yards away. An hour later, the father of three, who had been the state's NAACP field director, was pronounced dead.

I n the ten weeks following the shooting death of Medgar Evers, there was a total of 758 racial demonstrations and 14,733 arrests in 186 American cities. One of the demonstrations occurred in mid-June when approximately three thousand people assembled outside Bobby Kennedy's office to protest the shortcomings they perceived in the Justice Department's approach to civil rights. The attorney general emerged from within to address the crowd. Pointing out that the demonstration was unnecessary, he claimed that the president's recent speech amply demonstrated the administration's ongoing commitment to the black movement.

British journalist Nigel Hamilton, then an intern for the *Washington Post* and later a Kennedy biographer, witnessed the scene: "RFK had no charisma at all. He was terrified; his whole body was shaking, and his voice was shaking, too. I was struck by the smallness of Bobby Kennedy, how short and tiny he looked. When he started to speak, no one could see him, even though he was standing on top of the steps. So someone brought a small ladder, the kind with two or three rungs. He started to get up on it, but was trembling so badly that the ladder started to shake and several of his aides had to hold it steady. He spoke in a quavering voice that could barely be heard."

Bobby did not sway the demonstrators, particularly those carrying placards accusing the Justice Department of racial discrimination in its own hiring practices. Despite the attorney general's sincere efforts at integration, scant progress had been made. Bobby could say little, save to cite percentage gains over the record compiled by the Eisenhower administration. When one protester shouted that he saw precious few blacks exiting the Justice Department's doors, the attorney general could only sputter, "Individuals will be hired according to their ability, not their skin color."

Perhaps the low point of Robert Kennedy's relations with activists of the civil rights movement came two months later, when the Justice Department handed down indictments related to events in Albany, Georgia.

According to an FBI investigation, black field hand Charlie Ware was in handcuffs on July 10, 1961, when Baker County sheriff L. Warren "Gator" Johnson shot him three times in the neck. ("This nigger's coming on me with a knife! I'm gonna have to shoot him," radioed the lawman to his office as he fired from point-blank range.) But a county grand jury indicted Ware, who miraculously survived the bullets, for felonious assault on the sheriff. Unable to make bail, Ware languished in jail for over a year before trial. His lawyer, C. B. King, a black resident of Albany who gave the town's white establishment little peace, refused to leave Ware's fate to the discretion of the state authorities and filed a suit in federal court charging Johnson with violation of Ware's civil rights.

The shooting set in motion the Albany Movement, a two-year campaign seeking desegregation and universal suffrage in the southwest Georgia town. Among the targets of the demonstrators were three white-owned grocery stores that served Albany's black neighborhood but reserved their better jobs for whites only. So, in the spring of 1963, when a federal jury took less than ninety minutes to find Gator Johnson not liable, courtroom spectators recognized among the all-white panel a familiar face—it belonged to Carl Smith, owner of one of the offending markets.

The following week, protesters set up a picket line outside Smith's store. But the demonstration's expected ending—dispersal of the line by the police coupled with the usual arrests—marked only the beginning of the response by the town's whites to the day's happenings, and, indeed, to the entire two years of upheaval. A lawyer in Albany's most prominent firm contacted the local bar association, the FBI, the trial judge and Burke Marshall to charge that the blacks in front of the store were attempting to punish the storekeeper for his role in the court case, thus violating federal statutes against intimidation of jurors. Other lawyers in the firm included the town's mayor and a close political associate of the state's two U.S. senators, Richard Russell and Herman Talmadge.

For months, blacks had been pleading in vain with federal authorities to investigate the many instances of brutality inflicted upon their number by the town's police, including the beating of a pregnant woman whose child was stillborn a month later. But within days of the white allegations concerning the grocer, more than thirty FBI agents arrived. The G-men found little evidence to support the charges of juror intimidation, especially since protests had taken place at Smith's store before the trial as well as after, and his establishment wasn't the only one to draw such attention. Nevertheless the Justice Department soon swore in a special grand jury and sent a force of U.S. marshals into the town's black neighborhoods to serve subpoenas.

One of the witnesses brought before the panel was Joni Rabinowitz, a white Antioch College student who had arrived that spring to work with the Albany Movement. Her father, a leftist New York attorney, recalled that his daughter had been unaware of the real reason she'd been summoned. "Joni assured me that this was a friendly grand jury," said Victor Rabinowitz, "that it was formed in response to the demands by SNCC for a federal investigation, and that everybody in Albany understood as much. Now, that wasn't all the case. The FBI agents who had been down there had not been interviewing the SNCC people but instead had been interviewing the opposition." Despite testimony that the young Rabinowitz was not among the picketers at Smith's store, she and eight others were indicted.

The indictments were announced in early August by the attorney general himself. Although many in the Justice Department vehemently opposed the action, RFK was unwilling to offend the white southerners involved, a Kennedy-appointed segregationist judge among them. Rabinowitz was the only one to be charged with the "crime" of picketing the former juror's establishment; the others were slapped with various contrived charges that included perjury. The proceedings were plainly an attempt at political coercion: in addition to the young white student whose indictment was meant to frighten others like her from civil rights work in the South, the defendants included several blacks who had played key roles in the Albany Movement. RFK underscored his commitment to the indictments by sending senior Justice Department lawyers to help the U.S. attorney for Georgia prosecute the case. His efforts, however, yielded meager results: Joni Rabinowitz was convicted on the district level, but her conviction was overturned on appeal; of the remaining Albany defendants, three were convicted of misdemeanors, five were completely vindicated.

After the Freedom Rides, after Ole Miss and the University of Alabama, after Birmingham and the meeting with James Baldwin, Robert Kennedy still could not bring himself to take a decisive stand in defiance of white racist opinion. "For the Kennedys to take on the southern establishment at that point was just not in the cards," said Victor Rabinowitz. "Bobby—well, we despised him. I mean, he was at the very lowest level."

I n early June 1963, Martin Luther King announced plans for a massive March on Washington to be held in August. The huge demonstration, uniting civil rights forces from all sectors of the movement, would put pressure on the current administration to vigorously support the public-accommodations legislation it was about to propose. It was further aimed at Congress, where a southern filibuster of the bill was expected in the Senate.

The Kennedys were not eager for the capital to be flooded by the hundred thousand marchers forecast by King. Once JFK announced the bill, he tried to convince the civil rights leader that discreet presidential persuasion, not a noisy public rally, was the best means of seeing it through Congress. But King would not be moved. The attorney general also took part in the effort to dissuade King, and in late June he appeared on NBC's *Meet the Press*. When moderator Lawrence Spivak opened the interview with a question about the march, Bobby, according to an FBI memo written the next day, "was most emphatic in opposing such action and stated Congress should not be faced with such pressure while debating legislation."

Walter Fauntroy, then director of the Washington bureau of King's Southern Christian Leadership Conference and later the District of Columbia's nonvoting representative to Congress, remembered attending a planning session for the march during the first week of July. "When I returned to Washington with the responsibility for coordinating the arrangements," noted Fauntroy, "I met with Bobby and he was, quite frankly, frightened to death. He said, 'You really shouldn't do it. You'll give right-wing extremists an excuse to precipitate violent situations. It will be a debacle. The Klan will be there and the Nazis. They could do so many things where you've got a hundred thousand people all together. There could be riots.'*

"But I argued it would be a classic display to the world of the efficacy of our First Amendment. It could be a model, it could be historic. And he, because the march was inevitable, finally decided to work with us.

"And I'll never forget, he was so helpful. The word got out to most of the federal agencies, including our District of Columbia government, that the president's brother wants you to cooperate and see to it that this event comes off. We had commitments and cooperation from the Parks and Planning Commission, the Metropolitan Police Department, the Capital Police, the Parks Police, the National Guard, the army, the intelligence agencies. As a result, by the time the march was two weeks off, conservative newspapers were saying that it was the Kennedy boys who were staging the event."

Despite his grudging public cooperation on the gathering's logistics, Bobby remained a private critic. Marietta Tree, a Kennedy appointee to the UN Human Rights Commission and the wife of anti-Cuba CIA operative Desmond FitzGerald, sat next to the attorney general at a dinner party held at Averell Harriman's Georgetown residence on August 27, the night before the march. The conversation turned to Bayard Rustin, chief organizer of the rally and a homosexual. "Bobby was terribly contemptuous of Rustin," recalled Tree. "He referred to him as 'that sad old black fairy.' And he was frightfully scornful of Martin Luther King. Said he'd lost some of his influence, and that he wasn't really a serious person. . . . Naturally I expressed my dissent with Bobby that evening because I thought the march was a very important and wonderful thing, and was rousing the Congress and the country to look at the plight of the black in America. I was horrified that the attorney general could talk this way." RFK had little use for Tree's opinion. "He was very contemptuous of me, because he put me into a category, which I resented deeply, of being a softy, a fuzzy-minded liberal, etc. Well, it is all the more ironic that toward the end of his life he became so strongly pro helping the blacks, helping the disadvantaged and the poor."

The following day, as the Kennedys watched on television, Martin Luther King spoke of his dream. As successful as the march was, King

---

* RFK had long counseled civil rights leaders against holding demonstrations in favor of supporting Justice Department legal actions. Fauntroy summarized Bobby's argument: "Better to take the kind of money and the kind of energy you're planning to spend bringing these people together, and instead use the resources to fight voting-rights abuse and to get people to the polls. Because if you get them to the polls, *they* can change the system."

had made a miscalculation in its planning: the hundred thousand he'd predicted turned out to be a quarter million.

I n December 1961, talking to a British reporter, Robert Kennedy had belittled the internal Communist threat so dear to the inquisitional heart of J. Edgar Hoover. So it is little surprise that a month later, when the director sent over a memo warning that a top adviser to Martin Luther King was also a top agent of the Soviet Union, the attorney general paid it little heed.

Not so Byron White. The deputy attorney general could hardly wait for RFK to leave town on February 1 before moving on Hoover's tip.* On February 2, he called Courtney Evans into his office to assert "that definitely some action should be taken," according to Evans's memo of the conversation. The acting attorney general in RFK's absence, White requested the Bureau's file on the allegedly Red civil rights activist, Stanley Levison, a New Yorker who was King's closest white friend. Evans approached Hoover, but the director refused White access, saying that the material was too important to disclose. The truth of the matter was that the director could not supply the evidence against Levison without revealing it to be flimsy and exaggerated.

Robert Kennedy was already familiar enough with J. Edgar Hoover to know that his overheated alarm about Levison was fueled by his hatred for King, whose race he considered suitable for little more than shining shoes and whose "dreams" he considered a challenge to the very order he had dedicated himself to maintain. But after he returned from overseas, the attorney general reconsidered Hoover's bias against the civil rights movement, and in mid-March he approved a request from the director to place wiretaps on Levison's telephone. (Hoover also planted bugs in Levison's office—federal statutes stipulated that he didn't require the attorney general's authorization for the placement of hidden microphones.)

On June 22, 1963, just ten days after JFK's passionate address on civil rights, Martin Luther King visited the White House. Expecting to press his case for more presidential leadership on what JFK had called a "moral issue," King was blindsided by consecutive attacks on the subject of Levison and another aide similarly tainted, Jack O'Dell. First, he met with Burke Marshall, who tried to enlighten him as to his friends' true

---

*RFK, accompanied by Ethel, spent the entire month on an international goodwill tour. They visited fourteen countries and logged thirty thousand miles, predominantly in Europe and the Far East.

identities. Unconvinced, he was hurriedly shuttled to Bobby for further browbeating. Finally the president himself took King for a Rose Garden stroll. Hinting at FBI coverage of the civil rights leader—"I assume you know you're under very close surveillance"—John Kennedy urged King to jettison his two associates.

The claims of the three officials to King were preposterous—listening devices had been in place on Levison for fifteen months with no evidence whatsoever to support the FBI's accusation that Levison was "a paid agent" of the Kremlin and O'Dell was the "number five Communist in the United States." Yet the stranglehold that J. Edgar Hoover had on Bobby and his brother seemed to be tightening. The director had just told the Kennedys he had become aware of the Campbell-Giancana connection. And the brothers had good reason to fear the harm Hoover could do them by revealing even a whiff of Communist influence over the civil rights movement—a movement much of the public deemed a Kennedy plot. Moreover, as Taylor Branch points out in *Parting the Waters,* his authoritative history of the civil rights years, King's crusade threatened to tear apart the fragile political coalition that had carried Jack and Bobby into office. Were King to admit his movement's contamination, the Kennedys would gain an edge over him, much as the FBI director held leverage over the brothers by his knowledge of their sex lives. Bobby was learning the director's lessons well. The week before the meeting with King, he had called Hoover to arrange a special FBI briefing on guidelines for warning the civil rights leader without compromising the Bureau's sources. As Branch writes, "For once, Kennedy was pushing Hoover about the threat of domestic subversion instead of vice versa."

The role reversal continued. In July, King informed Kennedy that he would not move against Levison without proof of the aide's subversive ties. Maintaining the secrecy of FBI files, Bobby could present only an absurd suggestion, made through Burke Marshall, comparing Levison to Rudolf Abel, the Soviet master spy who had stolen American nuclear secrets. King, sensing the Kennedy-Hoover tug-of-war, offered a deal: he would cease direct communication with Levison, but continue to consult him through intermediaries. That way, FBI snoops would believe the two men had ceased contact. To deliver his proposal to Marshall, King sent his lawyer, Clarence Jones, whose marriage to a Caucasian woman coupled with his apparent spinelessness nettled Bobby to no end.

When Marshall reported King's proposal, RFK was outraged. The civil rights leader had been warned by the president himself and had refused to act, and now he had the effrontery to suggest that he and the attorney general conspire to deceive the FBI. What's more, Jones had told Marshall of JFK's tip-off to King about Bureau surveillance; were that warning to become known to Hoover, the Kennedys' relationship with the director could become even more perilous. As soon as Burke Marshall left the room, Bobby picked up the telephone to call Courtney Evans. The attorney general ordered the installation of wiretaps on both King and Jones. In the past, requests for taps had come from Hoover to RFK. The idea to tap the nation's premier civil rights leader, however, originated with Bobby.

Evans advised caution: "I . . . raised the question as to the repercussions if it should ever become known that such a surveillance had been put on King," he wrote in his memo of the call.

"The AG said this did not concern him at all; that in view of the racial situation, he thought it advisable to have as complete coverage as possible."

The FBI paperwork for the devices came through within a week and Bobby approved the tap on Jones right away. But he held on to the form regarding King's surveillance for two days. By requesting the tap, Bobby had implicitly lent his endorsement to Hoover's version of the King story. Yet he evidently flinched at making this final, written commitment to the director's view, for he sent the form back unsigned, thus withholding authorization for the tap.

Bobby's disposition of the matter would change, however, and one factor in the shift had nothing to do with the rights of African Americans or the supposed infiltration of King's Southern Christian Leadership Conference by Communists. As so often was the case with the Kennedys, it had to do with sex.

For Ellen Rometsch, Capitol Hill provided a more bountiful environment than her native East Germany, which she'd left in 1955. She moved to Washington in 1961 as the wife of a West German army sergeant assigned to his country's embassy and soon became a frequent guest at the Quorum Club, an exclusive downtown watering hole part-owned by Lyndon Johnson's protégé Bobby Baker. (Baker, top aide to Johnson when LBJ was Senate majority leader, had stayed on in the post with the Texan's successor, Mike Mansfield of Montana.) Rometsch became one of the more popular habitués of the club, appreciated for her eager-to-please "party girl" personality, her seductive outfits (like low-cut dresses and fishnet hose) and her dazzling looks, which some of the powerful legislators she met there compared to those of Elizabeth Taylor.

Bill Thompson, a railroad lobbyist, took Rometsch to meet his friend

President Kennedy, and Jack "sent back word," said Baker, "it had turned out to be the best time he ever had in his life. That was not the only occasion they met. She saw him again. It went on for a while."

Topping her list of eminent intimates with the president of the United States made the young German a bit giddy, and she shared news of her good fortune with friends. That loquaciousness became the instrument of her undoing and by July 1963 the FBI had begun to monitor her fun. The FBI had become interested in more than her proficiency at having a good time; her country of origin, as well as her husband's position at the embassy, gave Hoover's men reason to suspect espionage. With the Novotny-Chang revelations linking Jack to Britain's Profumo case still fresh, Robert Kennedy acted quickly; in August, Rometsch and her husband were quietly deported back to West Germany.*

Less than a month after Ellen Rometsch's departure, a new Washington scandal emerged. An unhappy vending-machine contractor spoke out about the favors he thought he'd paid for, but not received, from Bobby Baker, and the intricate web of Baker's arrangements around town began to unravel. The rapidly appearing revelations focused on Baker's activities as Capitol Hill's leading influence peddler, but his involvement in many of the city's more prominent sex lives lurked beneath the surface as Congress opened an investigation of the mess.

With his brother's link to the Baker affair threatening to become public any day, RFK on October 7 received a renewed request by the FBI to tap King. Three days later, he signed the form authorizing the surveillance on King's Atlanta home and New York office. On October 21, Bobby approved a Bureau request for four more taps on King.

Following his triumphant march and stirring speech in August, Martin Luther King's national stature had grown ever larger, and Bobby's need for information on him had grown ever more vital. Yet having authorized the eavesdropping to acquire that intelligence, RFK had eliminated any and all remaining means he had to control Hoover. The attorney general admitted as much to Evans the day he signed the form: granting the FBI agent's point of three months earlier, Bobby emphasized that disclosure of the taps would be disastrous; clearly, RFK realized he had armed the director with political dynamite to use at his whim. With the Rometsch scandal brewing, Robert Kennedy could stand up to neither Hoover's abhorrence of King, nor his own desire to outflank

---

* Ellen Rometsch wasn't the only woman deported by Attorney General Robert Kennedy. Marita Lorenz, who possessed an American passport, was deported to Venezuela in 1964 because of an alleged onetime romance with Fidel Castro.

Hoover. He later said there would have been "no living with the Bureau" had he withheld his approval.

Although he had gotten his way on the King wiretaps, the FBI director would give Jack and Bobby no rest. He pounced on the Rometsch affair, his position strengthened by the knowledge that Jack wasn't the only Kennedy to have enjoyed the lovely German's charms. "Information has been developed that pertains to possible questionable activities on the part of high government officials," read a Bureau memo dated October 26. "It was also alleged that the President and the Attorney General had availed themselves of services of playgirls." The same day Hoover received that report, a Saturday, the *Des Moines Register* ran a front-page story titled "U.S. Expels Girl Linked to Officials." Written by Clark Mollenhoff, a journalist as friendly with the FBI director as he was with the attorney general, the article stated that the Bureau had "established that the beautiful brunette had been attending parties with congressional leaders and some prominent New Frontiersmen from the executive branch of Government. . . . The possibility that her activity might be connected with espionage was of some concern, because of the high rank of her male companions." The story also mentioned that Senator John Williams, a conservative Republican from Delaware, "had obtained an account" of Rometsch's doings—an account later determined to consist of a set of documents from the FBI. Williams vowed to present his findings, including a list of the woman's "government friends," the following Tuesday to the Senate Rules Committee, the body investigating Bobby Baker. The Kennedys had only recently managed to dodge the bullet of the actual Profumo affair. Now this homegrown version of the British scandal seemed about to release a career-ending cannonade.

The appearance of the article on a weekend and in a small-town newspaper gave Bobby some room to maneuver. He telephoned LaVern Duffy, his investigator during his work for the Senate committees, and ordered him on the next airplane to West Germany. Rometsch, the *Register* story had noted ominously, was rumored to be angry that "important friends" had forced her to leave the United States. Duffy had been instructed to make sure she kept her mouth shut. He succeeded in his mission—letters Rometsch later wrote thanked him for the money he gave her and promised, "Of course I will keep quiet."*

---

*Duffy, himself one of Rometsch's lovers, gave her (he told the current author) a total of $65,000, "all of it Kennedy money." The overriding fear among the Kennedys was that Rometsch, being East German, could possibly have been a Communist spy. It is worth noting that the FBI files linked JFK, RFK *and* Lyndon Johnson with the sultry brunette. All three were apparently involved with her at roughly the same time.

RFK subsequently called Jack, and the brothers agreed that in order to "control" Senator Williams before Tuesday's hearing they needed the help of the Senate brass: Mike Mansfield and his Republican counterpart, Everett Dirksen of Illinois. The Kennedys knew, however, that only one man could guarantee the two senators' cooperation.

Early Monday morning, RFK told Courtney Evans to alert the director to be prepared for a meeting. The proud young attorney general did not use the buzzer behind his desk to summon the older man; instead he rose and walked down the hall to Hoover's office. He brought with him an urgent plea: Hoover must warn Mansfield and Dirksen that a full airing of the Rometsch case would implicate so many members of both the legislative and executive branches as to inflict serious damage on the integrity of the national government.

The director let the supplicant burn. The Bureau had already compiled a comprehensive memo on the matter, he noted, and the attorney general was free to read the document to the senators himself. RFK continued to press. The legislators were concerned mainly with possible security breaches, he said. (They had no business, he implied, being concerned with details of the Kennedys' private lives.) The director's personal assurances were imperative. (Hoover needed to let the legislators know that if the Senate played with this fire, members from both sides of the aisle would be badly burned.) Hoover offered but a hint of relief: he revealed that he had been given a phone message from Mansfield and would shortly return the senator's call.

Bobby then turned the discussion to civil rights. After inquiring about the Bureau's progress in solving a recent church bombing in Birmingham, he mentioned an FBI report released the previous Friday characterizing King as "an unprincipled man," one who "is knowingly, willingly, and regularly taking guidance from communists." When he'd read the report, which Hoover had disseminated throughout the government in an effort to discredit not only King, but also the Kennedy brothers who he believed coddled him, Bobby had been livid. Now, the best the attorney general could muster in the director's presence was that even though the document did not expressly label King a Communist, many people might conclude he was one from reading it. The smug director would only reply that the report was "accurate and supported by facts."

After Bobby left his office, Hoover telephoned Mansfield, who requested that the director meet him and Dirksen that afternoon. Following their conference, which took place at Dirksen's home, Mansfield telephoned the president. Hoover, he said in a state of disbelief, had named names, dates and locations. His briefing not only implicated the chief executive, but also tied senators from both parties to a host of favors arranged by Baker, including cash, cruises and women. The next day, Senator Williams confined his remarks to Baker's financial sins. Hoover's shock therapy had worked.

Meanwhile, the taps on Martin Luther King had been activated. The overheard conversations revealed the civil rights leader to be, like the Kennedys, an adroit navigator of political shoals. They also disclosed another side of King to which all three Kennedy brothers could relate. Roswell Gilpatric recalled reading transcripts in which King discussed a number of sexual liaisons, with both black and white women. One of his more frequent escorts was Phyllis Daitch, a white schoolteacher from Alabama in her mid-twenties.* Agents of the Bureau tracked her down; they described her as a green-eyed blonde with an hourglass figure. King had described her as "a piece of tail who can go all night long."

Through early 1963, despite all the information in Hoover's files on the Kennedys, the brothers had made little secret within high government circles of their intention to replace the FBI chief. The director would in 1965 turn seventy, the mandatory retirement age for federal employees, and JFK would not issue the executive order needed to retain him. "The way it came to me," reminisced William Hundley, "was that the president had said to Bobby, 'I can't do it now. But when I'm re-elected I'm going to get rid of him, make him boxing commissioner or something.' And when I'd bitch to Bobby about Hoover, he'd say, 'Wait, just wait.' That kind of comment kept getting back to Hoover."

On October 29, the day after he'd rescued the Kennedy brothers from probable impeachment over the Rometsch affair, and less than three weeks after Bobby had approved the initial tap on King, the director asked the attorney general about the rumors he had heard concerning termination of his employment. RFK assured him the gossip was baseless. Over lunch at the White House two days later, the president repeated his pledge, and within the next twenty-four hours, Bobby approved the director's request to tap Bayard Rustin.

J. Edgar Hoover wasn't going anywhere.

In late 1963, when Lyndon Johnson became president, he predicted privately that his support of civil rights would cost the Democrats the South for years to come. He buried Barry Goldwater in 1964, but the

---

* Phyllis Daitch committed suicide in 1969, one year after the assassination of Martin Luther King.

Arizonan's inroads into the former Confederacy marked the beginning of the historic shift of white southerners to the party of Lincoln—a change that by the 1990s has produced a Congress as dominated by southern Republicans as its predecessor of a generation ago was controlled by Dixie Democrats. (The transformation was aided in no small way by the 1968 presidential campaign of the governor whose national career began when he stood up to Bobby in the schoolhouse door.)

Lyndon Johnson, the son of dust bowl Texas who was distrusted by blacks in the 1960 campaign, sacrificed his party's future to the greater good of equal justice, using his famous legislative skills to see consequential civil rights bills enacted throughout his administration. John Kennedy, the privileged New Englander who was ultimately embraced by blacks in 1960, did not show similar foresight or courage.

And his brother walked right beside him. Early in the administration, Bobby told Georgians he would enforce the law. And in some of the instances in which he was called upon to act—during the Freedom Rides, at Ole Miss and the University of Alabama—Robert Kennedy did apply the force of the federal government to protect citizens' rights, albeit not as vigorously as civil rights advocates wished. Still, he could not bring himself to place the full weight of his office, and of his family, behind the civil rights cause. With the Albany Nine, he gave blacks reason to see the federal government as just another purveyor of the white justice they had already so long endured. And, most egregiously, for reasons mixing political belief and family secrets, RFK unleashed against Martin Luther King and others the police power of the state in the person of the most curious—and the most dangerous—man in America, J. Edgar Hoover.

On righting the wrongs done the descendants of slaves, Bobby the moral absolutist butted heads with Bobby the political operator, fierce defender of his brother's office. On the preeminent moral issue of his attorney generalship, the moral absolutist gave way to his lesser self.

18

MARILYN

Happy birthday . . . Mr. Pres . . . i . . . dent
Happy birthday . . . to you.
—Marilyn Monroe, May 19, 1962

Hollywood's most beguiling star was all whisper and curves and sex that night as she congratulated John Kennedy two days past his forty-fifth birthday. No more than a handful of the fifteen thousand loyal Democrats at the Madison Square Garden fund-raiser could have known that the nation's chief executive and the screen goddess singing to him had been sleeping together on occasion for three years. And even fewer could have suspected that JFK wasn't the actress's only lover listening to her musical tribute from the arena's presidential box. Robert Kennedy, seated beside the older brother he revered, had only recently become intimate with the blonde lusted after by males from Tallahassee to Tehran. Not three months after the president's birthday party, Marilyn Monroe would lie dead in her Brentwood bedroom. During those last eleven weeks, her life would be intricately intertwined with the life of the attorney general of the United States.

Since their initial walk on Peter Lawford's private stretch of California beach in 1957, and their initial episode of sex at Frank Sinatra's California home in 1959, Jack and Marilyn had connected a number of times on both West Coast and East. But Bobby, too busy managing Jack's nomination to meet the star during the 1960 Democratic convention, didn't make her acquaintance until February 1, 1962, when he and Ethel spent the night in Los Angeles on the first leg of their fourteen-country goodwill tour. The Lawfords threw a dinner party that evening honoring RFK and invited, among others, their good friend Marilyn. (Also on the guest list was an actress RFK had already met, Kim Novak.) The following day, Marilyn described the gathering in a letter to the teenage son of her most recent ex-husband, playwright Arthur Miller. The attorney general, she wrote, "is very intelligent, and besides all that, he's got a terrific sense of humor. . . . When they asked him who he wanted to meet, he wanted to meet me. So I went to the dinner and I sat next to him, and he isn't a bad dancer, either." When not doing the foxtrot together, they discussed issues of the day, with the thirty-six-year-old attorney general complimenting the thirty-five-year-old actress for asking questions "that the youth of America want answers to."

At the end of the meal, the fascinated government official called his disabled father in Florida to brag that he had sat next to Marilyn Monroe. The actress likewise spoke to the ambassador, a man who had known a movie star or two himself, and afterward sent him a letter. In response, Bobby's sister Jean wrote Marilyn from Palm Beach to thank her for the "sweet note to Daddy" and to quip, "Understand that you and Bobby are the new item! We all think you should come with him when he comes back East!" (How much Jean knew about the *old* item—Marilyn and Jack—has never been revealed.)

Bobby and Ethel flew to Honolulu, en route to Tokyo, the morning after the Lawfords' party. Upon his return to the States at the end of February, RFK immediately contacted his new friend. Bobby and Marilyn first made love during late winter or early spring. For the time being, however, Marilyn remained the president's girl.

"She was crazy about Jack," recalled Peter Lawford. "She devised all sorts of madcap fantasies with herself in the starring role. She would have his children. She would take Jackie's place as first lady. The fact that he was president allowed her to attach a lot of symbolic meaning to the affair. It had been merely a lark for him, but she really fell for the guy, for what he represented. In her depressive and currently doped-out state, she began to fall in love with him—or she convinced herself she was in love, which is basically the same thing.

"Besides telephoning Jack at the White House, she used to send him copies of her love poetry, most of it written early in her career. Then one day she told me she had actually telephoned Jackie at the White House. For all her romanticism and masochism, Marilyn could also be a mean little bitch. Everybody wrote her up as being the poor, helpless victim, but that wasn't necessarily always the case.

"According to Marilyn, Jackie wasn't shaken by the call. Not outwardly. She agreed to step aside. She would divorce Jack and Marilyn could marry him, but she would have to move into the White House. If Marilyn wasn't prepared to live openly in the White House and assume all the responsibilities that came with being first lady, she might as well forget about it.

"In fact, Jackie was infuriated by the call, and for some reason blamed Frank Sinatra for it. She couldn't easily blame me because I was family, so she took it out on him. She and Sinatra had always been on decent terms. He visited the White House, Hyannis Port, Palm Beach. Jack and Jackie hosted him aboard [Joe's yacht] the *Honey Fitz*. But this marked the end of it for Jackie. Sinatra was no longer welcome at the White House, or in any of the other Kennedy bastions."

Shortly after the first lady stopped talking to Sinatra, the rest of the first family cut off contact as well. The attorney general, hot in pursuit of mafiosi like Sam Giancana and Johnny Roselli, advised his brother that the gangsters' favorite vocalist made poor presidential company, and Jack agreed.

The president's decision to distance himself from Sinatra came just as he was preparing to spend the weekend of March 24–26 at the singer's Palm Springs compound. The planned excursion, timed to coincide with a trip by Jackie to India and Pakistan, spurred on the prospective host to a flurry of home improvement: Sinatra added several rooms to his already mammoth house, some cottages for the Secret Service and a concrete landing pad to accommodate the president's helicopter. The proud property owner could hardly have been expected to enjoy hearing that his hospitality would now be rejected, so the president, a ready delegator of awkward tasks, asked the attorney general to see that Sinatra got the news.

Bobby passed the job to Lawford. "So I rang up Sinatra," recounted the British actor, "and laid it out. I blamed it on security, said that the Secret Service felt his place would be difficult to secure. Sinatra knew bullshit when he heard it. He telephoned Bobby Kennedy and called him every name in the book and a few not in it. He told RFK what a hypocrite he was, that the Mafia had helped Jack get elected but weren't allowed to sit with him in the front of the bus.

"Jack, meanwhile, had made arrangements to spend the weekend at Bing Crosby's Palm Springs home. This blew Sinatra's mind. The other singer wasn't even a goddamn Democrat. Sinatra unfairly blamed the whole thing on me. It ended our friendship. I heard later that he grabbed a sledgehammer and tore apart the heliport he'd built for Kennedy."

Despite the Republican singer's chaste public image, the president went ahead with the less-than-chaste activities he'd planned for his stay with the Democratic singer of seamy public image. Most people who came to Crosby's place for the party the crooner threw that weekend spent the evening either at poolside or wandering in and out of the hacienda-style residence. Only a handful were invited to a cottage where the Leader of the Free World was holding court. Although JFK wore a turtleneck sweater, his attire was nonetheless more formal than that of his companion for the night. Marilyn Monroe was covered by only a bathrobe as she and the president made no attempt to hide their intimacy. No one who saw the couple could doubt that later on they would take their night's rest in the same bed.

It was Peter Lawford's idea to have Marilyn sing for the finale of the president's birthday gala in May. Executives at Twentieth Century-Fox, however, did not share the actor's party spirit. Shooting had just begun on *Something's Got to Give,* a big-budget CinemaScope film costarring Marilyn with Dean Martin, and the studio's considerable investment seemed to be in jeopardy. Pleading illness, the actress appeared on the set only on the rarest occasions. And much of the footage director George Cukor shot of her when she did show up proved unusable, for she slurred her lines in what producers described as a kind of "hypnotic" slow motion. Studio heads were not pleased that their star, too sick to make the movie her contract demanded, seemed healthy enough to fly to New York for the president's birthday celebration. Bobby Kennedy placed a telephone call to Milton Gould, then chairman of Twentieth Century-Fox's executive committee. "He wanted us to release Marilyn for a few days so she could attend JFK's party," said Gould. "I told him it was impossible. We were way behind. RFK got very angry and abusive and banged the phone down on me. He called me a 'no-good Jew bastard,' which I didn't like very much." Soon Marilyn was on a plane flying east.

Marilyn had asked her couturier, Jean-Louis, to create her dress for the evening. At a cost of seven thousand dollars, the designer had fashioned a gown of flesh-colored mesh studded with rhinestones. Skintight, the garment would somehow have to be slipped on; underneath, Marilyn would wear nothing at all. She called the creation "skin and beads," although few people saw the beads.

According to James Spada's biography of Peter Lawford, *The Man Who Kept the Secrets,* Marilyn arrived at the Garden well before showtime with her hair already set. But to apply the finishing touches she took RFK's recommendation and called in Mickey Song, who had just given haircuts to both Kennedy brothers. While the stylist was plying his trade—including the placement of a flip curl on the star's right side—he observed Bobby pacing to and fro outside the open dressing-room door. Eventually, the attorney general stepped inside and ordered the hairdresser to leave. Song complied and Bobby closed the door. When it opened twenty minutes later, RFK emerged and Song found Marilyn inside, her hair disheveled. "Mickey," she giggled, "you've got to help me get myself together."

The encounter apparently did not calm the actress's stage fright; for she drank heavily while waiting for her cue and had to be pushed on-stage after emcee Peter Lawford's introduction. Celebrities like Henry Fonda, Jack Benny and Ella Fitzgerald were among the packed house waiting expectantly as Marilyn took thirty seconds to catch her breath. She then looked toward the president and began to sing "Happy Birthday." (Ethel had joined Bobby and Jack for the party, but Jackie passed the evening at her Virginia retreat, Atoka, evidently uninterested in hearing her husband serenaded by the woman who planned to evict her from the White House.) The countless rhinestones on Marilyn's dress glittered in the spotlights as she musically seduced not just the birthday boy, but the thousands of other men in the arena and the millions watching on television.

After finishing the number, Marilyn launched into a specially written version of "Thanks for the Memory,"* then led the audience in a birthday chorus. A huge cake was wheeled toward the actress, and the president soon appeared onstage to cut it. "I can now retire from politics," he joked to the crowd, "after having had 'Happy Birthday' sung to me in such a sweet, wholesome way."

With the show over, the party adjourned only long enough for a few of the more important participants to relocate to a private affair hosted by Arthur Krim, president of United Artists. As much a hit there as she had been at the larger affair before, the beautiful actress captivated no one more than Bobby. Wrote Adlai Stevenson, "My encounters [with Marilyn, that evening] were only after breaking through the strong defenses established by Robert Kennedy, who was dodging around her like a moth around the flame."†

Later that night, Marilyn wished JFK an even happier birthday in one of the bedrooms at the Kennedy suite in the Carlyle. But the actress

---

*Thanks, Mr. President,
  For all the things you've done,
  The battles that you've won,
  The way you deal with U.S. Steel,
  And our problems by the ton,
  We thank you—so much!

†This excerpt from a Stevenson letter to his friend Mary Lasker appeared originally in Arthur Schlesinger's *Robert Kennedy and His Times* which, despite its grave attention to almost every aspect of RFK's political life, practically ignores Bobby's sexual relationship with Marilyn and completely ignores his other dalliances.

did not spend the night with the president. After Jack had taken his satisfaction, Marilyn found her way to another bedroom in the same suite, where she gave delight to her devoted moth, the attorney general of the United States.

Despite a birthday to remember—and despite the million dollars the actress helped raise for the Democratic Party that night—John Kennedy would never again sleep with Marilyn Monroe. Her erratic behavior no longer amused him; he'd tired of the actress's phone calls and love poems. Once again he delegated a distasteful task: he sent his brother to California to get Marilyn off his back.

When Marilyn had signed herself into New York's Payne Whitney Psychiatric Clinic in early 1961 she was expecting gentle treatment of her multiple addictions. Instead, the patient using the pseudonym "Faye Miller" was classified as potentially self-destructive and stripped of all her possessions, including her clothes. Locked in a room with barred windows, she was helpless to avoid the peering eyes of hospital workers who would crowd outside the cell hoping to catch a glimpse of the fallen sex symbol through the tiny pane of shatterproof glass in the door. When she screamed for release from her imprisonment, she was confined in a straitjacket. At last permitted to use the telephone, she called Joe DiMaggio, with whom she had remained close even after their nine-month marriage had dissolved in 1954. The former baseball great immediately arranged for Marilyn to be moved to Columbia Presbyterian Hospital, where she received more humane medical attention.

The cure didn't take, however. Depressed over her recent divorce from Arthur Miller, and terrified that age was diminishing her cinematic appeal, she relied on increasing doses of barbiturates to combat her chronic insomnia. Jeanne Carmen lived next door to the actress in an apartment building on Los Angeles's Doheny Drive. "We were sleeping pill buddies," recalled Carmen. "I wasn't a big drinker, but Marilyn used to mix the booze and the pills, and that's where you get in trouble. We weren't into other stuff—we tried cocaine once, and were bouncing off the walls; neither of us liked it. All we wanted to do was sleep. We took Seconal and Nembutal, both very potent sleeping pills."

Marilyn sought relief from her addictions, and her demons, through Ralph Greenson, a Los Angeles therapist noted as one of the nation's foremost practitioners of classic Freudian psychoanalysis. Greenson, who had also treated Frank Sinatra, began seeing Marilyn on a daily basis. Sometimes the sessions took place at Marilyn's home, but usually the two met at the psychiatrist's residence, where he reserved one room as an office. Before long, the strict boundaries of the doctor-patient relationship began to crumble. "My husband felt Marilyn needed a family," maintained Hildi Greenson, widow of the doctor. (Ralph Greenson died in 1979.) "He thought she was a waif who needed a home." Often, following her late-afternoon hour of therapy, Marilyn would join the Greensons and their two children for dinner. The famed actress spoke little of her film career. "Our conversations consisted mainly of small talk. She would tell me that she liked to help in the kitchen, which she did. She liked peeling potatoes, she liked doing the dishes. She said, 'That I'm good at. I had to do it in the foster homes all the time.'* These dinners came about because she would have no plans whatsoever for an evening.

"I felt sorry for her in many, many ways. She had an intensity in every direction. If she felt angry about something she would pound her chest. You heard it like a drum when she did it. She was a person of multiple moods and it could be that one day her mood was very good and another day you had a feeling she wasn't there because she wasn't paying much attention to you. She'd be very preoccupied with herself. You could feel these changes in mood, but I wouldn't say that I could see her getting better or getting worse—her mood swings were part of her personality."

Dinner-table discussions occasionally turned to politics. "She considered herself very much a liberal," said Hildi Greenson. "At the time she was here she had just been married to Arthur Miller, who, after all, is very much a liberal, and so was she. She used to call herself a Jewish atheist. That was something I thought was wonderful: 'a Jewish atheist.' "

Marilyn's interest in politics, and in politicians, led her to long dialogues with the Greensons' twenty-two-year-old son, Danny, a college graduate with a major in political science. Insecure in dealing with people (like Robert Kennedy) more educated than herself, the actress looked to Danny for coaching. "She very much wanted to learn, and she had very little background to go on," said Hildi Greenson. "New bits of information surprised her and made her wonder; she wanted to know more about them. She had a very inquisitive mind." It was Danny Greenson who helped her prepare the list of questions—on civil rights, Vietnam, the House Un-American Activities Committee—that had so charmed Robert Kennedy at his first meeting with her.

---

* Marilyn, whose given name was Norma Jean Baker, had been raised in a series of orphanages.

Marilyn also befriended Danny's sister, Joan. "She wanted to be pals with Joanie," said the twenty-year-old's mother; "she wanted to sort of adopt her as a younger sister. She could be very charming and, of course, this delighted my daughter. Joan had helped her practice singing 'Happy Birthday' for the president's birthday party. It was my daughter's idea, as far as I know, for Marilyn to sing it the way she did. 'Do it slowly,' she told her, 'don't just sing "Happy Birthday," do it very slowly.' " To her psychiatrist's wife and children, Marilyn made no overt reference to her involvement with the Kennedys. But, said Hildi Greenson, "I think she mentioned it in a very veiled way to my daughter. She told her that she was seeing someone she called 'the General.' It didn't mask the situation very much." ("General" is a common form of address for the attorney general.)

Although Ralph Greenson saw Marilyn practically every day, often for much longer than her hour of analysis, he considered the fragile star to need additional attention, and thus recommended that she accept a live-in companion. The Greensons had bought their house from its original owner, a woman named Eunice Murray, who at this time was in the employ of a psychiatric colleague of Dr. Greenson. Although not trained as a nurse, the sixty-year-old Murray nonetheless had experience working with troubled patients. Marilyn hired Eunice, and the two women soon began living together. The latter's job entailed preparing meals for Marilyn and acting as personal secretary.

For all her problems, Monroe felt optimistic enough in early 1962 to begin shopping for her first house. (Until then, she had lived her entire adult life in apartments and hotel suites.) "Marilyn loved our house," said Hildi Greenson. "And since Eunice Murray had built it, Eunice came in very handy when it came to Marilyn's new abode. The two of them went house hunting together. They found a house on Helena Drive in Brentwood, and then Eunice went with Marilyn to Mexico where they bought tile. They wanted it to be like the tile in our house, and if you were ever in Marilyn's house, you could see that her kitchen was tiled very much like ours." The actress's house resembled the Greensons' on the outside, as well—both were built in the Mexican style. And if Marilyn needed her doctor, she wouldn't have far to go: the two dwellings were only a mile and a half apart. (The Lawfords' home was located in the vicinity.)

Despite all the care the Greensons lavished on Marilyn, and all the trust she placed in each of the four family members, Ralph Greenson had little influence over the actress's bad habits. He cooperated in her care with an internist, Dr. Hyman Engleberg, but the patient's recalcitrance prevented the two physicians from fully exercising their collective medical wisdom. "The idea," said Hildi Greenson, "was that she was never to be said no to when she wanted a prescription, because the only thing that would happen was she would procure medication elsewhere and not inform her primary physicians about it. So whenever she asked for a drug she would usually get it."

Marilyn turned to both Greenson and Engleberg for prescriptions. Engleberg recounted the procedure he and Greenson followed in attempting to coordinate efforts: "I coordinated with Dr. Greenson as to her sleeping medication, but I didn't go over it with him if, say, I wanted to give her antibiotics for an infection. Nor would I tell him every time I gave her an injection of liver and vitamins. During the last movie she was making she developed a recurring sinus problem, and liver and vitamins boost resistance, they make you feel better. There may also be a positive psychological effect from getting an injection a couple of times a week."

When asked if he had told Dr. Greenson about Marilyn's last Nembutal prescription, the internist said: "As I said, I didn't notify Dr. Greenson about every prescription I wrote for Marilyn. I'm not a little busboy, you know. Regarding her sleeping medication, we were limiting the amount and, generally, I was following our mutual feeling about how much she should have."

Engleberg insisted he was always careful to restrict the number of Nembutal he prescribed: "As I remember, the most we ever gave her at one time was twenty-four." But when Engleberg viewed Marilyn's body just after her death, he realized how little control over his patient's treatment he'd actually had. "I was surprised to learn about the large assortment of sleeping pills which she had apparently bought on a recent trip to Mexico. It's my understanding that in Mexico in those days, you could walk into any pharmacy and buy any tranquilizers or sleeping pills you wanted. There certainly were lots of other pills that I had not prescribed. The coroner told me afterward that he'd found evidence of barbiturates such as Seconal and chloral hydrate. I knew nothing about any chloral hydrate. I never used chloral hydrate. Nembutal was the only sleeping-medication prescription I wrote for her."

Hildi Greenson maintained that her husband had been able to "turn the tide" of Marilyn's drug addiction. "She became less and less dependent on drugs," said the psychiatrist's widow.

On the night table of the bedroom in which Marilyn's lifeless body was found the morning of August 5, 1962, police counted fifteen bottles of pills.

For once, Robert Kennedy failed as his brother's keeper. Instead of cutting Marilyn off, Bobby drew her even deeper into his family's orbit. In his oral history for the JFK Library, Charles Spalding tells of how Bobby, years before meeting Marilyn, accidentally ran over a dog with his car and became terribly upset. "We must have spent three hours going up and down the road. We went into every single house for ten miles . . . until we finally found the owner. And Bobby explained what had happened and said how terribly sorry he felt and asked about the dog—could he replace it or was there anything possible that could be done?" In 1962, Bobby could not help but be smitten by Marilyn Monroe. Possibly this sometimes compassionate man saw the troubled actress as a wounded animal in need of his aid. For whatever combination of reasons, the attorney general fell in love with the film star.

"To John Kennedy, Marilyn was just another fuck," contended Jeanne Carmen. "I don't think he ever really cared about her the way Bobby did, and I don't think she was ever really in love with him. And he wasn't even good in bed; I can tell you that one firsthand, because I had him too. I don't know too many women out here who *didn't* sleep with Jack. He was a two-minute man. I think sex to him was just about another conquest.

"Now, Bobby was a different story. He was sweet, cute and playful, and he really cared about Marilyn. He treated her very well and I think he was in love with her, in his own little way.

"Even though Jack dropped her, Marilyn was obsessed with becoming first lady. She used to dance around the house like a belly dancer, singing, 'First lady, first lady!' She really thought she had a shot at it with Jack, but then also with Bobby, who wanted to be president himself at some point. She thought that if she were first lady it would bring her the power she craved, power she couldn't get just being a movie star. It would also make people take her seriously and accept her as intelligent and smart, which was something she was very sensitive about."

Marilyn's intellectual aspirations inevitably led to a disagreement between the lovers. "Bobby had a real rattlesnake side to him, too," Carmen continued, "and it came out when he saw that Marilyn was keeping a diary of some of the things he had said. He was furious. He grabbed the diary and threw it against the wall and screamed, 'Get rid of this!' That was the beginning of Bobby pulling away from Marilyn, because I think he started to realize how dangerous the relationship might really be to him and to his career.

"She kept a diary so she could remember things he said, so she could discuss them with him later on. Marilyn didn't want to look like a dumb blonde—and she wasn't. She was smart, she just wasn't educated. But she was forever reading books to learn more."

Marilyn became as enamored of the sensitive attorney general as she had been of the jaunty president. Instead of phoning the White House, she now dialed Bobby's private number at the Justice Department, and would chat amiably with Angie Novello whenever the boss wasn't around.

The couple met mostly in Los Angeles, often at Marilyn's home in Brentwood, often at the Lawfords'. Chuck Pick, a parking lot attendant who worked a party one night at Pat and Peter's place, recounted a Secret Service agent's ominous warning: "You have eyes but you can't see, you have ears but you can't hear, and you have a mouth but you can't speak. You're going to see a lot of things, but you have to keep your mouth shut." Bobby and Marilyn left the party together that night, with the attorney general behind the wheel of a white 1956 Thunderbird convertible.

Jeanne Carmen saw the lovers most often at Doheny Drive, where Marilyn kept her apartment even after purchasing her house. "There were lots of good times between Marilyn and Bobby," observed Carmen. "Bobby would drive straight into the garage at the building, go through the courtyard and across to her ground-floor apartment. There was no way anyone would even see him.

"I loved spending time with the two of them. We used to go to this nude beach, past Pepperdine.* We'd put Marilyn in a dark wig and sunglasses, and Bobby would have on a fake goatee and mustache with a baseball cap. We'd get into the convertible and they'd wave to people as we drove to the beach. Once we got there we sunbathed and walked by the water. Nobody seemed to recognize them.

"Bobby was quite a clean-living guy, really, but he and Marilyn both liked to live dangerously. They had that in common—being on the edge a little. I remember once I asked Bobby, 'Aren't you afraid someone might make a scandal?' And he said to me, 'I'm in love, I don't give a damn, and the whole world can go to hell!'"

The height of Robert Kennedy's romance with Marilyn Monroe lasted barely a month. As noted by Marilyn's biographer Anthony Sum-

---

* "Bobby wouldn't think anything about being nude in front of me, he was very relaxed about it," said Carmen. "But don't ask me about size, because I'm not about to tell you. The only one I'll tell you about is Frank Sinatra, because I've been with him, too. Well, you know how skinny he is—it's like a watermelon on the end of a toothpick!"

mers in his book *Goddess,* telephone records show that on June 25, just over five weeks after the president's birthday party, Marilyn ceased calling the attorney general's private office number and dialed the Justice Department's main switchboard instead. The call that day lasted but a minute, long enough for Marilyn to be told that RFK was on his way to Los Angeles as part of a national tour to fight organized crime.

Later that night, wearing gray slacks and a light blue dress shirt, Bobby drove up in a Cadillac convertible to the Lawfords' home, where he met Marilyn for dinner. The following day, he visited the movie star at her house. At some point toward the end of that second rendezvous, presumably, he told his lover that he had changed his office number and that she was never to call him, or the president, again. June 26 was the last time, until August 4, that Bobby and Marilyn were together.

Wigs and beards on the beach were not enough to disguise the Monroe-Kennedy link from those with an interest in knowing. "Marilyn's house was being bugged by everyone—Jimmy Hoffa, the FBI, the Mafia, even Twentieth Century-Fox," said Peter Lawford. "Jimmy Hoffa wanted to gather information on Monroe and the Kennedys for personal use; the FBI hoped to ascertain what Marilyn knew about Frank Sinatra's connections to the Mafia; the Mafia was curious as to what she knew about the FBI. As for Twentieth Century-Fox, who knows what they wanted?"

In fact, the first recording of conversations between Marilyn Monroe and Jack Kennedy took place at Peter Lawford's residence. "Fred Otash, the Hollywood investigator, had been hired to bug Lawford's house," maintained author Ted Schwartz. "So he went out there. But before he bugged it, just for the hell of it, he swept it and he detected a bug that was already in place. In other words, before he installed his own wire, he listened with somebody else's. It came courtesy of Howard Hughes, who had long been politically active on behalf of Richard Nixon, and who was determined to gather dirt on the Democrats." Republican-inspired electronic surveillance of the Lawfords' home and telephone lines—a convenient way to keep informed of the Kennedys' West Coast activities—had begun as early as 1959.

At times, Otash worked in tandem with Bernard Spindel, a surveillance expert on whom the main character in the popular 1970s film *The Conversation* was based. But the two also worked separately, creating a jumble of competing wires and microphones at Lawford's home and Marilyn's house and apartment. (MM's answering service was also tapped.) The breadth of curiosity as to the actress and her "friends" offered Spindel a pathway to easy cash. "Spindel was a crook among crooks," crooned Schwartz, "in that he would have a client and he'd get paid to install a wiretap, but there would actually be five clients for the same tape. Tapes from Spindel went to J. Edgar Hoover, the CIA, Jimmy Hoffa, and Mafia boss Carlos Marcello, as well as other notorious mob characters." Otash, not Spindel, serviced another client interested in recording Marilyn's conversations: the actress herself. She asked the investigator to help her tap her own telephone, apparently in hope of holding the Kennedys to at least some of their numerous promises.

By March of 1962, the surveillance was in full swing. Peter Lawford recalled listening to copies of some tapes that had been paid for separately by both the Mafia and the Teamsters: "You could hear the voices of Marilyn and JFK in addition to Marilyn and RFK. In both cases you could make out the muted sounds of bedsprings and the cries of ecstasy. Marilyn, after all, was a master of her craft."

At 3:10 A.M. on December 16, 1966, over four years after the actress's death, a squad of police officers and prosecutorial investigators showed up at Bernard Spindel's residence in the upstate New York town of Holmes. Armed with a search warrant, they removed a vast quantity of electronic equipment, as well as other materials. Spindel later said that the district attorney behind the raid "did the Kennedys a big favor. . . . They stole my tapes on Marilyn Monroe and my complete file."*

As comprehensive as the surveillance tapes were, they were not the only recordings to include intimate glimpses into the love lives of Marilyn Monroe and the two brothers. "At the behest of Dr. Greenson," said Lawford, "Marilyn was making 'free-association' tapes. Greenson had suggested she tape her daily thoughts while riding to and from appointments in the backseat of her limousine. In a kind of Joycean stream-of-consciousness mode, she carried forth on everyone and everything from Joe DiMaggio to Robert Kennedy. The tapes revealed—and I heard several of them—that she had fallen deeply in love with Bobby. She spoke about her desire to be married to him and to have his children. She also spoke about both Kennedys having jilted her, then passing her around like a football.

"What she failed to mention, or at least I never heard it, was Bobby's

---

* Robert F. Kennedy was senator from New York in 1966 and was, according to Fred Otash, "responsible for the raid on Bernard Spindel's house. He engineered this by leaning on certain upstate New York government officials." The tapes were never returned to Spindel. Police officials informed Spindel's attorney that the tapes had "mysteriously disappeared."

help in trying to settle a dispute with Lew Wasserman and MCA, her final theatrical agency. She wanted MCA to release her from her contract, and Bobby attempted to negotiate an agreement with Wasserman. After she died, MCA sued her estate for more than eighty thousand dollars."

The Jack-Marilyn-Bobby triangle may in fact have been a square. The fourth side of the polygon was Pat Newcomb, a woman who served as Marilyn's press agent and personal handler and who became one of the actress's closest friends. According to journeyman actor Ted Jordan (who played Burt the freight office clerk in *Gunsmoke* for twelve years), Marilyn and Newcomb had a relationship so close and competitive that it appealed to Marilyn's "other side"—her proclivity for lesbianism, an aspect of her character which more than one friend, biographer and psychotherapist has addressed. Jordan insisted that he was well qualified to discuss the actress's exotic orientation. "Marilyn . . . had an affair with my ex-wife, Lily St. Cyr, who worked as what some people called a high-class ballerina stripper." Journalist George Carpozi concurred as to Marilyn's bisexuality: "There's no question about it, she went both ways."

According to her psychiatrist, Marilyn said on the last day of her life that she'd had a serious altercation with Newcomb. The actress, Greenson reported, had been furious that her friend, who had spent the night before at the house, had slept well while she (Marilyn) had suffered her usual insomnia. But the argument may have included another subject: Robert Kennedy. "Newcomb had a habit of inching in on people who were hot and heavy for Marilyn," remarked Carpozi. "They had battles on the set of Marilyn's movies—*Some Like It Hot,* for example. They would have it out over the way Marilyn would get cozy with people and then Newcomb would come in and take over." Was Marilyn jealous that Newcomb had been pursuing her lover Bobby? That Bobby was after her lover Newcomb?*

Whether or not Bobby and Newcomb were lovers before Marilyn's death, they almost certainly appear to have become involved after the

---

*Greenson later wrote (as quoted by Anthony Summers in *Goddess*) that Marilyn "had an outright phobia of homosexuality, and yet unwillingly fell into situations which had homosexual coloring, which she then recognized and projected on to the other, who then became her enemy." He cited the actress's angry reaction when Pat Newcomb dyed her hair to display a streak similar in hue to Marilyn's own shade. "Marilyn instantly jumped to the conclusion that the girl was 'trying to take possession of her, that such identification means homosexual possessiveness.' She turned with a fury against this girl."

fact. Within days of the star's demise, Newcomb found herself in Hyannis Port; soon thereafter the Kennedy family bundled her off to Europe to keep her away from the press. (To conceal their involvement in Newcomb's movements, the Kennedys had Averell Harriman make her travel plans.) After a stay abroad of several months, she was given a job in Washington with the United States Information Agency.

In August of 1963, RFK wrote Newcomb a memorandum at her new office: "I have been trying to handle your work as well as mine while you were on vacation. I hope you enjoyed yourself." He signed the page, "Charlie Pleasant/(Robert F. Kennedy)."

Two months later the pair went horseback riding and had trouble with a horse. Shortly afterward, RFK sent Newcomb a handwritten letter:

Dear Pat,

I received the bill for your horse. They charged for the whole hour's ride and we three—you me and the horse—know you didn't ride half that time. I will point this out to them.

The bill was $2.50. If you would send me $1.25, I will generously pay the rest. I know you will insist on paying the whole thing but I think you should remember I rode your horse part of the time and the rest of the hour he was just standing around eating grass and so perhaps I can get a refund.

In any case, leave it up to me—just send me the $1.25 and Dad and I will handle the rest.

Love and kisses,

Charlie Generous

Newcomb responded with a question typed on a USIA letterhead: "Do you suppose that hostile horse hated women and I reminded him of his mother?" With that note she enclosed a check, written against her personal account at Washington's Riggs National Bank, for $1.25. It was made out to "Charlie Generous" and signed by "Bertha Bronco."

The playful exchange of messages between Pat and RFK continued long after their supposed relationship ended. Newcomb eventually went to work for the attorney general at the Justice Department (her office was only five doors away from RFK's, a not inconvenient arrangement), yet she has never revealed in public anything about her friendship with either Marilyn Monroe or Bobby.

B obby's farewell to Marilyn came at a bad time for the actress. Work on *Something's Got to Give* had continued to go poorly after her appearance at Madison Square Garden, and not even the heroics of Dr. Greenson could help. He and his wife had gone on a vacation, but, as Hildi Greenson recalled, they were unable to enjoy the trip: "There were constant telephone calls. We were in Israel and we received a slew of calls from both Marilyn and her studio people. Finally, when we arrived in Switzerland, my husband said, 'I promised them I'd come back to save the picture.'" Greenson's return to California accomplished little. Having had enough of Marilyn's antics, Twentieth Century-Fox fired her on June 8 and instituted a lawsuit against her for failing to meet her contractual obligations.*

With her career in apparent ruins—a perception made even more irrefutable to Marilyn by the thirty-sixth birthday she'd marked on June 1—the break with RFK led her deeper into despair and addiction. Pat and Peter Lawford attempted to cheer the dejected actress, but she would not be comforted. Bobby had promised to marry her, she told them; now he was gone. The Kennedys "use you and then they dispose of you like so much rubbish."

Said Lawford later, "On several occasions when Marilyn came over for dinner or a party, she stayed overnight, especially when she had too much to drink. One time I woke up very early in the morning and discovered her in a robe perched on the balcony staring at the swimming pool below. I went out and said, 'Are you all right?' Tears were rolling down her face. I led her in and made breakfast, and Pat and I consoled her for hours. She was completely down on herself, talked about how ugly she felt, how worthless, how used and abused." Medical records reveal that over the thirty-five days from July 1 until her death, she saw her psychiatrist on twenty-seven of them and her internist on thirteen.

Marilyn continued to telephone the Justice Department; RFK did not return her calls. Frustrated, she called Hickory Hill and spoke to Ethel, much to Bobby's dismay. And sometime in June or July the attorney general learned that his conversations with the actress had been anything but private—Lawford had been tipped off to the surveillance of his house by a disgruntled employee of Fred Otash. The attorney general had finally come to realize the danger he and his brother faced as a result of their association with such a famous and unstable woman.

---

* Dean Martin refused to work with any other leading lady, and the picture was never completed. The disaster of *Something's Got to Give,* added to the box-office flop of *Cleopatra,* led to financial disaster for Twentieth Century-Fox.

Hoping to calm their friend, the Lawfords suggested a change of scenery. But peace and quiet were not commodities in easy supply at the Cal-Neva, the Mafia–Rat Pack gambling resort to which Marilyn, Peter and Pat repaired for a mid-July weekend. Alcohol, however, was a specialty of the house, and Marilyn and her companions drank heavily. The actress had also stocked her suitcase with pills. She'd taken pills for so long, she told a fellow hotel guest, that only high doses had any effect.

Afraid to be alone, the actress left her telephone line open to the casino switchboard when she retired for the evening. When the operator heard arduous breathing, she notified the Lawfords, who rushed to find MM lying on the floor next to her bed, barely conscious. Peter and Pat alternated cups of coffee with walks around the room until Marilyn revived. Apparently, the overdose was accidental.*

Pat left Lake Tahoe for Hyannis Port, but Marilyn and Peter boarded Frank Sinatra's private airplane for Los Angeles. Both passengers were drunk during the flight, after which the actress, barefoot and reeling, entered a limousine to be driven home. Several members of the flight crew offered Peter Lawford a ride, but only blocks from the airport, the actor asked that the car be stopped. He got out and stepped into a telephone booth.

The recipient of his call was Robert Kennedy. Using the pay phone to avoid possible taps on his home line, Lawford reported to his brother-in-law that over the weekend Marilyn had threatened to hold a press conference to make public her affairs with the Kennedys. Lawford further informed RFK that the actress claimed to have evidence to document her case: in Tahoe, she had disclosed to Lawford that she had been recording her own telephone conversations. No longer the passive football, Marilyn intended to start tackling and talking—she had tapes of herself with the attorney general that the nation would love to hear. "When Bobby stopped taking Marilyn's calls," ventured Jeanne Carmen, "Marilyn was at first confused and hurt. But then she got angry and began acting like the woman scorned. She became frantic, saying things like, 'Fuck him, I'll show him. I'll tell the world.' "†

---

*The events that led to Marilyn's death, including the visit to Cal-Neva, are reported in detail in both Anthony Summers's Marilyn biography and in James Spada's biography of Peter Lawford. Both authors seem to feel that her overdose at Cal-Neva was accidental. In an interview with the current author, Peter Lawford said, "Marilyn had a death wish of sorts but didn't actually want to die, at least not in her more sane moments. In my opinion, she had manic-depressive tendencies and should have been on a different type of medication."

†In early 1996, a number of documents purportedly found in the files of the late

Marilyn continued to issue threats over the following weeks as Lawford did his utmost to assuage her. On Friday, August 3, he took the actress and Pat Newcomb to dinner at a favorite Italian restaurant. At home later, drunk, she resolved to speak to Bobby. An acquaintance had told her that the attorney general was scheduled to be in San Francisco that weekend before giving an address there on Monday to a meeting of the American Bar Association. She called Lawford to ask for a number where RFK would be staying. Although the actor didn't know, he thought his wife might, and he gave Marilyn the telephone exchange for the Kennedy compound in Hyannis Port where Pat was vacationing. The actress called Massachusetts. Pat Kennedy told her to dial San Francisco's St. Francis Hotel.

Marilyn left several messages at the establishment, where the lawyers' group had booked rooms for Bobby, Ethel and four of their children. But the attorney general was staying at the ranch of John Bates, a wealthy lawyer (and president of the California Bar Association) who lived some sixty miles south of town. Marilyn at last reached RFK; after a brief and somewhat caustic conversation, he agreed to see her the following day.

Marilyn had demanded a full-scale, face-to-face explanation from her lover as to why she had been abandoned; Bobby would now give it to her. On Saturday he flew to Los Angeles. From the airport he took a helicopter to the Twentieth Century-Fox lot where he was met by Peter Lawford. The two then drove to Marilyn's Brentwood home.

They arrived at about three in the afternoon. In anticipation of their visit, Marilyn had set out a buffet of Mexican food—guacamole, stuffed mushrooms, spicy meatballs—which she had ordered from a nearby restaurant, plus a chilled magnum of her favorite beverage, champagne. Lawford poured himself a glass and went out to the swimming pool so Marilyn and Bobby could talk. Within minutes he heard shouting. Bobby maintained he was going back to Lawford's house. Marilyn insisted that he spend the rest of the day alone with her.

"They argued back and forth for maybe ten minutes," said Lawford, "Marilyn (who had probably been drinking all day) becoming more and

---

Lawrence X. Cusack, a New York City–based attorney, indicated that JFK paid Marilyn Monroe in excess of $1 million in exchange for her silence over their affair, and her supposed knowledge of his ties to the mob. These documents found their way into the hands of Pulitzer Prize–winning journalist Seymour Hersh, who planned to use them in *The Dark Side of Camelot,* his book on the Kennedys. Hersh also used the documents to convince ABC-TV to produce a two-hour documentary based on his book. ABC later discovered the documents to be forgeries, thus raising serious questions as to the validity of Hersh's research techniques.

more hysterical. At the height of her anger she allowed how first thing Monday morning she was going to call a press conference and tell the world about the treatment she had suffered at the hands of the Kennedy brothers. At this point Bobby became livid. In no uncertain terms he told her she would have to leave both Jack and him alone—no more telephone calls, no letters, nothing. They didn't want to hear from her anymore.

"Marilyn presently lost it, screaming obscenities and flailing wildly away at Bobby with her fists. In her fury she picked up a small kitchen knife and lunged at him. I was with them at this time, so I tried to grab Marilyn's arm. We finally knocked her down and managed to wrestle the knife away. Bobby thought we ought to call Dr. Greenson and tell him to come over. The psychiatrist arrived at Marilyn's home within the hour."

Lawford eventually explained why Bobby turned to Greenson for help in solving this delicate matter: "The most surprising revelation of Marilyn's 'free-association' tapes was that in addition to her affairs with the Kennedys, she was also involved with Dr. Greenson, who appeared to be deeply in love with her. I myself knew nothing about any of this until after Marilyn's death, at which time I heard those portions of the tapes she'd made for Greenson in which she alluded to her affair with him. I also got hold of portions of the Mafia-Teamster tapes, and heard what seemed to be sounds of their [Marilyn and Greenson's] lovemaking. Greenson's wife, presumably, knew nothing about the affair.*

"Somehow [perhaps from Pat Newcomb] Bobby learned of Marilyn's liaison with her therapist. He had spoken to Greenson and convinced him that his star patient intended to disclose her romantic dealings not just with the Kennedys but also with her psychiatrist. This would certainly mark the end of the doctor's career; it would also very likely land him in prison. 'Marilyn has got to be silenced,' Bobby told Greenson—or words to that effect. Greenson had thus been set up by Bobby to 'take care' of Marilyn."

Ralph Greenson arrived at Marilyn's home around 4:30 P.M. Half an hour later, the actress called her friend Ted Jordan. "She told me about her fight with Bobby," Jordan recalled. "She said that Dr. Greenson, who was still there, had given her an injection to quiet her down, and that Lawford and Bobby Kennedy had already gone.

"Marilyn called me a second time that evening. She sounded a thousand miles away. She said Lawford had phoned her around seven and

---

* Hildi Greenson categorically denied that her husband had ever indulged in a sexual relationship with Marilyn. "It's just ludicrous," she said. "It's so dumb."

invited her over for some Chinese dinner and a little poker with friends. Bobby wanted her to come. But Marilyn suspected that once the poker game ended, Lawford would invite a couple of hookers over for Bobby and himself, and they would expect Marilyn to participate. 'I've had enough of that stuff,' she said.

"She mentioned she had taken sleeping pills earlier in the evening, which in addition to Greenson's shot and the alcohol would surely have done her in."

Greenson left Marilyn's house at approximately half past six and went with his wife to a dinner party. Over the next two or three hours, Marilyn made a few more telephone calls. Peter Lawford, perhaps suffering an attack of conscience, suddenly began to worry about Marilyn. Yet instead of calling her himself, he contacted Milton Rudin, who was not only the lawyer to both Monroe and Frank Sinatra, but also Ralph Greenson's brother-in-law. Remembered Hildi Greenson, "Apparently Lawford called Milt Rudin and said, 'Marilyn sounds kind of peculiar,' and Milt said, 'Okay, I'll check into it.' Milt then called the house and asked, 'Eunice, is Marilyn okay?' Eunice replied, 'Yes, she's fine,' or whatever; consequently, Milt never alerted my husband."

The Greensons returned from their dinner party and went to bed, only to be awakened at 2 A.M. by the telephone. Ralph Greenson picked up the receiver; his widow later remembered the call: "There wasn't much conversation on this side. He just said, 'Okay,' then hung up and began getting himself together to dash off. 'Eunice called,' he told me. 'Marilyn's door is locked and she can't get in.'

"I was very worried. My daughter and I went downstairs and sat around until my husband called and said that Marilyn was dead."

It took Dr. Greenson just five minutes to drive from his house to Marilyn's. Unable to open the door to the actress's bedroom, he and Eunice Murray walked outside to a window through which they could see the actress, perfectly still on her bed. Greenson broke the glass, lifted up the frame and climbed inside. He later reported that he'd found Marilyn lying facedown, clutching her telephone in her right hand.

Murray had also called Hyman Engleberg. The internist soon arrived, but, for some reason, the two doctors did not summon the police until nearly 4:30. Sergeant Jack Clemmons, watch commander of the West Los Angeles station, was the first officer to enter the house. Curiously, he found Eunice Murray doing laundry.

An autopsy conducted later that day by deputy medical examiner Dr. Thomas Noguchi found copious amounts of a wide array of barbiturates in Marilyn's blood and liver. An examination of her stomach contents revealed a number of not fully dissolved Nembutal capsules but no evidence of Seconal. Noguchi used a magnifying glass to check the decedent's entire body for evidence of needle marks; none was found.

Noguchi's futile search for needle marks has often been offered as proof that Marilyn received no injections on the immediate days prior to her death. Other physicians have noted that needle marks are often undetectable within hours after injection. Dr. Engleberg recalled seeing his patient on "Friday evening. It was to give her an injection of liver and vitamins. I frequently gave it in the buttocks, but sometimes in the upper arms, where you usually give intramuscular injections. This one was probably in the buttocks because that's the usual place I would put it." Since Noguchi failed to detect the site of Marilyn's injection by Engleberg on Friday night, it is entirely possible that he would have missed a subsequent injection by Dr. Greenson.*

If the autopsy proved inconclusive, so, thanks to Peter Lawford, was the evidence found at the death scene. Sometime during the early morning hours of Sunday, the actor entered Marilyn's home and removed items tying the now-dead star to his in-laws. Marilyn's diary, for example, has never been found. "Peter was torn between his loyalty to Marilyn and his loyalty to the Kennedys," commented Jeanne Carmen, "but in the end he chose the Kennedys. They were family, after all. I don't think Peter ever recovered from what happened. I think his whole life went downhill after Marilyn died."

According to Carmen, the actress's home wasn't the only location cleared of inconvenient information: "I went over to Marilyn's house around noon on Sunday and it was swarming with cops and newspaper reporters and photographers. They rushed up to my car as I drove in and I figured I should just get the hell out of there. So I drove to the beach to think, and during that time my place was broken into. They took documents and papers and old photographs."

Robert Kennedy left Los Angeles Saturday night, first using a helicop-

---

*John Miner, a lawyer and physician who attended Marilyn's autopsy as head of the Los Angeles district attorney's Medical-Legal Section, suggested another possible cause of the actress's death: "What was peculiar and odd was a discolored section of the large intestine. The area affected was in the sigmoid colon, which is not very far from where a substance would be introduced into the anus by enema. It's really by hindsight that I am concerned with this issue. The thought of her having been killed deliberately that way by someone—namely, murder—did not cross my mind at the time." Miner cautioned that his suspicion of fatal enema "is a theory, that's all it is." Yet he speculated that "if you wanted to kill somebody," that method would "leave no residue in the stomach." Miner further noted that tissue samples from the body were not saved and that stomach contents were never fully analyzed—circumstances he labeled "strange, very strange."

ter to fly from the Lawford beach house to the airport. On Sunday morning, near the Bates ranch south of San Francisco, he went to church, then took a horseback ride and played touch football. The following day, as planned, he addressed the convention of the American Bar Association. Like the audience at Madison Square Garden in May, the lawyers at the meeting were unaware of circumstances: they had no idea that their featured speaker, the attorney general of the United States, very likely had conspired in the murder of his former lover, the nation's premier cinema star.*

"Both Jack and Bobby had much to lose should Marilyn have gone public about her relationships with the two of them," declared Jeanne Carmen. "If they hadn't taken her out, she would have ruined both of them. I tried to warn her that these people didn't fool around, but she regarded it all as a big game. Even when we used to hang out with Johnny Roselli, the gangster, she used to say things to me like, 'Gosh, they actually *kill* people!' And I'd tell her, 'Yeah, like their friends, their mothers and anyone else who gets in their way.'

"But, you know, Marilyn was drinking a lot and taking pills, and I think her hold on reality was not so great. Marilyn never thought anything would happen to her. She was an innocent. She never believed she would get hurt."

H earing of his ex-wife's death early Sunday morning, Joe DiMaggio left his hometown of San Francisco on the first available flight to Los Angeles. Upon arrival he rode to the Miramar Hotel, near Marilyn's house, and checked into a suite with his son and two friends. The dead actress's half sister asked the retired ballplayer to arrange the funeral; he would insist on a quiet affair. He sat in his hotel room weeping, next to a pile of unopened telegrams. Said one of the friends with him, "He held Bobby Kennedy responsible for her death. He said that right there in the Miramar."

Three years later, at an old-timer's game at Yankee Stadium, Bobby was introduced to DiMaggio. Then a United States senator, RFK extended his hand.

Without a word, Joltin' Joe turned and walked away.

---

*Three days after Marilyn's death, RFK left San Francisco on a camping trip to Oregon with his children. Ironically, they were joined there by his early travel companion, Supreme Court Justice William O. Douglas.

19

DEATH OF A BROTHER

Just after taking office in 1961, Robert Kennedy had received an invitation to travel that dovetailed neatly with his brother's foreign-affairs objectives. For some time, American policymakers had been noticing that student riots around the world inevitably targeted the local embassy of the United States but ignored that of the Soviet Union. John Kennedy's administration wanted to counter America's image as stodgy defender of the colonialist status quo. But neither of the two senior officials charged with the execution of foreign policy—Secretary of State Dean Rusk and UN ambassador Adlai Stevenson, both born in the first decade of the twentieth century—seemed an effective candidate to sell his homeland as the vibrant champion of the liberation movements then transforming the globe. Instead, Robert Kennedy, far younger than these two elder statesmen, would take off the month of February 1962 from his duties as attorney general to act as an international representative in behalf of his country, his government and, most notably, his brother.

The invitation that prompted the trip came from Dr. Gunji Hosono, director of the Japan Institute of Foreign Affairs and a friend of the family since both he and Joe Kennedy were diplomats stationed in England before the war that made their countries enemies. After attending JFK's inauguration in January 1961, Hosono visited Bobby in the Justice Department to say that, despite anti-American riots in Japan the year before—disturbances that had forced Dwight Eisenhower to cancel a planned visit there—the Japanese were warmly disposed to their former adversaries. It was essential that they learn about the New Frontier, he said. Perhaps the new president could visit; if not, maybe the new attorney general could find the time.

Bobby begged off, citing the responsibilities of his job. But in the following months Hosono dispatched a barrage of letters and messengers urging the attorney general to accept. The U.S. ambassador to Japan, Edwin O. Reischauer, added his voice to the campaign of persuasion, and by spring RFK decided to go. Dean Rusk gave his blessing to the trip—perhaps heartfelt, perhaps more a recognition that he would be foolish to challenge the foreign-policy credentials of the first brother— and assigned further diplomatic business to be conducted in Indonesia and elsewhere.*

Following his February 1 send-off in Los Angeles by Marilyn Monroe, the attorney general—accompanied by Ethel, John Seigenthaler, the State Department's Brandon Grove, Jr., and ten American journalists— spent a day in Honolulu, where he drew headlines for capsizing a sail-boat, then flew to Tokyo. "A principal goal of the trip," the *New York Herald Tribune* quoted "State Department sources" as saying, "is to show the world through the President's thirty-six-year-old younger brother that there is a young, vigorous Administration in Washington." RFK's sched-ule alone was a testament to youth and vigor. Ambassador Reischauer recalled his role in preparing for the attorney general's visit: "We sent him a copy of his daily schedule, every minute occupied till 10 o'clock at night, and he wired back, 'Program looks fine. What do I do from 6 to 8 A.M.?' So we added those hours, as well. He roller-skated with workers, 6 to 8 A.M." RFK wanted a schedule that "got him out meeting the peo-ple," remembered John Seigenthaler. Although he did pay courtesy calls on officials of the Japanese government, RFK looked to avoid the stan-dard itinerary of the visiting dignitary: endless rounds of high-level con-ferences mixed with carefully scripted tours of industrial facilities. Instead, Bobby talked to farmers and workers, housewives and students. He dropped in on an electronics factory and a milk-processing plant. On the last of his six days in the country he viewed an early-morning exhibi-tion of the martial art of aikido. When the diminutive Japanese master asked him to participate, RFK passed, instead designating a hefty re-porter from *Life* magazine to take his place, and for the next ten minutes the instructor tossed the reporter around the gymnasium like a beanbag.

The "Japanese are a very formal people," noted Seigenthaler, "and

---

*The 1962 trip was neither the first nor the last diplomatic mission undertaken by the unconventional attorney general. In August 1961 he headed the U.S. delegation to honor the first anniversary of the independence of the Ivory Coast, formerly a part of French West Africa. And in December 1962, Bobby journeyed to Brazil to secure that country's cooperation in the administration's Latin American initiative, the Alliance for Progress.

they stand on ceremony. This trip, in that regard, was precedent breaking." Reischauer had warned that too "bustling" an attitude might deviate
too widely from rigid Japanese standards of propriety, but in reality the
young, informal American leader charmed the nation's citizens with his
fresh approach to diplomacy. "His sojourn was limited," editorialized a
leading Japanese newspaper, "but we feel certain that he must have obtained something which couldn't have been grasped by observing protocol only or going through regulation routines of casual interviews and
inspection tours. Daily he was on the go from morning till midnight,
going all over the place and meeting with common people everywhere."

The Japanese were equally enchanted by the energetic American official's energetic American wife, who told all she met, "Just call me
Ethel." Her first day in Tokyo began at 8:15 A.M. with a visit to the University of the Sacred Heart, whose mother superior had taught at Manhattanville College when Ethel was a student there. After attending a
calligraphy class and writing on the blackboard the Japanese characters
for "Japanese and American friendship," Ethel left with her eleven-car
motorcade to visit a hospital for crippled children. She then kneeled
through a three-hour, thirteen-course vegetarian luncheon at a Buddhist
temple, and afterward hosted a reception at the American embassy for
250 women—employees of the embassy and wives of male staffers. The
day continued with a visit to the home of a businessman related to Ambassador Reischauer's Japanese wife, followed by another embassy reception, this one attended by men, including the Japanese prime minister.
After attending a dinner hosted by the Japanese foreign minister, she
made an appearance on the Japanese version of the American television
show *What's My Secret?* In the course of the day, she wore four different
outfits—a red Chanel suit with black trim, a green Chanel suit, a yellow
gown from Christian Dior and a white lace dress from Balenciaga—each
with matching accessories.

Later in the week, Ethel gave a press conference. Asked "who counts
most," husband or children, she replied, "My husband, but the children
are a close second." She continued with an outline of her parenting practices: "I make each child read for half an hour every day, say grace before
and after every meal, say the rosary every day and read two chapters of
the Bible before going to bed. Television comes only after reading, although there is a morning science program they watch and the little ones
watch *Captain Kangaroo.*"

With regard to the trip, A. M. Rosenthal noted in the *New York
Times*, the "Attorney General of the United States spent six days in Japan
and hardly anyone asked him questions about the law." On the other

hand, Bobby did hold talks on one subject in which he had had extensive experience: labor relations. Seeking to counter impressions that America was a land where unfettered robber barons trampled workers underfoot, RFK met with Japanese union chiefs, including Akira Iwai, the "burly, confident chainsmoker," according to *Time,* who served as secretary-general of the leftist Sohyo federation. Bobby denied Iwai's contention that the United States was run by the Rockefellers and described efforts of the Kennedy administration to raise the minimum wage, extend Social Security and build public housing. The labor leader admitted to being "impressed," and praised the American for the "cyclone tour [which the] whole country had been watching on TV." He later said of his visitor, "He's bold, very active and frank. Not bad. In fact, pretty good, this fellow." Said another labor leader, "He is, as far as we know, the first high-ranking American official who refused to go on the hotel–palace–government office routine of visits in Japan. Kennedy was also the first man from Washington who sought to learn things which are not in books. All this is highly refreshing and welcome, an indication that something entirely new is cooking in Washington today."

Even more than laborers or labor leaders, students were the audience Bobby hoped to reach. He gave his first major speech of the trip at Tokyo's Nihon University, where, before fifteen thousand collegians, he sounded his theme of an enlightened cold war: "We have no intention of trying to remake the world in our image but we have no intention either of permitting any other state to remake the world in its image. . . . We call to the young men and women of all nations of the world to join with us in a concerted attack on the evils which have so long beset mankind— poverty, illness, illiteracy, intolerance, oppression, war."

The CIA had warned Bobby to expect a disruption from Marxist students at his next speech. He entered the auditorium at Waseda University, also in Tokyo, to cheers from four thousand students. As RFK approached the podium, however, a group of angry left-wing scholars began to jeer and stomp their feet. One of them, a red-faced, skinny boy, started screaming at the speaker. Finally, Bobby invited the student to join him on stage and offered him the microphone. "You present your views," he said, "and then allow me to present mine."

The youthful protester launched into a lengthy tirade, reciting, said John Seigenthaler, "every Communist assault he could think of on the United States government: imperialism, atomic bombs, nuclear proliferation, the whole bit." At last he stopped talking and took his seat. The American attorney general then began a point-by-point response to the harangue, when all at once the lights and sound went dead. Somebody handed Bobby a bullhorn and he continued to speak. "In my country," he said, "we respect the views of the young. Don't forget, we have a young president and an even younger attorney general."

The young attorney general had won over the crowd—and the nation—for by his nationally televised handling of the hostile university demonstrator he had proven himself to be anything but "the ugly American" the Japanese had expected. In the aftermath of the Waseda speech, huge crowds lined roads to catch a glimpse of the passing visitors. The New Frontier had indeed come to Japan.

There were several detractors of the trip at home, notably a Republican congressman (and future mayor of New York)—John V. Lindsay, from the city's silk stocking district—who criticized "highly placed amateurs" conducting diplomacy and suggested: "Far better that the man who holds the highest legal office in the country spend time familiarizing himself with the meaning of the rule of law." But in Japan the trip was considered, in Edwin Reischauer's words, "a smashing success."

On February 10, Bobby and his group departed Tokyo for quick stops in Taiwan, Hong Kong and Singapore before flying into Djakarta, Indonesia, two days later. The dictator of this tropical island nation, Achmed Sukarno, seeking to avoid offending his distinguished guest, had ordered all "Kennedy Go Home" graffiti painted over before the Americans arrived. And fearing embarrassing incidents, he housed the visitors in the presidential palace and surrounded them on their rounds with what Seigenthaler described as "a massive array of armed soldiers, shoving people out of the way, forcing them back." Despite Sukarno's precautions, Bobby somehow managed to connect with a few ordinary folk, reaching over bayonets to shake hands. "I must say," remarked Seigenthaler, "that by the end of the week [the Indonesians] were really going out of their way to embrace him." RFK visited various sites, including a bookstore, a road project and a fabric shop, where he purchased fifty yards of silk goods for his favorite sister-in-law, Jackie Kennedy.

Although RFK had spent little time with government officials in Japan, he had business to transact with Sukarno. On personal terms, the two men seemed to "hit it off," observed Howard Jones, the American ambassador to Indonesia. But for Bobby, the bonhomie was a show. He didn't care for Sukarno, he told associates, because of his use and abuse of women. In light of his own extramarital activity (and that of his brothers), this seemed a strange reason to criticize his host. He felt repelled, he said, by all the statues, paintings and pictures of nude women that decorated the presidential palace's interior. And when Sukarno treated his guests to a dance presentation given by his daughter and a few other young women, Indonesians in the back row of the audience informed the visiting U.S. reporters that two of the lovely dancers often gave private performances in the sixty-year-old leader's bedchamber.

In between social events, RFK and Sukarno discussed two specific issues. The first involved an ongoing dispute between Indonesia and its former ruler, the Netherlands, over West New Guinea, a Dutch possession which the Indonesians called West Irian. Recognizing that colonial rule over the territory had to end, Bobby hoped to avert war by encouraging negotiations between the two sides. Holland, too, saw the writing on the wall, but was willing to hold talks only if no preconditions were set—it was "a question of pride" with them, RFK explained. Indonesia, a country receiving substantial aid from the USSR, could not expect American support if it rushed to fight with Holland, a member of NATO. Bobby urged the Indonesian leader not to go to war over a mere point of procedure, and Sukarno listened. Six months after RFK's departure, an agreement was signed between the Netherlands and Indonesia, with the latter gaining control over the disputed territory. RFK had helped erase a vestige of colonialism from Third World Asia, and the Soviets could only fume: they soon called home the military advisers they had sent to Indonesia, since the war they had been training that country's army to fight had now been called off.

Bobby's second issue proved a more difficult sell. In 1958, Indonesian forces had captured Allen Pope, an American bomber pilot downed in an unsuccessful coup that had been mounted with CIA help, and in 1960 Sukarno's court sentenced the airman to death by a firing squad. The Kennedys were motivated less by concern for the flier's life than by fear of his wife: an attractive National Airlines flight attendant, she had visited Bobby to lament that her children were growing up without their father and had threatened to take her case to congressional Republicans always in search of new ways to badger the administration. She had also gone to see Sukarno and had apparently impressed him because when Bobby suggested to the autocrat that Pope be pardoned and released, Sukarno said he would consider the matter.

New York gossip columnist Cindy Adams, a close friend of Sukarno's, remembered him speaking about the Pope affair: "Pope was in prison awaiting execution. RFK, in several meetings with Sukarno, made a strong pitch to have the pilot released. Bobby didn't threaten Sukarno, but he let him know that it was important to the Kennedys that Pope be released. 'Pope's a CIA bastard,' Sukarno said to Bobby, and Bobby replied, 'In my country, he's considered a hero.' They had words, and both men stood their ground. But four months after Kennedy left Indonesia, Pope was quietly returned to the United States."

Before departing Djakarta, Bobby addressed students at a local public school. Entering the building, he was approached by a young Communist sympathizer. Without a word, the stranger wound up and threw an orange which hit Bobby in the head. As police took the man away, the unruffled speaker turned to his wife. "It could've been worse," he said. "He might have had a gun."

In Saigon, South Vietnam, President Ngo Dinh Diem's brother came to the airport to meet the Americans' plane. Before returning to the air, RFK spoke to reporters, making the point that "this is a new kind of war. It is war in the very real sense of the word, yet it is a war fought not by massive divisions but secretly by terror, assassination, ambush and infiltration." Bobby went on, informing the press that "President Kennedy has been extremely impressed with the courage and determination of the people of your country and he has pledged the United States to stand by the side of Vietnam throughout this very difficult and troublesome time. We will win in Vietnam and we shall remain here until we do."

In Thailand, Bobby met with both the prime minister and foreign minister, as well as a contingent of student leaders and factory workers. The Americans then departed for Rome, with refueling stops in Calcutta, India; Karachi, Pakistan; and Beirut, Lebanon. After a fifteen-hour journey, the travelers arrived in the Italian capital, where they had an audience with Pope John XXIII. Bobby later noted that he found the pontiff "an impressive man, with a wonderful humility and a fine sense of humor." When the aged prelate blessed the group, he assured the mostly non-Catholic journalists "that it was just a little blessing and wouldn't do them any harm." A midday repast at Alfredo's featured piles of food and bottomless wineglasses, and ended with the presentation to Ethel by the restaurant of a Vespa motor scooter. The madcap American wife dutifully started up her present and took off, speeding back and forth in the establishment's aisles, then exiting to orbit the small square outside, snarling Rome's traffic pattern as far as the Colosseum.

In West Berlin, where Bobby was to address the Free University, the Americans were joined by Teddy. The youngest of Joe Kennedy's sons, then planning his run for Jack's Senate seat later in the year, saw the trip as an opportunity to further his education: at meetings conducted by his big brother, he sat silently in the back row and took copious notes. While most Germans loved the Kennedys, the family's Irish American wit did not always jibe with the Teutonic sense of humor. After Mayor Willy

Brandt offered a dinner toast to "the president, government and people of the United States," Bobby responded, "That's the three of us—the president, that's my brother; the government, that's me; and [gazing in Teddy's direction] you're the people." Arthur Schlesinger, who was present at the banquet, reported in his RFK chronicle that the mayor didn't seem the least bit titillated by the comment. In fact, Schlesinger notes, Brandt later wrote that he regarded the Kennedy family's "political expansion with disquiet."

In Bobby's university address, he spoke of communism, capitalism, Karl Marx, George Washington, Germany, Russia and the United States. The words were less poignant than the manner in which he delivered them. He was accorded a standing ovation, as well as a meeting the following day in Bonn with West German chancellor Konrad Adenauer. After the meeting, Bobby flew to the Hague to report to the Dutch on his discussions with Sukarno. In Paris he saw the always acerbic Charles de Gaulle, and flew back to New York, then Washington, on February 28. Descending the ramp, Bobby fell to his knees, bent over and kissed the tarmac.

R FK wasn't the only unlikely diplomat to serve the Kennedy administration. In April 1961, State Department veteran Robert Murphy traveled to the Dominican Republic for talks with that country's strongman, Rafael Trujillo. Second in authority on the mission, at John Kennedy's behest, was the Hearst gossip columnist known as Cholly Knickerbocker.

Cholly Knickerbocker was the pen name of Igor Cassini, brother of Oleg, the first lady's designated White House dress designer. Ghighi, as Igor was known, had long been a Palm Beach pal of Joseph Kennedy's, and had often been pleased to provide the ambassador with introductions to beautiful women who knew how to delight not only the old man, but also his chip-off-the-old-block sons. His social ties to the family gave him more detailed knowledge of the Kennedy secrets than that available to most journalists; unlike others, Cholly Knickerbocker had always remained discreet.

Writing about the "jet set"—a term he coined—Ghighi Cassini had become friendly with Porfirio Rubirosa, one of its most notorious members. Although he was an aide to Gernalissimo Trujillo (and later the Dominican ambassador to the United States), Rubirosa's true fame rested on his reputation as a superbly endowed playboy, not as a statesman; and he had been married to the likes of Danielle Darrieux, Doris Duke, Barbara Hutton and Trujillo's youngest daughter, Flor de Oro, before landing his current life's partner, Odile Rodin, the French actress much appreciated by JFK and much resented by Jackie. Cassini had been married more than once himself. His latest spouse, Charlene, was the beautiful daughter of financier Charles Wrightsman, Palm Beach neighbor and financial supporter of the Kennedys. Former lawyer to the columnist's father-in-law was America's spymaster Allen Dulles, who occasionally formed one-third of a golfing threesome in Florida along with JFK and Cassini. Former boyfriend to the columnist's wife was America's president, John Kennedy, who had dated the future Mrs. Cassini before he and Jackie were wed.

During the first phase of the Kennedy administration, Porfirio Rubirosa told Cassini that the Dominican Republic had been teetering on the edge of a Communist takeover. The United States had recently severed diplomatic relations with the cruel and corrupt Trujillo regime. If American favor was not soon restored, said Cassini's lady-killing friend, the Caribbean would before long be polluted by another Cuba.

Ghighi passed the word to his chum Joe, who told his son Jack, who sent Ghighi with Robert Murphy to see if Trujillo was serious about implementing reforms that might give the hemisphere's superpower the fig leaf it needed to protect his regime. When the amateur and professional envoys returned, they informed their president that the dictator had indeed been giving the matter thought, since a few minor changes would hardly threaten the vast wealth he had accumulated in over three decades of rapacious rule. Speculation on the despot's intentions proved moot, however, for on May 30 he was gunned down by an eight-man military assassination team led by General Juan Tomás Díaz.

John Kennedy happened to be in France the day Trujillo was shot. And, as the protocol demanded, the vice president was in Washington. But Lyndon Johnson did not direct America's response to the Dominican turmoil. Upon hearing of the murder, the president's brother established a command post on the seventh floor of the State Department, with Robert McNamara and LBJ in attendance, and Chester Bowles representing the absent Dean Rusk. As *Time*'s Hugh Sidey reported, "On every decision the others always waited for a word from Bobby. On that day there was no hesitation from the attorney general. He wanted to get the word out on Trujillo's assassination immediately. The State Department's Roger Tubby was ordered to make a statement. 'Have we looked into this? Have we done that?' Bobby kept asking. He firmly supported sending a fleet of naval ships to lie out of sight offshore; he made certain that we had checked our moves with the Canadians; he urged that our people in the Dominican Republic be calmed down because by now the cables were approaching hysteria."

No catastrophe befell the Americans in the Dominican Republic. A year after the coup, Trujillo's successors opened the files of the former regime to inspection by American reporters, who would assert that Igor Cassini's interest in the Dominican Republic was not purely altruistic. Since 1959, documents seemed to show, the columnist had represented the Trujillo government in the United States through his public-relations firm, Martial and Company, and had gained access to some two hundred thousand dollars in payments hidden in a Swiss bank account. The attorney general indicted his father's friend for failing to register as an agent of a foreign government. Cassini's column was suspended by the Hearst organization, at the same time that Martial and Company's clients began to slip away.

Cassini proclaimed his innocence, insisting that his name appeared on the seemingly incriminating papers only because he had been offered the public-relations assignment, not because he'd accepted it; in fact, he said, he had turned it down and referred it to someone else. On March 31, 1963, his wife sent her former lover a letter: "Dear Mr. President, I have hesitated writing you before, but now I feel I must appeal to you." Bobby "seems to be hell-bent in punishing Ghighi. I cannot tell you how surprised and shocked I have been by Bobby's harsh and punitive attitude. . . . Ghighi still cannot understand why the son of a man whom he considered one of his closest friends for seventeen years . . . should now be determined to bring him down to total ruin."

The president, evidently moved by the letter, invited Cassini's lawyer, Louis Nizer, to the White House. Nizer recalled that the president showed "deep feeling for the Cassinis' plight, but he suggested I speak directly to Bobby."

At the Justice Department several days later, RFK greeted Nizer as a friend and even invited the celebrated attorney to go ice-skating with him that evening. (Nizer declined "with thanks.") Once pleasantries had been exchanged, however, RFK's "demeanor changed to sheer ugliness," according to Nizer. "He cussed and denounced Igor and I had to retort sharply that the facts did not warrant his anger." Nizer argued that his client's failure to register as a foreign agent was at worst "an innocent oversight," but "Bobby would not yield. He had to do his duty. Igor was not worth consideration. . . .

"The contrast between the two brothers was startling. Jack had responded with heart. Bobby with bile. Both were honorable, but feelings are part of honor. Heartlessness is not an essential ingredient of judicial or executive objectivity. A great official or judge must first be a noble man, and there can be no nobility without compassion." Oleg Cassini also commented on the different approaches of president and attorney general: "JFK wanted to charm his enemies, RFK to vanquish them."

On April 8, Charlene Cassini, who had become addicted to painkilling medication following a skiing accident, and had been suffering from depression since the recent deaths of her mother and a close friend, swallowed an overdose of sleeping pills. Emergency treatment kept the thirty-eight-year-old beauty alive for less than twelve hours; she died of heart failure the next morning.

When Nizer telephoned Cassini to report on the meeting with RFK, the bereaved widower responded with rage at the attorney general's intransigence. The columnist "threatened," said Nizer, "to tear the robe of respectability from Bobby, and proceeded to give me a bill of particulars. I interrupted and told him that his idea was unthinkable, and that if he really meant it, he would have to get another lawyer. We will win this case without having to resort to such tactics, I assured him."

Two weeks after the death of his client's wife, Nizer again called on the attorney general. Expecting to hear his host express sorrow over the suicide, Nizer was taken aback by RFK's opening words: "Now you have found out that your client is a blackmailer at heart." Observed Nizer, "He combined this condemnation with praise for my rectitude in curbing him. It was clear that my telephone talk with Igor had been tapped. I was stunned by this violation of law by the Attorney General." Despite his anger, Nizer "suffered in silence" as Bobby pressed on the attack. Finally the attorney general altered his tone to suggest that Nizer meet with Nicholas Katzenbach to work out a plea bargain.

The Justice Department eventually dropped three of four counts in its indictment, allowing Cassini to avoid jail by pleading nolo contendere to the remaining charge. In January 1964 he received his sentence: six months' probation and a ten-thousand-dollar fine. Cholly Knickerbocker never again wrote his column; Martial and Company dissolved. Igor moved to Milan, Italy, to work in his brother's fashion business. He remains there to this day.

"No prosecutor can act on all the violations brought to his office," claimed Nizer. "He must choose those cases for prosecution which will best serve the public interest. I could not understand why there had been such concentration on a matter of such little consequence." Nizer's minimizing of Cassini's offense was, of course, colored by his role as his client's lawyer. Yet he also failed to take into account the Kennedy doctrine of friendship. Robert Kennedy, Jr., summarized his father's teachings on the subject: "There are some values that transcend friendship. They are absolutes, and if they are broken, then the person that does it cannot be a true friend." Igor Cassini's crime was not a mere matter of law. Sent on a mission of national importance, he harbored a personal agenda which he concealed from the president. In Bobby's eyes, Cassini had used Jack. The family friend had betrayed the family.

W hile state dinners and gala concerts took place at the White House, the true social center of the Kennedy administration was Hickory Hill. On its broad lawns and sprawling patios, around its spacious swimming pool, true believers of the New Frontier gathered to celebrate their accomplishments and blow off steam. Joseph Tydings, during the early sixties a U.S. attorney from Maryland and later a U.S. senator, remembered visiting the estate "for tennis—played a lot of tennis—and parties—went to most of the parties then. It was a very gay period, loads of fun, loads of fascinating people. Bobby 'collected' personages and personalities in different fields, you know. Any time you'd go over there you'd have, well, a couple of Hollywood stars, or Max Taylor, or a professional football player or two. His parties were something else."

Ethel Kennedy made sure her guests enjoyed themselves. One evening, she had Harry Belafonte teach the twist to the revelers. When Robert Frost came for dinner, she passed out paper and pencils to his fellow guests for a poetry-writing contest. She set the table with a centerpiece of live bullfrogs one St. Patrick's Day, and another time supervised a game of hide-and-seek in which cabinet members found themselves stuffed into closets with their prettiest secretaries.

But the highlight of Hickory Hill parties was the sight of formally attired adults, often among the most influential in the land, winding up one way or another in the estate's swimming pool. At a party held in June of 1962 to fete Peter and Patricia Lawford, Ethel took a seat at a small table perched on a plank laid across the water. In she splashed, the *Washington Star* reported, "evening dress, shoes and all, when a chair leg went over the side." Two others took the plunge that night. Arthur Schlesinger, "wearing an impeccable light-blue dinner jacket," was pushed. As for Ethel's friend Sarah Davis, *U.S. News & World Report* asserted, "It's not clear whether she fell or was pushed, but the dip was not voluntary." The magazine also classified two guests as "near misses": astronaut (and future senator) John Glenn as well as Supreme Court Justice Byron White. At another party, Robert McNamara's technocratic dignity was thrown overboard due to a push by Ethel and/or Bobby and/or others joining in the spirit of the time and place. Pierre Salinger took his Kennedy baptism in stride: the tuxedoed press secretary bobbed to the surface with his cigar still in his mouth.

Joe Dolan of the Justice Department recalled one Hickory Hill occasion: "Bob and Ethel would have a party every year just before they took the family up to Hyannis for the summer. They would invite maybe a hundred, hundred and fifty people. It was a black-tie dinner, all over the lawn and down by the pool and all that. I happened to be at a table near the water when I saw Angie Novello standing on the top rung of the ladder leading to the slide. Three or four men were at the bottom of the slide shouting, 'Come on, Angie, go ahead! We'll catch you!' Well, you know what happened: she slid down and they didn't catch her.

"Ted Kennedy was standing by the side of the pool. He hadn't been one of those calling for Angie to go, he was just there. But he did one of the most gallant things I've known him to do. As soon as Angie went in, he dove in after her. They were the only ones that went into the pool that night, and it got into the newspaper the next day. I heard that the president called up Ethel and said, 'Ethel, if I don't read your name and Bob's name in the paper for another eight months, it will be just fine.' "

B obby and Ethel's Virginia homestead was also the original site of less raucous gatherings of the Kennedy faithful. A year into the new administration, Arthur Schlesinger proposed to Bobby that high officials and their wives meet with distinguished thinkers, writers and scientists to discuss issues that transcended the ordinary doings of the government. The first meetings were held at RFK's house; afterward, the "Hickory Hill seminars" moved to the residences of other participants. "We met in a way that was completely out of the normal channels of Washington," recalled Elspeth Rostow, wife of national security aide Walt Rostow and a professor of history and government at Georgetown University. "And whether we met, let's say, at Hickory Hill or at Arthur Schlesinger's or once in the White House or once in our house, what we'd have was people talking about issues which, by definition, had nothing to do with what they were working on during the day. That was the purpose of the Hickory Hill venture."

The list of those regularly invited—drawn up by Schlesinger and Bobby—included Robert McNamara, Roswell Gilpatric and Edward R. Murrow, along with their wives. Time-Life executive Donald Wilson and his wife frequently attended the sessions. Maxwell Taylor and his wife came occasionally, as did Teddy and Joan Kennedy. The Rostows were regulars, as were Treasury Secretary Douglas Dillon and his wife, whereas the Rusks, Sorensens and Bundys appeared only intermittently.

"There was no inner logic to the people who were asked," said Elspeth Rostow, "but it tended to be self-perpetuating once it got started. Participants listened to such lecturers as historian Elting Morison on Theodore Roosevelt or Rachel Carson, author of *Silent Spring*, on environmental pollution. We imported talent wherever it turned up, and the basis for being invited to speak was that you would talk on something that wouldn't involve the professional interests of anyone around." Although Jackie came occasionally, the president attended only once, when Sir Isaiah Berlin held forth on the subject of linguistics. JFK viewed the whole enterprise with amusement, seeing it as one of his earnest younger brother's "self-improvement" schemes. Following sessions, Jack would take pleasure in hearing gossipy rundowns of the proceedings, particularly when they featured philosophical disputes between his "traditional" Catholic sisters and Professor Schlesinger's high-grade intellectuals.

The president must have loved hearing the report on the seminar showcasing Oxford philosopher Sir Alfred Jules Ayer—one of the few sessions at which RFK had anything to say. "Bob was more of a benign host than an active participant," said Elspeth Rostow. "He had a good mind. I don't think he'd had as well-rounded an early education as Jack Kennedy. He didn't have the easy familiarity with the classics, for example, that comes from a certain kind of training. But he had a sense of discovering new ideas, and when he did discover them, he handled them well. Certainly, he was not a card-carrying intellectual, but he was a very bright person with a mind that was constantly exploring and expanding. I had a feeling he was growing, almost before my eyes.

"One of Bobby's most notable contributions to the series may have been proffered at Arthur's house when Freddy Ayer was talking logical positivism, a subject not exactly on everyone's lips in the 1960s. And being the provocateur that he was, Ayer was denying the existence of religion, politics—all the issues that concerned most of the people present. He said that although he *could* verify the reality of some highball glasses that were on the table, he could *not* verify the reality of religion.

"That became too much for Ethel Kennedy and, after he had finished his presentation, she entered the discussion, invoking the spirit of Saint Thomas Aquinas. This went on for quite a while, with Ayer rather amiably putting her down. It was a typical Oxford performance—he was having fun among the colonials. And Ethel was getting more and more indignant.

"Bob Kennedy was sitting by the British ambassador, and his head was in his hands because he was obviously unhappy about the direction of the discussion. And finally he said, in memorable tones, 'Drop it,

Ethel, drop it.' At which point she did. The conversation then proceeded to a discussion of Plato's parable of the cave and various other things, but Bob had no more to say. I think once he silenced Ethel he felt the family had made sufficient contribution to the dialogue."

Not all who breathed the rarefied atmosphere of the seminars were thrilled by the cerebral altitude. "I was not at the early ones," recalled Fred Dutton, a White House special assistant who later became assistant secretary of state for congressional relations, "but one I remember was held at Averell Harriman's Washington town house. George Kennan had just returned from a stint as ambassador to Yugoslavia. Robert McNamara was there, Randolph Churchill was there—it was a strange mix. I don't know, I thought these people had too many career responsibilities to be conducting the equivalent of an eighteenth-century French salon. Everybody thought it was wonderful, and it probably was somewhat stimulating—it gave you a broader picture than you derived from concentrating on your own special area. Yet I always considered it a bit precious. There was a certain amount of gamesmanship, although not at all on Bob's part; these were highly competitive people, and they were trying to posture and show off. In the status contests of the day, being in the Hickory Hill seminars was one of those silly little badges that were considered important. The sessions did lend an intellectual dimension to the everyday operation of government departments, but I often wondered why these people weren't all at home exhausted."

While the seminars were designed to give relief from the toil and drudgery of governing, some participants didn't leave business at the office. "There were some very vigorous discussions that went on in the seminars," remembered Secretary of the Interior Stewart Udall, a frequent attendee, "and some equally good private conversations, where you would discuss things relating to the administration's decisions, its activities. Of course, where you had a president's brother that was doing this, this gave it even more importance than it would have had . . . if simply some of the cabinet members had decided to meet informally. Bob Kennedy being as close to the president as he was . . . you could feel almost as if you were talking to him, you were talking with the president." When an official had failed to get his point across through normal channels, suggested Udall, the seminars, and the other gatherings that took place at Bobby's home, provided a useful setting for further lobbying. "That was one of the advantages of Hickory Hill and . . . the kind of lively social life that existed under the Kennedys. . . . Sometimes you didn't have to make an appointment and then go over to see somebody; you could simply get them off in a corner and do it casually and informally."

After his brother died, Robert Kennedy tried to preserve this particular corner of Camelot, but the seminars soon petered out. "Somehow," said Elspeth Rostow, "the spirit didn't last."

Labor pains struck Ethel Kennedy on July 4, 1963, as she was playing tennis at the family compound in Hyannis Port. Robert Kennedy placed a telephone call and a helicopter arrived to take her to Boston, where a police car drove her the last two miles to St. Elizabeth's Hospital. Six-pound fourteen-ounce Christopher George Kennedy was born by cesarean section later that Independence Day, exactly twelve years after the birth of his sister Kathleen, eldest of the children. "Christopher," said Lem Billings, "is an example of his mother's fortitude. Only Ethel Kennedy could give birth during a tennis match, then pick up her racket and finish the set."

Jacqueline Kennedy also spent the summer in Massachusetts, although she and her husband did not reside at Joe's estate. Citing their growing family and their need for presidential office space, they rented a home on Squaw Island, just half a mile away. The house belonged to Joe Kennedy's friend, the Irish crooner Morton Downey. Jackie was also carrying a child that summer, but her pregnancy did not end as joyfully as that of her ever-fecund sister-in-law: born two months prematurely on August 7, Patrick Bouvier Kennedy lived only two days.

Summer's end brought newborn Christopher and his seven siblings back to Hickory Hill, which had become the social center not only for the adults of the administration, but for the clan's next generation as well. "The Robert Kennedys were dominant over the other parts of the family," said author Lee Rainey, "and that primacy had a couple of sources. First, their sheer numbers. Second, their energy. So when all the cousins were hanging around at Hickory Hill, they absorbed the bedlam there.

"I'm not sure Caroline and John Jr. had much connection with the RFK kids. Jackie was not anxious to have her children overwhelmed by the Hickory Hill environment, and she quite consciously organized it so they weren't in that maelstrom all the time. The influence of Bobby on his nieces and nephews intensified after Jack died, but he was the natural leader even before, because he was much more child-oriented than his brother. To his children and their cousins, he was a much more accessible, approachable and immediate figure than the president was. He and Ethel, above all, created the Kennedy élan. Jack had a bad back and Jackie didn't want to play sports, so the touch football games, the tennis matches, the sailing and skiing trips were the product of Bobby and Ethel's insistence.* And because there were so many Robert Kennedy children, they became kind of the trunk of the tree and everyone else the branches. The non-RFK cousins were always "connecting" with and to the RFK kids—to their games, to their stature in the family—and measuring themselves against them. There were four or five layers of kids. The oldest cousins perpetually measured themselves against Joe. The next oldest against Bobby Jr. David was kind of free-floating—he compared himself to Bobby Jr., too. Then came the youngest generation. The five- and six-year-olds would dig up mounds of sand at the beach in Hyannis Port and sell it to tourists at a dollar per pail, justifying the price by calling it "Kennedy sand."

Steve Smith, Jr., described his uncle's role: "I remember him mostly on the river trips around the campfire. He was the general director of affairs. He'd organize the skits and the songs, and we'd all play charades. If you knew a joke, you'd tell it, or recite a poem, and if you did it well, he would be very generous in his praise."

Robert Kennedy wasn't only generous, however; he could be demanding. "He didn't coddle his children," maintained Gerald Tremblay, Bobby's old law school friend. "He didn't raise them so that they'd . . . come up and whine to him if something happened to go wrong. He never tolerated the kids crying and complaining. But he always treated them well, and gave them a lot of affection and a lot of direction.

"I never saw Bob really lose his temper with his children. . . . I have heard him raise his voice to get his point over, or give them orders, but I've never seen him lose his patience. If one of the children wasn't doing something fair, or quite up to the standards of the game they were playing, he'd let them know right away. He'd make them do it differently." One day, Bobby walked in on a raging food fight, recalled Joe, his oldest son, and the "only thing he said was that he was very disappointed in all of us. He made us feel like real rats."

"Kennedys never cry," RFK told his children time and again.† "Kennedys never give up." During winters, the family would ski in New Hampshire. Phil Stanton, a real estate agent from Waterville, recalled that "after the children had come down a slope, RFK would look at them. And if they weren't bruised, he'd send them back up. He wasn't happy

---

*RFK's children enjoyed the benefits of top-flight athletic instructors: Roosevelt Grier in football, Pancho Segura in tennis, Billy Kidd in skiing. These and other well-known professional athletes were regular members of Bobby's entourage.

†Playing on Bobby's famous family motto, Sarge Shriver once told his daughter Maria (wife of bodybuilder turned actor Arnold Schwarzenegger), "It's okay for Shrivers to cry."

unless they were black and blue." In a warmer season, Gerald Tremblay remembered, Bobby once insisted young Kerry jump off a cliff into a lake: "I think I understood the way he thought. After the kid did that . . . it would be pretty tough to scare that child again. . . . That's the way he brought up his kids, and I think that's the way his father brought him up. . . . He obviously felt that the method his father had used on him worked pretty well." Whenever neighbor Larry Newman watched the boys' football games, he couldn't help but notice their bloody noses. "They were pretty rough young kids. They were ultra competitive and they beat the hell out of one another."

"It seemed that Daddy never wasted time on elementary talk," remarked Kathleen, "such as how much the new car cost or where he was going to go for a haircut." But he did include his offspring in the grand events of history he helped to manage. When George Wallace took his stand in the schoolhouse door, David Kennedy not only watched the confrontation unfold on a television in his father's Justice Department office, he also received a letter from Dad about the incident. Michael received such a letter, too: "By the time you become attorney general," Bobby wrote the boy, "perhaps behavior like Wallace's will no longer be possible."*

Said Larry Newman, "I think [the children] believed there were two sets of rules governing the world: the one for the rest of *us* and the one for *them*." Kennedy exceptionalism entailed not only the responsibility shouldered by a future attorney general, but also unrelenting privilege. Since Bobby Jr. loved animals, his father had employees of the Bronx Zoo construct an elaborate terrarium, housing seventy-five species, in the Hickory Hill basement. On the rolling back lawn at the Virginia estate, the Green Berets had built an intricate obstacle course which the Kennedy children and various family guests utilized for training and pleasure.

Although Ethel cooperated in Bobby's program of character building, she softened its edges. "She was more protective . . ." said Gerald Tremblay. "Oh, much more so. Ethel was kind of tough herself—in sports . . . she'll do anything—but she has a lot of areas where she's quite fearful. She's scared to death of airplanes, just absolutely petrified of flying.† And a lot of things will scare her, but, boy, she's got gumption like you never saw!"

---

*In his RFK biography, Arthur Schlesinger also refers to these letters, both of which are located in the RFK papers at the JFK library. Ironically, David and Michael Kennedy would both die under tragic circumstances at an early age (see epilogue).

†An understandable phobia, considering the fate of her parents and, later, her brother.

The mistress of the huge household left most of the daily chores to her constantly changing staff of a dozen or so. But she did bring her inexhaustible energy to many of the standard tasks performed by the modern suburban housewife—overseeing meals, organizing parties, driving in car pools. The children in her car—whether her own offspring or those of another McLean mother—were quizzed by Ethel on current events. She graded the answers, always granting highest marks to those mentioning the president or attorney general.

Not all American children could reside in the luxury of Hickory Hill, but in mid-1963 RFK arranged for less fortunate youngsters to enjoy an amenity his own brood took for granted: he intervened to see that a Washington school open its swimming pool to summer use by neighborhood children. But when Bobby visited the site, the local recreation-department administrator's pride in the dignitary's appearance turned to mortification when the attorney general unleashed a barrage of questions in machine-gun fashion:

"How deep is the shallow end of the pool?" asked RFK.

"Three feet," the bureaucrat replied.

"What about children under three feet tall?"

"They can't use the pool."

"Why not use a wooden platform to raise the shallow end?"

"It would rot."

"Why wasn't the pool to be open on Sundays?"

"None of the pools was ever open on Sundays."

The attorney general said not another word to the hapless clerk before walking off. But Bobby's scowl quickly lifted. For "as he left the pool," wrote Pat Anderson in an *Esquire* magazine profile, "hundreds of Negro children ran after him, shouting his name and reaching out to touch him. Kennedy moved among them slowly, smiling, rubbing their heads, squeezing their hands, reaching out to the smaller ones who could not get near him."

Robert Kennedy loved children. To Steve Smith, Jr., receiving praise from his uncle was "the best feeling in the world. He had an empathetic quality that kids can sense. Either you have it or you don't, and kids can spot it."

At noon on Robert Kennedy's thirty-eighth birthday, Wednesday, November 20, 1963, his staff crowded into his Justice Department office to celebrate. Standing atop his desk, the honoree responded to the gathering's felicitations with an address, recalled Ramsey Clark, "which seemed rather funny at the time. He was proud, he said, to have accomplished so much at such a young age. And then he reeled off a list that included his battles with Roy Cohn and Jimmy Hoffa, his popularity in the South because of his civil rights policies, his prowess as a wiretapper. There was an obvious undertone of bitterness, which goes with the job. Being attorney general is a generally thankless task."

That evening, Bobby attended a presidential reception for the judiciary at the White House. After mingling on the main floor with magistrates and Justice Department brass—as well as the mailroom clerks and maintenance men whom other attorneys general had never bothered to invite to the annual affair—RFK joined Jack and Jackie upstairs in their living quarters. The president and first lady had argued before the reception—Jackie had taken her husband to task for his frequent womanizing—but now they had calmed down long enough to discuss their upcoming visit to Texas, where an intraparty feud threatened to disrupt that crucial state's effort in the coming campaign. With Ethel in tow, RFK left the White House and was driven to Hickory Hill, where his own birthday party was in progress. Bobby ended his day chatting with actor-dancer Gene Kelly; they sipped vodka and spoke until three in the morning. Kelly, who knew RFK through Peter Lawford, said, "Afterward, we sat in his library and talked about Marilyn Monroe. He kept saying how beautiful and intelligent she was. And the more we spoke, the more he drank."

On Friday, November 22, Robert Kennedy attended a late-morning meeting with Nicholas Katzenbach and Joe Dolan. "We spent an hour, hour and a half, going over some difficult judgeship vacancies," Dolan recalled, "and then the attorney general said, 'Well, I've got to go now.' He left us and was driven out to his house. He had Bob Morgenthau there, the U.S. attorney for New York, and Silvio Mollo, chief of Morgenthau's criminal division.

"I heard later that the purpose of having Morgenthau out there was to tell him that he, Bobby, planned to leave the attorney general's position in January to run the president's reelection campaign and that the president would name Morgenthau as attorney general. Plus, he and Jack would welcome Morgenthau's support for Mollo to take over the New York job."

RFK, Morgenthau and Mollo were joined by Ethel, and on that bright Indian summer day, the four sat by the swimming pool lunching on soup and sandwiches. At 1:43 P.M. the bathhouse telephone rang. Ethel got up to answer, then announced, "It's J. Edgar Hoover." Bobby took the call.

The FBI director told his boss that President Kennedy and Texas governor John Connally had been hit while touring Dallas in an "open car." Reported Hoover in his detailed memo of the conversation, "The Attorney General had not previously been advised of this." RFK demanded to know the president's condition. "I think it's serious," Hoover replied. The director's memo recounted the call's conclusion: "I asked the Attorney General if there was anything we could do at Dallas. He asked that we do whatever we could, and I told him we would get in touch with the Secret Service there."

Hanging up the telephone receiver, Bobby looked away from his guests and then covered his face with his hands. "Jack's been shot," he said. "It may be fatal."

The attorney general didn't wait for the FBI chief to contact Dallas, but instead he rushed back to the house and placed his own call. Unable to reach his old Harvard football comrade, Ken O'Donnell, he spoke with Clint Hill, the courageous secret service agent who had pushed Jackie Kennedy back into the Lincoln Continental and accompanied the stricken president to Parkland Memorial Hospital. The agent, Bobby later recalled (in his oral history for the JFK library), seemed himself distraught. "Is it serious?" Bobby asked. "I'm afraid it is." "Is he conscious?" "No." "Has a priest been called?" "Yes. We're doing everything we can, sir." "Then," RFK's account continued, "I said, 'Will you call me back?' and he said, 'Yes, I promise,' and then he called me back. . . ." At 2:10, when Hoover again telephoned, it was Bobby providing the update. Wrote Hoover, "I called the Attorney General to advise him that the President was in very, very critical condition. The Attorney General then told me the President had died."

Some friends and associates arrived, but Bobby soon stepped outside. United Press International reported later that day that "the attorney general was seen walking about the grounds of his Hickory Hill estate in McLean, Va., a suburb of the nation's capital.

"He walked alone, head down, shoulders hunched, his hands in his pockets.

"His favorite dog, a black Newfoundland called Brumus, trailed at his heels."

Robert Kennedy had lived his life as his father had taught him: for the glory of his brother. With the repeated firing of a rifle in Dallas, that brother, and that life, were gone.

20

KEEPER OF THE FLAME

As had Jack on August 1, 1944, with the death of Joe Jr., so Bobby on November 22, 1963, stepped up to a new position in the family: he was now Joseph Kennedy's eldest son. Within minutes of learning of his brother's death, RFK was on the telephone, taking command of the clan's response to the tragedy. Rose, in Hyannis Port, had already learned the news from a television screen watched by Joe's niece and caretaker, Ann Gargan. Mother and son agreed that the ailing old man should not be given the news just yet, so RFK called Teddy in Washington and assigned the junior senator from Massachusetts the task of flying to the Cape to tell Joe the next day. Bobby also called his sisters. Eunice, the one closest to Rose, would travel north with Ted. He couldn't reach Jean, but asked Steve Smith to relay her assignment: since she was the closest to Jackie, she would fly from New York to Washington to comfort the first lady upon her return from Dallas. Pat would take a plane to the nation's capital from California. Stas and Lee Radziwill would come in from London. Reliable Sargent Shriver would organize the funeral.

As Hickory Hill filled with people, Bobby seemed the least anguished among them. He tried to console those around him, including his own wife and children, by issuing words of confidence and comfort. John Mc-Cone, whom Bobby had asked to make the five-minute drive from CIA headquarters, later observed that "through this ordeal, as severe a trial as a man can go through, he never cracked. He was steely. Obviously he was seriously affected, but at no time did he lose his composure." RFK did not have time for his own grief this day.

The brother and son was forced to recall that he was also the attorney general of the United States when Lyndon Johnson called at 3 P.M. from

Texas. Once JFK had been pronounced dead an hour earlier at Parkland Hospital, Johnson had rushed back to Love Field to board Air Force One. The rest of the Kennedy party, led by Ken O'Donnell, had returned to the plane, too, and with an important cargo: the casket containing Jack's body. O'Donnell, thinking Johnson would fly home on the vice presidential plane that had brought him, ordered Air Force One to depart immediately. But a press aide shouted, "Tell O'Donnell he's not the commander in chief anymore. President Johnson is on the plane."

The nation's chief executive for sixty minutes, Lyndon Johnson, after conferring with several Texas congressmen, had decided to take the presidential oath before leaving the ground. And for guidance on the procedure he telephoned the nation's top officer of the law. Sounding harried, even frightened, LBJ told Bobby he suspected a worldwide plot in the works, so perhaps he ought to be sworn in at once.* Who could swear him in? he asked—what was the best way to do it? Although annoyed by Johnson's impatience, RFK said he would find out and get back to him.

The attorney general contacted his deputy, Nicholas Katzenbach, who checked with Harold Reis of the Justice Department's Office of Legal Counsel. Anyone who was authorized to administer federal and state oaths, said Reis, could administer the presidential oath, the wording of which could be found in the Constitution. Bobby called Johnson back with the information. To give him the oath, LBJ summoned Sarah T. Hughes, an old friend whom John Kennedy had appointed to the federal bench. However, no one on Air Force One could find a copy of the Constitution, so Katzenbach dictated the text to a secretary taking shorthand in the aircraft's staff cabin. Once Judge Hughes arrived, the new president addressed Ken O'Donnell. "Would you ask Mrs. Kennedy to come stand next to me?"

"You can't do that!" O'Donnell cried. "The poor kid has had enough for one day. You just can't do that to her, Mr. President!"

"Well, she said she wanted to do it."

"I don't believe that."

But when O'Donnell found the now former first lady, she agreed to stand by her husband's successor. "At least I owe that much to the country," she whispered. In her pink wool suit stained by blood and gore from

---

* LBJ's initial fear of a "worldwide plot" had caused a problem aboard Air Force One. According to air force Major Godfrey McHugh, Johnson, in his state of panic, had taken refuge in the plane's bathroom. "He was scared to death," said McHugh. " 'They're going to kill us. They're going to shoot down the plane, they're going to kill us all.' He'd gone berserk. I slapped him across the face, a quick one, and he seemed to regain his senses."

Jack's shattered skull, she watched as Lyndon Johnson raised his right hand to take the oath as the thirty-sixth president of the United States.

Air Force One took off. While the airplane was airborne, television networks announced that a suspect had been apprehended in connection with the president's murder. His name was Lee Harvey Oswald.

Despite the harsh words Ken O'Donnell had directed toward him earlier, LBJ now spoke to the Kennedy aide. "And," O'Donnell remembered, "he used the famous line that he used on every single staff member: 'I need you more than he ever needed you.' " While changing his shirt the new president continued: "You can't leave me. . . . You know that I don't know one soul north of the Mason-Dixon Line, and I don't know anything about those big city fellows. I need you. My staffers don't know anything. . . . They don't know anybody outside of Texas." "Noncommittal at the moment" in response to Johnson's plea, as O'Donnell afterward described himself, the aide later in the flight refused Johnson's request that he come to the front of the aircraft to talk to the president about matters of national security, opting instead to stay with Jackie. "That's fine," said Bill Moyers, Johnson's messenger and a Peace Corps organizer. "I don't blame you and the boss understands fully. No problem whatsoever."

Robert Kennedy went to the Pentagon, from which he would depart by helicopter with Robert McNamara and Maxwell Taylor for Andrews Air Force Base, where the presidential jet would land. He arrived at the airfield at 5:30 and secluded himself in a U.S. Army transport truck adjacent to the runway. Thirty minutes later, the plane bearing his dead brother touched down.

As the jumbo jetliner taxied to a halt a ground crew began wheeling a ramp toward the aircraft's front entrance, and Bobby ran up its steps while it was still in motion. He rushed inside the plane, "elbowing his way," recalled Jack Valenti, a Texas Democratic Party advertising man who became an aide in the LBJ White House, ". . . really racing through, neither looking to the right nor to the left to get to the back of the jet. The only thing that I noticed was that . . . he passed President Johnson without saying anything." RFK didn't stop until he reached his sister-in-law. "Hi, Jackie," he said softly, "I'm here."

Army personnel presently boarded the plane to remove the coffin, but Ken O'Donnell announced, "We'll take it off," and Jack's Secret Service detail loaded the casket onto a yellow forklift. In the crowd and the commotion, one person was ignored: the new president of the United States. The following afternoon, he complained to a cabinet member about the treatment he had received. "He said," according to the official's notes, "that when the plane came in . . . [they] paid no attention to him whatsoever, that they took the body off the plane, placed it in a vehicle, took Mrs. Kennedy along and departed, and only then did he leave the plane without any notice paid him whatsoever—'me, the goddamn President of the United States.' "

Bobby and Jackie accompanied the body to Bethesda Naval Hospital for the autopsy, then returned to the White House early Saturday morning while morticians prepared the president's remains for burial. At 4:34 A.M., the body, in a coffin of African mahogany, also arrived at the executive mansion. Following a brief Catholic service in the East Room, Bobby conferred with advisers and decided, in accord with Jackie's wishes, to keep the coffin closed throughout all ceremonial rites. At 6 A.M. he retired to the Lincoln Bedroom for a few hours' rest. After swallowing a sleeping pill provided by Charles Spalding, Bobby said, "Why now, God? Why now?"

As Spalding left the room and shut the door behind him, he heard his old friend's younger brother begin to weep. Yet Spalding could not bring himself to intrude upon Bobby's private grief. Gradually, the crying rose in pitch until it became a wail.

Robert McNamara arrived at Arlington National Cemetery in Virginia at 9 A.M. Saturday morning, November 23, to inspect a possible grave site for the fallen commander in chief. An hour later he stood in the White House East Room, where the coffin lay upon a specially constructed catafalque; there a low mass was led by Father John Cavanaugh, an old Kennedy family friend. Following the mass, Bobby, Jean and Pat, with William Walton, an artist and longtime associate of Jackie Kennedy, accompanied McNamara back to Arlington. The two sisters had favored burial in Boston, but as they stood in a driving rain, the tranquil majesty of the military graveyard convinced them that their brother should lie there among the nation's heroes. Jackie would visit later in the day to approve the precise location: on a slope leading up to the Robert E. Lee Mansion, directly in line with the Lincoln Memorial across the Potomac.

At half past two that afternoon, Lyndon Johnson convened his first White House cabinet meeting as president. Bobby arrived late. LBJ began with a silent prayer, then reiterated the phrase that had become his favorite refrain: I need you more than he did. Dean Rusk, the senior member of the cabinet, and Adlai Stevenson, the senior member of the Democratic Party, expressed their unqualified support for the nation's new leader. Robert Kennedy remained mute. The meeting lasted twenty-five minutes.

At 12:30 P.M. on Sunday, November 24, Bobby and Jackie entered the East Room. With the help of Major Godfrey McHugh, the commander of the honor guard standing watch, they lifted the lid of the wooden box containing John Kennedy's corpse. Inside, Jackie placed items of jewelry—her wedding ring, a bracelet he had given her, a set of gold cuff links she had given him—and a scrimshaw version of the presidential seal she had commissioned a Cape Cod artist to fashion for her husband. To this she added a ten-page farewell letter she'd written in the early-morning hours, a letter from Caroline (which Jackie had helped compose)—"Dear Daddy, We're all going to miss you. Daddy I love you very much. Caroline."—and some pencil scribblings from three-year-old John-John. Bobby removed his *PT-109* tie clasp. "He should have this, shouldn't he?" he said to his brother's widow. He placed it in the coffin, along with an engraved silver rosary given him by Ethel at their wedding. McHugh and RFK watched in silence as Jackie arranged the various articles the way she wanted them. She gazed at her husband's face. She began to stroke his hair and continued to caress it as the minutes ticked by. Sensing what she wanted, McHugh left the room and quickly returned with a pair of scissors. Jackie bent forward and carefully cut a lock of Jack's hair. Bobby slowly closed the lid of the coffin and the two mourners, both in tears, departed.

A few minutes later, Lyndon and Lady Bird Johnson met with the Kennedys in the Green Room. When Eunice Shriver greeted Mrs. Johnson she told the new first lady that the suspected murderer of John Kennedy had himself been shot. The assault had taken place at 12:21 P.M. and had been televised nationally by NBC. Lee Harvey Oswald was pronounced dead at 2:07 P.M. at Parkland Memorial Hospital, where the president had died some forty-eight hours before. Jack Ruby, a sometime nightclub owner and a Mafia hanger-on, had been Oswald's gunman.

JFK's coffin, draped in the American flag, was transported by procession from the White House to the Capitol Rotunda, where it would lie in state. Leading the line of march along Pennsylvania Avenue was the caisson bearing the late president. Drawn by six white horses, it was the same gun carriage that had carried the body of Franklin Roosevelt in 1945. Next came a horse, riderless, with boots reversed in the stirrups, a symbol of a fallen leader since the time of Genghis Khan. The limousine carrying Jackie, Caroline, John-John, Bobby and the Johnsons followed. Lady Bird Johnson later documented the scene in her personal memoirs: "Soldiers were marching, and always there was the sound of muffled drums in the background. Flags flew at half-mast. But most vivid of all was the feeling of a sea of faces all around us and that curious sense of silence, broken only by an occasional sob."

LBJ, Jackie and Caroline sat in the backseat, Bobby and Lady Bird Johnson in the jump seats. John-John moved among them. "We were a silent group as we rode along," Mrs. Johnson continued, "each wrapped in his own thoughts. The only light moments came from John-John, who jumped from the back to his uncle's lap to the front, until finally Bobby Kennedy said, 'John-John, be good, you be good, and we'll give you a flag afterward. You can march with Dave Powers, and you can give your Daddy a salute.' "

Chief Justice Earl Warren, Speaker of the House John McCormack and Senator Mike Mansfield delivered eulogies at the Capitol. Then "Lyndon went forward and laid a wreath at the foot of the casket. Mrs. Kennedy went over and knelt. I remember how carefully she . . . kissed the casket, and Caroline by her side simply put her little hand on the flag—sort of underneath the flag. John-John had disappeared. And then we left in separate cars."

At nine that evening, Bobby and Jackie visited the Rotunda again.

By 9 A.M., Monday, November 25, a quarter of a million people had filed past the catafalque on which rested John Kennedy's coffin. The details of the day had been approved by Jackie, but at 10:45 Bobby suggested a departure from the official schedule: a final moment of privacy with the deceased. For ten minutes, Robert, Jackie and Teddy Kennedy knelt and prayed before the coffin. Then the mahogany box was once again placed on the caisson. On foot Jackie and her two brothers-in-law led the assembled mourners—the new president and two ex-presidents (Eisenhower and Truman), the cabinet, the justices of the Supreme Court, leaders of Congress, 220 representatives of 102 foreign governments, close friends, extended family, prominent Americans, White House servants, contingents from all the armed services—to St. Matthew's Cathedral near the junction of Rhode Island and Connecticut Avenues. Military bands and choirs sounded hymns as sharpshooters posted atop buildings nervously eyed the route for signs of further violence.

Richard Cardinal Cushing, the archbishop of Boston who had married the late president and his wife in 1953, conducted the requiem mass. He concluded the service: "May the angels, dear Jack, lead you into Paradise. May the martyrs receive you at your coming. May the spirit of God embrace you, and mayest thou, with all those who made the supreme sacrifice of dying for others, receive eternal rest and peace. Amen."

Outside again, Jackie watched as the team of soldiers assigned to the coffin lashed the box to the caisson for the third and final time. The mourners left by motorcade for Arlington.

At the grave site, the marine band played "The Star-Spangled Banner," and then air force bagpipers played the dirge "Mist-Covered Mountain." Fifty F-105 fighter planes flew over the grave, followed by Air Force One. Colonel James Swindal, the pilot who had flown Jack on his travels around the world, dipped the presidential jet's wing as he passed overhead. Cardinal Cushing sprinkled holy water on the coffin, military rifle teams fired salutes and "Taps" resounded in the still air. With a nation watching on television, Jackie received the folded flag that had covered her husband's coffin; she then lit the eternal flame.

As the widow was leaving, Bobby said to her, "Say good-bye to General Taylor. He did so much for Jack." In *The Death of a President*, William Manchester described a photograph taken while Jackie spoke to Taylor, then chairman of the Joint Chiefs of Staff. Taylor, as well as the other Joint Chiefs standing nearby, "are at attention," Manchester wrote, "yet the most erect and militant figure there . . . is Robert Kennedy." Bobby and Jackie turned and walked down the hill, hand in hand, to their waiting car.

At the White House, the mourners reassembled. Haile Selassie of Ethiopia, Anastas Mikoyan of the Soviet Union, Charles de Gaulle of France, Prince Philip of Great Britain, and Willy Brandt of West Germany were among the visitors to offer the widow their condolences. Robert Kennedy's brave facade yielded to tears only when Eamon De Valera, president of Ireland, recited verses by nineteenth-century Irish poet Gerald Griffin: " 'Tis, it is the Shannon's stream, / Brightly glancing, brightly glancing!" the poem began.

Another White House guest was Aristotle Onassis, the Greek shipping magnate with whom Lee Radziwill had become intimately involved. After the 1963 death of Patrick Bouvier Kennedy, the infant's mother had joined Ari and her sister aboard his yacht, the *Christina*, for a cruise of the Greek Isles. In the course of the voyage, Jackie and Ari embarked on a friendship that culminated in their 1968 marriage, after the death of Bobby Kennedy.

By late evening, the guests had departed and the children had been put to bed. Bobby and Jackie were alone together in the family quarters on the executive mansion's second floor. After a few minutes, Bobby said to his sister-in-law, "Let's go and visit Jack."

Jackie gathered a bouquet from a large glass vase of assorted flowers she always kept on a hall table, and then she and Bobby were driven to Arlington by a Secret Service agent. The crowds had dispersed—a single military policeman stood guard over the fresh grave. The two mourners saw a green beret that had been placed by a member of the Special Forces on the branches of a nearby evergreen; an MP had left behind his black-and-white brassard, while a soldier of the Third Infantry had propped up his Old Guard ribbon and cockade. The flickering light of the eternal flame beckoned, as Jackie and Bobby kneeled. In the quiet of midnight, the two who had known and loved him best prayed for his soul. As they rose, Jackie arranged her flowers next to the grave, and the brother and the widow walked back to their car, bidding John Fitzgerald Kennedy farewell in his final resting place. In the backseat of the car, according to the Secret Service agent, Bobby and Jackie embraced. They said nothing as their driver slowly pulled away.

With his brother buried, with the foreign dignitaries gone, with the funeral and its distractions ended, Robert Kennedy sank into desolation. "I was shocked by his appearance," wrote William Manchester, who met with Bobby in early 1964 regarding the book to be written on Jack's death. "I have never seen a man with less resilience. Much of the time he seemed to be in a trance, staring off into space, his face a study in grief."

Joe Kennedy still lived but was disabled, so he who had become elder son had also become effective head of the clan, lending his strength to his stricken wife, mother, children, siblings, cousins, nephews, nieces, in-laws. "The whole family was like a bunch of shipwreck survivors," Lem Billings later remarked. "I don't think they could have made it at all without Bobby." RFK "seemed to be everywhere. He always had an arm around a friend or family member and was telling them it was okay, that it was time to move ahead." But Bobby himself could not move ahead. Consumed with despair, the attorney general neglected the nation's business in favor of his family's business, such as the answering of condolence letters and the establishment of his brother's presidential library.* RFK did not return to his job at the Justice Department until January 1964.

Joe Dolan recalled the first meeting he had with his boss after the assassination: "I came in to talk to him about judgeships, which is the thing I talked to him most about. He saw me coming across the room—it

---

*Bobby and Jackie investigated countless sites, including the Harvard University campus, and interviewed numerous architects before settling on I. M. Pei. The completed structure, located at Columbia Point in Boston, offered little shelf space and drafty outdoor wind tunnels; and in terms of design, it seemed woefully inappropriate for its purpose—a museum and research center dedicated to the life and times of John F. Kennedy.

was a big office—and when I got to him he put his arm around me. That was a very telling gesture. When they weren't on the campaign trail, none of the Kennedys were touchers, they didn't grab people. They didn't do the ol' politician's routine, where you shake with the right hand and put your left arm around the person's back. And they would recoil, physically, from anyone who swarmed on them. You could see they didn't like that. So, this was an unusual thing for him to do. And he didn't say a thing about Jack. We just started discussing the judgeships."

For months afterward, RFK couldn't bring himself to say the words "assassination," "death" or "Dallas." He spoke only of "the events of November 22." "Into the spring of '64," continued Dolan, "he was more subdued, he didn't make funny comments. Bobby Kennedy was one of the greatest persons I ever knew for situational humor. And a lot of it was self-deprecating, but there was much less of that in 1964."

Bobby's sense of humor did not forsake him altogether; rather, it took on a dark, mordant cast. Not long after Jack's death, Dave Hackett and RFK attended the burial of a mutual friend. "Hackett and I have so much experience at this thing," he said afterward, "that we're offering a regular service for funerals. We select readings and songs of utmost simplicity, and then we pick out a cheap casket to save the widow money. You know they always cheat you on a casket. We pick passages from the Bible and do all that's necessary to ensure an interesting and inexpensive funeral. This is a new service we can provide all our friends."

Dave Hackett and others could not fail to see the anguish behind the bitter jokes, but the fellowship of confreres could not keep Bobby from his dearest companions: his private, sacredly held memories of his brother. Some mornings, he would emerge from his Hickory Hill bedroom at 3 A.M., climb into his convertible and drive into the winter night with the top down, returning at dawn for breakfast and a shower before heading to the office. He wore articles of Jack's clothing—a cashmere sweater, a tweed overcoat, a leather jacket from PT duty—as if by covering his own body with the fabric that had covered Jack's he could preserve his contact with the absent brother's flesh.

Teddy Kennedy, unfortunately, provided little consolation. "Bobby didn't have anyone to counsel with," commented Andrew Oehmann, Jr., son of RFK's executive assistant. "He could share things with the president, his bigger brother, his older brother. But he didn't have the same feeling with Teddy. Teddy was still a kid, he hadn't grown up yet." Indeed, Robert Kennedy had only one brother. "When he said 'my brother,'" said Joe Dolan, "he meant the president. Always. I can remember one morning on the elevator. Teddy had said something that I thought was pretty stupid, and I remarked to Bob, 'Did you hear what your brother said?' And he stared at me with a funny look in his eyes and said, 'What?!' You could see that he was jarred when I said, 'what *your brother* said.' By using that phrase, I had brought Jack back to life."

Work meant less than before. Bobby was still attorney general, but now he was *only* attorney general, not the roving presidential alter ego who commanded the obedience of the secretaries of state and defense and the director of Central Intelligence. Currently he was one department head among many, deprived of his special mission as his brother's dogged defender and merciless enforcer. "It had been exciting at the Justice Department," said Oehmann, "it had been dynamic, it had been fun. And then it wasn't. Then it was more like work." Customary celebrations only reminded RFK of what he had lost. When columnist Mary McGrory, a Kennedy family devotee, encountered Bobby on St. Patrick's Day 1964, she could see that his "Irish eyes were not smiling." She recalled that she tried to cheer him up by speaking of his future: "It was something like, 'Well, you're young and you're going to be productive and successful. . . .' But before I could finish he just let out a yelp of pain and buried his head in my shoulder."

His career had been involved in politics and the law only incidentally; his real life's work had been his brother, but his brother no longer existed. In the past, when Bobby needed advice or direction, he turned to either his brother or his father (and sometimes both), but now one was dead and the other was an invalid, so he had to re-create himself without their help. Still, the elder son could not forget that he had been kid brother, and his new mission—his new self—would grow out of the old. In the months following the assassination RFK assumed a self-appointed role— keeper of the flame, consciously assigning himself the burden of ensuring that the "unfinished business" of his brother's tragically shortened administration did not go unaddressed. In death, Jack would grow into a martyr to the Kennedy "cause," even though in life he had scoffed at certain causes and the idealists who espoused them. Beneath the heroic rhetoric, the Kennedy administration had been supremely pragmatic and reactive: it had acted on behalf of civil rights only when a national movement forced its hand; it had publicly pursued organized crime while secretly soliciting its assistance in a plot to assassinate Fidel Castro; it had never questioned the cold war assumptions behind a deepening involvement in Vietnam. The humane "liberalism" of RFK's last years came to fruition only after the death of his brother. While he would remain an astute politician, RFK could now gradually allow the compassionate side of his nature a more forceful expression than ever was possible when Jack was alive to require compromise of principles for the sake of political advancement. By designating himself inheritor of Jack's "legacy"—a legacy he invented after the president's assassination—the eldest son, though grieving, was now free. In the last four and a half years of his life, Bobby Kennedy could be the person he, not Jack, dreamed of becoming.

The man of action became more thoughtful, seeking wisdom in literature. He read the plays of William Shakespeare, the novels of Albert Camus, the essays of Ralph Waldo Emerson, underlining passages that spoke to his tortured state, making marginal notations to help him understand the book he was reading and the world that had made him so sad. Jackie gave him a copy of classicist Edith Hamilton's popular rendering of ancient Hellenic civilization, *The Greek Way.** He likewise discovered the tragedies of Aeschylus. At Justice Department meetings, aides thinking he was staring at his lap in a daze realized he was immersed in a volume of modern French poetry. Two quotations found their way onto the wall over the fireplace in the Hickory Hill master bedroom. One was from Emerson: "Seek to persuade the sea wave to break—You will persuade me no more easily." The other was Hamilton's description of Aeschylus: "Life for him was an adventure, perilous indeed, but men are not made for safe havens."

His safe haven destroyed, RFK found insufficient solace in the nostrums he'd learned as a boy in church—thus his need for the existentialism of Camus, the fatalism of the Greeks. Ethel's faith was more basic, with fewer questions; as such, her ability to comfort her husband was diminished. Her friend Coates Redmon recalled conversations that would take place at Hickory Hill: "Someone would say, 'Well, what are we going to do about such-and-such?' You know, government talk. And Ethel would say, 'Well, Jack will take care of that. Jack's up in heaven and Jack's looking down on us and Jack will show us what to do.' She often said that. And one time Bobby sat back and said, audibly, to everyone, 'That was the wife of the attorney general of the United States. No more out of her.'" Bobby had always shaped his life around a simple

---

*Jackie gave Bobby another volume in 1964, *Plutarch's Lives,* which had been sent to her by poet Robert Lowell. In 1965 and 1966, Jackie and Lowell would occasionally see each other, and eventually she introduced him to her brother-in-law. "I think she wanted to educate Bobby by exposing him to somebody like Lowell," speculated TV newsman Blair Clark, a friend of both the poet and the former first lady. Bobby turned out to need less educating than Clark supposed. One day, the senator and the renowned man of letters engaged in a contest to see who could quote the most Shakespeare. Long a lover of the Bard's work—while showering, he often listened to Caedmon recordings of Shakespeare's poetry and plays—RFK won the competition hands down.

expression of faith: his devotion to his brother. Suddenly, the world seemed more complicated. "Why now, God? Why now?" RFK had cried out. Ethel still recognized the God they'd both come to know in childhood. To Bobby, He had become a stranger.

For the succor not available from the mother of his eight children, Bobby looked elsewhere. Jackie's friend Joan Braden, who had worked on the 1960 campaign, recalled RFK baring his grief to her. "My heart wrenched from complicated tugs of emotion," Braden said. "He had never seemed more vulnerable than the night [he met] me in Georgetown in early January 1963. My husband, Tom Braden, happened to be out of town. When Bobby asked me to bring him upstairs, I did. On the bed, we kissed. Then he got up to take off his tie. But I could not go through with it. He was hurt, silent and angry. Looking out the window, I watched his straight back under the streetlights as he walked toward his car. Why hadn't I done it? . . . Tom [Braden] would have understood, even if Ethel would not have."

On January 14, 1964, Bobby, Teddy and Jackie appeared on national television to thank the public for the hundreds of thousands of messages of condolence they had received. Bobby and Ethel then left immediately for the Far East. New trouble had arisen with Indonesia—this time, President Sukarno was engaged in hostilities with Malaysia—and some White House advisers had convinced Lyndon Johnson to approve Bobby, experienced in dealing with the irksome Asian leader, as a presidential envoy to the dispute. The sorrowful attorney general had as much desire to go as the mistrustful Johnson had to send him, but he left for Tokyo, where he conducted talks with Sukarno, then journeyed to Malaysia, and finally to Djakarta for more talks with the Indonesian. Although RFK helped broker a truce in the dispute, Johnson showed little interest in the trip's outcome after Bobby returned home on January 27. Unlike his predecessor, the new president didn't want or need two secretaries of state.

In Tokyo, RFK had returned to Waseda University, where a few years earlier he'd won a skeptical nation's affection by his deft handling of leftist hecklers. "President Kennedy," he now proclaimed to the students, "was more than just president of a country. He was the leader of young people everywhere. What he was trying to do was fight against hunger, disease and poverty around the world. You and I as young people have a special responsibility to carry on the fight." The message of January 1964 was almost identical to that of February 1962, with the same themes—youth, idealism—and the same soaring language. But there were two differences: now when Bobby spoke of his brother, he used the past tense; and when he challenged Japan's youth to fight the world's ills, he was also challenging himself to live up to his new, brotherless, purpose.

Bobby's despair was in no small measure a result of survivor's guilt. JFK had been warned of a climate of hatred in Dallas. Senator William Fulbright, the target of vicious attacks by the *Dallas News,* had declined several invitations to visit the city and had pleaded with JFK to do likewise. Byron Skelton, the Democratic National Committeeman from Texas, had written to Bobby on November 4, 1963, "Frankly, I'm worried about President Kennedy's proposed trip to Dallas." The city wasn't safe, Skelton argued. But political commitments had been made, and RFK, preparing for his brother's reelection campaign, had favored keeping them. Moreover, it was RFK who suggested that the president ride through the streets of Dallas in a car without using the specially outfitted bulletproof bubble top. "It will give you more contact with the crowd," he had said.

Bobby's advice to visit Dallas, however, weighed less heavily on him than did his conduct over the whole of his brother's term in office, for he had been the driving force in the Kennedy administration's most aggressive operations. He had pushed the government to hound the mob, to chase down Hoffa, to destroy Castro. He had "taken care" of Marilyn Monroe. Less than a day after Jack was declared dead, Bobby told Larry O'Brien, "I'm sure that little pinko prick had something to do with it, but he certainly didn't mastermind anything. He should've shot me, not Jack. I'm the one who's out to get them." News about Jack's assassin, and about the assassin's assassin, was not slow in coming. By the day of the funeral, Bobby knew that Lee Harvey Oswald had Communist ties and had demonstrated in New Orleans as a member of the Fair Play for Cuba Committee. He knew that Jack Ruby was a Dallas racketeer connected to the national Mafia. As John H. Davis observed in his book *Mafia Kingfish: Carlos Marcello and the Assassination of John F. Kennedy,* RFK "could not possibly have escaped the awful suspicion that his aggressive campaigns against Castro and the mob might have backfired on his brother."

The CIA's John McCone remembered conversations with the attorney general shortly after Jack's death: "He wanted to know what we knew about it and whether it had been a Cuban or perhaps Russian hit. He even asked me if the CIA could have done it. I mentioned the mob, but RFK didn't want to know about it. I suspect he thought it was the mob. He said, 'They'—whoever 'they' were—'should have killed me. I'm the one they wanted.' He blamed himself because of all the enemies he'd made along the way and also because he'd advised his brother to go to

Dallas." At the time of Jack's death, the pursuit of the Mafia was proceeding unabated. Indeed, when the telephone rang with J. Edgar Hoover's word of Jack's shooting, RFK was awaiting another call: one supplying news of the verdict in the federal trial of New Orleans godfather Carlos Marcello. (The don was acquitted that day.)

Over the next year, Bobby kept his distance from the Warren Commission, the blue-ribbon panel, headed by the chief justice, created to look into the assassination.* J. Edgar Hoover, whose Bureau was a key investigative arm of the commission, sent the attorney general none of the raw materials developed by FBI agents during the probe, but neither did Bobby seek to acquire them. Earl Warren's group issued its final report to Lyndon Johnson on September 24, 1964. Oswald and Ruby, the document concluded, had both acted alone. Did RFK maintain his odd detachment from the inquiry into his brother's death—an inquiry for which he, as master of the FBI, had significant official responsibility—because he was too heartbroken to dwell on the grisly details? Or did he fear that a truly comprehensive investigation might uncover details of Marcello and Roselli, Giancana and Campbell, Monroe and Castro? Was his brother's assassination the act of a solitary lunatic, or an expertly devised reprisal for the administration's efforts and Bobby's vendettas?† At a champagne party following Jimmy Hoffa's court convictions in early 1964, a glum RFK said, "There's nothing to celebrate." The labor leader had gloated after Jack's death, "Bobby's just another lawyer now." Hoffa

---

* The other members of the commission were U.S. senators Richard B. Russell, Democrat of Georgia, and John Sherman Cooper, Republican of Kentucky; U.S. representatives Hale Boggs, Democrat of Louisiana, and Gerald Ford, Republican of Michigan; Allen Dulles, former CIA director; and John J. McCloy, former president of the World Bank.

† Privately, RFK expressed dismay over the Commission's report, telling LaVern Duffy it was "impossible that Oswald and Ruby hadn't known one another." Recently issued assassination files (CIA and FBI) indicate that on November 23, 1963, the day after his brother's death, RFK had telephoned Harry Ruiz-Williams, a CIA operative, at the Ebbitt Hotel, 8th Street N.W., in Washington, D.C., a CIA-operated safehouse used primarily to house Cuban exiles. After speaking with Ruiz-Williams, RFK talked to journalist Haynes Johnson, who was also at the Ebbitt, telling Johnson he suspected CIA-backed anti-Castro forces of having been involved in his brother's death. Bobby later told Duffy the same thing. "Those Cuban cunts are all working for the mob," said Bobby. "They blame us for the Bay of Pigs, and they're trying to make this look like a Castro-Communist hit. I don't buy it. And I don't trust those guys at the CIA. They're worse than the Mafia." In the end, said Duffy, "Bobby simply didn't want to know who did it. But at the same time, he couldn't put it behind him. He wanted to bring his brother's murderers to justice, but he didn't have the strength to do it. He must have felt tremendous guilt over his failure to act."

was only one of the attorney general's enemies with a motive to see the president eliminated.

Jim Garrison, the flamboyant New Orleans district attorney who challenged the Warren Commission's conclusions, recalled a telephone conversation he had with RFK in 1964: "I told him some of my theories. He listened carefully, then said, 'Maybe so, maybe you're right. But what good will it do to know the truth? Will it bring back my brother?' I said, 'I find it hard to believe that as the top law man in the country you don't want to pursue the truth more ardently.' With this he hung up on me."*

(Indications of a second gunman and a mob-controlled hit have grown considerably over the years. The House Select Committee on Assassinations, which convened in 1979, acknowledged the likelihood of a "second gunman" theory. Then, in May 1997, Gerald Ford publicly admitted that in 1975, while president of the United States, he had suppressed certain FBI and CIA surveillance reports that indicated that JFK had been caught in a crossfire in Dallas, and that John Roselli and Carlos Marcello had orchestrated the assassination plot. Roselli resented the fact that the Kennedys had tapped the Mafia for campaign contributions, then used the mob for vote-control purposes at the same time that RFK continued to persecute and prosecute leaders of the group. Marcello's animosity toward RFK [and thus the Kennedys] began in 1961, when the attorney general made him a primary target in his massive drive against crime, essentially "kidnapping" him in an effort to have him deported.)

Suspicion of conspiracy was not Bobby's only motivation to avoid a thorough probe into Jack's death; the attorney general's efforts to avoid certain disclosures about his brother—and to control those he couldn't avoid—began only hours after the shooting. As physicians at Bethesda Naval Hospital conducted the autopsy on the president's body during the night of November 22 and into the early morning of the twenty-third, Bobby and Jackie spent part of the night in a private suite on one of the facility's higher floors. Dr. George C. Burkley, the White House physician who had accompanied the president to Dallas, represented the family at the postmortem. "I supervised the autopsy," he remembered, "and kept in constant contact with Mrs. Kennedy and the members of her party. . . . I made trips back and forth . . . and talked to her on a number of occasions." Dr. Pierre Finck, a surgeon at the procedure, later said that one of the high-ranking military officers present instructed him not to

---

* RFK not only didn't pursue the facts behind his brother's assassination, he went so far as to disband the Organized Crime Task Force, which he had earlier formed to probe Mafia and mob activities, including Teamster racketeering and overt police corruption.

dissect the track of the bullet wound in the president's back. The order, Finck maintained, originated with "the Kennedy family." Most likely, Bobby and Jackie meddled with the autopsy to avoid exposure of the dead president's adrenal glands, atrophied from Addison's disease. Revealing that infirmity would lay bare the deception Jack and his family had perpetrated over the years by portraying his outward image as one of robust health.

RFK's attempt to limit the investigation into Jack's death continued. Immediately following the autopsy, a variety of forensic materials— photographs and X rays, 119 microscopic tissue slides, 58 slides of blood smears taken during JFK's senatorial and presidential years, as well as the president's chemically preserved brain—were moved from Bethesda Naval Hospital to the Executive Office Building, next door to the White House. Though technically in the custody of the Secret Service, the materials, and the locked file cabinet into which they had been sequestered, were controlled by Dr. Burkley. The materials remained stored in that location for nearly a year and a half, with neither the Warren Commission nor the FBI examining them before the commission filed its report.

In April 1965, with Congress debating a bill calling for the government to acquire certain pieces of evidence relating to President Kennedy's death, Bobby directed Burkley to transfer "the file cabinet's contents" from the custody of the Secret Service to the care of Evelyn Lincoln for "safekeeping" at the National Archives. Lincoln, working temporarily at the Archives on the indexing of her late boss's papers there, stored the items in a footlocker, which Angie Novello removed, on Bobby's order, four weeks later. Novello, according to Davis, then placed the footlocker in a storage space the Archives had been making available as a courtesy to RFK.

In November 1965, Congress enacted the law calling for the acquisition of forensic evidence related to JFK's autopsy. Several months thereafter, Ramsey Clark, who had become Lyndon Johnson's attorney general, asked RFK to comply with the new statute. Although Bobby was generally uncooperative, he agreed, after prolonged discussion with Clark, to release the items. On October 29, 1966, Burke Marshall, representing the late president's estate, signed an agreement with the government to donate to the National Archives the autopsy materials in the estate's possession. Parties to the deal also approved an inventory of the items; the list included the X rays and photographs, the tissue slides and the remains of JFK's brain. But when officials at the National Archives were given the key to the footlocker a few days later, they discovered that although the majority of the photos and X rays were present, pictures of the brain and of the interior cavity of his chest—that is, those showing the sites of the gunshot wounds—were gone. The tissue and blood slides had also disappeared, as had the stainless steel container holding the brain itself.

In the late 1970s, the House Select Committee on Assassinations concluded that "circumstantial evidence tends to show that Robert Kennedy either destroyed these materials or otherwise rendered them inaccessible." The probable reason the panel cited for RFK's actions was that the materials "would be placed on public display in future years in an institution such as the Smithsonian." But was defense of Jack's dignity in death the only reason? Or did Bobby fear that forensic evidence might point to more than one gunman, a conclusion that could lead to disclosure of the deepest secrets of the Kennedy administration? Was he still looking to avert public knowledge of the president's Addison's disease? Or of his amphetamine use?

The Kennedy myth had grown large since Jack's death. The truth could not be permitted to tarnish it.*

S omeone was sitting in John Kennedy's chair.

Despite the gulf separating Jack's East Coast sophistication from Lyndon Johnson's Texas earthiness, JFK had liked his vice president. LBJ's drawl, his outlandish stories, his barnyard vocabulary, had amused the urbane president. And Jack had sympathized with the plight of his fellow politician: once the domineering leader of Congress, Johnson had found himself in a ceremonial post with little more power, as he put it, "than the frigging Queen of England." He would ultimately claim that he loathed being second in command; he loathed it mainly because he was expected to fulfill only one major function: to show the president unswerving loyalty. "I never heard Lyndon Johnson criticize John Kennedy in any way, publicly or privately, while he was vice president," insisted George Christian, an LBJ aide who would become White House

---

*RFK's probable involvement in the disappearance of autopsy materials may well have been politically motivated. His own political future would have been in danger had his family's dealings with the Mafia been revealed. He pursued organized crime figures on the one hand, and courted them on the other. And those he did pursue, such as Carlos Marcello, were often the target of illegal Justice Department activity. In April 1961, shortly after he became attorney general, Bobby authorized an operation which resulted in the kidnapping of Marcello by Immigration Department agents and his immediate deportation from New Orleans to Guatemala City. Returned to the United States, Marcello could in fact have been the brains behind the murder of JFK. He was once quoted as having said, "I got the wrong Kennedy."

press secretary in 1967. "If anything, he went in the other direction. In conversation, he always referred to JFK as 'the president': 'The president did this, the president did that.' Bobby, on the other hand, was a thorn in his side. That's what LBJ always perceived him to be, and for good reason, I think. Bobby just didn't have any use for him whatever."

LBJ's fealty to Jack hadn't altered Bobby's opinion of the man. Whereas the vice president's coarseness inspired affection in Jack, Bobby's reaction was pure disgust. The attorney general could never let go of the grudge he had formed, for mostly unexplainable reasons, at the 1960 convention. Joe Kennedy had said years before, "When Bobby hates you, you stay hated." LBJ stayed hated.

Johnson knew that he was the butt of ridicule among what he called "the Bobby crowd," who referred to the vice president and his wife, in a phrase coined by Jackie, as "Colonel Cornpone and his Little Porkchop." The candid Texan begged for approval from the reserved New Englander. "Bobby, you just can't abide me, can you?" he said on one occasion during a weekend visit with the Kennedys at Camp David. RFK did not expend much energy trying to understand the proud, complicated man loyally serving his brother. Just two weeks before Jack's assassination, Bobby's friends gave him an LBJ voodoo doll into which all delightedly stuck pins. "LBJ courted him," Christian continued, "tried to appease him, tried to get on his better side. Johnson reached out to Bobby, but I never saw any evidence that Bobby reached out to him. I really believe, and in fact I'm damn sure, that if Bobby Kennedy had made an effort to be generous to Lyndon Johnson, Lyndon Johnson would have loved it. I mean, that just was the way Johnson was. If Bobby had treated him with some respect, instead of going around calling him Colonel Cornpone, it would have been entirely different."

Vice President Johnson no doubt also heard rumors that his ambitions and those of the attorney general were likely to clash in the future. "I remember a conversation I had with JFK in the spring of 1963," said Charles Bartlett, "when Kennedy remarked, 'Who do you think the nominee will be in 1968? Bobby or Lyndon?' I didn't have the feeling from this question and some others which he asked that John Kennedy was particularly thrilled by the fact that Bobby had decided that he would try to succeed him." In addition, Bobby's Justice Department was investigating LBJ's former associate Bobby Baker. RFK had no evidence of wrongdoing on the vice president's part, but Johnson couldn't help but feel that the attorney general would be overjoyed to be able to reel in an even bigger fish than Baker.

The unfriendly relationship between the two men began moving toward outright hostility within minutes of Jack's death. For it was Lyndon Johnson who insisted on being sworn in as president while Air Force One was still in Dallas, though in fact (according to the Constitution), he automatically assumed the position the moment of JFK's death. Ken O'Donnell typified the attitude of what quickly solidified into the Kennedy side of the feud. "There's no question in my mind," he said, "that Lyndon Johnson wanted to be sworn in by Judge Sarah T. Hughes, an old family friend, and he was afraid somebody was going to take the thing away from him if he didn't get it quick."

The lines were quickly drawn. On December 13, 1963, RFK met with Richard Goodwin and Arthur Schlesinger. Among the subjects they discussed was LBJ's selection of a fellow Texan for the State Department's top position for Latin American affairs. The following day Schlesinger in his journal called the appointment "a declaration of independence, even perhaps a declaration of aggression, against the Kennedys." Later he was to write: "Of course, it was ridiculous. We tried to perpetuate the myth by convincing ourselves that we were good and that LBJ was evil. I remember one time Bobby telling me he was convinced that Lyndon was behind his brother's death. 'Come on, Bob. Get real,' I said. His other theory had it that Richard Nixon and Howard Hughes were somehow involved. He hated them both. 'Nixon's a true slimebucket,' he said. 'And I should've investigated Hughes years ago.'"

LaVern Duffy visited Bobby at Hickory Hill. "The day I saw him," observed Duffy, "he began bitching about how Lyndon Johnson had no intention of helping the down-and-outers in this country. 'Now that we're out,' he lamented, 'the Negroes don't have a voice in government. Nobody gives a damn about them. My brother cared, but this guy could care less.'" John Kennedy had lost little sleep over the plight of America's underprivileged, but Bobby was wasting no time in revising history, transforming his consummately political brother into a beacon of altruism. One man was standing in the way of the completion of Jack's unfinished business—business the late president had never cared to begin.

"Let us continue," Lyndon Johnson exhorted the nation just after the assassination. Wrapping himself in the myth of his predecessor's idealism, the new president quickly applied his formidable legislative skills to the passage of a program of social-welfare legislation the likes of which JFK never treated with much more than lip service. "It was the damnedest performance the first few months," insisted Harry McPherson, an attorney who served Johnson in the Senate and the White House. "It was a spectacular performance." And it was a performance that contrasted with the stagnation that had set in before Jack's death. "The legislative ma-

chinery had ground down," said McPherson, "everything had begun to
stop, Kennedy was unable to get anything done." RFK considered his
brother's legacy in a different light, constantly grumbling that Johnson
was merely capitalizing on JFK's popularity, enacting programs that the
Kennedys had envisioned without giving them the credit they deserved.

Lyndon Johnson tried to bring Bobby and his family around. From
the day of the shooting, he maintained a solicitous concern for the dead
president's widow, hoping that by reaching out to her he might reach out
to her brother-in-law. He told her to take all the time she needed before
moving out of the White House. After she did leave—on December 6
she and her children relocated to a house temporarily vacated by the
Averell Harrimans at 3038 N Street in Georgetown—the new president
and new first lady sent her a stream of friendly notes and flowers, as
well as gifts for John-John and Caroline. "Jackie assured me that Lyndon
Johnson had just been marvelous," said Charles Bartlett, referring to a
conversation that took place within days of the funeral. "She said she felt
she had put on him tremendous burdens and that he had been im-
mensely thoughtful. She said, 'Of course, I've always liked Lyndon Johnson. I feel that he has been very generous with me. Bobby gets me to put
on my widow's weeds and go down to his office and ask for tremendous
concessions like renaming Cape Canaveral after Jack, and he has come
through on everything." The space center in Florida was renamed by
LBJ's executive order just a week after the assassination. When Jackie
soon bought her own house—at 3017 N Street, across from the Harrimans'—the president made a surprise appearance at the housewarming
party organized by Bobby and Ethel.

"I was truly touched by his generosity of spirit," Jackie remarked
years later, recalling Johnson's "incredible warmth." Still, the recent
widow and the new president had different needs. Franklin Roosevelt,
Jr., was at Jackie's residence when LBJ telephoned with one of his frequent invitations to attend a White House function—invitations that
Jackie, unwilling to return to the scene of so many memories, always
declined. After the call, recounted Roosevelt, Jackie "was fuming. 'It was
Lyndon,' she said. 'He said to me, "Sweetheart, listen, Lady Bird and I
want to see you over here at our next White House dinner party. Jack
was a great man, but you've got to start living again."' She was furious,
and not just about his condescending attitude toward Jack. 'How dare
that oversize, cowpunching oaf call me sweetheart,' she said. 'Who the
hell does he think he is?'

"The next time I saw the president I told him he had hurt Jackie's
feelings. 'How do you figure that?' he asked. 'Well, Mr. President, I don't

think she appreciates being called sweetheart.' Johnson drew himself up to his full height and said, 'I'm tired as hell of this bullshit. Where I come from, we call the ladies sweetheart, and the ladies call their gentlemen honey. I've bent over backwards for that woman. I've done cartwheels and deep knee squats, and all I get is criticism.'"

Bobby's wider family—of aides, staffers and sycophants—never gave LBJ even the qualified deference offered by Jackie. "There was sort of an arrogant disregard of Johnson by the attorney general's staff," said Bartlett. "I frankly think he took quite a lot. I think these fellows were awfully impressed by themselves and had a sort of 'we're it and you're not it' attitude towards LBJ." Those Kennedy men who stayed on with the new president—people like McGeorge Bundy, Robert McNamara and even brother-in-law Sargent Shriver, who would head LBJ's War on Poverty—were considered by RFK to be outright turncoats. "He honestly believed," said McGeorge Bundy, "that if you were fully in the Kennedy administration you had a continuing allegiance that should, in certain circumstances, be more important to you than your allegiance to the existing president. And I didn't see it that way." RFK similarly enlisted his children's support. "Lyndon Johnson was rather a nemesis to the family while we were growing up," reminisced Bobby Jr. "In retrospect, he was one of the best presidents we ever had, but during the heat of battle, the kids all regarded him as some kind of ogre."

"I think President Johnson made every effort after the assassination of President Kennedy to get along with the Kennedy family," commented Clark Clifford, an adviser to Democratic presidents, "and in almost every instance his overtures were rejected, and rejected in a manner that was thoroughly offensive and insulting. I thought the attitude of Robert Kennedy and the other members of the family was inexcusable, and I think President Johnson tried to the best of his ability to work out some basis to get along with RFK. He was gracious and courteous and handled it in statesmanlike fashion and Kennedy and his followers rejected him at every turn.

"The Kennedy family considered President Johnson an interloper. President John F. Kennedy had been elected to the spot; they saw themselves in the position which they liked a great deal for a full eight years, by which time maybe some other member of the family would be ready to receive the mantle as it was passed on, so they just had stars in their eyes about the future and they loved the light and all that went with it. And then suddenly all their hopes were dashed and they looked upon President Johnson as a usurper of the job that really belonged to them.

Their attitude was exceedingly immature and one of the more unattractive chapters in the life of that particular family."

Bobby's power had shrunk. When a crisis arose in January 1964 over the Panama Canal, the attorney general who had been his brother's most trusted foreign-policy adviser became miffed because he wasn't consulted. The new president also showed little interest in RFK's pet project, the harassment of Fidel Castro. Johnson left Bobby to run the Justice Department, but made it clear that the attorney general was no longer the administration's chief consultant. LBJ, too, drew a line in the sand. As Bobby disapproved of former Kennedy attendants who served Johnson too faithfully, so, said George Christian, "Johnson did not like people who were close to him in the White House to have too good a relationship with Bobby. That was part of the problem that Bill Moyers and President Johnson had. Bill had some relationship with RFK, dating back to Moyers's Peace Corps days, and Johnson didn't like his press secretary to be that close to Bob Kennedy."

Fanning the flames that were scorching Bobby and his new nemesis was Bobby's old nemesis, the director of the FBI. J. Edgar Hoover wasted little time in adjusting to the new realities of power in post-Dallas Washington. Not long after November 22, he disconnected the telephone line which ran from his office to that of the attorney general. He removed Courtney Evans as his liaison to the White House and instead put in Cartha DeLoach, a personal friend of Johnson aide Walter Jenkins. He stopped sending FBI vehicles to pick up Bobby when the attorney general visited agency offices around the country. "For that matter," said Ken O'Donnell, "he ceased communicating with Bobby, reporting instead directly to LBJ."

The director kept the president up-to-date on almost every conversation held between one Kennedy partisan and another, even when the discussions involved subjects as mundane as travel and vacation plans. On a more serious level, Hoover would subsequently report that a secret meeting had taken place among RFK's cohorts for the purpose of arranging Johnson's replacement by Bobby as the 1964 Democratic presidential nominee. "J. Edgar," said Charles Bartlett, "who hated Bobby, was doing what he could to make sure that the president was convinced that there existed a Kennedy conspiracy. The problem is that the Kennedy thing was such a far-flung movement that there were people who were emotional about the president in almost every city in the country, and there was always somebody who would say something and make a move on behalf of Bobby, and this would inevitably drift back to LBJ. So it became possible to depict the thing as a sort of a coordinated conspiracy. My impression dealing with Bobby was that this was just the way it happened, it wasn't anything that he was necessarily stirring up, it wasn't that he had any real desire to undermine the president. I felt that it was just a series of coincidences which made it look more sinister than it was on RFK's part, and I suspected that Johnson's hatred of Bobby probably didn't go as deep as Bobby believed it did."

Nonetheless, if Bobby wasn't looking to mount an outright palace coup, he did little to extinguish his followers' resentment of the usurper. "LBJ made some overtures to Bobby Kennedy," said George Christian. "That's why I think he would have loved it if Bobby had said, 'Mr. President, you are the president, and my brother is dead. He's not here, and consequently you have unyielding loyalty. We're going to march on together and carry his program out.' I don't think he did that. I believe he sat in the attorney general's office and grieved. He couldn't bring himself to saddle up and move on."

In the wake of the assassination, Bobby informed his allies that he intended to stay on as attorney general through 1964's presidential balloting. "We've got about a year," he informed Franklin D. Roosevelt, Jr. "Once Lyndon wins the general election, we'll have even less influence than we do now." Over time, however, he came to reconsider his plans. He told Larry O'Brien at one point that he would consider becoming LBJ's vice presidential running mate. Observed O'Brien, "That RFK would seriously contemplate such a move was, considering the bristling animosity between the two men, a measure of Bobby's deep confusion in the months following his brother's death."

People began recommending Bobby for the second slot on the coming year's ticket long before the soil had settled on Jack's grave. On December 3, 1963, RFK heard that several New England politicians, including Thomas J. Dodd of Connecticut, were considering endorsing him for the job. Bobby was soon taking straw polls among his friends. A few days later, LBJ addressed the issue in a conversation with one of those friends, Ken O'Donnell. Noted O'Donnell: "Over the telephone, the now president told me he wasn't necessarily opposed to putting Bobby on the ticket. 'Hey,' he said, 'whatever it takes.' I had no illusions, however, about the possibility of an LBJ-RFK ticket. It was about as likely as the Second Coming, maybe less so."

In early January, Paul Corbin, the outspoken operative who had attached himself to the Kennedys in 1960, began organizing a write-in campaign for Bobby as vice president in February's New Hampshire primary. Despite RFK's denials, Johnson was convinced that the attorney general was behind Corbin's actions. Bobby waited until only a few days before the balloting to issue a public disclaimer, declaring himself a "non-candidate." The non-candidate nevertheless received 25,900 votes in the New Hampshire primary, with LBJ pulling in only a few thousand tallies more.

Although Ethel and his three sisters encouraged him to seek the vice presidential slot, RFK had spoken privately to Jackie about the possibility of running for U.S. senator from New York. Except for Jackie, who had become his almost constant companion, he shared his plans with nobody, not even his most trusted associates; one result of his silence was confusion among the ranks of his staff. "As strange and weird and impossible as that might have been," maintained Bobby's aide at the Justice Department, John Nolan, "he was really interested in running for vice president with Johnson. He would have done it." John Richard Reilly thought the movement to secure Bobby the nomination was a product not of the potential candidate's desires, but rather of the desires of his followers: "You have to remember that in politics there are a lot of jockeys and they're always looking for a horse. And when the Kennedy people lost their president, they needed a mount. In truth, Bobby had little desire to run with Johnson, and Johnson had even less desire to run with Bobby."

"If Bobby ever had been a serious contender," said Franklin D. Roosevelt, Jr., "the Republicans soon made him politically expendable. When Barry Goldwater, the unelectable right-winger, defeated Nelson Rockefeller, the moderate governor of New York, in June's California primary, the polls indicated that LBJ would win the presidential election even if he ran with a Golden Retriever."

The man who had managed a president's election had no trouble comprehending the meaning of Goldwater's victory. He called a meeting at Hickory Hill to tell his brain trust that he would resign as attorney general and run for the Senate from New York. He planned, however, to delay his announcement so as to maintain the influence of the Kennedy faction over the process and thus swing the vice presidential nomination over to a liberal like Hubert Humphrey. He also hoped thereby to exercise more sway over the Democratic Party's political platform.

When LBJ heard of Bobby's decision to remain in the running, he became infuriated. According to one of Johnson's White House aides, the president railed against Bobby, insisting he'd had enough of "all those goddamn Kennedys. I'm also," he added, "sick and tired of the press, the Vietnam War, the problems in Nicaragua, the civil rights movement, the whole fucking agenda." Threatening to step down as chief executive, the embattled president went so far as to draft a three-page resignation statement, which Lady Bird finally persuaded him to throw away.

Although he agreed to run in the coming election, Johnson was determined once and for all to rid himself of his arch enemy. To accomplish this mission he began calling party leaders to quiz them about telling Kennedy he wasn't on the ticket.

On July 21, he called Chicago mayor Richard Daley, a strong John Kennedy supporter in 1960, and asked him to help quell any Robert Kennedy enthusiasm by informing party leaders that Johnson needed a midwesterner (like Hubert Humphrey), not a New Englander, on the ticket. Southerners, he remarked, can't stand Kennedy—"and that's the only region where I can use some help."

"All right, I'll do that," Daley said, but cautioned against rejecting Kennedy too soon and risking a split in the party.

A day later, Daley called Johnson after apparently talking directly to RFK. "Maybe you're right in doing it [telling Kennedy's he's out]," Daley ventured.

Within the week, Barry Goldwater was anointed by his party in San Francisco's Cow Palace, and President Johnson asked RFK to visit him at the White House. The hour-long meeting took place on July 29, the president formally informing Bobby that he would bypass him for the vice-presidential spot. Commending his visitor on his performance at the Justice Department, he indicated that RFK might wish to either stay put or relieve Adlai Stevenson as ambassador to the United Nations. Other opportunities were likewise dangled, including the possibility that Bobby might run LBJ's presidential campaign, a prospect which interested him no more than any of the others. Before leaving, the Attorney General just happened to bring up a routine matter of Justice Department business: Bobby Baker, and the need to decide how to proceed with a case involving misappropriation of government funds. Johnson, somewhat to RFK's surprise, defended his longtime friendship with Baker.

The meeting over, Bobby took Ken O'Donnell to lunch. "You ought to be treating me," remarked RFK, "because I'm practically out of work." The results of the meeting hadn't come as a surprise to Bobby, claimed O'Donnell, "and perhaps they came as something of a relief. He and Johnson were anathema. He told me about the time, in 1961, he'd visited LBJ at his Texas ranch. They'd gone deer hunting on the property. 'He does it at night,' said Bobby. 'He turns on a spotlight and the deer come out of the woods and gather in the clearing, and then he opens fire. That bastard is some sportsman, let me tell you.'

"A week later Bobby received a telephone call from Johnson. The president wanted him to announce that he had withdrawn from the vice presidential running without any prodding from LBJ. In other words, that he had volunteered to withdraw. Johnson didn't want to take the heat for killing the nomination. Bobby refused to play along, and that's when Lyndon came up with his idea to tell the world that he would exclude all cabinet members from consideration for the position. 'I think he actually believes his own bullshit,' said Bobby. 'At least when I tell a lie, I know I'm lying.' "

On Tuesday, August 25, Bobby took to the steps of Gracie Mansion, the official residence of New York City's mayors, to announce his candidacy for the United States Senate from the state of New York. On the twenty-sixth of August, he appeared before the Democratic National Convention in Atlantic City, New Jersey, to introduce a film about his late brother.

The film had originally been set for Tuesday, but Lyndon Johnson did not want his convention stolen away from him. "In 1960," recalled John Treanor, Jr., a Kennedy advance man, "Adlai Stevenson had stormed the convention hall in Los Angeles, hoping that the massive demonstration for him would sway the delegates. LBJ had a recollection of that taking place out there, so it was no wonder he didn't want Bobby doing the same thing." Johnson delayed Bobby's appearance until Thursday night, when the balloting for the nominations—LBJ for president, Hubert Humphrey for vice president—had been completed. And in case the schedule change alone didn't throttle the Kennedy cabal, the president asked J. Edgar Hoover to post a squad of his best agents around the convention site to keep a close eye on Bobby and his friends. The director sent twenty-five men who relayed frequent reports on their findings to the chief executive. The occupant of the Oval Office was taking no chances.

Bobby arrived in Atlantic City with Jackie and they began their stay with a sentimental journey, visiting thirteen delegations—of states that had been critical to the 1960 nomination—to thank them for their efforts on behalf of Jack. "Wisconsin and, of course, West Virginia led the list," said Ken O'Donnell, "and they gave little speeches to each one of them."

Then came time for the film. After Scoop Jackson introduced Bobby, the delegates rose and started to applaud and cheer. "Mr. Chairman . . . Mr. Chairman . . ." RFK said repeatedly, trying to begin his speech. But the emotional outpouring only intensified. After twenty-two minutes, the pandemonium finally subsided and Bobby spoke.

He opened by expressing his gratitude to all of the delegates to the

Democratic National Convention and the supporters of the Democratic Party for all their work on behalf of President John F. Kennedy. He placed his brother in a grouping of great Democratic presidents going back to Jefferson, and praised Jack's record at home and abroad; he noted that Jack had been "committed to the young people not only of the United States but to the young people of the world."

He quoted words that had been suggested to him by Jackie: "When I think of President Kennedy, I think of what Shakespeare said in *Romeo and Juliet*:

> "When he shall die
> Take him and cut him out in little stars
> And he will make the face of heaven so fine
> That all the world will be in love with night,
> And pay no worship to the garish sun."

He forged ahead: "I realize that as individuals, and even more important, as a political party and as a country, we can't just look to the past, we must look to the future.

"So I join with you in realizing that what started four years ago—what everyone here started four years ago—must be sustained; it must be continued." He sounded the expected trumpet call in support of Johnson ("the garish sun"?) and Humphrey, exhorting the delegates to stand behind the nominees, "just as you supported John Kennedy." RFK then asked his audience to recall, as they watched the film, "that President Kennedy once said: 'We have the capacity to make this the best generation in the history of mankind, or make it the last.'

"If we do our duty," the fallen leader's brother went on, "if we meet our responsibilities and our obligations, not just as Democrats, but as American citizens in our local cities and towns and farms and our states and in the country as a whole, then this generation of Americans is going to be the best generation in the history of mankind.

"President Kennedy often quoted from Robert Frost—and said it applied to himself—but we could apply it to the Democratic Party and to all of us as individuals:

> "The woods are lovely, dark and deep.
> But I have promises to keep
> And miles to go before I sleep,
> And miles to go before I sleep."

Dead, the charismatic politician had become the romantic visionary, and the Kennedy legend was reborn. RFK, before Dallas Jack's conscience and alter ego, would now carry his brother's torch to New York and beyond. He had found his calling. He was coming into his own.

21

THE SENATOR AND
MRS. KENNEDY

The captain of the *Caroline* refused to fly in the thunderstorm covering Massachusetts the night of June 19, 1964, so Edward Kennedy chartered another, smaller airplane to take him to Springfield, where he
would receive his party's nomination to run for a full Senate term in
November. The senator never reached his destination. In the ensuing
crash near Southampton, Massachusetts, both the pilot and Teddy's aide
Edwin Moss were killed. Teddy suffered several shattered vertebrae and
a punctured lung.

Shaken by the accident that came so soon upon Jack's death, RFK
worried about his parents. "How much more do they have to take?" he
cried the day after the accident, as he and Ed Guthman walked in a park
near the hospital to which Ted had been taken. "I just don't see how I
can do anything now. I think I should just get out of it all. Somebody up
there doesn't like us." For a time, Robert Kennedy considered leaving
politics. But when he visited West Germany and Poland the last week in
June—he helped dedicate a memorial to Jack in West Berlin and met
with Poland's cardinal in Warsaw—the enthusiastic crowds he encountered helped convince him to hold steady in his quest to continue his
brother's work. He also received encouragement closer to home. "Jackie
sat down and wrote him a letter," recalled Lem Billings, "a most feeling
letter, in which she implored him not to give up, not to quit. She told
him she needed him and that the children, especially John Jr., needed
him as surrogate father, as somebody they could turn to, now that their
own father was gone. And another thing—and this is the most vital in the
long run—was how much the country still needed him. It was time, she
wrote, to honor Jack's memory—not continue to mourn it. They would

both, herself included, be negligent in their responsibilities to that memory if they collapsed. Jack would want them both to carry on what he had stood for, and died for—she through the children, Bobby through public service."

As Bobby made the transition from attorney general to senator, from mourner to active participant once more in the nation's affairs, he would rely increasingly on the support and affection of his late brother's wife. And as Jackie moved from first lady to grieving widow to independent woman and single mother, she would look to her late husband's brother as her reservoir of strength, her fount of recovery.

Bobby's doubts about remaining in public life dissolved soon after his return from Europe, and with the vice presidency an ever more unlikely prize, he set his mind to the contest in New York. The experienced political manager analyzed the situation in detail. He authorized statewide polling, which showed him defeating the Republican incumbent, Kenneth B. Keating. Correctly, he identified a major liability in the race— that he would be perceived as an outsider, a "carpetbagger," exploiting for his own ambitions a state in which he had no roots. And with remarkable accuracy, he predicted the course of the campaign: "I'll draw huge crowds as I go to different parts of the state for the first time. All the attention will be on that, and it will last for about three weeks. I'll hit a low point around the first of October. The question will be whether I can turn it around and regain momentum."

He also determined that he needed the support of both sides in the struggle then prevailing within New York's Democratic Party. From Jack's campaign in 1960, RFK had strong ties to the regular leadership. But his high-handed tactics over the years had offended members of the "reform" segment. The liberal-minded reformers mistrusted Bobby for all the usual reasons—his earlier support of Joe McCarthy, his questionable methods in hunting down Jimmy Hoffa, his general usurpation of power-mongering schemes during his term as attorney general, his espousal of a left-wing ideology at the same time that he adopted a dictatorial, often conservative manner. Additionally, RFK was the Kennedy most identified with the consciencelessness of the father. Many of the Jews among the reformers feared that he shared the ambassador's anti-Semitism.

RFK set out, in his own words, "to mend the fences." "Shortly before he announced for the race, we had a meeting of the reformers at the home of one of my colleagues," said Ronnie Eldridge, a Democrat from Manhattan's West Side who became a member of the New York City Council. "It was a lovely apartment, and we were all waiting for this ruthless, aggressive person to arrive. Instead, this very shy person walked in. There was a famous artist's portrait of his brother hanging in the foyer, but he never looked up at it."

Albert Blumenthal, another guest that evening, and a Democratic assemblyman who later ran for mayor of New York, recalled that as the meeting got under way Bobby appeared "very nervous. It hadn't occurred to me that somebody with his background in public life would ever get that nervous. We had expected the big bad wolf, but what we got was this skinny, little guy with a rather high Bugs Bunny voice. He seemed concerned about making a good impression. He was gentle but also very impassioned, the kind of person who adopted a cause and then stuck to it. He wasn't your ordinary politician."

RFK made friends at the meeting. "I was thrilled with him," said Eldridge. Blumenthal remarked that "although Bobby won over many members of the reform group that evening, there were those who expressed concerns. One issue that came up was America's involvement in Vietnam and the role that John F. Kennedy played in the conflagration. Bobby, of course, defended his brother's actions, but it's possible our views influenced RFK's eventual decision to oppose our intervention in Vietnam."

Blumenthal later met alone with Bobby: "We discussed the fact that by running in New York he would be perceived as something of a carpetbagger. 'I can't very well run in Massachusetts,' he joked, 'because I'd never beat Teddy. Besides, the only difference between New York and Massachusetts is that New Yorkers lie a lot more.' I told him I tended to agree with his theory."

To familiarize himself with the problems of his new state, Bobby took a crash course, reading books about New York as well as thirty-six position papers prepared for him by outside experts and assembled by William vanden Heuvel, a prominent New York attorney and public servant who had served as a special assistant to him at Justice. To meet New York's less than rigorous residency requirement, he had Steve Smith procure for him a two-year lease on a three-story, twenty-five-room farmhouse in Glen Cove, Long Island. The property was ideal for a family that enjoyed swimming: in addition to its private beach on Long Island Sound, it featured a heated Olympic-size swimming pool.

RFK sought, and won, the endorsement of New York's mayor, Robert F. Wagner, who straddled the regular and reform factions. In announcing his candidacy at the mayor's mansion, Bobby addressed the carpetbagging issue directly: "I have an obvious problem in coming in from out of state. It's going to be tough to win. I recognize that some voters have misgivings about considering a man for high office who has left the state and who has only recently returned." He noted—perhaps convincing no one but himself—his ties to the state: he had, after all, lived in Riverdale (in the Bronx) and in Bronxville (in Westchester County) as a boy. "But I do not base my candidacy on these connections. I base it on the belief that New York is not separate from the nation in the year 1964. I base it on the fact that the greatest state in the Union must play a leading role at the federal level and I wish to play a part in that effort."

For campaign staff, Bobby started by raiding the Justice Department: William vanden Heuvel, John Nolan, Walter Sheridan, Angie Novello, Dave Hackett (who had worked with RFK on problems on juvenile delinquency). Two young department lawyers, Adam Walinsky and Peter Edelman, came to the effort as speechwriters and policy advisers, working with vanden Heuvel and Milton Gwirtman, a Washington lawyer with ties to Teddy. William F. Haddad, a former Peace Corps official and former New York newspaperman, directed the Volunteers for Kennedy organization. The loyal Kennedy men—and they were all men; the campaign had virtually no women in positions of substantial responsibility—coexisted uneasily with local operatives. For example, Steve Smith managed the campaign, but ceded the title of chairman to R. Peter Straus, president of New York radio station WMCA.

By the time the state party convention took place on September 1 at the Seventy-first Regiment Armory in Manhattan, only one other Democrat had announced his candidacy for the Senate seat. "There was some resentment against Bobby for coming in from the outside," remarked New York state senator Manfred Ohrenstein, a reformer, "because here you had this very respectable candidate, Samuel Stratton, who was an independent Democratic congressman from upstate, clean-cut, fairly progressive. I felt badly about Stratton, I really did, because he was a good guy and a good congressman. But he couldn't approximate what Bobby Kennedy would bring us. Bobby was someone who looked at problems nationwide, he'd participated in the civil rights battles with his brother, the president. I didn't feel great about how we were giving up on Stratton, but he would have been just another junior senator. I thought Bobby Kennedy represented an extraordinary opportunity for New Yorkers." The unlucky Stratton received 153 nominating votes from the convention delegates to Bobby's 968.

At 5 A.M. on September 2, RFK opened his campaign with the New York politician's traditional first stop: the Fulton Fish Market in lower Manhattan. He then flew to Washington to resign as attorney general. Three thousand students from all over the District of Columbia gathered at Cardozo High School to bid Bobby farewell with their homemade signs and marching bands. Following this event, RFK met at the White House with LBJ to formally withdraw from the cabinet position he had never even wanted. Their hour-long conference was described by the *New York Times* as having been "reasonably cordial."

As Bobby had predicted, the New York senatorial campaign began in a wave of euphoria. With polls predicting a landslide RFK victory, he undertook a three-week tour of the state, starting Labor Day weekend. Everywhere he went, crowds were enormous. Four thousand people jammed the town square in Stuyvesant, a quaint village with a population of less than a thousand. In Buffalo, 150,000 lined the streets as Bobby's motorcade drove downtown from the airport. ("The Kennedys always felt Buffalo was a second home," he kidded the businessmen of the Buffalo Club. "My brother felt that way, although I'm not quite sure why.") A day later, eighteen hours of campaigning ended with a visit to Glens Falls (population: 21,000). The stop had been scheduled for eight in the evening; the *Caroline* landed at half past one in the morning, yet three thousand people and two high school bands waited to greet him at the airport. "Win or lose," he promised them, "I shall return to Glens Falls."

As in Buffalo, the first-time candidate continued to pepper his speeches with a sense of humor, advising the citizens of a shoe-making town that with eight children—and another on the way—"I can practically support this place single-handedly." He appealed to the self-interest of an organization of dairy farmers by pointing out that his large family ate large breakfasts.

Advance man John Treanor, Jr., recalled the mood around the state: "He had wild crowds, even more demonstrative than they had been for Jack and Jackie, and for Jack and Jackie people had gone bananas. But they never manhandled Jack the way they did Bobby. He always wore a pair of cuff links—they were gone by nine o'clock in the morning. His shirt would be black right to the elbows. His hands were covered with scratches, which became infected, from people grabbing at him, scraping him with watches, rings, fingernails.

"Ordinarily, for a politician to get his way from point A to point B isn't that much of a problem. You get ten big policemen with helmets on to form a phalanx. We discovered early on in Bobby's campaign that that didn't work because the police helmets acted as a homing device for ten thousand people who'd start pushing toward him. We used to sit and plan how to get him from this table to that door, talking about ropes and directions, but we discovered that if one of us led him and another was right behind him holding onto his belt, we could sort of snake him through the crush of people.

"I remember one time I saw an old hand with a couple of rings on it—a woman's hand—reach over my shoulder to the back of Bobby's head and grab a handful of his hair. His head snapped angrily, with a look of absolute anguish. That's what people did to him.

"He didn't like it, he didn't like any part of it, but he'd wade into the crowd. That's not to say he wasn't antsy at times. I remember sitting in a motorcade up in Schenectady, and it started to rain. The kids were there on bicycles, wanting autographs and bumper stickers. The procession hadn't started and he was very unhappy sitting up on the boot of this convertible. I wasn't even in charge of it, but he grabbed me afterward and said, 'Don't you ever again leave me in a motorcade like that sitting in the rain.' He was mad as a wet hen."

In the frenzy of excitement that greeted Bobby's entry into the race, his opponent seemed almost superfluous. Ken Keating might as well have been given his job by central casting. Ruddy-faced, with a thick head of white hair and a resonant voice, the Rochester resident was well liked by New Yorkers. As a congressman during the fifties he'd been known as relatively conservative, but since his election to the Senate in 1958 he had moved leftward, emulating the liberalism of the state's top two Republicans, U.S. senator Jacob Javits and Governor Nelson Rockefeller. Moreover, he had deftly managed to bridge the chief divide in the bifurcated state. "Keating was a popular and nationally known senator," observed John Nolan. "He had an ingratiating manner, folksy enough to keep people upstate, where he was from, satisfied that he was one of them. Plus, he assiduously cultivated the New York City community by indefatigable traipsing from one temple to another, one celebration to another—bar mitzvah, birthday, anniversary, christening. He was all over the place. When campaigning he never really said anything, he would just go around and smile and shake hands and say, 'Hello. How are you? Nice to see you. Hello. How are you? Nice to see you.' The trouble for Bobby was that it all seemed very effective."

Nevertheless, confronted by the phenomenon of the Kennedy campaign, with Bobby invoking the spirit of his late brother at every opportunity, the affable but ordinary Keating at first seemed overmatched. "We expected from the Kennedys a claim so close to divine," wrote Murray Kempton in *The New Republic*, "that we cannot call it pretension. If the Attorney General has a wound so great that, not to heal him but just for a little while to relieve him, he must be made a Senator, then we owe him nothing smaller." Eric Sevareid of CBS News commented that Keating, "a palpable, flesh and blood human being, is fighting witchcraft, a symbol of adulation and sorrow, memory of the deepest mass emotion of recent years, a fabulous ghost returned to earth."

But, as Bobby correctly assayed, by late September the tide had turned. Whereas RFK had attracted voters' sympathy on account of his grief over Jack, Keating began to win sympathy for his predicament as underdog. "We have a right to consider it an insult to our intelligence to believe that New Yorkers can be captured by a whirlwind courtship of a few weeks," said Jacob Javits. "And it is especially an insult when such a whirlwind candidate seeks to displace an outstanding public servant like Ken Keating, who does not deserve such a fate." Jewish voters, who usually composed a large percentage of the Democratic vote in the state, were still a problem for Bobby, partly because of the sins of his father, partly because of what one Kennedy follower termed "a great uneasiness, a fear, as one person put it, of the tough Irish kid that beat him up on the way to school each day."

Although Bobby never gave public cause for suspicions of anti-Semitism on his own part, Jewish New Yorkers were not entirely mistaken when they perceived bigotry in the candidate's family. And such prejudice was not limited to the Kennedy patriarch. Charles Guggenheim, who had been hired to make a film on RFK for the campaign, met Ethel Kennedy for the first time when he visited Hickory Hill to acquire some still photographs for his project. "As I was about to leave, I thanked her," he recalled. "I don't know how it came up but it was the time when the polls were showing that they were in trouble with the Jewish group . . . and I remember she made a comment that didn't endear me to her at that time. She said, 'You know, it's your people who are giving us all the trouble; it's your people who are giving us all the trouble.' "

Among the New York reformers, there were some Jews as well as non-Jews who could not bring themselves to back Bobby. Led by writer Gore Vidal and television journalist Lisa Howard, 120 of them formed Democrats for Keating, warning that Bobby, the supposed champion of progressivism, was in fact "anti-liberal and disturbingly authoritarian."

In his recent memoir *Palimpsest,* Gore Vidal noted that Lisa Howard was reputed to have been a lover of Fidel Castro. One day at Democrats for Keating headquarters, she was hectoring the senator on a point of politics. Vidal intervened, saying, "Lisa, for Christ's sake, leave him alone. He's a Republican. But at least he's not Bobby, who's been trying to kill your friend Castro all these years." Vidal also wrote that during the campaign he was approached by a "stout, bald Italo-American with a large diamond ring," a man Vidal presumed to be a member of the Teamsters.

In a "thick New Jersey accent," the "hood" presented information about two instances of alleged misconduct by RFK: a sexual liaison with a minor, and his threat to bring deportation proceedings against an Englishwoman in order to suppress her claim to have had affairs with both him and Jack. Not wanting to deal with the "material" the Teamsters were offering, Vidal and Howard declined to pursue the tips.

In addition to the difficulties posed by recalcitrance among normally Democratic voters, Bobby's campaign was plagued by internal problems. For once, a Kennedy campaign lacked strong leadership, since the best political manager on the team had to concentrate on being the candidate. "It was total disorganization," recalled John Seigenthaler. "Dave Hackett was screwing up royally. . . . Steve [Smith] did an impressive job, especially considering he hadn't worked in this particular area before, but his staff wasn't very good.

"I recall spending three goddamn nights trying to make a determination about campaign material, whether you use this photograph or that one. Lem Billings was in on some of those damn discussions, and he could drive you crazy. You'd get into a serious discussion about a picture and you'd agree that it was a good picture and he'd come in with something like, 'Well, that looks like Sneaky Fox.' That's a direct quote, 'That looks like Sneaky Fox.' That blows that discussion wide open. Once you've said it you could see that in the photo RFK did look like 'Sneaky Fox.'"

Deprived of Bobby's experienced direction, the campaign committed elementary errors. Edward Costikyan, a New York lawyer active in the Democratic Party, remembered a meeting that he and other local pols attended one Saturday morning at Steve Smith's apartment: "The Kennedys had really been very slow about coming up with literature and stuff. They didn't quite understand why we needed it and how our captains used it, and they didn't consult anybody. They came up with a brochure that looked like a comic book. None of us had known about it in advance, and those of us who finally saw it were appalled.

"There were so many things wrong with it. It weighed too much, for one thing. You've got to give people literature that they can carry, and these things were big, heavy packets. What's more, they had the wrong theme. They said, 'Put Bobby Kennedy to Work for New York.' And all of us said, 'That's the wrong theme. It ought to be, 'Support Johnson, Humphrey and Kennedy,' or something to that effect."

Putting Bobby "to work for New York" suggested that even as the country's top lawman, he hadn't gone to work for New York in the past. Photographs in the bulky campaign pamphlet showed the candidate in his rolled-up shirtsleeves, as if he were a freelance consultant whose services the voters were thinking of retaining, a hired gun who would move on as soon as a better job (e.g., the presidency) beckoned. "The biggest liability," said Costikyan, "was that he was a carpetbagger." And it was a liability because, as John Treanor noted, "he was a carpetbagger to all intents and purposes, and everybody knew it." The race at the top of the ticket in New York was not in doubt. Keating, Javits and Rockefeller had all refused to endorse Barry Goldwater; Lyndon Johnson was far ahead of his opponent in the state polls. Sooner or later Bobby would have to take advantage of the president's strength.

The main problem with Bobby's campaign wasn't disorganization or carpetbagging or slogans or perceptions of anti-Semitism. It had to do with Bobby. He had chosen to run on his brother's record, not his own—and not even his opponent's. "He didn't want to attack Keating," observed John Nolan, "because he thought that Keating was old and kindly, and Bobby was young and thought to be aggressive and—what was that word?—ruthless. He didn't want to reinforce those perceptions, so he laid off. The campaign started off pretty well, with high—in fact, total—recognition. And then it just sort of went downhill. And after several weeks, the campaign was not going well at all."

Bobby began to see the paradox implicit in his new self-definition as inheritor of Jack's legacy. Struggling to create his own identity, he had not yet found that part of himself which he could merge with the myth of his brother to present a candidate voters would accept as a full-fledged vehicle of their desires. With his elegiac speeches quoting Dante and George Bernard Shaw, he offered, as Murray Kempton wrote, "not so much a choice as an echo." RFK understood the meaning of the delirium that greeted his campaign. "He would come back from the streets of New York," said Milton Gwirtzman, "and remark, 'They treat me like I'm a Beatle.' It was adulation. He knew it was cult stuff. He had become an icon. People who had a strong feeling of admiration for his brother could express it by going out on the boulevards to cheer Bobby. He realized it wasn't anything he had done." During a break in a day's events in Buffalo early in September, Ed Guthman expressed optimism based on the enthusiastic crowds. "Don't you know?" the candidate responded. "They're here for him—they're here for him."

Other than recounting his brother's record, Bobby generally had little to say. Paralyzed by his reputation as attack dog, halfway through the campaign he was still publicly praising Keating's performance as senator. New York voters were not buying the pastel nostalgia Bobby seemed to be selling. "Come on, Bob. Get with it!" Steve Smith chided the candidate. "You're blowing it. You're letting this thing slip away."

But Bobby hadn't been "with it" for some time. Shortly after RFK's death in 1968, Adam Walinsky would reminisce about "how much [Bobby had] really been affected and how much of his life and his outlook and his character and his sense of public action were shaped by President Kennedy and by the fact that he had been killed. . . . And as I reflect on it now, I see that some of that streak of fatalism, acceptance, whatever, and that curious detachment about his own career and his own future, for the most part, came from the sense that he had had the best; whatever he attained for himself, whether he got to be president or not, nothing could ever compare to the excitement he felt in the days of Camelot. There was a feeling that the world would never be young again, that all joy had been cut and severed."

With less than a month to go before Election Day, the polls had Johnson ahead of Goldwater 65–35 in the state, whereas Kennedy was trailing Keating 47–53.

Although there were fourteen rooms in the brick town house Jackie bought on N Street, she was not comfortable there. She "had become Washington's number-one tourist attraction," said Franklin Roosevelt, Jr. "Morning, noon and night the street clogged with people peering in at her and the children. They would line up on both sides of the street. As Jackie walked down the block, they just stood watching, almost reverently. The local police and Secret Service had to clear a path through the crowd so she could move. Women were always breaking through police lines trying to grab and hug the children as they went in and out. Tourists actually camped on her doorsteps, eating box lunches, leaving behind empty Coca-Cola bottles and sandwich wrappers. The most daring would approach the house and try to peek in through the windows to catch a glimpse of Jackie or the kids. By her dignity and grace, Jackie had led a nation in mourning. Now, sightseeing buses added her home to their itineraries, and press photographers roosted at her doorstep. It had become a nightmare," Roosevelt said.

"It was terribly sad," agreed Robert McNamara. "Here she had been elevated to the position of mythical folk heroine, yet she remained practically a prisoner in her own home. She couldn't go out for a walk or a bite to eat without being mobbed. I once took her to a restaurant in Georgetown for lunch. People at neighboring tables stared; waiters and waitresses stared. I kept praying that nobody approached her for an autograph."

Jackie's house was becoming her fortress. Often, she would retreat within its walls, remaining in bed long hours, taking sedatives and antidepressants by day and sleeping pills by night. She began to follow in the footsteps of other Kennedy spouses, such as Ethel and Joan, smoking and drinking—great quantities and without stop. Yet in her despair, as always, she could count on her brother-in-law. "Bobby was the central, core figure in Jackie's life after the death of her husband," stressed Roswell Gilpatric, who would later become one of her beaux. "She had no brother, her husband had been killed. Bobby undertook to help her normalize an existence. He acted *in loco parentis*, seeing that John-John and Caroline were included in family gatherings." Bobby attempted to fill in as father to Jackie's now fatherless offspring. In short order, he was also performing another of Jack's roles.

Rumors that Bobby and Jackie had initiated a sexual relationship began to circulate around Washington society within months of the assassination. "I'd say I'm ninety-nine percent sure they had an affair," said Coates Redman. "You used to go to dinner parties and talk to people who lived near where Jackie lived on N Street just after Jack died. Bobby was constantly there. All hours. And you could see how they might have had a mad, morbid attraction to each other under the circumstances, because they were the two persons most wounded by the president's death.

"In the early months of '64, when Bobby was still deeply brooding, a friend of mine went to dinner at Hickory Hill. She was desperate to try to make conversation with him. She just couldn't think of anything that wouldn't offend him. After all, he was not exactly a chatty guy. So she said, 'I was noticing those wonderful pictures in your den. And I just love the picture of Jackie.' And he brightened up. She continued, 'It's the most attractive picture of her I've ever seen.' And Bobby said, 'Oh, I think so, too. Doesn't she look beautiful? Thank you for saying so.' So they got to talking. The only thing he seemed to want to discuss was her."

To escape the Washington fishbowl, in February 1964 Jackie spent a weekend in New York, staying at the Carlyle. Soon she was back for another visit, during which she accompanied Bobby to the Waldorf Towers for a visit with Herbert Hoover, the ex-president who had briefly been Bobby's boss a decade before. At Easter, she took her children to Stowe, Vermont, for some skiing with Bobby, Teddy and their families. Then she left Caroline and John-John with their cousins and flew to the Caribbean.

Ethel didn't make the trip to socialite Bunny Mellon's house overlooking Half-Moon Bay in Antigua, but Bobby did. Also in the group were Lee and Stas Radziwill and Charles Spalding. Jackie and Bobby picnicked and water-skied. They played pop records and, wrote Diana DuBois in her biography of Lee Radziwill entitled *Her Sister's Shadow,* "turned the volume way up in the hope that it would shake their pain and lift their spirits. Bobby in particular kept playing the same records over and over again."

The crowds continued to torment Jackie after she returned to Washington from her brief holiday; so did the memories in the city where she and Jack had once reigned as queen and king. Bobby Kennedy and Lee Radziwill both suggested she move to New York. In Gotham's bustle, she could find the anonymity she longed for. In addition, she would be more at home in the international city of New York than she ever could be in the company town that was the nation's capital. The former first lady didn't dawdle over her decision. In late spring 1964, she put her Georgetown house up for sale, and also unloaded Wexford, her weekend retreat in Virginia. For two hundred thousand dollars, she purchased a fifteen-room cooperative apartment at 1040 Fifth Avenue, at the corner of Eighty-fifth Street, three blocks from the Metropolitan Museum of Art. While her new residence was being renovated, she stayed at the Carlyle.*

"Jack would always say to his wife," commented Bobby's Hyannis Port neighbor Larry Newman, " 'If you need anything when I'm away, get hold of Bobby and Bobby will take care of it.' " Now that Jack was dead, Jackie relied on Bobby more than ever. And, as industrialist Robert David Lyon Gardner pointed out, her needs were not only emotional: "The children—John-John and Caroline—had millions in their trust fund. It was that money that paid for their schools and for the apartment on Fifth Avenue. Jackie, their mother, could live there, but it was against the terms of the trust for her to buy a dress, or even a handkerchief. So Bobby gave her an allowance of fifty thousand dollars a year, a pittance considering the situation but better than nothing."

Once Bobby followed Jackie to New York, their relationship continued to deepen. Sometimes they were indiscreet. "A friend of mine had a room opposite them in a New York hotel," said film producer Susan Pollock, "and saw them, on two consecutive days, go into their room at night

---

*Accompanying Jackie to New York as personal assistants were Pamela Turnure and Nancy Tuckerman, who during the White House years had been the first lady's press secretary and social secretary, respectively. Jackie hired Turnure for the New York job— and had kept her on in Washington throughout the Kennedy administration—even though she knew that the young woman had enjoyed an extended sexual liaison with JFK, which began during the summer of 1958 and continued into the White House.

and then leave together early in the morning. You can look at people and tell if they've been intimate. My friend could tell."

The lovers connected most often in Manhattan. "Bobby had a driver named Jim," recalled Polly Feingold, who worked on the Senate campaign. "He was a white-haired, blue-eyed, retired Irish cop. He idolized the Kennedys, but on one occasion he became fed up with Bobby. It was the rich person's syndrome, you know, 'Someone will take care of it. Someone will watch out for me.'

"He told me that on this particular night he dropped Bobby off at about ten p.m. at Jackie's apartment on Fifth Avenue. Bobby said, 'I'll be down in a little while.' Jim dozed off behind the wheel and woke up at around two. Bobby still hadn't come down. He finally appeared at four a.m., looking rather disheveled, as if he'd just gotten out of bed. And from the grin on his face and the twinkle in his eye, it was obvious he had done just that. 'I'll be going back upstairs, so you can go home now.' Jim wasn't overly pleased about having had to wait all those hours, but he didn't mind that his boss seemed to be having such a pleasant time."

New York City wasn't the only familiar Kennedy venue where Jackie and Bobby pursued their affair. "I was staying in a house next to the Kennedy compound in Palm Beach in 1964," said socialite Mary Harrington. "I was looking out a window on the third floor and could see onto the Kennedy property. There was Jackie, beside the house, sunbathing on the grass, wearing a black bikini bottom with no top. Then Bobby, wearing a white swimsuit, emerged from the house and knelt by her side. As they began to kiss, he placed one hand on her breast and the other between her legs, on the outside of her bikini bottom. After a few minutes she stood up and wrapped a towel around her breasts and shoulders. Together, Bobby and Jackie disappeared into the house."

The widow and the brother clung to each other in the grief they shared. When Bobby leased a home in Glen Cove, Jackie rented one just minutes away. The devoted equestrienne boarded her mounts at the nearby estate of Bruce Balding, a favorite investment counselor of wealthy Long Islanders. One day, according to Diana DuBois, "Balding entered the stable and found Jackie and Bobby locked in a passionate embrace. As soon as they saw him they broke apart."

Bobby could not help but compare his brother's wife to his own. Whereas Jackie was fey and beautiful, Ethel was substantial and plain. Jackie was worldly; she had hosted memorable White House evenings honoring classical musicians and poets; Ethel was parochial; she had never outgrown the system of belief she had formed at the convent schools of her girlhood. Although Jackie was the mother of two children, she had never become defined by her domestic role. In Paris, Jackie had charmed Charles de Gaulle by her knowledge of French history. Ethel had gone to Japan and spoken of Captain Kangaroo. Jackie loved antiques and art. She almost never played touch football or pushed anyone into a swimming pool. The ways of "Old Moms," as Ethel kiddingly called herself, had been well suited to those of her athletic, family-oriented husband. After all, he *did* play touch football and he *did* push people into pools. But for a time after Jack's death, only Jackie seemed to understand his pain, for only she suffered as he did.

Ethel caught on to the affair, and she did not hide her knowledge from members of her family. Mary DeGrace, who worked for seventeen years as a laundress for Bobby and Ethel on the Cape, recalled an exchange overheard by one of her coworkers: "Katherine, an elderly maid employed by Ethel, was present one day when Teddy Kennedy came into the house, went toward Ethel and bent over to give her a kiss. She pushed him away and told him, 'There will be no situation here like Bobby and Jackie.'" According to Meribelle Moore, a Skakel family friend, the wronged wife called on one of her brothers for help, asking that he appeal to Bobby to stop sleeping with Jackie.

"I was always amazed that the Jackie-Bobby love affair remained under wraps as long as it did," insisted writer Truman Capote, who became a frequent escort of Jackie's in the New York of the mid-1960s. "Nobody talked about it, but everybody who was anybody knew about it. They carried on in public like teenagers. I used to see them at Le Club all the time, holding hands, kissing, dancing as close as two leaves stuck together in a storm. They were lovebirds in every respect. Bobby was crazy about her. He wanted to ditch Ethel and marry Jackie, but she understood this would mark an end to his political career and she turned him down.

"Another reason for not wanting to get married is that Jackie had become extremely cynical about the institution. John Kennedy had been nothing but trouble—daily assignations and a lifetime of venereal disease. The last thing Jackie wanted to do at the time was start all over again. Which is not to say she wasn't up for a little romance."

Early in 1965, RFK and Jackie escaped the New York winter for a few days at the opulent estate of the very private Audrey Zauderer in Round Hill, the most exclusive area of Montego Bay, Jamaica. Kathryn Livingston, a New York magazine editor, spoke to Zauderer years later about the visit: "When I began the conversation, Audrey was evading—consciously or unconsciously—the subject of Bobby and Jackie's relationship. 'Jackie came down here with John-John,' she said, 'and I had to put up with all those Secret Service people.' And Bobby? 'Bobby also came,' she replied, 'and I don't know what happened.' She went on like this for a while, so I finally came out and asked bluntly, 'Well, do you think there was a romance between Jackie and Bobby?' And she stopped and she had this little smile as if I had really hit on it. She gave a very strong nod of her head, indicating yes."

"I suspect," wrote Gore Vidal of Jackie, "that the one person she ever loved, if indeed she was capable of such an emotion, was Bobby Kennedy. As Lee had gone to bed with Jack, symmetry required her to do so with Bobby."*

By mid-1965, the widow and the brother ended the sexual component of their relationship. But they remained close, bound by the eternal flame of their devotion to Jack, as if neither knew where their love for him ended and their love for one another began. Carl Killingsworth, an NBC television executive who dated Jackie during the late 1970s, after Aristotle Onassis had died, recalled that in her apartment on Fifth Avenue he saw only one family photograph on prominent display. It stood on top of the grand piano. It was a picture of Bobby.†

Four weeks into the Senate campaign, Bobby held a question-and-answer session with approximately two thousand students at the Columbia University gymnasium on Broadway and 116th Street. Filmed for television, the encounter represented a turning point in Bobby's campaign. Students always brought out the best in him, and true to the pattern he appeared to come alive. "I finally realized I was in a horse race," RFK said later, "and I wasn't necessarily the favorite."

Eventually, the 1964 Kennedy operation began to resemble prior Kennedy efforts. "The 'Kennedy magic' consisted of an excess spending of money,' cracked Ed Costikyan. For the final five weeks of the effort, Bobby's campaign hired, at a cost of one hundred thousand dollars, a freelance television news crew to follow him wherever he went. Every

---

*Symmetry also apparently required that RFK and Jackie share a bedroom in the New York apartment of Steve and Jean Smith, or so claim recently released Secret Service files. The same files indicate that on at least two occasions RFK and Jackie stayed in an apartment occupied by Peter Lawford at Manhattan's Sherry-Netherland Hotel. "Pat [Kennedy] and I were no longer together," said Lawford, "so I had moved temporarily to New York. Bobby and Jackie needed a place to stay, so I let them use my apartment."

†RFK, who had become somewhat friendly with Richard Burton and Elizabeth Taylor, brought Jackie together with Burton. Lem Billings went along once when Burton, RFK and Jackie met for drinks at the Plaza Hotel. "Burton kept encouraging them to get married," recalled Billings. "Finally, Jackie changed the subject by insisting that Burton, who was crocked, recite something from Shakespeare. Burton complied."

evening, two airplanes flew unedited film footage to broadcast news-rooms in all corners of the Empire State. By Election Day, 98 percent of stations in the state had used the film the campaign had provided.

The campaign supplemented the free airtime on news telecasts with a massive dose of paid advertising. The commercials did not begin run-ning in high volume until October. "Bob believed that the voters did not begin to focus on how they would cast their ballots until the final weeks of a campaign—'after the World Series,'" Ed Guthman later claimed.* The success of the Columbia University appearance shaped the entire body of RFK's ads, for when he spoke extemporaneously, voters could behold the intelligence and intensity that abounded beneath a sometimes remote and imperious exterior. Like the highly successful thirty-minute film from the university, the shorter commercials showed the candidate in give-and-take sessions—often filmed in shopping-center parking lots with "average" citizens. The spots generally tried to soften Bobby's cut-throat image by featuring shots of him with his children and then preg-nant wife.

The campaign used money in other ways that were familiar to the political clan of Joseph Kennedy. "Customarily," reflected Ed Koch, "be-fore Election Day, the candidate would send the leader of a political organization an envelope containing a check to cover the cost of food, drinks and so on for poll watchers." Koch, who became a congressman and then New York City's mayor, was in 1964 head of the Village Inde-pendent Democrats, a reform group. "So RFK's campaign sent down two men to our clubhouse. Since I was head of the organization, they asked me to step outside with them. They handed me an envelope. I looked inside and it contained cash, lots of it. In fact, there were thousands of dollars, as opposed to the usual check for five hundred or so." The gener-ous supply of funds the campaign spread around the state meant that the local party clubhouses could be stocked with whatever their leaders and treasurers desired—including, at times, liquor and prostitutes.

Another key to the so-called Kennedy magic was a staff at the ready that Bobby could cause to disappear in one place and instantly reappear in another. Local leaders had been assigned the task of distributing cam-paign literature wherever the candidate spoke. But one day Bobby saw no leaflets at any of the four rallies he attended in Brooklyn. He told an aide, "Call Joe Dolan and see if he'll come up here. If anybody can get this job done, I know he can." The next morning, Dolan resigned his post

*The St. Louis Cardinals defeated the New York Yankees in seven games in October 1964.

as assistant deputy attorney general and arrived in New York by noon. Within hours, fifty thousand leaflets were ready for dispersal.

Whenever the local organization failed to complete an assignment, Kennedy people did not hesitate to step in. Four years earlier, Jack's discerning campaign manager had mounted a drive to register new voters, particularly blacks and Puerto Ricans. The 1964 campaign entrusted local leaders with a similar effort. But many city pols, threatened by the prospect of an increasingly minorities-dominated electorate, balked. So Kennedy workers went into the neighborhoods themselves. Their drives yielded thousands of new voters.

"Bobby was an uptight sort of campaigner," said John Treanor. "The only time that he seemed at ease while campaigning was when he was with minorities—blacks, Hispanics, disabled people and the like. Ethnic crowds turned him on and vice versa." Herman Badillo, the Puerto Rican leader who in 1965 would be elected borough president of the Bronx, spoke of campaigning with Bobby in 1964: "He got up and said, 'You have to vote for me for senator because I've retired from my job as attorney general and if I don't get elected I'll have to go on welfare. And you Puerto Ricans, you have large families just like I do—you know how it is.' He could get away with something like that. Nobody felt offended, they knew he was joking, that he was sympathetic to them. Anybody else they would have booed.

"Bobby knew how to joke and how to relate to people. He understood what a lot of people in that campaign didn't, that poor people want to touch you. It isn't so much what you say as it is having physical contact. You can't just go on television. Poor people want to see a person and shake hands with him. He understood that. John Kennedy had the bearing of a patrician, but seeing Bobby, you wouldn't know he came from a wealthy background. He looked like he was from any Irish family in New York. Aside from the Boston accent, he didn't have a patrician air about him at all. He related to Puerto Ricans as if he were one of them, and that's why he got such firm support."

RFK also did well with New York's black voters, thanks in large measure to a visitor from Mississippi. The New York State chapter of the NAACP convened in Buffalo for two days in early October, with Keating scheduled to speak the first night and Bobby the next morning. In his address, Keating said little that was critical of his opponent's civil rights record. But his text contained the assertion that RFK had "abandoned his post at the Department of Justice with an unfinished task before him." Following the speech, reporters questioned the senator about the charge; he replied that he stood by the accusation.

Seated nearby as Keating delivered his remarks was the next featured speaker, Charles Evers, who had replaced his slain brother, Medgar, as director of the NAACP's Mississippi chapter. Evers had been told that the New York branch was strongly considering an endorsement of Keating, and had been asked to abide by that decision. Rising to speak, however, Evers discarded his prepared text and said: "Robert Kennedy has done more for minority groups in Mississippi than any other attorney general. We don't need someone who will talk civil rights and go along, we've had that. We need action. We need young blood and Kennedy is the one man who cared." New York's NAACP officials claimed to be outraged by Evers's comments and declined to converse with Evers following his speech, but the group remained neutral in the Senate race.

If New York's African American leaders didn't embrace Bobby, the majority of black voters did. Arthur Hirson, a teenage volunteer for the campaign, later remembered "standing on a street corner on Fulton Street in Brooklyn. And a black woman came up to me and said, 'I don't ever want this man to be elected. Because if he is, someone will kill him. He's too good to black people.'" However, Bobby's public demeanor toward blacks seems not always to have matched some of his private utterances, at least according to Gene Scherrer, a high-ranking Los Angeles–based police officer who acted as liaison between the LAPD and the Kennedys. Scherrer, who often traveled with RFK, testified that "when he was speaking to blacks, he used one tone, but behind closed doors in the company of aides and intimates he used derogatory, obscene language when it came to Afro-Americans. 'What do those goddamn niggers want from me?' he used to say. He also called them 'coons.' Yet this may have been pure Irish bravado, a kind of suburban prejudice rather than overt racism. I suppose we'll never know."[*]

D emocratic politico Manfred Ohrenstein analyzed the political appeal of Robert Kennedy and of all the Kennedys: "They had an incredible feeling about politics and political choreography. Their genius was that they were able to meld all sorts of people together. They had an attraction to us, the reformers, because they were willing to be activists on the issues. On the other hand, Bobby recognized that there was a local organization, and he was willing to do business with them. It was like, How do you put blue-collar steelworkers together with blacks interested in civil rights?

[*]A number of people accused RFK of using similar terminology when privately discussing Jews. According to Truman Capote, "He often referred to Jews as either 'kikes' or 'yids.' I found it revolting. He was just like his old man."

"They brought with them the ethos of the Catholic Church, not as churchgoing Catholics but as committed Catholics nonetheless, people brought up in the church. So that this whole group of blue-collar people—Irish and Italians—felt comfortable that this was one of theirs, that the Kennedys understood where they came from, these people who had pulled themselves up by their bootstraps, people to whom religion was an important means of elevating themselves and of keeping their families together. That's what the Kennedys represented to them. And so they accepted their progressivism because they weren't some wild, Jewish West Side radicals like we were. They were safe liberals. The Kennedys had this ability to communicate to blue-collar Catholics that they understood their concerns, just as they could communicate with poor blacks.

"They represented a successful immigrant family. Their people came from Ireland a hundred years ago and now they've got entrée all over the world. So to working-class voters, the Kennedys were the expression of their best hope, yet still people who could communicate with them. And to the blacks, they represented a kind of urban liberalism that seemed to denote an understanding of where the blacks were, even though the black experience was not part of the Kennedy experience. They had this magical ability to fuse all these different strains together."

Keating's heavy-handed attempt to turn black voters against Bobby was but one in a series of blunders the upstate resident committed as he tried to navigate the tribal streams of downstate politics. "Somewhat unaccountably," remarked John Nolan, "Keating altered course midstream by launching a negative campaign offensive which for its time was very advanced and very aggressive, and it was definitely pitched to voting blocks of New York City. I have always attributed it to a guy named Herb Brownell, who was manager of Keating's campaign and had been a manager for Eisenhower. A New York lawyer who'd served as U.S. attorney general, Brownell was a pushy, astute, hard-hitting politician. Without these developments, I guess Bobby maybe would have won, but it would have been much closer and more difficult."

To win over Italian-Americans, Keating charged that as attorney general, his opponent had gone after only Mafia crime figures to the exclusion of every other race and religion. "Kennedy makes a big production of [Mob informant] Joseph Valachi's testimony," remarked Keating, "but what did we hear of Bobby Baker? Very little. President Johnson's best friend commits outrageous acts of fraud, and the attorney general of the United States does nothing."*

* Joseph Valachi, a member of the Genovese crime family, became a government

But Jews were the audience for most of Keating's attacks. He ran newspaper ads with the headline "Why Nasser Is for Kennedy." (Gamal Abdel Nasser was at the time president of Egypt, a country still an enemy of Israel.) And in a late-September speech to a group of chemical workers in Newark, New Jersey, he cited the case of General Aniline.

In March 1963, the Justice Department (encouraged by RFK) had granted a Swiss holding company $60 million in disputed assets of the General Aniline and Film Corporation, a chemical firm with German interests that had been taken over by the U.S. government during World War II. Keating charged that the Swiss corporation (Interhandel) was in fact no more than a front for I.G. Farben, "the chemical arsenal for Nazi Germany." No Jew could miss Keating's implication: that the attorney general had rewarded manufacturers of poison gas for Hitler's death camps.

Keating's verbal attack on RFK elicited a letter to Kennedy from Richard Neustadt, a professor of history and a former consultant to JFK. "It gives you the justification for attacking him for a change," wrote the historian. Bobby took the cue. "I never have heard of a charge as low as this one," he ventured at a press conference from the Carlyle Hotel the following morning. "I expected more from Mr. Keating." Bobby insisted the charge was untrue. "I'm not pro-Nazi. I lost my brother and brother-in-law to the Germans. The idea that I would turn over money to the Nazis is ridiculous." Bobby's staff did some quick research. "A check of the records," recounted John Nolan, "found that the agreement had been subject to congressional approval and that Keating had voted for it on the floor of the United States Senate, not once but three times. It was perfect counterattack material."

The candidates had exchanged roles: now Bobby was the righteously aggrieved party, and Keating the hatchet man. "I thought my opponent had more class," RFK told the *New York Post* with only two weeks left before balloting. Said Nolan, "Keating, who had really been in his element the way he started the campaign, suddenly found himself confronted with this intense controversy and with a now unleashed Bobby Kennedy, who could be quite formidable. Bobby challenged him to back up what he had said about Valachi, to back up what he said about General Aniline, to either acknowledge or disown the Nasser ad. It had a big turnaround impact on the campaign."

---

informer in 1962 in order to avoid facing the death penalty for murdering a fellow inmate while serving time in the Atlanta Penitentiary. Valachi's testimony proved helpful in the Justice Department's campaign against organized crime.

Previously, Bobby's carpetbagging had been the campaign's key issue; now, the subject had been changed to his advantage. "There were a lot of things about New York State that he didn't know despite the cram courses," Nolan continued, "and there were a lot of jokes about it. He'd mispronounce the name of a place, he didn't know all the issues, he'd never been in the town of Auburn before. All that stuff. But if you're going to talk about his record as attorney general—about the Valachi hearings or the General Aniline settlement or any of those things that he knew and understood—then you're on his turf. He was on solid ground and he knew it. Those decisions were defensible and he loved defending them."

The previously tepid race heated up with the approach of Election Day, as each candidate vied to prove the other was no liberal. Bobby, in a brochure denouncing "The Myth of Keating's Liberalism," accused the senator of voting against civil liberties, labor and the War on Poverty, and opposing aid to education, housing and the Third World. "By right-wing standards," the pamphlet blared, "Keating is an ultra-conservative." Keating growled that RFK had supported legislation to curb civil liberties, had installed segregationist judges and had first sought backing in the state's Democratic Party not from the reformers, but from the old-line bosses. Bobby simply had no business running for senator from New York. "I am troubled," said Jacob Javits on behalf of his colleague, "by the arrogance and cynicism of a young man who dares to come into New York State, not to *serve* our state, but to *use* it as a political stepping stone."

But differences over issues did not decide the race so much as a piece of political theater. And once again, Keating proved himself an unwitting master of farce. Early in the campaign, the Republican had challenged Bobby to a debate, but RFK, convinced he could win the election without a televised confrontation, refused. A week later, he changed his mind. So, too, did Keating. Both men continued to vacillate. Finally, WCBS-TV, the CBS-owned station in New York City, offered them an hour of airtime for a debate on the evening of October 27, just one week before Election Day. This time representatives for the candidates couldn't agree to a format, and negotiations between the two sides broke down only hours before the proposed broadcast.

At the Carlyle when the talks were halted, Bobby received word that Keating had purchased half an hour of airtime on the same station for that night, beginning at 7:30 P.M., and planned to "debate" an empty chair to dramatize the Democrat's supposed refusal to appear. RFK called the station and asked to buy a thirty-minute segment to directly follow Keating's but was rebuffed. He decided to take his request to a higher authority: network president William Paley, who happened to be an excellent friend of Jackie Kennedy. RFK's call to Paley, in California, and Paley's call to his station in New York promptly netted Bobby his time.

But then, as Peter Edelman recalled, "Some of RFK's advisers during an afternoon meeting at the Carlyle proposed that he consider 'storming' the television studio during Keating's appearance and force him into a debate. I, personally, thought it a good idea." "I remember being up in that suite at the Carlyle in one of the bedrooms," said Adam Walinsky, "and all of these people sitting around, and all going back and forth on 'Should you? Shouldn't you? Should you? Shouldn't you, show up when Keating has the empty chair?' Then I remember him just saying, 'Well, look, I've just got to do it, that's all, or else I'm not a serious candidate.' "

Bobby Kennedy and his aides arrived at the CBS-TV studio in Manhattan at 7:27, three minutes before airtime. "I'm here to debate," RFK told the uniformed guard posted at the door to the Keating set. "Senator Keating has invited me to debate."

"I'm sorry, I can't admit you," responded the keeper of the gate.

"Senator Keating said he would have an empty chair for me. I'm here and I want to go in."

"Mr. Keating has purchased this time and I have orders not to let anybody enter."

Television and newspaper cameras recorded the confrontation at the door, while inside Keating opened his broadcast in a burst of self-pity: "I wanted this debate for the benefit of the people of New York and also for my own sake because I know a face-to-face meeting between my opponent and myself would expose his ruthless attempt to destroy my lifetime career." At Bobby's request, studio technicians held up a sign for Keating to see: "Kennedy's here." But the Republican would not acknowledge his rival's presence. At this juncture, a network attorney appeared outside to tell RFK once and for all that he would not be admitted to Keating's show since it was a paid political broadcast. "In that case, kindly remove the empty seat from the stage," RFK demanded for all journalistic witnesses to hear, "and ask Senator Keating to withdraw his remark about my not showing up."

Bobby finally retreated to the studio that had been reserved for his own use, expecting to admit Keating to *his* broadcast coming up at eight. But the white-haired senator (who had neither removed the empty seat nor retracted his remark) panicked. As he emerged from his studio just after ending his program, he brushed past a cluster of waiting reporters, photographers and cameramen. With the journalists trailing him, he began to speed up. He turned a corner, dashing past an array of television props—furniture and artificial trees—which his aides threw in the way of the pursuing pack. The fox ran through a doorway, down two flights of stairs and out of the building, as the hounds chased behind him.

"It mattered not what either candidate said on their programs," Ed Guthman later noted. "It mattered not that the next day the newspapers impartially reported what had happened. Television cameras had photographed the drama—Bob standing outside the studio door, demanding to be let in, and Keating fleeing the scene with fake palm trees hurtling through the air behind him. Millions of voters *saw* that, and for all practical purposes the race was over."

There was still time for Keating to commit one final bungle, and on October 30 he seized the opportunity by arranging to debate his opponent at last. With an hour telecast appearance of his own set for that evening, this one on NBC, the Republican knew that Bobby was scheduled to be a guest late that night on *The Barry Gray Show,* a highly popular New York City radio program. Keating demanded that he be invited as well, much to the delight of the strategists ensconced at the Carlyle. "Of course," Peter Edelman remembered, "everybody in the room saw it the same way, that here was the debate, that Keating had boxed himself in, that he had, in effect, accepted a debate without even knowing it, and that we could have the debate, have it late at night, avoid the problem of a television confrontation between the abrasive Bostonian whippersnapper and the white-haired senatorial-looking fellow; that it would murder his hour on television earlier, which nobody would watch because they were going to listen to the radio debate, and Keating's major NBC-TV spot would get no coverage in the press the next day because all the coverage would be the debate itself. So it was just marvelous all the way around."

Each candidate submitted questions for the host to pose to the other debater, and RFK drew on his recent diplomatic mission to the Far East to throw Keating a curve. " 'I want to ask him what his policy is towards Sabah,' " Edelman recalled Bobby instructing his aides minutes before going on the air. "We said, 'What's Sabah?' And he said with great superiority, 'Sabah is an island in Indonesia which the Indonesians have been fighting with the Malaysians about.' So we put that on the list, and, of course, Keating had no idea what Sabah was and avoided the question by stating that he encouraged independence and sovereignty around the world."

If RFK gladly made the most of the openings provided by an outclassed Keating, he only reluctantly capitalized on the benefits bestowed by another, more fortunate politician. "As big or maybe even bigger than Keating's problems," said John Nolan, "was the realization that Lyndon Johnson, running against Barry Goldwater, was going to rack up the biggest presidential win in recent history. And that majority had been building and building and building, so midway Bobby really, really had to swallow hard and change the theme of the campaign." "Put Bobby Kennedy to Work for New York" became "Get on the Johnson, Humphrey, Kennedy Team." Pamphlets and placards pictured Bobby with the president, and the shirtsleeves of the manager-for-hire gave way to the business suit of the company man.

Late in October, RFK and LBJ barnstormed the state. "You had to feel sorry for both of them," said Lem Billings, who also made the trip. "They were stuck with each other for 48 hours, and it drove them nuts. Johnson would throw that heavy arm of his around Bobby, who reached his shoulder, and he'd tell the crowd, 'I want you to elect ma boy here! I want you to elect ma man!' And then Bobby would have to sing Lyndon's praises, proclaim him the greatest president in the history of the universe, the greatest humanitarian, the whole nine yards. There would be a sea of arms reaching out for Bobby, and this didn't sit well with Lyndon. It ended in Brooklyn, and after their last appearance together, Bobby said to me, 'I've got to get to a phone so I can call Ethel-bird.'"

Hubert Humphrey came to New York, too. Bobby could not have been pleased to hear the Minnesotan, who had taken the spot he had perhaps wanted on the national ticket, praise the former attorney general for his "great contributions to the Kennedy-Johnson administration." Humphrey later recounted with amazement the tour he and Bobby took through Manhattan: "I'd never seen anything quite like it. We were in one of these motorcades rumbling down Fifth Avenue and cutting across town on one of the crosstown streets. And people were just ecstatic. They literally tore at Bobby Kennedy, and I remember women were tossing their shoes into the car. And at the end of the tour there was a girdle, or a garter belt, or a girdle—I guess it was part girdle, part garter belt—lying on the floor of the car, and I said to Bobby, 'You're a magician. How did you do that?' I'd never seen such excitement as he generated in that particular tour."

RFK won election to the Senate by some seven hundred thousand votes. LBJ's margin in New York State was 2 million greater; nationally, he won by a historic landslide. In Bobby's victory speech to several thousand cheering supporters gathered at the Statler Hilton Hotel he called the vote "a mandate to continue the efforts begun by my brother four years ago . . . and a vote of confidence for Lyndon Johnson and Hubert Humphrey." As candidates customarily do, he listed people to whom he owed a debt of gratitude: Averell and Mrs. Harriman, Mayor Robert Wagner, state party chairman Billy McKeon, Mayor John Burns of Binghamton, R. Peter Straus and his wife, Ellen, and Steve Smith. Just a few months earlier, LBJ had briefly wondered if he could not be elected without help from the brother of the man he'd replaced. As it turned out, it was the brother who needed the help and the usurper who gave it.

S hortly before Christmas 1964, Ronnie Eldridge attended a meeting at the Carlyle Hotel with the senator-elect and members of the New York City Board of Education. The purpose of the gathering was the planning of a holiday party for schoolchildren to take place at the Theodore Roosevelt School in East Harlem. "And Bobby was saying," Eldridge recalled, "that he wanted to have some kindergarten kids. For which one board member said, 'No, children that young will get too excited and wet their pants.' Speechless, Bobby stared at the man for nearly a minute. And I'll never forget, he then looked at me and said, 'Is this what it's all about?' I said, 'Yes, this is what the board of education is all about.'

"Anyway, we held the party. A friend of mine and I made the decorations, and they were spectacular. And the show was studded with stars—Carol Channing, Soupy Sales, Sammy Davis, Jr., like that. We brought all these kids down and they all received presents we'd gotten donated.

"The party took place on a Saturday afternoon. And that night there was to be a screening of a film to which we were invited as a token of appreciation for our work on the party. The film turned out to be about the assassination—it began with the funeral procession. And before we left for the screening, Mike Cohen, a West Side coordinator, got a telephone call from one of Bobby's people: Had any of us seen the senator-elect's tweed overcoat? Because he'd lost it and it was his brother's. It was the president's."

22

A NEW LIFE

At noon on January 4, 1965, Edward Moore Kennedy, the thirty-two-year-old senator from Massachusetts, still recovering from his airplane crash of the previous June, took the oath of office alongside his thirty-nine-year-old sibling, the new senator from New York. The two surviving sons of Joseph Kennedy would maintain close family ties as they went about their work, but they would pursue the nation's business, and their own careers, in dissimilar styles: the younger would concentrate on mastering the Senate's legislative arts, the older would seek to perform on a far wider stage.

During his first two years in the Senate, Teddy had won the grudging respect of his colleagues by dint of his determination and hard work. Now he was eclipsed, for there was another Kennedy present—an older Kennedy, with a higher profile in national affairs. "I've got to take second spot to Bobby for now," Ted told his staff. When the two senators traveled on the *Caroline,* it was RFK who sat in "the president's chair," the seat Jack had always occupied. When *Newsweek* was planning a cover on the two brothers, Ted agreed to pose for a joint picture, but Bobby claimed he was too busy. The senator from New York did, however, demand that the stock photograph used by the magazine show him—falsely—to be taller than his younger brother.

Initially, at least, the two men coordinated their work efforts to maximize their influence. Soon, however, each of them set out on a separate course. "Robert Kennedy, although he had been attorney general, turned down the Judiciary Committee because Edward Kennedy was on it," remarked Milton Gwirtzman, who worked for Ted. "He did not turn down the Labor Committee (on which Teddy served), but they made

399

sure to be on different subcommittees. . . . I think they decided that by taking on separate assignments, they increased their individual effect on legislation and on the public. The fact that a Kennedy was involved and working in one area guaranteed that said area would suddenly become the focus of press attention. The country didn't need both of them working on the same issue."

For Ted Kennedy, work in the Senate provided its own reward. He had a reputation for being "a senator's senator." For his part, Bobby soon became frustrated by life in the collegial, slow-moving body. As attorney general and first brother, RFK had been used to having his own way on his own terms. Now, as a freshman senator, he had to wait his turn in committee hearings while questions were asked by members who, though more senior than he, had not honed their interrogational skills on the likes of Jimmy Hoffa. "That's how it's done around here, Robby my boy," Ted chided him.

"The general sense I have . . ." observed political journalist Joseph Kraft, "is that Bob was not awfully happy in the Senate, that he felt it was a talking place rather than a doing place. He would frequently talk of how little it was in his style. He referred, often contemptuously, to things that were going on as 'five or six old men sitting around.' "

Dun Gifford, an assistant on Ted Kennedy's staff, overheard RFK telling his brother, "If only I were a member of the club, Teddy, the way you are, they'd take my amendments.' In a funny way," said Gifford, "Ted just plain did his homework better than Bobby did. Bobby, I think because of his life at Hickory Hill with all the children, because of the demands on his time, be it Jackie or the other members of the family or anything to do with John Kennedy's memorials—that [were] always interviews with the press—endured more drain on his time than there was on Ted's." (The burden at home grew heavier during Bobby's Senate tenure: Matthew Maxwell Taylor Kennedy was born January 11, 1965, and Douglas Harriman Kennedy, Bobby and Ethel's tenth child, was born March 24, 1967.)

Teddy, said Gifford, rose "every single morning" at 6:30 and "read the newspapers and he read everything in his briefcase." He'd have breakfast with his staff and review the amendments to be considered that day by the Labor Committee. "We'd just fill him full of it. He'd ask us questions, and we'd play the cross-examination game. . . . Teddy didn't want to go in there unless he damn well knew what he was talking about."

Bobby, on the other hand, "just trusted much more that he could ad-lib it, that he knew about it and that he could speak to the need for it and that the technical people would take care of the language." In presenting legislation to the Labor Committee—concerning, for example, poverty in the slums—Gifford noted that RFK would say, " 'We just have to do something. This amendment's going to do it.' And [another senator] would say, 'How?' And he'd say, 'Well, it's going to do it. Don't worry about it, it'll do it.' " Dave Burke, Teddy's top aide, recalled that amid such confusion the younger Kennedy "would hand [RFK] a note saying, 'I don't care about the other fellows, I understand it, Bobby,' which would just break him up in the middle of his presentation."

Humor was the intra-Kennedy language, and the two senators spoke it to one another as though the Senate were just another Kennedy living room. "Whenever they were there together," said Gifford, "on just every occasion, they needled each other, privately and sometimes out loud in the presence of other senators. There was frantic note passing back and forth. . . . Everybody would be shocked at the informality. . . . The two brothers always had an enormously good time together." Although staffers and other lawmakers were "looking at them, and . . . buzzing in their ears to do this and that," the senators Kennedy shared "a really private world between the two of them. . . . Only they understood the allusions, only they understood the references to jokes in passing."

Teddy, a veteran of the Senate compared to Bobby, delighted in referring to his older, more prominent brother as "the junior senator from New York." But he knew that Bobby was the Kennedy next in line for the national spotlight. Adding a hundred thousand dollars of personal funds to the amount allotted by the nation's taxpayers, RFK assembled a crackerjack staff, the stars of which were Adam Walinsky and Peter Edelman. RFK's chief speechwriter and chief legislative tactician, respectively, the two by 1967 "were getting to be famous in their own right . . ." said Gifford. "And they sort of liked that, and they reveled in it." Neither made any attempt to hide his views or his intelligence. "Adam," Gifford remarked, was "an outgoing, brash, gregarious, outspoken individual. Peter . . . is very passionately committed to the things he is involved with, and outspokenly so."

Yet it was the less flashy staff of the senator from Massachusetts that achieved the concrete legislative results. "Teddy," said Gifford, "and therefore [his staff], were more interested in getting the stuff on the books, whether anybody knew about it or not; Bob remained interested in making a case publicly and gaining credit for it. For every thing RFK put on the books, Ted put five—things no one has ever yet heard of, but which are quietly accomplishing things. Other senators knew that." Still, the headlines went to Bobby. "We clearly were in the back of the bus and that was the constraint that we just plain operated under."

Frank Valeo, secretary of the Senate in the mid-sixties, remembered Bobby as "pleasant and reserved, essentially quiet and withdrawn. I had the impression that he had no deep interest in the Senate and that his mind was set on something else out there. I think he was primarily using the Senate as his platform. No piece of legislation that he sponsored comes to mind, but even if you have no impact on the Senate itself, the word goes abroad. So if you're moving toward the presidency, you'd certainly want to make speeches in the Senate on foreign affairs."

During the 1960s, Senate majority leader Mike Mansfield actively sought to enhance the Senate's role in shaping foreign policy. "However," remarked Valeo, "the difference between Mansfield's speaking on foreign policy and Bobby Kennedy's speaking on foreign policy was that the whole world, especially the press corps, knew Mansfield was not going to be president and they weren't sure about Bobby Kennedy. That's the basic distinction."

The distinction was not lost on Lyndon Johnson, who hoped to remain president himself for two elected terms. Joe Dolan, who worked in Washington as RFK's administrative assistant, recalled that LBJ "tried to arrange votes in the Senate that were important to New York and on the same day as the vote make an appearance in New York, so that Robert Kennedy would have to either miss the vote in the Senate or not appear with Johnson in New York. Then the press would write that Bobby was petty enough not to accompany the president in New York.

"I was friends with the White House liaison to the Senate. And I used to call him up whenever we heard that there was a vote coming up in the Senate on an issue important to New York. I'd say, 'Where's he goin'?' He'd say, 'What do you mean?' And I'd say, 'Well, I bet he goes to New York.' And he would! Or they'd announce that the president was going to New York. And I'd call up and say, 'What bill are you bringing up in the Senate?' It happened over and over."

After his election to the Senate, Ted Kennedy successfully asserted control over the Democratic Party in Massachusetts. Bobby made desultory efforts to do the same in New York; when the party balked, he dismissed it as a "zoo." Although he went through the motions his position required, he had larger interests than standing side by side with unimaginative, if hardworking, local pols like Abraham Beame, the party's candidate for New York City mayor in 1965, and Frank O'Connor, who ran for governor in 1966. By his own definition, his "greatest triumph" in local politics was in helping to elect a man to the "monumentally insignificant" position of judge in the surrogate court, a post entailing the probation and execution of wills.

In his first two years as senator, Teddy had focused on legislation to aid New England airlines and fisheries. He had thus initiated the process by which he hoped to make the Senate his home for years to come. Bobby had no wish to be hopelessly mired in the minutiae of budgets, urban planning, taxes. It was no accident that for his maiden speech to the Senate, he chose as his topic the proliferation of nuclear weapons.* From the start, RFK saw himself as a national senator. Although early in his term he did not speak, publicly or privately, of higher ambition, his colleagues and the press regarded him as a president-in-waiting. Even if he didn't admit it to himself, by the way he did his job and by the agenda he advocated, he appeared determined to recapture for his family what had been lost that day in Dallas.

The national senator wasted little time before stepping into the international arena. In November 1965, Bobby took advantage of a Senate recess to visit Latin America. The three-week trip, which originated with an invitation to speak in Brazil, brought Bobby and his party—Ethel, Adam Walinsky, William vanden Heuvel, Richard Goodwin, Thomas Johnston (the manager of his New York office), John Seigenthaler and assorted others—to Peru, Chile, Argentina, Brazil and Venezuela. Bobby would be received in those countries with much of the fanfare normally accorded a head of state. America's actual head of state, Lyndon Johnson, was not pleased with the travel plans of his princely rival. The briefing the State Department gave Bobby prior to the trip suggested to Frank Mankiewicz, soon to be RFK's press secretary, that there was a good deal of resentment at the very top toward the planned expedition.

In Lima, Peru, RFK's first stop, he visited factories and schools, attended a bullfight and a soccer match, went to receptions and white-tie banquets. Most of all, though, he spent time among the poor. "He wanted to see the slums," recalled Pedro San Juan, an RFK aide who had served in the protocol office of the Kennedy White House. "And in Lima we saw *slum* after *slum* after *slum*. And, you know, one slum in Lima's just like another. And I kept saying, 'Why are we seeing only slums? What do we get from seeing such need?' He did the same thing in Chile, he did the same thing in Argentina. Each stop in the itinerary involved going to see poor people.

"He was motivated by the world's need to be conscious of the enor-

---

*The 1963 nuclear test ban treaty between the United States and the Soviet Union had been one of JFK's proudest achievements. It seemed in character for RFK to pick up where his brother had left off.

mous amount of poverty and suffering in the Third World. He needed to
see this and he wanted to understand it. As a matter of fact, during our
trip to Latin America we offended a lot of people in power who wondered, 'Why the hell are you spending so much time with all these dirty
people?' The senators in Peru thought he was too young. They didn't like
his entourage, they thought our shoes were filthy because we'd just come
from a slum. They thought his hair was disheveled and that he was not
being respectful of the fact that he was in the Peruvian senate. His view
was that he had seen what he had come to see and now he was going to
drop by the senate, but he didn't really care much about these senators,
who were all octogenarians anyway. So there wasn't a great deal of chemistry there. The same business occurred in Chile."

In Concepción, Chile, he descended eighteen hundred feet with a
group of coal miners, fifteen hundred feet into the earth by elevator, then
took three subterranean pulley trains a total of six miles to the end of a
dark, dusty shaft. Neither Chilean security officers nor U.S. embassy officials were eager to see the visiting senator trust his safety to the miners,
who were members of a staunchly Communist union. Those in RFK's
party were no more comfortable with the expedition. "There were forty
of the miners to just a few of us," said San Juan. "They could have killed
us. At the beginning they hated him, but when we came out we could
have made them our personal guard because they thought he was won-
derfully heroic and courageous and great. Throughout the trip, there was
that sense of the dramatic, that knowledge of how to get a crowd to be
on his side."

RFK's interest in the continent's downtrodden, and his openness in
discussing relations between his land and the lands to its south, were not
what Latin Americans expected from a prominent visitor from Washington. Still, there were times when he seemed every bit the gringo. "He
didn't have a very clear grasp as to what country he was in," San Juan
continued. "He thought Peru was Chile, and so on—that they were all
the same. But you couldn't say in Argentina what you were saying in
Peru. So when I was interpreting, there were times when Bobby said
something that shouldn't have been said in that particular milieu and I
just changed it in the Spanish.

"We were in Cusco, Peru, where RFK was to speak at a school named
after the great Peruvian writer of the early seventeenth century, Garcilaso. We were out on the balcony, before the microphone, and I wrote
Bobby a note reminding him to mention Garcilaso. He looked at it, nodded his head, and said in his Boston accent, 'Yes, and I want to mention
Garkilayko, the great politician and great statesman of Peru after whom

the school is named.' And I translated it as, 'I want to mention Garcilaso, the great writer.' He didn't say that, but nobody knew the difference. And he didn't know I changed the words. If he had, he would have gotten angry."

On occasion, San Juan was the one who got angry: "We were at a little Andean village about forty miles north of Cusco. It was an amazing place. The people of that region chew coca, from the plant that contains cocaine, and their eyes are glazed. Women have their first child when they're fifteen or so, and then die at around thirty-five of old age. Because of the coca and the altitude, they never stop hemorrhaging. They think it's perfectly normal to bleed constantly. I thought it so strange that this group of North Americans came into this village, understanding nothing.

"Finally, toward the end of the visit, we were treated to a dance performed by the village women. They were accompanied by drums, harps and flutes. The music was amazingly delicate, and they did a dance which was so coy and so wonderful. I was mesmerized. I mean, they were putting their souls into it. And all of a sudden, Bobby turns around and says to me, 'We gotta go.' And it was like a bolt of lightning had struck me. I said to him, '*You can't move!*' 'What?' he said. I said, 'You cannot move, you cannot blink. You have to stay glued to this spot and listen to this and watch it. Because you'll hurt their feelings enormously and destroy everything you've done if you leave now.' And I thought the next thing would be that I'd get a punch in the nose. But he sat there like a little schoolchild who's been scolded. And we stayed another twenty minutes until the dance was finished. 'Now you can go,' I said. And he said, 'Thank you.' To him, and to the rest in his party, it was just a funny Indian dance.

"If you got mad at him for the right reason, he wasn't vindictive. He'd shut up about it. On several occasions, when I lost my cool because something had gone wrong, he overlooked it. But then I said to myself, 'Don't push your luck,' because he could be brutal. I remember one day in Peru he became enraged because some apartments built through the America's Alliance for Progress had gone to upper-middle-class people, not to those who deserved them. At the embassy there was an American counselor who had a reputation as a conservative. The guy had nothing to do with the program, but Bobby just picked on him mercilessly and wouldn't let him open his mouth. This counselor realized that if he defended himself, he was a dead duck. Bobby became a tiger, sharpening his claws on the back of his prey until he'd shredded him to bits. It was a cheap shot. Bob had a bad temper and he could be very nasty. That was one of his less admirable traits."

RFK's travels in Latin America seemed in part to represent—if only unconsciously—an act of atonement for his past as spearhead of Jack's anti-Castro campaign. Ty Fain, an official with the American embassy in Mexico City, recalled RFK's visit there to dedicate the John F. Kennedy Memorial Condominium Project, a housing development sponsored by the Alliance for Progress and financed in part by a loan from the AFL-CIO: "The embassy people were not happy that he wanted to meet with leftist Mexican labor leaders and intellectuals. Their policy was, 'Don't have anything to do with these guys, they'll screw you, they'll try to embarrass you.' The American embassy considered these agitators to be nothing but Russian agents capable of any act of violence, including murder.

"Kennedy felt that our policy in Latin America had to encompass a willingness to deal with the Latin American left. If we didn't find a way to approach them, we were going to be in big trouble. He wanted to reach out to them; he wanted to understand their point of view. Remember, this happened to be a time when relations between Cuba and the U.S. were particularly rotten, and Cuba was the leader of revolutionary ferment. Many of the liberals, the progressives, were leftists, socialists. The labor leaders, the students, they were looking for guidance, and Kennedy kept making the point to them that the U.S. was progressive, forward-looking, not an easy claim to make considering the Kennedy administration's stance vis-à-vis Fidel Castro."

Never one to be stymied by apparent contradictions, RFK plunged ahead. "With these people," continued Fain, "he would get into the subject of Mexican education and how it works, into the history of the Mexican labor movement, into the relationship of Mexican labor to U.S. corporations. He'd listen intently, then find some point at which the U.S. and Mexico either collided or got along. He'd elaborate on what we should be doing, then ask them, 'What do you think?' I've worked in a lot of Latin countries, but this was dialogue I've seldom heard expressed between an American politician and the Latins. He knew how to ask questions."

On November 20, 1965, Bobby celebrated his fortieth birthday in São Paulo, Brazil, with a buffet supper party at the villa of Mildred Sage, the American diplomat who had arranged RFK's Brazilian itinerary. Sage's birthday present had been a battery-operated model airplane, described by Ethel as "a U-2 sent by Lyndon Johnson to spy on my husband." The next day in Recife, a hundred thousand people watched Bobby stop his motorcade, climb onto the roof of a car and announce to the crowd that what Brazil needed is what every country in the world needed: more jobs, more schools, more hospitals. On the 22nd, the second anniversary of Jack's death, Bobby spoke to orphaned children at a community center in Bahia. "More than anything," said William vanden Heuvel, "Bobby liked young children."

On an airplane that evening, he sat in the last seat, his body slumped over and his eyes glistening with tears.

D uring the fall of 1965, the National Union of South African Students (NUSAS), an anti-apartheid group, asked Robert Kennedy to address its members at an Affirmation Day ceremony scheduled for the following spring in Cape Town. The country's white-supremacist regime, not pleased to be visited by the former U.S. attorney general known for his role in racial desegregation, waited six months before granting Bobby a visa.

RFK soon began perusing a variety of materials on South Africa and arranged meetings with American experts on the country and on the continent as a whole. (He would also visit Tanzania, Kenya and Ethiopia.) He asked Adam Walinsky to write a speech for the NUSAS event, then summoned Allard Lowenstein, a New York liberal with ties to NUSAS, to look over the draft. Finding the initial version timid, Lowenstein urged RFK to mince no words in confronting the racism of apartheid. Bobby called in Richard Goodwin to work with Lowenstein on the speech's revision.

When Bobby arrived in South Africa, the government's hostility toward him was apparent. Forty foreign journalists, mostly American, who had planned to cover the trip had been denied entrance to the country. Ian Robertson, NUSAS's director, had been "placed under a three-year ban," i.e., his personal and professional contacts had been severely constricted. And the nation's prime minister, Dr. Hendrik Verwoerd, had announced that he would not meet with the visiting American. One South African newspaper reflected the suspicions of the nation's white establishment: "There are those who say that his purpose is purely to advance his political ambitions at home, that he wishes to capture the Negro vote in his campaign for the Presidency by championing the cause of the Black man in the last outposts of White domination."

A crowd of two thousand greeted Bobby and Ethel as they disembarked from their plane at Johannesburg's Jan Smuts Airport in the late evening of June 4, 1966. Cries of "Go home, Kennedy" were intermingled with cheers. "We are, like you, a people of diverse origins," he told the gathering. "And we too have a problem, though less difficult than yours, of learning to live together, regardless of origins, in mutual respect for the rights and well-being of all our people. . . . I come here to South Africa to exchange views with you . . . on what we together can do to meet the challenges of our time." With that, a man in his twenties approached RFK and spat in his face. He was arrested and taken away.

Over the four days of his visit, RFK exchanged views with newspaper editors and opposition leaders. His first afternoon in the country, he took lunch at the American ambassador's residence in Johannesburg, then strolled around an affluent white neighborhood, introducing himself along the way to the black servants tending the residents' gardens: "I'm Robert Kennedy from the United States and this is my wife Ethel." At dinner that night, a contingent of white Afrikaner businessmen complained to Bobby that he didn't understand the political situation in South Africa, where Blacks represented the vast majority. "We feel put upon," said an industrialist. "If you feel put upon," retorted the visitor, "what must they feel?"

Disobeying the authority of his host country, RFK paid a visit to Ian Robertson, presenting the banned student leader with a copy of *Profiles in Courage* inscribed by both Bobby and Jackie. Suspecting that Robertson's flat was bugged, Kennedy proceeded to jump up and down on the floorboards, claiming that the vibrations would disrupt the listening devices for a few minutes. "How do you know that?" Robertson asked. "I used to be attorney general," RFK replied. Bobby met with novelist Alan Paton (*Cry, the Beloved Country*), also persecuted by the regime, then helicoptered to the small remote farm to which the government had restricted Zulu chief Albert Luthuli, a recent winner of the Nobel Peace Prize. To the aged Luthuli, whose words South Africans were forbidden to quote, he gave a portable phonograph and a recording of some of Jack's speeches.

He toured the black township of Soweto. The group walked through great masses of people, and Bobby found himself making speeches from the steps of a church, from the hood of a car and standing on a chair in the middle of a school playground. "Master, master," many called to him. "Please don't use that word," he told them.

Bobby spoke to overflowing audiences of white students at universities in Durban and in Johannesburg. Firmly but respectfully, he urged South Africans of all races to "commit their every resource of mind and body to the education and improvement and help of their fellow man." When one young questioner suggested that black Africans were too primitive and too violent to be trusted with self-government, Bobby replied that "no race or people are without fault or cruelty. Was Stalin black? Was Hitler black? Who killed forty million people just twenty-five years ago? It wasn't black people, it was white." Another student declared that the Bible mandated black servitude. "But suppose God is black?" RFK replied. "What if we go to Heaven and we, all our lives, have treated the Negro as inferior, and God is there, and we look up and He is not white? What then is our response?"

Although most newspapers in South Africa did their best to ignore Bobby, the more liberal English-language press gave the trip front-page coverage. The touring American legislator had become "a kind of third political force in the country in less than a week," wrote Anthony Delius in the *Cape Times*. For a change, RFK wasn't being perceived as a political opportunist using racism to advance his own career, but rather as an American hero bearing a message from the heart. The *Rand Daily Mail* sang his praises in a glowing editorial: "Senator Kennedy's visit is the best thing that has happened to South Africa for years. It is as if a window has been flung open and a gust of fresh air has swept into a room in which the atmosphere has become stale and fetid." In bearing "his message of confident, unashamed idealism" to South Africa's young people, whom most of the globe considered pariahs, RFK had helped them again feel "part and parcel of the great tradition of the contemporary world." The editorial concluded with words to the visitor: "Thank you a thousand times for what you have done for us. Come back again. You have a place in our hearts."*

The highlight of Bobby's trip was his speech for Affirmation Day at the University of Cape Town. It took him forty-five minutes to make his way through the throng of students gathered to hear him the evening of June 6. Jameson Hall seated only fifteen hundred people. The remaining seventeen thousand who had turned out were forced to listen over loudspeakers set up on the campus lawn and in adjacent academic buildings.

The address was perhaps the finest of his life. In the most memorable section he quoted Archimedes—"Give me a place to stand, and I will move the world"—and then said:

> It is from numberless diverse acts of courage and belief that human history is shaped. Each time a man stands up for an ideal, or acts to improve the lot of others, or strikes out against injustice, he sends forth a tiny ripple of hope, and crossing each other from a million different

---

* U.S. newspapers also reported extensively on Bobby's visit—so much so that one of his fellow senators became "jealous." "Dear Bobby," a note from Ted to his returning brother began, "I am sick and tired of hearing about your trip to Africa. For me to get my name in the papers I am currently planning a night excursion to McLean VA to release Brumus from the county pound."

centers of energy and daring those ripples build a current which can sweep down the mightiest walls of oppression and resistance.

It is from this speech by Robert Kennedy that words were taken and etched into the stone wall facing his grave at Arlington National Cemetery.

At hearings of the Migratory Labor Subcommittee early in his term as senator, RFK listened to accounts of the hardships endured by itinerant farmworkers in Appalachia. Soon a witness appeared representing a group of landowners. When the man not only objected to every possible proposal to help the laborers but also admitted that his organization could suggest no ways to ameliorate the distress, Bobby dressed him down: "To be opposed to a minimum wage, to be opposed to legislation which would limit the use of children, to be opposed to collective bargaining completely—to oppose all that without some alternative makes the rest of the arguments you have senseless."

The last time Bobby had berated a witness from management over a labor situation had been 1958. Then, as John McClellan's chief counsel, he had become furious at an executive from the Kohler Company for his defense of the working conditions at the firm's plant in Sheboygan, Wisconsin, where the United Auto Workers was conducting a strike. As attorney general, Bobby had been in a position to stand up for the rights of workers, but had been too preoccupied with the prosecution of corruption in the upper ranks of the labor movement to concern himself with the daily grind of workers on the line. By this juncture, however, Jimmy Hoffa had been convicted and RFK no longer had to fight his dead brother's political battles. He had initially seen the depths of the nation's poverty while campaigning with his brother in West Virginia in 1960. At the Justice Department his official responsibility had been the enforcement of laws; yet he had found spare time and had used it to lead not a public war on poverty, but a secret war on Cuba. Now, though, he was free to adopt a new and more giving stance. In his three and a half years as senator, he would seek out America's disadvantaged, moving from ghetto to barrio to shantytown to work camp. In the hurt that had lingered within him since Dallas, he would reach out to those of his countrymen for whom despair seemed a birthright. Nominally, Bobby's passion to serve America's underclasses was an expression of the Kennedy legacy he had inherited from Jack. In fact, it was the core of the legacy Bobby himself was constructing, a legacy light-years removed from that which he had created as an angry young rebel molesting Third World female drug pushers and victims in then cold-water tenement dwellings.*

At the beginning of 1966, Walter Reuther of the UAW convinced RFK to travel with the Migratory Labor Subcommittee to Delano, California, where the United Farm Workers had spearheaded a strike of itinerant grape pickers, urging a national boycott of grapes picked by nonunion workers. The senator made the journey reluctantly—"Lord, why am I doing this?" he grumbled to Peter Edelman on the plane west—although he soon became convinced the trip had been necessary.

RFK would later call Cesar Chavez, the leader and founder of the UFW, "one of the heroic figures of our time." A rebel but also a pacifist, Chavez seemed to Bobby the Chicano counterpart to Martin Luther King. The son of the tycoon and the son of migrant farmworkers had much in common: both were committed Catholics, highly intelligent, stubborn, strong, and moralistic. Chavez's workers earned less than $1.50 a day; Chavez himself accepted a salary of only $5 per week.

At the subcommittee hearings, RFK listened to the county sheriff brag that he had prevented trouble by arresting strikers before they were able to commit crimes. Senator George Murphy of California, the former Hollywood song-and-dance man, was also a subcommittee member. "Although I was a Republican and not overly impressed by this particular movement, I couldn't believe the sheriff. I remember saying something facetious to him, like, 'It's too bad you weren't around before the Watts riots.' The Los Angeles ghetto had erupted the previous summer and, of course, if he had arrested everyone in Watts there would have been no riot. Bobby was in a state of shock. 'I didn't realize you could arrest somebody in this country *before* they violated the law,' he said. 'Maybe I ought to reread the Constitution.'

"Bobby had gone out to California to meet with Chavez and with Dolores Huerta, Chavez's second-in-command, and with the strikers. He supported them at a time when nobody else would, which was quite interesting considering he'd once been McCarthy's doughboy. And he supported Chavez's uprising with such conviction I felt it would work against him if he ever ran for president. He would be considered to be a revolutionary."

RFK's position, according to Murphy, was that "the workers were eventually going to be organized, and the sooner the growers recognized this, the sooner things would normalize. Bobby lambasted the growers

---

*Lem Billings commented on another aspect of RFK's dualism. "As a father," he said, "Bobby could be very tough but also very tender, very harsh but very loving."

during the hearings, not always justifiably but certainly vociferously. He would not quit."

Jacob Javits, who had opposed RFK during his senatorial race against Kenneth Keating, joined him in 1967 on a trip to an upstate New York migrant agricultural workers' camp. "I gained some respect for Kennedy that day," said Javits. "The workers in the camp, most of them Black, were living in old schoolbuses whose seats had been torn out and replaced with mattresses. Naked infants were crawling around amid rodents and litter. These people were earning three dollars a day to pick celery. Then the boss showed up and pointed a shotgun at Bobby. 'You're nothing but a goody-goody trying to gather headlines,' he said. 'And you're an animal whose ass I'm going to fry in a court of law,' Kennedy replied. On the way back to New York City, where we were both headed that evening, he said: 'I've rarely seen such squalor. Only the American Indian lives like that.' And that's when he started telling me of his crusade on behalf of the Native American. Some time later, I accompanied him to a Five Nations reservation, government-funded, near Syracuse, New York. And he was right: their living conditions were sub-human."

Stewart McClure, chief clerk of the Labor Committee, remembered being called into Bobby's Washington office one day: "I was astounded. It looked like the inside of a tepee. He had tomahawks and wampum belts and bows and arrows, a whole panoply of Indian objets d'art and artifacts and books on Indian life. And he said to me, 'Do you think Senator Hill' "—Lister Hill, Democrat of Alabama, the committee chairman—" 'would let me have a subcommittee on Indian affairs? That Bureau of Indian Affairs is a scandal and Indian education is a disaster.' " The Bureau of Indian Affairs was properly the business of another committee, but education was part of Labor's mandate. Bobby soon got, and chaired, his own subcommittee on Indian education, which helped to get legislation passed that eventually improved the situation.

"Marlon Brando talked about the plight of our First Americans," said Larry O'Brien, "but Robert Kennedy did something about it."

In April 1967 Bobby and the Labor Subcommittee on Poverty visited the Mississippi Delta, where the mechanization of cotton production and changes in local surplus-food programs had devastated black sharecroppers. Hearings featuring local officials making excuses did not interest the junior senator from New York. "He wanted to see the area for himself," said Secretary of Agriculture Orville Freeman, "so he went down to Cleveland, Mississippi, with Charles Evers, Peter Edelman, a bunch of reporters and a TV crew, and they worked their way deep into the Delta. When Bobby returned to Washington, he told me these people were starving, and he needed an allocation of emergency funds to get them fed.

"He described what he'd seen there—the shacks, the vermin, the catatonic children with hollowed cheeks and bloated bellies, the ancient grandmother whose body had wasted away, the starved pig with a half-eaten rat hanging out its snout. 'I can't adequately communicate the horror of the place,' he said to me. 'It smelled of urine, of vomit—you couldn't breathe without gagging.' I contacted President Johnson to try and raise some temporary funds; Johnson's response: 'We've already got a Green-Stamp Program.' "

Before Jack's death, the world beyond the Kennedys had been to Bobby little more than a territory to conquer, a wasteland that demanded mastering for the common good of the American populace. Presently he began to recognize that he had much to learn from the least of his fellow Americans, and he seemed to grasp that his insulated Kennedy upbringing may have been too protective. "If I hadn't become a United States senator, I'd rather be working in Bedford-Stuyvesant than any place I know," he assured a meeting concerned with the disadvantaged Brooklyn neighborhood. "I wish I'd been born an Indian," he told the Comanche wife of a Senate colleague. "If I hadn't been born rich, I'd probably be a revolutionary," he said to a reporter from Latin America. "I'm jealous of the fact that you grew up in a ghetto. I wish I'd had that experience," he informed journalist Jack Newfield, a native of Brooklyn.

Few who heard Bobby complain about his comfortable childhood would have minded being raised in homes and on estates so large they were called "compounds." Yet surprisingly few suggested to the senator that he tended with some of his remarks to sound condescending.

Sam Yorty, however, administered a blunt dose of reality. At a Senate hearing in 1966 on urban renewal, the Los Angeles mayor was one of a number of big-city chief executives to provide testimony. RFK criticized Yorty, who had supported Johnson for president in 1960, over the circumstances endured by his city's African Americans. "And Bobby said to me," recalled Yorty, " 'Mayor, I hope the blacks will have the same opportunity growing up that you and I had.' And I said, 'Well, Senator, I hope they have the same opportunity I had, but they'll never have the same opportunity you had.' "

A lifetime of privilege may have left Bobby unprepared for all he was discovering. Nonetheless, his transformation in the years following his brother's death seemed real. Fred Dutton, one of RFK's closest confidants during the sixties, reflected on the change: "In the fifties, Bob had the reputation of being a conservative, traditional Catholic in American politics. Catholicism was always important in his life, but it was much more an intellectually and emotionally present force in the younger Bob Kennedy. I'm not saying he wasn't a good Catholic to the end, but I'm saying there was a lot of ferment going on. If you look at the progression from that early stage in his life to where he ended up, it was a huge personal movement—somewhat politically motivated, but I don't think most of it was.

"He needed to live experiences. He didn't get them out of books as much as he got them from real life. In 1961 and 1962, he and his brother were not—the Kennedy people don't like to admit this—at the front of the civil rights parade. But he was somebody who was very much in transit. The civil rights movement was a precipitating cause, Vietnam was a precipitating cause, some opportunism for his own political advancement was a cause. And when he went to the Mississippi Delta and saw the true poverty of the blacks, when he went to the Indian reservations and saw the enormous poverty there, he became radicalized.

"His inner passions were evolving, changing. He was going through what might best be described as a kind of metamorphosis, transforming himself from a political terrorist to a humanitarian peacemaker."

B obby maintained a senatorial office in Manhattan, but, revealed aide Carter Burden, "he only came into the office about a dozen times in the two and one-half years that I was there." Rather, he worked out of his apartment at 870 United Nations Plaza, on Manhattan's East Side. Ed Koch remembered visiting him there: "It wasn't a large apartment. They would use the downstairs lobby as a waiting room. You would be called upstairs—an assistant escorted me up—and then, slowly, you would advance through the apartment until you met Robert in the living room. He was boyish and very informal. At this meeting he didn't wear a tie. He had just finished eating some fried eggs and he had egg stains all over his face and shirt."

Leading writers were among the most frequent visitors to RFK's urban home. Besides Jack Newfield, Bobby befriended journalists Pete Hamill and Jimmy Breslin. Truman Capote lived in Bobby's building; the two neighbors would occasionally drop in on each other for drinks. Capote noted Bobby's charismatic quality. "At social functions," said the author, "he would enter the room and the other guests would instantly fasten on him. They would go on talking to each other, but they weren't listening. Instead, they were watching RFK. They concentrated on his every move. They would eavesdrop on his conversations and try to engage him in idle chitchat, which is something he wouldn't often do."

Authors from Norman Mailer—who met him only briefly and liked him—to Gore Vidal—who never ceased despising him—tried to understand RFK in print. John Cheever dropped in, as did Art Buchwald, William Styron, and Tennessee Williams. Soviet poets Yevgeny Yevtushenko and Andrei Voznesensky saw him during stateside visits, the latter commenting on RFK's "inquisitiveness" and "outspoken candor." From closer to home, American poet James Dickey likewise showed up.

"I visited RFK during a stay in New York," reminisced Dickey. "I'd given a reading at the 92nd Street Y and Kennedy gave a cocktail reception at his home in my honor. He seemed quite animated that evening, perhaps because Jackie was also present. The three of us traded views on politics and poetry. I began quoting some lines from *Julius Caesar* and I suddenly couldn't remember how they went. To my amazement, Bobby completed the passage. He wasn't like any politician I'd ever met."

Bobby had been an unusual attorney general; he was a rare United States senator, as well. His appearance—long, unruly hair, rumpled suits—baffled his fellow legislators. "He looks like a damned beatnik," groused Thurston Morton, Republican of Kentucky. But even more unnerving to his colleagues was the effort he made to comprehend the cultural ferment and social upheaval of the 1960s. He talked politics with New Left leader Tom Hayden, he discussed Bob Dylan with protest singer Phil Ochs. At his Washington office he received Allen Ginsberg, the beat poet and counterculture hero. Following the meeting, Ginsberg called RFK "savvy and serious," and said, "we spoke about Russian literature, alternative lifestyles, education, urban politics and drugs. I asked if he'd ever sampled pot. He said he hadn't, but I don't know that I believed him. I asked whether the poverty situation in the country would improve. 'It'll get worse before it gets better,' he speculated. I left, and then I remembered something I'd wanted to do. When I returned, I found him in the outer office. I took out my harmonium and chanted a rendition of Hare Krishna. When I finished, he said, 'Now what happens?' I told him it was an incantation for the preservation of the planet. He smiled. 'Maybe you ought to play it for the fellow up the street,' he said. 'He needs it much more than I do.' He pointed in what I assumed was the direction of the White House."

Not all the people with whom RFK socialized during his Senate years were prizewinning poets or acclaimed urban journalists. "Personally," observed Peter Edelman, "I never saw what he saw in somebody like Andy Williams, who I think is really a dopey guy. But there was a side to Robert Kennedy which liked that kind of stuff—you know, the bright lights. No question about it—he'd go out to fancy New York restaurants with his pals and so on, and sometimes looked bored, but he kept on doing it. And he'd go to Los Angeles and stay at Andy Williams's house and go to a lot of glittery Hollywood parties and receptions.* I don't think he would have done that if he didn't enjoy it in his own peculiar way. So that side of him I never quite understood. It's just that we were always sort of purist about him—this was *our* Bobby and he was a Kennedy, and what did we know? He was more famous and classy than any of them. But I think he derived some satisfaction from those things. It's just that the particular ones sometimes, like Andy Williams, who was really such a dummy. . . . Kennedy told me once that Williams couldn't remember the words to any songs, that he always has to have a whatchamacallit—TelePrompTer—to tell him the words to the songs. And Andy's wife, Claudine, was also no genius."

Ethel Kennedy loved the inoffensive crooning of Andy Williams, who in the early 1960s starred in a weekly television variety show. So she had Bobby telephone the singer to invite him and his raven-haired wife, Paris-born actress Claudine Longet, to join them in Palm Springs for a long weekend.† Soon, the two couples became the best of friends: they went boating together off the Cape, took ski vacations in Sun Valley, sailed the Caribbean. Williams and Longet partied at UN Plaza and Hickory Hill. They filled their Beverly Hills mansion with snapshots of the Kennedys, and named the third of their three children Robert after Bobby.

The Kennedys and the Williamses shared more than vacations. "I heard that Andy Williams knew about the affair between Claudine and Bobby," noted Cathy Griffin, a private investigator based in Los Angeles. "But Andy so idolized Bobby that he didn't say anything or try to interfere in any way." According to Peter Lawford, as reported by his last wife, Williams may have been too "preoccupied" to object. The late actor insisted not only that Bobby had a short-lived, passionate affair with

---

*One of these "glittery Hollywood parties" took place at the home of Rock Hudson. To Bobby's amazement, most of the men at the affair (including Hudson) were dressed in drag.

†Claudine Longet married Andy Williams in 1961, when she was nineteen and he was thirty-one. The singer got his young wife's career started, helping her land a series of guest appearances in such television shows as *Dr. Kildare* and *Combat*. She would also appear in a number of forgettable films. Longet became best known, however, for a feat she performed off camera: in 1977, after her divorce from Williams, she was convicted of criminally negligent homicide in the shooting of her paramour, professional skier Vladimir "Spider" Sabish, at his chalet in Aspen. Claiming the gun went off accidentally, she served a jail term of just thirty days.

Longet, but also that Ethel and Williams were very attracted to one another. Said Patricia Seaton: "Peter went skiing with them one time in Aspen and saw the two of them falling all over each other, at the same time that Bobby and Claudine were falling over each other. Ted Schwartz, who coauthored a book I wrote about my late husband (*The Peter Lawford Story*), heard a similar report: he mentioned to me that he interviewed somebody who claimed that the four of them were drunk one night in Aspen, and Ethel was practically getting it on with Andy while Claudine was doing the same with Bobby."

Longet wasn't the only entertainer seen with Senator Robert Kennedy. "Bobby, like his father and his brothers, loved making it with movie stellars," maintained Truman Capote. "The bigger the name, the better. He met Shirley MacLaine in 1960, when she was a supporter of Jack. (She'd been introduced to JFK by Frank Sinatra.)

"My guess is that Shirley and Bobby were merely close buddies. That wasn't necessarily the case with other actresses of note. Mia Farrow, for instance, might well have been a lover of Bob's. She and RFK spent a good deal of time together. She was very young and married to Frank Sinatra at the time. It led to the dissolution of Mia's marriage to Sinatra. Sinatra loved Jack Kennedy but hated Bobby. He constantly referred to Bobby as 'the punk.' "

In the fall of 1967, Frank Sinatra ordered his wife to leave the California set of *Rosemary's Baby* and join him on the New York location of *The Detective,* a film in which the two were to costar. With her work on *Rosemary's Baby* unfinished, Farrow refused. That evening she went to the Factory, L.A.'s trendiest discotheque, with a group that included Bobby.* When Sinatra heard that his young wife had spent most of the night dancing with the man who had come between him and a president, he immediately ordered his lawyer to draw up divorce papers. The attorney served them to Farrow at her trailer on the Paramount lot.

Another young, blonde actress with whom the senator spent time was Candice Bergen. In early autumn 1965, RFK and Bergen attended a dinner party at Jackie's New York apartment, and Bobby, whose sexual affair with his sister-in-law had recently ended, apparently took a jealous interest in a trip Bergen was about to take to the Far East. From her Manhattan home on East Sixty-eighth Street, the actress wrote her hostess a note of thanks:

---

*Among the owners of the Factory were Sammy Davis, Jr., Peter Lawford, Tommy Smothers, Paul Newman and Pierre Salinger (John F. Kennedy's former White House press secretary).

Dear Mrs. Kennedy—

Thank you for a lovely dinner which brought the summer to an end in
warmth and nostalgia. Also—please tell the Senator that while I'm on
my trip I shall try to compile a list of how I spend my Saturday nights in
Tai Pei.

Sincerely,

Candice Bergen

In late January of 1967, RFK traveled to Europe for talks with leaders
of England, France, Italy and West Germany. In Paris, he was the guest
of honor at a dinner party held at the home of Hervé Alphand, France's
ambassador to Washington. Actresses Shirley MacLaine and Catherine
Deneuve were among the many guests, as was Candice Bergen, who was
at the time making a film in Paris. "The dinner was very lively and gay,"
remembered Alphand. "Bob loved dancing." Before leaving Paris, Bobby
dined with Bergen again, this time without the crowd. The rendezvous
found its way into the local society pages. "Senator Kennedy," reported
Edgar Schneider in the *Paris Presse,* "could not resist the pleasure of
seeing Candice. . . . Tired of the official banquets and political meetings,
Mr. Kennedy decided that nothing could be more agreeable to end his
stay in Paris than an intimate dinner in a cozy place in Saint-Germain-
des-Prés. So Bobby very candidly asked Miss Bergen to share his last
evening."

Schneider went on to say that Bergen had brought to the dinner her
small dog, which she'd acquired in the Canary Islands. "The dog spent
the meal under the table. When the two humans finished their dessert,
one of them—a United States senator—bent underneath the table to
retrieve the pooch so that all three of them could leave."

"Bobby and Candice Bergen didn't take too much trouble to hide
what they were doing," insisted Coates Redman. "They were not being
furtive; they made it obvious." Said Capote, "Candice had that Waspish,
preppy look that appealed to all Kennedy men. And like Shirley
MacLaine and Mia Farrow, she always struck me as rather bright. Bobby
wasn't so much into bimbos as his two brothers were. He had lengthier,
more serious affairs. Therefore, he was more choosy."

Not all the women the choosy senator chose were famous. During a
barbecue at Hickory Hill, according to Jerry Oppenheimer (*The Other
Mrs. Kennedy*), he took off for a motorcycle ride with Polly Bussell, a
recent Radcliffe graduate whom Bobby had hired to work in his Washington office after meeting her at the Martha's Vineyard home of writer

William Styron. Television journalist Douglas Kiker, who was present at the cookout, told Oppenheimer that both Bobby and his blonde companion were clad only in bathing suits as they rode to a wooded area nearby and parked the bike.

They were interrupted when a McLean police car drove up. As Kiker had it, when RFK saw the cruiser he darted into the trees, leaving Bussell in her bikini to face the representatives of the law. Only after the officers escorted Bussell back to Hickory Hill did Bobby emerge to make his own way back. Bussell later denied that she and the senator were up to anything more than sight-seeing; it was just an innocent ride on a motorcycle, she told Kiker. Kiker saw in Bobby's abandonment of Bussell a precursor of Chappaquiddick.*

The sexual revolution of the 1960s had little to teach the Kennedy men, who had been enjoying the benefits of free love for decades. But in the try-anything spirit of the time, Bobby may have indulged in an experiment that, even for his lusty family, broke new ground. In *Palimpsest*, Gore Vidal ruminated on RFK's sexuality: "Between Bobby's primitive religion and his family's ardent struggle ever upward from Irish bog, he was more than usually skewed, not least by his own homosexual impulses, which, [Rudolf] Nureyev once told me, were very much in the air on at least one occasion when they were together. 'Nothing happen,' said Rudi. 'But we did share young soldier once. *American* soldier. Boy not lie . . . *maybe.*' Rudi gave his Tatar grin, very much aware, firsthand, of the swirls of gossip that envelop the conspicuous. Yet anyone who has eleven children must be trying to prove—disprove?—something other than the ability to surpass his father as incontinent breeder."

According to Janet Villella, a prima ballerina with the New York City Ballet during the 1960s, the Russian dancer's assertion that "nothing happen" between him and Bobby was not entirely accurate. Villella recalled an evening she spent at Arthur's, an Upper East Side discotheque operated by Sybil Burton, the Welsh actress and former wife of actor Richard Burton: "I saw Bobby arrive that night with Jackie. Later on, as I went to make a phone call, I saw RFK and Nureyev in a telephone booth. They were kissing passionately."

---

*On July 18, 1969, Senator Ted Kennedy drove twenty-eight-year-old blonde Mary Jo Kopechne from a party to the ferry on Chappaquiddick, an islet off Martha's Vineyard. Teddy's 1967 Oldsmobile went off a bridge into the water. Teddy escaped; Kopechne, who had worked for a short time as Bobby Kennedy's secretary, drowned. Teddy did not report the accident to authorities for more than nine hours. An interview with a friend of Kopechne by the current author revealed that Mary Jo had engaged in a brief affair not with Ted Kennedy, as many suspected, but with Bobby.

Despite such escapades, rules to be flouted by Kennedys were still to be obeyed by everyone else. Gerald Tremblay remembered that one night in South America RFK became angry at a reporter for the *Washington Star* when he noticed the journalist "playing footsies with this married gal. It irritated Bob and it irritated him enough to say something about it to the reporter. That gives you an idea of how he felt about morals."

Despite all his wanderings, Bobby always came home to his wife. Even though she was no movie star, "Old Moms" could single-handedly raise a roof. In March 1966, she and her husband attended a party in Washington to mark the resignation of McGeorge Bundy from the Johnson administration. "Ethel Kennedy wowed 'em with the frug the other night," a newspaper account of the shindig began, referring to a popular dance of the sixties. She "wowed 'em" with her outfit, as well. "To the amazement of the other ladies at the party who showed up in their best floor-length chiffon and *peau de soie,* Ethel, Sen. Robert Kennedy's wife, wore a short-short dress of shiny black-and-white vinyl with rhinestone shoulder straps. While 'The Decadents' pounded out frenzied Beatle music 'til dawn, Ethel figuratively tore up the dance floor with her snow-white Courrèges boots.

" 'She had the Courrèges of her convictions,' quipped *Washington Post* columnist Maxine Cheshire the next morning."

The women in his office were younger, the film actresses he met were more glamorous, but RFK cherished his life's companion. "It was kind of known," said journalist Marie Ridder, "that when Ethel was on an airplane with Bobby, even though she was a very nervous flyer, he felt better. I so often picture them getting on various planes, his arm, not exactly around her, but on her shoulder. There were rumors about other women. I was on the airplane when Candy Bergen got on, and I presume he did have a flirtation or even an affair with her. But it had no meaning to him. His devotion was to Ethel. She was his partner. She was his love. Oh, absolutely."

On a bleary day in early February 1966, Bobby Kennedy toured one of New York City's most disadvantaged neighborhoods, Bedford-Stuyvesant, a black section of Brooklyn. As he walked along the rubble-strewn streets, past shabby storefronts and rubbish-filled building lots, he told an aide that the scene reminded him of the Warsaw Ghetto. But later, at a meeting with community leaders, his compassion was met with scorn. "You don't really give a damn," said one skeptic. "You're like all the others."

RFK hardly appreciated the hostile reception. "I don't need this shit," he grumbled during the car ride back to Manhattan. "I could be down in Palm Beach catching some sun and sipping a Mint Julep. I don't need to hear that I'm like every other goddamn politician." But Bobby had never been able to resist a challenge, and in his role as a U.S. senator he decided to make the community a testing ground to see what could be done for America's urban poor.

Within a period of several months, Bobby and his staff developed a plan. A board of local residents would work to determine where efforts were needed and how they should be applied. But the senator also decided to tap the muscle, money and expertise of the city's business elite, and in so doing he departed markedly from the previous ways of his family. "John Kennedy just didn't understand businessmen," said Roswell Gilpatric, "and he never developed much rapport with them. Joe Kennedy, though wealthy, never had been a standard businessman, he was very much a loner in the financial community. Robert, however, made it a point to work with business leaders, to develop one-on-one relationships with those whom you wouldn't expect to be interested in working with Robert Kennedy." RFK reached out to people like André Meyer of the investment banking house Lazard Frères, Thomas J. Watson of IBM and James Oates of Equitable Life Insurance to form a Manhattan-based board of white business leaders to work with the community-based black board. Gilpatric joined the otherwise mostly Republican group, as did his fellow Kennedy administration alumnus C. Douglas Dillon (JFK's secretary of the treasury). Bobby also placed Jacob Javits on the panel.

Bobby saw flaws in the top-down approach used by Lyndon Johnson in his formally titled War on Poverty. Investment banker Benno C. Schmidt, a partner in J. H. Whitney & Company, recalled that Bobby "was very dissatisfied with the progress that had been made, with the programs that were in effect, particularly with the federal programs, and he felt that this was a problem to which we had to find some better solution or it would destroy this nation. He also felt that the solution had to be found at the local level. He proposed to try to set up in Bedford-Stuyvesant a model operation where we could by trial and error learn some of the answers, and provide a format which could be used in other cities." The answers would not come from Washington, the senator believed. "Each community had its own problems and RFK felt that the only hope of solution was an attack on the problems at the community level with each community bringing to bear on its problems all the resources of the federal government, the state government, the city government, and particularly the private sector, both at the business and the philanthropic level."

To lead the local board, Bobby chose Franklin Thomas, a native of Bedford-Stuyvesant who had been working as New York's deputy police commissioner in charge of legal matters. Thomas, who went on to become the first black man to head the Ford Foundation, recalled that some of the initial, short-term projects included putting young Bed-Stuy residents to work: "We organized the youngsters into teams and taught them simple tasks of repairing broken cement sidewalks and doing welding and painting and minor carpentry. That first summer we went out and organized blocks so that at least fifty percent of the area's residents would agree to have improvements made to the exterior of their homes at a nominal cost of twenty-five dollars and in return promise that they would do a similar amount of work on the interior of their homes and use local labor to accomplish same. It was a little tough getting started, but once it got going it became a booming, visible success."

The long-term strategy, noted Thomas, was "development," as opposed to "protest": "Protesters would say, 'We need a thousand housing units for low-income people,' and the city or state or feds might respond to that. Development says, 'We need a thousand units and we're going to identify the sites, acquire the land, put together the financing, etc. We're not turning over the process to third parties to produce those thousand housing units. We want to find out what it takes to produce them and to be central participants in that production.'

"So what happened is you'd have mortgage pools out here that were run by community people and you had commitments from banks and insurance companies. You had business finance and you had housing renovation. You also had community health centers, legitimate theater, a performing-arts company. We managed to build a shopping center and leased a space to major commercial tenants."

Every second week, Thomas would meet with Bobby. "The problems," said Thomas, "centered on incredibly difficult personalities whom I was trying to grapple with. On some of them, he didn't have any more clue than I did. He'd say, 'You tell me if you think a call from me would help or hurt.' "

For all the help he offered the people of Bedford-Stuyvesant, their ways sometimes confounded Bobby. Thomas R. Jones, a community leader and a New York civil court judge, explained that social pressures on African American men led to "a larger and larger role being played by black women. . . . However, the white society—the dominant society—doesn't have that kind of orientation; it operates on the basis of the leadership of men." Jones remembered a conversation he had with RFK after a meeting with local residents: "The senator said to me, 'Judge Jones, you know, I have never been dealt with as rudely and as abruptly, by anybody—even my worst adversaries—than I have been dealt with by some of the women of Bedford-Stuyvesant. They take particular delight in abusing me, in accusing me, in harassing me. I . . . I . . . don't know what to do, but I just can't stand it.' And he flushed and his face turned beet red."

Bobby's ardor for the project led him to make unreasonable demands. "He would see a vacant block in Brooklyn," commented Eli Jacobs, Mayor John V. Lindsay's liaison to the enterprise, "and he would say, 'I want a building there.' And he'd come back several weeks later, and there'd be no building, and he couldn't understand why the building hadn't been built in that intervening period, however short it was." On another occasion, RFK demanded that the substandard collection of garbage in the area be improved—a commendable objective but an impossible one, according to Jacobs, due to the inexorable bureaucracy of the city's sanitation department. "It wasn't likely to happen. Frank[lin Thomas], who understood Kennedy psychology better than I, looked him straight in the eye and said, 'We will do it, Bob. I will get the job done.' Well, needless to say, we didn't get the job done."

"Robert Kennedy wanted action, not explanations," Jacobs noted. "But you have also to remember—and I think this reflected naïveté on the senator's part—we were not sovereign, we were not the City of New York. We were a well-intentioned project with worthy goals . . . but we were not the sanitation department. . . . The mistake he would make in contexts like that would be to assume that we could press buttons and make things happen. . . . He had a utopian and unrealistic set of notions."

If unrealistic in his expectations, Bobby, with his passion and commitment, inspired even greater passion and commitment from those around him. "All the businesspeople, including some who previously hadn't met him, worked like crazy," remarked Franklin Thomas. André Meyer, famous for megadeals, teamed up with Citibank chairman George Moore to recruit banks and insurance companies for a mortgage pool worth $65 million. Thomas Watson induced his company, IBM, to set up a factory in the neighborhood. RFK refused to take no for an answer. Eli Jacobs recalled a visit Bobby made to David Unich, the president of Macy's, to see about locating a store in Bed-Stuy's new shopping center: "Unich indicated that they hadn't studied the matter and he didn't think they should. And after Robert Kennedy stared at him long enough, Unich agreed to assign several of his staff to consider the merits of the project."

Sometimes by intimidation, more often by words and by example, Bobby energized people. "I remember the first day I got on the job I was called in to work at four o'clock in the morning to help type up a speech," said Angela Cabrera, a secretary in Bobby's New York office. "And our reward was that we would go with the senator where he would make the speech. And that's the first time I really met him one-to-one. That was incredible.

"You wanted to be with the senator, you knew he was doing good things and that you were in the presence of a great man. That's the way we felt.

"The press would always be around. And they would say, 'How are you girls so full of energy at four o'clock in the morning?' And one young lady said, 'We take loyalty pills.' The senator heard that, and for Christmas he gave each of the four of us a little gold pill (from Tiffany's). On one side it said, 'Loyal,' and on the other it said, 'RFK, one a day.' It was wonderful, it only encouraged us more. We broke our backs. I was always the last one to leave that office, but it just didn't matter. You did what you had to do."

"What set Bobby apart," said Roswell Gilpatric, "was his ability to inspire others, to make people believe they could accomplish everything they wanted to accomplish. He had that special quality which is so rare among human beings—he made you understand that if you tried hard enough, you could actually succeed."

The Bedford-Stuyvesant organization still exists today. The neighborhood remains beset by inner-city ills, and the IBM plant closed in the early nineties. But development projects continue, as does Medgar Evers College, a school that originated at a meeting of federal, state and local educational officials with the corporate Bed-Stuy board, convened by Bobby at the Manhattan headquarters of CBS. And nationwide, according to Franklin Thomas, "there are presently some two thousand such organizations patterned on the Bedford-Stuyvesant model." Seen in this light, Robert Kennedy's initiative has to be considered a leap in the right direction.

The highest unclimbed mountain in North America as of early 1965 did not have a name until the Canadian government decided to call it Mount Kennedy in honor of the late president. The National Geographic Society suggested that Jack's two surviving brothers join in the initial assault on the peak. Although he would have enjoyed making the climb (or so he claimed), Teddy was still nursing his back injury. Bobby had no such excuse, although most people would consider an aversion to heights and an utter lack of mountaineering experience ample reason to decline the offer. The prospect of a physical trial, combined with an act of homage to Jack, meant that Bobby had no choice but to accept.

In March 1965 RFK flew to the small Yukon outpost of White Horse for a day of training with the two leaders of the expedition, Jim Whittaker and Barry Prather, veterans of Mount Everest. The men then flew by helicopter to their base camp, 8,400 feet up the slope. "And as we flew over these magnificent mountain peaks in a military helicopter," recalled Malcolm Taylor, a writer and photographer hired by the National Geographic Society to cover the climb, "we were all looking out the windows from a perspective a mountain-climber doesn't have, flying up and dipping and soaring over the summits, and going down into these glacial valleys. We were all saying things like, 'Wow! Hey, look at this!' And here's Kennedy with a thick paperback book, right in his face." It was a volume by Winston Churchill. "He kept leaning toward the window where he could get enough light to read, while the rest of us were completely overwhelmed by these magnificent mountains and glaciers. I thought, 'Well, maybe he just doesn't care about mountains.' Some of us are into mountain-climbing and others aren't. He wanted to get there, get up that mountain, do what he came to do, get out, and return to civilization."

The party took three days to ascend. Through wind tunnels and up glaciers, Bobby climbed as second man on a three-man rope, with Whittaker taking the lead. Nights, with temperatures as low as twenty below zero Fahrenheit, the men huddled in tents pitched in snow caves. "In my contact with him," Taylor continued, "he stayed completely to himself, very focused, very intent, no banter, no kidding around." When the men approached the summit, at 13,900 feet, Whittaker said, "Senator, the climb is yours, take the lead." As the rest of the party stayed behind, Bobby walked the final fifty yards to the top. There he planted an American flag, a *PT-109* tie clip, a Kennedy family flag and a copy of JFK's inaugural address.* He crossed himself, and after a few moments returned to the others. His solitude at the windswept summit was not pure—helicopters hovered above, covering the feat for American news organizations. A photograph of the event appeared on the following week's cover of *Life* magazine.

* In 1956, Joseph Kennedy asked authorities on heraldry to create a flag for his family. The experts came up with a design that featured three gold helmets on a black background. They told the ambassador that the motif could be traced to early Kennedy forebears in Ireland.

"I've had more fun in my life," RFK said later of the climb. Still, the expedition was but one of the feats of daring Bobby undertook as senator. He had always been athletic, and had never been less than fearless. But in the wake of Jack's death, he moved beyond touch football to what seemed a conscious effort to tempt fate. "He was forever thumping his chest," maintained Lem Billings. "It was as if he wanted to say, 'Okay, Death, you just try it. I dare you!' "

On the last full day of his November 1965 stay in Brazil, Bobby and two in his party canoed into a tropical deluge at dusk to go fishing. As they disappeared into the jungle, the native guides, who had prudently chosen to remain ashore, predicted the three gringos would never return. They did, with four fish. The next morning, to keep on schedule for Venezuela, he arose at 3:30 A.M., then with four guides paddled down-river, in waters infested with carnivorous fish, to the spot where he was to meet an amphibious plane. William vanden Heuvel remembered that "when the canoe foundered in the rapids, Kennedy jumped overboard and pushed the boat forward. Splashing along in the river, he mimicked Walter Cronkite in declaring: 'It was impossible to pinpoint the exact time and place where he decided to run for president. But the idea seemed to take hold as he was swimming in the Amazonian river of Nha-mundá, keeping a sharp eye peeled for man-eating piranhas. Piranhas have never been known to bite a U.S. senator.' "

During the winter months, RFK raced down torturous ski slopes in New England and the West. Summers, beginning in 1965, he took his family on whitewater rafting trips. Once, on the Salmon River in Idaho, he left the raft and clambered into a kayak—he had never been in a kayak before—to take the final, most difficult, seven miles of rapids himself. "We went rafting on the Colorado River together," recalled George Plimpton, "and once we hit the rapids, Bobby began diving into the on-rushing water like a salmon swimming upstream. It was photographed by the press." While horseback riding with Jackie, he suddenly stood up in his saddle and dismounted by doing a forward flip. Journalists docu-mented many of his daredevil accomplishments, yet Bobby's adventures were more than exercises in political public relations. Jack was dead; only by his defiance of death could Bobby show he deserved to be alive. In-deed, the publicity served his deepest aim, for to prove his courage he needed not only to reveal it to himself, but also to brandish it before the world.

Pedro San Juan recounted a visit by Bobby to a student rally at a soccer stadium in Santiago, Chile: "The Trotskyite, Spartacist and Maoist students were there in force, and also a lot of Communists. And the

Spartacists were not allowing him to talk. They were yelling and screaming and throwing rocks and large copper coins at us. And I was there on the platform with Bobby, and with William vanden Heuvel, John Seigenthaler and Barney Angelo of *Time* magazine. And I was saying, 'Why is everybody getting hit by the coins except Bobby? Why doesn't he get hit so we can get out of here? I'm not Bobby Kennedy, hit *him*, for God's sakes.'

"Next he decided he wanted to go and talk to the ones in the balcony who were the biggest noisemakers. And they were waving to him, extending their arms, saying, 'Come on up, we'll lift you.' And he wanted to be lifted up so he could talk to them. And I said to Seigenthaler, 'Is he crazy? They'll lift him halfway and drop him. They hate him! These guys really hate him!'

"Well, he wanted to go, and some people tried to put him up there, but they couldn't reach, thank God. Then a couple of Communist students—not Spartacists—said to us, 'Does he really want to talk? We'll take care of it for you.' So the Communists started kicking out the Spartacists. And Bobby remarked to me, 'Let's get those students to stop fighting.' And I said, 'They're fighting to get rid of the agitators so you can speak.' So they cleaned them out and he gave his speech. And by the way, the Communists applauded him wildly.

"Time and again he exhibited that type of bravery, that type of total disregard for his safety. He really didn't care. His Senate office was at Constitution Avenue. And I said to him one day, 'I think you may have been told this, but you can be seen from the street. Somebody with a gun could come here and pick you off without anybody being able to stop him. He wouldn't have to come into the building, he could just shoot you through the window.'

"Well, he became livid, he became enraged, he said he hadn't asked for my opinion, that when he wanted my opinion on his safety he would ask for it, that it was none of my damn business and he would sit anywhere he damn pleased, and was there anything else I wanted? And I told this to Joe Dolan and he said, 'You shouldn't have mentioned that, he gets furious every time.' Now, that indicated to me that he had a complex, that he didn't want anyone to think he feared being shot, the same as his brother. He did some dumb things. We could have been killed in that Chilean mine, we could have been murdered by those students."

Bobby's office received dozens of threatening letters and telephone calls each month. The FBI documented other dangers and warned him about "copycat" murderers. Nevertheless, even as he more and more vocally adopted positions guaranteed to inflame the obsessions of the deranged, he refused to take the security measures urged on him by his friends. He continued to travel in open-topped cars, even though his brother had been murdered in one, and he eschewed plainclothes body-guards who might separate him from the multitudes crowding around him as though his touch conferred healing and renewal.

In a motorcade one day, Bobby turned pale when he thought he heard shots. A moment later, realizing that the noise had only been that of a car's backfiring, he said out loud, "Sooner or later." Noted San Juan, "He had to prove he was no less capable of taking it than his brother was. He wasn't going to be afraid. And of course, that's how he died. He never should have walked into that hotel kitchen alone."

23

WAR

Robert Kennedy's most remarkable achievement as senator was the voice he gave to his increasing concern for America's poor. His most remarkable failure was his delay in using that voice to air his increasing doubt about America's war in Vietnam. As he and Jack had come late to the struggle for civil rights, so Bobby would come late to the struggle to end the war. He is today remembered for his anti-Vietnam stance. But for the first two years of Lyndon Johnson's escalation of American involvement in Southeast Asia, RFK remained cautious while others were bold, elusive while others were frank, ambiguous while others were straightforward. His conduct over Vietnam stemmed, as did his actions so often during his life, from an odd mixture of motivations both personal and political—for Bobby, the two spheres were never far apart.

When the issue of Vietnam came up during Bobby's campaign for the Senate, he did not deviate from the policy established by his brother. "In my judgment," RFK said, "the war has to be won in South Vietnam."

But private misgivings arose just months later, after the February 1965 attack by the Vietcong on the American air base at Pleiku. Following the incident, Lyndon Johnson initiated the bombing of North Vietnam and decided to send large numbers of American troops to fight the war that had to that point been waged primarily by the army of South Vietnam, with the aid of American "advisers." In April, Bobby went to see the president to urge that he consider a pause in the bombing. It couldn't hurt, RFK told Johnson; it might help. LBJ assured the senator that the idea was under consideration. It wasn't.

Convinced that the United States had no choice but to escalate its efforts, the president requested an additional $700 million for the fighting, telling Congress it was being asked not just to pass a "routine appropriation," but to give its vote of confidence to an overall policy that left "scant room for deviation." With his advisers, Bobby weighed the pros and cons of voting against the measure; he announced his decision in a speech to the Senate on May 6. He outlined three possible directions in Vietnam. Withdrawal would be unacceptable: "Such a course would involve a repudiation of commitments undertaken and confirmed by three administrations. It would imply an acquiescence in Communist domination of South Asia." Escalation "would be a deep and terrible decision. . . . The course of enlarging the war would mean the commitment to Vietnam of hundreds of thousands of American troops." Bobby advised the third option, negotiation, but only against the backdrop of American resolve: "We must show Hanoi that it cannot win the war, and that we are determined to meet our commitments no matter how difficult." Just how the United States could meet its commitments, "no matter how difficult," without escalation, he did not say. He would not take the political risk of being perceived as letting down the soldiers in the field. Only three senators voted against the appropriation. Bobby was not one of them.

Adam Walinsky and Peter Edelman had opposed the war from the start, and they worked to bring Bobby to their side. Concerning the war's negative aspects, the senator needed little prodding. He recognized that a burgeoning conflict would only rend the nation and at the same time divert resources from those Great Society programs designed to benefit the poor and the sick. In a commencement address at New York City's Queens College in June of 1965, he spoke with admirable candor and perspicacity about relations between the globe's haves and have-nots: "The developing world's revolution is directed against us—against the one-third of the nation that diets while others starve; against a nation that buys eight million new cars a year while most of the world goes without shoes; against developed nations which spend over one hundred billion dollars on armaments while the poor countries cannot obtain the ten to fifteen billion dollars of investment capital they need just to keep pace with their expanding populations." In the same speech he went on to defend the right of students to protest the war, as they had begun to do at Berkeley and other university campuses. In an apparent effort to modify his stance, he speculated: "It is not helpful—it is not honest—to protest the war in Vietnam as if it were a simple and easy question, as if any moral man could reach only one conclusion. Vietnam admits no simple solution."

Four weeks later, Bobby spoke at the International Police Academy, an institution established during his brother's presidency, as part of RFK's counterinsurgency program, to train police in Third World countries to combat communism. In his address, RFK sought to contrast his own approach to wars of liberation with the campaign of massive firepower being mounted in Vietnam by Lyndon Johnson. The senator emphasized that successful rebellions were best fought by political, rather than military, means: "The essence of counterinsurgency is not to kill, but to bring the insurgent back into the national life." He seemed by this time to have lost heart in the facet of counterinsurgency that he had so enthusiastically advanced while attorney general: violence, carefully planned and brutally applied.

On November 18, 1965, RFK and Peter Edelman flew to Los Angeles and toured the riot-scarred streets of Watts. Later that day Bobby held a press conference at the University of Southern California. He supported the rights of student antiwar demonstrators and said of the burning of draft cards, "I don't agree with it personally, but I understand it as an action taken by a person who feels very strongly about this matter." When asked by a reporter how he felt about one student group's declaration advocating the donation of blood to the North Vietnamese, RFK responded, "I'm in favor of giving blood to anybody who needs it. I'm in favor of them having blood." George Wallace and Barry Goldwater both called Bobby's comments the words of a "traitor," while the *Los Angeles Times* went so far as to suggest that he might possibly be "a spy for North Vietnam."

On Christmas Day, responding to hints of enemy interest in negotiations, LBJ temporarily halted the bombing of the North. Privately, RFK urged Johnson to extend the moratorium, and when the bombing was resumed at the end of January he suggested in the Senate that such a policy could only "hurt the United States." But when fifteen colleagues—among them Frank Church of Idaho and George McGovern of South Dakota—asked him to join them in signing a letter to the president protesting the bombing, Bobby refused.

George McGovern attributed Bobby's decision not to sign to ego: "Perhaps he didn't want to be just another name on a list. He wanted to cut out a role for himself as an individualist. There was the human factor of his own ego and the feeling that he was a national figure whose efforts should not be mixed with that of other dissenters, though he was one himself."

With each step toward active dissent, no matter how tentative, RFK attracted a storm of criticism; he was, after all, presumptive heir to the throne—and presumptively "conniving" to regain the throne. These attacks reached a high point in February 1966. On the fourth of that month, with American troops in Vietnam numbering over two hundred thousand, William Fulbright's Senate Foreign Relations Committee opened public hearings on the war. RFK followed the proceedings closely on television, and often attended them as a spectator, standing in the back of the room. "What he found in those hearings," revealed journalist Joseph Kraft, "was that these people kept avoiding the big question. The question was: how do we end the war? Nobody seemed to have an answer."

The former Rackets Committee interrogator decided to provide some of his own responses. Counterinsurgency wouldn't work and neither did the strategy of overwhelming megatonnage. Thus on February 19, reaffirming an earlier opinion, RFK made public a press release calling for the admission of the National Liberation Front—the political arm of the Vietcong—"to a share of power and responsibility . . . [in] hope of a negotiated settlement."

Two days later, the *Chicago Tribune* captioned its editorial "Ho Chi Kennedy," and many other periodicals ran equally negative assessments. The administration unleashed a concentrated attack on the senator. From the Far East, where he had gone to promote his boss's policy, Vice President Hubert Humphrey accused Bobby in a *New York Times* interview of "writing a prescription for the ills of Vietnam that includes a dose of arsenic. It would be [tantamount to] putting a fox in the chicken coop."

RFK suddenly pulled back from his position, issuing "clarifications," attempting to make the ridiculously fine point that he had advocated including the NLF only in negotiations, not in any coalition government that might result from such talks. Its rival humbled, the Johnson administration moved to avoid a total break. Bill Moyers, LBJ's latest press secretary, emphasized common elements in the approaches of Bobby and the president—the NLF might, said Moyers, be allowed to participate in an interim government. Johnson, still looking to be reelected in 1968, did not wish to provoke Bobby to outright antagonism.

For the remainder of 1966, the chastened junior senator from New York retreated into silence on Vietnam. His staff continued to counsel him toward open opposition. Others, too, encouraged him to speak out, including Ethel, Jackie, and Joan Kennedy. He discussed the issue with his Senate colleagues and appreciated the most vocal of the body's dissenters. "He was especially high, as I remember it," said George McGovern, "on Frank Church and on me. I think he regarded us as two of the more thoughtful critics in the Senate, and he told me as much on more than one occasion." But in public Bobby would only express "reservations" and call the matter "complex."

By year's end, the U.S. commitment to Vietnam had increased to 389,000 troops, and peace demonstrations were growing in size and fervor. Americans who opposed the war looked to Bobby as their natural leader and were disappointed by his inertia. Allen Ginsberg wrote RFK imploring him to step forward once more, calling him "the nation's last great hope." Liberal journalist I. F. Stone tried to embarrass Bobby into action, penning an article for his weekly newsletter, which he titled: "While Others Dodge the Draft, Bobby Dodges the War."

Frank Mankiewicz, Bobby's press secretary as of early 1966, remembered the senator explaining that he was reluctant to oppose the war publicly because such a course "wouldn't accomplish anything." Indeed, whatever Bobby advocated, LBJ would do the opposite—"to spite me," RFK told Larry O'Brien. If Bobby "made a pitch to decrease the bombing," said Ken O'Donnell, "Johnson stepped it up. If Bobby said, 'Don't send in troops,' LBJ dispatched fifteen thousand more." Moreover, Bobby believed that everybody "realized what his position was anyway, that he would merely be grandstanding to repeat himself."

In fact, Bobby's position remained more or less a mystery through 1966. His frustration at being unable to slow the escalation was no doubt one cause of his reticence, but there were others. Polls showed that the large majority of the nation was not prepared to abandon its support of the war, and Kennedys had always prospered by forming broad coalitions, not by leading basically unformulated movements. To safeguard his career he had to tread lightly, for many in the press, as Larry O'Brien later asserted, viewed criticism of the war by Bobby "as a political rather than a spiritual consideration." Since his election to the Senate, Bobby had maintained close ties to the big-city bosses he had so successfully cultivated for Jack. But LBJ remained head of the party. Were Bobby to take on the president, few Democrats would choose the side of the young upstart with the obvious ulterior motives.

RFK's disinclination to break publicly with the president, even though the two men had privately despised each other for some time, can be seen in his behavior in a matter apparently wholly unrelated to the war in Southeast Asia. Shortly after Jack's death, the Kennedy family authorized historian William Manchester to write an account of the assassination and the events surrounding it. In 1966, Manchester's book (*The Death of a President*) was ready to go to print, and Manchester had signed a lucrative contract for excerpts of the work to appear, in several installments, in *Look* magazine. As late as July of that year, Bobby gave his blessing to both the book and magazine versions, but before either could appear, Jackie objected irately to the arrangement with *Look*. Sections of the manuscript "might be printed out of context," she argued. Her privacy and that of her children were at stake.

Jackie's position quickly expanded, from opposing the serialization to quarreling with the content of the book itself, and Bobby soon took up her cause. Neither the senator nor the widow ever read the entire manuscript, but they assigned top Kennedy attendants—John Seigenthaler, Richard Goodwin, Ed Guthman—to comb through it and pressure a resistant Manchester to make changes. In December, Bobby and Jackie filed suit to prevent the book's publication, either in whole or in part. When Manchester sought refuge from the front-page controversy in a Manhattan hotel room (en route to a European vacation), RFK banged on the door and demanded admittance. Once inside, he shrieked at the author, going so far as to threaten physical violence. The senator and his former lover eventually dropped the suit after Manchester agreed to a number of modifications and to donate a percentage of his royalties to the John F. Kennedy Library in Boston.

RFK received credit in the press for acting the gallant knight, rushing to defend his sister-in-law's dignity. And the passages which Jackie disputed did include intimate details of the first couple's married life: Jack walking around in his undershorts before retiring, Jackie examining her face for wrinkles. Bobby supported Jackie's protests, but his own objections centered on the book's depiction of his relations with Lyndon Johnson. Manchester later recalled RFK's "protective attitude toward LBJ," reasoning that "Bobby and his political advisers decided that some of the passages in the book might be used against Bob if he should run, as they all assumed he eventually would, for national office." Were a Kennedy-authorized book to treat the president shabbily, Bobby would appear petty and vindictive. Publicly alienating the president and his friends was no way to go about succeeding him.*

---

*Previously, Bobby had angrily forced Red Fay, JFK's old PT boat buddy who'd served as undersecretary of the navy, to delete an inordinate percentage of his manuscript of *The Pleasure of His Company* (1966). The book was innocuous enough, but RFK complained that the personal details Fay had revealed about the late president (including sexual innuendo) tended to "diminish" his memory. Bobby's fifteen-year friendship with Fay never recovered from the dispute.

At heart, Robert Kennedy was a loyalist.* Dean Rusk, Robert McNamara, Walt Rostow, Maxwell Taylor—the architects of Lyndon Johnson's war—had been builders of the New Frontier. While senator, Bobby continued to seek the counsel of both McNamara, who had privately given up on winning the war even as he publicly continued to insist victory was near, and Taylor, who served as ambassador to South Vietnam in 1964–65 and remained a true believer. "It had always seemed to me," said George McGovern, "that right until the end he had the highest regard for McNamara and Taylor and great personal affection for both of them. I don't know why he continued to have such a high regard for their judgment, in view of how wrong they were on Vietnam, but, nevertheless, he did. To the best of my knowledge, he went to his death thinking that Taylor and McNamara were two of the ablest men ever to serve in government. I had a very high regard for their brilliance and their ability, but I was always somewhat puzzled as to why he continued to seek them out for advice."

But the most prominent of the New Frontiersmen who had helped John Kennedy begin America's war in Vietnam was Bobby himself. "Let every nation know," announced JFK at his inauguration, "whether it wishes us well or ill, that we shall pay any price, bear any burden, meet any hardship, support any friend, oppose any foe to assure the survival and the success of liberty." Author David Halberstam commented, "The Kennedy people had taken over from the Eisenhower people, who were flabby and soft; the Kennedy people saw themselves as eggheads, but tough. . . . And Bobby was very important in this thing. There was a way somehow that they were going to do this; it was going to be an American decade of intellectualism harnessed to toughness."

To battle communism in the Third World, the Kennedy administra-

---

* RFK could at times be somewhat less than loyal. When he heard that Jackie Kennedy had given Evelyn Lincoln, JFK's personal secretary, several items of historic interest—including President Kennedy's handwritten journals from a 1951 trip to Eastern Europe, a personalized silver Tiffany calendar marking the Cuban missile crisis, and JFK's Hermès black-leather briefcase—he became enraged. "He showed up at my house and insisted I return the items," Evelyn Lincoln told the current author. "I told him Jackie had given them to me. He said he didn't care, they belonged to the family and would eventually be placed in the John F. Kennedy Library. At one point he picked up a vase and threw it, flowers and all, against the wall. I asked him to leave. He said he would return with a warrant for my arrest. I said to him—this was 1966—'Bobby, your days as attorney general are over. Why don't you concentrate on being a good senator?' He continued to send me Christmas cards and never again mentioned the incident, at least not to me. Frankly, he could be a real boor."

tion embraced "flexible response," a concept, said educator James C. Thomson, Jr., in part cooked up by "social scientists ensconced up at MIT and Harvard, racking their feeble brains through the fifties trying to find some 'answer' to guerrilla warfare since, admittedly, air power and bombing and the like weren't the answer. Now, you add to that the Kennedy family ethic of toughness, touch football, sexuality, the cult of vigor. Robert Kennedy was sold, to some extent, a bill of goods—the notion of counterinsurgency."

As mastermind of America's counterinsurgency efforts, RFK had overseen the first applications of U.S.-made napalm and chemical defoliants—sometimes from planes flown by American pilots—to the jungles and villages of South Vietnam. Notes from insurgency group meetings reveal that when the organization's members discussed the defoliation program, designed to destroy crops and livestock the enemy might use, they expressed no interest in the campaign's results. Rather, they focused only on whether Operation Hades, as the venture was initially called, or Operation Ranchhand, as it was euphemistically renamed, had the approval of the South Vietnamese military. "Untroubled about the consequences of those initiatives," said John White, "government leaders initiated a decade of destruction in Vietnam. The barbarism of our conduct in Vietnam, which gave fire to an intense antiwar movement during the Johnson Administration, started with these little-noticed programs of the Kennedy Administration."

And Bobby had led the way. "He had been a great enthusiast for clandestine operations," commented George Ball of the State Department, the in-house critic on Vietnam for both JFK and LBJ, "and we disagreed completely on Vietnam because he was at that time pushing JFK strongly for it and I was very much against it. He was fascinated by the idea of clandestine operations, counterinsurgency. I thought it was all nonsense."

Senator Kennedy's mute public posture on LBJ's Vietnam policy was matched by a private reticence about the role Attorney General Kennedy had played in the war's origins. "He was rather reluctant to discuss that period," said author Norman Mailer, "other than to say that he was one of those involved in supporting the policy." Bobby was well aware, to his shame, that his predicament over Vietnam was partly of his own making.

When John Kennedy gave his inaugural address, there were 685 American military advisers in Vietnam. When he was buried, just weeks after his administration cooperated in the overthrow and murder of South Vietnamese president Ngo Dinh Diem, there were over 16,000. John and Robert Kennedy had led America to the shores of the quagmire in which by late 1966 it stood waist deep. Before Dallas, JFK did send a few ambiguous signals that he intended to withdraw U.S. forces following the 1964 election. The preponderance of evidence, however, suggests that had he lived, he would have maintained, and intensified, American involvement. Interviewed by the press only a few months after Jack's death, RFK stated that "the president felt that there was a strong, overwhelming reason for being in Vietnam and that we should win the war in Vietnam." Asked if JFK had ever considered pulling out, Bobby's reply was an unequivocal "No."*

Concerning assertions that John Kennedy was preparing to leave Vietnam, Leslie Gelb remarked, "I don't believe that for a minute, I mean not for a minute." Gelb, the former foreign-affairs columnist for the *New York Times,* worked in the sixties for the Defense Department. "Everything that you can lay your hands on, other than a remark thrown off to Senator Mansfield, another remark to Kenney O'Donnell, everything else pointed in the direction of his being prepared to do whatever was necessary not to lose." After-the-fact claims by Kennedy acolytes to the contrary are not credible, insisted Gelb. "There's just a startling difference between the early memoirs written by those who were close to him and the later memoirs. If you look at what Arthur Schlesinger and Ted Sorensen wrote about Kennedy and Vietnam right after they left government, they all said Kennedy was committed to sticking it out. They all quoted those interviews JFK gave to [Walter] Cronkite and [David] Brinkley as symbolic of the president's views at the end of his life. But by the end of the sixties, early seventies, they rewrote it themselves. I trust the earlier accounts."

For Bobby to criticize the war now, forcefully and forthrightly, would be to confess his own guilt in the national catastrophe rapidly unfolding. And it would be to admit the flaw in the "legacy" left by his beloved brother. Lyndon Johnson had no doubt he was following the inheritance left him by his predecessor. For had there been no escalation, he ranted to historian Doris Kearns, "there would be no Robert Kennedy out in front, leading the fight against me, telling everyone that I had betrayed

---

* Recently unclassified files pertaining to the Special Counterinsurgency Group reveal that in late 1962, the Kennedy administration asked the CIA to prepare a report on the prospects of a major military offensive by the United States in Vietnam. The resultant document (May 29, 1963) called for a massive increase of counterinsurgency war games; it also concluded that "We are [currently] winning the war in Vietnam. Current statistical indicators reflect favorable trends, and the most significant development is the increase in volume of spontaneous intelligence provided by the people. This is because the Government is now providing them with security from the Viet Cong."

John Kennedy's commitment to South Vietnam. That I had let a democracy fall into the hands of the Communists. That I was a coward. An unmanly man. A man without a spine. Oh, I could see it coming all right. Every night when I fell asleep I would see myself tied to the ground in the middle of a long, open space. In the distance, I could hear the voices of thousands of people. They were all shouting at me and running toward me: 'Coward! Traitor! Weakling!' "

Even the mild disapproval Bobby had directed toward him through 1966 drove Lyndon Johnson to rage. The president was haunted by the ghost of John F. Kennedy, and by the ghost's living representative. Vietnam would be the New Frontier's (as well as the Great Society's) most lasting legacy.

Among the meetings RFK held during his ten-day European trip that began in late January of 1967 was a session in Paris with Étienne Manac'h, the Far East desk officer of the French foreign ministry. Speaking in French, Manac'h told Bobby that the North Vietnamese would engage in negotiations with the Americans if the bombing of the North were halted. John Gunther Dean of the State Department, who acted as the non-French-speaking senator's interpreter for the conversation, recognized the significance of the diplomatic nuance: the North Vietnamese were waiving other, previously declared preconditions to talks. But Bobby, whose mind may have been wandering to his dinner with Candice Bergen, apparently missed the point. "I remember the State Department fellow was very excited," Bobby later told Frank Mankiewicz, "and wrote it all down and, as we were driving away in the car, said to me, 'Well, I think that was extremely important what he said.' So I said, 'Well, yes, I'm sure it was very important.' But you know the way those fellows are, they're always talking like that. And then before I left Paris, the State Department fellow showed me a cable that he was going to send and wanted to know if I had agreed that it was an accurate account of our conversation. Well, I had no idea whether it was an accurate account of our conversation or not. I mean, if he said it was, then I assumed it was because Manac'h spoke in French. So I said, 'Sure, I suppose it was.' "

After marking the cable to indicate the senator had approved it, Dean sent it to the State Department: a department employee read it and promptly leaked it to *Newsweek*. The *New York Times* managed to procure a copy of the cable, and before Bobby had arrived home the newspaper released a front-page story stating that Senator Kennedy, negotiating on his own, had received a "peace feeler." President Johnson, already angry that his rival had been abroad conferring with foreign leaders, assumed that RFK had gone to *Newsweek* with the wire in order to force him to the negotiating table.

Back in Washington amid the uproar, Bobby decided he should speak to Johnson to clear up the misunderstanding. On February 7, two days after his return from Europe, RFK visited the chief executive. The two men fought, Johnson accusing Kennedy of leaking the story to "that God-awful *Newsweek* magazine." Bobby countered: "With all due respect, I believe the leak came from somebody in your State Department." "My State Department," rejoined the president. "It's your fucking State Department, not mine!" Victory in Vietnam was imminent, LBJ continued. He had plans to escalate the bombing. Bobby urged him to consider de-escalation, in fact a complete halt to bombing, followed by negotiations (as overseen by an international commission) and the formation of a co-alition government (which would hopefully conduct elections). "There just isn't a chance in hell that I would do that," said LBJ. "Not a chance in hell."

The argument raged on, the president threatening to "destroy" Bobby politically—"and all your dumbassed dove friends. You'll be dead in six months. I'll fucking bury you!" After a few more insults, Bobby rose and said: "I don't have to take this shit from you." RFK didn't walk out just yet. Nicholas Katzenbach and Walt Rostow tried to quiet the tempers—but the meeting soon broke up with the senator grudgingly agreeing to tell the press that he had not brought home any peace initiative.

"I seldom saw him shaken," Peter Edelman said of his boss, "but he came back shaken from that encounter." Bobby had seen and heard enough. The president's invective convinced him that he no longer had reason to conceal either his opposition to the war or his feud with the war's commander. He asked Adam Walinsky to draft a major speech taking issue with Johnson's policy and calling for the peace plan he had described to the president during their confrontation.

Anticipation over Bobby's planned address mounted during the ensuing days and weeks, as the senator gave hints of what was to come: On February 10, in a talk at the University of Chicago on America's China policy, he denied that the Chinese had inspired the Vietnamese Communists to fight; on February 26, speaking before the liberal group Americans for Democratic Action, he blamed the war for dividing the nation's generations. The *New York Times* featured a story in expectation of RFK's Vietnam speech, and LBJ launched a preemptive attack on it through appearances by administration officials on a bevy of television news programs. When the day for the address arrived, LBJ, in an attempt to divert coverage of the event, gave three impromptu speeches and held a press conference. The president's lightly veiled efforts only drew more attention to RFK's long overdue antiwar declaration.

Walinsky's original text had been reworked by Peter Edelman, Burke Marshall, Arthur Schlesinger and others. Frank Mankiewicz and Richard Goodwin completed it on March 1, the day before its delivery, not stopping until four the next morning. Bobby had left them only half an hour earlier.

Edelman recalled reading the final version: "Kennedy came in and said, 'Am I dove enough for you?' And I said, 'No,' because . . . the criticism had been muted and the stuff really about the fact that the whole war was foolish had been muted and so on and so forth. And Kennedy was sticking to the position [that] he was neither for escalation nor for unilateral withdrawal, but was for negotiation. And you know, there was still that premise that . . . what we were fighting for made some sense, if it were done right. And by that time I was off that."

At 4 P.M., March 2, 1967, RFK spoke before a packed Senate chamber and gallery. He began by acknowledging "the grave and painful responsibility borne by the president of the United States. As he must make the ultimate decisions, he is also entitled to our hopeful sympathy, our understanding, and our support in the search for peace."

He then looked back. We are not here "to curse the past or to praise it," he said. "Three presidents have taken action in Vietnam. As one who was involved in many of those decisions, I can testify that if fault is to be found or responsibility assessed, there is enough to go round for all— including myself."

Bobby laid on a generous supply of jingoist boilerplate: "The fault rests largely with our adversary. He has pursued relentless and unyielding conquest with obdurate unconcern for mounting desolation." A Harris poll taken just prior to the speech reported 70 percent of the nation still in support of LBJ's policy. Bobby felt compelled to express his fundamental loyalty to his country and its soldiers.

Yet the main point of the speech was not the enemy's responsibility, but our own: "It is not just a nation's responsibility but yours and mine. It is we who live in abundance and send our young men out to die. It is our chemicals that scorch the children and our bombs that level the villages."

RFK followed this by outlining his proposal for peace, concluding:

And if we pursue this program, it will at least help us to know we have done everything we can be expected to do, that we have let neither pride nor fear deter us in the quest for peace. We owe no less to ourselves, our people, and to those whose land we both protect and ravage. The stakes are very high: They are the home of the child in a jungle village, the hunger of a man driven from his farm, the life of a young American even now preparing for the day's battle. There is great principle, and there is also human anguish. If we can protect the one and prevent the other, then there is no effort too great for us to make.

Bobby had not, as Peter Edelman had wanted him to, condemned the very idea of Americans fighting in Vietnam, an idea that had originated in the councils of the Kennedy administration, when RFK had been the nation's virtual co-president.* But he had at last begun to do penance for the war he had helped inflict on his country. By his speech, Bobby made clear that he considered Vietnam now to be Lyndon Johnson's war. It was a Kennedy war no longer.

---

* "It's fair to say," noted Ken O'Donnell, "that Robert Kennedy spent nearly as much time in the Oval Office as Jack, and sometimes more. As President Kennedy's appointments secretary, I was certainly in a position to know."

24

THE CHALLENGE

In mid-September 1967, Allard Lowenstein, the thirty-eight-year-old liberal activist from New York, paid a visit to Hickory Hill. That summer, he had begun to mount a movement to "Dump Johnson in '68." Now he was urging Robert Kennedy to lead the effort by running for LBJ's job. Toppling the president was not only necessary, argued Lowenstein to the senator and the Kennedy intimates present, it was also feasible: Johnson could be defeated in the early primaries, and if he were, he might quickly bow out of the race. "I wholeheartedly agree," said RFK. "Lyndon's a coward and a quitter, but I'd have problems if I ran against him. People would accuse me of personal malice, of splitting the party, of running not because I disagree with his policies but simply because I hate the man. I'd be dead in the water before I began. You'll have to find some other sacrificial lamb to oppose him." Bobby's arguments were well formed—he'd been mulling over a challenge to Johnson for months.

Since his Vietnam breakthrough speech on March 2, Kennedy had continued to offer statements on the subject. In April, he rose in the Senate to criticize a policy based on achieving a peace by destroying the enemy through "the systematic use of bombs and military intervention." Battlefield conduct was not the only aspect of the war he condemned. In mid-March, before faculty and students at the University of Oklahoma, he was asked his stand on educational draft deferments. He replied that he opposed them: while he possessed the funds to send his own children to college, it was a clear moral wrong that a young man's fate should rest with the size of his parents' checkbook. "There was an explosion of hissing and booing," reported Oklahoma senator Fred Harris, who attended the speech and later wrote about it.

442

"Let me ask you a few questions," said RFK. "How many here support continuing the deferments?" The audience cheered loudly. "And how many of you support an escalation of the war?" Again, the young people approved. "Let me ask you one final question. . . . How many of you who voted for the escalation of the war also voted for the exemption of students from the draft?" Grasping the significance of Bobby's words, the audience emitted a "giant gasp," as Harris noted, followed by a standing ovation.

Campus turmoil over the war, in addition to unprecedented urban disorder—during the summer of 1967, Newark, Los Angeles and Detroit had led the list of cities to erupt—created in the minds of many Americans an image of a disintegrating nation. To Bobby's dismay, Lyndon Johnson had little response to the crisis of the cities. The vision of his Great Society seemed to be fading before the realities of financing a massive land war half a world away from the poverty and strife of America's ghettos. "I suppose I am dissatisfied with our society, our country," Bobby said on *Meet the Press* in August. Americans agreed, and they began looking to Bobby for help: three days after Allard Lowenstein's visit to Hickory Hill, a national poll gave the senator from New York a twenty-four-point edge over the president.

On October 8, Pierre Salinger gathered several of Kennedy's advisers at the Regency Hotel in New York. The purpose of the meeting, which RFK himself did not attend, was to discuss the issue of a presidential bid. Ted Sorensen counseled most forcefully against a run—Bobby should bide his time, said the speechwriter; he should wait until 1972. Nothing was decided, except to authorize Joe Dolan to begin sounding out party leaders around the country.

While Bobby and his circle dithered, one "sacrificial lamb" had decided to take up Lowenstein's challenge. Senator Eugene McCarthy of Minnesota had threatened to run against Johnson if no one else did, and on November 30 he stopped waiting and declared his candidacy. McCarthy's bold entry made Bobby see the risks of his own caution. George McGovern received a telephone call from Kennedy "in which he expressed concern that I would make an early commitment to McCarthy and that others would do the same—and this would make it difficult for anyone else to enter the race at a later point. I think he wished he had announced for the presidency himself," said McGovern, "because he observed that the country couldn't possibly endure another term of Lyndon Johnson."

Although he expressed private rage over LBJ, in public he continued to denounce only the man's politics. His attacks, however, were more lethal in nature than those he had previously levied. In November, when a majority of students in his audience at a Catholic women's college in New York City called for more bombing, he exploded: "Do you understand what that means? It means you are voting to send people, Americans and Vietnamese, to die. Don't you understand that what we are doing to the Vietnamese is not very different than what Hitler did to the Jews?" When, shortly thereafter, Robert McNamara was squeezed out of the Department of Defense and into the chairmanship of the World Bank, Bobby felt that the administration had lost its strongest internal brake on further escalation.

On December 10, there was another meeting at RFK's inner sanctum. William vanden Heuvel hosted a luncheon at his New York home, with Ted and Robert Kennedy, Ted Sorensen, Richard Goodwin, Fred Dutton, Pierre Salinger, Ken O'Donnell and Arthur Schlesinger in attendance.* Schlesinger and Goodwin favored an immediate candidacy, but the senator from Massachusetts argued that Bobby had no chance of dethroning Johnson and should wait until 1972, when his nomination would be assured. Bobby countered that four years to prepare for a campaign would also be four years to accumulate more enemies. Furthermore, a reelected LBJ would work night and day to keep RFK from succeeding him. As the meeting broke up Bobby sighed, "We haven't decided anything, so I guess I'm not running."

RFK and his advisers recognized that support moving toward Gene McCarthy would be difficult to recapture, and a race against the incumbent would, at best, be problematic. Early in 1967, Bobby had asked Barrett Prettyman, a Washington lawyer who had been his special assistant at the Justice Department, if he should run. "I told him that the reason I was opposed to it," recalled Prettyman, "was that I thought Lyndon Johnson would go to any lengths to see him defeated and that I didn't put it past the president to do anything, from manufacturing gossip on down, in order to scuttle him, and that I was very much afraid that, in view of the power of the presidency and the power particularly to manipulate events, I thought he was doomed to failure." LBJ, feared Bobby, would escalate or de-escalate the war according to the demands of politics. Even the members of the antiwar faction in the Senate offered

---

*RFK lightheartedly assigned the initials "K.P.I" to identify his circle of followers: Kennedy Political Industries. It amazed Roswell Gilpatric, among others, that RFK could elicit such loyalty from many of the same people who had supported JFK: "Some of these fellows seemed to have no lives of their own; they existed simply to keep the Kennedy machinery clicking. That always struck me as somewhat sad."

Bobby little encouragement; many were up for reelection in 1968 and were loath to incur the president's wrath. Among party chieftains nationwide, Joe Dolan could turn up only one—Jesse Unruh, boss of California—to offer firm backing. Bobby did hear that Mayor Daley of Chicago had come to see the war as folly—a dear friend of his had lost his nineteen-year-old son in battle. But even the boss of bosses was not ready to abandon a sitting president of his own party.

To Bobby, a run seemed doomed to failure. It would split the Democrats and lead to the worst possible outcome, the election of Republican front-runner Richard Nixon. Above all, he worried that the American people would see the race not as a contest over issues, but rather, he told questioners on *Face the Nation* in late November, as "a personality struggle," in which "an overly ambitious figure [was] trying to take the nomination away from President Johnson, who deserves it because of the fact that he is not only president but served the Democratic Party and the country as president for four or five years." Bobby could not bring himself to step forward: "I expect that [President Johnson] is going to receive the nomination and I will support him."

Many friends and acquaintances of Robert Kennedy urged him to jump in. "While most of us agreed with Gene McCarthy's opposition to the war," Manfred Ohrenstein remembered of his fellow reform Democrats in New York, "we all felt he was totally unqualified to be president. I used to characterize him as a great poet, and I didn't want a poet to be president. We were constantly arguing with Bobby that he had to run, because a primary fight between Gene McCarthy and Lyndon Johnson made no sense. We were not really for Gene McCarthy for president."

By January, Bobby's indecision induced other admirers to take a harder line. Greek film star Melina Mercouri flirted with RFK at a United Nations cocktail party, then told him she admired men who took chances in life. Grace Kelly, a secret lover of JFK, offered to return from Monaco to campaign for Bobby if he ran. Abe Ribicoff, former secretary of Health, Education and Welfare under JFK sent Bobby a Western Union: "It's now or never." André Meyer pledged untold financial support in the event RFK joined the campaign. "What truly jolted Bobby," said Joe Dolan, was a placard he saw a student carrying when he spoke at Brooklyn College; it read: "ROBERT KENNEDY—HAWK, DOVE OR CHICKEN?"

Lyndon Johnson didn't doubt that Bobby would run, and he dreaded the prospect. "The last thing LBJ wanted," said Abe Ribicoff, "was to go down in history as the man who occupied the Oval Office between two Kennedy administrations. Like most politicians, he had an enormous ego,* as did Bobby." RFK's candidacy would confirm LBJ's worst night-mare. The native of Texas ranch country described to Doris Kearns his recurrent dream of being restrained in a chair in the middle of a cow pasture: "I felt that I was being chased on all sides by a giant stampede. I was being forced over the edge by rioting blacks, demonstrating students, marching welfare mothers, squawking professors, and hysterical report-ers. And then the final straw. The thing I feared from the first day of my presidency was actually coming true. Robert Kennedy had openly announced his intention to reclaim the throne in the memory of his brother. And the American people, swayed by the magic of the name, were dancing in the streets."

One solution to Bobby's dilemma would have been to support Mc-Carthy. But for all RFK's contempt of Lyndon Johnson, he held the sena-tor from Minnesota in only slightly higher regard. "Kennedy didn't like McCarthy," recalled Peter Edelman. "That . . . I think went back to 1960 when McCarthy tried to shaft John Kennedy.† And of course, how people had regarded John Kennedy and what they had done either for or against him was a tremendous touchstone in Robert Kennedy's life. . . . So he had this general antipathy toward McCarthy. He felt, I think with some justification, that McCarthy was less than totally honest in his politics in the Senate Finance Committee, that he may not have taken bribes, but he had certainly represented the special interests of certain groups, and one supposed that that was how his campaign coffers got filled since he wasn't personally a wealthy man. Secondly, it was perfectly obvious that Eugene McCarthy was a lazy senator, that you could not count on him to show up for votes when you needed him and that sometimes he would even vote against you. . . . And so [RFK] remarked from time to time that McCarthy was lazy and didn't do anything."

The senator from Minnesota was disdainful in return. "McCarthy had known John Kennedy since 1949 when they were both in the House of Representatives," noted journalist Al Eisele. "And while he respected Kennedy, he resented all the advantages he'd had. McCarthy was not only Catholic like Jack, he had matriculated at and subsequently taught in a select Benedictine college. He considered himself more expert than

---

*LBJ's ego took on a multitude of forms. Once at a 1965 meeting with J. Edgar Hoover and several agents, the subject of President Kennedy's prolific womanizing arose. Exercised, LBJ unbuttoned his trousers, reached inside, withdrew his penis and thumped it atop a glass coffee table. "Now tell me," he said to those gathered, "do you think Mr. Kennedy could ever have measured up to the size of that motherfucker?"

†Edelman refers to the rousing nominating speech McCarthy gave on behalf of Adlai Stevenson at that year's Democratic convention.

John Kennedy on subjects both political—like history—and spiritual—like philosophy. But the rich handsome New Englander, renowned among his colleagues as a playboy, had garnered fame as the nation's premier Catholic politician while the provincial Midwesterner, who approached his faith with sober obligation, remained obscure. Now the intellectual Minnesotan with the surprisingly elegant wit was facing Jack's younger brother, who convened seminars to be taught the elements of higher learning that McCarthy had acquired as a youth, and without the benefit of enrollment at Harvard. RFK loved poetry. McCarthy wrote poetry."

Still, as Eugene McCarthy was mounting his campaign, he was under no illusion that he could match RFK in terms of the national stature so vital to an attempt at ousting a sitting president. Near the end of 1967, said Peter Edelman, McCarthy met with Bobby and "told him . . . obviously not thinking of himself as a tremendously serious candidate at that point . . . and thinking Kennedy would be better, 'If you get into it, I'll get out.' "

But Bobby would not get into it. Ethel, Jean Smith, Goodwin, Schlesinger and Unruh were urging him to run, but his brother and most of the professional political operatives in the Kennedy orbit were urging him to stay put. He was at a loss. Cosmetics heir John Revson overheard a conversation Bobby had during this period at a New York City restaurant. "Gee," Bobby told his dining companion, "I wish my ailing father were able to speak so that he could tell me what to do."

On January 23, 1968, the day North Korean forces captured the *Pueblo,* an American vessel engaged in intelligence operations, RFK had lunch with actor Rod Steiger and director Mike Nichols, both of whom encouraged him to declare his candidacy. "I can't do it," RFK told them. "That evening he telephoned his father in Palm Beach," said Ken O'Donnell. "He told Joe he wasn't going to run. Rose came on the line and said his father would support any decision he made. Bobby then prepared a press release stipulating that he would not oppose Lyndon Johnson under any 'conceivable circumstances.' When Joe Dolan heard that, he prevailed upon Frank Mankiewicz to get Bobby to change 'conceivable' to 'foreseeable,' a less definitive stance. Dolan, Adam Walinsky and Peter Edelman all informed Bobby that under the circumstances they saw little point in continuing to work for him; they wanted to find another way of defeating Johnson. Allard Lowenstein, who'd already begun working for McCarthy, came by and rubbed more salt in Bobby's wounds. 'You could've become president,' he told him, 'but you don't have the balls.' "

An event soon took place that shifted RFK's perspective. On January 30, North Vietnamese and Vietcong forces loosed a surprise attack throughout the South. The offensive began just as the people of Vietnam were celebrating the lunar new year. They called the holiday "Tet."

W hen the Communist enemy stormed the U.S. embassy in Saigon, the American people finally saw through the rosy fantasies of imminent victory Lyndon Johnson and his generals had been spinning. The American and South Vietnamese armies quickly recovered their footing, but the Tet offensive ended LBJ's credibility for good.

Also gone was Bobby's caution—at least oratorically. On February 8, 1968, he spoke to editors, writers, and sales personnel at a book-industry luncheon in Chicago. "Our enemy," he proclaimed, "savagely striking at will across all of South Vietnam, has finally shattered the mask of official illusion with which we have concealed our true circumstances, even from ourselves." We cannot, he added, "win a war which the South Vietnamese cannot win for themselves." As before, he did not call for withdrawal, but instead for immediate negotiations. "The best way to save our most precious stake in Vietnam—the lives of our soldiers—is to stop the enlargement of the war, and the best way to end casualties is to end the war." Jeff Greenfield, then a twenty-four-year-old speechwriter for RFK, described the address as "wholly different in tone from anything he'd ever said on Vietnam—no attempt to preserve the bridges to the administration that was so much a part of the other speeches. . . . The February 8 speech was simply an angry statement of a man who was . . . disgusted with the way the policy was going."

A month later, Kennedy was further distressed when he heard from the Pentagon's Daniel Ellsberg that the Joint Chiefs of Staff had responded to Tet with a request that an additional 206,000 troops be sent to Vietnam to join the half million already there. "The fact is that victory is not just ahead of us," Bobby said in the Senate on March 7. "It was not in 1961 or 1962, when I was one of those who predicted that there was a light at the end of the tunnel. There was not in 1963 or 1964 or 1965 or 1966 or 1967, and there is not now. Moreover, there is a question of our moral responsibility. Are we like the God of the Old Testament that we can decide, in Washington, D.C., what cities, what towns, what hamlets in Vietnam are going to be destroyed?" Bobby railed against "the corruption of the South Vietnamese regime," then, for the first time in public, lashed out directly at LBJ. "When this [corruption] was brought to the attention of the president, he replied that there is stealing in Beaumont,

Texas. If there is stealing in Beaumont, Texas, it is not bringing about the certain death of American boys."

As they witnessed the transformation in the senator's attitude, RFK's advisers also noted a shifting electorate. "Our best friend in New Hampshire was Bill Dunfey, a national committeeman up there," said Joe Dolan. "And he and I had thought Bobby would win the New Hampshire primary. And when I told Bobby so, he kind of screwed up his face.

"That was before Tet. Johnson was popular in New Hampshire. The state had a lot of veterans—from Korea, World War II—and the war in Vietnam was not regarded as badly there as in other places. But after Tet—I think Tet shifted everything around."

Tet shifted everything around for Eugene McCarthy, too. His thus far uninspired and uninspiring campaign metamorphosed into a sacred quest—a "Children's Crusade," so called for the legions of college students who trekked to the Granite State on behalf of the white knight doing battle with the evil king. They cut their hair and changed their clothes to make themselves "Clean for Gene" as they set about wooing flinty New Hampshirites two, three and four times their age. Even before Jack's death, Bobby had made of the young a special constituency. Now they were flocking to another suitor.

Bobby seemed to intuit that history was summoning him, and that so far he had failed to heed the call. Theodore White remembered a telephone conversation he had with Bobby late one night: "He said he'd been reading his mail and that hundreds of college students had written letters encouraging him to run. 'If you don't listen to them,' I said, 'you'll lose them.' 'Do you think I should run?' he asked. 'Indeed, I do.' 'Maybe I should. I'm not as gung-ho as I ought to be, but on the other hand I can't take another dose of that war-crazed cowpuncher.'"

The New Hampshire primary would take place on March 12. Three days before, RFK traveled to Iowa to appear at a political dinner for the state's governor, Harold Hughes. After the meal, Bobby conferred privately with Hughes, as well as the Democratic governors of Missouri, Kansas and North Dakota. John Seigenthaler and John Reilly, the Chicago operative who'd worked with Bobby in 1960, sat in on the meeting. "They had all come up at the suggestion of Hughes," Reilly remembered, "and they were trying to convince him to run. Well, he was reluctant, standoffish from the importuning, and they kept after him. I think they left the meeting feeling they hadn't gotten very far. And afterward Bobby turned to us, Seigenthaler and myself, and said, 'What the hell were you guys just sitting there for?' And we said we didn't think it was our role to stick our nose into the conversation with four governors. And he said,

'That's the trouble.' And I said, 'What do you mean?' And he said, 'I don't have anybody who plays me, I don't have anybody who does what I did for Jack. I used to ask, "How many votes do you have for Jack?" and you guys aren't doing that for me.'"

He said the same to others. "I don't have anybody to do for me what I did for my brother," Peter Edelman remembered RFK as complaining. Just as John Kennedy had had a younger brother, so now did Bobby. "I think [RFK] looked to [Ted] for political advice," said Edelman, "but not with a great deal of confidence. . . . He would always talk to Teddy before he did anything that was major, if for nothing else [than] to tell him that he was going to do it. But, you know, it just wasn't the same thing. He and John Kennedy had grown up together and been partners for a long period of time. And Teddy had never been a partner of his. He and Teddy . . . had had separate political careers." Teddy could never be Bobby's Bobby.

Ted continued to oppose the candidacy into March. He realized, however, that his brother was not likely to follow his advice. Barrett Prettyman recalled discussing the issue with the senator from Massachusetts: "While Ted had a great number of reservations about Bob running, I think [he] probably felt at that point that he sensed in Bob a compulsion to do it, and that Bob would never really be at peace with himself if he didn't and, I think for that reason, felt it had to be done. And that was more or less the conclusion that I had come to."

From Iowa, Bobby flew to California. Violent incidents had taken place in response to the struggles of the United Farm Workers, and Cesar Chavez had staged a hunger strike as penance. Now the union leader was about to break his fast at a Catholic mass in Delano, to which he had invited Bobby. A huge crowd turned out to witness the event. Paul Schrade, a United Auto Workers organizer who would imminently become the labor vice chairman of RFK's campaign, recalled Bobby passing Chavez the communion bread, then telling the press that he had come to California "to pay homage to a modern-day hero." After the ceremony, said Schrade, "Bobby made his way through a surging crowd, down a path to his waiting car where he shook hundreds of hands and talked to people who basked in the reflection of his bright smile. Then I lost sight of him. Dolores Huerta later told me that at a certain point his mood suddenly darkened. Before stepping into his car, he pointed to some guy and without explanation said, 'That man wants to kill me.'"

Bobby flew from California to New York, where he met with Ken O'Donnell and Roswell Gilpatric to discuss the prospect of entering the race. "He felt if he did enter, McCarthy would bow out," said Gilpatric.

"I didn't agree with him." RFK also spoke to Joseph Rauh, one of the founders of the liberal group Americans for Democratic Action, who suggested that the senator endorse McCarthy in New Hampshire. "Such a move," Rauh told RFK, "might make McCarthy more amenable to quitting should you decide to enter." "That may be true," responded Bobby, "but I can't endorse somebody I don't believe in."

As it developed, McCarthy didn't require Kennedy's endorsement. On March 12, the voters of New Hampshire cast 49.6 percent of its ballots for LBJ (all in the form of write-in votes) against 41.9 percent for a previously little-known Midwestern senator. The president's margin was far less than expected. Moreover, due to the vote's distribution, the now well-known senator walked away with twenty of the state's twenty-four convention delegates.

In one sense, the New Hampshire vote liberated Bobby, said Ken O'Donnell, it "freed him from the fear that his entry would be regarded by the professionals in the party as a party-splitting act. After all, it was quite clear from the results in New Hampshire that the party was already hopelessly split. Conversely, the fact that McCarthy had done so well gave birth to a problem Bobby hadn't anticipated. It became known as 'the McCarthy Problem,' and part of the dilemma was not only that many Democrats had already cast their lot with McCarthy but that McCarthy was going to be in there for the duration of the campaign. Not that McCarthy on his own could win—he couldn't—but he could certainly make life more difficult for our man."

According to LaVern Duffy, RFK spent the night of March 12 at the Carlyle with "an exquisitely stacked blonde from Sweden who had been featured in *Playboy*." Duffy claimed he'd made the arrangements directly with Hugh Hefner, "who'd extolled the lady's virtues. As far as I know, Bobby had no complaints."

The following morning, said Duffy, "RFK flew to Washington and met with Eugene McCarthy. He congratulated McCarthy and then informed him he was considering entering the campaign. McCarthy, who had no intention of withdrawing, did offer a compromise: in exchange for RFK's endorsement, he would agree to serve but one term as president and would then try to ensure that Bobby was elected to succeed him." Bobby later told Peter Edelman he thought the offer represented the height of *chutzpah*.

RFK countered with a proposition of his own: he would support McCarthy in Wisconsin, where the filing deadline for the primary had already passed, in exchange for McCarthy's backing elsewhere. McCarthy, who had joined the battle while the senator from New York sat on the sidelines twiddling his thumbs, wasn't interested in striking a deal.

Bobby flew back to New York that afternoon to attend a meeting of his aides and advisers at the home of Stephen Smith, the purpose of which was to decide on a course of action regarding Bobby's candidacy. Recapping the session, Barrett Prettyman recalled that Burke Marshall favored RFK's immediate entry into the race, whereas Ted Sorensen as before adopted a more tentative stance. Arthur Schlesinger suggested an alliance with McCarthy similar to what Bobby had presented as an option earlier in the day. "To be perfectly frank," remarked Prettyman, "there were some views from Arthur Schlesinger that struck me as naive and impractical, and others at the gathering shared my reaction. Joining forces with the McCarthy team was a plan that had no basis in practical politics; it just didn't seem feasible."

Prettyman added that "for the entire first half of the evening we were under the assumption that we were there to help RFK render a decision, but then . . . when somebody switched on the television and we watched the Walter Cronkite Report, we discovered that the decision had already been made. RFK had taped the Cronkite interview while still in Washington and all but announced his candidacy. 'What the hell are we debating here?' said Ted Kennedy. 'He's made up his mind.' There was a good deal of laughter."

There remained one final stepping stone. Lyndon Johnson had indicated prior to the New Hampshire primary that he would consider the possibility of appointing a presidential commission to study the military situation in Vietnam and to propose an acceptable solution. One idea, suggested Johnson, would be for RFK to head such a commission and to recommend the names of other potential members.

"I told Bobby it was absurd," said Ken O'Donnell, "that in the end Johnson would never agree to the formation of a Vietnam Commission. Nevertheless, the morning following the Cronkite Report, Kennedy and Sorensen flew to Washington to meet with Clark Clifford, the new secretary of defense, at the Pentagon. Bobby presented Clifford with his list of prospective commission members, and Clifford practically laughed them out of his office. LBJ concurred: he could not allow a committee to dictate foreign policy."

The final obstacle had been removed and on Friday evening, March 15, Schlesinger, vanden Heuvel, Walinsky, Greenfield, Dutton, Sorensen and Lowenstein descended on Hickory Hill to prepare an announcement of candidacy for the following day. They were greeted not only by Bobby and Ethel but by an assortment of revellers, including filmmaker George

Stevens, Jr., humorist Art Buchwald and mountaineer Jim Whittaker. "There was a party going on," said Fred Dutton, "and Bob had us in his office across the hall working on the statement. Arthur Schlesinger, Ted Sorensen and Adam Walinsky each came with a draft. And Bob would make an appearance at the party, then come back to us. His manner of operation was well represented by this ridiculous, eclectic, disorganized evening.

"Walinsky, Sorensen and Schlesinger all had huge egos. Nobody was going to back off of his draft. Bob and I and a couple of others tried to do a patch-up job—'We'll take this paragraph from this draft, that paragraph from that'—but the authors weren't going to agree. Finally, at one o'clock Bob said, 'I've got to get to bed, you all keep going. You know what I want. I'll be up at six-thirty and I want to see a draft ready by then.'"

In the interim, Ted Kennedy had been dispatched to Green Bay, Wisconsin, where Eugene McCarthy was campaigning for that state's upcoming primary. The senator from Massachusetts had been commissioned to explore one more time the idea of cooperation between the two candidates. In order to maximize the possibility of stopping Johnson, Ted planned to say, the two peace candidates ought to split up the next string of primaries, avoiding direct competition until California on June 4. When the Minnesota senator heard that Ted hoped to confer with him, he informed his wife, Abigail, that he had no desire to entertain the visitor and was going to bed.

Teddy arrived just after 2 A.M. and the weary candidate was awakened, reluctantly, by his wife. McCarthy, in a blue terry-cloth robe, sat on his bed and listened as Ted spelled out his political proposal. At best the meeting was unfriendly, at worst it was hostile. McCarthy wanted nothing to do with the scheme. Neither did Mrs. McCarthy. After thirty minutes, she stood and showed their visitor to the front door.

At 6 A.M., Ted showed up back at his brother's residence, where, only a few hours before, the advisers had finally gone to sleep. Ted woke them up with news of his failed mission: "Abigail said no."

The men rose and worked on the final draft, which included language urging Kennedy supporters in Wisconsin, Pennsylvania and Massachusetts—states whose primary deadlines Bobby had already missed—to vote for McCarthy. A barber arrived and trimmed the soon-to-be candidate's hair. He showered, then put on a plain blue business suit.

The group (including Ethel) drove downtown. At 10 A.M. on March 17, 1968, St. Patrick's Day, Bobby stepped behind the lectern at the Senate Caucus Room, where Jack had announced his race for the White

House eight years and two months before. "I am announcing today my candidacy for the presidency of the United States," began Joseph Kennedy's eldest surviving son. "I do not run for the presidency merely to oppose any man but to propose new policies. I run because I am convinced that this country is on a perilous course and because I have such strong feelings about what must be done, and I feel that I'm obliged to do all that I can."

25

PLAYING TO WIN

$\mathbf{T}$he campaign took off in a whirlwind. Within the first two weeks, Bobby traveled from Kansas to Alabama to Tennessee to New York to California to Oregon to Idaho to Utah to Nebraska to Colorado to Indiana to New Mexico to Arizona. Initially, he concentrated on college campuses, trying to win back the many students and other young people he had lost to McCarthy by virtue of his delay in joining the race.

People greeted the newly declared candidate with a frenzy rarely seen, even in presidential campaigns. Joining Bobby in Topeka, Kansas, Jimmy Breslin wrote in the *New York Post* (March 18, 1968) about the thousands of spectators, who in their desire to get close to RFK, began tearing at his shirtcuffs, at the buttons on his suit jacket, at his tie: "They reached for his hair and his face. He went down the fence, hands out, his body swaying backwards so that they could not claw him in the face, and the people on the other side of the fence grabbed his hands and tried to pull him to them."

In 1964, when he ran for the Senate, the delirium of the crowds had surprised RFK; now he made it the starting point in his strategy. The excitement on the streets, he was betting, would arouse voters watching on television, who would give him victories in the handful of primaries he could still enter. Those victories would impress the party moguls, who still controlled most of the delegates to the convention, set for Chicago in August 1968. And one mogul was the key to all the rest. "What about Daley?" Jimmy Breslin asked Bobby. "He's the whole ball game," RFK replied.

Mayor Richard Daley's importance to the campaign could not be overestimated. "Daley hated the war," said Theodore H. White, "and so

455

did Bobby. And Daley had worked with the Kennedys in 1960 to get JFK elected president. But to gain Daley's current backing RFK had to start winning primaries, and to win the remaining primaries he had to prove to the world that he was more than a mere imitation of his late brother."

Bobby's campaign got underway with a torrent of verbiage directed at Lyndon Johnson. At Kansas State University the day after his declaration of candidacy he preached that the war in Vietnam had "divided Americans as they have not been divided since your state was called Bloody Kansas. . . . I regard our policy there as bankrupt. . . . I am concerned that, at the end of it all, there will only be more Americans killed; more of our treasure spilled out; and because of the bitterness and hatred on every side of this war, more hundreds of thousands of Vietnamese slaughtered; so that they may say, as Tacitus said of Rome: 'They made a desert and called it peace.' " In Los Angeles six days later he said that "for almost the first time the national leadership is calling upon the darker impulses of the American spirit—not, perhaps, deliberately, but through its action and the example it sets—an example where integrity, truth, honor, and all the rest seem like words to fill out speeches rather than guiding beliefs." Robert Kennedy had hated Lyndon Johnson for years. Finally, he was letting the public know it.

The Los Angeles speech in particular drew the ire of the press. "When a war becomes a flaming political issue," wrote Robert Donovan of the *Los Angeles Times,* "the line between debate and demagoguery becomes a thin one." America was looking for relief from stress; Bobby, in his fervor, and in the fervor of those who turned out to see him, seemed almost an Old Testament prophet threatening to rain down destruction upon a wicked nation.

Even so, the most searing criticism of the most recent Democratic candidate had to do with chronology. "I'd been in New Hampshire with McCarthy," recalled journalist Dan Blackburn, "and when Kennedy announced right after the primary, a lot of reporters were genuinely outraged at the timing. It was as though he'd let McCarthy test the water, and when the water turned out to be a reasonable temperature, he plunged in." Bobby tried to defend his delay. "He argued—and it was an argument that, at least, you couldn't dismiss out of hand—that if he had gone into New Hampshire and taken on Johnson initially, it would have been set up as a Johnson-Kennedy fight with a lot of personal overtones that would have all but buried the major issues." Blackburn showed more understanding than many. "Sorry I can't join you," Murray Kempton said in a telegram to Teddy, who had invited him to a cocktail party. "Your brother's announcement makes clear that St. Patrick did not drive all the snakes from Ireland."

Most indignant of all was Eugene McCarthy. "McCarthy, who was Black Irish, was a pretty good hater, anyway," said Al Eisele. "And he became terribly angry that Bobby jumped into the race when he did, because he thought that Kennedy had exploited what he'd done in New Hampshire." Asked about his new rival, the eloquent Minnesotan spoke of politicians "willing to stay up on the mountain and light signal fires and dance in the light of the moon, but none of them came down." Most of McCarthy's supporters followed his lead.*

While tempers flared on the campaign trail, at the White House a sudden complacency had set in. For several months, Lyndon Johnson had been telling advisers that he was weighing not running for another term. Now he was discussing the possibility more openly. He had even begun saying kind things about RFK. When special assistant Joseph Califano voiced the opinion that RFK would win the election if Johnson pulled out, the president responded, "What's wrong with that? Bobby would support many of the Great Society programs we initiated."

Johnson saw a nation divided and recognized that he had become the focus of its discontent. His own internal commission of wise men—Dean Acheson, McGeorge Bundy, Cyrus Vance—had all advised that the war was unwinnable. And New Hampshire had demonstrated that his political fate was perilous at best. The Wisconsin primary was next, on April 2, in anticipation of which, his aides warned him that McCarthy would win two to one. Were Johnson to pull out of the race now, he could maintain that he was leaving of his own volition; were he to wait until after the Wisconsin balloting, he would seem to all to be responding to a decisive repudiation by voters of his own party.

At 9 P.M. on Sunday, March 31, the president addressed the nation on the subject of Vietnam. "I am taking the first step to de-escalate the conflict," he said. He ordered a reduction in the bombardment of North Vietnam, and announced that he would send Averell Harriman as his personal representative "to any forum, at any time, to discuss the means of bringing this ugly war to an end."

Thirty-five minutes into his address, he changed the subject:

> Fifty-two months and ten days ago, in a moment of tragedy and trauma, the duties of this office fell upon me. I asked then for your help

---

*The animosity between the two sides never healed. "Even today," said Democratic consultant Ted Van Dyk in his interview for this volume, "the people who worked in the McCarthy and Kennedy campaigns from '68 all hate each other."

and God's, that we might continue America on its course, binding up our wounds, healing our history, moving forward in unity, to clear the American agenda and to keep the American commitment for all our people.

United we have kept that commitment. United we have enlarged that commitment.

What we won when all our people were united just must not be lost in suspicion, distrust, selfishness, and politics among any of our people.

Believing this as I do, I have concluded that I should not permit the presidency to become involved in the partisan divisions that are developing in this political year. With America's sons in the field far away, with America's future under challenge right here at home, with our hopes and the world's hopes for peace in the balance every day, I do not believe that I should devote an hour or a day of my time to my personal partisan causes or to any duties other than the awesome duties of this office—the presidency of your country.

Accordingly, I shall not seek, and I will not accept the nomination of my party, for another term as your president.

But let men everywhere know, however, that a strong, a confident, and a vigilant America stands ready tonight to seek an honorable peace— and stands ready to defend an honored cause—whatever the price, whatever the burden, whatever the sacrifice that duty may require.

Thank you for listening.

Good night and God bless all of you.

The operative sentence had gone by so fast, viewers in living rooms across America did double takes. Lyndon Johnson had withdrawn from his nightmare.

"We were flying back from Arizona to La Guardia," recalled Fred Dutton, "and when we arrived somebody came on the plane and told Bob and me that Johnson had pulled out. As we got off, the press wanted all kinds of comment, but we didn't want to give any. We hadn't expected Johnson to pull out. It was a real shocker.

"We jumped into a car and drove to his apartment at UN Plaza. The first thing he did was he picked up the phone and started calling all over. He called Mayor Daley, he called David Lawrence, who was the political boss of Pittsburgh, and so forth. On the one hand he hated making phone calls like that, but at this moment of importance he spent about two and a half hours calling every key Democrat who had been holding back and had felt he had to go with the president."

Peter Edelman remembered that "the initial reaction" to LBJ's withdrawal "was that it made things easier. You know, it was electrifying." But when few of the pols Bobby called were willing to give their support, "we realized that it was a little more complicated, and that whether people liked Humphrey or not"—Vice President Hubert Humphrey was expected to run, in Johnson's place, as the establishment candidate—"they were not about to jump on the Kennedy bandwagon just like that. . . . So that from initial elation we realized that in many ways it had become harder." Even though "we were no longer trying to unseat an incumbent president, a task labeled by political pundits as impossible, we also had lost our sitting duck, and that became clear quite quickly. . . . The animus just didn't flow against Hubert Humphrey the way it did against Lyndon Johnson. And as a matter of fact . . . because people couldn't hate Lyndon Johnson anymore, Robert Kennedy became the focus of a lot of hate, a lot of . . . floating hostility in the country." The passions Bobby had been stirring up by his rallies and speeches could now circle back toward him.

With Johnson gone, continued Edelman, "there became a much more acute need to look for issues." For in his speech Johnson had not only removed himself from the race, he'd also, by his peace initiative, nullified the crux of the Kennedy campaign: Bobby had called for negotiations to end the war; the president was now pursuing them. RFK thus had "lost his issue, his thing, his reason for being in the whole thing in a way, although he obviously had much broader concerns about the country. But he was a little stupefied. He was doing it very nicely, going along attacking Johnson and loving it, and didn't need to be told what to say, didn't need to be primed. . . . Well, now he lost all that."

McCarthy had "lost" the war issue, too, but he relished RFK's predicament. "Bobby will have to shoot straight pool now," he said at a press conference. "As long as he was banking his shots off Lyndon it was a different game."

The day after LBJ's withdrawal, his rivals suddenly became charitable toward him. "The president's action reflects both courage and generosity of spirit," intoned Bobby. McCarthy said that Johnson "merited the admiration of the entire nation." On April 2, the Minnesotan won 56.2 percent of the vote in Wisconsin to LBJ's 34.6.

"I respectfully and earnestly request an opportunity to visit with you as soon as possible to discuss how we might work together in the interest of national unity during the coming months," said Bobby in a telegram to Johnson. The president's immediate reaction to the request was not so florid: "I don't want to see that miserable little mick." Despite the slur, he received the senator at the White House on April 3.

"Senator Kennedy came in with Ted Sorensen," reported Walt Rostow. "Charlie Murphy [counselor to the president] and I were there with President Johnson. . . . That was the morning we got some sort of a first indication from Hanoi of a possibly positive reply to the president's speech. There was a briefing on the situation in Vietnam, and then, at Senator Kennedy's instigation, a probing as to what President Johnson's position in the campaign would be. President Johnson clearly didn't intend to be out campaigning or overtly throwing his weight around, but he reserved his rights as a citizen. He made it clear that he felt very close to Vice President Humphrey, and, in a sense, answered Senator Kennedy . . . by saying, 'On balance, I'm going to support Vice President Humphrey.' " Bobby asked LBJ to let him know if he planned to take an active role.

"President Johnson agreed to do that," noted Rostow. "Next he started to speak in a most touching way about his connection with President Kennedy; how he had worked with him. He felt that President Kennedy had dealt with him A-plus from his end, and he was probably a B-minus vice president, because it was a hard job. He thought that Hubert had done a better job as vice president in the sense of being able to live with its constraints. Then he described his attitude toward President Kennedy and the family, and his loyalty to the Kennedy people and cabinet, and to their programs and commitments. He felt like a junior partner whose senior partner had died, and he had to move in." LBJ stated that he had worked to carry on the policies of the Kennedy administration. However, despite all his efforts on behalf of civil rights and education, he had managed to alienate blacks and young people alike. Still, he had done his best. He "said very quietly that 'Somewhere up there President Kennedy would agree that I've done so.' This evoked from Robert Kennedy a rather remarkable, and I think sincere statement: he could vouch for that, that their differences had been overestimated. President Johnson said, 'If you sat here, your views would be very much more like mine than they've been, so that the differences have been overdone.' " "You are a good man," Bobby told the president before leaving. "That was a rather stirring occasion," recalled Rostow. "I suspect it was the last occasion those two men talked with each other."

Indiana's May 7 primary was the first such contest Bobby had decided to enter, and on Thursday, April 4, a day after his sentimental session with LBJ, RFK made an afternoon appearance at Ball State University in Muncie, Indiana. He spoke about an end to the war in Vietnam, a higher minimum wage and the need for better understanding between the races. Following a brief question-and-answer period in which he expressed his belief that "the vast majority of white people have good intentions toward minorities," he rode to the airport for the short flight to Indianapolis. About to board his plane, he received a telephone call from Pierre Salinger: Martin Luther King had been shot in Memphis. On landing, he learned that King had died.

"He recoiled when he heard the news," said one observer, "as though he'd been the one struck by the bullet that took King's life." RFK's initial comment: "Good gracious! Will this crap never end?"

Scheduled to speak that evening in the heart of the Indianapolis ghetto, Bobby was advised by the local police chief that such a venture was fraught with danger.

"When they hear the news, they'll riot," said the police chief.

"I'm going to speak," RFK replied, "and I don't want a police escort."

Two thousand people had gathered in the chill of the early spring night to listen to Robert F. Kennedy. Word of King's death had not yet reached them as RFK, somber and gaunt in a black overcoat, mounted a flatbed truck. He had discarded a speech he had originally written for the occasion. "I wanted to speak to them from my heart," he would tell his wife, who had stayed behind in their hotel suite.

An expression of pain was etched in his face as he addressed the crowd. "I have bad news for you," he began, "for all our fellow citizens, and people who love peace all over the world, and that is that Martin Luther King was shot and killed tonight."

A collective gasp could be heard, followed by cries of anguish and disbelief. Bobby continued:

> Martin Luther King dedicated his life to love and to justice for his fellow human beings, and he died because of that effort.
>
> In this difficult day, in this difficult time for the United States, it is perhaps well to ask what kind of a nation we are and what direction we want to move in. For those of you who are black—considering the evidence there evidently is that there were white people who were responsible—you can be filled with bitterness, with hatred, and a desire for revenge. We can move in that direction as a country, in great polarization—black people among black, white people among white, filled with hatred toward one another.
>
> Or we can make an effort, as Martin Luther King did, to understand and to comprehend, and to replace that violence, that stain of bloodshed that has spread across our land, with an effort to understand with compassion and love.

For those of you who are black and are tempted to be filled with hatred and distrust at the injustice of such an act, against all white people, I can only say that I feel in my own heart the same kind of feeling. I had a member of my family killed, but he was killed by a white man. But we have to make an effort in the United States, we have to make an effort to understand, to go beyond these rather difficult times.

My favorite poet was Aeschylus. He wrote: "In our sleep, pain which cannot forget falls drop by drop upon the heart until, in our own despair, against our will, comes wisdom through the awful grace of God."

What we need in the United States is not division; what we need in the United States is not hatred; what we need in the United States is not violence or lawlessness, but love and wisdom, and compassion toward one another, and a feeling of justice toward those who still suffer within our country, whether they be white or they be black.

So I shall ask you tonight to return home, to say a prayer for the family of Martin Luther King, that's true, but more importantly to say a prayer for our own country, which all of us love—a prayer for understanding and that compassion of which I spoke.

We can do well in this country. We will have difficult times. We've had difficult times in the past. We will have difficult times in the future. It is not the end of violence; it is not the end of lawlessness; it is not the end of disorder.

But the vast majority of white people and the vast majority of black people in this country want to live together, want to improve the quality of our life, and want justice for all human beings who abide in our land.

Let us dedicate ourselves to what the Greeks wrote so many years ago: To tame the savageness of man and to make gentle the life of this world. Let us dedicate ourselves to that, and say a prayer for our country and for our people.

On the fringes of the crowd there appeared to be some growing hostility. Several youths yelled "Black Power!" and raised their fists in defiance. But for the most part, the crowd dispersed and went home. "That's what he asked them to do," said Peter Edelman, "and that's what they did."

RFK's extemporaneous speech was the second used for Bobby's epitaph at Arlington.

Bobby telephoned Coretta Scott King later that night. She told him she hoped to travel to Memphis in the morning, retrieve her husband's body and accompany it back to Atlanta. RFK offered to make a plane available and subsequently instructed his aides to charter an aircraft for the mission.

"There was some concern within the organization [the SCLC]," Coretta King recalled, "as to whether or not this was quite the proper thing to do. I said, 'I don't really see anything wrong, period; one friend to another friend.' " RFK also arranged for additional phones to be installed in her home.

On April 6, RFK attended a memorial service for King in Washington, by the Reverend Walter Fauntroy, an associate of the slain leader. The nation's capital had been hit hard by the tragedy.* Following the service, Fauntroy accompanied Bobby on a walk through the streets. "There were fires everywhere," the minister recalled. A crowd gathered behind RFK as he walked. "And at that time," noted Fauntroy, "he said something to me that was very, very disturbing. It just silenced me. I asked him how the campaign was going. And he said, 'I fear that a gun stands between me and the White House.' And I was just stunned, because here we were only three days after King's death, and he was talking like that. Almost two months later to the day he was gone.

"Martin, Malcolm X, Bobby and John. In a matter of four or five years, a whole generation of leadership was wiped out."

Twenty-four hours later, Bobby attended King's funeral in Atlanta. All the other (declared and undeclared) presidential candidates from the major parties attended—Nixon, Humphrey, McCarthy, Nelson Rockefeller—but Lyndon Johnson (presumably having had his fill of assassinations) stayed home. Following the service at Ebenezer Baptist Church, the mourners hiked six miles to Morehouse College, King's alma mater. His jacket slung over his shoulder, RFK marched next to Sammy Davis, Jr. "Sammy and Bobby received more cheers from the crowd," said Walter Fauntroy, "than all the rest of us combined."

Earlier, Mrs. King had asked Bobby if Jackie could attend. Bobby replied, "This would be very hard for her because of her own experiences; but if it meant anything to you perhaps she would try to come." Bobby spoke to his sister-in-law, emphasizing the importance of her presence; although hesitant, in the end the former first lady did come.

Just before King's death, Jackie had run into Arthur Schlesinger at a New York dinner party. "Do you know what I think will happen to Bobby?" she asked him. "The same thing that happened to Jack. . . .

---

*In the aftermath of King's assassination, there were uprisings in more than a hundred American cities. Forty blacks were killed and thousands injured. Nearly 100,000 federal troops and National Guardsmen were dispatched by Johnson to contain the riots.

There is so much hatred in this country, and more people hate Bobby than hated Jack. . . . I've told Bobby this, but he isn't fatalistic, like me."[*]

"**B**obby campaigned without benefit of security," said Larry O'Brien. "He had one or two private bodyguards, but he eschewed the Secret Service detail to which he was entitled. Although on the face of it this seemed quite extraordinary—and dangerous—he obviously had his reasons. In the first place, he wanted to appear fearless, not at all cowed by the assassination of his brother; secondly, his personal style was to reach out to the people, to place as few obstacles as possible between himself and the crowd; third, he never had a great deal of faith in the Secret Service—after all, look at what they'd done for Jack: not a goddamn thing." If someone wanted to "get" him, they'd get him. . . .

Despite the agency's failure to protect John Kennedy, Bobby's decision to campaign without proper security made little sense. The hard-core right-wing press had issued a call to arms—"RFK MUST DIE!" screeched the headline of one Bible Belt periodical. In Washington, D.C., the FBI arrested a man who had been impersonating RFK, checking in and out of hotels and while there signing his vouchers, "Senator Robert F. Kennedy." Another arrest took place at New York's JFK International Airport—a man, carrying a concealed gun, had followed Bobby to his departure gate. Death was everywhere in the air.

Bobby announced for the presidency in the same room as did Jack, but the similarity ended there. The older brother's campaign had been planned for years; extensive groundwork had been laid. When Bobby declared his candidacy, he had virtually no machinery behind him, no organization in place. Quickly, then, he had to make up for lost time.

The veterans from 1960 were paired with the new breed from Bobby's senate staff plus the activists RFK had met around the country. "One of the problems in RFK's campaign," commented Fred Dutton, "was that Bob was always trying to mesh the old-timers with some of the new peace-movement types and civil rights leaders. The key Kennedy operators from before had been Larry O'Brien, Ken O'Donnell and Ted Sorensen. And this time they all had very active roles; I'm sure they thought they were ruling the world. But the Senate staff—Walinsky and Edelman—really made up the inner team.

---

[*] Schlesinger records Jackie's fateful comments in *Robert Kennedy and His Times*, p. 921. It should be remarked, however, that despite her concern for Bobby's safety, she did give him public support. Her appearance at Martin Luther King's funeral was nothing if not a sign of her devotion to Bobby.

"In my opinion, Bob sort of downgraded the old JFK crew—Sorensen, O'Brien—and elevated his younger people. He avoided titles so it wouldn't look like the newer guys were superseding the senior guys. Even our business cards had no titles." The effect was chaos. "Who the hell makes decisions around here?" asked Ken O'Donnell on one occasion. Steve Smith vowed to execute a major reorganization following the June 4 primary in California, when, it was assumed, there would be breathing space.

Dutton traveled with Bobby. Salinger and Mankiewicz divided the press responsibilities. Dave Hackett reprised his role as keeper of the card files on delegates, who, as usual in Kennedy campaigns, enjoyed a variety of favors, licit and illicit.

Further down the organizational line, the Kennedy campaign hired practically anyone it could find. Ty Fain remembered a telephone call he received from Fred Dutton's law office in early April: "And the voice on the phone said, 'The senator fondly remembers his time with you in Mexico and would like to have you on his campaign.' Apparently, my name was in some file. I'm sure they made hundreds of these calls." Fain took a leave of absence from his present position with the Los Angeles branch of the American Bank and went to RFK headquarters in New York. "So I was given a tour of the building and taken in to see Dave Hackett. And Dave Hackett summoned Ted Sorensen. The three of us met and they asked a few questions. 'Where are you from?' 'Originally from Texas,' I said, 'but I don't know anybody there. I've been gone for fifteen years.' And they said, 'You're perfect. You know your geography and you know your state and you're a Texan and you have no commitments.' I tried to say no, but they said, 'You'll be the Texas coordinator.' Then someone else came in and said, 'Well, we've got things to do in New Mexico that are urgent, and Arizona, too.' So Hackett said, 'All right, you're *Southwestern* coordinator.' 'What does that mean?' I asked. 'It means that you get votes there.' 'How do I do that?' 'I don't know, we'll figure it out.'

"I had no experience before that on any campaign. None whatsoever."

The organizational disarray, however, diminished neither the number nor the ardor of the throngs that turned out to greet RFK. Staid, Midwestern Indiana went wild for the New York New Englander. "Indiana's my home," said Dan Blackburn, "that's where I grew up. If somebody had told me that Bob Kennedy would have drawn those kinds of crowds there, I'd have had real trouble believing it. On the motorcade from South Bend to Gary, we couldn't go anywhere. We were hours late. People would jam the roads to see him and crowd around. Bill Barry"—the former FBI agent who, more or less, constituted Bobby's entire security staff—"was holding on to him most of the ride with both arms to keep him from being pulled from the car.*

"After a while we began to recognize certain people. There were some in the crowds who would wait until he'd gone by and then they'd jump in their cars wherever they had left them, race along somehow, knowing the back roads, and wind up ahead of us in the next town. This went on for hours. I've never seen anything like it, the emotional outpouring never stopped."

Despite their creed of impartiality, some journalists were swept up in the wave of affection. "If you were a photographer," recalled Bill Epperidge, who took pictures for *Life*, "even if you didn't love him for his political ideas, you had to love him for the way he handled crowds and just the way he was. He was one of the more photogenic people you'd ever want to see.

"Bobby was not manicured, he didn't have a public-relations firm. He had a couple of advance people, but Bobby was Bobby. He was a real person, he was a human being, he was himself. I mean, you take any contemporary politician—they're all manufactured by a PR firm. So it's a bore to photograph them. Also, the security is such that you can't get close. As for Bobby—if you wanted to ride in his car you'd say, 'Senator, can I ride in your car this trip?' 'Sure, fine, come on.' And we'd do that. If the television guys wanted to stand up on the hood of his car, that was fine. His press secretary was Frank Mankiewicz, but that didn't mean anything. You didn't have to go through Frank."

Dan Blackburn recalled that "before the campaign ended, many of the reporters covering it told their assignment desks that they had to be taken off because they were losing their objectivity. They said they liked the man too much. It's certainly useful to have terrific access. Yet you've got to keep remembering that you're probably being used by the guy. I think for a lot of us it just got too hard after a while."

One day in late April, the campaign took to the rails for a whistle-stop tour of Indiana along the legendary Wabash Cannonball line. At one depot, a handful of reporters failed to make the train because Bobby had ended a speech without his usual closing, a quotation from George Bernard Shaw: "Some men see things as they are and say, 'Why?' I dream of

---

*On occasion, RFK used personal friends as members of his very limited security force, among them former football player Rosey Grier and Olympic gold medalist Rafer Johnson.

things that never were and say, 'Why not?' " From that day forward, it was agreed that Bobby would introduce his closure with the words "As George Bernard Shaw once said . . ." "As soon as we heard the name Shaw," noted Dan Blackburn, "we knew we had better clamber aboard the old press bus."

At each of the small towns along the train ride, a banjo ensemble performed "The Wabash Cannonball." On the train's press car, a number of journalists made up their own version of the song. "I was lugging my guitar around Indiana," said David Breasted, a reporter with the campaign. "David Halberstam had broken into the newspaper business on the *Nashville Tennessean,* and he had a real appreciation for country music. Anyway, we just got going. And he threw in verses, and others would contribute a line here and there. And someone—I don't know who, it might have been Jules Witcover—wrote them out on his portable typewriter.

"We got it down, and I played it through, and it was well received by the originators as well as whoever else was around. And it wasn't long before Frank Mankiewicz heard about it and went back and told Bobby that there was trouble afoot. When we composed it, the understanding was that the song wouldn't get off the train. But we should have known better, because in actuality it made fun of Bobby. And Mankiewicz could tell that they had to get with it and listen to it or it would wind up on the six o'clock news without them.

"So Bobby came and sat down in our car, looking suspicious, with a smile pasted on his face. And I started to play. And all of a sudden this CBS cameraman stood up and started shooting Bobby. Anyway, we went through the whole thing and there was general laughter all around":

> Old Hubert's got Big Business, Big Labor and Big Mouth,
> Aboard the Maddox Special, a'comin' from the South.
> Lyndon's got him preachin', so ecu-meni-call,
> But soon he'll be a'heavin' coal on The Ruthless Cannonball.
>
> So here's to Ruthless Robert, may his name forever stand,
> To be feared and genuflected at by pols across the land.
> Old Ho Chi Minh is cheering, and though it may appall,
> He's whizzing to the White House on The Ruthless Cannonball.

"There were seven verses in all," added Breasted. "I can't remember all of them, but I do recall Bobby flashing his best campaign smile and saying something like, 'Well, I'll be damned.' He knew that we'd scored. And that night, the song wound up as the lead-in music for the campaign segment on *The CBS Evening News.*"

If uncomfortable about the prospect of becoming the frequent target of journalistic parody, Bobby nevertheless retained a sharp sense of humor. He would tell audiences that President Johnson had recently advised him, "Go west young man, go west." Then, after a meaningful pause, he'd add, "But I was in California at the time."

His wit was most wicked when its subject was most gruesome. "On one plane ride," noted Bill Epperidge, "the senator was sitting next to John Glenn, with Glenn by the window. And we hit some turbulence. We hit air pockets that were knocking everybody all over the place. And the senator loosened his seat belt and stood up and said, 'I have an announcement to make: Colonel Glenn is scared.' And then he sat down. It just broke us up." Dan Blackburn remembered a similar flight: "We were in a small plane and there was lightning dancing all around. We were bumping all over the place. And Bobby looked at us, the reporters, and said, 'You know, if we go down, you guys are all going to be in small print.' "

Bobby's wife did not share his carefree approach to air travel. "Ethel hated landing in planes," said Epperidge. "And whenever we had to land she would sit next to somebody—often a photographer—and hold that person's hand. She required this."

On one flight, however, her nerves were calmed by a mix of music and alcohol. "We were flying back to Washington from Omaha, where we'd had a rally," remarked David Breasted. "And Ethel was sitting in front of me. Like all of us, she'd had a few drinks. And she wanted to hear some songs. I got out the guitar and began to play. She requested soft rock, calypso, Kingston Trio hits, stuff like that. And people were running up and down in the aisle. Ethel was kneeling on the seat ahead of me, singing away. 'The Sloop John B' was one of the tunes we did.

"When we were about to land, the captain put on the seat belt sign and announced that we had to prepare for landing, but nobody paid the slightest bit of attention. Ethel was no exception. I had put away my guitar, but she was singing at the top of her lungs and didn't stop until we pulled up to the gate."

Ethel traveled with the campaign only part-time. "With all due respect," said Fred Dutton, "when Ethel was there she was always a problem. If you've worked in campaigns, the candidate's wife may look great in public but she's a pain in the ass behind the scenes. After all, you have to arrange for somebody to do her hair every morning and it just complicates the entire operation. My guess is that two-thirds, three-fourths of the time we were traveling with just Bob."

Washington Post columnist Maxine Cheshire wrote about Ethel's needs just after Bobby's campaign began: "As with most politicians' wives on the road, Ethel's hairdo is her biggest problem at the moment. She took along a fall, but getting it combed and adjusted proved to be just as much trouble as her own hair.

"Fortunately, she also took along a friend who is skillful with a comb and brush. Astronaut Scott Carpenter's wife, Rene, doubled as traveling companion and hair-dresser."

Rene Carpenter and several other friends were dubbed "ladies-in-waiting" for the help they provided Ethel at home and on the trail. Liz Stevens, wife of director George Stevens, was "lady-in-waiting," assigned to look after the children; Kay Evans, married to Washington political columnist Rowland Evans, supervised Ethel's household; and Sarah Davis, wife of stockbroker Spencer Davis, took care of the would-be first lady's wardrobe.

A former first lady was rooting for Bobby's success. "Won't it be wonderful when we get back in the White House?" she said. Hearing the remark, Ethel glared at her sister-in-law. "What do you mean *we*?" she asked.

Jackie presented a problem for Bobby. In the months before her brother-in-law's candidacy, she was seen more and more often in the company of Aristotle Onassis. A few days after RFK's announcement, the self-made shipping tycoon was interviewed in Paris on the subject of his new companion. "She's being held up as a model of propriety, constancy and of so many of those boring American female virtues," he said. "She's now utterly devoid of mystery. She needs a small scandal to bring her alive. A peccadillo, an indiscretion. Something should happen to her to win our fresh compassion. The world loves to pity fallen grandeur."

Bobby was not pleased that "the Greek"—as he and Ethel referred to Onassis—was looking for a "small scandal" in the family just as the presidency seemed within reach. Confronting Jackie, he was told that she and Onassis had discussed marriage but had reached no decisions. A few days later, Ethel and Joan, Teddy's wife, visited Jackie in New York to implore her not to marry Onassis. Such a union, to a divorced non-Catholic with a reputation not only as a philanderer but as a tycoon with questionable business ethics, would bring the family the wrong kind of publicity at a crucial time. Soon, Bobby visited on his own. "There's nothing wrong with Onassis," he said to his sister-in-law. "I'm sure he's the sweetest fellow on earth. But it might be taken the wrong way. And I won't get a second chance."*

---

* In a lighter vein, RFK also evidently told his former lover that marrying Onassis "will cost me at least five states."

According to Truman Capote, "Jackie wasn't bowled over by Bobby's reasoning. After all, the Kennedys weren't exactly generous toward her when it came to monies. JFK's last will and testament, executed while he was still senator, left her about a million dollars—enough for most of us, but not for Jacqueline Bouvier Kennedy. She had to go to Bobby whenever she needed anything, and although RFK was always ready to authorize funds for Jackie, it placed her in a difficult position.

"Jackie's threats to marry Onassis may at first have been a means of shaking down the Kennedys for more money. She was then dating Roswell Gilpatric [the former State Department official]. In fact, she had become something of a home-wrecker, insofar as Gilpatric's wife left him when she found out about Jackie."

Said Roswell Gilpatric of the situation: "Jackie and I had just returned from a vacation in Mexico when some New York newspaper, I think the *Daily News*, ran an item linking Jackie and Ari Onassis. I didn't give it much thought because Ari, who by the way had known Joe Kennedy since 1946, was still seeing Maria Callas—and I was with Jackie. Later, of course, Jackie dumped me and married him. But that only happened after Bobby's assassination."

When RFK failed to elicit a positive response from his sister-in-law, he turned to André Meyer, who had become Jackie's close friend and financial adviser. "What Bobby didn't know," said Truman Capote, "is that André and Jackie had enjoyed a brief affair, although Meyer, like Gilpatric, also had a wife. Meyer wanted to get rid of his wife and marry Jackie, but she had other ideas. Yet he did manage to convince her to postpone any plans to wed Onassis, at least until after the 1968 presidential election. Strangely enough, Onassis wound up contributing a large sum to Bobby's political war chest. He also gave Bobby and Bobby's staff the keys to his vast offices at Olympic Towers, the building he owned in Manhattan. And that's where Kennedy and his advisers held many of their later strategy sessions. In other words, RFK had nothing personally against Onassis—he just didn't want him as a member of his family."

Bobby "rewarded" Jackie for consenting to delay the Onassis nuptials by giving her, claimed Capote, a check for five hundred thousand dollars (always the joker, RFK actually gave his sister-in-law two five-hundred-thousand-dollar checks; he signed one of them "Nelson Rockefeller").

Another family member troubled Bobby as he campaigned: his son David. With his parents away so much of the time, the twelve-year-old took to acting out his frustrations at the expense of Hickory Hill's neighbors. Jack Kopson, a construction supervisor whose property abutted on Bobby's, noticed that his house was becoming a nightly target for pranks and vandalism. He had found garbage on his steps and cherry bombs in his mailbox. Once a firecracker had been placed on a windowsill, then set off. Kopson suspected that David Kennedy was among a number of neighborhood youths responsible for the mischief, and on April 12 he approached the youngster. Trying to scare him, Kopson fired his shotgun into the ground less than a yard away from the boy's feet.

A month later, David and a young friend were caught by the local police force for heaving rocks at a passing car and causing an accident. The driver of the vehicle dropped his complaint but only after the Kennedys and the parents of the other youth agreed to compensate the victim for his trauma and damages. On the campaign stump in Indiana, RFK told reporters that David had apologized for what he'd done. The senator insisted his son "meant no harm" and had always been "a source of pride and joy" to the family. When Bobby returned to Hickory Hill, however, according to Bob Galland, a college student who'd been hired to help with the children, he and Ethel were upset less over David's throwing of the rock than they were over his being caught at it.

Out on the campaign, Ethel displayed her customary boundless energy. During a three-hour layover in Snowball, New Mexico, she made six runs of the local ski slopes even though pregnant with her eleventh baby.* RFK, too, fit in sports when there was time. "Bob played as hard as he worked in the campaign," noted Fred Dutton; "the intensity never entirely let up. If he needed to let off steam, he was likely to go play a hard game of tennis, and ram it down somebody's throat, or play a hard game of touch football."

Sometimes, though, the candidate pursued a quieter kind of relaxation. "Often he attended mass," said Dutton, "during the week as well as on Sunday. And I think that was Bob retreating into himself, maybe even reassuring himself of lifelong habits. Usually, he'd go with a few people. I'm not Catholic, but I went several times. Bill Barry would often go—there were always three or four of us. We'd finish someplace and he'd say, 'We've got twenty-five minutes,' and he'd visit a church. Sometimes he'd go to mass and take communion, other times he'd just sit in there and pray."

Interviewed by Jean Stein and George Plimpton for *American Journey,* their oral history of Robert Kennedy, *Newsweek* correspondent John J. Lindsay recounted an incident that took place on the campaign trail.

---

*Bobby and Ethel's last child, Rory Elizabeth Kennedy, was born December 12, 1968, more than six months after her father's death.

One evening a group of reporters sat over drinks while assessing Bobby's chances of winning the White House. "Do you think he has the stuff to go all the way?" asked Jimmy Breslin. "Yes, of course he has the stuff to go all the way," responded Lindsay, "but he's not going to go all the way. The reason is that somebody is going to shoot him. I know it and you know it, just as sure as we're sitting here—somebody is going to shoot him." There was a stunned silence around the table, and then, one by one, each agreed. Added Lindsay, "He's out there now waiting for him."

The last great romance of Robert Kennedy's life was with Kristi Witker, a bouncy, buoyant twenty-one-year-old with long blond hair, hypnotic blue eyes, and a beguiling figure. "I was twenty-one, but I looked and felt about twelve," Witker acknowledged. "I wore micro-miniskirts and had a good sense of humor. Among other things, I provided Bobby with relaxation and relief from the tension and anxiety of the campaign itself. I helped him unwind. He'd be restless and grumpy after giving a speech, so I would sit with him and we would talk until he felt better again."

Witker, who would later become the evening news anchor at WPIX-TV channel 11 in New York, was then working for *American Heritage* magazine. "The editors," she said, "had decided to produce a book of photographs and text on Robert F. Kennedy. My assignment was to cover him on his run for the presidency."

She joined the campaign during the Indiana primary: "He was giving a speech, and I got in by flashing my driver's license rather than a press pass, which I didn't have. I was nervous and shy but I wanted to make myself look important, so I sat down on a folding table. Bobby started speaking, and the table collapsed. There I was on the floor, having created this tremendous noise and everyone, including Bobby, was staring at me. It was the last thing I'd wanted to do."

That evening, the fledgling political writer managed to procure a seat for herself in the press section of RFK's private aircraft. "I had wanted to introduce myself to Bobby," she remarked, "but I didn't know exactly how to go about it. I'd prepared a little introductory speech to give when I first met him. Anyway, we were in midair and I was standing in the aisle talking to some reporter when somebody tapped me on the shoulder. I turned around and it was Bobby Kennedy. He said, 'Hello, my name is Robert Kennedy. And who are you?'

"Although his approach seemed direct, he was surprisingly reserved, even remote at times. He always appeared to be a little bit ill at ease, a strange quality considering his chosen career. I've covered a number of political campaigns over the years, but I never encountered another candidate like Bobby. He had the mien of a gawky, awkward teenager. Jack had been poised and polished, outgoing, extremely handsome; Bobby looked like a kid—small, rumpled, longish hair, quite often with a big grin on his face. This child-like veneer was part of Bobby's charm. Unlike other politicians, he was real, genuine. This is what drew the crowds—his seeming vulnerability. Almost despite himself, he (like Jack) had tremendous charisma.

"From the moment we met, I felt awe-struck, star-struck. I fell passionately in love with him. I knew there was no marital future for us. To divorce Ethel Kennedy would have been political suicide. We once discussed the prospects of our relationship—if Bobby had reached the White House, he would have made me assistant press secretary, something of that sort."

According to Kristi Witker, Bobby talked extensively about death, so much so that she (as well as others) became paranoid. "Because of what had happened to Jack, because Bobby sounded so much like him and was therefore reminiscent of him (although vastly different in manner), his aides and friends worried. All of us began to look at the surging crowds in a searching way. I found myself gazing up at rooftops, at windows, at people's hands in the crowd. 'It could happen again?' I asked myself. I used to worry that Bobby would be killed in the same way as his brother."

Idealistic and in love, Witker would watch helplessly as the maddening crowds enveloped the forty-two-year-old candidate. "I was very naïve," she said. "I would say to Bobby, 'If anything happens, I'll save you. I'll throw myself in front of you. I'll protect you.' Bobby would look at me and grin like a little boy. 'If they want to kill me,' he'd say, 'they'll kill me.' "

Faced with an ever-expanding list of Hollywood stellars who supposedly had been involved with JFK—Grace Kelly, Janet Leigh, Rhonda Fleming, Arlene Dahl and Monique Van Vooren were among the most recently cited—RFK made certain that his own conquests were of lesser note. Langdon Marvin, who had been an aide to JFK, and who had procured numerous women for his boss, recalled doing the same for Bobby. "He was running for president, and while he evidently had a steady lover or two," said Marvin, "he suddenly became as sexually insatiable as Jack had been. I provided a gaggle of women—airline hostesses, starlets, secretaries, and others. RFK had a penchant for nymphettes—underdeveloped women with unformed personalities. I called them the Kennedy Pack, after Frank Sinatra's Rat Pack. Once, when Bobby stayed at the Carlyle, I sent him three fifteen-year-old private high school girls. 'That's the best present anybody ever gave me,' he said. Afterward, he told me he'd watched the girls having sex amongst themselves.

"Bobby's faithful little coterie of followers wanted the world to believe that he was pure as snow, but RFK was a good old 'chippie-chaser.' One by one, he dated almost all of the 'boiler-room' girls, the entourage of young women who worked for him on the campaign trail.

"In January 1964, not long after Jack's death, RFK asked me out to Hickory Hill. There, he handed me a packet of letters—maybe a dozen or so—and told me to 'get rid of them.' I should have saved them but I didn't. I didn't even read them. He admitted to me later that they were love missives both he and Jack had received from Marilyn Monroe."

R FK's groping for a campaign theme following the March 31 withdrawal of Lyndon Johnson lasted only days, remembered Peter Edelman, "because Martin Luther King was killed on April the fourth, and it was very clear to us that somebody had to begin speaking to the issues which resulted in his death." Bobby would place at the center of his appeal the concerns that had been occupying him since he'd been elected to the Senate: poverty and race. John Bartlow Martin, who had once co-managed Adlai Stevenson's presidential campaign and who now joined the RFK camp, remembered him stalking the state of Indiana "and talking about poverty in Appalachia, poverty in Brooklyn, poverty in Watts, poverty on the Indian reservation. Poverty, poverty, poverty. Racism, racism, racism. I don't think half the people who heard him had any idea what he was talking about. But he said it with such conviction, such fervor, that they at least listened, which is more than I can claim for any other politician in America."

RFK seemed determined to awaken a complacent nation. On college campuses, he continued to declare his opposition to student draft deferments. Before eight hundred students of the Indiana University medical School, he outlined a plan to extend medical care to the urban and rural poor. When he asked for questions, the future physicians let him know that they considered the health of the poor to be of lower priority than their own ability to practice medicine in an unfettered marketplace. "Where are you going to get all the money for these federally subsidized programs you're talking about?" one medical student asked.

"From you," he shot back. "Let me say something about the tenor of that question. . . . I look around this room and I don't see many black faces who are going to be doctors. . . . A responsibility of civilized society is to let people go to medical school who come from ghettos. You don't see many people from the ghettos or off the Indian reservations in medical school. You are the privileged ones here. It's easy to sit back and say it's the fault of the federal government, but it's our responsibility too. It's our society, not just our government, that spends twice as much on pets as on the poverty program. It's the poor who carry the major burden of the struggle in Vietnam. You sit here as white medical students, while black people carry the burden of the fighting in Vietnam. That's not right and that's not just."

When RFK spoke publicly of the war, he called for negotiations, not withdrawal. But privately, he voiced a different intention. "Sometimes, at the end of the day," recalled Bill Epperidge, "Bobby would slip down and find the photographers at the bar. And he'd sit down and talk about what he was *really* feeling. And one thing I remember specifically that he said was that when he was elected president, we were out of there. Immediately." Other insiders reported similar conversations.

RFK campaigned in the primaries with an eye to the convention and the general election. He never doubted he would defeat Eugene McCarthy. Therefore, in order to preserve the goodwill of McCarthy supporters, so that he could gain their loyalty once the primaries had ended, he for the most part refrained from attacking the Minnesotan. The same could not be said with regard to Hubert Humphrey. The vice president did not formally enter the race until April 27. "Robert Kennedy made much of the fact that Humphrey had dodged the primaries," said Ted Van Dyk, an aide to Humphrey. "He didn't dodge them. Johnson quit too late to allow us to get in. We had no option but to go without the primaries." Nineteen sixty-eight was the last year in which a majority of convention delegates were chosen not through primaries, but by state party caucuses and the leaders who ran them. Humphrey would seek the nomination by appealing less to the public than to the pols.

The vice president was absent from the states where Bobby was competing against McCarthy, but Bobby attacked Humphrey nonetheless, labeling him a surrogate for Lyndon Johnson and the administration's policies. He also assailed Humphrey for remarking, during his speech declaring his candidacy, that he intended to pursue "the politics of happiness, the politics of joy. And that's the way it's going to be, all the way, from here on in!" "It's such a stupid, simpleminded thing to say," Bobby told Ken O'Donnell, "that I don't know what to make of it." He told a gathering of students at Temple University in Philadelphia that "any man who finds joy in Martin Luther King's recent slaying or in the score of young men brought home from Vietnam in body bags each week is not a man I want to see as president of the United States."

The Humphrey forces took umbrage at Bobby's interpretation. "In his announcement speech," noted Van Dyk, "Humphrey had quoted a favorite passage of his from John Adams about the spirit of public happiness and public service. Robert Kennedy twisted it, in all his campaign speeches, to say that at a time of war and dreadful poverty, Humphrey was just a vapid, silly, happiness candidate. It was a very below-the-belt, stop-at-nothing kind of campaigning."

Hubert Humphrey, probably the nation's foremost traditional liberal, was running as the candidate of the labor unions and party regulars. At the same time, he was well liked by American Jews, who, despite their small numbers nationwide, constituted sizable Democratic voting blocs in both California and New York, the last two primary states. "Bobby couldn't understand why he wasn't more popular with Jewish voters," said Abe Ribicoff. "He telephoned me and asked what I perceived the problem to be. 'Maybe it's your old man,' I told him. 'But that business with my father happened thirty years ago,' he said. 'In the meantime, nobody has been more supportive of Israel than I have.' I don't think he ever comprehended what 'that business' with his father was all about."

If Bobby Kennedy and Eugene McCarthy agreed on the necessity of ending the war in Vietnam, they nevertheless had vastly different styles of presentation. Bobby was earnest and intense; McCarthy was ironic, nonchalant. Bobby seethed; McCarthy floated, above passion, above politics. "Do you think you'd make a good president?" a reporter asked him. "I think I'd make an adequate president," he replied. The antipolitician appeared to disdain the office he sought. He claimed, perhaps justifiably, that both JFK and LBJ had misused the powers of the Oval Office. McCarthy proposed to be a president who limited his own power, returning large pieces of authority back to Congress and serving but a single term. To his supporters, McCarthy seemed unassailable. He neither carried Bobby's baggage—in particular, the association with another midwestern senator named McCarthy—nor did he have the benefit of the Kennedy money and machine. He had entered the race first, courageously, and appealed to intellect, not emotion. McCarthy's followers tended to be richer, whiter, and better educated than Bobby's.

Blair Clark, Eugene McCarthy's campaign manager (and a former friend of JFK), acknowledged that McCarthy "did not court the minority vote because he knew that Bobby already had it sewn up. We realized it would be a waste of time to campaign in the ghetto, so we stayed away.

RFK had very effectively cornered the minority market, if I can put it in such gauche terms."

But RFK also engaged in a calculated appeal to the white working class. The Kennedys had always done well among blue-collar Catholics; now Bobby sought to capitalize on that tradition. In Indiana, he began adding to his speeches a call for "law and order." The national press reacted skeptically, referring to a "new, conservative Kennedy," and the younger members of his staff—including Walinsky and Edelman—opposed the tactic. The members of the Kennedy team who had been there before felt otherwise. "When speaking to white audiences," said Ken O'Donnell, "he emphasized the call for order, just as to black crowds he accented the fight for equality. I regarded the shift a sage response to a nation yearning for calm." Others, however, saw it as further evidence of the old, amoral Bobby. First, it seemed, he had stood idly by while Eugene McCarthy "got rid" of Lyndon Johnson, and now he was pandering to white backlash at the same time that he was presenting himself to blacks as a modern-day Lincoln. Formerly known by his opponents for his cutthroat ruthlessness, RFK now became known as a hard-nosed opportunist.

"If being termed an opportunist meant having a broader-based constituency," said Fred Dutton, "it was a worthwhile trade-off. America was in huge ferment at that time, and it required a passionate political figure to stay ahead of the trends. In mounting Bob's 1968 campaign we attempted to put together the anti-Vietnam forces and the civil rights forces with the hard hats, the redneck whites. The majority of blacks in this country were too radicalized for that kind of coalition, the majority of rednecks too bigoted, but a mainstream major politician had to try to put these elements, which had been coming apart, back together again. In our private discussions as we traveled around and in our speechwriting, we were looking for a way to bridge the George Wallace vote and the civil rights and peace movements.* And if that had happened, if Bobby had lived, the Democrats would not have slipped from power as they did, and America would not have had to endure the Nixon-Reagan regimes.

"You're not going to solve the race problem, in my opinion, just by satisfying the blacks or even by recognizing, in a pure principled way, the extent of inner-city poverty, because you're not going to get the main-

---

* George Wallace, Alabama's governor, broke from the Democratic party to mount a third-party run in the general election on a states' rights populist platform. He won five southern states, taking forty-five electoral votes and 13.5 percent of the popular vote.

stream whites to go along. It's probably not a solvable problem, even over a long period of time, and maybe it was hubris on our part to think we could in 1968. But we thought that we had to both take from the left and siphon from the Wallace movement as much as we could. That's what 1968 was all about."

The transformation of Bobby's political persona during the last years of his life moved many to admiration. "I think he became more thoughtful and perceptive and sensitive after the death of his brother," said George McGovern. "I think it was time for him to come to terms with himself in a way that he hadn't before." But others have remained dubious. John P. Roche, an aide in the LBJ White House, said, "I didn't like him. I didn't trust him. The word I always thought of in connection with Bob Kennedy was *demonic.* I don't think he knew a principle from a railroad tie." And author Nicholas von Hoffman, a biographer of Roy Cohn, said, "I see a very ruthless man who would do whatever he thought he needed to do to get from point A to point B, a man who finally showed himself to have no fixed beliefs. I see a man who ultimately abandoned his McCarthyism for the pursuit of higher office. I see a man who supported the war, then turned around within two years. When the tide changed, he changed, that's my view of him. If there ever was a man who was reading the polls, it was this man."

Many traditional liberals were reluctant to accept Bobby, because as he emerged from his metamorphosis he did not conform to their example. "He jumped over the whole sort of New Deal liberal thing that everybody in New York was caught up with," commented Allard Lowenstein, "because he was really not a liberal at all in any of the traditional senses that you might define the term." Frank Mankiewicz remarked that when Bobby in his last years made an "intensive study and analysis of the social classes and the way people live in America, particularly the poor . . . he was learning what most of the liberals accepted with their mother's milk and had never bothered to reexamine. And he was aware of the fact that, after all, he hadn't been out there on the frontiers fighting for increased social security benefits and public housing and minimum wages and civil rights acts early on." Now, he was making such efforts, "but from a slightly different vantage point, from what he thought was a more sophisticated and a better understanding of the country and its needs than they had, even though they had reached [these] positions ahead of him."

RFK's work in Bedford-Stuyvesant had been a harbinger of his attitude. Dissatisfied with the central government's massive hand in local affairs, he looked to invest more power in communities. Two weeks before his death, Bobby spoke in California of a "new politics" which recognized "that federal spending will not solve all our problems, and that money cannot buy dignity, self-respect, or fellow feeling between citizens." The first priority of his administration, he said, would be "the creation of dignified jobs, at decent pay, for all those who can and want to work." And he would remake public-assistance programs, so they would provide "adequate help to those who cannot work, without the indignities and random cruelties which afflict the present welfare systems."*

Theodore White asked Adam Walinsky how Bobby's approach differed from Barry Goldwater's attack on the federal government in 1964. Said White: " 'Simple,' Walinsky told me, '—Barry wanted to leave local institutions as they were, with local power as it was; we want to transfer more power to local institutions and change them at the same time.' " Unlike Goldwater and subsequent Republican haters of the central authority, Bobby was advocating not just the return of power to those who'd had it, then lost it to Washington, he was looking to give power to people who'd never had power before.

"Bridging the gap between the different segments of the population," said Fred Dutton, "was Bob's concept, but his ideas were more feels and gropes than articulated. His speechwriters—the Walinskys and Edelmans—could verbalize it, but this you didn't want to entirely verbalize. If you did, if you put it together, you'd lose the Wallace people, you'd lose the blacks. But it was not just something under the surface, it was a major effort. We thought there was no point in running in primaries if all you won were the primaries. This was McGovern's problem in 1972, McCarthy's problem always. To win the primaries, they positioned themselves too far out. There's no point in running unless you are always positioning yourself for the general election, because if you zig too much one way in the primaries and then zag too much the other way in the general you've lost your credibility. In the 1968 primaries, we were being driven to the left by the civil rights movement, by the students, by the crowds that turned out, by the emotionalism of that period and by the volatility of the issues.

"The campaign looked unruly. To middle-class Americans it looked like Kennedy's supporters were people who were a bit off the wall. How was that handled? We began to change the scheduling, to change the kinds of crowds we had. When we would go on campuses, Bob would

---

* "Bobby genuinely wanted to help people and heal the nation," said Kristi Witker, "and thereby heal himself. At the time of his death, Bobby was still mourning the death of his brother."

take on the white middle-class kids who were accepting college defer-ments rather than going to war. One, he believed it. Two, he was trying to point out their contradictions. It demonstrated he wasn't just uncriti-cally going along with all the anti-Vietnam people.

"Bob became more passionate, more principled, more idealistic, more polarized toward the end, but he remained essentially a pragmatist. He believed that if you want to be merely a do-gooder, then become a preacher, a teacher, a missionary. Become a private citizen who works in the community. But if you go into politics, see that you bring along fifty-five percent. See that you know how to work your way through the laby-rinth, sorting out which ideas you choose in order not only to improve your times but also to advance yourself. Kennedy had no problem with that. He was not just into bettering the world, he was advancing the Kennedy banner. He wanted to do good, but he was also a power animal. He didn't want to be a hero. He wanted to win."

On May 7, the Democratic voters of Indiana gave Bobby 42.3 percent of their ballots, to 27.4 percent for McCarthy; Governor Roger D. Brani-gan, running as a stand-in for Humphrey, garnered 28.7 percent. On the same day, the voters in the District of Columbia gave RFK a clear 2–1 victory over Humphrey: 67 percent to 33 percent. Hubert Humphrey ("Bump the Hump" read a bumper sticker proudly displayed by ardent Kennedyites) promptly took to the airwaves to assure the viewing public, in his high-pitched, nasal twang, that "winning a primary isn't every-thing."

"Everything considered," RFK responded in the press, "I'd rather win a primary than come in second. My family believes that winning is better than losing."

In the rural state of Nebraska, Bobby recycled a joke he'd told farmers in upstate New York in 1964: "Ten children and two adults consume a lot of milk, eggs, and other agricultural products." Eugene McCarthy's name was on the ballot in the state, but his campaign pulled out early, thus diminishing Bobby's victory. Nebraska was the only state in which RFK won a majority of votes cast: 51.7 percent to McCarthy's 31. Oregon was next, and both men would campaign there at full steam.

The Beaver State wasn't exactly Kennedy territory. "It's one big sub-urb," observed Ken O'Donnell, "with a surprisingly high percentage of college graduates. A good place for McCarthy to pick up support." Un-employment was low and the population was overwhelmingly (98 per-cent) white. Bobby's sermons on poverty and hunger fell on deaf ears; the indifference of his audiences, after the mad enthusiasm elsewhere, left him frustrated and depressed. After leaving one such gathering—a group of electronics employees near Portland—Bobby could only shake his head. The workers, he said, were the strangest he'd ever met. "When Bobby would drive into Watts or someplace like that," commented Fred Dutton, "he'd say, 'Boy, these are my kinds of people.' He was looking not just for their support, but also for some electric charge back and forth, an emotional jolt. But in Oregon, on his way to an all-white, middle-class audience, he'd say, 'This ain't my group.'"

McCarthy thrived in the well-heeled state, and he made hay over the one substantive issue which divided him from his rival: gun control. Since Jack's death, Bobby had favored federal legislation to restrict ownership of firearms. McCarthy opposed such regulation, and he made his stance no secret in a state where the Second Amendment was held on a par with the Ten Commandments. Even more than gun control, McCarthy hit his stride by making an issue of Bobby himself. The Minnesotan had grown so resentful of Kennedy that he had failed to congratulate him after his victories in Indiana and Nebraska. Now he referred to RFK in his speeches as a "spoiled little rich kid who can't run this race without his dog, his astronaut and his father's millions."

In his own neat address, RFK said, "I don't mind his taking issue with Dad's money, but let's leave Freckles out of this. That cocker spaniel goes everywhere with me."

Unfriendly demographics and a caustic adversary were not Bobby's only problems in Oregon. Many voters—especially those belonging to the Teamsters, the state's largest union—still remembered the investigations Bobby had conducted there while working for John McClellan. Terry Schrunk, then Portland's mayor, had been indicted as a result of those probes. Later, he had been acquitted. In 1968, he was still mayor. Schrunk, an enormously popular figure in the Northwest, had it out for RFK. "By strange coincidence," recalled Ken O'Donnell, "there were traffic jams in Portland whenever Bobby campaigned there. As a result he couldn't get around. And there wasn't a policeman in sight to help clear the route."

Bobby did not handle the stress of Oregon well. "I remember quite vividly," said Peter Edelman, "that day he came back to Portland and we went to these factories [and] he realized that the thing wasn't so good. And we didn't get along with each other very well that day. . . . He knew it wasn't my fault, and yet he was just sort of griping about everything. And then he went out to a Democratic convention at a public high school that night . . . and it was a very festive occasion, and they had all their balloons and it was really very colorful. And he . . . wouldn't take it seriously, because they were just . . . kids. And on another occasion . . . he would have probably thought it marvelous. But the result [was] he was awful and he left a bad taste in their mouth, and they nominated Humphrey because they felt Bobby had treated them condescendingly."

He could treat his aides shabbily, too. Edelman recalled a day in a Portland hotel when the campaign's discussion over whether RFK should debate McCarthy coincided with press reports describing Adam Walinsky's harmonica-playing ability: "Ethel was carrying on at Bobby. You know, she was inside the room screaming about something or other, whatever it was and, of course, she could be extremely excitable. And while most of the time she behaved well, she could be a real shrew sometimes, too. And people had been after him all day to debate McCarthy, and he seemed reluctant and so Adam Walinsky, on behalf of himself and me, had made a pitch at a meeting with Pierre Salinger and Larry O'Brien, both of whom initially supported Bobby's position, and really kind of turned them around." At approximately six or six-thirty, a time when Bobby usually took a nap, one of the people who had met with Walinsky "went in to tell [RFK] that it was the belief of this group that the matter ought to be reopened again. Meanwhile, Adam and I were standing out in the hall talking to John Lewis and Earl Graves, who were there to see him about something else.* And we were laughing, and a little bit loudly, and it either disturbed his sleep or whatever, so he came out in the hall in his underwear. . . . And he made [a remark] about Walinsky playing his 'goddamn harmonica' all the time, and didn't he have anything better to do, he could at least go and ring doorbells or else go home. And, you know, I was really mad. I thought that was very inconsiderate and very nasty to say to somebody who'd been so devoted, but I didn't say anything. Adam started toward the door, and he slammed the door in Adam's face."

Bobby did not debate McCarthy in Oregon. "Except for Oregon, RFK felt he held the overall lead," said Edelman, and "didn't want to raise McCarthy into a candidate of equal stature." Plus, there was "some worry about how well he would do in it. . . . [He] hadn't had time to prepare." Bobby's trouble explaining his refusal to debate was reminiscent of Ken Keating's blundering in New York four years earlier. Indeed, Blair Clark recalled an encounter between McCarthy and Kennedy at the Portland Zoo, which ended "with Bobby scurrying in the direction of the nearest exit to avoid a face-to-face meeting with his adversary. Mc-

---

*John Lewis, a hero of the Freedom Rides, later became a congressman from Georgia. Earl Graves, of Bedford-Stuyvesant, became a leading black businessman.

Carthy later called him a coward." In the course of a local radio broadcast, he challenged Kennedy to a duel: "Choose your weapon—sabers or
quills." RFK's retort: "Let's meet at dawn in front of the gorilla cage and
trade insults."

No Kennedy had ever been beaten in an election prior to May 28,
1968, but Oregon showed itself immune to the Kennedy magic. McCarthy won the day with 44.7 percent to Bobby's 38.8. RFK was shaken.
The real winner, he told a reporter, was Hubert Humphrey, "because
McCarthy won't get the Democratic nod under any circumstances."
Then, in a lighter tone: "Perhaps I ought to consider sending Freckles
back home to Hickory Hill."

The next day, RFK toured Los Angeles, which he dubbed his "Resur-
rection City" after he received the kind of ecstatic welcome he had
been accorded before his outings one state to the north. California, with
its large black and Hispanic populations, provided a natural environment
for his appeal. Cesar Chavez had launched a massive voter registration
drive, and Jess Unruh put the state party's apparatus to work on Bobby's
behalf. Prominent New Frontiersmen and other eastern liberals came
out to canvass McCarthy campus strongholds. Steve Smith took charge
of the southern half of the state, establishing headquarters in Los
Angeles, while John Seigenthaler managed the northern half from San
Francisco.

The frenetic pace of the Kennedy campaign turned even wilder in
California, the nation's biggest electoral prize, with 174 delegates and a
winner-take-all format. From Watts to Modesto, from a meeting with
black militants to a fund-raiser with movie stars, Bobby traversed the
state night and day, telling his joke about his hungry family—who loved
to eat whatever product was locally grown—and holding forth about the
war, law and order and, most centrally, poverty. Meanwhile, campus disturbances were ravaging Stanford, in Palo Alto, as well as Columbia University, in New York, where a group called Students for a Democratic
Society (SDS) took over administration buildings and closed down the
school. Demonstrations and sit-ins took place at Berkeley and the University of Chicago. Abbie Hoffman, crown prince of the yippie subcul-
ture, called for an end to higher education. A militant organization, the
Black Panthers, threatened to destroy "white supremacist America."
Near San Francisco, saboteurs blew up three utility towers, thus depriv-
ing thirty thousand homes of electricity. Bobby was the object of adulation, but he was also the target of hostility. "DID 20,000 AMERICANS DIE
FOR A COALITION IN VIETNAM?" asked the placard of a war supporter.

"Fascist pig!" shouted a left-wing student just before he threw a punch at the candidate's head. He missed.

"Against this background on every nightly television show in California stormed the Kennedy," wrote Theodore White in *The Making of the President 1968*. "Not the elegant cool John F. Kennedy as America remembered him. But the exhausted Robert F. Kennedy, his emotions rubbed raw, disturbing the tranquility of the evening with his vision of America and the passionate hope of making it a country without miseries."

On Saturday, June 1, the rivals finally met in a televised debate. The San Francisco event produced few fireworks, as the two men concurred on the majority of issues. Screenwriter-novelist Jeremy Larner, who had become McCarthy's chief speechwriter, remembered only two points of difference: "McCarthy said if elected he would get rid of J. Edgar Hoover as FBI director. RFK, aware of the sex files on his family that Hoover possessed, made no such commitment. The only other topic that produced drama was urban policy. And in this area, Kennedy showed himself to be the more knowledgeable of the two."

McCarthy proposed that poor blacks be dispersed from ghettos, while Kennedy called for reconstruction of the existing neighborhoods, a program similar to the Bedford-Stuyvesant project. "What you suggest," said McCarthy, "is nothing more than another form of apartheid." "I'm not against poor people leaving the ghetto," responded RFK, "but simply to take citizens out of their homes and plop them down in a different neighborhood doesn't address the issue. It makes no sense."

According to newspaper and television call-in polls, RFK swept the debate by a clear two-to-one margin. "And a good thing," said Ken O'Donnell, "because after his defeat in the Oregon primary, winning California became virtually an imperative." On June 2, Bobby and Ethel, six of their children, their dog Freckles and an entourage of aides, friends, relatives and reporters moved into the Ambassador Hotel in downtown Los Angeles.

On Monday, June 3, the day before the balloting, Bobby rose early and met with his advisers in his hotel quarters (room 516, the Royal Suite, on the fifth floor) to review plans for an eleven-hundred-mile barnstorming tour, which in the final hours of the California campaign would take the candidate from L.A. to San Francisco, Long Beach, Watts, Venice, Santa Monica, San Diego, then back to L.A.

From the San Francisco airport, their first stop of the day, RFK's motorcade drove to one of the city's oldest neighborhoods: Chinatown. Kristi Witker, seated in a car close behind the candidate and his wife, described the scene there as one of "churning, burning humanity closing in on Bobby, their hands grabbing his hands, his arms, several of the onlookers trying to hurl themselves into his convertible. I said something about all the cuff links he'd lost to crowds during the campaign. 'Nixon's worn the same pair of cuff links since 1945,' responded Dick Dragne, one of Bobby's assistant press secretaries. We both laughed. Then suddenly there was a sharp popping sound that made our words echo and the streets seem to spin. Ethel had reached out and pulled Bobby down beside her. My first thought was, 'My God, it can't be . . . it just can't be.' And it wasn't. Someone said, 'It's firecrackers.' Ethel and Bobby sat up, and the street stopped spinning. But I remember that stark, stark feeling of terror."

Huge thunderous ovations greeted Bobby at the remainder of his rally stops. As the candidate stood at a makeshift podium in Long Beach, an unshaven, longhaired male bystander ran up and screamed, "Hey Mr. Kennedy, who killed your brother?"

Sunny skies had turned to mist by the time they reached Santa Monica. Night had fallen as they arrived at San Diego's El Cortez Hotel. In the middle of his San Diego address, Bobby stopped speaking abruptly and sat down at the edge of the stage with his head in his hands. Rafer Johnson, Bill Barry and Rosey Grier rushed to his side and led him off-stage—he had been seized by stomach cramps.* He returned shortly afterward to finish his speech, closing with the all-too-familiar lines of George Bernard Shaw, "Some men see things as they are . . ." "By the way," he then stammered, "I just wanted to let the members of the Fourth Estate know that we're done for the evening."

The press and stalwarts on RFK's campaign team partied late that night in the Kennedy suite at the Ambassador Hotel. Bobby and Ethel were absent: they and their children had gone to Malibu to stay with film director and family friend John Frankenheimer, with whom they periodically visited whenever they were in the area.

---

*RFK's stomach cramps were accompanied by nausea and dizziness. Despite repeated daily shots of vitamin B-12, the candidate was suffering from exhaustion.

26

JOURNEY'S END

Pierre Salinger: "Ten days before the California primary, I went to dinner at the home of one of the state's most powerful Democratic leaders, Paul Ziffren, and his wife, Mickey. There, I ran into a friend, the French writer Romain Gary. After dinner, Gary approached me and said, 'You know, your guy will be killed.'

"I had managed to push the idea of assassination to the back of my mind. Suddenly, I was directly confronted with it. 'Why do you think so?' I said.

" 'He's too irresistible a temptation for the American paranoiac personality, too much provocation, too rich, too young, too attractive, too happy, too lucky, too successful. He arouses in every "persecuted" type a deep sense of injustice.'

"The subject came up a few days later in Malibu, where Bobby was resting at the home of film director John Frankenheimer. Gary was there, too, with his wife, [actress] Jean Seberg. He put the subject to Bobby. 'What precautions are you taking?'

"Bobby, who knew what he meant because I had already reported the conversation to him, shook his head. 'There's no way to protect a candidate who's stumping the country. No way at all. You've just got to give yourself to the people and trust them. From then on, it's just that good old "bitch luck." ' Bobby took a sip from a glass of orange juice. 'In any event, you have to have luck on your side to be elected president of the United States. Either it's with you or it isn't. I'm pretty sure there'll be an attempt on my life sooner or later. Not so much for political reasons. I don't believe that. Just plain nuttiness. That's all. There's plenty of that around. We live in a time of extraordinary psychic contagion. Someone should make a study of the traumatizing effect caused by the mass media—which dwells on and lives by drama.'

"It was obvious that Bob wanted to change the subject, and he did. He talked to Gary about [political affairs in France]. But then he returned to the subject of the assassination. 'How many attempts have there been on the life of Charles de Gaulle?' he asked.

" 'Six or seven,' Gary replied.

" 'I told you: luck,' Bobby said. 'You can't make it without that old bitch luck.' "

Robert and Ethel Kennedy slept late the morning of June 4, primary day, while their children frolicked on the Frankenheimers' private beach. Theodore White, who joined the Kennedys for lunch and later wrote about it for *Life,* recalled that "it was a windy, overcast afternoon. The sea was rough, but the kids were dashing in and out of the water. David went in with his father, and suddenly this wave came and just enveloped them. They disappeared beneath the surf for a few anxious moments, and when they reemerged Bobby had hold of his son. David was spitting up sea water, and Bobby had sustained a cut over his eye.

"We went up to the swimming pool, near the house, for lunch and were joined by Fred Dutton and Richard Goodwin. After lunch, Bobby dozed off in a beach chair, while I called CBS-TV for early projections on the outcome of the vote; the first exit polls gave RFK a forty-nine percent share, enough to win because besides McCarthy there were four or five other candidates on the ballot."

RFK presently awoke and went to his bedroom for a few additional hours of sleep. Around three, Ethel suggested to Bob Galland, the children's twenty-one-year-old companion, that he take the youngsters back to the Beverly Hills Hotel, where they would be staying that night in two bungalows.

At six-fifteen, Kennedy and Dutton were driven by John Frankenheimer from Malibu to the Ambassador Hotel, where in RFK's suite the campaign brain-trust would monitor returns and, they hoped, celebrate the triumph that would catapult their man to his party's presidential nomination. Ethel, slower in dressing, would follow in a separate vehicle.

As Frankenheimer cruised along the Santa Monica Freeway, attempting to make the thirty-minute trip in half that time, Bobby said, "Hey, John, take it slow. I want to live long enough to enjoy my impending victory."

Sirhan Bishara Sirhan was born to Jordanian parents in Jerusalem on March 19, 1944. When Palestine was partitioned to create the new nation of Israel, his father, Bishara Sirhan, lost his job in the local waterworks, and the Sirhans fled their home to spend nine years as indigent refugees in nearby lands. In 1957, the family emigrated from Jordan to the United States under the sponsorship of a church in Pasadena, California, with passage paid by the United Nations Relief and Welfare Agency. Unable to obtain gainful employment in California, Bishara Sirhan abandoned his family and returned to Jordan, where he remarried and purchased an olive grove.

In 1968, Sirhan Sirhan, an unemployed welfare recipient, applied for a junior license to become a jockey at racetracks in Southern California. For reasons never specified, the California horse racing commission rejected the application. The cause of all his troubles, Sirhan later avowed, was the state of Israel.

At seven, with an hour to go before the polls closed, Bobby arrived at the Ambassador Hotel and took an elevator to the fifth floor. Teddy, Jean and Pat were already there, as were Goodwin, Ted Sorensen, Jesse Unruh, Jimmy Breslin, Pete Hamill, Kristi Witker and others. (The Shrivers were in France, to which Sarge had recently been appointed U.S. ambassador.) All were drinking and watching television news updates: victory appeared imminent.

The Embassy Room, a vast ballroom on the second floor of the hotel (currently utilized primarily for banquets, functions, luncheons and receptions) had been decorated with hundreds of banners, balloons and posters. The space had begun to fill rapidly with supporters, reporters, campaign workers and TV camera crews (many of those in attendance wore "ALL THE WAY WITH RFK" campaign buttons).

At the same time, Bob Galland placed a telephone call from the Beverly Hills Hotel and reached Nicole Salinger, Pierre's wife. Galland proposed that the youngest children, Max (three years old) and Christopher (four), remain at the bungalows under the aegis of Diane Broughton, another family caretaker, while he brought Kerry (eight), Michael (ten), Courtney (eleven) and David to the Ambassador Hotel. Mrs. Salinger called Ethel and soon Galland and his four charges left by limousine to join the party.

South Dakota also voted on June 4. Bobby had spent only a few days chasing the state's twenty-six delegates, concentrating on the much richer treasure to the west. Nor had McCarthy expended much energy there. As in all other states, Hubert Humphrey was not on the ballot. But Lyndon Johnson was, in effect acting as a stand-in for his vice president. Bobby took 49.5 percent of the vote to 30 percent for Johnson and 20.4 percent for McCarthy.

The polls in South Dakota closed before those in California. George McGovern, who represented the heartland state in the Senate, spent the night of June 4 there. "South Dakota was Humphrey's native state," noted McGovern, "and McCarthy had been born in North Dakota. Then both went on to become senators next door in Minnesota. For Bobby to get about as many votes as they did combined seemed truly quite remarkable.

"Bobby called me from California the night he was killed—just a few minutes before, in fact—really pleased with the results from South Dakota. He was especially happy with the Indian precincts, some of which he carried a hundred percent.

"The last time he visited South Dakota, I introduced him to an audience. And I referred to 'The Impossible Dream,' the song from *Man of La Mancha*. Late that night, as he was having a nightcap, he seemed to be kind of pensive. He didn't speak for a long time. Then he said, 'Do you really think it's impossible?' 'What do you mean,' I said. 'You talked tonight about the impossible dream.' I said, 'Well, I just think it's going to be awfully tough. It's very hard to win a nomination under these circumstances. I think Humphrey has a big lead on you in the delegate search, so it's proper to speak of it as a dream, even an impossible dream. But I still think it's worth the effort.' He said, 'I hope so. There are a lot of people hurting out there. I would like to think that this campaign would give them some kind of a lift, too.' "

Advance man Thomas Shack: "Several days prior to the election, Ethel Kennedy arrived for a rally in Rapid City, South Dakota. Andy Williams was there, too. After the event, we drove her back to the airport, where she would board her flight to go to California to be with the senator. In the backseat with her was a woman reporter from a local radio station who'd asked to do an interview. I sat in the front with one of the campaign people. It was a fifteen-minute ride.

"It began as a classic interview: What does Mrs. Kennedy think about this? What does Mrs. Kennedy think about that? Then, out of the blue, the reporter said, 'Do you think it's likely that Senator Kennedy will be assassinated?' Now that's a rather hair-raising question to ask a wife. Mrs. Kennedy froze up. 'No, I never think about it,' she said.

"I couldn't believe the woman had asked that question. But then she continued: 'Well, in light of what happened to *President* Kennedy, and since Senator Kennedy is so readily accessible to crowds, don't you think it's a possibility that he could be assassinated?' I mean, she persisted on the topic. It was tasteless and aggressive, and Ethel remained frozen. I kicked myself for allowing the woman to interview her. When I put Ethel on the airplane, I apologized to her. 'Well,' she said, 'you can't control the questions.' "

The moment the balloting in California ended, the television networks began reporting that Bobby would win the state. "I was sitting on a bed up there in the Royal Suite," recalled reporter Dan Blackburn. "And oh! Oh! He was one happy camper. Ethel seemed so excited. She sat on another bed, bouncing up and down. She bounced with sheer excitement and delight and energy and radiance." Bobby lit a cigar and gave interviews—to NBC's Sander Vanocur and CBS's Roger Mudd, among others.

"Bobby was on his way to the nomination," said labor liaison Paul Schrade. "Before we went downstairs we were talking about it and making plans. I tried to get him to call [UAW chief] Walter Reuther because I thought contact ought to be made right away, but we couldn't locate him at the time."

Steve Smith scheduled a series of meetings to map out the campaign's further reorganization. Dave Hackett delivered the latest count of delegates: Humphrey, 944; Kennedy, 524½; McCarthy, 204; undecided, 872. Thirteen hundred twelve delegates were needed to nominate. Hackett's goal by opening day of the convention was 1,432 for Bobby and 1,153 for Humphrey.

Seeking a bit of quiet in the busy suite, Bobby pulled Richard Goodwin into a bathroom. "I have to get free of McCarthy," he remarked. "While we're kicking each other's ass, Humphrey's racing around the country picking up delegates. I don't want to stand on every street corner in New York for the next two weeks competing in the New York primary. I've got to spend time in other states, talking to delegates before it's too late."

Goodwin, who had briefly worked for the McCarthy operation during Bobby's period of indecision, now took it upon himself to telephone other Kennedy allies still with McCarthy to see if any of them might jump ship. Robert Lowell refused; John Kenneth Galbraith equivocated; Allard Lowenstein agreed to join RFK but felt he had to discuss the matter with Gene McCarthy first.

Pierre Salinger: "As the coordinator of press operations for the campaign, I remained downstairs in [the Embassy Room] where we had set up facilities for the press, and where, win or lose, Robert would make a speech to supporters and campaign workers later in the evening. Whenever reports came in from South Dakota or various parts of California I would relay them to him in his suite.

"From the start, it looked good, and by 11 P.M. I was able to assure the candidate that he could come down and make a victory speech with the confidence that he had won the California primary."

Kristi Witker: "I'd spent the evening drifting in and out of Bobby's hotel suite, some of the time sitting on the floor in front of the TV next to four of his children, all of whom watched the screen intently while sipping Coca-Cola.

"At one point, Eugene McCarthy's face suddenly appeared on camera as he gave a brief and grudging concession speech, vowing that he had 'just begun to fight.' A few minutes later, I bumped into Bobby in the corridor outside the suite. 'What did you think of McCarthy just now?' I asked, and he answered quickly, 'I'm not surprised—but I can only win with the help of those people [McCarthy supporters]. It'll depend on how many put more stock in principle than in personality.'

"I saw Bobby again around eleven. He stopped and whispered, 'We're having a victory party at The Factory afterwards—will you come?' I felt elated that he had won in California. It promised to be a wonderful night."

Dan Blackburn: "I conducted the last interview Bobby ever gave, up in his hotel suite. And then, at 11:45 P.M., we all left the suite together and surged toward the fifth-floor elevators. Bill Barry, Rafer Johnson and Ethel were among those who accompanied Bobby. We emerged from the elevator on the second floor and headed for the ballroom."

By ten-thirty, Ethel had suggested that Bob Galland return with her four children to the Beverly Hills Hotel. Back at the bungalow, Galland gave the kids a snack and allowed them to stay up and play with a tiny spider monkey they had acquired as a present earlier in the day from John Frankenheimer. After a while, Kerry, Michael and Courtney went to bed (Max and Christopher were already asleep in a second bungalow, as was Diane Broughton). Galland and David sat down to watch the scene at the Ambassador on television. David continued to play with the monkey.

Ted Kennedy spent primary night with an aide at a rowdy celebration in a San Francisco nightclub. There was a good deal of pushing and shoving, yelling and screaming. The Massachusetts senator nearly became embroiled in fisticuffs with one inebriated Democrat who accused him of shamelessly flirting with his wife.

Sometime after eleven, the aide suggested to his boss that they leave. Ted agreed. The two men returned to the Fairmont Hotel, on elegant Nob Hill, where Robert Kennedy's younger brother had booked a fourth-floor suite. The hotel had been the site of Ted's last meeting with Bobby, two days before.

"**B**ob wouldn't let Bill Barry carry a gun," said Dan Blackburn. "Bob wanted him there to look after Ethel more than after him, particularly in crowd situations."

"Barry was along with Bobby as, kind of, security," said Bill Epperidge. "But he was his sole security. That was it. And so, that night, Barry was all the security Bobby had."

Bobby had met Barry while attorney general. "As attorney general," said Epperidge, "you've got an FBI agent for a driver, and Barry would drive him when he was in New York. Well, Bill Barry, being a really nice guy, became friends with the family. When J. Edgar Hoover found out his agent had grown close to Bob Kennedy, he had Barry transferred down South, to Mobile or someplace like that. So Barry told Hoover, 'I quit.'" In 1968, the former G-man, then working as a bank vice president, was asked to travel with the RFK campaign as its security officer.

Once engaged, however, Barry received little cooperation from Bobby. RFK would allow his friend to help him through crowds, but he refused all of Barry's efforts at meaningful protection. Even mild precautions would interfere with the flesh-on-flesh contact the candidate so needed from his admirers. Moreover, even the most sensible avoidance of danger seemed to signal to Bobby that he wasn't strong enough or brave enough or Kennedy enough to follow in his brother's footsteps.

In his oral history for the JFK Library, Barry recalled that during a stopover in Lansing, Michigan, in April 1968, a police officer had informed him that a man carrying a rifle had been spotted entering an office building across the street from RFK's hotel. (The man was later determined to be an insurance company employee planning to leave on a hunting trip after work.) Unaware of the man's identity at the time, Barry ordered that RFK's car be parked in the hotel garage so the candidate would be driven off without having to walk out onto the street. When he learned of the precaution, Bobby laced into Barry. "Don't ever do anything like that again!" he shouted. "Don't make any decisions or changes without my permission. I make the decisions around here. If somebody's going to shoot me, they'll shoot me. But I'm not sneaking around like a thief in the night."*

Nor would Bobby accept help from the police. "RFK was very concerned about image," said Gene Scherrer, the Los Angeles Police Department official assigned to work with RFK. "He didn't want his followers—the poor, the blacks, the ethnic groups, the liberals—to see him surrounded by police types. I argued with him about it the last day, but he told me not to come to the Ambassador that night."

"The police can be very rough," observed Los Angeles newsman Jim Wrightson. "If you give them a job, they perform it to the letter. They push people around, they push the press around. The whole spirit of the RFK campaign had to do with openness. You enlist the police and they whisk you into your car and out of your car, and they form a cordon so you can't get close to people. It belies the whole spirit."

The Los Angeles Police Department was especially inimical to that spirit. "Sam Yorty offered protection to the Kennedy campaign but was told thanks but no thanks," Wrightson continued. "The police chief at the time was William Parker, who had a reputation as a tough guy, tough on civil rights. A bad guy, a really bad guy. And Sam Yorty wasn't exactly a Kennedy fan, you know. He couldn't be. I'm sure that Yorty and Chief Parker thought Kennedy was a rich big shot with no regard for the law. They hated him."

Dan Blackburn: "There had been all kinds of threats to Bobby, but Bobby didn't want the LAPD. The campaign had endured extremely bad treatment by Sam Yorty and the police department. They'd made a point of messing with the motorcade, making it clear that this campaign was not welcome in Los Angeles."

The bad blood between RFK and Sam Yorty ensured that the LAPD was not a presence at the Ambassador Hotel the night of June 4. The one exception, Gene Scherrer, appeared at the hotel that evening (despite RFK's admonition to the contrary) only because he had "a premonition—I don't know why, I just did."

"I traveled everywhere with Hubert Humphrey," remarked Ted Van Dyk. "I was kind of his constant companion, adviser and aide for the

---

*David Ormsby-Gore (Lord Harlech), British Ambassador to the U.S. during the Kennedy Administration, had always been a close friend to RFK. But on one occasion, in May 1968, when Ormsby-Gore suggested that Bobby beef up his personal security force, the presidential candidate became enraged. "He used profanity the likes of which I never heard before," said Ormsby-Gore. "He went out of his head. I have no idea what he thought he had to prove to the world. It cost him his life."

last two years of his vice presidency. And I recall, incredibly vividly, the night that Robert Kennedy was killed. We were driving from the airport in Denver. It was the end of a long day—we'd been in several time zones—and I said, 'Mr. Vice President, what would you like to see happen tonight?' And he said, 'I want Robert Kennedy to win decisively.' That startled me. I already knew we were on our way to winning at the convention, but if Kennedy were defeated in California, it would have made it clear-cut and unequivocal that Humphrey had the nomination.

"I said, 'I'm surprised to hear that. Why do you say so?' 'Well,' Humphrey said, 'Robert Kennedy and I understand each other, we're both essentially straight-line liberal Democrats. If I'm nominated, he'll unquestionably support me. And if by some fluke he were nominated, I'd support him. We'd have no problem, we're out of the same shell. However, if Gene McCarthy wins in California, he'll plague both of us and make our lives miserable all the way to Election Day.' And of course, he'd known Gene McCarthy all his life.

"The critical point for us in stopping the Robert Kennedy candidacy was the Pennsylvania caucus, which selected a huge delegation. And we swept that. Kennedy got almost nothing. The only thing that could keep him going was if he won every primary and came rolling into the convention. But he lost in Oregon, which derailed the thing. So, essentially, the losses in Pennsylvania and Oregon ended Robert Kennedy's campaign. He went on to win California, of course, but it wouldn't have done anything for him. The mythology of the time says that he would have been nominated had he not been assassinated. But it was never in the cards."

What if? The question haunts any discussion of the Kennedys. Would Jack have withdrawn from Vietnam? Would Bobby have been elected president? For Ted, too: What if there had been no Chappaquiddick? Would he have reached the White House?

Van Dyk may have been overconfident in June of 1968. Humphrey did lead in delegates, but as the California returns were coming in, Bobby spoke to Richard Daley. Daley wished him luck and hinted that if early indications of a Kennedy victory in the Golden State turned out to be accurate, the Illinois delegation would support RFK at the convention. Had the boss of Chicago given his nod to Bobby, other bosses and other delegations would have followed. "Daley means the ball game," RFK had said.

Had Bobby lived, he might or might not have captured his party's nomination. But the catastrophe of the Chicago convention—the blood in the streets, the rancor in the hall—would certainly not have occurred. Humphrey was right: had the vice president won the nomination, Bobby would have supported him in the fall, and vice versa. Sometime after Chicago, Eugene McCarthy issued a lukewarm endorsement of his fellow Minnesotan in the contest against Richard Nixon, but otherwise he stayed aloof from the campaign. Had Bobby lost the nomination to Humphrey, he would have fulfilled his responsibility as a leader of his party and as head of his family. Whatever his disappointment, he would have stumped with at least outward enthusiasm for the Democrats' standard-bearer.

Even as a failed candidate for the nomination, RFK would have commanded sufficient loyalty within the party, and respect around the nation, to have been able to compel Humphrey to moderate his stance on Vietnam. Such suasion might have balanced LBJ's pressure on his vice president to toe the administration's line, and could thus have saved Humphrey from his inability to distance himself from Johnson's war—a failure that surely contributed to his defeat.

With either RFK or Humphrey as the Democrats' candidate, the disastrous rending of the party that took place after Bobby's death would have been avoided. The party's fall effort would have focused on its core issues and its opponent, not on making up for the images from Chicago that frightened a nation already sick of chaos. The Democratic Party was still America's majority party in 1968. The realignment toward the Republicans had yet to occur; voting Democratic was still a habit for a nation whose youngest voters were born only a few years after the passing of Franklin Roosevelt.

Richard Nixon outpolled Hubert Humphrey by only half a million popular votes in November of 1968. It cannot be assumed that Bobby would have won the White House had he lived. But it is fair to say that Richard Nixon owed his election to Sirhan Sirhan.

B y the time Robert Kennedy appeared before the cheering throng at the ballroom of the Ambassador Hotel, the tally of the balloting was almost complete. The final result would be 46.3 percent for Bobby and 41.8 percent for McCarthy, with 11.9 percent going to the unpledged slate.

Stepping before the microphones, Bobby thanked Steve Smith, Cesar Chavez, Jesse Unruh, Paul Schrade, Rafer Johnson, Rosey Grier, Freckles, Ethel and Don Drysdale, who that very night had hurled a record-breaking sixth-straight shutout for the Los Angeles Dodgers. "I'm not doing this in any order of importance," he said.

He continued: "I am very grateful for the votes that I received—that all of you worked for . . . in the agricultural areas of the state, as well as in the cities . . . as well as in the suburbs. I think it indicates quite clearly what we can do here in the United States. The vote here in the state of California, the vote in the state of South Dakota: Here is the most urban state of any of the states of our union, and South Dakota, the most rural state of any of the states of our union. We were able to win them both."

He was interrupted by applause. People shouted "Bobby Power" and "Kennedy Power."

He resumed: "I think we can end the divisions within the United States. What I think is quite clear is that we can work together in the last analysis. And that despite what has been going on with the United States over the period of the last three years—the divisions, the violence, the disenchantment with our society, the divisions, whether it's between blacks and whites, between the poor and the more affluent, or between age groups, or over the war in Vietnam—we can start to work together again. We are a great country, an unselfish country and a compassionate country. And I intend to make that my basis for running over the period of the next few months. . . .

"So, my thanks to all of you, and it's on to Chicago, and let's win there."

As the crowd roared, Bobby waved, then gave the V-for-victory/peace sign. With a quick smile, he left the platform. A press conference had been arranged and would ensue in the Colonial Room, an area usually reserved for smaller-scale affairs. To avoid the crush in the ballroom, RFK would take a shortcut through the kitchen.

P edro San Juan: "I wasn't there, but Frank Mankiewicz told me that actually Rosey Grier was supposed to go into the kitchen first. However, Ethel was pregnant, and, therefore, couldn't easily climb off the platform, which was about three feet high. And so when Bobby and Rosey stepped off, and they started walking to the kitchen, Ethel said, 'I can't get down.' Rosey came back and helped her down and Bobby walked into the kitchen by himself." Bill Barry also stopped to assist Ethel, as did George Plimpton, the more recent addition to RFK's campaign team.

"If Bobby hadn't gone in so fast," San Juan continued, "somebody else would have been shot, or somebody would have seen Sirhan sitting there with a gun in his hand and the tragedy might have been averted. I also wonder how Sirhan knew that RFK was going to go to his press conference by way of the kitchen. Who tipped him off?"

B ill Epperidge: "My office said, 'Look, tonight we want you to stick right with him. Ask him if you can be right in his party.' So upstairs in his suite I caught him and said, 'Look, Senator, my magazine has asked me to stick as close as I can to you tonight.' And he said, 'Fine, you're with us.' And there was another cameraman, Jimmy Wilson of CBS. CBS had decided to move him to another campaign, but Jimmy didn't like it so he had resigned from his job that day. And he said to the senator, 'Since it's my last day on the job, I'd like to be right with you tonight.' And the senator said, 'Fine.'

"So Jimmy and I were the two with the immediate party. Consequently, when he came off the platform and went back through the kitchen we were supposed to have been in front of him. We would always be in front of the candidate. As it happened, though, we weren't. We had to kind of scramble to catch up.

"The press had already gone through the hotel kitchen ahead of him. When he got to the press conference he intended to tell the reporters that there was to be a party that night at the Factory, a happening place in those days. Everybody was invited."

P aul Schrade: "I got off the platform during his speech and walked into the kitchen area. When he came by he said, 'Paul, I want you and Jess [Unruh] with me,' meaning at the press conference. The print reporters wanted him right after his victory speech. So I turned around and saw Jess and said, 'Come on, Bob wants us with him.' "

K arl Uecker, the hotel's assistant maître d', accompanied Bobby into the kitchen. "I had the impression that RFK should have been going in the other direction," said Frank Burns, a campaign organizer, "but somebody had obviously changed the plan, so I hurried to catch up with him. He had stopped to shake hands with two busboys—actually, I think it's more accurate to say that they had stopped him, moving in front of his path with their arms out, and Senator Kennedy, being a politician, was going to shake hands. So I had just caught up with him, and was a step or so past him. And I'd turned around facing the same way as he, toward the busboys. I was just off his right shoulder, a matter of inches behind him."

At 12:15 A.M., Wednesday, June 5, 1968, Sirhan Sirhan lifted a .22-caliber Iver-Johnson Cadet revolver toward the back of RFK's head and shouted, "Kennedy, you sonofabitch." "The noise was like a string of firecrackers going off," said Burns, "it wasn't in an even cadence. In the process, a bullet must have passed very close to my left cheek because I can remember the heat and a sort of burn. I remember an arm coming toward us, through the people, with a gun in it. I was putting together the burn across my cheek, the noise and the gun and I was thinking, 'My God, it's an assassination attempt.' I turned my head and saw the gun and quickly looked back to the senator and realized he'd been shot because he'd thrown his hands up toward his head as if he was about to grab it at the line of his ears. He hadn't quite done it. His arms were near his head and he was twisting to his left and falling back. And then I looked back at the gunman, and at that moment he was almost directly in front of me. He was still holding the gun and coming closer to the senator, pursuing the body so that the arc of the gun was coming down to the floor as the body was going down."

P aul Schrade: "I turned around and Bob was shaking hands with these kitchen workers and a thought went through my mind: 'We've got a president. A person who understands and has all this wonderful support.' I was in a state of euphoria because we'd won, so I didn't even know I'd been shot. I got a bullet in the head and passed out."

Apart from Bobby, five people were wounded by the gunfire, none fatally.

F rank Burns: "I went straight into the gunman—there were about three of us who grabbed him at once. The gun arm was off my left shoulder. I didn't grab the arm, I don't know why. Karl Uecker had him from behind, and someone else had him, too. He pulled all three of us around in a circle." Within seconds, as the assailant continued to discharge his weapon, Rafer Johnson, Roosevelt Grier and George Plimpton joined the struggle to subdue him. "After we stopped whirling and had come to rest against the steam table, I remember Bill Barry coming up, and we were trying to get Sirhan off his feet. Everybody was pulling him in a different direction, with the result that he was still standing up. Barry was yelling that we had to get him flat, so I took off my belt and bent down and put it around his legs so he could be lifted up and put on the table. Then I got back up on top of the steam table to try to find out where the gun was, and also to make sure that nobody killed Sirhan in the process. I would say that Jess Unruh and I spent most of our time being concerned that we'd have another Oswald, and we were really screaming and yelling about that."

Bill Epperidge: "I met Bill Barry in the Denver airport about five years later. And he said, 'You know, I'm a pretty strong guy.' Of course, he's a trained FBI agent. 'I have never hit anybody so hard in my whole life as I hit Sirhan, and he didn't even move. I tried to get the gun down, the gun wouldn't move.' It was like he was catatonic."

George Plimpton: "I caught up to Bobby just after he entered the kitchen area, and I was a few yards behind him when the horror began. As the shots rang out, I acted on pure instinct. Somebody yelled, 'Get the gun, get the gun!' I surged forward and came face-to-face with Satan himself: Sirhan looked like the Devil. As long as I live, I shall never forget those utterly cold, utterly expressionless eyes of his. I grabbed hold of his gun hand, but I couldn't wrest the goddamn weapon out of it."

Altogether, Sirhan had fired eight bullets, emptying his eight-chamber revolver. The men holding him in place protected him from the angry crowd.

Kristi Witker: "Following the victory speech, there were prolonged shouts and cheers from his supporters, after which Bobby and his immediate contingent headed for the doors. We had been moving in one direction, when suddenly we started in another. Once we hit the hotel kitchen area—I didn't realize at the time that's what it was—I grabbed hold of George Plimpton's coattails and held on. We were right in back of Bobby. And then there was a loud sound of balloon popping, and more balloons—or firecrackers. 'Please oh please,' I thought, 'let it be firecrackers—just like in Chinatown.' But almost immediately, a man nearby crumpled to his knees. His hair looked wet. There was a high-pitched scream. Another scream. People were running in all directions. A man next to me clutched his stomach. Someone was whining in an almost inhuman voice, 'Oh no, oh no. Not again. Oh no.'

"The idea of assassination had been in the air for months. It had happened to Jack, it could as easily happen to Bobby. When it did happen, however, it came as a total shock. There were two very distinct series of *pop-pop-pop . . . pop-pop-pop-pop-pop*. Three *pops*, then five—eight in all. One lunatic gunman with, it later emerged, a lunatic political agenda. While everyone around me scattered, I remained frozen in place. Time, it seemed, had stopped.

"I saw the gunman standing, pointing the gun and firing. I remember at least two people, Rafer Johnson and Rosey Grier, grabbing the gunman's arm but not succeeding in getting the gun away from him. It was as though the gun and his arm were fused. He just kept standing there and shooting.

"I heard a mix of voices. Steve Smith was shouting in the distance, 'Please clear the area. Please don't panic. Everything is all right.' But of course everything wasn't all right. Once they had the gunman in hand, I heard someone cry, 'Kill him—kill him—kill him now.'

"I looked down and saw Bobby lying on the ground. He was staring directly at my eyes. The expression in his eyes was not one of recognition, but of resignation. 'Well, they finally got me,' he seemed to be saying. We had discussed this moment many times before, he and I, and now it had happened, and I had been unable to do a thing to save him."

F rank Burns: "People were screaming, there were television and camera lights and flashbulbs going off, and just pandemonium." Police arrived to carry Sirhan away by his arms and legs. In the struggle for the gun, he had suffered a broken finger and a sprained ankle.*

Steve Smith had called for a doctor over the ballroom's public-address system.

T wo ambulance attendants arrived with a rolling stretcher. "Don't lift me, don't lift me," Bobby whispered. "Oh, no, no . . . don't," he said as they gently raised him to the gurney. He soon lost consciousness.

Bobby was quickly wheeled to an elevator, as Ethel, Jean Smith, Fred Dutton, Bill Barry and a few others went along. When they arrived at the waiting ambulance, one of the medics, Max Behrman, said that only Ethel would be allowed to ride to the hospital with the patient, but Dutton clambered into the back next to Ethel, while Bill Barry and *Look*'s Warren Rogers sat in the front with the driver. As the ambulance sped toward Central Receiving Hospital, a mile away, Behrman tried to place an oxygen mask over the patient's nose and mouth. Ethel screamed at him to leave her husband alone. However, when Bobby's breathing became more labored, she allowed Behrman to apply the mask.

At Emergency Room 2, Bobby was lifted onto a padded aluminum table. He had minimal pulse and blood pressure. A doctor slapped Bobby on the face and called his name, but received no response. However, he was able to locate a heartbeat. The physician allowed Ethel to listen through his stethoscope so that she would know her husband was still alive.

Doctors administered heart massage and a shot of adrenaline. They connected Bobby to life-support machinery.

*Sirhan's .22 revolver ended up in the hands of Gene Scherrer, who was photographed by the press holding the weapon. "Because I wasn't supposed to be there that evening," said Scherrer, "the *Los Angeles Times* referred to me as the man who wasn't there."

Father James Mundell, a lay priest and a Kennedy friend, waited in a corridor outside the emergency room, his path blocked by a security guard posted there by the hospital. Ethel emerged from the room, frantic in her demand that the priest be admitted. She pushed the guard aside and Mundell followed her. After giving Bobby Absolution, Mundell was joined by a second priest, Thomas Peacha, who performed last rites.

Half an hour later, doctors decided to move Bobby to Good Samaritan Hospital, ten blocks away. There surgeons would attempt to remove two bullets: one, which had entered behind the right ear, was lodged in the right hemisphere of the cerebellum (brain); another had entered the right armpit and lodged in the back of the neck, just short of the cervical vertebra. A third bullet had also entered the right armpit but had exited from the front of the right shoulder without striking any bony structure or leaving any lead fragment in its track.

At 1 A.M., Bobby was transferred by ambulance to Good Samaritan. Jean and Pat waited with Ethel while Bobby was taken to the operating room on the ninth floor. The stricken candidate's wife soon received a telegram from President and Mrs. Johnson. "We grieve and pray with you," it said.

"**R**obert Kennedy must be assassinated . . ." wrote Sirhan Sirhan in a notebook found after the shooting by the LAPD. "My determination to eliminate RFK is becoming more the more [*sic*] of an unshakable obsession." He vowed to kill the senator by June 5, the first anniversary of the Arab-Israeli Six Day War.*

No one can doubt that Sirhan Sirhan fired a gun at Bobby in the kitchen of the Ambassador Hotel the night of the 1968 California primary. But theories abound as to conspiracies behind the murder. Philip H. Melanson, director of the Robert F. Kennedy Assassination Archives at Southeastern Massachusetts University, has suggested Sirhan was a "Manchurian Candidate," programmed to kill by "a professional expert or experts working for, or in the shadow of, U.S. intelligence." Another conspiracy buff, Robert D. Morrow, has tied Sirhan to SAVAK, the Shah of Iran's secret police. Among those looking for a complex explanation to what seems a simple story, speculation is most heated over the so-called "woman in the polka-dot dress," allegedly seen standing near Sirhan just before the shooting began. Afterward, according to a young campaign

---

* Sirhan Sirhan's notebooks and other personal possessions were confiscated from a house he shared with his mother and two brothers at 696 East Howard Street in Pasadena, a suburb of Los Angeles.

worker, the woman ran down the front steps of the hotel in the company of an unidentified man. "We shot him!" the witness claimed to have heard her say. The woman was never heard from again.

Gottfried Isaac, a lawyer who represented Sirhan in his court appeals from 1970 to 1978, raised the possibility of a second gunman: "There was no question that Sirhan had been there, had a gun and was firing. But the question is: Did a bullet from the muzzle of the gun held in the hand of Sirhan Sirhan actually kill Senator Kennedy? Or, for that matter, strike him? And we came to the conclusion that it had not." Bernard Fensterwald, a lawyer interested in the assassinations of the 1960s, claimed that eleven bullets were fired in the hotel kitchen—three more than were held by Sirhan's gun.

John Miner, in 1968 head of the Medical-Legal Section of the Los Angeles district attorney's office, discounted the various theories: "I attended the autopsy. I made sure that physical evidence was preserved and turned over to the investigating agency, which was the LAPD. The investigation was unbelievably complete. Can you imagine? Forty qualified officers spending six months, concentrating on just one individual. There has never been that thorough an investigation of a crime.

"His reason for the murder? The motivation was that of a little man out to kill a big man and to thereby make himself big. He had a hatred of Kennedy and of Israel and the Jews. He thought killing RFK would make him a hero to the Arabs and also throughout the world because of the importance of the man who would have very likely become president of the United States.

"There was no second gun, only the shots fired by Sirhan. There was no conspiracy."

On April 17, 1969, after a three-month trial, Sirhan Sirhan was convicted of first-degree murder. The jury imposed the death sentence. Ted Kennedy, the last surviving son of a tragedy-inflicted family, petitioned the district attorney's office to reduce the sentence. For his part, Sirhan Sirhan filed a pro forma appeal requesting clemency. While the appeal was in progress, the California Supreme Court abolished the state's death penalty. On June 17, 1972, Sirhan's sentence was commuted to life imprisonment.

Periodic requests for parole have been denied. At this writing, Sirhan Sirhan remains behind bars at Soledad Prison in the state of California.

B ack in their suite at the Fairmont Hotel, Ted Kennedy and Dave Burke turned on the television set to watch Bobby's victory party. The announcer was talking about a shooting at the Kennedy rally. "We were lucky to get out of there," said Burke, not surprised that the San Francisco celebration had turned ugly.

But Teddy wasn't paying attention to his aide. He stared at the television, listening as Steve Smith asked everyone to remain calm and to please vacate the area as soon as possible. Burke suddenly realized that the shooting had taken place not in San Francisco but in Los Angeles.

Ted said only, "We have to get down there," nothing more. Burke rushed to the hotel desk to obtain assistance in making arrangements for transportation. Considering the hour and the urgency to leave, the logistics were complicated; he wound up using the telephone in the assistant manager's office. In between calls, Burke raced up to the suite three or four times. Teddy just stood in the room, in front of the blaring television set, his jacket off, not uttering a word.

At 1:15 A.M. the two men left the hotel for a nearby air force base. A military jet flew them to Los Angeles. Throughout the flight, Teddy maintained his silence.

Jack Micay, a college student in 1968, later a producer of television documentaries: "A day or two before the California primary, a friend and I were on the street in San Francisco when Robert Kennedy's motorcade passed by. He was sitting in a convertible and he seemed most charismatic, like some bronze god.

"So we volunteered to canvass the day of the election and were assigned to a poor part of San Francisco near the Tenderloin. That night, we went to the party downtown. There was a big room full of people and they had televisions on the stage so we could watch the results. Ted Kennedy spoke and thanked people for their help.

"Later, we watched as Robert Kennedy gave his speech. And then he got shot, on television, live. The whole place went berserk. There was total pandemonium. I remember that Willie Brown, then a state assemblyman and later the assembly speaker, picked up a chair and threw it at the TV.

"We hitchhiked down to Los Angeles and arrived there the day after he died. The streets were deserted, there was a pall over the city."

Pierre Salinger recalled that he remained in the ballroom as Bobby left the platform following his speech. Then: "Suddenly people were rushing away from the kitchen. I fought my way past them and saw Robert on the ground. I was certain he was dead. I thought, *Not again?*

"An ambulance took Kennedy to a hospital. I had no car, and there were no taxicabs. A man on a motorcycle stopped and offered me a ride. My wife, Nicole, was with me. We both got on and roared across the city to the hospital."

R oswell Gilpatric: "I was with Jackie Kennedy the night that Robert got shot. She and I went to a rally for him here in New York. I saw her back to her home at 1040 Fifth Avenue, and left around eleven, eleven-thirty. Of course, it was only eight-thirty in California.

"For some reason I turned on the radio in the middle of the night, three or four o'clock, and got news of the shooting. So I called up Jackie and she was awake, she'd already gotten word. She asked me to come up." In London, Stas Radziwill had also heard the news bulletins. He had called Jackie to tell her what had happened and to say that he would be on the first available flight to New York.

"Jackie was determined to go to California," Gilpatric continued. "So I called up Tom Watson of IBM and got him to lend her his private jet. He and I took her out to the airport."* Jackie waited for Radziwill to arrive; together they flew west.

Upon their arrival in Los Angeles, they were met by Charles Spalding. "What's the story?" asked Jackie. "I want it straight from the shoulder."

"He's dying," Spalding replied.

T y Fain, Southwest coordinator for the campaign: "We were at RFK headquarters in Albuquerque, New Mexico, watching the Los Angeles celebration on television. He had won the primary and was going to win the nomination and then the presidency. We were going to resolve so many problems, we were going to eliminate poverty and racism in our lifetime. We had dreams of mythic proportions. And then in a burst of gunfire, it was all blown away for us.

"I left Albuquerque and flew to Los Angeles, where I was not needed for anything. Bobby was still alive, so I went to the hospital. There were tens of thousands of people and police lines and TV cameras and flood-lights. Nobody was talking, I'll never forget that. And those lights—all those people's faces were illuminated. They were just staring at the white exterior of the hospital."

---

* According to Gilpatric, Jackie's only comment en route to the airport was, "No! It can't have happened. It can't have happened. Tell me it hasn't happened." "Although Jackie seemed shaken on the way to JFK," said Gilpatric, "by the time we arrived, she had gotten hold of herself."

Journalist Al Eisele: "Hubert Humphrey was at the Air Force Academy in Colorado when he heard that Kennedy had been shot. And Muriel Humphrey turned to him and said, 'It's all over for us.' She saw, she instinctively sensed, that Bobby's fate would befoul the political atmosphere and thus ruin her husband's chance to be president."

Ted Van Dyk: "In the middle of the night I was shaken awake by David Gartner, a personal aide to the vice president. And Dave said, 'Humphrey says get up, Robert Kennedy's been shot.' And I said, 'David, that's a sick joke.' He said, 'No, no, Robert Kennedy's been shot.'

"So I got up and Humphrey was absolutely distraught, he was just absolutely beside himself with anxiety and concern. And we then received a telephone call from Steve Smith and Pierre Salinger in California. They said, 'There's a brain surgeon we trust in Boston. Could you arrange for a private plane to fly him to Los Angeles? Because Robert Kennedy's still alive and there's a possibility of saving him.'

"Humphrey called up the commanding general of the air force, who happened to be there at the academy. And Humphrey said, 'Will you please dispatch this plane?' The general said, 'I surely will.'

"Ten minutes later we received a call from an aide in the White House: President Johnson had canceled the plane because Humphrey had no authority to send it. The fact was, Johnson preferred Robert Kennedy dead.

"It was one of the most heinous acts I've ever experienced in my life, and it all but broke Humphrey's heart. He canceled his speech the next day and flew back to Washington."

Rose Kennedy arose at 6 A.M. on June 5 to attend mass at St. Francis Xavier Roman Catholic Church in Hyannis Port. As she was getting dressed she turned on the television. Only half listening, she sensed (she later told Mary Sanford) that somewhere there had been an accident, perhaps during some sort of victory celebration. Then Ann Gargan came in and told her that Bobby had been shot.

Ted soon called and spoke to his mother and father. Afterward, Joe, seated in his wheelchair, wept. Rose went to mass and prayed for her son.

Back home, she retired to her bedroom and flipped through albums of family photographs. Several hours later, wearing sunglasses and a red cloth coat, she exited the house and stood in the driveway bouncing a small rubber ball against the door of the garage. When she noticed that she was being watched by a horde of reporters, she said, "I've got to do something or I'll go mad."

Peter Lawford watched Bobby's victory speech on a television set at the Factory, waiting for the party that would take place there later that night. When he heard Steve Smith's call for a doctor, he turned to a friend and said, "He's had it." He rose from his chair and left the club.

At the Beverly Hills Hotel, Bob Galland and David Kennedy watched the scene at the Ambassador. "Oh God," David gasped, "they got Dad. They got my father."

The two left their bungalow and trudged the nearby streets for over an hour, ending up back on the hotel grounds, behind the swimming pool. Galland then entered the lobby to ask the night clerk for an additional key: he felt that David could more easily relax if left alone. Galland sat next to David on the bed, until the boy finally dozed off. He then returned to the other children to make sure they were still asleep.

Back at Hickory Hill, fourteen-year-old Bobby Jr. had viewed the early election returns on television, retiring only after his father had been declared the probable victor. He awoke at 7 A.M., got dressed and went downstairs to retrieve the newspaper from the front lawn. "RFK SHOT!" read the headline of the *Washington Post*. Racing inside, RFK Jr. turned on the television. Later that morning, having spoken briefly by telephone with his mother, he shredded the pages of the newspaper and threw the heap into the living room fireplace. Also at Hickory Hill was the youngest of the Kennedy offspring, fourteen-month-old Douglas.

By midafternoon, the two oldest of the brood, fifteen-year-old Joe and sixteen-year-old Kathleen, had reached Hickory Hill from their respective New England boarding schools. In the early evening, Bob Galland and the half dozen younger children arrived, accompanied by John Glenn, who had arranged for an air force jet to carry them east.

That night, Bobby Jr., Joe and Kathleen flew to Los Angeles aboard a plane provided for their private use by Lyndon Johnson. Accompanying the three children were Lem Billings and a pair of Secret Service agents.

Seeing no brain-wave activity, doctors at Good Samaritan Hospital harbored little hope for Bobby's survival.

Nonetheless, at 3:15 A.M., a team of five surgeons, headed by Dr. Henry Cuneo, commenced a three-and-a-half-hour operation in a last-ditch effort to save the patient's life. Detective Sgt. Daniel Stewart of the LAPD and another policeman stood guard outside the operating room. "I'd already been told by one of the doctors," said Stewart, "that Bobby didn't have a prayer in the world."

Dan Blackburn: "We set up a pressroom in the hospital, and we put in microphones and lights. Frank Mankiewicz would come in and do a briefing periodically."

After completion of the operation, at 7:25 A.M., Mankiewicz entered the makeshift press room and informed reporters that although surgeons had removed almost all of the bullet fragments that had penetrated RFK's brain, Bobby's vital signs were impaired and showed little chance for improvement.

Bobby lay in the intensive care recovery room. Ethel stood next to him. She whispered in his ear; he did not respond.

On Wednesday evening, Frank Mankiewicz reported that physicians attending the senator were worried by his continuing failure to show improvement following surgery and were describing his condition as "extremely critical." The press secretary concluded his brief statement by noting that there would be no further bulletin until early the next morning.

The family and friends who had convened at Good Samaritan Hospital quietly discussed what all knew to be a hopeless situation. Also they eased their pain. "One of the Kennedy people brought in some liquor by a back entrance," reported Daniel Stewart. "They put it on a medical trolley and wheeled it around. Within the hour, they were all pretty far gone. Steve Smith was the worst. He's obviously a mean drunk, and he started pushing people around. I mean physically pushing them around. He had to be restrained."

At 10:00 P.M., Kathleen, Joe, and Bobby Jr. stood by their father's bedside. Tubes and lifelines connected the wounded figure to the latest in medical machinery. "I held his hand," RFK Jr. said later. "His head was bandaged and his eyes blackened. I knew he had little or no chance."

About 1:15 A.M., Thursday morning, Bobby's doctors met with Ethel, Jean, Pat, Jackie and Ted. They informed the Kennedys that from the beginning there had been no brain activity. A mechanical ventilator was keeping the senator alive. "Is there any hope of recovery at all?" asked Ethel. "None," responded Dr. Cuneo. "Then turn it off," she said.

Ethel remained by her husband's bedside as an attendant disconnected the life-support apparatus. Bobby continued to breathe on his own for a few minutes, then gradually stopped.

Frank Mankiewicz made the announcement. The official time of death was 1:44 A.M., Thursday, June 6, 1968, twenty-five and a half hours after Sirhan Sirhan had raised his pistol. Robert Francis Kennedy was forty-two years old.

L yndon Johnson had sent Air Force One to Los Angeles to bring the body back to New York. After an autopsy, Bobby's remains were taken to the aircraft.* Despite his bad back, Teddy helped load the casket on board. He sat beside it, alone, the entire cross-country journey.

At 9 P.M., Air Force One arrived at La Guardia Airport. After a brief prayer from New York's archbishop, Terence J. Cooke, the body and the family were transported to St. Patrick's Cathedral on Fifth Avenue, where thousands had gathered outside. At ten, the coffin was carried into the church. The Kennedys then left, but Ted soon returned. He remained all night, along with six family friends who formed an honor guard around the bier.

At 5:30 A.M., June 7, members of the public began walking through the cathedral to view the closed coffin of African mahogany. At 6:45, Ted rose from his pew in the eleventh row and joined the line of mourners. He filed past his brother, then followed the others out onto the street. At times during the day, the line of people outside the church stretched to a mile and a half; some waited seven hours to enter. The body lay in state until five the next morning.

That day, Congress approved legislation, proposed by Lyndon Johnson, authorizing Secret Service protection for major presidential candidates. The president signed the bill and it went into effect immediately.

B eginning just before 10 A.M., Saturday, June 8, Richard Cardinal Cushing, assisted by a representative of Pope Paul VI, said a solemn pontifical requiem mass for Bobby at St. Patrick's Cathedral. Archbishop Cooke was a principal celebrant. Over two thousand people attended, including Lyndon Johnson, Hubert Humphrey, Eugene McCarthy, Richard Nixon, Nelson Rockefeller, Cary Grant, Averell Harriman, Walter Reuther, Coretta Scott King, Barry Goldwater and Ralph Abernathy. Tens of thousands of mourners flooded the immediate area surrounding St. Patrick's.

The service lasted two hours. Leonard Bernstein conducted the Adagietto from Mahler's Fifth Symphony. Andy Williams sang "The Battle Hymn of the Republic."

But the highlight of the morning had to be the eulogy delivered by

---

*The autopsy was performed on July 6, from 3 A.M. to 9:15 A.M., in the basement autopsy room at Good Samaritan Hospital. It was conducted by Dr. Thomas Noguchi, chief medical examiner for Los Angeles County, and two of his assistants. Dr. Noguchi had previously officiated in the autopsy of Marilyn Monroe. Among those present at RFK's autopsy were representatives of the LAPD, the sheriff's office, the Secret Service and the FBI.

Teddy. He spoke of his family's love for his brother, then read passages from Bobby's 1966 Day of Affirmation speech in South Africa.

He closed with words composed for him by Milton Gwirtzman. "My brother need not be idealized," said Joseph Kennedy's eldest surviving son, his voice and body trembling, "or enlarged in death beyond what he was in life, to be remembered simply as a good and decent man, who saw wrong and tried to right it, saw suffering and tried to heal it, saw war and tried to stop it. Those of us who loved him and who take him to his rest today pray that what he was to us and what he wished for others will someday come to pass for all the world. As he said many times, in many parts of this nation, to those he touched and who sought to touch him: 'Some men see things as they are and say, Why? I dream things that never were and say, Why not?'"

After the funeral train ride from New York to Washington, D.C., Bobby's family accompanied the casket to its burial site at Arlington National Cemetery. Some of the Kennedy children carried flowers and some of them also carried candles. The fifteen-minute graveside ceremony was a simple religious one without military trappings. Ethel had requested that there be no gun salutes or troops.

A final, brief burial liturgy was given by Archbishop Philip M. Hannan of New Orleans, who substituted for Richard Cardinal Cushing of Boston, stricken ill during the train ride to Washington.

The Kennedy family stood quietly, motionlessly as John Glenn, serving as a pallbearer, folded the American flag that had draped Bobby's coffin and handed it to Ted Kennedy. Ted turned it over to Joe Kennedy, eldest son of the slain candidate, who gave it in turn to his dazed mother. The Harvard University band then played "America."

One by one, the numerous members of the family, adults and children, knelt to kiss the mahogany casket at the end of its journey, under a magnolia tree sixty feet southeast of John F. Kennedy's grave. Bobby and his brother had been brought together again, forever and at last.

EPILOGUE

PROMISES TO KEEP

One day after Robert Kennedy's burial, Jacqueline Kennedy fell apart. Her demeanor throughout the funeral service at St. Patrick's Cathedral in New York, aboard the funeral train to Union Station in Washington, D.C., and during the burial ceremony at Arlington had been as exemplary as her behavior during the four days following JFK's assassination. "After Bobby's death, Jackie became alarmingly distraught," said Roswell Gilpatric. "It shocked me because she'd seemed so composed after JFK's death. And also I'd heard that while bringing RFK's body back east from Los Angeles on Air Force One, she and Ethel had sat together and calmly mapped out plans for the funeral. But when I saw her, a day or two after the funeral, Jackie seemed highly agitated, even unbalanced. Among other things, she kept referring to Bobby as her husband. She became very imperious, barking orders as if she were still first lady. It was as if Jackie could take one such tragedy, but not two."

Jackie's anger and anguish in the wake of Bobby's assassination knew no bounds. "I hate this country," she announced. "I despise America and I don't want my children to live here anymore. If they're killing Kennedys, my kids are number-one targets."

On October 20, 1968, amid an avalanche of personal and public excoriation, the former first lady married Aristotle Onassis on Skorpios, his private island in the Ionian Sea. "If you marry that man, you'll fall off your pedestal," Truman Capote had warned Jackie prior to the betrothal. "Better to fall off than be frozen there," she'd responded.

Larry O'Brien recalled that "the Kennedys all despised Onassis. Jack, in fact, always suspected Jackie of having been involved with the tycoon. 'She's tired of my screwing around, so she's stepping out on me with the pirate,' he used to say. But it wasn't true—nothing of that sort went on with Onassis until after JFK's death. The only man I suspected Jackie of being involved with other than her husband during his presidential term was Gianni Agnelli, the Italian industrialist. And I think even when Jack was alive, she felt a great deal for Bobby. Whenever she mentioned him, she practically glowed. After Bobby's death, Onassis seemed inevitable."

After Bobby's death, Onassis did seem inevitable. As Roswell Gilpatric put it, "With all his wealth and private islands and yachts, Onassis could give Jackie a sense of security. She'd felt that her source of safety and strength, Robert Kennedy, had been taken away from her.

"Then, too, Jackie didn't get along very well with the rest of the Kennedy clan. She didn't want Caroline and John Jr. to grow up in the Kennedy glare. She hoped to bring up her children in Europe, away from the Kennedys and away from what she at that time perceived as a most dangerous climate. As it turned out, Caroline and John Jr. did grow up in America. But, as everyone knows, she kept them as far away as she possibly could from the rest of the clan, especially from Ethel and Ethel's eleven children. 'Ethel,' Jackie said to me about two years after Robert's death, 'is a dysfunctional parent.' "

Bobby's death shook the very foundations of Ethel Kennedy's being. She became not only a "dysfunctional parent," she became a dysfunctional person. Truman Capote encountered her at a Manhattan cocktail party late in 1970. "She seemed to be in a stupor," he said. "She looked terrible. She was no great beauty to begin with—in fact, she was very plain-looking—but that evening she had obviously gotten drunk and was stumbling around bumping into people, her face puffy and dry, her hair matted with dirt and standing on end. She was out of it."

Doris Lilly attended a charity event in Washington, D.C., nearly a year later. There she found herself in conversation with "an inebriated Ethel Kennedy. She was slurring her words while expressing her disdain for Jackie Onassis, the former Jacqueline Kennedy. 'That girl is too much, she's just too much,' said Ethel. 'Do you know that Ari's people [employees] refer to her as "super-tanker," because he paid as much for her as he would've for an oil freighter. She's too much, that girl, too much.' Ethel kept imbibing while we were talking. Finally, she had to be helped out of the restaurant. She could barely move."

Ethel's emotional breakdown following her husband's murder had a chilling effect on the lives of their children. "There were times," said Larry O'Brien, "when she appeared to be in full control. She would sit at the head of the dinner table—Joe usually sat at the other end—and she would lead discussions on current events, just as Bobby had done. There were regular activities for the kids: swimming, sailing, football, baseball, tennis. They'd go white-water rafting, a reenactment of the July 4th expeditions organized every year by RFK. Then there would be occasional guests at Hickory Hill—John Lennon, the Jefferson Airplane, Country Joe and the Fish. On other occasions, however, Ethel lost control of herself and the brood. Things began to break down. The children lacked proper supervision. The place looked more like a Skakel house than a Kennedy home. On one visit, I actually saw rats darting about in the kitchen. Bobby Jr. would, I learned, trap and skin them. There were bats in the attic. The family pets (including a giant tortoise from Kenya) excreted all over the house." Hickory Hill smelled, said another frequent visitor, "like a fucking zoo."

There was not only a complete lack of supervision, but a lack of discipline. "Bobby had been a strict disciplinarian," continued O'Brien. "When any of the children acted up, he'd set them straight. But Ethel grew up in a household bereft of discipline and lacked the mind-set to impose it on her own kids. When the kids had problems—particularly drug- and alcohol-related—she'd ship them out to friends and relatives. She didn't want the responsibility."

One of those Ethel turned to for help was Lem Billings, whose Upper East Side Manhattan cooperative apartment soon became a home away from home to several of the older RFK boys; allowing Billings to become involved in the upbringing of her children only made matters worse. For all his good intentions, JFK's former prep school chum and perpetual houseguest was not the man for the job.

Lawrence J. Quirk, a writer who worked for JFK in his 1946 congressional campaign, knew Billings well. "In later years, he asked me to ghost his autobiography," said Quirk. "Then he decided against the project. I felt sorry for him—everybody did. He was very insecure. He had been in love with Jack Kennedy since their days together at Choate, and Kennedy loved the idea of being loved. After JFK's death, Lem became extremely depressed. After Bobby's death, he went completely to pieces.

"Lem wanted to become a kind of surrogate dad to RFK's children, a role model, but instead of guiding them and elevating them to his level, he descended to theirs. His apartment became what in street vernacular is known as the 'corner candy store'—an LSD, hash, pot, coke and heroin den.* Lem often plied the kids with drugs and became a rampant user

---

*Lem Billings died in 1981. He bequeathed his cooperative apartment to RFK Jr. Before taking possession of the dwelling, Bobby called in a New York realtor, who found it littered with floor-to-ceiling piles of old newspapers and magazines as well as an arsenal of drug paraphernalia. In addition, the floors and carpets were covered with urine stains and human excrement.

himself. He was closest to Bobby Jr., but he was also close to David as well as Chris Lawford, the son of Peter and Pat Kennedy Lawford. All three of them were addicted to drugs and hooked on booze."

"One of the problems," acknowledged Quirk, "is that Lem was gay," which in a strange way only endeared him all the more to the Kennedy family. The clan embraced him. He went shopping for clothes with Rose and her daughters, and he became a confidant to the Kennedy men. He knew where all the bodies were buried. "What wasn't so wonderful, I suppose," added Quirk, "is that Lem and Jack Kennedy indulged in an ongoing sexual relationship. It started at Choate and continued until the day JFK died. That's what Billings told me, and I have no reason to disbelieve him. He revealed that Jack had always been on the receiving end. In other words, Lem serviced him. Jack, of course, like his father before him, was a hedonist and a sex addict. He was basically straight, and by simply allowing himself to be orally pleasured without in any way reciprocating, he could rationalize the act. In the World According to John F. Kennedy, anything went."

Truman Capote also knew Lem Billings: "I didn't care for him. I used to see him at Studio 54. He would often be high on one drug or another, bragging about how he used to give JFK blow jobs in the Lincoln Bedroom. Big deal! If it meant getting off, Jack Kennedy would have inserted his dick in a cement mixer."

Whatever the nature of the friendship between Lem and Jack, there is little question that the presence of Billings only added to the family's mounting woes. In 1970, at age sixteen, Robert Kennedy, Jr., was arrested in Barnstable, Massachusetts, for possession of marijuana. He and his cousin Robert Sargent Shriver III (also arrested) were both placed on probation. Influenced by Billings, Bobby Jr. seemed unable to curb his addictions.* He was arrested again in 1983, this time for possession of 6.2 grams of heroin. Facing a term of two years in prison if convicted, he received a suspended sentence in exchange for entering a drug rehabilitation center and working in a community service program.

To his great credit, Robert Jr. eventually saved himself. His love of the outdoors and a degree from the University of Virginia School of Law (from which both his father and Uncle Ted Kennedy had graduated)

---

* According to Patricia Seaton, Peter Lawford's widow, Lem Billings would regularly show up at Peter's house in Los Angeles to pick up marijuana and cocaine for RFK Jr. "Bobby visited us in 1978," said Seaton. "He was wearing an old, rumpled suit that had belonged to his father. He told us his closets and dressers were filled with his father's clothes: shirts, pants, shoes, undershorts, the entire wardrobe."

brought him to Riverkeeper, an environmental protection group located in Westchester County, New York, whose major accomplishment was the cleaning up of the Hudson River and the Hudson River valley. Bobby Kennedy, Jr., teaches prelaw today at Pace College and is chief prosecuting attorney for Riverkeeper.

Following his arrest for possession of heroin, RFK Jr. purportedly became an outpatient at Four Winds, a drug rehabilitation and psychiatric facility in Katonah, not far from the home he would subsequently share with his second wife and four children in Mount Kisco, New York. The former director of the drug unit at Four Winds, a clinical psychologist named Kent Cunow, noted that "being the son of a martyr is never easy. And while it's convenient to blame Ethel Kennedy for her son's difficulties, I don't imagine that raising eleven children without benefit of a husband is a very pleasant or simple task.

"On the other hand, it's safe to say that not everybody with problems turns to heroin as a solution. The Kennedys were blessed with phenomenal wealth and power. They own horses, boats, sprawling homes. They have none of the everyday financial burdens the rest of us face. Instead of going to jail for possession of drugs, they went to Harvard. And all of this is part of the dilemma. Their privilege was often used for the good of the country, but it also imbued them with an intolerable arrogance, the sense that they were impervious to the rules and regulations that govern the majority of the population."

Nothing speaks more to Cunow's point than the death of Mary Jo Kopechne at Chappaquiddick, just over a year after the assassination of Robert Kennedy. "People have forgotten some of the specifics of the case," said Doris Lilly. "Ted Kennedy's car went into the water at 11:15 P.M. on July 18th, but it was not until mid-morning of the following day, long after Mary Jo's body had been found in Kennedy's submerged car, that he reported the incident to the police. He claimed afterwards that he'd been in a state of shock the night before, but the record indicates that after he returned to his hotel room at about 2:30 A.M., he proceeded to make some seventeen telephone calls, though none to the police. He did manage to call his cousin Joe Gargan—he asked Gargan to say that *he* had been driving the car at the time it went off the bridge. Gargan refused."

Ted attended Mary Jo's funeral in Pennsylvania accompanied by his wife Joan, Ethel Kennedy and Lem Billings. Shortly thereafter, Joan suffered a miscarriage. Ted pled guilty to the charge of leaving the scene of an accident and received a suspended sentence of two months in jail.

Mary Jo's parents admitted they had unanswered questions about what had happened the night of their daughter's death.

"I'd known Mary Jo Kopechne since 1965," observed Doris Lilly. "She'd been part of the Robert F. Kennedy election staff in 1968, and after the assassination we began working on an article (never completed) about RFK. She admitted that she'd been in love with him and that they'd had an affair during the early months of 1968. This didn't surprise me. Bobby wasn't exactly the choirboy that everybody thought he was. He had dozens of affairs, some longer-lived, some shorter. And Mary Jo had all the prerequisites: youth, vibrancy, intelligence. She was a sweet, sweet child. She deserved far better than to end up a passenger in the hands of somebody like Ted Kennedy. I wouldn't trust that man to walk my dog in the park. And, then, he actually had the audacity in 1980 to run for president. I mean his conduct on the night of Mary Jo's death was indefensible. The tragedy raised serious questions regarding the character of Ted Kennedy, questions which will never be answered."

Questions about Ted Kennedy's demeanor were asked not only by the American voting public but by the younger members of his family. "I'll never understand what motivated him that night," David Kennedy said to the current author in 1982. "But Ted's behavior at Chappaquiddick sickened me."

David Kennedy, the least fortunate of RFK's sons—but probably the most sensitive, intelligent and virtuous of the lot—had not only witnessed the assassination of his father on television but had endured premonitions of the murder in the form of harrowing nightmares. Always fragile, David withdrew almost completely after the death of his father. Introduced to drugs and alcohol by Bobby Jr., he soon began to surpass his brother in this department. "Drugs were the only area in which I felt competitive," David quipped by way of humor.

"As a young child, David was interested in wild flowers," said Larry O'Brien. "He'd be out in a field gathering dandelions, while the rest of the family engaged in a murderous game of touch football. His father would gently chide him about it, as would his brothers and sisters. But following RFK's death, David's siblings mocked and made fun of him."

Life at Hickory Hill and at the house in Hyannis Port during the years of David's youth was at best traumatic. Investigative reporter Leo Damore, who lived not far from the Kennedy Compound in Massachusetts, placed the blame for all the troubles on Ethel Kennedy's shoulders. "Had David been born forty years before, his mother would've insisted on having had him lobotomized," said Damore, a reference to Joe Kennedy, Sr.'s, treatment of his daughter Rosemary. "Like Joe, Ethel couldn't deal with weakness of any kind. In her eyes, David's inability to cope represented a real failing. She couldn't handle it.

"Ethel is a piece of work—the worst mother in the world. She never grew up. She was moody as hell, always screaming and yelling, castigating the employees and berating the kids. Her house was a pigsty, the drug capital of all time. Ethel was such a lousy parent, and her children so out of control, that Stephen Smith moved his family away from the Kennedy Compound and into a rented house in the Hamptons. Robert Kennedy, Jr., once stood up at an A.A. meeting on Cape Cod and said that when he was a kid, he used to go to bed at night and pray that he wouldn't wake up until he was 35 years old. That's how bad it was growing up in Ethel's house."

Richard Burke, who joined Ted Kennedy's staff as an aide in 1971, felt that by then, "Ethel Kennedy's family was totally dysfunctional. She had distinct mental problems and couldn't communicate with the children.

"A bad situation had been further intensified because there wasn't a man around the house. Ted Kennedy, due to his own shortcomings, couldn't do for Bobby's kids what Bobby had done for Jack's. Andy Williams, divorced from Claudine Longet, saw a good deal of Ethel. But Williams had his own children, as did Ethel's next beau, football player Frank Gifford. So that left Lem Billings, whose claim to fame was that he had been to the mountaintop with Jack Kennedy, but who simply couldn't make it on his own. It boggled the mind that people as loving and levelheaded as Sargent and Eunice Shriver didn't say a word about the obviously detrimental bond between Ethel's offspring and Lem.

"The combination of Lem Billings and the wretched environment at Hickory Hill took its toll. Beyond all else, few of Ethel's employees ever hung around very long. The kids had a different caretaker every other week. They went through nannies as fast as Saddam Hussein disposed of generals. The boys just tore them up and spat them out. They sexually harassed the women caretakers, physically attacked them. They even went after Theresa Fitzpatrick, who had been hired to look after Ted Kennedy's children.

"All the Kennedys—not just Ethel and her kids—developed grave problems after Bobby's death. It was as if the trunk of the tree had been chopped down, and the branches followed. Ted Kennedy did little more than party and sleep around, Joan would go on two- and three-day drinking binges and pass out in the backseat of her car. Their daughter Kara, at age fourteen, began to experiment with drugs, ran away from home and ended up in a halfway house. Teddy Jr. developed bone cancer and had to have his leg amputated, and nobody in the family wanted to know about it. They detest and fear illness, which is why they ignored David Kennedy. Bobby Jr. and David were perpetually high on something, usually pot. They harvested marijuana plants outside their house at Hyannis Port. You'd go into the house in the morning and the place would reek of pot. Ethel didn't have a clue, she didn't know what it was.

"I've got to believe that the excessive amount of drugs consumed by both David and RFK Jr. fried their brains to a crisp. Nevertheless, they were extremely bright boys. They shot heroin, which they either scored themselves or procured via Lem Billings. Ethel, meanwhile, was guzzling booze and taking sedatives. She would run up thousands of dollars in charges for services and merchandise, and when the bills arrived at her house she would either not open them or throw them away. One merchant threatened to sue her for eleven thousand dollars. I became fiscal director for Ted Kennedy's successful 1978 campaign for reelection to the Senate, and my first job entailed straightening out Ethel's finances.* RFK's oldest son Joe, by the way, managed that campaign. He couldn't stand his mother; neither could David or RFK Jr. They'll deny it today, naturally, but at the time it was true."

According to Jerry Oppenheimer, Ethel Kennedy's biographer, her employees and staff members were so put off by her bad temper and unending rages that they called Hickory Hill "Horror Hill." In one instance, Ethel attacked a newly hired maid. "You stupid nigger," she shrilled, "you don't know what you're doing."

Another family retainer, Mary DeGrace, worked for Ethel at Hyannis Port. "I did laundry for Mrs. Kennedy from 7:30 A.M. to 5:00 P.M., five days a week every week of summer for seventeen years. It took five or six years before she realized I had a name. I received minimum wage during the entire period of employment and received a gift only once—a picture of Bobby Kennedy. Because they paid so little, and because of Mrs. Kennedy's aggressive nature, the help was always leaving. During one ten-week stretch, she had thirteen cooks. In the years following Robert Kennedy's death, as the children grew up, I used to find pot in the laundry, in their pants pockets, especially with young David, the one who later overdosed. I would chuck it and tell Ena, Ethel's nursemaid for

* Mary Hayes, editor of *Aspen Times,* noted that every Christmas following her husband's death, "Ethel Kennedy would bring some of her kids to Aspen to go skiing. She wouldn't pay her bills (to restaurants, caterers or landlords) unless they sued. She used to rent condominiums in town but people stopped renting to her. The Kennedys would trash the place, they had wild parties. She finally bought her own condominium."

many years. Ena, who was Costa Rican, had seen Ethel through most of her eleven children. You couldn't tell Ethel. You couldn't even tell Ena. If I turned it over to Ena, she would hide it from Ethel.

"After seventeen years, Ethel and I had words over her laundry bill. She thought I was sending out too many things to be cleaned. I washed and ironed shirts, towels, underpants, pillow cases, even dungarees. Who irons dungarees these days, especially with a crease down the middle of the pants leg? The washing machine ran from the minute I arrived until after I left, when one of the other maids took over. But we sent out larger items—sheets, blankets, draperies. One day, Ethel came into the laundry room and told me, 'You must be in cahoots with the laundry man. My laundry bill so far this year comes to $700, and you're going to pay for it!' So I told her she could wish with one hand and shit in the other and see which one got filled up first. Then I threw down the iron and walked out the door."

Ethel Kennedy resided in a twilight zone, a make-believe empire with glossy photographs of her "late-and-great" husband plastered all over the bathroom walls, their favorite love songs piped into the lavatory through built-in stereo speakers, RFK's memory kept alive by the secret visits she paid at night to his grave site at Arlington Cemetery. Although she remained true to the Kennedy flame, she continued to spin off in all directions at once, mistreating her children, abusing the help, alienating former friends and other members of the Kennedy clan. Her son David characterized his own existence in her household as "hell on earth."

After attending a series of boarding schools and dropping out of Harvard, David Kennedy made headlines for the first time in 1979, when he was arrested in a seedy Harlem hotel, the Shelton Plaza, while transacting a narcotics deal with a trafficker whose friend then started a fight with him. He received a suspended sentence for drug possession and enrolled in a drug treatment program—not the first he had been in, nor the last. Over the next few years, he would go from one drug program into another.

His hair slick with grease and at times hanging below his shoulders (as did RFK Jr.'s), David seemed restless, unable to carve a niche in the Kennedy family or find a key to his future. Nor could anyone seem to help him. His brother Joe tried but failed. So, too, did Kathleen, his eldest (and probably most sensible) sibling.

In 1981, David began dating Pamela Page, a spunky and articulate debutante from New Orleans. "David and I met through a friend," she said. "He visited me in New Orleans, and we had a great time together. We then saw each other in New York. Over Christmas vacation, we went skiing in Aspen. In all, we went out for approximately a year. Toward the end, he invited me to come to Hickory Hill. Caroline Kennedy and other family brothers and sisters were there, all of them running hog wild. Ethel wasn't around. There was no adult supervision, by which I mean no members of the second generation of Kennedys.

"At night, David and I slept in the same room but in separate beds, twin beds. He'd take a handful of all different kinds of pills, swallow them, say good-night, roll over and go to sleep. There was no sex, although there had been on previous occasions. When we were in bed on the second night, he said to me, 'You're not as good as the daughter of Ben Bradlee.' I assumed he meant that I wasn't as good a sexual partner. So I jumped out of bed, threw on some clothes, ran to my car and drove off. He came after me in his car. It became a chase scene through the deserted, late-night streets of suburbia. Finally, I lost him.

"I saw him two or three times more before we broke up for good. He was really very cute, extremely cute, but very fucked up. I wasn't surprised by his death."*

Peter Collier and David Horowitz interviewed David for their bestseller, *The Kennedys: An American Drama,* eliciting his full cooperation. Although his siblings subsequently used the term "traitor" to define his betrayal of the Kennedy code of silence, beyond discussing the personal lives of his brothers and sisters, David divulged details of his own life. One detail involved his romantic attachment to Rachel Ward, the highly attractive British actress. Wearing a cast on his leg (having broken his ankle in a rare attempt at touch football with his cousins) and once again injecting himself with heroin (despite a recent stay in a methadone clinic), David entertained Rachel by taking her to such New York discotheques as Xenon and Studio 54. When he wound up on the locked psychiatric ward at Massachusetts General Hospital in Boston, Rachel was his only visitor. They shut the door and made love in his private room.

"One step forward, two steps backward . . . two steps forward, one step backward—my life is spent marshmallowing [*sic*] along, accepting a certain negativity." These lines (from a David Kennedy letter to the current author) were written in late March 1984. A month later, having been

*Another girlfriend of David Kennedy, Ryan Rayston of Greenwich, Connecticut, recalled that "he turned me on to drugs and took me on a drug-buying binge in South America. I was a student at Dartmouth College, and we used to go skiing together. I also saw him in Palm Beach. Despite his drug addiction, David was a darling, very gentle, extremely sweet, not like other members of the clan."

released from a drug rehabilitation center in Minnesota, David flew to Palm Beach to visit his grandmother, Rose Kennedy. Checking into room 107 at the Brazilian Court Hotel, around the corner from posh Worth Avenue, twenty-nine-year-old David embarked on a nonstop woman and alcohol binge. On April 25, paramedics were called to his room by the hotel operator. He had expired only hours before. The autopsy revealed excessive amounts of cocaine, Demerol and Mellaril in his digestive tract. Authorities later arrested two bellhops at the Brazilian Court in connection with the sale of the cocaine. David was laid to rest alongside his grandfather Joseph P. Kennedy in the family plot at Holyhood Cemetery in Brookline, Massachusetts.*

As the eldest male of his generation, Joseph Patrick Kennedy II was expected to carry on the family traditions, a point made explicit in a letter his father (RFK) wrote him on the day of President Kennedy's funeral: "You are the oldest of all the male grandchildren. You have a special and particular responsibility now which I know you will fulfill. Remember all the things that Jack started—be kind to others that are less fortunate than we—and love your country." What Joe didn't realize is that he would be expected to assume his new role as early as 1968. He embarked on his ascent in auspicious fashion.

In the summer of 1973, at the age of twenty-one, he overturned a jeep on Nantucket while driving his brother David and David's then-girlfriend, Pam Kelley, to the ferry. The accident, caused by Joe's extreme recklessness, bore a similarity to Teddy's carnage at Chappaquiddick. Joe had his driver's license revoked; Pam Kelley was permanently crippled and would never walk again.

A poor student ("He's dyslexic and not very bright," said Richard Burke), Joe enrolled at the University of Massachusetts (Boston campus) and, after much struggle, managed to graduate in 1976. Three years later, having accomplished little, Joe married socially prominent Sheila Brewster Rauch of Philadelphia, whom he had known for ten years. On October 4, 1980, they became the parents of twin sons, Joseph and Matthew, and moved into an old farmhouse on Massachusetts's South Shore, in suburban Boston.

In 1986, Joe Kennedy fulfilled his father's expectations by running for

---

*An investigation into the death of David Kennedy conducted by the Palm Beach Police Department included an interview with Caroline Kennedy, who had arrived in Palm Beach the evening before her cousin's demise. According to the report, Caroline claimed she had no knowledge that David was "suffering from any illness or taking any drugs."

and winning the retiring Tip O'Neill's congressional seat from his home state—JFK had captured the same seat exactly forty years before. In 1988, "the reluctant prince," as family members had dubbed Joe, ran and won again.

"Young Joe idolized Ted Kennedy," said Lawrence Quirk. "Ted drank, Joe drank. Ted had an automobile accident, Joe had an automobile accident. Ted Kennedy got a divorce, Joe Kennedy got a divorce." Ted and Joe Kennedy II both inherited Joe Kennedy, Sr.'s vigor (and money) but evidently not his searing intelligence. Teddy and Joe II—different generations, similar styles—are equally self-destructive.

In March 1989, Joe Kennedy announced that he and his wife were filing for divorce. "This has been a very painful day for me and my family. As a father, my principal desire is to assist my children through the most difficult time in their lives."

In a recently published personal memoir, *Shattered Faith,* Sheila Rauch detailed some of the abusive tactics employed by Joe Kennedy in forcing her to agree to an annulment of their marriage. At the same time that Rauch's book emerged in print, the congressman declared his intention to run for governor of Massachusetts.

"Politically speaking, an annulment is preferable to a divorce," said television documentary producer Brent Zacky. "But after two children and all those years together, there are no grounds for an annulment. It's pure bullshit. It makes Joe Kennedy look absurd."

The annulment, the memoir, and a new slew of Kennedy family scandals (including William Kennedy Smith's 1991 Palm Beach trial for rape) signaled the possible end of Joe's gubernatorial candidacy. The final bell tolled for Joe when his brother and campaign manager, Michael Lemoyne Kennedy, admitted late in 1997 to being an alcoholic and having had an extramarital affair with a fourteen-year-old baby-sitter. The baby-sitter and her family, in an effort to avoid unwanted publicity, refused to press charges against Michael for statutory rape. Michael's wife, however, Victoria Gifford, daughter of Frank Gifford, Ethel Kennedy's former beau, separated from her husband and instituted divorce proceedings. Their three young children were shifted to and fro between separate households.

In a personal miniessay on the perils of temptation, John F. Kennedy, Jr., in the pages of his magazine, *George,* referred to his cousins Joe and Michael as "poster boys for bad behavior" who "chased an idealized alternative to their life."

In a press conference the day after the magazine's publication, Joe Kennedy angrily retorted, "Ask not what you can do for your cousin, but what you can do for his magazine." Less than two weeks later, on August 24, 1997, Joe Kennedy, his second wife Beth by his side, renounced his run for the governor's office.

Scandal presently evolved into travesty. Four months after his brother's announcement, on December 31, Michael Kennedy, aged thirty-nine, perished in a skiing accident while vacationing with other family members, including his children, in Aspen. Michael's fatal end, widely documented in the media (the deceased's visage graced the cover of *Newsweek*), was again the result of a bravado and hubris that seemed almost endemic to Bobby's young. Michael died while playing a version of ski football wherein a small projectile is tossed back and forth from one player to another while the participants ski without poles or headgear down a difficult run, usually at dusk. Michael had just caught a pass when he smashed head-first into a tree.

Disclosures about Michael in the aftermath of his demise added further embarrassment to a clan already burdened by an overflow of negative press coverage. Much touted for his directorship of the Citizens Energy Corporation, a nonprofit organization founded by Joe Kennedy II that provided heating fuel for the needy, it developed that Michael had for years been setting aside a huge salary for himself, nearly $350,000 in 1996 alone. Another dismaying revelation had to do with Ethel Kennedy. Endlessly reckless and heedless, it was she who had encouraged the game of ski football that ultimately killed her son. Despite warnings about the dangers of the sport from members of Aspen's ski patrol, Ethel had suggested that Michael videotape a game of ski football to be used as a means of countering the negative publicity he had received for his ill-advised adventure with the underage baby-sitter. Michael's last run was captured on videotape by one of his children.

"If there's a weak strain in that family, it has got to be the sons of Robert F. Kennedy," literary agent Marianne Strong ventured. "David is dead. Michael is dead. Joe has dishonored himself. RFK Jr. has been resuscitated, but he has never lived up to his potential.

"The others are even less successful. Christopher [age thirty-four] is a drone in the family business, an executive vice-president for the Merchandise Mart in Chicago. Max [thirty-three] is going to UCLA for a degree in business administration. And Douglas [thirty-one], the supposed journalist, has left writing jobs at both the *Boston Herald* and the *New York Post* because they've run what he considers to be critical stories on his family. Some journalist!"

Harsh as Marianne Strong's assessment may be, there appears to be more than a modicum of truth at work. With such opportunity at hand as the Kennedys possess, one must truly wonder what has gone wrong with Bobby's boys. Equally wondrous, however, are the impressive accomplishments of RFK's four daughters. As a group, they have more than risen to the occasion. And in so doing, they have somehow managed to avoid the crush of controversy that has besmirched the personal lives and careers of their male counterparts.

Kathleen Kennedy Townsend, forty-six, mother of four, is a lawyer and presently the lieutenant governor of Maryland. Her husband, David Townsend, teaches in the Great Books program at St. John's College.

Courtney Kennedy Hill, forty-one, mother of one, is married to Paul Hill, who was imprisoned for fifteen years on charges of IRA terrorism and murder. He was set free when a British court admitted that he had been framed and his confession manufactured by the prosecution. A human rights advocate and fund-raiser, Courtney served as United Nations representative in eastern Europe for pediatric AIDS.

Kerry Kennedy Cuomo, thirty-eight, mother of three, is wed to Andrew Cuomo, secretary of housing and urban development, and the son of Mario Cuomo, former governor of New York. Kerry, founder of the Robert F. Kennedy Center for Human Rights, is an attorney and a human rights activist.

Rory Kennedy, twenty-nine, born after the death of her father, is a prize-winning documentary filmmaker. A radical feminist, she lives in New York City.

For better or worse, the Kennedy family is unlike any other family in the United States. Perhaps RFK put it best when he said to his children over dinner one evening at Hickory Hill: "Do you know how lucky you kids are to be born a Kennedy?" Then, with a twinkle in his eye, he remarked: "As Kennedys, you must answer the call—with vigor and valor. After all, you guys have promises to keep. And miles to go before you sleep. And miles to go before you sleep." He paused again, then added: "Now will somebody please pass the salt."

SOURCE NOTES

When and where possible the author has provided source notes within the body of the text. The following notes are included to supplement the textual references. Also included are occasional comments of an extraneous but informative nature. Author interviews (more than a thousand for this book) were conducted either by the author himself or by members of his staff. In almost all cases, the interviews were either typed and transcribed, or more than one person assisted with the interview. Oral histories, unless otherwise indicated, are almost all housed at the John Fitzgerald Kennedy Library, in Boston, Massachusetts.

Of the numerous books devoted to the subject of the Kennedys, several have proven to be of great value for the purpose of this biography and therefore merit special mention. Arthur M. Schlesinger, Jr.'s *Robert Kennedy and His Times* was particularly useful as both a political record and a chronology of RFK's month-to-month activities. Jerry Oppenheimer's *The Other Mrs. Kennedy* is an extremely well researched biography of Ethel Skakel Kennedy, with shrewd insights on the relationship between Bobby and Ethel. *The Kennedys: An American Drama*, by Peter Collier and David Horowitz, provides telling record of the lives of the third generation, with particular emphasis on the children of Robert and Ethel Kennedy.

Since chapter notes are usually of interest to a select few, the author has chosen a more general mode of source identification, as opposed to very specific page or line notations. For those who wish more detailed information, it should be pointed out that more than sixty banker boxes of material (including tapes and transcribed interviews) have been given by the current author to the rare book and manuscript collection at the State University of New York at Stony Brook, Stony Brook, New York.

PROLOGUE: THE FUNERAL TRAIN

Author interviews for the Prologue were conducted with Kirk LeMoyne "Lem" Billings, Russell Baker, Stewart McClure, Dan Blackburn, Joseph Crangle.

Concerning Pete Hamill and Shirley MacLaine: the statements by Hamill and MacLaine in the prologue appeared originally in Jean Stein and George Plimpton's *American Journey: The Times of Robert Kennedy*, an oral history conducted with those who rode RFK's funeral train from New York City to Washington, D.C., on June 8, 1968.

In 1977, two years after the death of Aristotle Onassis, Pete Hamill and Jackie became involved in a brief romance. Their relationship may well have ended because of an article Hamill had written for the *New York Post*, excoriating Jackie for her 1968 marriage to Onassis. The *Post* had at first killed it, but when Hamill began dating Jackie the newspaper ran bits and pieces on "Page Six," their gossip section. Jackie stopped seeing Hamill soon thereafter.

1. BEGINNINGS

Author interviews for this chapter were conducted with Earl Blackwell, Ida Large, Larry O'Brien, David Kennedy, Judge James Knott, Ken O'Donnell, Marianne Strong, George Vigouroux, Doris Lilly, Mary Sanford, Earl E. T. Smith.

Kennedy and Fitzgerald family background materials were obtained from the archives of the *Boston Globe, Boston Herald, New York Times, Chicago Tribune.*

A trove of materials on the early Kennedys and Fitzgeralds can also be found at the John Fitzgerald Kennedy Library and at the Boston Public Library.

2. RFK: THE THIRD SON

Author interviews for this chapter were conducted with Mary Sanford, Algernon Black, Barbara Guest, Peter Barton, Lem Billings, Judge James Knott, Robert Green, George Vigouroux, Martha Phillips, Marianne Strong, June Carter, William Unis, Ruth Blackburn Leonovich, Ruth Holmes Korkuch.

Teddy Kennedy on his mother's "mean right hand": see *People Weekly*, "The Last Matriarch," February 6, 1995.

Useful general texts for this chapter included Arthur Krock's *Memoirs: Sixty Years on the Firing Line*; Arthur M. Schlesinger, Jr.'s *Robert Kennedy and His Times*; Nancy Geiger Clinch's *The Kennedy Neurosis*.

3. LIKE FATHER, LIKE SON

Author interviews for this chapter were conducted with Cecil Parker, Lady Diana Cooper, Alexander Schnee, Pierce Kearney, Martin Evarts, David Hackett, George B. McCutcheon, Samuel Campbell, Jr., Hugh M. Watson, Nigel Hamilton, Mary Gimbel.

Oral histories consulted for this chapter: John J. Hooker, David Hackett, Robert F. Kennedy.

"Dear Bob: your father has . . .": Franklin D. Roosevelt Presidential Library, Hyde Park, NY.

Barbara Hutton: For a more detailed account of the Joseph Kennedy–Barbara Hutton encounter see C. David Heymann, *Poor Little Rich Girl*, pp. 183–184.

"I am so disappointed . . .": Rose Kennedy letter, JFK Library.

Samuel Adams: See *People*, June 6, 1988; also, Patricia K. Lawford, ed., *That Shining Hour*, p. 5.

David Hackett: See Schlesinger, *Robert Kennedy . . .*, p. 98.

"A selection of comments from his grade reports . . .": RFK's Milton School grade reports were sold at auction at New York's Omni Central Hotel, October 10, 1991.

"I don't know where I got . . .": RFK to Joseph and Rose Kennedy, JFK Library.

"The folks sent . . .": See Nigel Hamilton, *JFK: Reckless Youth*, p. 627.

Information on Joseph Kennedy as American ambassador to Great Britain has been retrieved from the Department of Records, Scotland Yard, London, England.

4. HARVARD DAYS, RESTLESS NIGHTS

Author interviews for this chapter were conducted with Edward Zak, Paul Alcott, Haven W. Hammond, Peter Dalton, Lem Billings, Paul "Red" Fay, Charles Glynn, Nicholas Rodis, Wally Flinn, Francis Boyd, Paul Lazzaro, the Duke of Devonshire.

Oral histories consulted for this chapter: Dave Powers, Lem Billings, William Brady, Jr.

"I think you have developed . . .": Schlesinger, *RFK*, p. 57.

". . . was rather rough": Ibid., 66.

For information on JFK's 1946 political campaign, the author consulted the following books: Schlesinger, *RK*, pp. 68–69; Paul Fay, *The Pleasure of His Company*, pp. 156–157; Nancy Geiger Clinch, *The Kennedy Neurosis*, p. 270; Joan and Clay Blair, Jr., *The Search for JFK*, p. 471.

RFK in U.S. Navy: Bates College Library records; U.S. Naval Institute; Veterans Administration, Department of Medicine and Surgery.

The relationship between RFK and Joan Winmill is explored in great detail by Jerry Oppenheimer in *The Other Mrs. Kennedy.*

RFK's courses, grades and instructors at Harvard and at Bates College are from grade reports at JFK Library and from Schlesinger. Also from Schlesinger are the partial texts of two letters from RFK to Dave Hackett and an RFK letter to Lem Billings. The two notes from JFK to RFK are from the Kennedy family papers, JFK Library, as is the letter from RFK to his parents.

5. ETHEL SKAKEL KENNEDY

Author interviews for this chapter were conducted with Mortimer Caplin, Neil Alford, Robert Cooley, Kenneth Crawford, Livingston Fairbanks, Harry Hicks, David Parrish, Larry O'Brien, Truman Capote, Doris Lilly, Charles Spalding, John Davis, George Crossman, Thomas Wilson, Marianne Strong, William Guerry, June B. Birge, Lester Persky, Arthur Arundel, Diana DuBois, Arthur Scott, Lem Billings.

Oral histories consulted for this chapter: Gerald Tremblay, Charles Spalding, Mary Davis, Mortimer Caplin, J. Walter Yeagley, Robert F. Kennedy.

Gerald Tremblay: in addition to Tremblay's oral history, the author used an interview with him which appeared in Patricia Kennedy Lawford's *That Shining Hour*, pp. 29–30.

Ancestral information and material on the Skakels was located at the JFK Library, Boston University Rare Book and Manuscript Collection, Harvard University Libraries, and at the University of Virginia School of Law.

The Manhattanville College Yearbook provided information on Ethel Skakel Kennedy's alma mater.

"How can I fight God?": See Schlesinger, *RK*, 88; Oppenheimer, *The Other Mrs. Kennedy*, p. 126.

RFK and University of Virginia School of Law Student Legal Forum: information located at University of Virginia School of Law archives (letter from RFK to Colgate Darden included in same files).

Newspaper archives consulted for this chapter include those of the *New York Times*, New York *Daily News*, *New York World-Telegram*, *Chicago Tribune*, *Chicago Herald-American*, *Boston Globe*, *Boston Post*, *Greenwich Time*, *Washington Post*, *Cavalier Daily* (University of Virginia newspaper).

Jerry Oppenheimer's *The Other Mrs. Kennedy* proved to be an invaluable source on all aspects of Skakel family background, as well as on Ethel Kennedy's education and childhood. In tandem with interviews and newspaper reports of the day, it also helped the current author to map out the early days of the marriage between RFK and Ethel. Oppenheimer's detailed (often touching) biography contains photographs of young Ethel that show her to be far prettier than she would later become. Other sources for chapter 5 include Arthur Schlesinger's *RK*, pp. 95–99; David Lester, *Ethel: The Story of Mrs. Robert F. Kennedy*; Laurence Leamer, *The Kennedy Women: Saga of an American Family*.

6. McCARTHY & CO. (PART ONE)

Author interviews for this chapter were conducted with Joseph Gargan, Larry O'Brien, John Harlee, Endicott Peabody, David Zimmer, Tom Bolan, Langdon P. Marvin, Jr., Morton Downey, Jr., LaVern Duffy, Red Chandor, Ralph de Toledano, Francis Flanagan, Stewart McClure, Larry Newman, Kenneth Crawford, Ken O'Donnell, Joan Darling, Amy Brandon, Roy Cohn, Lem Billings.

Oral histories consulted for this chapter: William Walton, Norman Ramsey, Theodore G. Klumpp (Herbert Hoover Presidential Library), William H. Orrick, Jr. (University of California at Berkeley), Henry Jackson, Ruth Young Watt, Roy Cohn.

Periodicals referred to in this chapter include the *New York Times*, *Life*, *Harvard Crimson*, *Boston Globe*, *Spy Magazine*.

The author consulted the following volumes for this chapter: Larry O'Brien, *No Final Victories*; Doris Kearns Goodwin, *The Fitzgeralds and the Kennedys: An American Saga*; Richard J. Whalen, *The Founding Father: The Story of Joseph P. Kennedy*; Ralph G. Martin, *A Hero for Our Time*; Nicholas von Hoffman, *Citizen Cohn: The Life and Times of Roy Cohn*; Gail Cameron, *Rose*; Stein and Plimpton, *American Journey*; Schlesinger, *RK*; Richard H. Rovere, *Senator Joseph McCarthy*; Robert F. Kennedy, *The Enemy Within*.

Prime sources for information on RFK's involvement with Senator Joseph McCarthy in chapters 5 and 7 were Arthur Schlesinger, *RK*, and Richard H. Rovere, *Senator Joseph McCarthy*. Schlesinger's extremely thorough biography has utilized the most telling excerpts from the most important accounts of the day—repetition of some of these extracts is almost unavoidable. What is less evident in Schlesinger's text is a point of view. A massive collocation of facts—Schlesinger had access to materials unavailable at the time to others—he draws few conclusions, which in the long run may have been for the best.

"You haven't been elected to anything": Schlesinger, *RK*, p. 106.

Salary raise and *Boston Post* article: Ibid., p. 109. *Boston Post* article appeared April 12, 1953.

Excerpts from the two McCarthy speeches before Congress: See *Congressional Record*, May 14, 1953, and May 19, 1953. Slightly altered versions of the same excerpts are also quoted by Schlesinger in his RFK biography.

Senator Stuart Symington: Details concerning Symington's role in this matter can be found in McCarthy files at the Dwight D. Eisenhower Presidential Library. See also Schlesinger, *RK*, p. 111.

"Did somebody": *Boston Traveler*, May 26, 1953.

" 'Shocking policy' ": Schlesinger, *RK*, pp. 111–112. See also Permanent Subcommittee on Investigations, *Control of Trade Hearings*, pt. 2, 146. Also: *Boston Herald*, July 1, 1953.

Cohn, McCarthy and G. David Schine: See Robert F. Kennedy, *The Enemy Within*; Schlesinger, *RK*, pp. 112–113; Richard Rovere, *Senator Joseph McCarthy*; FBI McCarthy files.

RFK's letter of resignation to McCarthy: RFK papers, JFK Library.

Commission on Reorganization of the Executive Branch: Commission paper, Herbert Hoover Presidential Library. Second Commission papers are located at Dwight D. Eisenhower Presidential Library. See also Schlesinger, *RK*, p. 115.

7. McCARTHY & CO. (PART TWO)

Author interviews for this chapter were conducted with Roy Cohn, LaVern Duffy, Morton Downey, Jr., Robert Arum, Doris Lilly, Lem Billings, Charles Bartlett, Peter Lawford, Zsa Zsa Gabor, Ken O'Donnell, Larry O'Brien.

Oral histories consulted for this chapter: Roy Cohn, Thomas Winship, Charles Spalding, William O. Douglas, Robert F. Kennedy.

Periodicals used: the *New York Times*, *New York Post*, *New York Daily News*, *Washington Post*, *Boston Globe*.

The author consulted the following volumes for this chapter: Sidney Zion, *The Autobiography of Roy Cohn*; Schlesinger, *RK*; Rovere, *Senator Joseph McCarthy*.

"Robert Kennedy has got to be watched": FBI files.

Fort Mammoth inquest: Roy Cohn interview. Roy Cohn also spoke to the author about his confrontation with RFK during the Hearings, as reported in this chapter.

"Minority Report": See Schlesinger, *RK*, p. 122. Also: Senate Special Subcommittee on Investigations, *Charges and Countercharges*: Report., 83 Cong. 2 Sess.

"The Senate should take action": Schlesinger, Ibid.

JFK's speech regarding McCarthy: The undelivered draft is located in the JFK papers, JFK Library.

8. THE McCLELLAN COMMITTEE

Author interviews for this chapter were conducted with Ken O'Donnell, Howard E. Shuman, Paul Tierney, Bob Novak, Ralph Dungan, Bob Riley, LaVern Duffy, Strom Thurmond, Charles Bartlett, Howard Diller, William G. Hundley, Courtney A. Evans, John K. Mintz, Mel Finkelstein.

Oral histories consulted for this chapter: John Sherman Cooper, William O. Douglas, Mercedes H. Douglas (Eichholz), Charles Spalding.

An informative interview with John McClellan appears in *That Shining Hour*, edited by Patricia Kennedy Lawford.

The following periodicals were consulted for this chapter: The *Washington Daily News*, *New Bedford* (Mass.) *Sunday Standard Times*, *U.S. News & World Report*, New York *Daily News*.

Volumes consulted by the author for this chapter include: William O. Douglas, *The Court Years*; Schlesinger, *RK*; Russell Baker, *The Good Times*.

RFK correspondence quoted or paraphrased in this chapter can be found at the JFK Library.

"Speaking as a mother . . .": Ethel Kennedy quote, New York *Daily News*, September 22, 1955.

"If there is a rotten situation": RFK to McClellan, December 1, 1954, JFK Library. Also quoted in Schlesinger, *RK*, p. 124. See Schlesinger as well for information on the Peress and Communist infiltration of defense plant cases. The Talbott case is likewise discussed by Schlesinger but Charles Bartlett in an interview with the current author provided the background information herein contained.

RFK's comments regarding his trip with Justice Douglas are largely culled from journals he kept on the trip, as well as articles and letters he wrote. The sources for this material is the JFK Library.

9. HICKORY HILL

Author interviews for this chapter were conducted with Bob Novak, Howard Diller, George Bell, George Plimpton, George Smathers, Gore Vidal, Pat Brown, Charles Spalding, Ron Cutler, Leo Damore, Cary Grant, Frank Ogden, David Kennedy, John Bartlow Martin, Diana DuBois.

Oral histories consulted for this chapter: Eugene Anderson, Dave Powers, John Sharon, G. Mennen Williams (University of California, Berkeley), Pat Brown (University of California, Berkeley), Peter Cloherty.

Periodicals referred to in this chapter include the *New York Times*, *Miami Herald*, *New York Herald-Tribune*, *Chicago Tribune*, *Boston Globe*, *Washington Post*.

Information on the deeds to Hickory Hill (as well as the deeds themselves) can be found at the JFK Library.

One source used by the author for information on the death of Ethel Kennedy's parents was Oppenheimer, *The Other Mrs. Kennedy*, pp. 174, 176. It should be noted that Ethel Kennedy was pregnant with David at the time of her parents' deaths.

The source for the relationship between Lee Radziwill and JFK is Gore Vidal's *Palimpsest: A Memoir*. The same volume discusses several of Jackie's affairs during the period when JFK was senator, including one with actor William Holden. Earlier in *Palimpsest*, Vidal describes how Jackie purportedly lost her virginity, an event which took place in an elevator during the future first lady's junior year abroad, when she was a student at the Sorbonne. According to Diana DuBois, Lee Radziwill's biographer, the man in the elevator was writer John Marquand, Jr., who throughout his life always denied the story. The story, however, appears to be accurate.

A number of anecdotes on life at Hickory Hill can be found in Jean Stein and George Plimpton's *American Journey: The Times of Robert Kennedy*.

Tip O'Neill's comments in this chapter are from his autobiography, *Man of the House*, written with William Novak.

Ethel Kennedy and LSD: See Martin A. Lee and Bruce Shlain, *Acid Dreams: The Complete Social History of LSD: The CIA, the Sixties, and Beyond*. For RFK's position regarding 1966 LSD hearings, see *Organization and Coordination of Federal Drug Research and Regulatory Programs: LSD*—Hearings before the Subcommittee on Executive Reorganization of the Committee on Government Operations, United States Senate, May 24–26, 1966, pp. 72–75.

"If you were in trouble": Although this quote has appeared in print many times, it appears to have originated with Schlesinger, *RK*, p. 143. Schlesinger also writes that it was RFK who arranged to have the infant buried at the family plot in Brookline.

Background information on Adlai Stevenson's presidential campaign in this chapter comes in part from John Bartlow Martin's *Stevenson and the World: The Life of Adlai Stevenson*.

George Plimpton on Hickory Hill: See Stein and Plimpton, *American Journey*.

10. HOFFA

Author interviews for this chapter were conducted with James P. Hoffa, George Smathers, Tom Bolan, Roy Cohn, Russell Baker, Ronald Goldfarb, Joseph Rauh, Jr., Joe Konowe, Chuck O'Brian, Joe Dolan, Pat Brown, Ken O'Donnell, Larry O'Brien, John Bartlow Martin, LaVern Duffy.

Oral histories consulted for this chapter: Peter Cloherty, Roy Cohn, Robert F. Kennedy, Jack Conway.

Useful information on Jimmy Hoffa and the Teamsters came from the American Labor Archives at Wayne State University Library, Detroit, Michigan.

Publications consulted for this chapter include *Newsweek*, *Life*, *Look*, *Portland Oregonian*, *Detroit Free Press*, *New York Daily News*.

Volumes consulted by the author for this chapter include: Victor Lasky, *Robert F. Kennedy: The Myth and the Man*; Robert F. Kennedy, *The Enemy Within*; Walter Sheridan, *The Fall and Rise of Jimmy Hoffa*; Tip O'Neill, *Man of the House*; Theodore Sorensen, *Kennedy*; Allan H. Ryskind, *Hubert*. Arthur Schlesinger's chapter on Hoffa in his biography of RFK was used for background information, as was Clark Mollenhoff's *Tentacles of Power*.

The author is grateful to Chuck O'Brian for making available his unpublished manuscript concerning his life-long affiliation with Hoffa.

"Paper locals": See Schlesinger, *RK*, p. 165.

"Listen, Bobby": Schlesinger, *RK*, p. 166.

John McGovern: See RFK papers, JFK Library; Schlesinger, *RK*, p. 187.

"Madder really": RFK, *The Enemy Within*, p. 278.

"I used to love": See Victor Lasky, *Robert F. Kennedy: The Myth and the Man*, p. 119.

"At birth": RFK's article, "Hoffa's Unholy Alliance," appeared in *Look* on September 2, 1958. It became—together with other articles and additions—the basis for his book *The Enemy Within*.

11. "EMOTIONAL, JUVENILE BOBBY"

Author interviews for this chapter were conducted with Daniel Patrick Moynihan, George Smathers, Joseph Foley, Paul Tierney, Mary Sanford, Herman Badillo, Perry Gildes, Charles Spalding, Ken O'Donnell, Polly Feingold, Samuel E. Neal, Franklin D. Roosevelt, Jr., Lester Persky, John Knowles, John Richard Reilly, Mary Harrington, Charles Peters, Philip Hoff, Lee Rainey, Hubert C. Little, Peter Lawford, Joseph Tydings, Joe Alsop, Robert Lewis, Arthur Arundel, Theodore H. White.

Oral histories consulted for this chapter: Daniel Patrick Moynihan, G. Mennen Williams (University of California, Berkeley), Chester Bowles (Columbia University Libraries), Louis Martin, John Richard Reilly, Charles Spalding, David Hackett, Joseph Tydings, Robert F. Kennedy, Franklin D. Roosevelt, Jr.

Periodicals consulted for this chapter include *Penthouse, Playboy, Time, Life, Look, Esquire, Washington Post, Baltimore Sun*.

Among the books consulted for Chapter 11 are Victor Lasky, *JFK: The Man and the Myth*; Budd Schulberg, *Making Pictures: Memories of a Hollywood Prince*; Lawrence F. O'Brien, *No Final Victories: A Life in Politics—John F. Kennedy to Watergate*; Walter Sheridan, *The Fall and Rise of Jimmy Hoffa*; Tip O'Neill, *Man of the House*.

Bailey and DiSalle: See Kenneth P. O'Donnell and David Powers, *"Johnny, We Hardly Know Ye,"* pp. 150–151.

"They say the Humphrey campaign": See Schlesinger, *RK*, p. 212.

For background information on the 1960 presidential race, see Theodore H. White, *The Making of the President, 1960*.

"Nobody asked me if I was a Catholic": O'Donnell and Powers, *"Johnny,"* pp. 106–107.

"I can't afford": Schlesinger, *RK*, p. 216.

"young, emotional, juvenile Bobby": Ibid.

12. HONORARY BROTHER

Author interviews for this chapter were conducted with Ovid Demaris, Franklin D. Roosevelt, Jr., Ken O'Donnell, Theodore H. White, William McCormick Blair, Jr., Mary Harrington, Joseph Tydings, Peter Lawford, Dore Schary, George Smathers, Janet DesRosiers, Gene Scherrer, Paul Schrade, Hugh Sidey, Joan Braden, Daniel Patrick Moynihan, Langdon P. Marvin, Jr., Joe Gargan, John Seigenthaler, Herman Badillo, Harris Wofford, Lewis Martin, Larry O'Brian, George B. McCutcheon, Charles Bartlett, John Richard Reilly, John Bartlow Martin.

Oral histories consulted for this chapter: Peter Lisagor, William A. Geoghegan, David Hackett, Joseph Tydings, Tracy S. McCraken, Daniel Patrick Moynihan, John Richard Reilly, India Edwards (Harry S Truman Presidential Library).

Periodicals consulted for this chapter include the *Washington Post, Atlanta Constitution, Chicago Daily News, New York Post, New York Times, New York Daily News, New York Herald-Tribune, New York Journal American, Vanity Fair*.

Volumes consulted for this chapter include Judith (Campbell) Exner as told to Ovid Demaris, *Judith Exner—My Story*; Tip O'Neill, *Man of the House*; John Bartlow Martin, *Adlai Stevenson and the World: The Life of Adlai Stevenson*; Robert Dallek, *Lone Star Rising: Lyndon Johnson and His Times, 1908–1960*.

With respect to Sam Giancana, the author made ample use of the FBI investigatory files, Federal Bureau of Investigation, Washington, D.C. Further information on Giancana can be found in *Double Cross: The Explosive Inside Story of the Mobster Who Controlled America* by Sam and Chuck Giancana, respectively the mobster's brother and nephew.

Sam Giancana's testimony is quoted by Arthur Schlesinger in his RFK biography on pages 177–178. The original source is: Senate Select Committee on Improper Activities in the Labor or Management Field. *Investigation of Improper Activities in the Labor or Management Field: Hearings*, 86, Cong., 1 Sess.

With respect to the 1960 presidential election, Franklin D. Roosevelt, Jr., remarked to the current author: "Over the years, there have been numerous accusations that the Kennedys 'bought' the vote by dispersing moneys to various party bosses, and by plying them with booze and women, but that's not *buying* a vote— that's the political system as it exists today in America. As for the other frequently levied charge about their using the Mafia to stuff ballot boxes, it's true that Joe and Jack Kennedy both met during this period with Sam Giancana—for whatever it's worth, Giancana couldn't successfully stuff a turkey, let alone swing an election. This doesn't exonerate the Kennedys, but on the other hand, it doesn't make them mass murderers. Not that I condone such activities, but they're a fact of life."

During the presidential campaign, most of JFK's female companions were drawn from that transient pool known in his camp as "the Kennedy girls," the models, hostesses and college cheerleaders recruited in every city, county and state by the candidate's advance men to add sparkle and zest to the race. Janet DesRosiers, the stewardess aboard the *Caroline*, felt that had Jackie done more campaigning with Jack, the opportunity and need for such dalliances would have been greatly reduced.

"The trouble is that Jackie didn't enjoy campaigning," said DesRosiers. "She found the pace too hectic and didn't care to rub shoulders with Mr. and Mrs. John Doe. When she did campaign, she remained aloof, quiet, alone. She was very reserved. I think Jack might have tried to encourage her more. She represented a large part of the Kennedy image-making machine, and it must have been disconcerting for him that she didn't accompany him more often or generate greater enthusiasm or buoyancy when she did accompany him.

"One of my functions as stewardess, which could not have pleased Jackie very much, were the neck and shoulder massages I gave JFK every day. Give somebody a massage and people automatically assume there's something going on. But somebody had to do it. He worked himself into knots, toiling interminable hours, rising at 4 A.M. to shake hands at some remote airplane gate in subzero weather. The man gave as many as thirty speeches a day, seven days a week, three weeks at a clip.

"He had voice and back problems. The massages helped his back. David Blair McCloskey, a Boston University professor, was his speech therapist and voice coach. McCloskey gave him exercises to strengthen his vocal cords and ordered me to keep him quiet once he boarded the plane. I gave him a pad, and he communicated by pen."

Preserved for posterity by Janet DesRosiers, several of JFK's midair notes provide intimate glimpses of his fixation on sexual fulfillment. Expressing himself on the possibility of defeating then–vice president Richard Nixon in the national election, he wrote: "I suppose if I win, my poon days are over"—"poon" being a familiar navy term for sexual activity. Another day he scribbled: "I suppose they are going to hit me with something before we are finished"—an apparent reference to his expectation that the Nixon camp would try to exploit his extramarital affairs. On the back of a business envelope, he coldly noted: "I got into the blonde." He also expressed his plans in case he failed to win the Democratic nomination: "If I lose—around the world in 180 days." He evidently had in mind an expanded version of the Mediterranean bacchanalia that had followed his 1956 defeat at the Democratic National Convention in Chicago.

For the record, it should be noted that prior to becoming JFK's personal "masseuse," Janet DesRosiers had performed more or less the same function for his father. According to *Vanity Fair* (November 1997), Janet had been Joe Kennedy's private secretary as well as his mistress.

Information on RFK's involvement with the selection of LBJ as JFK's running mate and RFK's direct dealings with LBJ at the convention comes from Schlesinger, *RK*, pp. 224–230; Collier and Horowitz, *The Kennedys*, p. 331; Theodore H. White, *The Making of the President, 1960*. Interviews with many of those notated above supplemented these secondary sources.

"Gentlemen, I don't give a hoot": Quoted in Schlesinger, *RK*, p. 228. Original source is *Time*, October 10, 1960. Also, author interview with Ken O'Donnell.

Martin Luther King and the Kennedys: See Schlesinger, *RK*, pp. 230–237 and Taylor Branch's *Parting the Waters: America in the King Years 1954–63*.

Seigenthaler: "But don't fret" and "Well, you'll have to make sure": See Schlesinger, *RK*, p. 234. Seigenthaler's words in this instance were provided to the current author by Ken O'Donnell, who had spoken to Seigenthaler shortly after the exchange took place.

Information on Martin Luther King and JFK and RFK's telephone calls on his behalf is from Branch, *Parting the Waters*.

13. ATTORNEY GENERAL

Author interviews for this chapter were conducted with Abraham Ribicoff, Lem Billings, Jim McCartney, Bob Novak, Theodore H. White, George Smathers, Clark Clifford, Harris Wofford, George Carpozi, Jr., Peter Lawford, Phil Stern, Kenneth McKnight, Arthur Goldberg, C. Douglas Dillon, Robert McNamara, George McGovern, Orville Freeman, Evelyn Lincoln, Red Fay, Ken O'Donnell, John Richard Reilly.

Oral histories consulted for this chapter: Harris Wofford, Philip Elman, Abraham Ribicoff, Louis Martin, John Seigenthaler, Tracy S. McCraken, Clark Clifford, John Richard Reilly, David Hackett, William A. Geoghegan, Lee Loevinger, Joe Gargan, Patricia Collins, William O. Douglas, Stewart Udall (University of Arizona Library), India Edwards (Truman Library).

Periodicals consulted for this chapter include: the *New York Times*, *Washington Post*, *Boston Globe*, *Wall Street Journal*, *Time*, *The New Republic*, *The Nation*, *Saturday Review*, *Atlantic Monthly*.

Information concerning Harris Wofford's disdain for Byron White can be found in Taylor Branch, *Parting the Waters: America in the King Years 1954–63*.

Discussions between JFK and his father regarding RFK becoming attorney general: see RFK OH, JFK Library.

LBJ's reaction to RFK as attorney general: LBJ personal papers, Lyndon Baines Johnson Presidential Library.

JFK, RFK and Seigenthaler breakfast meeting: John Seigenthaler OH, JFK Library. See also Schlesinger, *RK*, p. 249, as well as Collier and Horowitz, *The Kennedys*, p. 256.

"If Bobby Kennedy was one . . .": *New York Times*, November 29, 1960. See also Schlesinger, *RK*, p. 251.

Dick Russell: Robert Gene Baker with Larry L. King. *Wheeling and Dealing: Confessions of a Capitol Hill Operator*, pp. 120–121.

"You have, as I understood it . . .": Schlesinger, *RK*, p. 253.

"To Bobby—who made the impossible possible . . .": Collier and Horowitz, *The Kennedys*, p. 357. See also Schlesinger, *RK*, p. 250.

Patricia Collins: Ovid Demaris, *The Director*, p. 197.

The author referred to the following books for chapter 13: Theodore H. White, *In Search of History*; Clark Clifford, with Richard Holbrooke, *Counsel to the President*; Tip O'Neill, *Man of the House*; Janet Leigh, *There Really Was a Hollywood*; Collier and Horowitz, *The Kennedys*; Schlesinger, *RK*.

14. HIT LIST

Author interviews for this chapter were conducted with William G. Hundley, Howard Diller, Roy Cohn, Ronald Goldfarb, Jay Goldberg, Edwyn Silberling, Patrick Anderson, Ken O'Donnell, Larry O'Brien, Victor Navasky, Robert Arum, Kenneth Crawford, John Mintz, John Richard Reilly, Robert Hinerfeld, Courtney A. Evans, Chuck O'Brian, Doris Lilly, Nicholas von Hoffman, Thomas B. Curtis, James P. Hoffa, Joe Konowe, Tom Bolan, Joe Gargan, Ramsey Clark.

Oral histories consulted for this chapter: Robert F. Kennedy, Irving Younger, Roy Cohn, John Richard Reilly, Ronald Goldfarb, Edwyn Silberling, William G. Hundley.

Useful information for this chapter was derived from the FBI investigatory files, Federal Bureau of Investigation, Washington, D.C. The author also consulted files of the Department of Justice, Criminal Division, Washington, D.C.

Among the books consulted in this chapter were Victor Navasky, *Kennedy Justice*, Schlesinger, *RK*; Sorensen, *Kennedy*; Zion, *The Autobiography of Roy Cohn*; Von Hoffman, *Citizen Cohn*; Exner, *Judith Exner—My Story*; Ronald Goldfarb, *Perfect Villains, Imperfect Heroes: Robert Kennedy's War Against Organized Crime*.

Stories abound concerning RFK's so-called "Hit List." Journalist Doris Lilly recalled eating lunch with Roy Cohn. "I stupidly brought up Robert Kennedy. Roy almost choked on his food. 'Don't mention that motherfucker while I'm eating,' he said. 'Every time I hear his name I want to puke.'"

There is no question that Robert Kennedy engendered hatred among his enemies. John Mintz, general counsel to the FBI, noted: "RFK's age. inexperience, lack of respect for authority, and lack of respect for J. Edgar Hoover, rankled the director of the FBI to no end. He would have done anything to get rid of him."

FBI tour guides: Victor Navasky, *Kennedy Justice*, p. 8.

"It is ridiculous": Schlesinger, *RK*, p. 276.

"That sneaky little son of a bitch": Richard Nixon, *RN: The Memoirs of Richard Nixon*, p. 595.

Hoover's "Hate List": Schlesinger, *RK*, p. 280.

Get Hoffa Squad: Ibid., p. 300.

Physical surveillance of Hoffa: Justice Department Files, Organized Crime Section. Also FBI files.

Hoffa indictments and trials: Ibid. See also Schlesinger, *RK*, pp. 300–301.

Roy Cohn and J. Edgar Hoover: the most useful books were Sidney Zion, *The Autobiography of Roy Cohn*, and Nicholas von Hoffman, *Citizen Cohn*.

15. SEX

Author interviews for this chapter were conducted with Marty Benker, Mel Finkelstein, Lawrence J. Quirk, Doris Lilly, George Plimpton, Blair Clark, Truman Capote, James Spada, Fred Otash, Morton Downey, Jr., Coates Redman, Peter J. Sharp, Earl E. T. Smith, Marianne Strong, Al Hirschfeld, Patricia Seaton, Ruth Jacobson, Tom Jacobson, Kenneth McKnight, Michael Samek, Charles Spalding, George Smathers, Eddie Fisher, Pierre Salinger, Edward McDermott, Ray Strait, Leslie Devereux, Francis Lara, Claude Pepper, Irving Mansfield, Toni Bradlee, Oleg Cassini, Igor Cassini, Tony Sherman, Stanley Tretick, Lem Billings, Robert Hinerfeld, Courtney A. Evans, Purette Spiegler, Janet DesRosiers, Langdon P. Marvin, Jr., Ralph Ginzburg, Anthony Summers, Philip Nobile.

Oral histories consulted for this chapter: Robert F. Kennedy, Robert Hinerfeld.

Judith Meredith divorce case: See Anthony Cook, "The Man Who Bugged Marilyn Monroe," *Gentlemen's Quarterly*, October 1990. Also, James Spada, *Peter Lawford: The Man Who Kept the Secrets*, pp. 284–287.

FBI/Department of Justice files were used for information on JFK amphetamine use, as well as on alleged romance between RFK and unnamed El Paso girl.

Courtney A. Evans memo: FBI files, Washington, D.C.

RFK–Lee Remick romance: See Lawrence J. Quirk, *The Kennedys in Hollywood*, pp. 306–309.

JFK and Max Jacobson: Ruth Jacobson, widow of Dr. Jacobson, made available to the current author an unpublished memoir by the late physician, as well as tapes, appointment books and court documents belonging to Jacobson.

Profumo case: See Anthony Summers, *Official and Confidential: The Secret Life of J. Edgar Hoover*, pp. 305–312; Stephen Dorril, *Honeytrap*; Phillip Knightley and Caroline Kennedy, *An Affair of State*. Information also derived from criminal investigation files, Scotland Yard, London.

RFK and Novotny: See Simon Bell, Richard Curtis, Helen Fielding, *Who's Had Who?* Novotny later admitted being a heroin addict and having had a lengthy relationship with a female physician. She died in London in 1981.

Suzy Chang: See FBI files, as well as Heymann, *A Woman Named Jackie*, p. 372.

Regarding the affair between Pierre Salinger's wife and JFK: See Robert Sam Anson, "Secrets and Lies," *Vanity Fair*, November 1997.

Periodicals consulted for this chapter include *New York Journal-American*; *News of the World*; *London Times*; *Club International*; *Palm Beach Life*.

Other volumes consulted for this chapter: Anthony Summers, *Goddess: The Secret Lives of Marilyn Monroe*; James Spada, *Peter Lawford: The Man Who Kept the Secrets*.

16. CASTRO

Author interviews for this chapter were conducted with George Smathers, George McNamara, Thomas Moorer, James J. Angleton, Louis Oberdorfer, Mike Miskovsky, Richard Goodwin, Godfrey McHugh, Walt Rostow, Roswell Gilpatric, Arthur Lundahl, Truman Capote, Lem Billings, Mark A. Allen, Edward McDermott, Ken McKnight, John Nolan, Evelyn Lincoln, Michael Samek, Ken O'Donnell, Charles Bartlett.

Oral histories consulted for this chapter: Chester Bowles (Columbia University

Libraries), Maxwell Taylor, Hanson Baldwin, Robert Amory, Walt Rostow (LBJ Library), Isaiah Berlin, Nicholas Katzenbach, Richard Helms (CIA), Richard Bissell (CIA), David Murphy (CIA), McGeorge Bundy.

Counterinsurgency information: See counterinsurgency investigative files, Department of Justice, Washington, D.C.

See FBI files, Department of Justice, Criminal Division (Washington, D.C.), for information on memorandum from J. Edgar Hoover to RFK regarding Sam Giancana (December 11, 1961).

For information on Operation Mongoose: See CIA departmental files, CIA, McLean, Virginia.

Meetings between RFK and KGB agent Georgi Nikitovich Bolshakov are fully documented by Michael R. Beschloss in *The Crisis Years: Kennedy and Khrushchev, 1960–1963*. For a more informed portrait, see Ben Bradlee, *Conversations with Kennedy*.

Other volumes consulted for this chapter include Evan Thomas, *The Very Best Men: Four Who Dared: The Early Years of the CIA*; Anthony Summers, *Official and Confidential*; Robert F. Kennedy, *Thirteen Days*; Ernest R. May and Philip D. Zelikow, eds., *The Kennedy Tapes: Inside the White House During the Cuban Missile Crisis*; Dean Rusk, *As I Saw It*; David Halberstam, *The Best and the Brightest*; Warren Hinckle and William Turner, *Deadly Secrets: The CIA–Mafia War Against Castro and the Assassination of J.F.K.*; John H. Davis, *Mafia Kingfish: Carlos Marcello and the Assassination of John F. Kennedy*.

Of the books listed above, the Evan Thomas volume proved particularly useful in terms of background material. Perhaps the most valuable document was provided by the U.S. Government Printing Office: *Alleged Assassination Plots Involving Foreign Leaders: An Interim Report of the Select Committee to Study Government Operations with Respect to Intelligence Activities*, 1975.

In 1975, following the Church Committee on "alleged" assassination hearings, Congress passed a law prohibiting U.S. government complicity in the assassination of foreign leaders. "If we continue to engage in such activities," said former CIA director Richard Helms, "we are going to quickly lose more presidents." In defense of Operation Mongoose, however, Helms stated, "When you engage in terrorist activities, you occasionally have to do business with people you wouldn't want to invite for dinner." These comments were made by Helms in a documentary on the CIA broadcast on the Discovery Cable Network, November 26, 1997. They appear to give license to Robert Kennedy's deployment of mafiosi in the attempted assassination of Fidel Castro.

James J. Angleton of the CIA insisted that Operation Mongoose "should have been called 'the Kennedy Vendetta.' It was retaliation in kind for the humiliation the Kennedys had suffered at the Bay of Pigs, an operation whose failure JFK partially blamed on the CIA as well as the Joint Chiefs of Staff. He blamed everyone, that is, but himself. And don't forget, the Kennedys had two hideaways—one on Peanut Island, off the coast of Florida, the other somewhere in the Blue Ridge Mountains. While they would have been safe in their luxury bunker, presumably watching World War III on television, the rest of us would have burned in hell."

See Evan Thomas, *The Very Best Men*, pp. 396–398 (notes section) for an excellent overview (utilizing FBI documents) of RFK's involvement in Operation Mongoose and his knowledge of the CIA's use of Mafia figures in the attempted assassination of Castro. Thomas also provides information on p. 271 of JFK's desire after the Bay of Pigs disaster to name RFK director of the CIA. His discussion of CIA magnates such as Richard Bissell, Ed Lansdale, Richard Helms, Desmond FitzGerald and Thomas Parrott, as well as former FBI agent Robert Maheu, proved extremely useful for this chapter. Of all the books that deal with the complex operation known as Mongoose none is better written or illuminating than *The Very Best Men*, upon which the author has drawn for appropriate details, including such topics as the Maheu-Roselli meeting, the Bissell–Allen Dulles meeting and the Bissell-Giancana meeting.

17. CIVIL RIGHTS

Author interviews for this chapter were conducted with Samuel Herman, Arthur Goldberg, Gene Scherrer, Victor Navasky, Theodore Hesburgh, Ramsey Clark, Fred Dutton, Jack Greenberg, Larry O'Brien, James Farmer, Roger Wilkins, Theodore H. White, Victor Rabinowitz, Kenneth B. Clark, David Filvaroff, Roswell Gilpatric, Ralph de Toledano, C. Douglas Dillon, George Plimpton, Walt Rostow, Elspeth Rostow, John Doar, Milton Gwirtzman, Louis Oberdorfer, Nigel Hamilton, Walter Fauntroy, Courtney Evans, Algernon Black, George Smathers, Claude Pepper, John Mintz, Harris Wofford, LaVern Duffy, Mike Mansfield, Jacob Javits.

Oral histories consulted for this chapter: Robert F. Kennedy, John Richard Reilly, John Seigenthaler, Joseph Tydings, Stewart Udall (University of Arizona Library), Donald Wilson, Maxwell Taylor, Isaiah Berlin, Edwin O. Guthman, Marietta Tree (Columbia University Libraries), Clark Mollenhoff, Walt Rostow (LBJ Library), James Farmer (LBJ Library).

The most valuable published resource on RFK's involvement in the civil rights movement was Taylor Branch, *Parting the Waters: America in the King Years 1954–1963*. Other books consulted include Schlesinger, *RK*; Peter Collier and David Horowitz, *The Kennedys: An American Drama*; Summers, *Official and Confidential*.

Periodicals consulted for this chapter include: *Atlanta Constitution, Washington Post, Life, Look, Newsweek, The New Yorker.*

Useful information on RFK's relationship with Martin Luther King, Jr., can be found at Martin Luther King, Jr., Center, Atlanta, Georgia.

Additional materials for this chapter were located in the FBI files, Civil Rights Division, as well as in the Department of Justice files, Department of Justice, Washington, D.C.

One of RFK's first major talks as Attorney General: See Taylor Branch, *Parting the Waters*, pp. 414–415. See also Schlesinger, *RK*, p. 315.

A group of thirteen blacks and whites: Schlesinger, *RK*, pp. 316–317.

Mr. Greyhound: RFK and George Cruit (local Greyhound superintendent) conversation: May 15, 1961, RFK papers, JFK Library. See also Schlesinger, *RK*, p. 318.

"I never thought we would reach the point": Peter Maas, "Robert Kennedy Speaks Out," *Look*, March 28, 1961. See also Schlesinger, *RK*, p. 316. The current author has slightly revised the words for the sake of editorial purposes.

RFK and Ross Barnett: See Burke Marshall Civil Rights files, JFK Library; see also Branch, *Parting the Waters*, pp. 651, 656–657; and Schlesinger, *RK*, pp. 342–343. The same sources were used for the telephone conversation between JFK and

Barnett which is reported in detail in this chapter ("Governor, this is the President"/ "our poultry program").

James Meredith: See Burke Marshall files, as well as Branch, *Parting the Waters,* pp. 652–657.

"I haven't had such an interesting time . . ." and "The Attorney General announced today . . .": Branch, *Parting the Waters,* p. 657.

RFK and James Baldwin: See Schlesinger, *RK,* pp. 355–360, and Branch, *Parting the Waters,* pp. 810–813.

Ellen Rometsch: the Rometsch affair, long written about by Kennedy biographers, is fully documented in recently released FBI and CIA files.

Martin Luther King, Jr.–Phyllis Daitch affair: newly released material on Martin Luther King, Jr., FBI files.

18. MARILYN

Author interviews for this chapter were conducted with Hildi Greenson, Hyman Engleberg, Jeanne Carmen, John Miner, Gene Scherrer, Ted Schwartz, Christopher Mankiewicz, Stanley Tretick, Peter Lawford, Patricia Seaton, Cathy Griffin, Fred Otash, Ted Jordan, Anthony Summers, George Carpozi, Jr., Charles Spalding, Leo Damore, Doris Lilly, Cord Meyer, Jr., Blair Clark, Victoria Pryor, Jack Clemmons, Truman Capote, Ronald Carroll, Raymond Strait, Marianne Strong, George Smathers.

Hyman Engleberg: a portion of Dr. Engleberg's comments can be found in the 1982 reinvestigation of MM's demise ("The Threshold Examination of the Death of Marilyn Monroe")—this report, prepared by Ronald Carroll, assistant district attorney in Los Angeles, was submitted in December 1982 to John K. Van De Kemp, district attorney of Los Angeles.

Jeanne Carmen interviews: in addition to the interview provided for this book, interviews with Jeanne Carmen can be found in Anthony Summers, *Goddess,* and James Spada, *Peter Lawford: The Man Who Kept the Secrets.* Both volumes provide insightful examinations of the RFK–Marilyn Monroe affair. Spada's book is particularly useful for its coverage of Marilyn at JFK's Madison Square Garden birthday bash. *Goddess* contains material on every aspect of the JFK-MM-RFK triangle, including (but not limited to) the Jean Smith letter to MM ("I understand that you and Bobby are the new item") and Ralph Greenson's writings re MM's feelings about lesbianism.

Peter Lawford: The current author spoke to the actor in 1983, a year before his death, for a biography of Jacqueline Kennedy Onassis (*A Woman Named Jackie: An Intimate Biography of Jacqueline Kennedy Onassis*). At that time, Lawford described in full the details of the RFK–Dr. Greenson conspiracy to "subdue" Marilyn. Unable, however, to locate Mrs. Hildi Greenson in order to confirm the existence of tapes MM had made for Dr. Greenson, the author quoted only a segment of the Lawford interview in the Jackie biography. Mrs. Greenson, interviewed for the current biography, confirmed the existence of the tapes identified by Lawford. This biography contains Lawford's comments in toto. It should further be noted that Lawford never informed his last wife, Patricia Seaton, of the details concerning RFK's involvement in MM's death. "If he discussed it with you," said Seaton to the current author, "he probably did so because he felt guilt over Marilyn's death. Perhaps this was his way of confessing his own part in the macabre events. I do know that he often expressed regret over his failure to take on more responsibility. Maybe he felt he could have saved her, but instead he may have unwittingly made the situation worse." Said Peter Lawford, "I certainly think Marilyn would have held a press conference. She was determined to gain back her self-esteem. She was unbalanced at the time—and Bobby was determined to shut her up, regardless of the consequences. It was the craziest thing he ever did—and I was crazy enough to let it happen."

George Smathers, the Florida senator and friend of JFK, claimed that he was sent to Hollywood by the president to help quiet Marilyn down. He evidently failed in his mission, because Bobby Kennedy soon took charge and ultimately fell in love.

Marilyn Monroe in tears at Peter Lawford's house: see Summers, *Goddess*. Summers also discusses MM's obsessive fear of homosexuality. Other themes and anecdotes alluded to in this chapter can be found in Ted Jordan, *Norma Jean: My Secret Life with Marilyn Monroe*; Stein and Plimpton, *American Journey*; Patricia Kennedy Lawford, ed., *That Shining Hour*; Schlesinger, *RK*.

John Miner: following MM's death, Ralph Greenson read to Miner from his notes on Marilyn and played him excerpts from several of her tapes. Apparently Marilyn would read to Greenson from her diary, including sections she had written about the Kennedys. It is likely that Peter Lawford, having confiscated Marilyn's diary (along with other personal possessions), eventually turned it over to Robert Kennedy. The long-lost "red diary" has never emerged.

Pat Newcomb: One of the sources for information on Patricia Newcomb's relationship with JFK, RFK, and MM was Peter Lawford. Newcomb had known Peter and Pat Kennedy Lawford long before she met Marilyn Monroe. The morning after MM's death, Newcomb (who worked for public relations specialist Arthur P. Jacobs) drove to Marilyn's house only to find it overrun by members of the press. Highly agitated, she began screaming at them, calling them "vultures." Thereafter, she spent a period with the Kennedys at Hyannis Port, before venturing abroad. Upon her return, she decided to move to Washington, procuring employment with the United States Information Agency, for which she organized film festivals. After JFK's assassination, Newcomb joined the staff of former White House press secretary Pierre Salinger in his bid to become senator from California, a campaign allegedly financed (at least in part) by Robert Kennedy. Salinger lost to S. I. Hayakawa, and Newcomb returned to Washington, this time as an employee with the so-called "Special Unit" of the Justice Department, a division presided over by RFK personally.

Correspondence between RFK and Pat Newcomb: Confidential source.

"Something's Got to Give": a TV documentary aired in the early 1990s on the making of *Something's Got to Give* contained out-takes which show Marilyn Monroe to be in far better shape (mentally and physically) than her bosses at Twentieth Century-Fox wanted to admit. A number of people who knew her at the time, however, including Peter Lawford, found her behavior erratic. "She looked good part of the time," said Lawford, "but for the most part appeared to be incoherent. On many occasions, she could barely remember her lines." In any case, there is no question that Marilyn was being blamed, at least in part, for the "sins" of Elizabeth Taylor, who was being paid $1 million (to Marilyn's $100,000) to star as Cleopatra, in Fox's film by the same title, then being shot in Rome. Taylor, who had fallen in love with her costar, Richard Burton, caused Fox tremendous financial strain as a result not only of her salary but also because of her tardiness, absences, illnesses, and suicide attempts. ET, whose survival techniques far exceeded Marilyn's, lived to see better days; Monroe did not.

The Dark Side of Camelot: Seymour Hersh's 1997 volume on JFK regurgitates and recycles a slew of anecdotes already recounted in previous Kennedy tomes. ("Some of these stories are so old," said Marianne Strong, "they've grown whiskers.") Within the dross, however, there are several nuggets, including an extract from one of the "stream-of-consciousness" tapes made by Marilyn Monroe for her psychiatrist, Dr. Ralph Greenson: "Marilyn Monroe is a soldier. Her commander in chief is the greatest and most powerful man in the world. The first duty of a soldier is to obey her commander in chief. He says do this, you do it. He says do that, you do it. This man is going to change our country. . . . It's like the Navy—the President is the captain and Bobby is his executive officer. Bobby would do absolutely anything for his brother and so would I. I will never embarrass him. As long as I have memory, I have John Fitzgerald Kennedy." For all her espoused devotion, Marilyn evidently had a change of heart. On the day of her death, she was prepared to "embarrass" not only the captain but the executive officer as well.

19. DEATH OF A BROTHER

Author interviews for this chapter were conducted with John Kenneth Galbraith, Joseph Tydings, Saul Rotter, John Seigenthaler, Robert McNamara, Oleg Cassini, Igor Cassini, Louis Nizer, Phil Stanton, Larry Newman, Gerald Tremblay, Joe Dolan, Lee Rainey, Fred Dutton, Walt Rostow, Elspeth Rostow, Gene Kelly, Norman Mailer, William Manchester, George Plimpton, Theodore H. White, Roswell Gilpatric, Dean Rusk, Lem Billings, Mike Mansfield, William Manchester, Cindy Adams, Ramsey Clark.

Oral histories consulted for this chapter: Robert F. Kennedy, Joseph Tydings, Howard Jones (LBJ Library), Gerald Tremblay, Donald Wilson, John Douglas, Edwin O. Reischauer, John Seigenthaler, Nicholas Katzenbach, Maxwell Taylor, Stewart Udall (University of Arizona Library), Chester Bowles.

Stewart Udall: See Stewart Udall papers, University of Arizona Library.

The following periodicals proved useful for this chapter: *Time, Life, Look, US News & World Report, Newsweek, Esquire, Saturday Evening Post, Washington Post, Washington Star, New York Times, New York Herald-Tribune, New York Post, Asahi Shimbun Tokyo, Yomuri*.

Ambassador Edwin O. Reischauer: See Reischauer OH (JFK Library) and Schlesinger, *RK*, p. 610 (author has combined the two sources and lightly edited the final version). RFK's world tour is also detailed in Schlesinger's *RK*, as well as in the American press of the day. Other useful texts consulted for this chapter include: Robert F. Kennedy, *Just Friends and Brave Enemies*; Igor Cassini with Jeanne Molli, *I'd Do It All Over Again*; Louis Nizer, *Reflections Without Mirrors: An Autobiography of the Mind*; William Manchester, *The Death of a President*.

"We have no intention . . .": Schlesinger, *RK*, p. 608. RFK's complete speech (Nihon University, Tokyo, February 6, 1962) located in RFK papers, JFK Library.

RFK and Sukarno: See Schlesinger, *RK*, pp. 611–615.

Hickory Hill seminars: *Ibid*., pp. 638–639.

Pat Anderson: Pat Anderson, *Esquire*, April 1965.

November 20, 1963: See Schlesinger, *RK*, pp. 653–654; William Manchester, *The Death of a President*.

November 22, 1963: See Schlesinger, *RK*, pp. 654–655. Manchester, *The Death of a President*; assorted articles in various publications including *New York Post, Esquire, Saturday Evening Post*. Also used was RFK OH (JFK Library).

J. Edgar Hoover memo regarding conversation with RFK concerning JFK assassination: FBI files.

At the time of JFK's death (November 1963), there was talk among Kennedy insiders of dumping LBJ as a running mate in the 1964 election. Ethel Kennedy made repeated recommendations that there be a Kennedy–Kennedy ticket, RFK to fill the vice-presidential slot. It is doubtful, however, that such a plan would have passed muster with either the president or the attorney general. Events, in any case, eliminated further conjecture.

20. KEEPER OF THE FLAME

Author interviews for this chapter were conducted with Jim Garrison, Jack Valenti, Charles Spalding, John H. Davis, Stephen Birmingham, William Manchester, Theron Raines, Charles Bartlett, John Treanor, Jr., Blair Clark, Ken O'Donnell, Joan Braden, Coates Redman, Andrew Oehmann, Jr., Joe Dolan, Lem Billings, John Nolan, John Richard Reilly, Red Fay, George Christian, Theodore H. White, Godfrey McHugh, Larry O'Brien, Ramsey Clark, LaVern Duffy, Franklin D. Roosevelt, Jr.

Oral histories consulted for this chapter: Robert F. Kennedy, John McCone, Edwin Guthman, Charles Bartlett, Clark Clifford, George Christian, George Burkley, Harry McPherson (LBJ Library), Homer Thornberry (LBJ Library), Jack Valenti (LBJ Library), Ken O'Donnell, John Jay Hooker, Charles Spalding, McGeorge Bundy.

Periodicals consulted for this chapter include *USA Today, Washington Post, Dallas News, Time, Life, Look, The Realist*.

The following volumes were useful in the preparation of this chapter: John H. Davis, *Mafia Kingfish: Carlos Marcello and the Assassination of John F. Kennedy*; Manchester, *The Death of a President* and *Controversy and Other Essays in Journalism, 1950–1975*; Collier and Horowitz, *The Kennedys*; Stephen Birmingham, *Jacqueline Bouvier Kennedy Onassis*; Paul B. Fay, Jr., *The Pleasure of His Company*; Lady Bird Johnson, *A White House Diary*; Schlesinger, *RK*; Heymann, *A Woman Named Jackie*; Stein and Plimpton, *American Journey*; Harrison Rainie, *Growing Up Kennedy: The Third Wave Comes of Age*; Clark Clifford, with Richard Holbrooke, *Counsel to the President*; Lyndon Baines Johnson, *Vantage Point: Perspectives of the Presidency, 1963–1969*.

Also reviewed for this chapter were recently released files from both the FBI and the Department of Justice, Criminal Division.

Regarding LBJ running for president in 1964: LBJ tapes (released July 1997), LBJ Library.

The current author had access to the outtakes of Paul B. Fay, Jr.'s *The Pleasure of His Company*, housed at Boston University Library's Rare Book and Manuscript Collection. The author similarly had access to the outtakes of William Manchester, *The Death of a President*, housed in the same collection. The latter were deposited at BU by *Look* magazine, which had acquired first-serial rights to *The Death of a President*. When Jackie initiated legal action, both *Look* and the book publisher (Harper & Row) agreed to excise segments of the manuscript. It is these segments that were made available to the current author.

Events in Dallas and aboard Air Force One: See Manchester, *The Death of a President*; Heymann, *A Woman Named Jackie*.

Charles Spalding overhearing RFK weeping: See Schlesinger, *RK*, p. 658. Schlesinger's is a somewhat different version of this anecdote.

Jackie and RFK visit JFK's grave: See Manchester, *The Death of a President*, pp. 693–694.

"President Kennedy was more than just president": RFK papers, JFK Library.

"Bobby's just another lawyer": Schlesinger, *RK*, p. 664.

"I was shocked by his appearance": Manchester, *Controversy*.

RFK's efforts to limit the investigation into JFK's death; his probable destruction of forensic materials: see John H. Davis, *Mafia Kingfish*, pp. 289–293.

RFK and J. Edgar Hoover following JFK's assassination: See Schlesinger, *RK*, pp. 678–680.

New Hampshire primary: See Schlesinger, *RK*, pp. 700–703, as well as Theodore H. White, *The Making of the President, 1964*.

RFK and LBJ meeting: See Schlesinger, *RK*, as well as Lyndon Johnson, *Vantage Point*.

21. THE SENATOR AND MRS. KENNEDY

Author interviews for this chapter were conducted with Charles Guggenheim, Jacob Javits, Dan Blackburn, Herman Badillo, Arthur Kirson, Diana DuBois, John Treanor, Jr., Robert McNamara, William J. vanden Heuvel, Susan Pollock, Truman Capote, Larry Newman, Coates Redman, Polly Feingold, Marianne Strong, Carl Killingsworth, Kathryn Livingston, Peter Manso, Mary DeGrace, Mary Harrington, Abe Hirschfeld, Roswell Gilpatric, Blair Clark, Ronnie Eldridge, William Haddad, Milton Gwirtzman, John Nolan, Ed Koch, Ross Graham, Manfred Ohrenstein, Joseph Kraft, Ed Costikyan, Franklin D. Roosevelt, Jr., Robert David Lyon Gardiner, Gene Scherrer, Diana Trilling, Lem Billings, Peter Lawford.

Oral histories consulted for this chapter: Robert F. Kennedy, Jacob Javits (State University of New York at Stony Brook), Thomas Watson, Donald Wilson, Hubert Humphrey (LBJ Library), John Seigenthaler, Charles Guggenheim, Adam Walinsky, Peter Edelman, Albert Blumenthal (Columbia University Libraries), Kenneth B. Keating (Columbia University Libraries), Milton Gwirtzman, Bill Walton, Richard Wade.

Periodicals consulted for this chapter include the *New York Times*, *New York Post*, *New York Herald-Tribune*, *The New Yorker*, *The New Republic*.

Books consulted for this chapter include Schlesinger, *RK*; Cary Reich, *Financier: The Biography of Andre Meyer*; Vidal, *Palimpsest*; Edwin O. Guthman, *We Band of Brothers*; Stein and Plimpton, *American Journey*; Diana DuBois, *In Her Sister's Shadow*.

The Kenneth B. Keating white papers on RFK (located at the Columbia University Libraries) are a collection of unsupported accusations concerning Kennedy's sometimes questionable deportment during his years as attorney general. There is

also a significant amount of material on Keating in the Jacob Javits Collection, located at the SUNY at Stony Brook. The best overall volume on the RFK-Keating
battle is Guthman's *We Band of Brothers*, which contains an excellent general description of Keating.

Hubert Humphrey: Hubert Humphrey Collection, Minnesota Historical Society.

Regarding RFK–Jackie Kennedy romance: For the record, it should be noted
that TV and film producer Susan Pollock met with the current author and literary
agent Marianne Strong at New York's Russian Tea Room in May 1995 to discuss
Pollock's interest in purchasing the film rights to the book at hand. It was in the
course of this meeting that Pollock recounted the RFK-Jackie anecdotes included in
this chapter. She subsequently offered to purchase film rights, but the author sold
them instead to producer Lester Persky. Pollock then tried to deny what she had
told both the author and Marianne Strong. Giving an interview, however, is somewhat akin to losing one's virginity: once the deed is done, it's done. Hence, the
author feels justified in including Pollock's commentary. In addition to sources used
in text, the author made use of newly released Secret Service files, Secret Service,
Washington, D.C.

Glens Falls and shoemaking town: Different versions of these RFK senatorial
campaign anecdotes appear in Schlesinger, *RK,* pp. 722–723.

"A great uneasiness . . .": Ibid., p. 725.

"It was total disorganization": This Seigenthaler OH and several other oral histories quoted in this section have been lightly edited by the author for the sake of
clarity.

"Come on, Bob. Get with it!": Steve Smith to RFK. Related to author by Lem
Billings.

With less than a month to go before Election Day: According to Schlesinger,
RK, p. 723, John F. Kraft, RFK's personal pollster, showed a closer race than those
conducted by other pollsters. On October 6, Kraft had Johnson leading Goldwater
60–40 in New York and Keating ahead of Kennedy 51–49.

Charles Evers: See Guthman, *We Band of Brothers,* p. 307, as well as Schlesinger, *RK,* p. 724.

Keating, RFK and Italian vote: See Guthman, *We Band of Brothers,* and Schlesinger, *RK,* pp. 724–725.

General Aniline case: See Guthman, *We Band of Brothers,* pp. 100–101, 300–
303; Schlesinger, *RK,* pp. 724–725.

22. A NEW LIFE

Author interviews for this chapter were conducted with Pedro San Juan, Stewart
McClure, Ty Fain, Sam Yorty, John Nolan, Roswell Gilpatric, George McGovern,
Malcolm Taylor, Milton Gwirtzman, George Plimpton, Angie Cabrera, Ed Koch,
Larry O'Brien, Ken O'Donnell, Joe Dolan, Betty Beale, Truman Capote, George
Murphy, Marie Ridder, Mary Harrington, Allen Ginsberg, James Dickey, Cathy Grif-
fin, Coates Redman, Hervé Alphand, Patricia Seaton, Janet Villella, Fred Dutton,
Norman Mailer, Benno C. Schmidt, Franklin Thomas, Lem Billings, Jacob Javits,
Ted Schwartz, Peter Lawford, Algernon Black, Gerald Tremblay, Joseph Kraft, Mike
Mansfield, C. Douglas Dillon, William vanden Heuvel, Orville Freeman, Fred Dut-
ton, Richard Goodwin.

Oral histories consulted for this chapter: Peter Edelman, Sam Yorty (U. Cal., Berkeley), Joseph Kraft, Carter Burden (Columbia University Libraries), Eli Jacobs (Columbia University Libraries), Benno C. Schmidt (Columbia University Libraries), John English (Columbia University Libraries), Thomas Jones (Columbia University Libraries), Allard Lowenstein (Columbia University Libraries), K. Dun Gifford, Wes Barthelmes, Gerald Tremblay, Robert F. Kennedy, Frank Mankiewicz, Fred Dutton.

The following periodicals were consulted for use in this chapter: *Washington Star*, *Washington Post*, *New York Times*, *Wall Street Journal*, *Rand Daily Mail*, *Cape Times*, *Paris Presse*, *The New Yorker*, *Life*, *Look*, *Saturday Evening Post*.

Volumes consulted for this chapter include Schlesinger, *RK*; Stein and Plimpton, *American Journey*; Oppenheimer, *The Other Mrs. Kennedy*; Gerald Clarke, *Capote: A Biography*; Kitty Kelley, *His Way: The Unauthorized Biography of Frank Sinatra*; Vidal, *Palimpsest*; Jacques E. Levy, *Cesar Chavez: Autobiography of La Causa*; Cary Reich, *Financier: The Biography of Andre Meyer*; Jack Newfield, *Robert Kennedy: A Memoir*; Patricia Seaton Lawford, *The Peter Lawford Story*; Edwin O. Guthman and C. Richard Allen, eds., *RFK: Collected Speeches*; Collier and Horowitz, *The Kennedys*; William vanden Heuvel and Milton Gwirtzman, *On His Own: Robert F. Kennedy 1964–68*; Richard Cummings, *The Pied Piper: Allard K. Lowenstein and the Liberal Dream*; Gore Vidal, *Palimpsest*; Margaret Laing, *The Next Kennedy*.

"That's how it's done around here": Comment reported to author by Lem Billings.

Information on Ted Kennedy's personal style as senator comes from a number of sources, including Collier and Horowitz, *The Kennedys*.

RFK's Latin American trip: See Schlesinger, *RK*, pp. 749–753; also Guthman and Allen, eds., *RFK: Collected Speeches*.

Ian Robertson: Schlesinger, *RK*, p. 802.

"We are, like you, a people of diverse origins": See Guthman and Allen, eds., *RFK*, p. 234. Original source for quote is the *Rand Daily Mail*, June 9, 1966.

"I'm Robert Kennedy": *Cape Times*, June 10, 1966.

"Master, Master": vanden Heuvel and Gwirtzman, *On His Own*, p. 160.

"To be opposed . . .": Schlesinger, *RK*, p. 851.

"If I hadn't become a United States Senator . . .": The RFK quotes in this paragraph are from Schlesinger, *RK*.

RFK trip to Mississippi Delta: RFK, "Suppose God Is Black," *Look*.

"Personally, I never saw what he saw . . .": This section of Peter Edelman's OH has been lightly edited by the current author for the sake of clarity.

RFK, Ethel, Claudine Longet and Andy Williams: A very complete and accurate account of the friendship between these two couples can be found in Oppenheimer, *The Other Mrs. Kennedy*, pp. 398–399. See also Lawford, *The Peter Lawford Story*, p. 87. In addition to the apparent affair between RFK and Longet, Patricia Seaton Lawford (in an interview with the author) discussed the less plausible aspect of an Andy Williams–Ethel Kennedy romance. That these two "fell over each other" seems very possible; that they had an affair appears to be a much more remote possibility. Ethel and Andy did not become romantically involved until well after RFK's death.

RFK and Mia Farrow: See Kitty Kelley, *His Way: The Unauthorized Biography of Frank Sinatra*, pp. 378–379.

Candice Bergen note to Jacqueline Kennedy: October 9, 1965, White House social files, JFK Library.

Jerry Oppenheimer anecdote regarding RFK and Polly Bussell: Oppenheimer includes several other interesting stories in *The Other Mrs. Kennedy* (pp. 240–243) which speak to Bobby's voracious sexual appetite. Jeannie Martin, ex-wife of Dean Martin, describes a girlfriend of hers trapped in a room alone with RFK at a party, while Ethel lingered in an adjoining room. The errant husband locked the door and threw his intended conquest onto a couch. At a Hawaiian theme party given by Roswell Gilpatric and his then wife Madelin, Bobby was spotted sitting on the floor next to one of the Hawaiian dancers, his hand between her legs. Imbued with a double standard, RFK lambasted Ethel at a private party in Greenwich, Connecticut, calling her "a whore" in front of others for dancing with a wealthy New York businessman.

Bedford-Stuyvesant: Among other sources, see Schlesinger, *RK*, pp. 845–850.

RFK and literary acquaintances: Schlesinger, *RK*, pp. 879–882. The Dickey and Ginsberg sequences are based on personal interviews.

Mimicked Walter Cronkite: This episode and descriptions of other dangerous athletic endeavors on RFK's part are detailed at various points in Schlesinger, *RK*, and in vanden Heuvel and Gwirtzman, *On His Own*. The bulk of this material, however, is taken from personal interviews and oral histories.

23. WAR

Author interviews for this chapter were conducted with Roswell Gilpatric, George McGovern, George Ball, Philippe de Bausset, Robert McNamara, Frank Valeo, John B. White, David Halberstam, Walt Rostow, William Manchester, Red Fay, Norman Mailer, Joseph Kraft, Evelyn Lincoln, Ken O'Donnell, Larry O'Brien, Allen Ginsberg.

Oral histories consulted for this chapter: George McGovern, Allard Lowenstein (Columbia University Libraries), Leslie Gelb (LBJ Library), George Ball (LBJ Library), Frank Mankiewicz, Peter Edelman, Robert F. Kennedy.

Periodicals consulted for this chapter include the *New York Times*, New York *Daily News*, *Chicago Tribune*, *Los Angeles Times*, *Washington Post*, *Boston Globe*, *Wall Street Journal*, *I. F. Stone Weekly*, *Time*, *Newsweek*.

Volumes consulted for this chapter include Schlesinger, *RK*; Bruce Miroff, *Pragmatic Illusions: The Presidential Politics of John F. Kennedy*, William Manchester, *The Death of a President* and *Controversy and Other Essays in Journalism, 1950–1975*; Fay, *The Pleasure of His Company*; Doris Kearns, *Lyndon Johnson and the American Dream*; Stein and Plimpton, *American Journey*; Jack Newfield, *Robert Kennedy: A Memoir*; David Halberstam, *The Best and the Brightest*; Victor Lasky, *RFK: The Myth and The Man*; Guthman and Allen, eds., *RFK: Collected Speeches*; Guthman, *We Band of Brothers*; Lyndon B. Johnson, *Vantage Point*.

Excerpts from RFK speeches regarding Vietnam: All of RFK's Vietnam speeches, (including that of March 2, 1967) unless impromptu, can be found in his papers at the JFK Library. In addition, see Edwin O. Guthman and C. Richard Allen, eds. *RFK: Collected Speeches*, pp. 127–128, 132–135, 265, 288–299, as well as Schlesinger, *RK*, pp. 788–798.

"To a share of power and responsibility": RFK, Vietnam papers, JFK Library. See also Schlesinger, *RK*, p. 793.

"Ho Chi Kennedy": *Chicago Tribune*, February 21, 1966. Reprinted in Schlesinger, *RK*, p. 794.

"Writing a prescription": *New York Times*, February 22, 1966.

I. F. Stone: See Schlesinger, *RK*, p. 298. Original source *I. F. Stone's Weekly*, October 24, 1966.

David Halberstam and James C. Thomson, Jr.: Both quotations (in slightly altered form) appear in Stein and Plimpton, *American Journey*.

"There would be Robert Kennedy": Doris Kearns, *Lyndon Johnson*, pp. 251–252 (same LBJ quotation reprinted in Schlesinger, *RK*, p. 800).

Etienne Manac'h: See John Gunther Dean State Department files, U.S. State Department, Washington, D.C. Further details on the Manac'h-RFK meeting and on the subsequent RFK-LBJ encounter can be found in Guthman and Allen, eds., *RFK*, p. 290, and in Schlesinger, *RK*, pp. 825–828.

Notes from meetings of the Special Group, Counterinsurgency Program: Attorney General Files, Justice Department, Washington, D.C.

Information for this chapter has come from a variety of government archives, including the FBI, CIA, Counterinsurgency Group (Department of Justice) and the State Department.

24. THE CHALLENGE

Author interviews for this chapter were conducted with William vanden Heuvel, Theodore H. White, Joe Dolan, John Richard Reilly, Manfred Ohrenstein, George McGovern, Ross Graham, John Revson, Diana DuBois, Al Eisele, Eugene McCarthy, Dan Blackburn, Barrett Prettyman, Fred Dutton, Ty Fain, Walt Rostow, Bill Epperidge, Morton Downey, Jr., Joseph Rauh, Jr., Cathy Griffin, James Spada, Paul Schrade, David Hackett, Clark Clifford, Peter Lawford, Roswell Gilpatric, Franklin D. Roosevelt, Jr., Larry O'Brien, Ken O'Donnell, Abe Ribicoff, Lem Billings, Allen Ginsberg, LaVern Duffy, Blair Clark.

Oral histories consulted for this chapter: Robert F. Kennedy, Barrett Prettyman, Frank Mankiewicz, Peter Edelman, Walt Rostow (LBJ Library), Allard Lowenstein (Columbia University Libraries), George McGovern, Fred Harris, Joe Dolan, James Loeb, Joseph Rauh, Fred Dutton.

Periodicals consulted for this chapter include the *New York Times*, New York *Daily News*, *Village Voice*, *Time*, *Newsweek*.

Volumes consulted for this chapter: Schlesinger, *RK*; Theodore H. White, *The Making of the Presidency 1968*; Walter Cronkite, *A Reporter's Life*; Eugene McCarthy, *Up 'Til Now: A Memoir*; Levy, *Cesar Chavez: Autobiography of La Causa*; James MacGregor, *Edward Kennedy and the Camelot Legacy*; Kearns, *Lyndon Johnson and the American Dream*; Newfield, *Robert Kennedy*; Stein and Plimpton, *American Journey*; vanden Heuvel and Gwirtzman, *On His Own*; Johnson, *Vantage Point*; Fred H. Harris, *Potomac Fever*; Robert F. Kennedy, *Just Friends and Brave Enemies*.

Excerpts from RFK speeches: See Edwin O. Guthman and C. Richard Allen, eds. *RFK: Collected Speeches*. See Guthman and Allen for occasional commentary on RFK speeches as well.

Lowenstein visit to Hickory Hill: See Newfield, *Robert Kennedy*, pp. 185–186. RFK's comments to Lowenstein in the current book, however, differ somewhat from Newfield's account. They are based on an author interview with Larry O'Brien to whom RFK recounted the conversation. See also Schlesinger, *RK*, pp. 886–887.

October 8, 1967 meeting: Ken O'Donnell interview. Meeting also described in Schlesinger, *RK*, p. 891.

Speech at the University of Oklahoma: Fred Harris, *Potomac Fever*; Fred Harris OH; Guthman and Allen, eds., *RFK: Collected Speeches*, p. 299.

"Don't you understand what that means"; Schlesinger, *RK*, p. 885.

"A personality struggle": Guthman and Allen, eds., *RFK: Collected Speeches*, pp. 300–301.

December 10, 1967 meeting: Schlesinger, *RK*, pp. 894–895.

"I felt that I was being . . .": Kearns, *Lyndon Johnson and the American Dream*, p. 343. See also Schlesinger, *RK*, p. 931.

"Our enemy, savagely striking . . .": See Guthman and Allen, eds. *RFK: Collected Speeches*, p. 307.

Jeff Greenfield, Ibid., p. 312. See also the New York *Daily News*, February 9, 1968.

March 7, 1968 speech: Guthman and Allen, eds., *RFK: Collected Speeches*, pp. 313–314; Schlesinger, *RK*, p. 906.

LBJ sex anecdote (asterisked note): Related to current author by former secret service agent who, for obvious reasons, wishes to remain anonymous.

"Abigail said no": The Teddy quote appears in Theodore White, *The Making of the President 1968*; James MacGregor Burns, *Edward Kennedy and the Camelot Legacy*; Schlesinger, *RK*.

Wisconsin, Pennsylvania and Massachusetts: Schlesinger, *RK*, p. 920.

25. PLAYING TO WIN

Author interviews for this chapter were conducted with Langdon Marvin, Fred Dutton, Larry O'Brien, Walt Rostow, John Treanor, Jr., George Plimpton, Walter Fauntroy, Dan Blackburn, David Breasted, Bill Epperidge, Kristi Witker, Theodore H. White, Jack Valenti, Eugene McCarthy, Thomas Shack, Truman Capote, Roswell Gilpatric, John Bartlow Martin, Ted Van Dyk, Ty Fain, John B. White, Marianne Strong, Nicholas von Hoffman, Rowland Evans, Jr., Lester Persky, Paul Schrade, George McGovern, Brent Zacky, Lem Billings, Ken O'Donnell, Blair Clark, Mike Mansfield, Abe Ribicoff, Jeremy Larner.

Oral histories consulted for this chapter: Peter Edelman, Walt Rostow (LBJ Library), Allard Lowenstein (Columbia University Libraries), Marietta Tree (Columbia University Libraries), Frank Mankiewicz, George McGovern, John P. Roche, Fred Dutton, Theodore C. Sorensen, John Seigenthaler, William Barry.

Periodicals consulted for this chapter include the *New York Times*, *New York Post*, New York *Daily News*, *Village Voice*, *Chicago Tribune*, *Chicago Sun-Times*, *Los Angeles Times*, *Washington Post*, *D.C. Examiner*, *Dan's Papers*, *Boston Herald*, *Miami Herald*, *San Francisco Chronicle*, *Women's Wear Daily*, *American Heritage*, *Newsweek*, *Esquire*.

Volumes consulted for this chapter include White, *The Making of the President 1968*; Frank Brady, *Onassis: An Extravagant Life*; Branch, *Parting the Waters*; Collier and Horowitz, *The Kennedys*; McCarthy, *Up 'Til Now*; Schlesinger, *RK*; Jules Witcover, *85 Days: The Last Campaign of Robert F. Kennedy*; Guthman and Allen, eds., *RFK: Collected Speeches*; Theodore C. Sorensen, *The Kennedy Legacy*; Oppenheimer, *The Other Mrs. Kennedy*.

"He's the whole ball game": Jimmy Breslin, " 'Daley Means the Ball Game,' Bobby says," *Chicago Sun-Times*, March 26, 1968.

Kansas State University and Los Angeles speeches: Guthman and Allen, eds., *RFK: Collected Speeches*, pp. 324–325; p. 338.

Murray Kempton telegram: JFK Library.

Joseph Califano: Schlesinger, *RK*, p. 930.

"Bobby will have to shoot": Jules Witcover, *85 Days: The Last Campaign of Robert F. Kennedy*, p. 134; Schlesinger, *RK*, p. 936.

Ball State University and Martin Luther King assassination: See Guthman and Allen, eds., *RFK: Collected Speeches*; pp. 355–357; Schlesinger, *RK*, pp. 939–940.

RFK's Indianapolis speech on King: Tape and transcription of this speech can be found in RFK papers, JFK Library.

RFK telephone conversation with Coretta Scott King: Schlesinger, *RK*, p. 941; see Coretta Scott King interview, Stein and Plimpton, *American Journey*, pp. 256–257.

Martin Luther King funeral: Schlesinger, *RK*, p. 943. See Reverend Walter Fauntroy interview, Stein and Plimpton, *American Journey*, p. 261.

"As George Bernard Shaw once said": The quote, a paraphrase from Shaw's *Back to Methuselah*, was first used by John F. Kennedy when he addressed the Irish Parliament in the summer of 1963. See Jules Witcover, *85 Days*, p. 161.

"Do you know what I think?": Schlesinger, *RK*, p. 921. Other sources for Jackie Kennedy–related material in this chapter are Frank Brady, *Onassis: An Extravagant Life*, pp. 169–173, and Heymann, *A Woman Named Jackie*.

"Old Hubert's got Big Business": All of the "Cannonball" verses can be found in Witcover, *85 Days*, pp. 162–63. See also Schlesinger, RK, p. 953.

Rene Carpenter and several other friends: Oppenheimer, *The Other Mrs. Kennedy*, p. 209.

David Kennedy's behavioral problems: See Oppenheimer, *The Other Mrs. Kennedy*, pp. 313–316.

Jerry Oppenheimer's interview with Bob Galland, the young caretaker hired to look after the RFK children, is an illuminating document on life at Hickory Hill during the 1960s.

John J. Lindsay: Stein and Plimpton, *American Journey*, p. 293. Also reprinted in Schlesinger, *RK*, p. 968.

Kristi Witker: In addition to the interview accorded the author for this book, Witker is interviewed in *Dan's Papers*, August 29, 1997.

"From you . . .": See Witcover, *85 Days*, p. 165; Schlesinger, *RK*, p. 948; Guthman and Allen, eds., *RFK: Collected Speeches*, pp. 342–343.

"Politics of happiness, politics of joy": See Schlesinger, *RK*, p. 950.

A "new politics": See Guthman and Allen, eds., *RK*, p. 385.

Hubert Humphrey notations: See Hubert Humphrey Collection, Minnesota Historical Society, Minneapolis, Minnesota.

Oregon primary: See White, *The Making of the President 1968*; Witcover, *85 Days*; Schlesinger, *RK*, pp. 972–973.

Student: "Fascist!": See Schlesinger, *RK*, p. 966. Also, Guthman and Allen, eds., *RFK: Collected Speeches*.

RFK-McCarthy TV debate: *New York Times*, June 2, 1968.

Information on various RFK death threats in this chapter is derived from newly released FBI files, FBI, Washington, D.C.

26. JOURNEY'S END

Author interviews for this chapter were conducted with Kristi Witker, Dan Blackburn, Thomas Schack, Marie Ridder, James Spada, Frank Burns, Paul Schrade, Gene Scherrer, Bill Epperidge, George Plimpton, Jim Wrightsman, Pedro San Juan, Lem Billings, Roswell Gilpatric, Ty Fain, Al Eisele, Ted Van Dyk, Daniel Stewart, Jack Micay, Francesca Hilton, Mary Sanford, Gottfried Isaac, Jim Garrison, Ramsey Clark, Philip H. Melanson, John Miner, Dan Moldea, Bernard Fensterwald, Jr., Truman Capote, Richard Goodwin, Theodore H. White, Pierre Salinger, John Kenneth Galbraith, Peter Lawford, Rosey Grier, David Ormsby-Gore.

Oral histories consulted for this chapter: Robert F. Kennedy, Frank Mankiewicz, William Barry, Fred Dutton, Allard Lowenstein (Columbia University Libraries).

Periodicals consulted for this chapter include the *New York Times*, *Jerusalem Post*, *Boston Globe*, *Cape Cod Standard-Times*, *Los Angeles Times*, *Dan's Papers*, *Life*, *Look*, *Time*, *American Heritage*, *McCall's*, *Newsweek*.

Volumes consulted for this chapter include Schlesinger, *RK*; White, *The Making of the President 1968*; Collier and Horowitz, *The Kennedys*; Vidal, *Palimpsest*; James Spada, *Peter Lawford*; Philip H. Melanson, *The Robert F. Kennedy Assassination*; Oppenheimer, *The Other Mrs. Kennedy*; Stein and Plimpton, *American Journey*; Guthman and Allen, eds., *RFK: Collected Speeches*; Witcover, *85 Days*; vanden Heuvel and Gwirtzman, *On His Own*; Joe McGinnis, *The Last Brother*; Robert Blair Kaiser, *"RFK Must Die!"*

Pierre Salinger on Romain Gary: See Schlesinger, *RK*, p. 968; Stein and Plimpton, *American Journey*, pp. 293–294; Salinger unpublished mss.

Theodore White on RFK at Frankenheimer home: Schlesinger, *RK*, p. 980; Oppenheimer, *The Other Mrs. Kennedy*, p. 324; Richard N. Goodwin article on RFK's last day in *McCall's*, August 1970; Theodore H. White, "The Wearing Last Weeks and a Precious Last Day," *Life*, June 21, 1968; Theodore White interview with author.

"At six-fifteen": Schlesinger, *RK*, p. 980.

Bob Galland placed a telephone call . . . to Nicole Salinger: Oppenheimer, *The Other Mrs. Kennedy*, p. 324.

The latest count of delegates: Schlesinger, *RK*, p. 981; vanden Heuvel and Gwirtzman, *On His Own*, pp. 391–392.

"I have to get free": A somewhat different version of the RFK quotation in the current book appears in Schlesinger, *RK*, p. 981. The Schlesinger biography, same page, also contains a reference to Richard Goodwin's telephone calls to Kennedy allies working for McCarthy.

By ten-thirty, Ethel had instructed Bob Galland: Oppenheimer, *The Other Mrs. Kennedy*, p. 325. David Kennedy witnessing his father's assassination on television: Ibid., pp. 327–328. See Oppenheimer also for Rose Kennedy reaction to RFK's assassination as well as Galland's activities at the Beverly Hills Hotel. Collier and Horowitz, *The Kennedys* also proved a useful source for this section.

Ted Kennedy's whereabouts during RFK's assassination: Joe McGinnis, *The Last Brother*, pp. 445–447.

William Barry Oral History: See also Schlesinger, *RK*, p. 969.

Don Drysdale's record-breaking sixth straight shutout: Oppenheimer, *The Other Mrs. Kennedy*, p. 326.

RFK Jr. at Hickory Hill: Ibid., p. 331. See also Collier and Horowitz, *The Kennedys*.

Ethel Kennedy's deportment at Good Samaritan Hospital: Ibid., pp. 330–333.

Kathleen and Joe Kennedy at New England boarding schools: At the time of RFK's death, Kathleen was attending the Putney School, Putney, Vermont, while Joe went to Milton Academy, the same school previously attended by his father.

During the campaign, Kristi Witker asked Bobby to give her notes he had made for a campaign speech, to be used for the article she was then writing for *American Heritage*. The first lines of the two-page document she received (on yellow, lined legal paper) contained the now-ironic headings: "Violence/Lawlessness; Enemies of the System . . ." Unwittingly, RFK had penned his own epitaph.

Sirhan wounded five others, none fatally: Paul Schrade, 43, of Los Angeles, was in satisfactory condition at Kaiser Foundation Hospital following a two-hour operation to remove brain fragments from his skull; William Weisel, 30, of Washington, D.C., an American Broadcasting Company Associate News Director, was also in satisfactory condition at Kaiser Foundation Hospital, where he underwent surgery for removal of a bullet in his abdomen; Ira Goldstein, 19, of Encino, California, a Continental News Service reporter, was treated at Encino Hospital for a bullet wound received in his left thigh; Mrs. Elizabeth Evans (age unknown), of Saugus, California, a Kennedy supporter, was in good condition at Huntington Memorial Hospital, where she was treated for a scalp wound; Irwin Stroll, 17, of Los Angeles, was in good condition at Midway Hospital, where he was treated for a wound in the lower part of his left leg.

John F. Kennedy had been as fatalistic about the possibility of assassination as Bobby would later become. According to Gore Vidal's memoir, *Palimpsest*, JFK once said to him: "If the assassin is willing to die, it couldn't be simpler." RFK's assassination, in fact, was just that—the case of a gunman willing to die. Unlike the JFK assassination, where there is every indication of a conspiracy (Lee Harvey Oswald shot Kennedy from a concealed location), RFK's murder points to a typical political hit wherein the killer (Sirhan Sirhan) shoots his victim at close range and is willing to either be killed or, at the very least, apprehended. In so doing—and in acting alone (there is not a scintilla of material evidence to the contrary)—Sirhan sought martyrdom. Instead, he conferred it upon Bobby.

In addition to John Glenn, RFK's pallbearers were: Robert F. Kennedy, Jr., Stephen Smith, John Seigenthaler, Lem Billings, James Whittaker, W. Averell Harriman, Rafer Johnson, C. Douglas Dillon, Bill Barry, Robert McNamara, David Hackett and David Ormsby-Gore (Lord Harlech).

EPILOGUE: PROMISES TO KEEP

Author interviews for this chapter were conducted with Roswell Gilpatric, Doris Lilly, Truman Capote, Larry O'Brien, Ken O'Donnell, Kent Cunow, Lee Rainey,

Lem Billings, Richard Burke, Harrison Rainie, Ted Schwartz, Patricia Seaton, Peter Lawford, Mary Sanford, Franklin D. Roosevelt, Jr., Leo Damore, Jamie Auchincloss, Bob Davidoff, David Kennedy, Robert Kennedy, Jr., Pamela Page, Laurie Cooper, Marianne Strong, Lawrence J. Quirk, Mary DeGrace, Peter Manso, Mary Hayes, Brent Zacky, Ryan Rayston.

Recent articles used by the author for the epilogue include Deborah Sontag, "Robert Kennedy's Children," *New York Times*, June 15, 1997; Michael Shnayerson, "Inside the Kennedy Clan," *Vanity Fair*, August 1997.

David Kennedy and Rachel Ward: See Collier and Horowitz, *The Kennedys*.

David Kennedy's death: See Town of Palm Beach [Florida] Police Department Investigatory Report on the Death of David Anthony Kennedy, April 25, 1984.

"You are the oldest of all the male grandchildren": Schlesinger, *RK*, p. 660. Letter located in RFK papers, JFK Library. Other RFK letters to his children that appear in this volume can also be found in RFK papers, JFK Library.

Lem Billings and JFK sexual relationship: See Lawrence J. Quirk, *The Kennedys in Hollywood*.

Ethel's racial slur and description of her bathroom at Hickory Hill: See Oppenheimer, *The Other Mrs. Kennedy.*

The Kennedys weren't the only scandal-ridden family around. On October 31, 1975 (Halloween), the bludgeoned and bloodied body of fifteen-year-old Martha Moxley was found in the woods in back of Rushton Skakel's home in Greenwich, Connecticut. The last person to be seen with Martha prior to her death was seventeen-year-old Tommy Skakel, Rushton's son. Rushton Skakel was a brother of Ethel Skakel Kennedy; Tommy was her nephew. The murder weapon, a golf club, which had been located at the scene of the crime, matched a set of clubs later found in the home of Rushton Skakel. The murder sent shock waves through the wealthy community and made national headlines. Despite what appeared to be an abundance of evidence, the Greenwich Police Department never charged Tommy Skakel with the crime. To this day, it remains unsolved, supposedly because of Skakel family money and Kennedy family influence. The case was reopened in late 1997, by which time many of the Police Department's files had disappeared—"mysteriously," according to police officials. It is hoped that DNA-related tests on the corpse of Martha Moxley will reveal the identity of the murderer. Tommy Skakel remains a prime suspect, as does his younger brother, Michael, who earlier that last evening had also been seen with the victim.

"Promises to Keep": Robert Frost had been one of John F. Kennedy's favorite poets. RFK had quoted from "Stopping by Woods on a Snowy Evening" during his speech at the 1964 National Democratic Convention when talking about his brother. Following JFK's assassination, Bobby read Frost's collected works and committed several of his favorite poems to memory.

AUTHOR'S NOTE

In 1962, while an undergraduate at Cornell University, I became involved in Democratic Party politics. Through family contacts I subsequently met Ken O'Donnell, and through O'Donnell such Kennedy stalwarts as Larry O'Brien, LaVern Duffy and Lem Billings. In 1968, I worked for Robert F. Kennedy, supporting his presidential bid by helping to register future voters in New York City. The dream died in early June of that year.

—CDH

BIBLIOGRAPHY

A Concise Compendium of the Warren Commission Report on the Assassination of John F. Kennedy. Introduction by Robert J. Donovan. New York: Popular Library, 1964.

Report of the Warren Commission on the Assassination of President Kennedy. Introduction by Harrison Salisbury with additional material prepared by the *New York Times.* New York: Bantam, 1964.

White House History. Journal of the White House Historical Association.

The Witnesses: Excerpts from the Warren Commission's Hearings. New York: McGraw-Hill, 1964.

Abel, Elie. *The Missile Crisis.* Philadelphia and New York: J. B. Lippincott, 1966.

Abernathy, Ralph David. *And the Walls Came Tumbling Down.* New York: Harper and Row, 1989.

Abramson, Rudy. *Spanning the Century.* New York: William Morrow, 1992.

Adler, Bill. *The Kennedy Children.* New York: Franklin Watts, 1980.

———, ed. *The Kennedy Wit.* New York: Citadel, 1964.

———, ed. *A New Day.* New York: New American Library, 1968.

———, and Bruce Cassiday. *RFK: A Special Kind of Man.* Playboy Press, 1977.

Adler, Richard, with Lee Davis. *You Gotta Have Heart.* New York: Donald Fine, 1990.

Agee, Philip. *Inside the Company: CIA Diary.* New York: Stonehill, 1975.

Albert, Judith Clavir, and Steward Edward Alberts. *The Sixties Papers. Documents of a Rebellious Decade.* New York: Praeger, 1984. (excerpt)

Alsop, Joseph W., with Adam Platt, *"I've Seen the Best of It." Memoirs.* New York: W.W. Norton, 1992.

Alsop, Stewart, *The Center.* London, England: Hodder and Stoughton Ltd., 1968.

Ambrose, Stephen E. *Nixon: The Triumph of a Politician, 1962–1972,* vol. 2. New York: Simon & Schuster, 1989.

Anderson, Jack. *Washington Expose.* Washington, D.C.: Public Affairs Press, 1967.

Anger, Kenneth. *Hollywood Babylon II.* (excerpt) New York: E.P. Dutton, 1984.

Anson, Robert Sam. *"They've Killed the President."* New York: Bantam, 1975.

Ashman, Charles. *Connally: The Adventures of Big Bad John.* New York: William Morrow, 1974.

———, and Rebecca Sobel. *The Strange Disappearance of Jimmy Hoffa.* New York: Manor, 1976.

Aumont, Jean-Pierre. *Sun and Shadow.* New York: W.W. Norton, 1977.

Austin, John. *Hollywood's Unsolved Mysteries.* New York: Shapolsky, 1990.

Bacall, Lauren. *By Myself.* New York: Ballantine, 1980.

Baker, Robert Gene, with Larry King. *Wheeling and Dealing: Confessions of a Capitol Hill Operator.* New York: W.W. Norton, 1978.

Baker, Russell. *The Good Times.* New York: William Morrow, 1989.

Baldridge, Letitia. *Of Diamonds and Diplomats.* Boston: Houghton Mifflin, 1968.

Ball, George W., *The Discipline of Power.* Boston: Little Brown, 1968.

Barlett, Donald L., and James B. Steele. *Empire: The Life, Legend, and Madness of Howard Hughes.* New York: W.W. Norton, 1979.

Bauer, Stephen, with Frances Spatz Leighton. *At Ease in the White House.* Secaucus, N.J.: Carol Publishing Group, 1991.

Belin, David W. *Final Disclosure: The Full Truth about the Assassination of President Kennedy.* New York: Charles Scribner's Sons, 1988.

Bell, Simon, Richard Curtis, and Helen Fielding. *Who's Had Who?* New York: Warner, 1990.

Bender, Marilyn. *The Beautiful People.* New York: Coward-McCann, 1967.

Bennett, Arnold. *Jackie, Bobby and Manchester.* New York: Bee-Line, 1967.

Benson, Michael. *Who's Who in the JFK Assassination.* New York: Citadel, 1994.

Bergen, Candice. *Knock Wood.* New York: Linden, 1984.

Bernstein, Irving. *Promises Kept. John F. Kennedy's New Frontier.* New York: Oxford University Press, 1991.

Bertagna, Joe. *Crimson in Triumph: A Pictorial History of Harvard Athletics, 1882–1985.* Lexington, Mass: Stephen Greene, 1986.

Beschloss, Michael R. *The Crisis Years: Kennedy and Khrushchev, 1960–1963.* New York: Edward Burlingame, 1991.

Bevington, Helen. *Along Came the Witch: A Journal in the 1960's.* New York: Harcourt Brace Jovanovich, 1960.

Bigler, Philip. *In Honored Glory: Arlington National Cemetery, The Final Post.* Arlington, Va.: Vandamere, 1987.

Bird, Kai. *The Chairman: John J. McCloy, the Making of the American Establishment.* New York: Simon and Schuster, 1992.

Birmingham, Stephen. *Jacqueline Bouvier Kennedy Onassis.* New York: Grosset and Dunlap, 1978.

Bishop, Jim. *The Day Kennedy Was Shot.* New York: Funk and Wagnalls, 1968.

———. *A Day in the Life of President Kennedy.* New York: Random House, 1964.

Blackwell, Earl. *Celebrity Register.* Townson, Md.: Times Publishing Group, 1986.

Blakey, G. Robert, and Richard N. Billings. *Fatal Hour.* New York: Berkley, 1992.

Blight, James G. *The Shattered Crystal Ball: Fear and Learning in the Cuban Missile Crisis.* Savage, Md.: Rowman and Littlefield, 1990.

———, and David A. Welch. *On the Brink. Americans and Soviets Reexamine the Cuban Missile Crisis.* New York: Hill and Wang, 1989.

Block, Herbert. *The Herblock Gallery.* New York: Simon and Schuster, 1968.

Blum, John Morton. *Years of Discord: American Politics and Society, 1961–1974.* New York: W.W. Norton, 1991.

Boller, Paul F. *Presidential Wives.* New York: Oxford University Press, 1988.

Bouvier, Kathleen. *To Jack with Love.* New York: Kensington, 1979.

Braden, Joan. *Just Enough Rope: An Intimate Memoir.* New York: Villard, 1989.

Bradlee, Benjamin C. *Conversations with Kennedy.* New York: W.W. Norton, 1975.

———. *A Good Life: Newspapering and Other Adventures.* New York: Simon and Schuster, 1995.

Brady, Frank. *Onassis. An Extravagant Life.* New Jersey: Prentice-Hall, 1977.

Bragg, Melvyn. *Richard Burton.* Boston: Little, Brown, 1988.

Branch, Taylor. *Parting the Waters: America in the King Years 1954–63.* New York: Simon and Schuster, 1989.

Brauer, Carl M. *John F. Kennedy and the Second Reconstruction.* New York: Columbia University Press, 1977.

———. *Presidential Transitions: Eisenhower through Reagan.* New York: Oxford University Press, 1986.

Brennan, Rev. J. F. *The Evolution of Everyman: Ancestral Lineage of John Fitzgerald Kennedy.* Dundalk: Dundalgan, 1968.

Brill, Steven. *The Teamsters.* New York: Simon and Schuster, 1978.

Brodie, Fawn. *Richard Nixon: The Shaping of His Character.* New York: W.W. Norton, 1981.

Brown, Gene, ed. *The Kennedys: A New York Times Profile.* New York: Arno, 1980.

Brown, Peter Harry, and Patte B. Barham. *Marilyn: The Last Take.* New York: Dutton, 1992.

Brown, Stuart Gerry. *The Presidency on Trial: Robert Kennedy's 1968 Campaign and Afterwards.* Honolulu: University Press of Hawaii, 1972.

Brown, Walt. *The People v. Lee Harvey Oswald.* New York: Carroll and Graf, 1992.

Browne, Arthur, Dan Collins, and Michael Goodwin. *I, Koch.* New York: Dodd, Mead, 1985.

Browning, Frank, and John Gerassi. *The American Way of Crime.* New York: G.P. Putnam's Sons, 1980.

Brownstein, Ronald. *The Power and the Glitter.* New York: Pantheon Books, 1990.

Brugioni, Dino A. *Eyeball to Eyeball: The Inside Story of the Cuban Missile Crisis.* Edited by Robert F. McCort. New York: Random House, 1991.

Bruno, Jerry. *The Advance Man.* New York: William Morrow, 1971.

Buck, Pearl S. *The Kennedy Women.* New York: Pinnacle, 1970.

Burke, Richard E., with William and Marilyn Hoffer. *The Senator: My Years with Ted Kennedy.* New York: St. Martin's, 1992.

Burner, David, and Thomas R. West. *The Torch Is Passed: The Kennedy Brothers and American Liberalism.* New York: Atheneum, 1984.

Burns, James MacGregor. *Edward Kennedy and the Camelot Legacy.* New York: W.W. Norton and Co., 1976.

Burrows, Nanette Grant, Jane Cohhan, and Whitney McKendsee Moore. *Academy Days. A History of Greenwich Academy from 1826 to 1986.* Canaan, N.H.: Phoenix Publishing, 1987.

Califano, Joseph. *Governing America.* New York: Simon and Schuster, 1981.

Cameron, Gail. *Rose. A Biography of Rose Fitzgerald Kennedy.* New York: G.P. Putnam's Sons, 1971.

Campbell, James. *Talking at the Gates: A Life of James Baldwin.* New York: Viking Penguin, 1991.

Capell, Frank A. *The Strange Death of Marilyn Monroe.* The Herald of Freedom, 1964.

Carey, Robert G. *The Peace Corps.* New York: Praeger Publishers, 1970.

Caro, Robert A. *Means of Ascent. The Years of Lyndon Johnson.* New York: Alfred A. Knopf, 1990.

———. *The Power Brokers: Robert Moses and the Fall of New York.* New York: Vintage Books, 1975.

Caroli, Betty Boyd. *First Ladies.* New York: Oxford University Press, 1987.

Carpozi, George, Jr. *The Hidden Side of Jacqueline Kennedy.* New York: Pyramid Books, 1967.

Carr, William H. A. *JFK: An Informal Biography.* New York: Lancer Books, 1962.

Carroll, Peter N. *Famous in America.* Dutton, 1985.

Cassini, Igor, with Jeanne Molli. *I'd Do It All Over Again.* New York: G.P. Putnam's Sons, 1977.

Cassini, Oleg. *In My Own Fashion.* New York: Simon and Schuster, 1987.

Chafe, William H. *Never Stop Running.* New York: Basic Books, 1993.

Chandler, David Leon. *Brothers in Blood. The Rise of the Criminal Brotherhoods.* New York: E.P. Dutton, 1975.

Chern, Margaret Booth. *The New Complete Newfoundland.* New York: Howell Book House, 1976.

Cheshire, Maxine, with John Greenya. *Maxine Cheshire, Reporter.* Boston: Houghton Mifflin, 1978.

Chester, Lewis, and Godfrey Hodgson and Bruce Page. *An American Melodrama: The Presidential Campaign of 1968.* New York: Viking, 1969.

Chisholm, Anne, and Michael Davie. *Lord Beaverbrook: A Life.* New York: Alfred A. Knopf, 1993.

Christian, John G., and William W. Turner. *The Assassination of Robert F. Kennedy: A Searching Look at the Conspiracy and Cover-up 1968–1978.* New York: Random House, 1978.

Clark, Kenneth B. *King, Malcolm, Baldwin.* Middletown, Conn.: Wesleyan University Press, 1985.

Clarke, Gerald. *Capote: A Biography.* New York: Simon and Schuster, 1988.

Clay, Jim. *Hoffa! Ten Angels Swearing.* Beaverdam, Va.: Beaverdam Books, 1985.

Clifford, Clark, with Richard Holbrooke. *Counsel to the President.* New York: Random House, 1991.

Clinch, Nancy Gager. *The Kennedy Neurosis.* New York: Grosset and Dunlap, 1973.

Clooney, Rosemary, with Raymond Strait. *This for Remembrance.* New York: Playboy Press, 1977.

Colby, Gerard. *Dupont Dynasty.* Secaucus, N.J.: Lyle Stuart, 1984.

Collier, Peter, and David Horowitz. *The Fords.* London, England: Collins, 1988.

———. *The Kennedys: An American Drama.* New York: Summit, 1984.

Connally, John, with Mickey Herskowitz. *History's Shadow.* New York: Hyperion, 1993.

Cook, Fred J. *The Nightmare Decade.* New York: Random House, 1987.

Cooney, John. *The Annenbergs.* New York: Simon and Schuster, 1980.

Corry, John. *Golden Clan: The Murrays, the McDonnells and the Irish American Aristocracy.* Boston: Houghton Mifflin, 1977.

———. *The Manchester Affair.* New York: G.P. Putnam's Sons, 1967.

Costello, John. *Ten Days to Destiny.* New York: William Morrow, 1991.

Crenshaw, Charles A., with Jens Hansen and J. Gary Shaw, *JFK: Conspiracy of Silence.* New York: Signet, 1992.

Cronkite, Walter. *A Reporter's Life.* New York: Alfred A. Knopf, 1996.

Crosby, Donald F. *God, Church, and Flag: Senator Joseph McCarthy and the Catholic Church, 1950–1957.* Raleigh: University of North Carolina, 1978.

Cummings, Richard. *The Pied Piper: Allard K. Lowenstein and the Liberal Dream.* New York: Grove Press, 1985.

Curran, Robert. *The Kennedy Women.* New York: Lancer, 1964.

Curtis, Charlotte. *First Lady.* New York: Pyramid, 1962.

Curtis, Tony, and Barry Paris. *Tony Curtis: The Autobiography.* New York: William Morrow, 1993.

Cutler, John Henry. *"Honey Fitz."* New York: Bobbs-Merrill, 1962.

Dallas, Rita, with Jeanira Ratcliffe. *The Kennedy Case.* New York: G.P. Putnam's Sons, 1973.

Dallek, Robert. *Lone Star Rising: Lyndon Johnson and His Times, 1908–1960.* New York and Oxford: Oxford University Press, 1991.

Damore, Leo. *The Cape Cod Years of John Fitzgerald Kennedy.* Englewood Cliffs, N.J.: Prentice-Hall, 1967.

———. *Senatorial Privilege.* Washington, D.C.: Regnery Gateway, 1988.

Daniel, Lois, ed. *The World of the Kennedy Women: Profiles in Grace and Courage.* Kansas City: Hallmark Cards, 1973.

Daniels, Robert V. *Year of the Heroic Guerrilla.* New York: Basic Books, 1989.

David, Irene, and Lester David. *Bobby Kennedy: The Making of a Folk Hero.* New York: Dodd, Mead and Co., 1986.

———. *Good Ted, Bad Ted: The Five Faces of Edward M. Kennedy.* New York: Birch Lane Press: Carol, 1993.

Davis, John H. *The Kennedys: Dynasty and Disaster 1848–1983.* New York: Mc-Graw-Hill, 1984, 1992.

———. *The Bouviers.* New York: Farrar, Straus and Giroux, 1969.

———. *Mafia Dynasty: The Rise and Fall of the Gambino Crime Family.* New York: HarperCollins: 1993.

———. *Mafia Kingfish: Carlos Marcello and the Assassination of John F. Kennedy.* New York: McGraw-Hill, 1989.

Davis, Kenneth S. *The Politics of Honor: A Biography of Adlai E. Stevenson.* New York: G.P. Putnam's Sons, 1957.

Davis, L. J. *Onassis: Aristotle and Christina.* New York: St. Martin's, 1986.

Davis, Patti. *The Way I See It.* New York: G.P. Putnam's Sons, 1992.

Davison, Jean. *Oswald's Game.* New York: W.W. Norton and Co., 1983.

Deakin, James. *Straight Stuff: The Reporters, the White House, and the Truth.* New York: William Morrow, 1984.

Deaver, Michael K., with Mickey Herskowitz. *Behind the Scenes.* New York: William Morrow, 1987.

Dees, Morris, with Steve Fiffer. *A Season for Justice.* New York: Charles Scribner's Sons, 1991.

Demaris, Ovid. *The Director.* New York: Harper's Magazine Press, 1975.

De Toledano, Ralph. *J. Edgar Hoover: The Man in His Time.* New Rochelle, N.Y.: Arlington House, 1973.

Detzer, David. *The Brink: Cuban Missile Crisis, 1962.* New York: Thomas Y. Crowell, 1979.

Deutsch, Armand. *Me and Bogie.* New York: G.P. Putnam's Sons, 1991.

Diamond, Edwin. *Behind the Times: Inside the New York Times.* New York: Villard, 1994.

Diamondstein, Barbralee. *Open Secrets: Ninety-four Women in Touch with Our Time.* New York: Viking, 1970. (excerpt)

Dickerson, Nancy. *Among Those Present: A Reporter's View of Twenty-five Years in Washington.* New York: Random House, 1976.

Dinerstein, Herbert S. *The Making of a Missile Crisis: October 1962*. Baltimore: Johns Hopkins University Press, 1976.

Dinneen, Joseph Francis. *The Kennedy Family*. Boston: Little, Brown, 1969.

Dirksen, Louella, with Norma Lee Growning. *The Honorable Mr. Marigold: My Life with Everett Dirksen*. New York: Doubleday, 1972.

Dittmer, John. *Local People: The Struggle for Civil Rights in Mississippi*. Urbana and Chicago: University of Illinois Press, 1994.

Divine, Robert A., ed. *The Cuban Missile Crisis*. Chicago: Quadrangle, 1971.

Donaldson, Scott. *Archibald MacLeish. An American Life*. Boston: Houghton Mifflin, 1992.

Donovan, Robert J. *PT 109*. New York: Crest, 1961.

————, and Ray Scherer. *Unsilent Revolution. Television News and American Public Life, 1948–1991*. New York: Woodrow Wilson International Center for Scholars and Cambridge University Press, 1992.

Dorril, Stephen. *Honeytrap*. London: Weidenfeld and Nicholson, 1987.

Dougherty, James E. *The Secret Happiness of Marilyn Monroe*. Chicago: Playboy Press, 1976.

Douglas, Kirk. *The Ragman's Son*. New York: Simon and Schuster, 1988.

Douglas, William O. *The Court Years, 1939–1975*. New York: Random House, 1980.

————. *Go East, Young Man. The Early Years: An Autobiography*. New York: Random House, 1974.

DuBois, Diana. *In Her Sister's Shadow: An Intimate Biography of Lee Radziwill*. Boston: Little, Brown, 1995.

Dugger, Ronnie. *The Politician*. New York: W.W. Norton, 1982.

Duncliffe, William J. *The Life and Times of Joseph P. Kennedy*. New York: Macfadden, 1965.

Eban, Abba. *Abba Eban: An Autobiography*. New York: Random House, 1977.

Ehrlichman, John. *Witness to Power*. New York: Pocket Books, 1982.

Eisele, Albert. *Almost to the Presidency: A Biography of Two American Politicians*. Blue Earth, Minn.: Piper, 1972.

Eisenhower, Julie. *Pat Nixon*. New York: Simon and Schuster, 1986.

English, David. *Divided They Stand*. Englewood Cliffs, N.J.: Prentice-Hall, 1969.

Epstein, Edward Jay. *Deception: The Invisible War between the KGB and the CIA*. New York: Simon and Schuster, 1989.

————. *Inquest*. New York: Viking, 1966.

Evans, Peter. *The Life and Times of Aristotle Socrates Onassis*. New York: Summit, 1986.

Evans, Rowland, and Robert Novak. *Lyndon B. Johnson: The Exercise of Power*. New York: Signet, 1966.

Evica, George M. *And We Are All Mortal*. Hartford, Conn.: University of Hartford Press, 1867.

Ewald, William B. *Who Killed Joe McCarthy*. New York: Simon and Schuster, 1984.

Exner, Judith, as told to Ovid Demaris. *Judith Exner: My Story*. New York: Grove, 1977.

Fairlie, Henry. *The Kennedy Promise*. New York: Dell, 1972.

Fallaci, Oriana. *Limelighters*. London: Michael Joseph, 1967.

Farber, Stephen, and Marc Green. *Hollywood Dynasties*. New York: Delilah, 1984.

Fay, Paul B., Jr. *The Pleasure of His Company*. New York: Harper and Row, 1966.

Felsenthal, Carol. *Power, Privilege and the Post: The Katherine Graham Story.* New York: G.P. Putnam's Sons, 1993.

Firestone, Bernard J., and Robert C. Vogt, editors. *Lyndon Baines Johnson and the Uses of Power.* New York: Greenwood, 1988.

Flammonde, Paris. *The Kennedy Conspiracy: An Uncommissioned Report on the Jim Garrison Investigation.* New York: Meredith, 1969.

Fonteyn, Margot. *Margot Fonteyn: An Autobiography.* New York: Alfred A. Knopf, 1975.

Four Days. Compiled by UPI and *American Heritage* Magazine. New York: American Heritage, 1964 and 1983.

Fox, Steven. *Blood and Power: Organized Crime in Twentieth Century America.* New York: William Morrow, 1989.

Franco, Joseph, with Richard Hammer. *Hoffa's Man.* New York: Dell, 1987.

Frank, Gerold. *Zsa Zsa Gabor: My Story.* Cleveland: World, 1960.

Franklin, Roger. *The Defender.* New York: Harper and Row, 1986.

Fraser, Nicholas, Philip Jacobson, Mark Ottaway, and Lewis Chester. *Aristotle Onassis.* Philadelphia and New York: J.B. Lippincott, 1977.

Friedman, Allen, and Ted Schwarz. *Power and Greed.* New York: Franklin Watts, 1989.

Friedman, Stanley P. *The Magnificent Kennedy Women.* Derby, Conn.: Monarch, 1964.

Frischauer, Willi. *Jackie.* London: Michael Joseph, 1976.

———. *Onassis.* New York: Meredith, 1968.

Fuller, Helen. *Year of Trial. Kennedy's Crucial Decisions.* New York: Harcourt, Brace and World, 1962.

Gabler, Neal. *Winchell: Gossip, Power and the Culture of Celebrity.* New York: Alfred A. Knopf, 1994.

Gadney, Reg. *Kennedy.* New York: Holt, Rinehart, and Winston, 1983.

Galbraith, John K. *Ambassador's Journal.* Boston: Houghton Mifflin, 1969.

———. *A Life in Our Times.* New York: Ballantine, 1989.

Galella, Ron. *Jacqueline.* New York: Sheed and Ward, 1974.

Gallagher, Mary Barelli. *My Life with Jacqueline Kennedy.* New York: David McKay, 1969.

Gallen, David. *Malcolm X. As They Knew Him.* New York: Carroll and Graf, 1992.

Gardner, Gerald. *Robert Kennedy in New York.* New York: Random House, 1965.

Gardner, Ralph. *Young, Gifted and Rich.* New York: Simon and Schuster, 1984.

Garrison, Jim. *A Heritage of Stone.* New York: Berkley, 1970.

———. *The Star Spangled Contract.* New York: McGraw-Hill, 1976.

Garrow, David J. *Bearing the Cross.* New York: Vintage, 1986.

Garthoff, Raymond L. *Reflections on the Cuban Missile Crisis.* Washington: Brookings Institution, 1989.

Gatti, Arthur. *The Kennedy Curse.* Chicago: Henry Regnery, 1976.

Gentry, Curt. *J. Edgar Hoover: The Man and the Secrets.* New York: W.W. Norton, 1991.

Getty, J. Paul. *As I See It: My Life as I Lived It.* New York: Berkley, 1986.

Giancana, Antoinette, with Thomas C. Renner. *Mafia Princess.* New York: Avon, 1984.

Giancana, Sam, and Chuck Giancana. *Double Cross: The Explosive, Inside Story of the Mobster Who Controlled America.* New York: Warner, 1992.

Gibson, Barbara, with Caroline Latham. *Life with Rose Kennedy. An Intimate Account.* New York: Warner, 1986.

———, with Ted Schwarz. *The Kennedys: The Third Generation.* New York: Thunder's Mouth, 1993.

Giglio, James N. *The Presidency of John F. Kennedy.* Lawrence: University Press of Kansas, 1991.

Gingras, Angele de T. *The Best in Congressional Humor.* Washington, D.C.: Acropolis, 1973.

Gitlin, Todd. *The Sixties: Years of Hope, Days of Rage.* New York: Bantam, 1987.

Gleason, Bill. *Daley of Chicago: The Man, the Mayor, and the Limits of Conventional Politics.* New York: Simon and Schuster, 1970.

Golden, Harry. *Mr. Kennedy and the Negroes.* New York: World, 1964.

Goldfarb, Ronald. *Perfect Villains, Imperfect Heroes: Robert Kennedy's War against Organized Crime.* New York: Random House, 1995.

Goldman, Eric F. *The Tragedy of Lyndon Johnson.* New York: Alfred A. Knopf, 1970.

Goldwater, Barry, with Jack Casserly. *Goldwater.* New York: St. Martin's, 1988.

Goodwin, Doris Kearns. *The Fitzgeralds and the Kennedys: An American Saga.* New York: Simon and Schuster, 1987.

Goodwin, Richard N. *Remembering America: A Voice from the Sixties.* Boston: Little, Brown, 1988.

Gordon, Gary. *Robert F. Kennedy, Assistant President.* Derby, Conn.: Monarch, 1962.

Goulden, Joseph C. *Fit to Print: A. M. Rosenthal and His Times.* Secaucus, N.J.: Lyle Stuart, 1988.

Graff, Henry F., ed. *The Presidents: A Reference History.* New York: Charles Scribner's Sons, 1984.

Graham, Hugh Davis. *The Civil Rights Era.* New York: Oxford University Press, 1990.

Granger, Bill, and Lori Granger. *Lords of the Last Machine: The Story of Politics in Chicago.* New York: Random House, 1987.

Gregory, Adela, and Milo Speriglio. *Crypt 33.* New York: Birch Lane, 1993.

Greene, Bert, with Phillip S. Schulz. *Pity the Poor Rich.* Chicago: Contemporary Books, 1978.

Gubernick, Lisa Rebecca. *Squandered Fortune: The Life and Times of Huntington Hartford.* New York: G.P. Putnam's Sons, 1991.

Guiles, Fred Lawrence. *Legend: The Life and Death of Marilyn Monroe.* Briarcliff Manor, N.Y.: Stein and Day, 1984.

Gulley, Bill, with Mary Ellen Reese. *Breaking Cover.* New York: Simon and Schuster, 1980.

Guthman, Edwin O. *We Band of Brothers.* New York: Harper & Row, 1971.

———, and C. Richard Allen, eds. *RFK: Collected Speeches.* Viking, 1993.

———, and Jeffrey Shulman, eds. *Robert Kennedy: In His Own Words.* New York: Bantam, 1988.

Guthrie, Lee. *Jackie, The Price of the Pedestal.* New York: Drake, 1978.

Hackett, Pat, ed. *The Andy Warhol Diaries.* New York: Warner Books, 1989.

Halberstam, David. *The Best and the Brightest.* New York: Random House, 1969.

———. *The Unfinished Odyssey of Robert Kennedy.* New York: Random House, 1968.

Haldeman, H. R. *The Haldeman Diaries*. New York: G.P. Putnam's Sons, 1994.

Hall, Gordon Langley, and Ann Pinchot. *Jacqueline Kennedy: A Biography*. New York: Frederick Fell, 1964.

Hamilton, Charles V. *Adam Clayton Powell, Jr.: The Political Biography of an American Dilemma*. New York: Atheneum, 1991.

Hamilton, Ian. *Robert Lowell. A Biography*. New York: Random House, 1982.

Hamilton, Nigel. *JFK: Reckless Youth*. New York: Random House, 1992.

Hampton, Henry, and Steve Fayer, with Sarah Flynn. *Voices of Freedom*. New York: Bantam, 1990.

Hannibal, Edward, and Robert Boris. *Blood Feud*. New York: Ballantine, 1979.

Harris, Bill. *John Fitzgerald Kennedy: A Photographic Tribute*. New York: Crescent, 1983.

Harris, David. *Dreams Die Hard*. New York: St. Martin's/Marek, 1982.

Harris, Fred R. *Potomac Fever*. New York: W.W. Norton, 1977.

Harrison, Rainie, and John Quinn. *Growing Up Kennedy*. New York: G.P. Putnam's Sons, 1983.

Haspiel, James. *Marilyn: The Ultimate Look at the Legend*. New York: Henry Holt, 1991.

Haygood, Wil. *King of the Cats: The Life and Times of A. C. Powell, Jr.* Boston and New York: Houghton Mifflin, 1993.

Heller, Deane, and David Heller. *Jacqueline Kennedy*. Derby, Conn.: Monarch, 1963.

———. *The Kennedy Cabinet: America's Men of Destiny*. Freeport, N.Y.: Books for Libraries Press, 1961.

Hemingway, Mary Welsh. *How It Was*. New York: Alfred A. Knopf, 1976.

Heren, Louis. *No Hail, No Farewell*. New York: Harper and Row, 1970.

Hersh, Burton. *The Education of Edward Kennedy*. New York: William Morrow, 1972.

Hersh, Seymour. *The Dark Side of Camelot*. Boston: Little, Brown, 1997.

Hess, Stephen. *America's Political Dynasties*. Garden City, N.Y.: Doubleday and Co., 1966.

Heymann, C. David. *American Aristocracy*. New York: Dodd, Mead and Co., 1980.

———. *Poor Little Rich Girl*. New York: Lyle Stuart, 1983.

———. *A Woman Named Jackie*. New York: Carol Communications, 1989.

Higgins, Trumbull. *The Perfect Failure: Kennedy, Eisenhower and the CIA at the Bay of Pigs*. Boston: W.W. Norton, 1987.

Higham, Charles. *Howard Hughes: The Secret Life*. New York: G.P. Putnam's Sons, 1993.

Hinckle, Warren, and William Turner. *Deadly Secrets: The CIA-Mafia War against Castro and the Assassination of J.F.K.* New York: Thunder's Mouth, 1992.

Hoffa, James R., as told to Oscar Fraley. *Hoffa: The Real Story*. New York: Stein and Day, 1975.

Hoffman, William, and Lake Headley. *Contract Killer*. New York: Thunder's Mouth, 1992.

Honan, William H. *Ted Kennedy: Profile of a Survivor*. New York: New York Times, 1972.

Hoopes, Townsend. *The Limits of Intervention*. New York: David McKay, 1969.

Hougan, Jim. *Spooks: The Haunting of America—The Private Use of Secret Agents*. New York: William Morrow, 1978.

Houghton, Robert A. *Special Unit Senator: The Investigation of the Assassination of Senator Robert F. Kennedy.* New York: Random House, 1970.

Hudson, James A. *The Mysterious Death of Marilyn Monroe.* New York: Volitant, 1968.

Hunt, Howard. *Give Us This Day.* New Rochelle, N.Y.: Arlington House, 1973.

Hurt, Henry. *Reasonable Doubt.* New York: Holt, Rinehart, and Winston, 1985.

Ions, Edmund S. *The Politics of John F. Kennedy.* New York: Barnes and Noble, 1967.

Isaacson, Walter, and Evan Thomas. *The Wise Men.* New York: Simon and Schuster, 1986.

Israel, Lee. *Kilgallen: A Biography of Dorothy Kilgallen.* New York: Delacorte, 1979.

Jacobs, Paul. *The State of the Unions.* New York: Atheneum, 1963.

James, Ann. *The Kennedy Scandals and Tragedies.* Publications International, 1991.

James, Ralph C., and Estelle Dinerstein James. *Hoffa and the Teamsters: A Study of Union Power.* Princeton, N.J.: D. Van Nostrand, 1965.

Jamieson, Kathleen Hall. *Packaging the President.* New York: Oxford University Press, 1984.

Jansen, Godfrey. *Why Robert Kennedy Was Killed: The Story of Two Victims.* New York: Third Press, 1970.

The Johnson Presidential Press Conferences. Vol. 1. Introduction by Doris Kearns Goodwin. New York: Earl M. Coleman, 1978.

Johnson, Lady Bird. *A White House Diary.* New York: Dell, 1970.

Johnson, Lyndon Baines. *The Vantage Point: Perspectives of the Presidency, 1963–1969.* New York: Holt, Rinehart and Winston, 1971.

Johnson, Sam Houston. *My Brother Lyndon.* New York: Cowles, 1969.

Johnson, Walter, ed. *The Papers of Adlai E. Stevenson.* Boston: Little, Brown, 1977.

Jones, Cranston. *Homes of the American Presidents.* New York: Bonanza Books, 1962.

Jordan, Ted. *Norma Jean: My Secret Life with Marilyn Monroe.* New York: William Morrow, 1989.

Junior League of Greenwich. *The Great Estates. Greenwich, Connecticut, 1880–1930.* Canaan, N.H.: Phoenix, 1986.

Kaiser, Charles. *1968 in America.* New York: Weidenfeld and Nicolson, 1988.

Kaiser, Robert Blair. *"R.F.K. Must Die!"* New York: E.P. Dutton, 1970.

Kalb, Marvin, and Bernard Kalb. *Kissinger.* New York: Dell, 1975.

Kane, Joseph Nathan. *Facts about the Presidents.* New York: H.W. Wilson, 1981.

Kantor, Seth. *The Ruby Coverup.* New York: Kensington, 1978.

———. *Who Was Jack Ruby?* New York: Everest House, 1978.

Kazin, Alfred. *New York Jew.* New York: Alfred A. Knopf, 1978.

Kearns, Doris. *Lyndon Johnson and the American Dream.* New York: Harper and Row, 1976.

Keeler, Robert. *Newsday. A Candid History of the Respectable Tabloid.* New York: William Morrow, 1990.

Kellerman, Barbara. *All the President's Kin.* London: Robson, 1982.

Kelley, Kitty. *My Way: The Unauthorized Biography of Frank Sinatra.* New York: Bantam, 1986.

Kennedy, Eugene. *Himself! The Life and Times of Mayor Richard J. Daley.* New York: Viking, 1978.

The Kennedy Presidential Press Conferences. Introduction by David Halberstam. New York: Earl M. Coleman, 1978.

The Kennedy Tapes: Inside the White House during the Cuban Missile Crisis. Edited by Ernest R. May and Philip O. Zelikow. Cambridge, Mass.: Harvard University Press, 1997.

Kennedy, John F. *Why England Slept.* New York: Wilfred Funk, 1961.

Kennedy, Robert F. *Apostle of Change.* Introduction by Douglas Ross. New York: Pocket Books, 1968.

―――. *Just Friends and Brave Enemies.* New York: Popular Library, 1962.

―――. *Promises to Keep.* Introduction by Edward Kennedy. Hallmark Cards, 1969.

―――. *The Pursuit of Justice.* New York: Harper and Row, 1964.

―――. *To Seek a Newer World.* Garden City, N.Y.: Doubleday, 1967.

―――. *Thirteen Days.* New York: W.W. Norton, 1969.

Kennedy, Rose Fitzgerald. *Times to Remember.* New York: Popular Library, 1960.

Kennedy, Sheila Rauch. *Shattered Faith.* New York: Pantheon, 1997.

Kimball, Penn. *Bobby Kennedy and the New Politics.* Englewood Cliffs, N.J.: Prentice-Hall, 1968.

Kissinger, Henry. *The White House Years.* Boston: Little, Brown, 1979.

Klagsbrun, Francine, and David C. Whitney, eds. *Assassination: Robert F. Kennedy—1925–1968.* New York: Cowles Education, 1968.

Klein, Edward. *All Too Human: The Love Story of Jack and Jackie Kennedy.* New York: Pocket Books, 1996.

Klein, Herbert G. *Making It Perfectly Clear.* Garden City, N.Y.: Doubleday, 1980.

Kleindienst, Richard. *Justice: Memoirs of an Attorney General.* Ottawa, Ill.: Jameson, 1985.

Knightley, Phillip, and Caroline Kennedy. *An Affair of State: The Profumo Case and the Framing of Stephen Ward.* New York: Atheneum, 1987.

Koch, Edward I. *All the Best: Letters from a Feisty Mayor.* New York: Simon and Schuster, 1990.

―――, with William Rauch. *Mayor.* New York: Simon and Schuster, 1984.

Koch, Thilo. *Fighters for a New World.* New York: Putnam, 1969.

Krock, Arthur. *Memoirs: Sixty Years on the Firing Line.* New York: Funk and Wagnalls, 1968.

Kwitny, Jonathan. *Vicious Circles. The Mafia in the Marketplace.* New York: W.W. Norton, 1979.

Laing, Margaret. *The Next Kennedy.* New York: Coward-McCann, 1968.

Lambro, Donald. *Washington: City of Scandals.* Boston: Little, Brown, 1987.

Lane, Mark. *Plausible Denial: Was the CIA Involved in the Assassination of JFK?* New York: Thunder's Mouth, 1991.

―――. *Rush to Judgment.* New York: Holt, Rinehart and Winston, 1966.

Lange, James E. T., Jr., and Katherine DeWitt. *Chappaquiddick: The Real Story.* New York: St. Martin's Press, 1993.

Lasky, Victor. *Robert F. Kennedy: The Myth and the Man.* New York: Pocket Books, 1971.

―――. *Arthur Goldberg: The Old and the New.* New Rochelle, N.Y.: Arlington House, 1970.

―――. *JFK: The Man and the Myth.* New York: Macmillan, 1963.

Latham, Caroline, and Jeannie Sakol. *The Kennedy Encyclopedia.* New York: New American Library, 1989.

Lattimer, John K. *Kennedy and Lincoln: Medical and Ballistic Comparisons of Their Assassinations.* New York: Harcourt Brace Jovanovich, 1980.

Lawford, Patricia Kennedy, ed. *That Shining Hour.* Privately published by PKL, 1969.

Lawford, Patricia Seaton, with Ted Schwarz. *The Peter Lawford Story: Life with the Kennedys, Monroe and the Rat Pack.* New York: Carroll and Graf, 1968.

Leamer, Laurence. *The Kennedy Women: The Saga of an American Family.* New York: Villard, 1994.

————. *Make-Believe: The Story of Nancy and Ronald Reagan.* New York: Dell Publishing Co., 1983.

Leary, Timothy. *Changing My Mind, Among Others.* Englewood Cliffs, N.J.: Prentice-Hall, 1982.

————. *Flashbacks: An Autobiography.* Los Angeles: J.P. Tarcher, 1983.

Lee, Martin A., and Bruce Shlain. *Acid Dreams: The Complete Social History of LSD: The CIA, the Sixties, and Beyond.* New York: Grove, 1985.

Leigh, Janet. *There Really Was a Hollywood.* Garden City, N.Y.: Doubleday, 1984.

Leigh, Wendy. *Prince Charming and the John F. Kennedy, Jr., Story.* New York: Dutton, 1993.

Lerner, Max. *Ted and the Kennedy Legend.* New York: St. Martin's, 1980.

Lesberg, Sandy. *Assassination in Our Time.* New York: Peebles, 1976.

Lesler, Stephan. *George Wallace: American Populist.* A William Patrick book. Reading, Mass.: Addison-Wesley, 1994.

Lester, David. *Ethel: The Story of Mrs. Robert F. Kennedy.* New York: Dell, 1972.

————. *Joan: The Reluctant Kennedy.* New York: Funk and Wagnalls, 1974.

Lester, Julius. *Revolutionary Notes.* New York: Grove, 1969.

Levy, Jacques E. *Cesar Chavez: Autobiography of La Causa.* New York: Norton, 1975.

Lewis, Anthony. *Portrait of a Decade.* New York: Random House, 1964.

Lewis, Finlay. *Mondale: Portrait of an American Politician.* New York: Harper and Row, 1980.

Lieberson, Goddard, ed. *John Fitzgerald Kennedy . . . As We Remember Him.* New York: Atheneum, 1965.

The Life and Death of Robert F. Kennedy. By the editors of *American Heritage.* New York: Dell, 1968.

Lifton, David S. *Best Evidence.* New York: Dell, 1980.

Lilly, Doris. *Those Fabulous Greeks: Onassis, Niarchos, and Livanos.* London: W.H. Allen, 1971.

Lincoln, Ann. *The Kennedy White House Parties.* New York: Viking, 1968.

Lincoln, Evelyn. *My Twelve Years with John F. Kennedy.* New York: David McKay, 1965.

Livingstone, Harrison Edward. *High Treason 2.* New York: Carroll and Graf, 1992.

Lopez, Enrique Hank. *The Harvard Mystique: The Power Syndrome That Affects Our Lives from Sesame Street to the White House.* New York: Macmillan, 1979.

Lorenz, Marita, with Ted Schwarz. *Marita.* New York: Thunder's Mouth, 1993.

Louis, Joe, with Edna and Art Rust, Jr. *Joe Louis: My Life.* New York: Harcourt Brace Jovanovich, 1978.

Lowe, Jacques. *Kennedy: A Time Remembered.* London, England: Quartet/Visual Arts, 1983.

———. *The Kennedy Legend.* New York: Viking Studio Books, 1988.

Lowenstein, Douglas, and Gregory Stone, eds. *Lowenstein: Acts of Courage and Belief.* New York: Harcourt Brace Jovanovich, 1983.

Maas, Peter. *The Valachi Papers.* New York: Simon and Schuster, 1968.

MacPherson, Myra. *The Power Lovers.* New York: G.P. Putnam's Sons, 1975.

MacRae, Sheila, with H. Paul Jeffers. *Hollywood Mother of the Year.* New York: Birch Lane, 1992.

Madsen, Axel. *Gloria and Joe.* New York: William Morrow, 1988.

Mahen, Robert, and Richard Hack. *Next to Hughes.* HarperCollins, 1992.

Mahoney, Richard D. *JFK Ordeal in Africa.* New York: Oxford University Press, 1983.

Mailer, Norman. *The Armies of the Night.* New York: Signet, 1968.

———. *Harlot's Ghost.* New York: Random House, 1991.

———. *Marilyn.* New York: Grosset and Dunlap, 1972.

———. *The Presidential Papers.* New York: Dell, 1963.

Manchester, William. *Controversy and Other Essays in Journalism, 1950–1975.* Boston: Little, Brown, 1976.

———. *Portrait of a President.* New York: Macfadden Books, 1964.

———. *The Death of a President.* New York: Harper and Row, 1963.

———. *One Brief Shining Moment.* Boston: Little, Brown, 1952.

Mangold, Tom. *Cold Warrior James Jesus Angleton: The CIA's Master Spy Hunter.* New York: Simon and Schuster, 1991.

Manso, Peter. *Mailer: His Life and Times.* New York: Simon and Schuster, 1985.

Marrs, Jim. *Crossfire: The Plot That Killed Kennedy.* New York: Carroll and Graf, 1989.

Martin, David C. *Wilderness of Mirrors.* New York: Harper and Row, 1980.

Martin, John Bartlow. *Adlai Stevenson and the World: The Life of Adlai Stevenson.* Garden City, N.Y.: Doubleday, 1977.

Martin, Ralph G. *A Hero for Our Time.* New York: Ballantine, 1983.

Matthiessen, Peter. *Sal Si Puedes. Cesar Chavez and the New American Revolution.* New York: Random House, 1969.

Matusow, Allen J. *The Unraveling of America.* New York: Harper and Row, 1984.

McCallum, John D. *Dave Beck.* Mercer Island, Wash.: Writing Works, 1978.

McCann, Graham. *Marilyn Monroe: The Body in the Library.* Rutgers, N.J.: Rutgers University Press, 1988.

McCarthy, Dennis V. N., with Philip W. Smith. *Protecting the President.* New York: William Morrow, 1985.

McCarthy, Eugene. *Up 'Til Now: A Memoir.* New York: Harcourt Brace Jovanovich, 1987.

———. *The Year of the People.* Garden City, N.Y.: Doubleday, 1969.

McCarthy, Joe. *The Remarkable Kennedys.* New York: Popular Library, 1960.

McClellan, John L. *Crime without Punishment.* New York: Duell, Sloane and Pierce, 1962.

McClendon, Sarah. *My Eight Presidents.* New York: Wyden, 1978.

McCullough, David. *Truman.* New York: Simon and Schuster, 1992.

McEvoy, Kevin, ed. *Two Kennedys.* New York: Paulist Press, 1969.

McGilligan, Patrick. *A Double Life: George Cukor.* New York: St. Martin's, 1991.

McGinnis, Joe. *The Last Brother.* New York: Simon and Schuster, 1993.

McGrory, Mary. "In Memoriam: John Fitzgerald Kennedy." *Washington Star*, November 23–26, 1969.

McMillan, Priscilla. *Marina and Lee*. New York: Harper and Row, 1977.

McNamara, Robert S. *In Retrospect: The Tragedies and Lessons of Vietnam*. New York: Times Books, 1995.

McPherson, Harry. *A Political Education*. Boston: Little, Brown, 1972.

Medland, William J. *The Cuban Missile Crisis of 1962: Needless or Necessary*. New York: Praeger, 1988.

Meese, Edwin III. *With Reagan. The Inside Story*. Washington, D.C.: Regnery Gateway, 1992.

Melanson, Philip H. *The Robert F. Kennedy Assassination*. New York: Shapolsky, 1991.

Mellon, Paul, with John Baskett. *Reflections in a Silver Spoon*. New York: William Morrow, 1992.

Messick, Hank, and Burt Goldblatt. *The Mobs and the Mafia. The Illustrated History of Organized Crime*. New York: Ballantine, 1972.

Michaelis, David. *The Best of Friends: Profiles of Extraordinary Friendship*. New York: William Morrow, 1983.

Midgley, Leslie. *How Many Words Do You Want?* New York: Birch Lane, 1989.

Miller, Hope Ridings. *Scandals in the Highest Office*. New York: Random House, 1973.

Miller, Merle. *Lyndon: An Oral Biography*. New York: G.P. Putnam's Sons, 1980.

———. *Plain Speaking: An Oral Biography of Harry S. Truman*. New York: Berkley, 1973.

Miller, Tom. *The Assassination Please Almanac*. Chicago: Henry Regnery, 1977.

Mills, Hilary. *Mailer: A Biography*. New York: McGraw-Hill, 1982.

Mills, Nicolaus. *Like a Holy Crusade*. Chicago: Ivan R. Dee, 1992.

Miroff, Bruce. *Pragmatic Illusions: The Presidential Politics of John F. Kennedy*. New York: David McKay, 1976.

Moldea, Dan E. *The Hoffa Wars: Teamsters, Rebels, Politicians, and the Mob*. New York: Paddington, 1978.

Mollenhoff, Clark. *Tentacles of Power*. Chicago: World, 1965.

Mooly, Sidney C., ed. *Triumph and Tragedy: The Story of the Kennedys*. New York: Associated Press, 1968.

Mooney, Booth. *LBJ: An Irreverent Chronicle*. New York: Thomas Y. Crowell, 1976.

Morella, Joe, and Edward Z. Epstein. *Paul and Joanne*. New York: Dell, 1988.

Morrison, Joan and Robert K. Morrison. *From Camelot to Kent State. The Sixties Experience in the Words of Those Who Lived It*. New York: Times Books, 1987.

Morrow, Robert D. *The Senator Must Die: The Murder of RFK*. Roundtable, 1988.

Murray, Eunice, and Rose Shade. *Marilyn: The Last Months*. New York: Pyramid, 1975.

Nash, Jay Robert. *Citizen Hoover. A Critical Study of the Life and Times of J. Edgar Hoover and His FBI*. Chicago: Nelson/Hall Company, 1972.

———. *Murder among the Rich and Famous*. New York: Arlington House, 1983.

Nash, Knowlton. *Kennedy and Diefenbaker: Fear and Loathing Across the Undefended Border*. Toronto: McClelland and Stewart, 1990.

Navasky, Victor. *Kennedy Justice*. New York: Atheneum, 1971.

Neff, James. *Mobbed Up*. New York: Dell, 1989.

Newfield, Jack. *Robert Kennedy: A Memoir.* New York: E.P. Dutton, 1969.

Newman, John M. *JFK and Vietnam: Deception, Intrigue, and the Struggle for Power.* New York: Warner, 1992.

Nixon, Richard. *RN: The Memoirs of Richard Nixon.* New York: Grosset and Dunlap, 1978.

Nizer, Louis. *Reflections without Mirrors: An Autobiography of the Mind.* Garden City, N.Y.: Doubleday, 1978.

Nobile, Philip. *Intellectual Skywriting: Literary Politics and the New York Review of Books.* New York: Charterhouse, 1974.

Noguchi, Thomas T., with Joseph DiMona. *Coroner to the Stars.* London: Corgi, 1983.

North, Mark. *Act of Treason: The Role of J. Edgar Hoover in the Assassination of President Kennedy.* New York: Carroll and Graf, 1991.

Oates, Stephen B. *Let the Trumpet Sound.* New York: Harper and Row, 1982.

O'Brien, Lawrence F. *No Final Victories: A Life in Politics, John F. Kennedy to Watergate.* Garden City, N.Y.: Doubleday, 1974.

O'Connor, Len. *Clout: Mayor Daley and His City.* New York: Avon, 1975.

O'Donnell, Kenneth P., and David F. Powers, with Joe McCarthy. *"Johnny, We Hardly Knew Ye."* New York: Pocket Books, 1973.

Ogden, Christopher. *Life of the Party: The Biography of Pamela Digby Churchill Hayward Harriman.* Boston: Little, Brown, 1994.

Oglesby, Carl. *The JFK Assassination: The Facts and the Theories.* New York: Signet, 1992.

———. *The Yankee and Cowboy War. Conspiracies from Dallas to Watergate.* Kansas City: Sheed Andrews and McMeel, 1976.

O'Neill, Tip, with William Novak. *Man of the House. The Life and Political Memoirs of Speaker Tip O'Neill.* New York: Random House, 1987.

Opotowsky, Stan. *The Kennedy Government.* New York: Popular Library, 1961.

Oppenheimer, Jerry. *Barbara Walters: An Unauthorized Biography.* New York: St. Martin's, 1990.

———. *The Other Mrs. Kennedy: Ethel Skakel Kennedy: An American Drama of Power, Privilege, and Politics.* New York: St. Martin's, 1994.

O'Reilly, Kenneth. *Racial Matters: The FBI's Secret File on Black America, 1960–1972.* New York: Free Press, 1989.

Oshinsky, David M. *A Conspiracy So Immense: The World of Joe McCarthy.* New York: Free Press, 1983.

Otash, Fred. *Investigation Hollywood.* New York: Henry Regnery, 1976.

O'Toole, George. *The Assassination Tapes: An Electronic Probe into the Murder of JFK and the Dallas Coverup.* New York: Penthouse Press, 1975.

Pachter, Henry M. *Collision Course. The Cuban Missile Crisis and Coexistence.* New York: Frederick A. Praeger, 1963.

Pack, Robert. *Edward Bennett Williams for the Defense.* New York: Harper and Row, 1983.

Paper, Lewis J. *The Promise and the Performance.* New York: Crown, 1975.

Paris, Barry. *Louise Brooks.* New York: Anchor Books/Doubleday, 1989.

Patterson, Thomas G. *Contesting Castro.* New York and Oxford: Oxford University Press, 1994.

Pearson, Drew. *Diaries: 1949–1959.* Tyler Abell, ed. New York: Holt, Rinehart, and Winston, 1974.

Perry, Bruce. *Malcolm: The Life of a Man Who Changed Black America.* New York: Station Hill, 1991.

Persico, Joseph E. *Edward R. Murrow: An American Original.* New York: Dell, 1988.

Peters, Charles. *Tilting at Windmills: An Autobiography.* Reading, Mass.: Wesley, 1988.

Peterson, Virgil W. *The Mob. 200 Years of Organized Crime in New York.* Ottawa, Ill.: Green Hill, 1983.

Podhoretz, Norman. *Making It.* New York: Random House, 1967.

Posner, Gerald. *Case Closed: Lee Harvey Oswald and the Assassination of JFK.* New York: Random House, 1993.

Powers, Thomas. *The Man Who Kept the Secrets: Richard Helms and the CIA.* New York: Alfred A. Knopf, 1970.

Prouty, L. Fletcher. *JFK: The CIA, Vietnam and the Plot to Assassinate JFK.* New York: Birch Lane, 1992.

Quirk, Lawrence J. *The Kennedys in Hollywood.* Dallas, Tex.: Taylor, 1996.

Rachlin, Harvey. *The Kennedys: A Chronological History.* New York: Ballantine, 1986.

Ragano, Frank, and Selwyn Raab. *Mob Lawyer.* New York: Charles Scribner's Sons, 1994.

Rainie, Harrison. *Growing Up Kennedy: The Third Wave Comes of Age.* New York: Putnam, 1983.

Rappleye, Charles, and Ed Becker. *All-American Mafioso: The Johnny Roselli Story.* New York: Doubleday, 1991.

Rather, Dan, with Mickey Herskowitz. *The Camera Never Blinks.* New York: Ballantine, 1977.

————, and Gary Paul Gates. *The Palace Guard.* New York: Warner, 1975.

Reagan, Nancy, with William Novak. *My Turn: The Memoirs of Nancy Reagan.* New York: Random House, 1989.

Reeves, Richard. *President Kennedy. Profile of Power.* New York: Simon and Schuster, 1993.

Reeves, Thomas C. *The Life and Times of Joe McCarthy.* New York: Stein and Day, 1982.

————. *A Question of Character.* New York: Free Press, 1991.

Reich, Cary. *Financier: The Biography of Andre Meyer.* New York: William Morrow, 1983.

Reid, Ed. *The Grim Reapers.* New York: Bantam, 1970.

Reston, James. *Deadline: A Memoir.* New York: Random House, 1991.

————. *Sketches in the Sand.* New York: Alfred A. Knopf, 1967.

Roberts, Allen. *Robert Francis Kennedy: Biography of a Compulsive Politician.* New York: Braden, 1984.

Robertson, Nan. *The Girls in the Balcony.* New York: Random House, 1992.

Robins, Natalie. *Alien Ink.* New York: William Morrow, 1992.

Roemer, William F., Jr. *Roemer: Man against the Mob.* New York: Donald I. Fine, 1989.

————. *War of the Godfathers.* New York: Donald I. Fine, 1990.

Rogers, Warren. *When I Think of Bobby: A Personal Memoir of the Kennedy Years.* New York: HarperCollins, 1993.

Rollyson, Carl E., Jr. *The Lives of Norman Mailer.* New York: Paragon House, 1991.
————. *Marilyn Monroe: A Life of the Actress.* Ann Arbor, Mich.: UMI Research, 1986.
Romero, Jerry. *Sinatra's Women.* New York: Manor, 1976.
Rooney, Mickey. *Life Is Too Short.* New York: Villard, 1991.
Roosevelt, Eleanor. *Eleanor Roosevelt's My Day,* Vol. 1. David Elmblidge, ed. Introduction by Frank Freidel. New York: Pharos, 1991.
Roosevelt, Elliott, and James Brough. *Mother R.: Eleanor Roosevelt's Untold Story.* New York: G.P. Putnam's Sons, 1977.
Roosevelt, Felicia Warburg, *Doers and Dowagers.* New York: Doubleday, 1975.
Roosevelt, Selwa "Lucky." *Keeper of the Gate.* New York: Simon and Schuster, 1990.
Ross, Douglas, ed. *Robert F. Kennedy: Apostle of Change.* New York: Pocket Books, 1968.
Ross, Shelley. *Fall from Grace: Sex, Scandal and Corruption in American Politics from 1702 to the Present.* New York: Ballantine, 1988.
Rovere, Richard H. *Senator Joe McCarthy.* New York: Harcourt, Brace, 1959.
Rowan, Carl T. *Breaking Barriers.* Boston: Little, Brown, 1991.
Rowe, Robert. *The Bobby Baker Story.* New York: Parallax, 1967.
Rusk, Dean, as told to Richard Rusk. *As I Saw It.* New York: W.W. Norton, 1990.
Russell, Dick. *The Man Who Knew Too Much.* New York: Carroll and Graf/Richard Gallen, 1992.
Rust, Zad. *Teddy Bare.* Belmont, Mass.: Western Islands, 1971.
Ryan, Dorothy, and Louis J. Ryan, eds. *The Kennedy Family of Massachusetts: A Bibliography.* Westport, Conn.: Greenwood, 1981.
Ryskind, Allan H. *Hubert.* New York: Arlington House, 1968.
Sable, Martin. *A Bio-bibliography of the Kennedy Family.* Metuchen, N.J.: Scarecrow, 1969.
Sahl, Mort. *Heart Lord.* New York: Harcourt Brace Jovanovich, 1976.
Sakol, Jeannie, and Caroline Latham. *About Grace: An Intimate Notebook.* Chicago: Contemporary Books, 1993.
Salerno, Ralph, and John S. Tompkins. *The Crime Confederation.* Garden City, N.Y.: Doubleday, 1969.
Salinger, Pierre. *With Kennedy.* New York: Doubleday, 1966.
————, Edwin O. Guthman, Frank Mankiewicz, and John Seigenthaler, eds. *"An Honorable Profession": A Tribute to Robert F. Kennedy.* Garden City, N.Y.: Doubleday, 1968.
Saunders, Frank, with James Southwood. *Torn Lace Curtain.* New York: Pinnacle, 1982.
Sauvage, Leo. *The Oswald Affair.* New York: World, 1966.
Schapp, Dick. *R.F.K.* New York: New American Library, 1967.
Schechter, Jerrold L., with Vyacheslav V. Luchkov. *Khrushchev Remembers. The Glastnost Tapes.* Foreword by Strobe Talbott. Boston: Little, Brown, 1990.
Scheih, David. *Contract on America.* New York: Shapolsky, 1988.
Schlesinger, Arthur M., Jr. *The Imperial Presidency.* New York: Popular Library, 1973.
————. *Robert Kennedy and His Times.* Boston: Houghton Mifflin, 1978.
————. *A Thousand Days.* Boston: Houghton Mifflin, 1965.
Schoor, Gene. *Young Robert Kennedy.* New York: McGraw-Hill, 1969.

Schulberg, Budd. *Moving Pictures: Memories of a Hollywood Prince.* New York: Stein and Day, 1981.

Scott, Peter Dale. *Crime and Cover-up.* Berkeley: Westworks, 1977.

———, Paul L. Hoch, and Russell Stetler, eds. *The Assassinations. Dallas and Beyond—A Guide to Cover-ups and Investigations.* New York: Random House, 1976.

Seagrave, Kerry, and Linda Martin. *The Continental Actress: European Film Stars of the Postwar Era.* Jefferson, N.C., and London: McFarland, 1990.

Seaman, Barbara. *Lovely Me: The Life of Jacqueline Susann.* New York: William Morrow, 1987.

Searls, Hank. *Young Joe, The Forgotten Kennedy.* New York: Ballantine, 1969.

Shadegg, Stephen C. *Winning's a Lot More Fun.* New York: Macmillan, 1969.

Shapiro, Doris. *We Danced All Night: My Life behind the Scenes with Alan Jay Lerner.* New York: William Morrow, 1990.

Shapley, Deborah. *Promise and Power.* Boston: Little, Brown, 1993.

Shaw, J. G., and Larry R. Harris. *Cover-up.* Cleburne, Tex.: J. Garry Shaw, 1976.

Shaw, Mark. *The John F. Kennedys: A Family Album.* New York: Greenwich House, 1983.

Shaw, Maud. *White House Nannie: My Years with Caroline and John Kennedy, Jr.* New York: New American Library, 1965.

Sheridan, Walter. *The Fall and Rise of Jimmy Hoffa.* Introduction by Budd Schulberg. New York: Saturday Review Press, 1972.

Sherman, Len. *The Good, the Bad and the Famous.* New York: Lyle Stuart, 1990.

Sherrill, Robert. *The Last Kennedy.* New York: Dial, 1976.

Shesol, Jeff. *Mutual Contempt: Lyndon Johnson, Robert Kennedy, and the Feud That Defined a Decade.* New York: W.W. Norton, 1997.

Shevey, Sandra. *The Marilyn Scandal.* London: Sidgwick and Jackson, 1987.

Shogan, Robert. *The Riddle of Power.* New York: Dutton, 1991.

Shulman, Irving. *"Jackie!"* New York: Trident, 1970.

Slatzer, Robert F. *The Life and Curious Death of Marilyn Monroe.* New York: Pinnacle, 1974.

Sloane, Arthur A. *Hoffa.* Boston: MIT Press, 1991.

Smith, Dwight C., Jr. *The Mafia Mystique.* New York: Basic Books, 1975.

Smith, Earl E. T. *The Fourth Floor: An Account of the Castro Communist Revolution.* New York: Random House, 1962.

Smith, Malcolm E. *John F. Kennedy's Thirteen Great Mistakes in the White House.* Smithtown, N.Y.: Suffolk House, 1980.

Sorensen, Theodore C. *Kennedy.* New York: Harper and Row, 1965.

———. *The Kennedy Legacy.* New York: Macmillan, 1969.

Spada, James. *Grace. The Secret Lives of a Princess.* Garden City, N.Y.: Doubleday, 1987.

———. *Peter Lawford: The Man Who Kept the Secrets.* New York: Bantam, 1991.

———. *The Spee Club of Harvard University.* Cambridge, Mass.: Stinehour, 1968.

Sparks, Fred. *The $20,000,000 Honeymoon: Jackie and Ari's First Year.* New York: Dell, 1970.

Speriglio, Milo. *The Marilyn Conspiracy.* New York: Pocket Books, 1986.

Spoto, Donald. *Marilyn Monroe: The Biography.* HarperCollins, 1993.

Stack, Robert, with Mark Evans. *Straight Shooting.* New York: Macmillan, 1980.

Stassinopoulos, Arianna. *Maria Callas: The Woman behind the Legend.* New York: Ballantine, 1981.

Steel, Ronald. *Walter Lippman and the American Century.* Boston: Little, Brown, 1980.

Stein, Jean, and George Plimpton, ed. *American Journey: The Times of Robert Kennedy.* New York: Harcourt Brace Jovanovich, 1970.

Steinbacher, John. *Robert Francis Kennedy: The Man, the Mysticism, the Murder.* Los Angeles: Impact, 1968.

Steinem, Gloria, with photographs by George Barris. *Marilyn.* New York: Henry Holt, 1986. (excerpt)

———. *Outrageous Acts and Everyday Rebellions.* New York: Signet, 1986. (excerpt)

Steiner, Paul. *175 Little Known Facts about J.F.K.* New York: Citadel Press, 1964.

Sterling, Clare. *Octopus: The Long Reach of the International Sicilian Mob.* New York: W.W. Norton, 1990.

Stern, Mark. *Calculating Visions. Kennedy, Johnson, and Civil Rights.* New Brunswick, N.J.: Rutgers University Press, 1992.

Stockman, David. *The Triumph of Politics. How the Reagan Revolution Failed.* New York: Harper and Row, 1986.

Stone, Oliver, and Zachary Sklar. *JFK: The Book of the Film.* New York: Applause, 1992.

Stoughton, Cecil. *JFK 1961–1963—The Memories of Cecil Stoughton, the President's Photographer.* Boston: W.W. Norton, 1973.

Stuart, Lyle. *The Secret Life of Walter Winchell.* New York: Boar's Head, 1953.

Sullivan, Frank. *Legend: The Only Inside Story about Mayor Richard J. Daley.* Chicago: Bonus, 1989.

Sullivan, Gerald, and Michael Kenney. *The Race for the Eighth.* New York: Harper and Row, 1987.

Sullivan, William C., with Bill Brown. *The Bureau: My Thirty Years in Hoover's FBI.* New York: W.W. Norton, 1979.

Sulzberger, C. L. *Fathers and Children.* New York: Arbor House, 1987.

———. *The Last of the Giants.* New York: Macmillan, 1970.

Summers, Anthony. *Conspiracy.* New York: McGraw-Hill, 1980.

———. *Goddess: The Secret Lives of Marilyn Monroe.* New York: Macmillan, 1985.

———. *Official and Confidential: The Secret Life of J. Edgar Hoover.* New York: G.P. Putnam's Sons, 1993.

Swanberg, W. A. *Luce and His Empire.* New York: Charles Scribner's Sons, 1972.

Swanson, Gloria. *Swanson on Swanson.* New York: Random House, 1980.

Tackwood, Louis E. *The Glass House Tapes.* New York: Avon Books, 1973.

Tamborrelli, J. Randy. *Sinatra: Behind the Legend.* Secaucus, N.J.: Carol, 1997.

Taub, William L. *Forces of Power.* New York: Grosset and Dunlap, 1979.

Teague, Michael. *Mrs. L: Conversations with Alice Roosevelt Longworth.* Garden City, N.Y.: Doubleday, 1981.

Teti, Frank. *Kennedy: The New Generation.* New York: Delilah, 1983.

Thayer, Mary Van Rensselaer. *Jacqueline Bouvier Kennedy.* New York: Doubleday, 1961.

———. *Jacqueline Kennedy: The White House Years.* Boston: Little, Brown, 1967.

Thimmesch, Nick, and William Johnson. *Robert Kennedy at Forty.* New York: W.W. Norton, 1965.

Theoharis, Athan. *From the Secret Files of J. Edgar Hoover.* Chicago: Ivan R. Dee, 1991.

Thomas, Evan. *The Man to See. Edward Bennett Williams Ultimate Insider: Legendary Trial Lawyer.* New York: Simon and Schuster, 1991.

———. *The Very Best Men. Four Who Dared: The Early Years of the CIA.* New York: Simon and Schuster, 1995.

Thomas, Lately. *When Even Angels Wept: The Senator Joe McCarthy Affair—A Story without a Hero.* New York: William Morrow, 1973.

Thompson, Nelson. *The Dark Side of Camelot.* Chicago: Playboy Press, 1976.

Tierney, Gene, with Mickey Herskowitz. *Self-Portrait.* New York: Wyden, 1979.

Tosches, Nick. *Dino: Living High in the Dirty Business of Dreams.* New York: Doubleday and Co., 1992.

Trewhitt, Henry L. *McNamara.* New York: Harper and Row, 1971.

Truman, Margaret. *Harry S. Truman.* New York: William Morrow, 1973.

Turner, William, and John Christian. *The Assassination of Robert F. Kennedy: The Conspiracy and Coverup.* New York: Thunder's Mouth, 1993.

Valenti, Jack. *A Very Human President.* New York: W.W. Norton, 1975.

vanden Heuvel, William J., and Milton Gwirtzman. *On His Own: Robert F. Kennedy 1964–1968.* New York: Doubleday, 1970.

Van Gelder, Lawrence. *Why the Kennedys Lost the Book Battle.* New York: Award, 1967.

Van Riper, Frank. *Glenn: The Astronaut Who Would Be President.* New York: Empire, 1983.

Velie, Lester. *Desperate Bargain: Why Jimmy Hoffa Had to Die.* New York: Reader's Digest Press, 1977.

Vickers, Hugo. *Cecil Beaton. A Biography.* Boston: Little, Brown, 1985.

Vidal, Gore. *Homage to Daniel Shays: Collected Essays, 1952–1972.* New York: Random House, 1972.

———. *Palimpsest: A Memoir.* New York: Random House, 1995.

Vizzini, Sal, with Oscar Fraley and Marshall Smith. *Vizzini.* New York: Pinnacle, 1972.

Von Hoffman, Nicholas. *Citizen Cohn: The Life and Times of Roy Cohn.* New York: Bantam, 1992.

Von Post, Gunilla, with Carl Johnes. *Love, Jack.* New York: Crown, 1997.

Wallace, Irving, and Amy Irving, David Irving, and Sylvia Irving. *The Intimate Sex Lives of Famous People.* New York: Delacorte, 1981.

Wallace, Mike, and Gary Paul Gates. *Mike Wallace's Own Story.* New York: William Morrow, 1984.

Walton, Richard J. *Cold War and Counterrevolution.* New York: Viking, 1972.

Warhol, Andy, and Pat Hackett. *POPism. The Warhol '60s.* San Diego: Harvest/HGJ Book, 1990.

Watson, Denton L. *Lion in the Lobby.* New York: William Morrow and Co., 1990.

Watson, Mary Ann. *The Expanding Vista. American Television in the Kennedy Years.* New York: Oxford University Press, 1990.

Wayne, Jane Ellen. *Grace Kelly's Men.* New York: St. Martin's, 1991.

———. *Marilyn's Men.* New York: St. Martin's, 1992.

Wecht, Cyril. *Cause of Death.* New York: Dutton, 1993.

Weinberg, Steve. *Armand Hammer: The Untold Story.* Boston: Little, Brown, 1989.

Weisberg, Harold. *Post Mortem.* Frederick, Md.: Harold Weisberg, 1975.

———. *Whitewash: The Report on the Warren Report.* New York: Dell, 1965.

———. *Whitewash II: The FBI–Secret Service Cover-up.* New York: Dell, 1965.

Weisbord, Marvin R. *Campaigning for President.* Washington, D.C.: Public Affairs Press, 1964.

Weiss, Murray, and Bill Hoffman. *Palm Beach Babylon.* New York: Birch Lane, 1993.

Welch, Neil J., and David W. Marston. *Inside Hoover's FBI.* New York: Doubleday, 1984.

West, J. B., with Mary Lynn Kotz. *Upstairs at the White House.* New York: Coward, McCann and Geoghegan, 1973.

Whalen, Richard J. *The Founding Father: The Story of Joseph P. Kennedy.* New York: New American Library, 1964.

White, Theodore H. *In Search of History.* New York: Warner, 1978.

———. *Breach of Faith: The Fall of Richard Nixon.* New York: Dell, 1975.

———. *The Making of the President 1968.* New York: Atheneum, 1969.

———. *The Making of the President 1964.* New York: Atheneum House, 1965.

———. *The Making of the President 1960.* New York: Atheneum House, 1961.

White, William S. *The Professional: Lyndon B. Johnson.* Boston: Houghton Mifflin, 1964.

Wicker, Tom. *JFK and LBJ.* New York: William Morrow, 1968.

———. *One of Us: Richard Nixon and the American Dream.* New York: Random House, 1991.

Williams, Juan. *Eyes on the Prize: America's Civil Rights Years, 1954–1965.* New York: Viking Penguin, 1987.

Wills, Garry. *The Kennedy Imprisonment.* Boston: Little, Brown, 1981.

Wilson, Earl. *Hot Times.* Chicago: Contemporary Books, 1984.

———. *Sinatra: An Unauthorized Biography.* New York: Macmillan, 1976.

Wilson, Frank J., and Beth Day. *Special Agent.* New York: Holt, Rinehart, and Winston, 1965.

Witcover, Jules. *Crapshoot: Rolling the Dice on the Vice Presidency.* New York: Crown, 1992.

———. *Marathon: The Pursuit of the Presidency, 1972–1976.* New York: Viking, 1977.

———. *85 Days: The Last Campaign of Robert F. Kennedy.* New York: Putnam, 1969.

Wofford, Harris. *Of Kennedys and Kings: Making Sense of the Sixties.* New York: Farrar, Straus, and Giroux, 1980.

Wolff, Perry. *A Tour of the White House with Mrs. John F. Kennedy.* New York: Doubleday, 1962.

Wright, Bruce. *Black Robes, White Justice.* New York: Carol, Lyle Stuart, 1987.

Wyden, Peter. *Bay of Pigs: The Untold Story.* New York: Simon and Schuster, 1979.

Youngblood, Rufus. *Twenty Years in the Secret Service: My Life with Five Presidents.* New York: Simon and Schuster, 1973.

Ziegler, Philip. *King Edward VIII: A Biography.* New York: Alfred A. Knopf, 1991.

Zirbel, Craig I. *The Texas Connection: The Assassination of President John F. Kennedy.* Scottsdale, Ariz.: Texas Connection Company, 1991.

ACKNOWLEDGMENTS

This book would not have been possible without the help of many individuals and institutions. First acknowledgment must go to my friends and literary agents, Georges and Anne Borchardt. Then I would like to thank my editors, Arnold Dolin and Elisa Petrini, and their able assistants, Lisa Hibler and Monica Ferrell, as well as attorneys Alexander Gigante and Eugene Girden for their careful libel reading of the manuscript. Steven Diamond did a fine job as photograph editor. Deborah Chiel was wonderful in her leadership of a large research team; her research and interviewing skills proved invaluable to the book. Pat Maniscalco filed and organized—in her uncanny fashion—an enormous bulk of materials related to every aspect of Robert Kennedy's life and times.

My thanks as well to Michael Takiff for his very adroit editorial and literary assistance. Jeanne Lunin (Heymann) helped to conduct interviews when the book was in its early stages. Rebecca Coughlan (Heymann) also did work on the project in its formative stage. Jane Ziegelman entered the picture at a later point and helped to complete a difficult job requiring patience and intelligence.

I am particularly grateful to an astute staff of researchers and interviewers that included Alexander Schnee, Roberta Fineberg, Joanne Green, Angela St. John Parker, Francis Broadhurst, Ann Conway, Cathy Griffin, Suzanne Freedman, Allan Freedman, Faith Gabriel, Mark Padnos, Leni Gilman, Lois Jacobini, Jack Owen, Melissa Kesler Gilbert, Peter Steere, Mark Alvey, Mildrade Charfils, Jim Claeys, Bridget Cox, Ruth Halliday, Beth Judy, Joan Barth, Paul Kangas, Sally Kline, Cheryl Miller and Kathryn Livingston. Christy Wise, "the dean of interviewers," a former press aide to the late Henry "Scoop" Jackson, covered Washington, D.C., like a blanket, convincing many to speak who ordinarily would not have. Another interviewer, distinguished criminal attorney Howard Diller, likewise acted the part of interviewee, recounting his days as an agent with the Drug Enforcement Agency.

Additional votes of gratitude go to Philip H. Melanson, who made available to the author his storehouse of information on the assassination of Robert F. Kennedy, and to John K. Mintz, a former counsel to the FBI, presently with Gibson, Dunn & Crutcher (Washington, D.C.), who handled a massive Freedom of Information legal request involving multivarious government agencies and departments.

On a personal level, I wish to acknowledge my great friend Gerry Visco, who was not only a companion but also a sage critic in helping to formulate later drafts of this volume. Julian de Rothschild bolstered my sagging spirits during the more difficult moments of this lengthy undertaking, as did Chickie the Siberian Husky, with whom I shared many a bucolic walk through Central Park. Then, I must express my gratitude to my mother, Renee K. Heymann, who has been there for me through not only this book but all the others. Finally, I would like to mention the late George Coleman, this book's first editor, who died far too young and unsung.

Numerous organizations and institutions provided documents, correspondence, oral history and written material of every description. While it is not possible to thank the individuals associated with each organization, I would like to express my gratitude to the following institutions: University of Alabama Libraries; American Jewish Archives; Amherst College Library; The Amistad Research Center; The Archdiocese of Boston; The George Arents Research Library (Syracuse University); Arizona Historical Foundation; University of Arizona Library; Arizona State University Library; The University of Arkansas Libraries; Assassination Archives and Research Center (Washington, D.C.); Associated Press and UPI offices (Athens, Greece); J. M. Atkins Library (University of North Carolina, Charlotte); Auraria Library (University of Colorado, Denver); The Bancroft Library (University of California, Berkeley); Bates College Library; Baylor University Institute for Oral History; Bentley Historical Library (The University of Michigan); Boise State University Library; Boston Herald Archives; Boston Public Library; British Broadcasting Corporation; The British Museum; Bronxville Historical Association; Brooklyn College Library; Brown University Library.

University of California, Los Angeles (The University Library, Department of Special Collections); California State Archives (Sacramento); Jimmy Carter Presidential Center; Central Intelligence Agency; Chattanooga-Hamilton County Library; University of Chicago Library; Clemson University Library; Columbia University Oral History Collection; Columbia University Rare Book and Manuscript Collection; Connecticut College Library (New London); Cornell University Libraries; Dartmouth College Library; Department of Labor Archives; Duke University Library; Dwight D. Eisenhower Library; The Earl Gregg Swem Library (The College of William and Mary); Ekstrom Library (University of Louisville); The Everett Dirksen Congressional Leadership Research Center; Federal Bureau of Investigation; Frank Melville, Jr., Memorial Library (State University of New York); The Free Library of Philadelphia; Gerald R. Ford Library; Greenwich, Connecticut, Historical Society.

The Gelman Library (George Washington University); Georgetown University Library; The Jean and Alexander Heard Library (Vanderbilt University); Herbert Hoover Presidential Library; The Houghton Library (Harvard University); University of Illinois at Chicago Library; University of Illinois State Historical Society; Illinois State University Library; Indiana State University Library; The University of Iowa Libraries; Lyndon Baines Johnson Library; Kansas State University Library; John Fitzgerald Kennedy Library; Kent State University Library; Margaret I. King Library (University of Kentucky) Martin Luther King, Jr., Center; Library of Congress (Manuscript Division); Los Angeles Police Department (Forensics); University of Maine Special Collections; Manhattanville College Library; Marquette University Library; The Commonwealth of Massachusetts State Library; University of Massachusetts; Maysles Films, Inc.; The Andrew Mellon Library (Choate Rosemary Hall); Miami Library; Minnesota Historical Society; University of Minnesota Libraries; University of Missouri Library (Columbia); Moellering Library, Valparaiso University; Mugar Memorial Library (Boston University); The Karl E. Mundt Historical and Educational Foundation; National Archives; National Archives of Canada; National Geographic Society; National Security Agency (Central Security Service); Department of the Navy (Naval War College and Naval Intelligence Command); Nebraska State Historical Society; University of New Hampshire Library; New Mexico State University Library; New Orleans Public Library; New York City Municipal Archives; New York Genealogical and Biographical Society; New York Public Library; New York University Library; The Archives of the University of Notre Dame; North Texas State University Libraries; Northwestern University Library.

Ohio Historical Society; Ohio State University Library; University of Oklahoma Library; Alexander S. Onassis Public Benefit Foundation; University of Oregon Library; Palm Beach Historical Society; City of Palm Beach Police Department; Pennsylvania Historical and Museum Collection; William R. Perkins Library (Duke University); Phillips Memorial Library (Providence College); Office of the Chief Postal Inspector; Princeton University Library; Priory School Library; Posey Library (Harvard University); Redwood Library and Athenaeum (Newport, R.I.); Walter P. Reuther Library (Wayne State University); Riley Library (Ouchita Baptist University); Riverdale Country Day School Library; University of Rochester Library; Franklin D. Roosevelt Library: The Rosenbach Museum & Library; Richard B. Russell Memorial Library (University of Georgia); St. John's University Library; St. Paul's School Library; Scotland Yard; Smithsonian Institution; South Dakota State College Library; Southern Massachusetts University Library; University of Southern Mississippi Library; University of Southwestern Louisiana Libraries; The Stanford University Libraries; State University (SUNY) at Stonybrook Library (Jacob K. Javitz Collection); University of Tennessee; Department of the Treasury; United States Secret Service; Harry S. Truman Library; Union College Library; U.S. Department of State; U.S. Naval Institute; University of Utah Library; Veterans Administration, Department of Medicine and Surgery; University of Virginia Law School Library; University of Virginia Library; University of Washington Libraries; Wayne State University Archives of Labor and Urban Affairs and University Archives; The Western Reserve Historical Society; West Virginia and Regional History Collection (West Virginia University); The State Historical Society of Wisconsin; University of Wisconsin at Stevens Point Library; Robert W. Woodruff Library (Emory University); University of Wyoming Library; Yale University Library.

A list of those interviewed for this book includes several interviews that first appeared in *A Woman Named Jackie: An Intimate Biography of Jacqueline Kennedy Onassis* (1989), by the current author. Approximately a dozen names have been omitted from the list by request of the interviewee.

Slim Aarons, Elie Abel, Bess Abell, David Achem, David Acheson, Beverly Acker, Joe Acquaotta, Cindy Adams, Bill Adler, Richard Adler, Jerome Agel, Paul Alcott, Diane Alden, Alexandre, Neil Alford, Mark A. Allen, Hervé Alphand, Joe Alsop, Calderon Augusto Alvarez, Arthur Amiot, Jr., Cleveland Amory, Chris Anderson, Jack Anderson, Patrick "Pat" Anderson, Bonnie Angelo, James J. Angleton, Army Archerd, Martin Arnold, Aileen Arthur, Robert Arum, Arthur Arundel, Joe Asbell, Agnes Ash, Linda Ashland, Roberta Ashley, Ed Asner, *Aspen Resident*, Ajit Asrani, Jamie Auchincloss, Janet Lee Bouvier Auchincloss, Bill Avery, Gerald Ayers.

Herman Badillo, Russell Baker, Letitia Baldridge, George Ball, Richard Banks, Robert Bannister, Peter Barton, Charles Bartlett, Stephen Bauer, Betty Beale, Edith Beale, Samuel H. Beer, Harry Belafonte, David Belin, Melvin Belli, Ray Bergen, Ray Berger, Dick Bergholz, Leonard Bernstein, Gabe Biaz, Kirk LeMoyne Billings, June Bingham Birge, Stephen Birmingham, Joey Bishop, Algernon Black, Dan

Blackburn, Earl Blackwell, William McCormick Blair, Jr., Tom Bolan, Julian Bond, Philip M. Boudreau, Bernard Boutin, Frank Bowling, Francis Boyd, Joan Braden, Toni Bradlee, Amy Brandon, David Breasted, Daniel Brewster, Frank Broadhurst, Earl Brown, Edmund G. (Pat) Brown, Alan Brownfeld, Jerry Bruno, Carter Burden, Richard (Rick) Burke, Frank Burns, John Burns, Richard Burton, Alec Byrne.

Angie Cabrera, Sherwood Cadwell, Herb Caen, Dr. Edgar Cahn, Gordon Caldwell, Joseph Califano, Jr., Samuel Campbell, Jr., Julie Cancio, Peggy Cannon, Cornell Capa, Mortimer Caplin, Truman Capote, Ari Caratsas, Jeanne Carmen, Sally Carpenter, William Carpenter, George Carpozi, Jr., Mike Carroll, Ronald Carroll, Hodding Carter III, June Carter, Igor Cassini, Oleg Cassini, Raul Castro, Anthony Celebrezze, Sr., Joseph Cerrell, William Chafe, O. Roy Chalk, Ken Chandler, Red Chandor, Tim Cheek, George Christian, Camille T. Christie, Mrs. Paul Christman, Sharon Churcher, Blair Clark, Dick Clark, Kenneth B. Clark, Ramsey Clark, Gerald Clarke, Jack Clemmons, Clark Clifford, Garry Clifford, Mrs. George Clifford, Chester V. (Ted) Clifton, Arthur Clarke, Art Z. Cohn, Roy Cohn, Bill (William) Colby, Barbara Coleman, George Coleman, Nancy Tenney Coleman, Dr. Robert Coles, John Collins, Mary Ann Mobley Collins, Frank Comerford, Bill Connell, John Constandy, Robert Cooley, Diana Cooper, John Sherman Cooper, Laurie Cooper, Norman Corwin, Ed Costikyan, Mel Cottone, Ruth Pollack Coughlin, Roderick Coupe, Carol Craig, Robert Craig, Barbara H. Crawler, Joseph Crangle, David Crawford, Kenneth Crawford, Countess Consuelo Crespi, George Crossman, Joan Crossman, Eloise Cuddleback, H. Cunningham, Kent Cunow, Charlotte Curtis, Thomas B. Curtis, Ron Cutler.

Rita Dallas, Peter Dalton, Leo Damore, Joan Darling, Herman Darvick, Lester David, Bob Davidoff, Jules Davids, Deborah Davis, John Davis, Ronald L. Davis, Emile de Antonio, Philippe de Bausset, John W. Dee, Hubert de Givenchy, Mary DeGrace, Ormande de Kay, Audrey del Rosario, Ovid Demaris, Couve de Murville, Helene Guillet de Neergaard, Dennis the Greek, Baron Alexis de Rede, Julian De Rothschild, Carmine de Sapio, Count Adalbert de Segonzac, Janet Desrosiers, Ralph de Toledano, Armand Deutsch, Joe Devers, Duke of Devonshire (Cavendish), Nancy Dickerson, James Dickey, Howard Diller, C. Douglas Dillon, Gladys Dise, John Doar, Muriel Dobbin, Marjorie Housepian Dobkin, Gary Doctor, Thomas Dodd, Gregg (Sherwood) Dodge, Carole Doheny, Joe Dolan, Sam Donaldson, Hebe Dorsey, Mrs. Morton Downey, Sr., Morton Downey, Jr., Elisabeth Draper, Charles Dresden, Robert Drew, Noreen Drexel, Diana DuBois, LaVern Duffy, Angier Biddle Duke, Paul Duke, Paul Duke, Jr., William Dunfey, Ralph Dungan, Frederick Dutton, Susan Duval, Judge Donald Duvall.

Lee Edwards, Al Eisele, Earl Eisenhower, Ronnie Eldridge, Mabel Elliot, Mrs. Ed Ellson, Bill Elvin, Dr. Hyman Engelberg, Lawrence Eno, Bill Epperidge, Edward Jay Epstein, Courtney A. Evans, Rowland Evans, Jr., Martin Evarts, George Michel Evica.

Ty Fain, Douglas Fairbanks, Jr., Livingston Fairbanks, Susan Falb, Joseph Fallon, James Farmer, Rev. Walter Fauntroy, Paul B. "Red" Fay, Polly Feingold, Justin Feldman, Bernard Fensterwald, Jr., Charles Ferris, Roger Fessanguet, David Filvaroff, Jerry Finkelstein, Mel Finkelstein, Peter M. Fishbein, Eddie Fisher, Murray Fisher, Alfred Bradley Fitt, Jeffrey Flach, Francis Flanagan, Wally Flinn, Joseph Foley, Andre Fontaine, Doris Ford, Dall W. Forsythe, Dorothy Fosdick, Molly Fowler, Fox 5 News, Ron Fox, Sanford "Sandy" Fox, Sonny Fox, James Free, Judy Freed, Alan

Freedman, Orville Freeman, Elizabeth McNamara Fretz, Grace L. Frey, C. Friend, Clayton Fritchey, Jacob D. Fuchsberg, Bill Fugazy, Peter Fuller, Vincent Fuller, Foster Furcolo.

Neal Gabler, Zsa Zsa Gabor, Helene Gaillet, Estelle Gaines, Steven Gaines, Alice Gaither, John Kenneth Galbraith, Betty Galella, Ron Galella, Robert David Lyon Gardiner, Joseph Gargan, Mary Teal Garland, Jim Garrison, David Garrow, Wilson R. Gathings, Judith Geddes, Robert W. General, Ann Geracimos, Jack Germond, Cecilia Parker Geyelin, Barbara Gibson, John Gibson, Rod Gibson, Jane Gilbert, Perry Gildes, Roswell Gilpatric, Mary Gimbel, Angele Gingras, Allen Ginsberg, Ralph Ginzburg, Andy Glass, Senator John Glenn, Charles Glynn, Tony Gobel, Arthur Goldberg, Jay Goldberg, Harry Golden, Ronald Goldfarb, Esq., Alan Goldstein, Barry Goldwater, Richard Goodwin, Senator Al Gore (now Vice President), Ross Graham, Joseph Grandmaison, Cary Grant, Janet Grant, Constantine "Castro" Gratsos, Earl Graves, Judith Gray, Peter Green, Robert Green, Jack Greenberg, Hildi Greenson, Nanette Grey, Roosevelt "Rosey" Grier, Gary M. Griffin, William Griffen, Cathy Griffin, Judge Erwin Griswold, Tony Gronowicz, Joy Gross, Judge William Guerry, Barbara Guest, Charles Guggenheim, Leo Guild, Milton Gwirtzman.

Lucien Haas, David Hackett, William Haddad, Tom Hailey, R. Hakin, David Halberstam, Kay Halle, Halston, Anne Hamilton, Nigel Hamilton, Haven W. Hammond, Alfred Hantman, Esq., John Harlee, Mary Harrington, Betty Harris, Laura Harris, V. V. Harrison, Jacques Harvey, Mrs. Anthony Hass, Arnie Hasselgrin, James Haught, Betty Bowling Haxall, Bowling Haxall, Mary Hayes, Sir Edward Heath, Ken Hechler, Stewart Hegleman, Peter Hegler, Richard M. Helms, Russell Hemenway, Deirdre Henderson, Thomas T. Hendrick, Peter Herdrich, Albert Herling, John Herling, Jerry Herman, John Hersey, Father Theodore Hesburgh, Charlton Heston, Jerry Hewey, Harry Hicks Esq., Gladwin Hill, Sonja Hillgren, Francesca Hilton, Robert Hinerfeld, Louise Hipkins, Abe Hirschfeld, Leslie Hixson, Philip Hoff, James P. Hoffa, Paul Hope, David Horowitz, Charles Horsky, Harold Hughes, William G. Hundley, John Hurley, Joe Hyams.

Paul Ilyinsky, Winchester F. Ingersoll, Jr., Harry Inman, Polly Irwin, Gottfried Isaac, Lois Jacobini, Ruth Jacobson, Dr. Thomas E. Jacobson, Cliff Jahr, Brandon James, Charles Jarrott, Jacob Javits, Joan Javits, Marion Javits, Lord Jenkins of Millieau, Evie Johnson, William Johnson, Bruce Johnson, Tom Johnston, Bobby Jones, Sr., Sally Jones, Ted H. Jordan, Jim Juliana.

Dr. Rolf Kaetenborn, James Kalafatis, Max Kampelman, Arthur Kaplan, Esq., Sheldon Kardiner, Jack Kassowitz, Robert Kastenmeier, Peter Kaye, Mimi Kazon, Pierce Kearney, Jack Nelson Kegley, Esq., Gene Kelly, David Kennedy, Robert Kennedy, Jr., Dr. Donald W. Kent, Jr., Ron Kessler, Andy Kilcar, Esq., Michael Kilian, Carl Killingsworth, Bob King, Kenny Kingston, Arthur Kirson, Nicholas Kisburg, Suzanne Perrin Kloman, Robert Knight, Judge James Knott, John Knowles, Edward I. Koch, Joe Konowe, Ruth Holmes Korkuch, Mary Lynn Kotz, Sarah Kovner, Joseph Kratt, Jerome Kretchmer, Katherine Krogness-Mixol, Peter Kumpa, Judge Theodore Kupferman, Jonathan Kwitny.

William Lacey, Roger Lajeunesse, Jack Lanahan, Mike Land, Ted Landreth, Burton Lane, Lynn Lane, Lester Lanin, Lew Laprade, Francis Lara, Ida Large, Jeremy Larner, Donald Larrabee, Mary Lasker, Nat Laurendi, Walter Lavendahl, Peter Lawford, Dave Lawrence, Paul Lazzaro, Stephen Leahy, Larry Leamer, Timothy Leary, Janet Leigh, Wendy Leigh, Tim Leimert, Masha Leon, Ruth Blackburn

Leonovich, Alan Jay Lerner, James H. Lesar, John W. Leslie, Samuel Leve, Russell Levine, Myra Levitt, Francis Levy, Jean Lewis, Mort R. Lewis, Robert Lewis, Doris Lilly, Anne Lincoln, Evelyn Lincoln, Saul Lindenbaum, Dan Lindsay, John Lindsay, John Linehan, Ron Linton, Herbert C. Little, Kathryn Livingston, Henry Cabot Lodge, Jr., Lee Loeringer, Robert Low, Jacques Lowe, Larry Lowenstein, Patrick Lucey, Arthur Lundahl, Renee Luttgen.

Phyllis Brooks Macdonald, Sue Macintosh, Harry MacPherson, Sheila MacRae, Norman Mailer, William Manchester, Christopher Mankiewicz, Irving Mansfield, Mike Mansfield, Peter Manso, George Markham, Don Marsh, Burke Marshall, John Bartlow Martin, Judge Baron Martin, Ralph G. Martin, Langdon P. Marvin, Jr., Christopher Mason, Paul Mathias, Rudy Maxa, Judge Armando "Dave" Mazzone, Susanna McBee, Carol McCabe, Joe McCaffrey, Dannis V.N. McCarthy, Eugene McCarthy, Jim McCartney, Helen McCauley, Diana McClellan, Sarah McClendon, David Blair McCloskey, Stewart McClure, John McCone, George B. McCutcheon, Edward McDermott, David McGough, George McGovern, Bill McGrane, Dell McGriff, Godfrey McHugh, Pat McKenna, William H. McKeon, Esq., F. Kenneth McKnight, Edward McLaughlin, Jr., Esq., Betty McMahon, Robert McNamara, Aileen Mehle (Suzy), Philip H. Melanson, Charles Merrill, Richard Meryman, Evelyn Metzger, Cord Meyer, Jr., Jack Micay, Mike Michaelson, A. Harry Middleton, Leslie Midgeley, Archie Miller, Geoff Miller, Hope Ridings Miller, James R. Mills, Wilbur Mills, Scott Milne, John Miner, John Mintz, Esq., Alexis Miotis, Milan "Mike" Miskovsky, Esq., Clarence Mitchell, Michael Mitchell, Dan Moldea, Thomas Monahan, Ruth Montgomery, Admiral Thomas Moorer, Peter Morrison, Esq., Ruth Mosse, Daniel Patrick Moynihan, George Murphy, Robert Murray.

Joe Naar, Victor Navasky, Bob Neal, Esq., James Neal, Samuel E. Neel, James Neff, Gaylord Nelson, Larry Newman, Khoi Nguyen, Eugene Nickerson, Russell Niguette, Sr., Esq., Louis Nizer, Esq., Philip Nobile, Dr. Thomas Noguchi, John Nolan, Bob Novak, Eugene Nuckols, Sam Nunn, Rudolph Nureyev, Helen Natura, Louis Oberdorfer, Chuck O'Brian, Lawrence F. "Larry" O'Brien, Ken O'Donnell, Andrew Oehmann, Jr., Frank Ogden, Manfred Ohrenstein, Grace Old, David Ormsby-Gore (Lord Harlech), Fred Otash.

Pamela Page, Katherine Pancol, Provi Parades, Henry Parish, Cecil Parker, Herbert Parmet, Fred Papert, David Parrish, Esq., Mrs. Henry Parrish II, Endicott Peabody, Larry Peerce, Mrs. Claiborne Pell, Paul Pepe, Ralph Pepe, Claude Pepper, Daphne Pereles, Lucia Perrigio, Lester Persky, Charles Peters, Martha Phillips, Robert Phillips, Bob Piolo, George Plimpton, Dr. Michael Polan, Stephen Pollak, Susan Pollock, Jane Poolsta, Dave Powers, Walter Pozen, Nathaniel Preston, Barrett Prettyman, Alan Pryce-Jones, Victoria Pryor, Michelle Putnam, Charles Quinn, Lawrence J. Quirk.

Victor Rabinowitz, Esq., Theron Raines, Harrison Rainie, Lee Rainey, Daniel Rappaport, A. H. Raskin, Joseph Rauh, Jr., Ryan Rayston, Kenneth Redden, Coates Redman, Matthew Reese, Carl Reich, John Richard Reilly, Harold Reis, Henry Reuss, John Revson, John Reynolds, Abraham Ribicoff, Helen Rich, Elliot Richardson, Stewart "Sandy" Richardson, Marie Ridder, John Rigas, Bob Riley, Patricia Riley, Charles Riser, Geraldo Rivera, Don Rizzo, Jilly Rizzo, Mead Roberts, Helene Rochas, Nick Rodis, Paul Rogers, Mitchell Rogovin, Franklin D. Roosevelt, Jr., Selma Roosevelt, Morris Victor Rosenbloom, Doris Rosenquist, John H. Ross, Elspeth Rostow, Walt Rostow, Dr. Saul D. Rotter, Dorey Roundtree, Esq., James

Rousmaniere, Lily Pulitzer Rousseau, Alan Rubenstein, George Rush, Dean Rusk, John Russell, Joy Rutherford, James Ryan.

Alice Sachs, Pierre Salinger, Michael Samek, Herman Samuel, Esq., Mary Sanford, Pedro San Juan, Arnold Sawislak, Louis Scarrone, Dore Schary, Raymond Lewis Scherer, Gene Scherrer, Fifi Fell Schiff, Aaron Schikkler, G. David Schine, Herb Schmertz, Patricia Schmidlapp, Benno C. Schmidt, Alexander Schnee, Gene Schoor, Richard Schotter, Paul Schrade, Charles Schwartz, Ted Schwartz, Arthur Scott, Patricia Seaton, John Seigenthaler, Carol Selig, Thomas Shack, Peter Jay Sharp, Carolyn Hagner Shaw, Martin Shepard, Tom Sheridan, Norman Sherman, Tony Sherman, Howard E. Shuman, Hugh Sidey, Edwyn Silberling, Esq., Samuel Silverman, Lori Slavin, Art Sloan, Eileen Slocum, Orville Slutzkey, George Smathers, Earl E. T. Smith, James H. Smith, Esq., Liz Smith, Robert Smith, Jane Snydam, Theodore Sorensen, Rosemary Sorentino, Thomas Sonder, James Spada, Charles "Chuck" Spalding, Milo Speriglio, Purette Spiegler, Mickey Spillane, Dr. Benjamin Spock, Baroness Garnett Stackleberg, Bill Stadiem, Phil Stanton, Jessie Stearns, Newton Steers, Judith Stecher, Peter Steere, Andrew Stein, Joseph Steine, Stanley Steingut, J. Warren Stephens, Phil Stern, Joseph Sterne, Daniel Stewart, John Stewart, Jennifer Stone, Joseph Stone, Rick Stone, Roger Stone, Ray Strait, Arnold Stream, Lyle Stuart, Mimi Strong, Anthony Summers, James Sundquist, Nelson Sutton, Frank Swoboda, Herb Swope, Jr.

Taki, George Tames, Auan Tannenbaum, Rosalyn Targ, Malcolm Taylor, Bruce Terris, Esq., Bob Thomas, Evan Thomas, Evan W. Thomas II, Franklin Thomas, Phillip Thomas, Strom Thurmond, Katherine Harris Tierena, Mary Tierney, Paul Tierney, Kathy Tollerton, Al Tomich, Jeanne Toomey, Nick Tosches, Dr. Janet Travell, John Treanor, Jr., Marietta Tree, Gerald Tremblay, Stanley Tretick, Diana Trilling, Esther Von Wagner Tufty, J. C. Turner, William Turner, Tom Turnipseed, Joseph Tydings, William Unis.

Jack Valenti, Frank Valeo, Richard Valeriani, John Valva, William S. vanden Heuvel, Ted Van Dyk, Barbara Van Dyke, Jeanne Murray Vanderbilt, Monique Van Vooren, Martin Venker, Rene Verdun, Gore Vidal, Alejo Vidal-Quadros, George Vigouroux, Janet Villella, Sue Vogelsinger, Nicholas von Hoffman, Diana Vreeland.

Helga Wagner, Phyllis Cerf Wagner, Malvin Waid, Robert Wallace, Walter Wallace, Eli Wallach, General Vernon Walters, Fanny Warburg, Andy Warhol, John Carl Warnecke, Harriet Wasserman, Alice Watson, Dr. Hugh M. Watson, Robert Watt, Jane Ellen Wayne, Alexandra Webb, Dr. Cyril Wecht, Joan Weeklyn, Mary Weinmann, Mrs. J. B. (Zella) West, John Whaley, Esq., Harvey White, John B. White, Theodore H. White, Jennifer Wiens, Roger Wilkins, Judge Paul Williams, Judge Richard Williams, Bob Willoughby, Allan Wilson, Thomas Wilson, Esq., James Wire, Jr., David Wise, Newton Wise, Kristi Witker, Harris Wofford, Esq., Stanley Wojcik, Dan Wolf, Esq., Virginia Wooster, Jim Wrightsman, Melvin (Mel) Wulf, Esq., Adam Yarmolinsky, Sam Yorty, Andrew Young, Elaine Young, Brent Zacky, Edward Zak, Jerome Zerbe, David Zimmer, Richard Zoerink.

INDEX